Criminology

JOHN E. CONKLIN
TUFTS UNIVERSITY

Criminology

THIRD EDITION

MACMILLAN PUBLISHING COMPANY
NEW YORK

Copyright © 1989 by John E. Conklin

PRINTED IN THE UNITED STATES OF AMERICA

All rights reserved. No part of this book may be reproduced or transmitted in any form or by any means, electronic or mechanical, including photocopying, recording, or any information storage and retrieval system, without permission in writing from the Publisher.

Earlier editions copyright © 1981, 1986
by John E. Conklin

Macmillan Publishing Company
866 Third Avenue, New York, New York 10022

Collier Macmillan Canada, Inc.

LIBRARY OF CONGRESS CATALOGING-IN-PUBLICATION DATA
Conklin, John E.
    Criminology / John E. Conklin. — 3rd ed.
      p. cm.
    Bibliography: p. 549
    Includes indexes.
    ISBN 0-02-323801-1
    1. Crime and criminals. I. Title.
  IN PROCESS (ONLINE)   88-7028
                             CIP

PRINTING: 2 3 4 5 6 7 YEAR: 9 0 1 2 3 4 5

Preface to the Third Edition

The most important new feature of this edition of *Criminology* is the Using Criminology box. Each chapter now contains at least one of these boxes, which show how the theories and findings of criminology have been applied to solving actual problems. These Using Criminology boxes deal with problems such as how to reduce the fear of crime, how to teach bullies to behave in nonaggressive ways, and how to prevent theft from stores.

In addition, each chapter contains at least one Cross-Cultural Perspective box. Boxes new to this third edition deal with the black market in Peru, dowry murders in India, and amputation as punishment in the Sudan. I believe that students gain much from looking at crime in other societies, and they find such cross cultural perspectives fascinating as well.

To make this edition of *Criminology* easier to read, the number of statistical tables has been reduced, with the conclusions to be drawn from the tables that have been dropped being summarized in the body of the text. Moreover, Chapters 5 ("Geographic and Temporal Dimensions of Crime") and 6 ("Social Dimensions of Crime") in the second edition have been reduced in size and combined into a single chapter (Chapter 5) in this edition. This revision reduces the amount of statistical material without any loss in the meaning of the statistical patterns that criminologists have uncovered.

Because many students in criminology courses have limited interest in the methods used by criminologists to carry out their research, the material in Chapter 2 of the second edition ("Methods of Criminological Research") has been cut significantly and integrated into Chapter 1. This section still introduces the student to some of the strategies of research used by criminologists and gives several examples of actual research projects, but the discussion is now much less detailed.

To introduce the student to the kinds of crimes that will be explored throughout the book, a new Chapter 2 ("A Typology of Crimes") has been added. This chapter includes a table toward the end that shows where each type of crime is later examined in the textbook. The book remains organized around a conceptual scheme rather than around types of crime (e.g., a chapter on property crime, a chapter on organized crime), which is a common way to organize textbooks in the field. I believe that a conceptual approach offers more to the beginning student in the way of tools and ideas with which to analyze criminal behavior than do texts that are divided into chapters on theories and then chapters on specific types of crime.

This edition has been completely edited for smoother reading. It includes more photographs and display tables that summarize material in the body of the text. Of course, all statistics have been updated, and use is made throughout of research that has been published since the last edition.

Important terms are listed at the end of each chapter and defined in a Glossary at the end of the book. Each chapter has a detailed but concise summary and an annotated list of suggested readings. References in the text are to the Bibliography at the end, which is followed by a Name Index and a Subject Index.

I would like to thank the following people for their comments and suggestions for this third edition: Bonnie Berry, *University of Washington;* David J. Dodd, *Montclair State College;* Gilbert Geis, *University of California–Irvine;* P.H. Harvey, *Colorado State University;* and Gary D. Hill, *North Carolina State University.* I would also like to thank Christine Cardone, Senior Editor at Macmillan, for her help and encouragement. Thanks are also due to Aliza Greenblatt for her professional production work on the book and to Ellen Falk for copyediting the manuscript.

J. E. C.

Author Biography

John E. Conklin is Professor of Sociology at Tufts University in Medford, Massachusetts.

Professor Conklin was born in Oswego, New York, in 1943 and was raised in Syracuse, New York. He is the father of four children—Christopher, Anne, Lydia, and Gillian—and is married to Sarah Belcher Conklin.

After earning a bachelor's degree, with honors in economics, from Cornell University in 1965, Professor Conklin attended Harvard University, completing his doctorate there in 1969. He then worked for a year at Harvard Law School's Center for Criminal Justice. He started teaching at Tufts University in 1970 and now offers introductory sociology, crime and delinquency, deviant behavior and social control, and sociology of law.

Professor Conklin's first book, published in 1972, was *Robbery and the Criminal Justice System,* a study based on data gathered in Boston. In 1973, he edited a collection of papers on organized crime, *The Crime Establishment*. In 1975, Macmillan published his study of community reactions to crime, *The Impact of Crime*. An examination of white-collar crime was published in 1977, entitled *"Illegal but Not Criminal": Business Crime in America*. Macmillan published the first two editions of *Criminology* in 1981 and 1986 and published two editions of *Sociology: An Introduction* in 1984 and 1987.

Contents

PART III

The Causes of Criminal Behavior   149

CHAPTER 6
Biological and Psychological Explanations of Crime   151

CHAPTER 11
Criminal Careers   330

PART IV
Reactions to Crime   357

CHAPTER 12
Community Reactions to Crime   359

CHAPTER 13

The Criminal Justice System   381

Boxes

Cross-Cultural Perspectives

Using Criminology

PART I

Introduction to Criminology

Chapter 1 introduces several basic concepts used in the study of crime and delinquency. We examine the social origins of the law — interest groups, public opinion, and expert evidence — and learn that crime is a social phenomenon rather than an intrinsic characteristic of behavior. The conceptual approach around which the book is organized is introduced, and an overview of later chapters is provided. We also look at several research strategies that criminologists use to study crime and delinquency.

In Chapter 2, a typology is presented to introduce four major kinds of crime that will be investigated throughout the book: conventional crime (both violent and property), white-collar crime, organized crime, and victimless crime.

CHAPTER 1

The Study of Crime

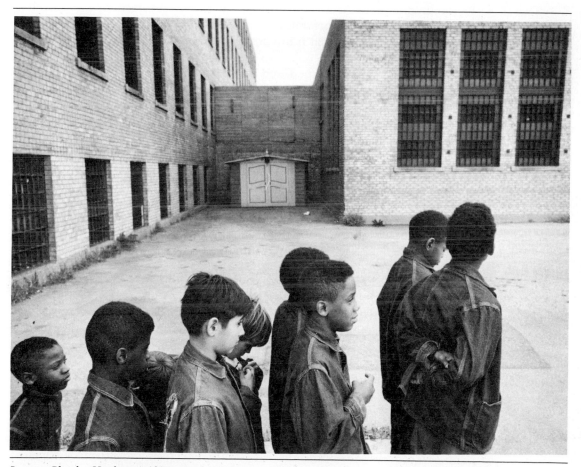

Source: Charles Harbutt Archive Pictures

We are all interested in crime. We watch police shows on television, go to movies that deal with crime, read mystery novels, and follow crime news on television and in the newspapers. The reasons for the broad appeal of crime as drama include escape, stimulation, relaxation, and the appeal of a "good-versus-evil situation where some sort of hero wins at the end through talent and, very importantly, morality" (Richard Meyers, cited in Pace, 1982: F9).

Television, radio, and newspapers rapidly disperse crime news throughout the nation and inform even the residents of relatively crime-free areas of the extent of crime in the society. Not only is news of crime more readily available today than in the past, but also the national organization of the media provides more dramatic crimes to report than was true in the past, when the population was smaller and news was more likely to be local. The media focus on attention-grabbing events, thereby bringing only the most sensational and bizarre crimes to public attention. As a result, people develop a distorted view of crime as inexplicably and unpredictably violent, even though petty larceny, burglary, auto theft, and commercial fraud are much more common than murder and rape.

Crime stories sell newspapers and are relatively easy to get. The crimes that appeal most to the press and their readers are those that are visible and spectacular, have sexual or political implications, can be presented in graphic — usually violent — terms, and seem to be the product of individual aberrations rather than social conditions (Chibnall, 1977). Crime news seems to be reported more as entertainment than as information.

A systematic study of televised crime based on observations of six weeks of prime-time programs in the United States in 1981 found that crime was rampant on television, with violent crime twelve times as common on television as in real life, and murder — the most common crime on television — one hundred times as frequent. After murder, the next most common crimes on television were robbery, kidnapping, and aggravated assault. The crimes most often experienced by the public — theft, burglary, car theft, and public drunkenness — showed up in television programs much less often than crimes of violence (Lichter and Lichter, 1983).

Not only are the kinds of crime that are actually committed portrayed in a distorted way on television, but those who commit crimes are also shown inaccurately. Compared with suspects arrested in actual crimes, criminals on television are older, more well-to-do, and more likely to be white.

Yet another distortion introduced by television concerns the consequences of crime. In real life, the chance of avoiding arrest for a serious crime is about four in five. On television, only 8 percent of offenders get away with their crimes. Television suggests that crime does not pay, but in fact most real crimes do not lead to an arrest, and even fewer lead to conviction and imprisonment. Television also conveys the impression that private detectives and citizens solve more crimes than the police, but in reality relatively few offenses are solved by people other than the police (Lichter and Lichter, 1983).

In distorting the nature of crime, the mass media may produce a higher level

Television, news + radio disperse crime news throughout the nation.

of anxiety among the public than would exist otherwise. Heavy watchers of television seem to be more likely than people who watch less television to see the world as violent, dangerous, and crime-ridden (Gerbner and Gross, 1977; Duffy, 1982).

The portrayal of crime in the mass media differs significantly from what criminologists have learned about patterns and causes of crime from their research. Sociologists, psychologists, economists, political scientists, biologists, and others who have studied crime in a systematic way have gathered empirical data to test their ideas and have revised those ideas to fit new information. In this book, we focus on sociological research, but we also draw on material from other disciplines that have studied criminals and criminal behavior.

The Nature of Crime and Delinquency

Before we define crime and delinquency, we need to become familiar with some concepts that sociologists use to describe social rules, the violations of those rules, and reactions to those violations.

Basic Concepts: Norms and Deviance, Laws and Crime

All societies have rules that govern behavior. These rules or *norms* make explicit certain social expectations about what is appropriate behavior for particular people in specific situations. Norms reflect the culture's *values* — those things that are considered worthy, desirable, or proper. For instance, the norm that we dress in our best clothes for a wedding or a funeral reflects the importance of the occasion and our desire to show respect for others. The norm against suicide reflects the value that cultures place on the preservation of human life.

Deviance, the violation of a norm, may be approved behavior (as with heroic acts during a battle) or may be disapproved behavior (as with cowardice). In other words, it is possible to deviate from a norm by "overconforming" (for instance, by turning in a hundred-page seminar paper) or by "underconforming" (for example, by turning in merely one page). Usually, however, deviance refers to disapproved or underconforming behavior.

Deviance in a disapproved direction is often met with a *sanction*, an effort to ensure future conformity to the norm and punish past nonconformity. One example would be a failing grade for a student who turned in a one-page seminar paper when a twenty-page paper was required. Another example is the sanctioning of suicide; for centuries, those who killed themselves were prohibited from being buried in consecrated ground, and often their property was confiscated by the state. Sanctions can be informal, including a critical glance or a spanking, or they may be formal, as in a military trial of a deserter or a criminal trial of an accused murderer.

Some informal social norms become legal norms. Through the political and judicial process, *laws* are passed and interpreted, and informal rules become formal laws. As a subset of norms, laws are written down and formalized by the political system. Over the past 150 years, problems once seen as private have increasingly been redefined as public matters warranting the intervention of such official agencies of the state as the police, the courts, and the prisons (Lane, 1967; Silver, 1967).

A *tort* is a civil wrong for which a plaintiff, or complaining party, can sue a defendant who is alleged to have caused the plaintiff harm. The outcome of civil cases is often monetary restitution or damages, with money paid to the victorious plaintiff by the losing defendant.

A *crime*, in contrast to a tort, is an act that violates the criminal law and is punishable by the state. A crime is considered an offense against the state rather than an act against a specific individual. This definition has its origins in medieval Great Britain, where the king replaced formal vengeance by victim against offender with sanctions by the state. Thus, today a robbery is dealt with by the courts as *State* v. *Jones* rather than as *Smith* v. *Jones*. Smith as the victim of the robbery might sue Jones, the alleged robber, in civil court to recover money for damages caused during the holdup, but this rarely happens. Instead, the offense would be dealt with in criminal court, with a prosecutor or district attorney acting on behalf of the state in bringing charges against Jones.

The Characteristics of Crime

Crime is behavior that is subject to legally defined punishment. Indeed, the French sociologist Emile Durkheim (1895, 1933) asserted in the late nineteenth century that punishment is the defining characteristic of crime and that other characteristics—such as social harm—are corollaries rather than defining traits. Punishable behavior includes a myriad of actions, from forcible rape to price fixing and from murder to pollution of the environment. Because crime includes so many diverse acts, it makes little sense to speak of "crime increasing" or "the typical criminal," without referring to specific crimes or specific criminals. However, many crimes have some common characteristics.

Crime usually involves *criminal intent*, the willed or conscious desire to commit an act that violates a criminal law. Prior to the twelfth century, the law did not include the idea of a guilty mind that formed criminal intent; guilt was then based simply on the causing of injury. Over time, the idea of intent was gradually introduced into the law, partly as a result of the influence of Christian teachings about sin and moral blame (McVisk, 1978). However, today not all acts designated as crimes involve criminal intent. Some crimes arise from negligence or recklessness. Others are strict liability offenses, meaning that there is no need to prove criminal intent in order to convict the defendant.

In most crimes, however, the law requires a causal connection among criminal intent, criminal conduct, and harm. For instance, an act that violates the law and causes harm may not be treated as a crime by the legal system if criminal intent is absent. This practice is based on the idea that punishment makes sense only if the violator of the law is responsible for his or her behavior. For intent to exist, an individual must have criminal capacity, or be in control of his or her own behavior. Capacity is lacking in people who act under duress, are legally insane, are too young to have criminal capacity (often defined as being under the age of seven), or are not legally adults (usually defined as being between the ages of seven and eighteen).

Juvenile Delinquency

People who violate the law but are not legally adults may be found delinquent by judges in juvenile court. Rather than being convicted of a crime, juveniles are adjudged delinquent. These delinquents may have committed an act that would be a crime if committed by an adult. The designation *juvenile delinquent* is also applied to those who commit *status offenses*, acts such as underage drinking, running away from home, or truancy, which are violations only because those who engage in them are below the age of majority.

The juvenile justice system was developed in the United States late in the nineteenth century, with the first juvenile court established in Illinois in 1899. The juvenile court was a product of efforts by the *child savers,* people committed to providing delinquent adolescents with help rather than punishment. The child savers saw nineteenth-century cities as breeding grounds for crime, especially by recent immigrants, and they tried to prevent juvenile misbehavior by taking young people from the cities and placing them in reformatories in small towns and rural areas. In theory, these reformatories would have the environment of a "healthy" home, and juveniles would be cured of their deviant behavior through education and retraining in middle-class values (Platt, 1977).

Today the label "delinquent" is applied to youthful offenders under the age of nineteen in one state, to those under the age of sixteen or seventeen in twelve states, and to those under the age of eighteen in other states. However, every state has also established some conditions under which juveniles can be prosecuted and punished as adults. This is a result of a widespread belief that fifteen- and sixteen-year-olds sometimes commit serious crimes knowingly, and that the juvenile justice system provides little punishment for them. Thus, in recent years the punishment of adolescent offenders has begun to replace the types of treatment favored by the child savers. One expert estimated that about 240,000 juveniles were held in adult jails in 1986, despite a 1974 federal law that required states receiving federal funds for juvenile programs to remove all juveniles from adult jails and lockups by 1988 or lose those funds (cited in Chambers, 1986). In 1986, there were thirty-three convicted murderers awaiting execution who had committed their capital offenses while under the age of eighteen; five of them had been only fifteen at the time of their crimes. Many critics believe such penalties to be unduly severe for young people, but U.S. Attorney General Edwin Meese 3d has commented, "You can have very vicious criminals at age sixteen" (cited in Ostrow, 1985).

In spite of this apparent growth in the harshness of penalties for young offenders, most states still emphasize treatment of juveniles rather than punishment for the specific acts they have committed. The offender's youth is thought to confer a kind of diminished capacity, and young criminals are thought to be more easily reformed than older ones.

Criminal Sanctions

In its ideal form, the criminal law is specific in nature, uniform in its application, dispassionate in its enforcement, and reflective of the culture's informal norms (Sutherland and Cressey, 1978: 5–8). Criminal law provides a way to control behavior by allowing or prohibiting certain behaviors for particular individuals in specific situations. Thus, in some circumstances a police officer can use lethal force to stop an escaping felon, but a private citizen generally is not permitted to kill an escaping felon. The same act is treated differently because each individual occupies a different status. The law is also specific to the situation. A victim who fears for his or her life during a crime may use lethal force in self-protection and have the action treated as justifiable homicide. However, people generally are not allowed to use lethal force to prevent a simple theft without having to face a charge of manslaughter or murder.

The criminal justice system imposes formal sanctions on those convicted of violating the law. The consequences of these formal sanctions differ from those of such informal sanctions as criticism or banishment from a group. Formal criminal sanctions include the loss of property through a fine, the restriction of freedom through probation, the loss of liberty through imprisonment or incarceration, and even the loss of life through execution.

Formal Laws and Informal Norms

Critical to the functioning of the criminal law is the consistency between formal laws and informal norms. In complex societies such as the United States, where many groups with different norms live side by side, it is inevitable that some laws will not be supported by all groups. Thus a significant proportion of the American public favors the legalization of marijuana, but most people continue to support existing laws that punish those who possess, sell, or use the drug. Even punishment for crimes that involve serious harm may not be fully supported by informal norms. For instance, in 1980 a Yemeni immigrant in California shot to death a fourteen-year-old boy found under the bed of his fifteen-year-old daughter, apparently because the boy had violated the father's strict moral code of Islam. Here the law conflicted with an informal norm about when it was acceptable to take another person's life. The Cross-Cultural Perspective describes a similar situation in contemporary Greece.

In simple tribal societies, informal norms often overlap to a great extent with the law. In these societies there is general agreement between popular attitudes toward right and wrong and the legal definition of crime. This makes for a stable society, even if it is one also characterized by stagnation and unresponsiveness to externally induced change.

A Cross-Cultural Perspective: "Crimes of Honor" in Greece

Conflict between informal norms and the law often characterizes societies undergoing social change. Industrialization and urbanization can divide a country between traditional rural areas and modern urban centers. A modern way of life involves greater reliance on a formal legal system, and the law sometimes conflicts with the standards of behavior in more traditional communities.

In Greece, a society that has a relatively low crime rate, about two-thirds of all murders involve the protection of "family honor." For instance, in a village coffee shop in front of a number of friends and relatives, a fifty year-old waiter shot and killed a young man who was to have become his son-in-law. The victim had abandoned the waiter's daughter just before the wedding, claiming that her dowry, a furnished apartment, was inadequate. The waiter denied being a murderer, saying he had simply done his duty to protect his family's honor.

A Greek professor of criminology explains these "crimes of honor" as follows:

> The feeling of being insulted is compounded by norms of a restricted society, where the prestige of the family is usually the key to public esteem and where the anonymity or broad-mindedness of urban centers is lacking. Resort to murder is the last attempt to regain respect in the eyes of the local community by showing that the offended person would stop at nothing to prove his righteousness. Under these circumstances cold-blooded murder becomes an honor.

The professor also points out that few Greeks adhere to these justifications for murder, and he attributes these crimes to "outdated and distorted values, . . . narrow-mindedness and lack of education." He states that these traits characterize the "least developed parts of Greek rural society," where most of the crimes of honor occur.

Greek law does not exempt these killings from punishment. However, the courts often take informal norms into account when these offenses are tried. One official in Greece's Justice Ministry describes the criminal justice system's effort to resolve differences between the law and informal norms as follows:

> Premeditated murder is murder and cannot justify different legislation, whatever provokes it. But in practice Greek courts unofficially take such traditionally established sentiments into consideration and can be lenient if the culprit has been provoked to extremes.

SOURCE: Based on "'Crimes of Honor' Still the Pattern in Rural Greece," *The New York Times*, February 10, 1980, p. 22.

In complex industrial societies, such as the United States, there is less overlap between the law and informal norms. If the lack of consistency between the two becomes too great, the government may resort to harsh sanctions against those whose actions conflict with the law. This conflict between the law and informal norms may undermine popular support for the government, but it can also keep a society flexible and responsive to change and new ideas.

The law is mostly likely to reflect informal norms in a society that has a "rule of law," a system in which the law is made through specified channels, announced to the public, and enforced consistently (Selznick, 1969: 11–18; Sutherland and Cressey, 1978: 4–12). Institutions that permit or encourage popular communication with lawmakers increase the consistency between informal norms and the law. Consistency is also greater when laws are effectively communicated to the public by lawmakers, through either the schools or the press; this socializes citizens in the law and encourages conformity to legal standards.

Social Origins of the Criminal Law

A detailed examination of all of the factors that influence the criminal law would require a massive book. Here we look at the social sources of the criminal law to which sociologists have paid particular attention.

Crime as a Social Phenomenon

Criminal law is a social phenomenon, and crime itself is a social product. Behavior defined as crime in one society may occur in a different society and not be regarded as suitable for punishment there.

We can see the social nature of crime by looking at variations in the legal definition of theft in different societies. Although most societies define theft of property as a crime, there are significant differences in the way this behavior is treated. In Norway, petty theft from a relative with whom the thief lives is not treated as a crime. In Colombia, thieves are exempted from criminal sanctions if they can show that they or their family had a pressing need for food or clothing, that there was no legal way to meet those needs, that no violence was used to perpetrate the theft, and that no more was taken than was necessary (Radzinowicz and King, 1977). The Soviet Union distinguishes between the theft of private property and the theft of socialist property, a distinction based on state ownership of land and the means of production (Chalidze, 1977; Shelley, 1981b; Simis, 1982). In industrial societies, taking a neighbor's property for personal use is generally regarded as a crime, but in some tribal societies one may actually be expected to take and use a neighbor's property in time of need. Understanding why one society permits such behavior while another condemns it as crime requires a careful study of the social structure, values, and level of economic development of each society.

Theoretical Perspectives on the Criminal Law

Two important theories of the development of the criminal law are the conflict perspective and the consensus perspective. Both emphasize the political and social nature of the law, but conflict theorists claim that the law benefits some groups to the detriment of others, and consensus theorists regard the law more as a reflection of popular agreement on standards of behavior.

A Cross-Cultural Perspective: The Black Market in Peru

In Peru, the executive branch—the President and the government departments— has used its power and resources to define many kinds of economic activity as illegal. Economic activity must meet the requirements of about 500,000 laws, executive orders, decrees, ministerial resolutions, and bureaucratic regulations. According to Mario Vargas Llosa, a Peruvian novelist, this "byzantine legal system seems designed to favor those already favored and to punish the rest by making them permanent outlaws" (p. 30). The multitude of laws has retarded economic development through legitimate channels, has encouraged bribery of government officials in order to circumvent legal restrictions, and has given rise to an extensive black market or "informal sector." According to Vargas Llosa, this black market is "the spontaneous and creative response of the impoverished masses to the state's inability to satisfy their basic needs" (p. 30).

In 1983, a research institute in Peru tried an experiment to document the difficulty and cost of registering a small workshop, one with two sewing machines. The researchers decided to pay no bribes unless failure to do so would shut down the shop. Bureaucrats solicited bribes on ten occasions, but the researchers had to pay bribes only twice to keep the shop operating. To register the shop took them nearly a year, cost them about $1,200 in expenses and lost wages, and required the full-time labor of four workers. Clearly, anyone of modest means would be unable to comply with the legal requirements of registering such a shop, thereby undermining economic development through legitimate channels and forcing anyone who used those channels to commit the crime of bribery. In many cases, such shops simply operate illegally, without being registered, thus contributing to Peru's large and growing black market.

In Lima alone, the black market supports more than 400,000 people, and four-fifths of the 331 markets there have been built by black market entrepreneurs. Half of the population of that city lives in housing built by the black market, and 95 percent of public transportation there is provided by the "informal sector." Such black market activity has become essential to the Peruvian economy and seems to be a more productive way of accomplishing economic goals than the legitimate market.

SOURCE: Based on Mario Vargas Llosa, "In Defense of the Black Market," *The New York Times Magazine,* February 22, 1987, pp. 28–47.

THE CONFLICT PERSPECTIVE   The *conflict perspective* sees criminal law as closely intertwined with the distribution of political power and economic resources in a society (Gordon, 1973; Taylor, Walton, and Young, 1973, 1975a; Balkan, Berger, and Schmidt, 1980; Inciardi, 1980b; Platt and Takagi, 1981). Conflict theorists argue that only certain behavior is legally defined as crime and that the people who control power and resources determine which kinds of behavior will be defined as crime and which kinds will be permitted (see the Cross-Cultural Perspective). The criminal law in a capitalist system thus reflects the will of the economic elite, and behavior that threatens the interests of that elite—such as theft and violence by the poor—will be harshly sanctioned (Reiman, 1984).

Some conflict theorists assert that criminologists should link the study of crime to the pursuit of social justice and the liberation of oppressed people (Krisberg, 1975; Schwendinger and Schwendinger, 1975). This view denies the "objective" nature of criminal behavior and regards offenders as victims of oppression. Property crime, for instance, is regarded as an effort to accumulate property as rapidly as possible, a goal highly valued in capitalist systems. These conflict theorists believe that criminology should be "normatively committed to the abolition of inequalities in wealth and power"; it should not try to find those factors that distinguish offenders from nonoffenders or seek ways to change people who violate the law (Taylor, Walton, and Young, 1975b: 44).

The conflict perspective claims that the criminal justice system in capitalist societies is biased against those who are disadvantaged by class or minority-group status. Conflict theorists argue that lower-class people are more likely than middle-class people to be watched by the police, arrested in suspicious circumstances, held in jail rather than released on bail, tried in court, found guilty, and given harsh sentences (Chambliss, 1969; Reiman, 1984).

The conflict perspective directs attention to the origin of the criminal law. Its critical approach forces criminologists to reexamine their premises and their conclusions. This perspective has also shifted attention from the "conventional crimes" of murder, rape, and robbery to white-collar crime and government corruption, even though conflict theorists have produced relatively few empirical studies of these offenses.

The conflict perspective does not explain why capitalist systems such as Japan sometimes have low crime rates, whereas socialist societies such as the Soviet Union seem to have significant amounts of crime (Clifford, 1976; Chalidze, 1977; Simis, 1982). Even if socialist nations did have low crime rates, this might be accounted for by the oppressive social control that exists in some totalitarian socialist states, rather than by the greater amount of social justice there.

THE CONSENSUS PERSPECTIVE In contrast to the conflict perspective stands the *consensus perspective*. This position claims that the criminal law represents social consensus or agreement about which kinds of behavior should be punished by the state. Consensus theorists propose that the law reflects shared values and norms held by all members of the society, rather than the norms and values of a particular group. Consensus is derived from discussion and compromise by elected lawmakers, rather than imposed on society by a group that controls political power or economic resources (Durkheim, 1895, 1933: 70–110).

Consensus theorists see crime as behavior that exceeds the society's limits of tolerance. In this view, crime is behavior detrimental to the public interest, rather than behavior detrimental to the narrow interests of organized groups that are able to influence the law. For the consensus theorist, the critical question becomes why some people do not share consensual values and thus violate the law, rather than why the law defines their behavior as criminal.

USING THE CONFLICT AND CONSENSUS PERSPECTIVES Probably the best way to view the criminal law is to examine the degree of consensus and the degree of conflict involved in the passage of a law, as well as the extent of public support for the existing law. Some laws reflect a widespread social consensus; for example, murder and rape are almost universally regarded as harmful acts that ought to be punished (Brown, 1952; Clifford, 1978). Other laws reflect the outcome of social conflict among groups; for instance, an antitrust law in the United States was the result of a victory by small businesses, labor, and farmers over large corporations (Quinney, 1970).

Conflict over a particular law can give rise to consensus about that law over time (Glaser, 1978: 15). For example, laws about predatory acts such as crimes against property and crimes of violence may be initiated through social conflict but perpetuated through consensus.

Social Sources of the Law

One important source of the criminal law is conflict between organized interest groups. A second source is public opinion, which can product changes in the law as attitudes shift over time. A third influence is expert evidence that points to the need for different criminal sanctions.

INTEREST GROUPS *Interest groups,* or people who organize to further their shared economic, political, or moral goals, are often able to use resources such as money and political power to translate their interests into law. Interest groups may be social classes or may be based on a shared economic goal, but often they have a moral rather than economic basis

Some interest groups base themselves on "moral indignation," a sense that those who "do wrong" should be punished for the sake of justice or for their own good. Sometimes moral indignation is aroused and organized by *moral entrepreneurs,* people who promote the idea that certain behavior is harmful and should be punished (Becker, 1973). One example was Anita Bryant's campaign to prevent and overturn local laws that guaranteed gays certain legal rights. Support for this antihomosexual movement came from people seeking to protect a particular way of life and set of values from those they felt were threatening it; the supporters' interests were not primarily economic in nature.

One law that was influenced in a relatively minor way by economic interests was the Prohibition Amendment that was in effect from 1920 to 1933. The most important support for making the sale of alcoholic beverages illegal came from temperance forces who sought to protect "the American way of life" from immigrants who supposedly drank and threatened that way of life. The advocates of prohibition sought to protect their position as exemplars of a particular life style, rather than to augment their economic well-being. Several factors led to the repeal of the Prohibition Amendment, including a lack of resources for

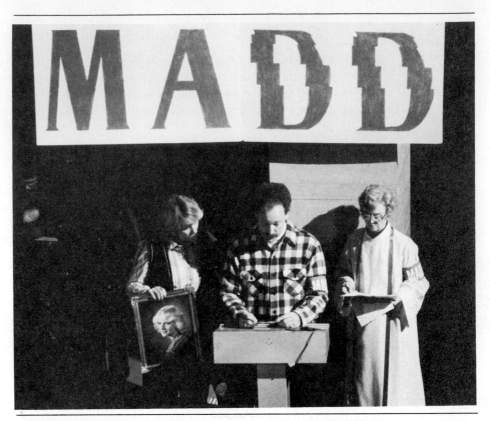

In recent years, moral entrepreneurs have argued forcefully that drunk driving should be regarded as a serious crime and punished more harshly. Here the grieving parents of a daughter killed in a car accident address a Mothers Against Drunk Drivers rally to arouse support for stricter laws on drunk driving. *Source: Michael Siluk/EKM— Nepenthe*

enforcing the law and the absence of popular support. Another reason for repeal was economic: New jobs and additional tax revenue that the liquor industry could provide appealed to a nation in the throes of the Great Depression.

Interest groups sometimes succeed in having a law enacted but then fail to get it enforced. The resources and influence of a group may be expended at the enactment stage so that there are no means left to press for enforcement once the law is passed. This was one reason for the failure of Prohibition; the "drys" were able to get the amendment passed but were unable to secure adequate funding, committed agents, and public support for the Prohibition Bureau (Gusfield, 1963).

PUBLIC OPINION Another important influence on the criminal law is public opinion. For example, popular response to brutal attacks on elderly victims by

FIGURE 1.1 Social Sources of the Law

young robbers led the New York state legislature to consider a special law under which offenders who assaulted and robbed the elderly would be given more severe penalties than criminals who attacked younger victims. A new category of crime defined by the age of the victim would have been created. The proposed law passed the state Senate and Assembly but was vetoed by the governor in 1977 (Fishman, 1978).

Popular opinion has kept laws against the use, sale, and possession of marijuana on the books, but in recent years in many states the moderation of public sentiments has led to a reduction in penalties for these offenses. The very definition of certain drugs as illegal is largely a result of ideological positions and moral attitudes held by the public. For example, alcohol and cigarettes are legal substances under most circumstances, even though their harmful effects have been demonstrated more clearly than have those of marijuana. Still, marijuana is seen by a majority of the public as a harmful drug that should be kept illegal, and alcohol and cigarettes are seen as substances that should be free of criminal sanctions.

EXPERT EVIDENCE Evidence collected and presented by experts who have a recognized claim to objectivity may, on occasion, influence the law. For example, research by Harvey Wiley between 1902 and 1906 on the harmful effects of food preservatives on people led to passage of the Federal Food and Drug Act of 1906, which established the Food and Drug Administration (Anderson, 1958). Another influence on this law was the scandal created by Upton Sinclair's novel *The Jungle* (1906, 1960), which revealed the filth that characterized meat-packing plants. Public opinion and interest groups also played a part in the passage of this law, but research evidence and a vivid, thinly fictionalized account of the consequences of no regulation convinced lawmakers to establish federal regulation of food and drugs.

Evidence presented by experts was also used to create a special category of criminal offender known as the sexual psychopath. In most states in which laws against these offenders were passed, a series of dramatic sex crimes had aroused public demand for the punishment and treatment of offenders. Psychiatrists

Using Criminology: Expert Witnesses and the Death Penalty

In the U.S. Supreme Court decision in *Furman* v. *Georgia* (1972), Justice Thurgood Marshall wrote that if people were fully informed about the nature of the death penalty, they would find it "shocking, unjust, and unacceptable." This "Marshall hypothesis" was put to the test in a 1984 case in which a sociologist and several other experts presented testimony to a jury in California.

In this case, a black man named Maxwell had been convicted by a jury of two counts of first-degree murder, acquitted on three other counts of murder, and had had five additional counts of murder dismissed because the jury could not agree on verdicts. The jury that found him guilty then had to decide in a separate trial, the penalty phase of the case, whether he should be sentenced to die or imprisoned for life.

To avoid the death penalty, Maxwell's court-appointed attorneys sought to educate the jurors about the exact nature of capital punishment, believing as Justice Marshall did that well-informed people would have difficulty imposing the death penalty. The defense team called as witnesses a correctional officer in charge of executions at San Quentin, a former death-watch officer, a former chaplain who had worked with Death Row prisoners, and a reporter who had witnessed executions. From their testimony emerged "a chilling glimpse of the life, final hours, and death of the condemned" (p. 128).

The defense attorneys also emphasized to the jurors that though guilt beyond a reasonable doubt was the basis for finding a defendant guilty as charged, to impose the death penalty they should be absolutely certain that the defendant had committed the crimes. Given that Maxwell had been convicted on only two of the ten counts of murder he had faced, the defense attorneys believed the jurors had some doubts about his actual guilt. They then sought to convince the jurors that no one should be executed if there were any lingering doubts at all.

To do this, they called sociologist Michael L. Radelet to testify about a research project on which he and philosopher Hugo Adam Bedau were working, a study of defendants who were innocent but had nevertheless been found guilty, and in some cases even executed. At the time of his testimony,

---

were often influential members of commissions that considered changes in the law, and they provided what was widely regarded as objective evidence on which to base laws that defined sex offenders as a group distinct from other criminals (Sutherland, 1950).

The Legalistic Definition of Crime

We have seen that the criminal law is affected by social influences such as interest groups, public opinion, and expert evidence. No behavior is intrinsically crimi-

Radelet had identified nearly one hundred cases in which defendants who had been sentenced to die were later shown to be innocent, and about a dozen cases in which doubts about guilt had surfaced only after execution. In most of these cases, the prosecution had admitted its own error.

Radelet met with the defense attorneys to prepare his testimony, focusing on what his research did and did not establish and trying to anticipate questions the prosecutor would ask. In reflecting on his role as a witness, Radelet says:

> I feel strongly that, while on the stand, answers must be given from a base of neutrality rather than as an advocate. Nevertheless, the defense in this case had an advantage over the prosecution because they had the time to figure out how best to use and direct my testimony, and for this they had my collaboration. To this extent, my role approached that of an advocate in the pretrial preparation of this case, even if it did not on the stand. On the stand, I adhere to a strict position of value neutrality, and I consider my personal opinions about the death penalty *and* the fact that I am serving as a defense witness totally irrelevant when deciding how to answer posited questions (p. 125).

The prosecutor was willing to admit Radelet's testimony about his research, but he had questions about the methods used in the study, about the way in which the innocence of defendants was ascertained, and about the frequency with which such errors occurred. The prosecutor tried to show that the project had limits by demonstrating that the researchers had not spoken to any homicide detectives, had not observed any death penalty jury trials, and had not tried to establish the reliability of the evidence used in those cases included as miscarriages of justice. Radelet acknowledged the weak links in the study, while maintaining that innocents had been executed and that the stakes of capital punishment in the absence of absolute certainty were very high.

The testimony of Radelet and the other witnesses was influential, for the jury voted unanimously against the death penalty and imposed a life sentence on Maxwell. Interviews by the defense attorneys with the jurors after their verdict in this penalty phase of the case showed that the expert testimony had shifted their opinion against the death penalty, for ten of the twelve jurors said they had favored execution after the first phase of the case in which they had found Maxwell guilty.

SOURCE: Based on Michael L. Radelet, "Sociologists as Expert Witnesses in Capital Cases: A Case Study," in Patrick R. Anderson and L. Thomas Winfree, Jr., eds., *Expert Witnesses: Criminologists in the Courtroom.* Albany: State University of New York Press, 1987, pp. 119–134.

nal; it must be defined as crime by the law. In this sense, both crime and the criminal law are social in origin.

Some criminologists would prefer that criminology focus primarily on the process by which criminal laws are created. For the most part, their work pays little attention to the content of criminal behavior or its causes (Quinney, 1970). In this book, we will spend more time examining the content and causes of criminal behavior than we do exploring the origin of criminal laws, while still recognizing that those laws are social in origin. This position treats crime in a legalistic way, beginning with the law's definition of crime and studying behavior that violates the law, rather than regarding the development of the law as the primary topic of study.

Some criminologists have criticized this legalistic approach, claiming that it implies an acceptance of the values of those who make the law (Becker, 1973; Platt, 1975). This is not necessarily the case, however, for it is certainly possible to recognize the existence of a body of criminal law and examine the content and causes of behavior that breaks that law, without at the same time giving one's moral support to that body of law or personally condemning behavior that violates it.

Sociologists who have sought to replace a legalistic definition of crime with one that is sociological or personal have encountered problems, for crime is by definition a violation of a legal norm rather than a violation of an informal norm, a "conduct norm," or a "human right" (Sellin, 1938; Platt, 1975; Schwendinger and Schwendinger, 1975). Nonlegal norms are less stable and certainly less easy to define than are criminal laws. Abandoning the study of violations of legal norms for the study of violations of informal norms leads either to the general study of deviant behavior or to a study of behavior that the individual sociologist happens to believe is wrong or immoral.

Criminology: The Study of Criminal Behavior

Criminology is a discipline that gathers and analyzes empirical data in order to explain violations of the criminal law and societal reactions to those violations. Because crime includes so many kinds of behavior, criminologists have developed *typologies,* or sets of categories of crimes and criminal careers. In the following chapter, we present a typology of crimes, and in Chapter 11 we look at typologies of criminal careers.

Rather than organize this book around types of crimes, with a chapter devoted to violent crime, another to property crime, and still others to different kinds of offenses, this book is organized around concepts and theories that criminologists have developed and used to explain different kinds of crime. For instance, robbery and price fixing are clearly different forms of behavior, as we make clear in Chapter 2, but both offenses might be explained by the concept of relative deprivation, the idea that people commit crimes when they believe they have less than others with whom they compare themselves and when they think they are rightfully entitled to more than they have.

The types of crime examined in the following chapter are repeatedly returned to throughout the book. We look at the financial, physical, and social costs of each type of crime. We investigate the social and economic sources of different offenses. We also explore in detail the needs and motivations of people who commit various kinds of crimes, the way they reduce their commitment to the law, the process by which they learn to commit crime, and the way in which they select opportunities to commit crime.

Needs and Motivations

The needs and motivations of people who engage in crime may be biological in origin, psychological in nature, or socially induced. Thus, a murder may be committed by one person because a brain tumor led to violence, by another person because of delusions about persecution by others, or by a member of a juvenile gang who is trying to impress peers by being tough.

Reducing Commitment to the Law

Having certain needs, desires, or motivations is a necessary but not sufficient reason to commit a crime. Because all people to some extent learn that they should abide by the law, potential offenders must reduce their commitment to the law before they violate it. The critical question becomes, "Why, in a society in which such actions are widely known to be criminal and severely punishable, are they committed?" (Walker, 1974: 61–62). People who violate the law are often only weakly attached to it and to people and institutions that support the law, including parents, teachers, and peers. Being unconcerned about the opinion of others who are committed to a conventional way of life makes it easier to neutralize the constraints of the law. People also neutralize the influence of the law by using rationalizations to justify their violations; for instance, they may claim that their circumstances make it acceptable for them to commit a crime.

Learning Skills to Commit Crime

Another factor critical to the perpetration of many crimes is the learning of skills needed to commit a crime. This learning may be from the general culture, from the mass media, from other criminals, or from noncriminals who convey values conducive to crime. Safecrackers must learn how to "blow" a safe or pick a lock. Armed robbers have less to learn, because holding a pistol and demanding money require few specific skills. Some offenders use specialized skills that they have employed for legitimate purposes to commit a crime; one example is an accountant who uses bookkeeping skills to embezzle funds from a company by manipulating the books.

Opportunities to Violate the Law

Given the need or desire to commit a crime, the reduction in commitment to the law, and the learning of the requisite skills, another factor needed before a crime can be committed is the opportunity to violate the law. Crime is sometimes situational in nature; that is, people who might not otherwise think of breaking the law may commit a crime if they are confronted with a tempting opportunity to make an illicit gain with little risk. Others systematically seek opportunities to commit profitable crimes, planning their offenses in advance and organizing a group of criminals to carry out illegal acts. Social change can increase opportunities for crime. For example, bank robberies have increased with the development of suburban branches that lack good security, and auto thefts have increased as the number of cars available to be stolen has grown.

Criminal Careers

Our conceptual scheme can help us to understand the reasons that people commit criminal acts. When individual acts of crime by an offender accumulate over time, we speak of a *criminal career,* a sequence of criminal acts that may lead an offender to change his or her self-concept, behavior, and commitment to a life of crime. An understanding of criminal behavior requires knowledge of the factors that give rise to individual acts that violate the law, but it also requires detailed information about the way that those acts add up to a criminal career.

Reactions to Crime

Society responds to crime in many ways. Some of these are institutional; for instance, the criminal justice system responds by punishing those who are convicted of violating the law. Other responses are less formal, such as the reaction of a bystander to a crime or community action against drug dealers.

COMMUNITY REACTIONS TO CRIME A community's social structure influences its amount of crime. Tightly knit neighborhoods are often able to keep the crime rate low by maintaining informal social control in an area. Public surveillance of the streets and willingness to call the police can deter potential offenders from violating the law or cause them to commit their offenses elsewhere. We look at informal social control as one response to crime and as a factor involved in the causation of crime. We examine the social conditions conducive to bystander intervention in a crime and explore collective reactions to crime such as citizen patrols and community action groups.

THE CRIMINAL JUSTICE SYSTEM A full understanding of the nature of crime requires attention to the criminal justice system: the police, the courts, and the prisons. What criminals do and how criminal careers develop are influenced by the agents of criminal justice (Pepinsky, 1980). We look at the way that the exercise of police discretion influences who is arrested and who is not. We look at the way that race and sex play a part in the processing of suspects.

The reactions of the criminal justice system to suspected offenders can push them into criminal careers or deter them from further crimes. However, there is much to learn about crime without limiting the analysis to the behavior of those who are found guilty in court. For instance, we can learn much about robbery by studying police reports of robberies that do not lead to arrest, and we can learn much from interviews with the victims of those robberies.

IDEOLOGICAL JUSTIFICATIONS FOR PUNISHMENT The formal responses of the criminal justice system to crime are based on several ideological justifications for punishment. These justifications reflect ideas about why offenders should be punished and what might be accomplished by punishing them.

Deterrence and Incapacitation. The "first line of defense" against crime is deterrence, the use of sanctions to prevent crime by raising the cost of crime to offenders. In this book we look at the assumptions that underlie the deterrence model and examine research on the effects of severity, certainty, and promptness of punishment on the deterrence of crime.

We also examine a rationale for punishment closely related to deterrence: incapacitation. Some people believe crime can be prevented if offenders are locked up for longer periods; keeping them off the streets is seen as a way to keep them from victimizing the public.

Retribution. When the threat of sanctions fails to deter crime, a second rationale for punishment usually enters the picture: retribution. This rationale does not suggest that punishment should try to reduce crime, but only that those who do wrong ought to suffer in return. Moreover, this philosophy of retribution states that suffering should be in proportion to the seriousness of the harm produced and the blameworthiness of the offender.

Rehabilitation. Throughout most of the twentieth century, the rationale for punishment that has dominated American penology is rehabilitation, the idea that convicted offenders should be reformed so they will not commit crime again. Recently, this model has lost some favor because considerable research has shown that treatment programs have been ineffective in changing offenders. We look at the way the police, the courts, and the prisons have been influenced by the idea of rehabilitation, and we evaluate the various treatment methods that have been tried.

Solving the Crime Problem

Conservatives, liberals, and radicals have proposed different ways to solve the crime problem, but in recent years most American political leaders have focused on reform of the criminal justice system as the best way to reduce crime. A second approach to crime reduction which has received less attention from politicians is situational crime prevention, the policy of making it more difficult for offenders to victimize people and property. A third approach, eradicating the causes of crime, has also received little attention from political leaders recently, but it may be the only effective way to reduce crime in the long run.

Ideally, criminology should begin with a description of criminal behavior, using crime statistics and interviews with offenders. It should then proceed to theories that explain the causes of crime, and conclude with policies derived from those descriptions and theories. Much criminological work does not take this form. It is either descriptive, nontheoretical, and lacking in policy analysis; or it is theoretical without empirical evidence or policy implications; or it prescribes policies but lacks supporting evidence and theoretical justification. The effort in this book is to integrate all three approaches—the descriptive, the theoretical, and the prescriptive.

Methods of Criminological Research

Criminologists have used different research strategies to study crime. Some offenses have posed knotty problems. For instance, criminologists have had a difficult time gaining access to people who engage in white-collar crime. However, in recent years criminologists have devised ways to study white-collar crime. They have used court records, data from regulatory agencies, autobiographical accounts, interviews with the few white-collar offenders in prison, and interviews with retired corporate executives (see, e.g., Clinard and Yeager, 1980; Clinard, 1983).

Even though the personal values of criminologists may influence the kinds of crime they decide to study and their research methods, it is possible to be relatively detached in the collection and interpretation of data. Stating a hypothesis and gathering data that might support or refute that hypothesis help to increase objectivity, even if the selection of the problem for study—for example, robbery or white-collar crime—reflects personal values.

In this section, we look in detail at four research strategies employed by criminologists, giving an example of each. This will give the flavor of how social scientists go about the task of studying crime. Then, we examine several other methods that researchers have also used to study criminal behavior and the criminal justice system.

Comparative and Historical Research

One way to illuminate the problem of crime causation is to study violations of the law in other societies and at other times. This process allows us to gain insight into the relationship between crime and factors such as level of economic development and rate of urbanization. *Comparative research* can be used to evaluate whether a theory of crime developed in one society also explains crime in other societies, that is, whether a theory is universally true or limited in scope. The comparative approach also helps to generate theory, for differences in crime from one society to another must fit a general theory of criminal behavior (Bennett, 1980).

Comparative research of this sort is uncommon. Crime has been studied in countries other than the United States, but researchers rarely collect data simultaneously in different countries so they can make direct comparisons (Beirne, 1983). Methodological problems with crime statistics gathered by the police, the courts, or the prisons also make comparisons difficult (Johnson and Barak-Glantz, 1983). Comparative research is hampered, too, by geographic, political, and linguistic barriers, by the lack of funding, and by the absence of a research tradition in some societies (Clifford, 1978; Kaiser, 1978). Moreover, criminologists from one society sometimes approach the study of crime in another nation with an ethnocentric bias or a theoretical preference that distorts their interpretation of the data (Johnson and Barak-Glantz, 1983).

Similar in some ways to comparative research in contemporary societies is *historical research*, which examines the same society at different times and looks at the ways that crime has changed with economic and social development. Historical research often requires reliance on nonstatistical material, although historical researchers have used official statistics from the past and have quantified material from historical documents. These researchers also use accounts by observers of the time, records of legislative hearings, narrative material from court files, and other documentary evidence to learn about crime in the past.

Historical studies put contemporary crime into perspective, show how people have reacted to crime in the past, and suggest problems that may be encountered by nations now undergoing social and economic change. For example, one review of historical research concludes that the recent upsurge of violent crime in Western societies is a deviation from a decline in violence that has been going on for more than a century (Gurr, 1981). A study of public reactions to crime in nineteenth-century Paris shows that the "law-and-order" movement in the United States during the late 1960s and early 1970s was not unique (Chevalier, 1973). One historical study that illuminates the nature of crime in today's developing societies is J. J. Tobias's *Crime and Industrial Society in the 19th Century* (1967).

TOBIAS'S STUDY OF CRIME IN NINETEENTH-CENTURY ENGLAND   J. J. Tobias's study of crime in industrializing England found that the crime statistics of that period were practically worthless for systematic study. As a result, he had to rely on parliamentary reports and contemporary accounts to piece together a picture of crime during this era.

Tobias discovered that crime rates were high early in the nineteenth century because social institutions had failed to respond to a sizeable increase in population; more specifically, there was a growth in the number of young people in the country, but no commensurate growth in employment opportunities. Migration from rural areas and small towns to larger towns and cities proved unsettling to many people, and these larger towns and cities provided ample opportunities for crime as well as anonymity, which reduced the risk of arrest.

During the nineteenth century, crime decreased as the social environment became more settled. Economic development increased job opportunities and raised incomes, and government resources were used to introduce social services for the disadvantaged. The police and the courts also changed over the course of the century, from a system that had a low rate of detection and severe penalties for the few offenders who were convicted, to one that had more lenient sentences but a higher rate of detection. Tobias argues that this change enhanced the deterrent effect of the law and contributed to the decline in the crime rate.

It is difficult to support Tobias's interpretation of these historical changes with precise data, but he provides convincing documentary evidence of the social changes that accompanied the long-term decline in the crime rate. His conclusions are also consistent with evidence about the changing nature of crime in societies that are now undergoing social and economic change.

Biographies

A fruitful way to study the sources of criminal behavior and the development of criminal careers is to examine in detail the experiences of a single offender. This *biographical method* reveals the needs and motivations of the offender, the way that commitment to the law is reduced, the way that criminal skills are learned, the obstacles encountered in pursuing a legitimate career and an illegitimate life style, the pattern of criminal activity over a lifetime, and the consequences of contact with the criminal justice system (Rettig, Torres, and Garrett, 1977).

One problem with the biographical method is that the criminal who is studied may not be representative of all offenders. Separating an offender's experiences into those that are idiosyncratic and those that are common to other offenders is a difficult undertaking that requires more information than can be provided by one criminal's biography. The richness of the account of one offender's life in crime thus sacrifices the representativeness provided by research on a sample of offenders, even though the biographical method often yields hypotheses that can be tested on a cross section of offenders.

Another problem with the biographical method is that offenders may intentionally or unintentionally distort their experiences. They may do this because of faulty memories, because they view the past in light of their present circumstances, or because they want to glorify and romanticize themselves to the interviewer (Rettig, Torres, and Garrett, 1977). This problem of distortion can be minimized by double-checking the accuracy of the account with the offender at different times or by interviewing friends and relatives of the offender (Klockars, 1974).

An early example of the biographical technique is Edwin Sutherland's (1937) study of "Chic Conwell," a professional thief who recounted his life of crime in great detail. William Chambliss (King and Chambliss, 1984) used a similar approach to study "Harry King," a "box man" or safecracker. Another valuable biographical study is the story of a heroin addict and thief named Manny (Rettig, Torres, and Garrett, 1977). The biographical method has also been used to good advantage by Carl Klockars in his study, *The Professional Fence* (1974), and by Darrell Steffensmeier in his book, *The Fence* (1986).

STEFFENSMEIER'S STUDY OF A FENCE   Steffensmeier initially met the fence, who is a middleman between thieves who steal property and members of the public who buy stolen goods, through the recommendations of several burglars he had been questioning as part of a study of female criminality. He interviewed the fence, whom he called "Sam Goodman," while the fence was serving time in prison for receiving stolen goods and on numerous occasions after his release.

In one chapter of *The Fence*, Sam tells how he became involved in criminal activity. He was self-reliant by the age of fifteen, working full-time and realizing that he was "out for a buck." His attraction to a fast life and hustling was reinforced by an uncle who led a similar life and had been in prison. From occasional petty theft, Sam graduated to burglary at age seventeen, being arrested and serving time in a juvenile reformatory. After his release, he worked full-time but continued to commit burglaries as part of a gang. Following his release from prison after another burglary conviction, he started to work for a furniture manufacturer. Eventually, he opened a secondhand furniture and antiques shop, though he continued to commit burglaries. Sam used his shop as a front to sell goods he had stolen. Other dealers began to pay him to upholster or doctor stolen goods for resale, and thieves began to bring him stolen merchandise. Sam's fencing took on larger-scale proportions after another prison term, and his burglaries became less frequent. Later he served time for receiving stolen goods, but after his release he seemed to become established more as a legitimate dealer in secondhand goods and antiques, though he did fence on a small scale. Steffensmeier's presentation of Sam's life illuminates the development of one criminal career, though Klockars's study of another fence shows quite a different pattern of criminal career development.

Steffensmeier looks at the way fences buy goods from thieves. Because of their greater experience and knowledge, fences tend to dominate thieves in the pricing of stolen goods. The thieves often need money quickly, have few options other than to agree to the fence's offer, and are under pressure to get rid of the stolen merchandise. However, fences must pay a fair price so that thieves will come back to them again with stolen goods.

Steffensmeier's study of Sam Goodman offers rich insights into the crime of fencing. Steffensmeier details the network in which the fence is embedded, and the way that the fence interacts with thieves, criminal justice officials, antiques dealers and collectors, truckers, dockworkers, competing fences, and many other people. Steffensmeier looks at the rewards of fencing, including money, reputation in the criminal community, excitement, and a sense of mastery over one's life. Another important contribution of this study is insight into the ways that Sam justifies his fencing. He claims that a fence is not the same thing as a thief, does little harm to the victims of theft, does not differ much from legitimate businesspeople, is able to operate only with the support of legitimate people, breaks no more rules than most people, and does a lot of good for others. Later in this book we will see that this process of justifying violations of the law is an important aspect of the development of criminal behavior.

Patterns of Crime

Another way to study crime is to look at it as a social phenomenon with a specific form or structure. This study of *patterns of crime* often involves the use of police statistics to determine where crime is committed, who commits it, who is victimized, and what are the major dimensions of the criminal act. Research of this kind looks at the spatial distribution of crime in a city, the social background of offenders and victims, relationships between offenders and victims, and the social processes that lead to crime.

This patterns-of-crime approach assumes that police records can provide a comprehensive and valid description of crime and its participants. However, as we will see later in the book, police statistics may not be very representative of all of the crime that occurs in a community. For instance, police records in Philadelphia, where this method has often been used, contain many details about those crimes that are reported to and recorded by the police, but there is evidence that a smaller proportion of all crimes that actually occur in Philadelphia are reported and recorded than is true for other large American cities (Skogan, 1976b: 111–112). Thus, Philadelphia crime statistics may not reflect the actual nature of crime in that city very well.

Patterns-of-crime studies are useful in describing the criminal act and in providing information on the prior arrest records of offenders and victims. However, they usually do not deal with the issue of crime causation in much depth. These studies do not tell us much about how offenders reduce their commitment to the law, learn criminal skills, or find opportunities to commit crime. The failure to interview offenders as a part of the study of patterns of crime is a major shortcoming of this research technique. In crimes such as homicide, where a high proportion of offenders are caught and convicted, much could be learned from interviews that cannot be discovered in police reports.

The patterns-of-crime approach has been used extensively at the University of Pennsylvania's Center for Studies in Criminology and Criminal Law, where Marvin Wolfgang pioneered the approach in his *Patterns in Criminal Homicide* (1958). Robbery and rape have also been studied using the same approach (Normandeau, 1968; Amir, 1971). A national study of four violent crimes in seventeen cities used a similar research strategy (Curtis, 1974).

WOLFGANG'S STUDY OF HOMICIDE   Wolfgang used police records on homicide from 1948 through 1952 in Philadelphia to analyze the race, sex, and age of homicide offenders and victims, the methods and weapons used to commit murder, the temporal and spatial patterns of homicide, the presence of alcohol in the offender and the victim at the time of the crime, the previous criminal records of offenders and victims, and the motives of offenders. He also explored the interpersonal relationships of offenders and victims, homicides committed during other crimes, and the extent to which victims contributed to their own murders. He looked at the solution of homicide cases by the police and at the court's disposition of charges against suspects.

One important finding that emerged from Wolfgang's research was that offenders and victims in homicide cases are often intimately associated with each other. For instance, about one-fourth of the homicides involved an offender and a victim who were relatives, and an additional 28.2 percent involved offenders and victims who were close friends. Homicides between strangers were relatively rare, accounting for only one-eighth of the cases. This finding helped to focus criminologists' attention on the interpersonal dynamics of intimate relationships as a factor that can lead to lethal violence.

Another important conclusion was that homicides frequently occur in a context that includes the use of alcohol. Alcohol was absent in the homicide situation in only 36.4 percent of the cases. In 43.5 percent of the murders, both the offender and the victim had been drinking, in 9.2 percent of the cases only the victim had been drinking, and in 10.9 percent of the cases only the offender had been drinking.

Wolfgang's study of homicide provides many other important findings. For example, he showed that most murders occur between an offender and a victim of the same race; murders of whites by blacks or of blacks by whites are relatively rare. He also found that murder rates were highest among young black males, a finding he later used to support his theory of a subculture of violence.

The Cohort Study

One problem with some research techniques is the lack of a time dimension; that is, little attention is paid to the way a criminal career develops over time or the way crime rates increase or decrease. One strategy that introduces a time dimension follows a carefully defined group of people who are in a common situation over a period of time. Such a group is called a *cohort*. A cohort of all the individuals born in a given year will experience similar events over their lifetimes, even though they may be affected differently by those events. For instance, all people born in 1915 experienced the Great Depression during their adolescence, although some were exposed to abject poverty during that era and others were relatively insulated from its effects.

The ideal way to carry out a cohort study is to begin to collect data at an early age for the members of a cohort and then follow them through adolescence and into adulthood. Such a study might take as long as twenty-five years to complete, if we assume that little crime is committed before the age of ten and that most offenders stop their criminal activities by the age of thirty-five. This kind of study would not have to rely solely on official records of delinquency or crime but could use questionnaires to measure violations of the law. Interviews could be conducted periodically to measure changes in the individual's social situation — for example, adjustment to school or family income — that might be associated with violation of the law. This long-term cohort study would yield much information on the causes of criminal behavior and the development of criminal careers that we cannot get from other kinds of criminological research (Farrington, Ohlin, and Wilson, 1986).

Cohort studies do have several drawbacks. They are expensive to conduct, because they take so long to complete, and thus researchers may have difficulty getting funding for such projects. Pressure on academic researchers to publish scholarly work may inhibit them from undertaking cohort studies that will not yield data for years. In addition, interviewing cohort members on a regular basis may interfere with the normal process of growing up.

In spite of such difficulties, several cohort studies have been done. An important early one was the Cambridge-Somerville Youth Study (Powers and Witmer, 1951; McCord and McCord, 1959; McCord, 1978, 1979, 1981). Another major cohort study has been carried out in England (West, 1969, 1982; West and Farrington, 1973, 1977), and a study of the relationship between juvenile delinquency and adult criminal careers has been done in Wisconsin (Shannon, 1982; Lab, 1984). One cohort study that has received much attention is reported in Marvin Wolfgang, Robert Figlio, and Thorsten Sellin's *Delinquency in a Birth Cohort* (1972).

WOLFGANG, FIGLIO, AND SELLIN'S COHORT STUDY OF DELINQUENCY Wolfgang, Figlio, and Sellin studied a cohort of all males born in 1945 who lived in Philadelphia continuously from the age of ten (the first age at which there were a significant number of arrests) until the age of eighteen (the age at which juveniles become adults). The researchers studied only boys because of "the greater incidence, frequency, heterogeneity, seriousness, and persistency of male delinquency" (Wolfgang, Figlio, and Sellin, 1972: 30). Records kept by the schools, draft boards, the police, and the juvenile courts were examined for all 9,945 boys in the cohort. All police contacts that resulted in a written report about a delinquent act were examined. A study of the experiences of some of those boys as adults has also been done (Wolfgang, 1974).

Wolfgang, Figlio, and Sellin looked at the characteristics that distinguished boys who had had contact with the police from boys who had had no such contact. Thirty-five percent of the boys had at least one contact with the police as a juvenile, but a mere 6 percent of the boys accounted for 52 percent of all of the police contacts in the cohort. This suggests that a policy that could keep this small group of chronic offenders from engaging in delinquency would have a major impact on the overall rate of juvenile delinquency.

Blacks and lower-class boys were more apt to have police contacts than were whites and middle-class boys. In fact, the likelihood that a black middle-class boy would have contact with the police was the same as the chance that a white lower-class boy would have. The cohort technique permitted such conclusions because nonoffenders as well as offenders were included in the study. Conclusions of this sort are not possible when the research strategy includes only people who have committed crimes.

Because the cohort they studied included only boys whose contact with the police was examined during the relatively tranquil period from 1955 to 1962, Wolfgang and his colleagues later decided to study a second cohort. This cohort of 27,160 included both boys and girls who were born in 1958 and lived in Philadelphia from 1968 to 1975, a time of turmoil that included the Vietnam War, increased drug use, and social protest. In comparing the two cohorts,

Wolfgang and his colleagues found that a similar percentage of each had had contact with the police, that in each cohort blacks were more likely than whites to have had such contacts, and that a relatively small proportion of each cohort accounted for most of the cohort's police contacts. The researchers did discover, however, that the members of the second cohort were much more likely to be involved in serious, costly offenses (Tracy, Wolfgang, and Figlio, 1985). Cohort studies can thus show how patterns of criminal and delinquent activity change over time.

Other Strategies of Criminological Research

Comparative and historical research, biographies, the patterns-of-crime approach, and cohort studies are but a few of the many strategies that criminologists have used to study crime and the criminal justice system. Other methods that have provided valuable information include the analysis of official and unofficial records, surveys, experiments, observation, and mathematical models and econometric techniques.

OFFICIAL AND UNOFFICIAL RECORDS   The records of the police, the courts, and the correctional system have been used to study how the police arrest suspects, whether there is racial discrimination in sentencing convicted offenders, and how parole boards decide to release inmates.

Unofficial records of crime have also proved useful. For instance, department store records have been used to study shoplifting, a crime that often is not reported to the police by store managers (Cameron, 1964). In recent years, private security forces have patrolled private and public spaces to an increasing degree, and the records of these firms may prove to be an important source of information for criminologists in the future.

SURVEYS   *Surveys* are studies in which samples of people who are representative of a larger population are asked a series of prepared questions. In Chapter 3, we will see that surveys have been used to measure the extent of crime in two ways, by asking people about their experiences as victims of crime and by asking them about their own involvement in criminal activity. Surveys have also been used to test theories of crime and delinquency, as we will see in Chapter 8 when we examine Travis Hirschi's (1969) use of survey data to test the control theory of delinquency.

EXPERIMENTS   *Experiments* are controlled studies in which people are treated in different ways to determine the effects of that treatment on their attitudes and behavior. One experiment created a "mock prison" and assigned subjects to be "inmates" or "guards"; this study contributed to our understanding of the social structure of prisons (Zimbardo, 1971, 1972; Haney, Banks, and Zimbardo, 1973; Zimbardo et al., 1973). Experiments have been used to evaluate the effectiveness of rehabilitation programs; one such study assessed the impact on inmates of group counseling (Kassebaum, Ward, and Wilner, 1971). A series of experiments conducted by Bibb Latané and John M. Darley (1970) has helped us understand why bystanders often fail to come to the assistance of victims of crime. Another important experiment tested the impact on ex-convicts' criminal behavior of providing them with financial assistance after they were released from prison (Rossi, Berk, and Lenihan, 1980).

OBSERVATION   One research method that has occasionally been used to study criminal behavior is *observation,* the careful and systematic watching of behavior. The difficulty in using this method stems from the fact that criminals want to keep their offenses secret and wait to commit their crimes until no witnesses are present. Nevertheless, observation has been used fruitfully by several criminologists. Francis Ianni (1972) examined the activities of an organized crime "family" for more than two years. Sociologists have observed the behavior of juvenile gangs (Miller, 1974; Horowitz, 1983). In a controversial study, Laud Humphreys (1975) observed homosexual acts by men in public restrooms. In another observational study, Patricia Adler (1985) spent six years investigating upper-level drug dealers and smugglers. Observational studies of the criminal justice system have also been productive, being used to study interaction between the police and suspects on the streets (Piliavin and Briar, 1964; Reiss, 1971; Skolnick, 1975; Black, 1980), as well as the operation of the courts, including the process of plea bargaining (Rosett and Cressey, 1976; Blumberg, 1979).

MATHEMATICAL MODELS AND ECONOMETRIC TECHNIQUES   A recent innovation in the study of crime is the use of mathematical models and econometric techniques. These are abstract formulations of the relationships among variables and are evaluated with data gathered from the police, the courts, and the prisons (Hellman, 1980; Fox, 1981a, 1981b; Phillips and Votey, 1981). These methods have been used to study the deterrent effect of punishment, including the death penalty, and to examine the relationship between crime and unemployment.

COMBINING RESEARCH STRATEGIES   Criminologists sometimes combine several approaches in their study of crime. This enables them to maximize the advantages and minimize the disadvantages of each method. Information that cannot be found in police records, such as how crime is planned, may be uncovered in interviews with offenders. Material that cannot be gathered by interviewing offenders, such as the overall distribution of crime in a city, can be found in police records. Klockars (1974) relied mainly on the biographical method in his study of the professional fence, but he also examined police arrest records, observed a fence at work, and read historical documents on fencing.

Criminologists thus use a variety of research methods to study criminal behav-

TABLE 1.1   Some Methods of
Criminological Research

1. Comparative and historical research
2. Biographies
3. Patterns-of-crime approach
4. Cohort study
5. Analysis of official and unofficial records
6. Surveys
7. Experiments
8. Observation
9. Mathematical models and econometric techniques
10. Combining research strategies

ior and responses to it by the criminal justice system. Each strategy of research can provide useful information if properly used, but none by itself can give us a complete picture of crime and the institutions that deal with it. As a result, in the following chapters we rely on research that has employed many different methods to study crime.

Summary

Criminology is the systematic study of violations of the criminal law (a set of formal norms that label certain behaviors legally punishable). Criminology also focuses on societal reactions to those violations of the law.

Crime includes a diversity of behavior, but most offenses are characterized by criminal intent that leads to behavior defined as socially harmful. People who are not thought capable of forming criminal intent, such as the legally insane, are not punished with criminal sanctions.

Crime and the criminal law are social phenomena, for behavior is socially defined as punishable rather than intrinsically criminal. This accounts for differences in the law from one society to another. Conflict theorists point to the criminal law as the social product of the domination of one group by another one that has more economic resources and political power. Consensus theorists see the law as the outcome of compromise and agreement among various groups.

The law has several social sources. One is interest groups, which are sometimes based on economic and political goals and sometimes based on the moral beliefs of an organized constituency. Moral entrepreneurs may work to get laws that support their own views written and enforced. In democracies, public opinion is another important source of the law. Occasionally, the expert evidence of specialists such as psychiatrists is used to write and interpret the law.

This book looks at a variety of types of crime, examining them within a conceptual scheme that focuses first on needs and motivations to commit crime and then on the ways that offenders reduce their commitment to the law before violating it. Offenders learn criminal motives and skills before violating the law, and they must find the opportunities to commit crime. When these factors lead to multiple crimes by the same person over time, we speak of a criminal career.

Reactions to crime can be informal or formal. Communities respond to crime with civilian patrol groups and citizen groups to improve the neighborhood, and bystanders may or may not respond to a crime they see in progress. The criminal justice system responds to crime in a formal way, and in doing so influences the behavior of offenders. Punishment has been justified as a way to prevent crime through threat (deterrence) or by locking up offenders (incapacitation), as a way to mete out penalties that are deserved (retribution), and as a way to reform offenders (rehabilitation).

Conservatives, liberals, and radicals have proposed different solutions to the crime problem. Over the past two decades, American political leaders have attacked the crime problem by trying to change the criminal justice system. Other approaches that probably would be more effective focus on situational crime prevention and on the eradication of the causes of crime.

Criminologists use many research strategies. Some employ the comparative method, looking at crime in two or more societies to test or develop theories. Historical work is a kind of comparative research, for it compares the past with the present, either explicitly or implicitly. Another useful method is the biographical approach. This method does not tell us how representative a particular offender is of all criminals, but it provides a richness of detail often missing from research based on official statistics or the survey method. Another method is the patterns-of-crime approach, one that uses police data to investigate the distribution of crime in time and space and to study offenders and victims. A very productive, but expensive and time-consuming, strategy is the cohort study. People who have a common characteristic — usually the same year of birth — are studied over time, allowing for the collection of data on criminal careers.

Many other research strategies have contributed to our knowledge of crime, as we will see in the following chapters. Unofficial records of crime, such as those kept on shoplifters by department stores, have been used by researchers. Surveys have been used to study victimization and self-reported crime, enhancing our knowledge of the nature and extent of crime beyond what official statistics can tell us. Experiments have been used to evaluate effects on offenders of prison treatment programs and financial assistance. Social scientists have engaged in systematic observation of criminals and their behavior to uncover information that may be difficult to gather in other ways. Sociologists and economists have also used mathematical models and econometric techniques to study crime in recent years. Many of these methods have been used to study the operation of the criminal justice system, as well as the criminal behavior with which it deals, and often several methods are used in combination by criminologists.

Important Terms

biographical method
child savers
cohort
comparative research
conflict perspective
consensus perspective
crime
criminal career
criminal intent
criminology
deviance
experiment
historical research

interest group
juvenile delinquent
law
moral entrepreneurs
norm
observation
patterns of crime
sanction
status offense
survey
tort
typology
value

Suggested Readings

JOSEPH R. GUSFIELD. *Symbolic Crusade: Status Politics and the American Temperance Movement.* Urbana: University of Illinois Press, 1963. A sociological analysis of how an interest group based on moral beliefs changed the law to prohibit the sale of alcoholic beverages in the United States.

TRAVIS HIRSCHI AND HANAN C. SELVIN. *Principles of Survey Analysis.* New York: Free Press, 1973. This book, originally titled *Delinquency Research,* takes a critical look at the use of survey research to study juvenile delinquency.

LAUD HUMPHREYS. *Tearoom Trade: Impersonal Sex in Public Places,* enlarged ed. Chicago: Aldine, 1975. The last sixty-five pages include several articles that deal with ethical issues confronted by sociological researchers, especially those who study deviants and criminals.

ANTHONY M. PLATT. *The Child Savers: The Invention of Delinquency,* 2nd ed. Chicago: University of Chicago Press, 1977. A sociological and historical study of the development of the juvenile justice system in the United States.

———AND PAUL TAKAGI, ED. *Crime and Social Justice.* London: Macmillan Press, 1981. A collection of essays by radical criminologists.

DARRELL J. STEFFENSMEIER. *The Fence: In the Shadow of Two Worlds.* Totowa, N.J.: Rowman & Littlefield, 1986. A rich biographical study of one fence.

JAMES Q. WILSON. *Thinking about Crime,* rev. ed. New York: Basic Books, 1983. An influential collection of essays by a conservative political scientist.

CHAPTER 2

A Typology of Crime

Source: AP — Wide World Photos

A theory that explains why murder is committed may not explain theft very well. A treatment method that works well for a rapist may be ineffective for a gangster. Because crimes and criminals differ from each other in important ways, criminologists have developed typologies, or sets of categories of crimes and criminals.

There is an important distinction between typologies of crimes and typologies of criminals or criminal careers. This chapter presents a typology of crimes, events in which an individual or an organization violates the law. In Chapter 11, we look at typologies of criminal careers, the sequences of crimes by individuals over time. There is a difference between the criminal career of a robber and the crime of robbery. As we will see later, most offenders are quite versatile in their choice of behavior, with relatively few criminals limiting themselves to a single offense such as robbery. More often we find an offender will sometimes commit robberies, other times commit burglaries, and occasionally may deal drugs. Because of the versatility of criminals, it is difficult to create typologies of criminal careers or criminals that accurately describe most offenders. We return to this problem in Chapter 11; in this chapter we limit ourselves to describing the main types of crimes examined throughout the book.

Our typology distinguishes among four major kinds of crime:

1. Conventional crimes
   a. Crimes of violence
      i. murder
      ii. forcible rape
      iii. robbery
      iv. assault
   b. Property crimes
      i. burglary
      ii. larceny
      iii. motor vehicle theft
      iv. fraud
      v. arson
      vi. vandalism
2. White-collar crime
3. Organized crime
4. Victimless crimes
   a. Drug use
   b. Gambling
   c. Prostitution
   d. Pornography

These types of crime and their subtypes are discussed briefly in this chapter, and in greater detail throughout the book.

Conventional Crimes

Conventional crimes are usually divided into two groups, crimes of violence (also called crimes against the person) and property crimes. Even this simple division creates a few problems. For instance, robbery is the theft of property from a person by force or threat of force, making it both a property crime and a crime of violence. Here we treat it as a crime of violence, because the use of force makes it a more serious crime than simple theft without violence. A second problem with the crime of violence/property crime distinction is that one crime event may involve multiple offenses. Thus, after committing a forcible rape the offender may steal the victim's car to get away. Law-enforcement officials would count only the more serious offense, forcible rape, in recording the crime. For the purposes of our typology, we would say that two different offenses occurred, a forcible rape and a motor vehicle theft.

Crimes of Violence

The four major types of violent crime are murder, forcible rape, robbery, and assault. Gangsters in organized crime may commit contract killings, and a few corporate executives have been convicted of murder for allowing their employees to work in lethal conditions. However, even when gangsters and executives commit violent offenses, we can speak of those crimes in terms of the four types that we examine here.

MURDER   *Murder and nonnegligent manslaughter* are defined by the Federal Bureau of Investigation as the willful killing of a human being. The taking of another person's life may fall outside this definition if it is excusable, such as an accidental shooting of a playmate by a child, or if it is justifiable, such as a police officer's shooting of a dangerous offender who is about to hurt someone.

Murder occurs more often between an offender and a victim who are known to each other than it does between strangers. In 1986, 15.7 percent of murders involved an offender and a victim in the same family; 40.1 percent involved boyfriends, girlfriends, friends, or other acquaintances; 1.4 percent involved neighbors; 13 percent involved strangers; and in 29.8 percent of the cases the victim-offender relationship was not known to the police (Federal Bureau of Investigation, 1987: 11). Overall, murders between offenders and victims who were known to each other outnumbered murders between strangers by four to one.

The marital relationship is sometimes conducive to murder, as we can see in the Cross-Cultural Perspective. In a study of marital homicide in Philadelphia, wives killed their husbands almost as often (forty-seven times) as husbands killed their wives (fifty-three times) (Wolfgang, 1958). A study using data from Houston found that thirteen husbands and common-law husbands killed their wives in 1969, and that twenty-four wives and common-law wives murdered their

Here Steve Benson, heir to a family cigarette fortune, arrives at a Florida prison after his 1985 conviction for the bombing murder of his adoptive mother.   *Source: Thomas A. Price—Fort Myers News—Press from Sygma*

husbands in that year (Lundsgaarde, 1977: 54). Women who commit murder seem to be more likely than male murderers to kill someone with whom they have an intimate relationship. This is probably especially true when traditional gender roles limit women's interaction to the home; it may be less often the case when women work outside the home and interact more with people outside the family.

The study of murder in Houston found that the criminal justice system's treatment of murderers depended on the relationship between the offender and the victim. Table 2.1 shows that strangers who committed murder were the least

TABLE 2.1   Criminal Justice Response to Different Kinds of Murders, Houston, 1969

Relationship between Offender and Victim	Number	Percentage Escaping Any Legal Penalty	Mean Prison Term of Those Convicted
Strangers	55	36%	27.9 years
Friends or asso-ciates	68	53%	10.1 years
Relatives	77	61%	7.6 years

SOURCE: Adapted from Henry P. Lundsgaarde, *Murder in Space City: A Cultural Analysis of Houston Homicide Patterns.* New York: Oxford University Press, 1977, p. 232. Reprinted with permission.

A Cross-Cultural Perspective: Dowry Murders in India

When Renu Puri married Rajesh Bhalla, in 1980, the Bhallas demanded as dowry about $7,000 (85,000 rupees) worth of jewelry and gold, a $1,000 stereo system, an $800 Panasonic television, two gold Omega watches worth more than $200 apiece, a $300 silver tea service, electric fans, steam irons, and twenty-one silk saris for the Bhalla women. Renu's father was an airline engineer and her mother a school supervisor, and such lavishness strained their resources. . . .

"Rajesh wanted to go to America to earn more money, but Renu refused to leave India," Mrs. Puri says. "That's how it started. Because she opposed him, he began demanding more dowry from us. He wanted a washing machine, and we gave him that. Then he demanded nine thousand rupees for a shopping trip to Hong Kong. He brought back a color TV and another 'music center,' and demanded that my husband pay the fourteen thousand rupees in customs duty for them. After that he tried to force Renu to make us transfer our property and home into his name, and when she wouldn't he began to beat her. He told her that she had ruined his life because she had kept him from going to America. Finally, he demanded a Toyota car. But how could we afford it? We had already given him everything we could."

In February of 1983 Renu's father received a phone call at his office. Renu, who had been a college beauty queen, lay in the hospital,

charred almost beyond recognition. Rajesh had doused her with kerosene and set her on fire. She died about a week later. (p. 21)

This type of crime, called a dowry murder, has increased in recent years in India, though its exact extent is unclear. One Indian sociologist estimates that in Delhi alone there were 690 deaths related to dowry disputes in 1983–1984. Police officials question such high estimates, saying that many burning deaths of young wives are accidents or suicides, rather than homicides by husbands or by members of the husband's family. Rajesh Bhalla is now serving a life sentence for murder, but he is the exception; few dowry murderers are imprisoned, and most are not even prosecuted. Indeed, few dowry murders are even officially recognized as crimes. Husbands have the right to waive a post mortem examination, and often the wife's body is cremated before anyone asks for an official investigation of the death. In some cases, bribes are paid to the police to declare such deaths as suicides. Some of these deaths are suicides, but a significant number are murders.

Traditionally, the dowry in India represented the daughter's share of the father's wealth, as only sons could inherit land. Since

likely to escape any punishment and received the longest prison sentences when convicted. Murderers who were friends or associates of their victims were more likely to escape punishment and were given shorter prison terms than strangers who committed murder. Finally, relatives who committed murder were the most likely to escape punishment and got the shortest sentences if convicted.

Law-enforcement officials say that one kind of murder that has become more common in recent years is the *serial murder*. This involves killers who slay strangers and then move on to other areas of the country in search of more victims. Serial murders occur over a period of time and differ from *mass*

1961, this practice has been illegal, and laws passed in 1983 and 1985 defined harassment over dowries as a crime. However, the definition of dowry in the law is still vague, and no effective way of enforcing the law has been developed.

A variety of social forces have given rise to dowry murders. Marriage in India has become increasingly commercialized, having never been based on romantic love, as in the West. Moral restraints exercised by caste and village have broken down with modernization and urbanization. Exposure to the high standard of living in industrialized nations has increased the materialism and acquisitiveness of India's middle class. Women are subordinate in the Indian social structure, so that even their own parents tend to blame them for their marital problems, rather than blame their sons-in-law. In addition, lack of access to educational and employment opportunities makes it difficult for women to become economically independent of their husbands.

A dowry is seen by men with aspirations to upward mobility, particularly by those who are well educated but lack good job prospects, as a way to get the goods and the money necessary to enter the middle class. A dowry becomes for these men a "shortcut to importance" (p. 24), a way to acquire the money to start a business or build a house. The bride becomes a means by which a man can extort money and possessions from her parents, who yield to him because they fear for their daughter's safety or are concerned they will get a reputation for being stingy. When the bride's parents eventually refuse the husband's demands, he may beat or kill his wife.

Dowry murders are also linked to the structure of the Indian family and to the culture's trait of avoiding psychological introspection. The husband's mother often sees the bride as an outsider to the family, and as a threat to alienate her son's affections. In a society that lacks the Western tradition of reflecting on one's feelings and motivations, husbands and their mothers tend to focus on the size of the dowry as the source of resentment and conflict within the family.

The presence in most Indian kitchens of kerosene for cooking offers husbands a handy means to commit murder, and one that allows others to see the burning of the wife as an accident or a suicide. This means of death also fits with the traditional practice of *suttee*, in which Indian widows threw themselves on the burning funeral pyres of their deceased husbands. The ambiguity that surrounds the cause of the burning deaths of young wives makes it difficult to determine the extent of this crime, but sociologists and feminists believe that dowry murder is a widespread and growing problem in Indian society today.

SOURCE: Based on Fergus M. Bordewich, "Dowry Murders," *The Atlantic Monthly* 258 (July 1986), 21–27.

---

murders, which involve the killing of several victims at the same time. The victims of serial murderers are often runaways, prostitutes, or the homeless. Serial murderers seem to be above average in intelligence, knowledgeable about police methods (which helps them avoid arrest), and personally charming (which helps them lure unsuspecting victims into lethal situations) (Levin and Fox, 1985; Leyton, 1986).

FORCIBLE RAPE According to the FBI, *forcible rape* is "carnal knowledge of a female forcibly and against her will" (Federal Bureau of Investigation, 1987:

331). However, some states now define forcible rape in sex-neutral terms, so that a sexual assault on a male victim, typically by another male, is defined as rape. Some states have also passed laws that distinguish among different degrees of sexual assault, with each carrying a different penalty and with the degree of the crime depending on the offender's intent, the nature of the sexual act, the amount of injury to the victim, and other circumstances of the crime.

Many forcible rapes are planned in detail, but some seem to occur spontaneously. One study found that nearly three-fourths of rapes were planned, with offenders deliberately trying to force the victim into sex. Another one-ninth of the rapes were partially planned, with vague plans being hastily made after an encounter with a potential victim. About one-sixth of the rapes were "explosive," with the offender having no earlier intention of committing a rape but perpetrating one impulsively when an opportunity presented itself (Amir, 1971: 141).

About half of all forcible rapes involve strangers, but some occur between offenders and victims who have close relationships. Three studies have found that the proportion of all rapes committed by total strangers to the victim ranges from 42 to 53 percent (Amir, 1971; Curtis, 1974; Timrots and Rand, 1987). Two of these studies found that 10 percent and 14 percent of the rapes occurred between an offender and a victim who had previously been intimately related, either as relatives, lovers, or close friends. The third found that 4 percent of the rapes were committed by relatives.

One relationship between the rapist and the victim that has received considerable attention in recent years is the rape of women by their husbands or ex-husbands. According to one study, one-seventh of women who have ever been married have been the victim of a rape, or attempted rape, by their husbands or ex-husbands (Russell, 1982). As of December 1984, twenty-seven states did not permit the prosecution for rape of a husband who was living with his wife. Other states have laws that define sexual violence as rape if it occurs between husbands and wives, whether they are living together or are separated. Rape in marriage is an underreported offense, and when it is reported the police often treat it as an assault, if they even deal with it as a crime at all.

ROBBERY *Robbery* is the theft of property from another person by force or threat of force. More severe penalties are usually meted out to robbers who are armed than to those who do not use weapons. Robberies can be divided into noncommercial robberies (purse snatches, robberies of individuals on the street, and robberies of individuals in a residence) and commercial robberies (cab holdups and robberies of commercial establishments).

Many robberies are planned only a few minutes before they occur, with offenders piecing together the elements of the crime by improvisation. One study found that more than 40 percent of juveniles and 25 percent of adults who committed robberies had not even intended to commit the crime before it occurred (Feeney and Weir, 1973). One example of an unplanned robbery involved a man who usually planned his offenses with a partner well in advance.

This man went into a liquor store to buy some beer, and when the clerk refused to sell to him because he was drunk, the man pulled a gun and demanded money. His partner outside in the car was taken by surprise because they had not planned a robbery, but he ran into the store to help. After the robbery, they drove away, but their license number was traced and they were arrested. When they had engaged in planned robberies, they had always stolen a car to avoid being traced (Conklin, 1972: 97).

Robbers often operate in loosely organized gangs. Members of the gang may have specialties, but most are quite versatile. The different roles and specialties of gang members must be coordinated so the group functions smoothly to carry out the robbery. One such role in the robbery gang is the "wheel man," who steals a car, maps an escape route, and drives to and from the robbery site. This role is critical in a robbery, because there is great risk in getting away from the scene of the crime in a car that cannot be identified. The wheel man may also act as a "lookout" or "peek man" for the gang, or he may leave the car and take an active part in the holdup. Occasionally the driver is hired for a fixed percentage of the profits, usually 10 percent. Some robbers who begin as "10 percenters" later join robbery gangs as full-fledged members (Conklin, 1972).

Robbers and their victims rarely know one another. Because thieves have access to the property of people they know well, they do not need to use force to steal from them. They can simply take the property by stealth in a larceny. In addition, a potential robber's need for cash can be explained to those with whom he or she is close, and so the would be robber may be given or loaned the necessary money rather than having to steal it. Concern for people whom they know well may lead robbers to think that if they must use force to steal, they might as well use that force against strangers rather than against relatives or friends. Moreover, strangers are less likely to be able to identify them to the police. Thus, it is not surprising that more than three-fourths of all robbers are strangers to their victims (Curtis, 1974; Hindelang, 1976; Timrots and Rand, 1987).

Two kinds of prior relationships do seem to give rise to robbery with some frequency: relationships between prostitutes and their clients, and relationships between homosexual partners who were previously strangers. A study in New York City found that one in five muggings — a colloquial term for strong-armed street robberies — involved a prostitute's client, a homosexual, or a chronic drunk (Burnham, 1968). A study of robbery in London revealed that one robbery in eight involved a "preliminary association of short duration between victim and offender (mainly for heterosexual or homosexual purposes)" (McClintock and Gibson, 1961: 16).

ASSAULT   An *assault* is an unlawful attack by one person on another. The FBI distinguishes between *simple assaults,* in which no weapon is used and no serious injury results, and *aggravated assaults,* in which the purpose of the attack is to inflict severe bodily injury and in which a weapon typically is used.

The exact relationship between victims and offenders in assaults is difficult to determine, because many assaults occur within the family and are not reported to the police, and perhaps not even to interviewers who conduct surveys about people's experiences as victims of crime. Fear of retaliation, embarrassment, and the desire to protect even abusive family members all contribute to the underreporting of family violence. As a result, assaults between spouses and parental violence against children are more common than is suggested by crime statistics (Steinmetz and Straus, 1980; Gelles, 1982).

In about one-fourth of the aggravated assaults reported to the police, the relationship between the victim and the offender is unknown. Of the cases in which the victim-offender relationship is known, about one-seventh occur between members of the same family and nearly one-third more involve lovers, friends, and acquaintances. Another one-fifth of aggravated assaults occur between strangers, and one-tenth involve a criminal and a police officer (Curtis, 1974).

Aggravated assaults that are reported to interviewers in surveys of victimization experiences involve strangers 56 percent of the time, a much higher proportion than is the case with aggravated assaults reported to the police. Of the aggravated assaults reported to the interviewers, 7 percent are by relatives and another 30 percent by acquaintances. In 5 percent of the cases, victim-offender relationships cannot be determined by interviewers (Timrots and Rand, 1987).

Property Crimes

Property crimes involve either the theft or the destruction of property. Theft can take the form of burglary, larceny, motor vehicle theft, or fraud. The destruction of property occurs in the crimes of arson and vandalism.

BURGLARY   *Burglary,* or breaking and entering, is unlawful entry of a building to commit a serious crime, usually the theft of property. A burglary might turn into a robbery if the burglar confronts the occupant of the building and uses force to steal, but most burglary involves no such confrontation. The targets of a burglary may be either private residences or commercial establishments such as stores and offices.

Often a burglary is planned before the offender enters the building (Reppetto, 1974). Burglars may examine the architecture of the building for ease of entry and escape. Often they first try to enter through an unlocked door, and only if that fails will they climb in through a window. They may seek a different target if they cannot make a quick entry. They look for alarm systems, occupants of the building, and nearby witnesses. Learning about police and security patrols in the area may also be a part of the planning of a burglary (Letkemann, 1973).

Although we might expect that there would rarely be a prior relationship between burglars and their victims, because the burglars would have access to the victim's property or would be able to ask for a loan, a 1985 study by the Department of Justice found that 42 percent of burglaries are committed by a relative, an acquaintance, or someone whom the victim would recognize (Greer, 1986).

LARCENY   *Larceny,* or theft, is the "unlawful taking, carrying, leading, or riding away of property from the possession of another" (Federal Bureau of Investigation, 1987: 331). The FBI excludes from this category motor vehicle theft, embezzlement, confidence games, and forgery, although these are forms of theft. Larceny differs from robbery in that it does not involve force or the threat of force, and it differs from burglary in that it does not require entry of a building. Some common forms of larceny are listed in Table 2.2.

   Some forms of larceny are carefully planned in advance, and other thefts are done on the spur of the moment. Shoplifting is carefully planned in advance by "boosters," or professional thieves, and even amateur "snitches" who steal for personal use may plan their thefts before entering a store (Cameron, 1964). Shoplifting often involves the intention to pick up certain merchandise, a plan to get out of the store, and a way to dispose of or use the stolen goods. Other thefts may not be planned; for instance, someone may be tempted to steal an unlocked bicycle or a coat left unattended in a movie theater.

   There is little reason to expect that there will be a prior relationship between thieves and their victims. Indeed, one survey found that 90 percent of the victims of personal theft were complete strangers to the perpetrators of the crime (Hindelang, 1976: 12).

MOTOR VEHICLE THEFT   *Motor vehicle theft* is often distinguished from larceny, of which it is actually one form. The reason for this is that car theft involves property of much greater value than is commonly stolen in other types of larceny, and often the car thief does not intend to deprive the owner of the property on a permanent basis. Most stolen cars are recovered, although the proportion that are never recovered has increased in recent years, apparently as the result of more thefts by professionals who strip the cars of their parts, repaint and sell them, or even ship them to other countries for sale.

   Fraud is the crime of obtaining money or property by false pretenses. This crime is similar to larceny, but it does not involve the physical taking away of property in the possession of the owner. Fraud may involve false or deceptive

TABLE 2.2   Some Common Forms of Larceny

Shoplifting
Bicycle theft
Pickpocketing
Theft from cars
Theft of car accessories
Purse snatching (without force)
Theft from vending machines
Theft from buildings

advertising in which customers lose their money by purchasing inferior or misrepresented merchandise. Deceiving the government about one's true income and underpaying taxes is a form of fraud. Faking an accident or a theft and collecting from an insurance company for a nonexistent loss is another. The fraudulent use of credit cards, whether it be a stolen card or one that is illegally made, is a form of fraud that has increased in recent years. Some forms of fraud are white-collar crimes, but this crime is also committed by people who are not white-collar criminals.

ARSON *Arson* is the willful burning of the building, motor vehicle, aircraft, or personal property of another person. This crime may also involve the intent to defraud an insurance company by filing a claim for the loss of one's own property through a deliberately set fire, though there are other motives for this crime, such as revenge. Arson is sometimes white-collar crime, but many fires are set by offenders of lower social standing.

VANDALISM *Vandalism* is the willful or malicious destruction, injury, disfigurement, or defacement of property without consent of the owner. Breaking the windows in an abandoned building is an act of vandalism that has little social significance, but vandalizing an important painting in a museum may ruin property of great economic and social value.

White-Collar Crime

The concept of white-collar crime was first introduced by sociologist Edwin Sutherland in a speech before the American Sociological Society in 1939 and elaborated on by him in a book ten years later. For our purposes, we modify his definition of *white-collar crime* slightly to include any illegal act, punishable by a criminal sanction, that is committed in the course of a legitimate occupation or pursuit by a corporation or by an otherwise respectable individual of high social standing (Edelhertz, 1970; Conklin, 1977).

One important aspect of this definition is that white-collar crime is *punishable*. Often it is not actually punished as a crime but is ignored or dealt with by a regulatory agency or civil court. What is important is that the offense might be punished under the criminal law. Another important aspect of the definition is that white-collar crime occurs in the course of legitimate activity; a corporate executive who murders his wife after an argument in the home has not committed a white-collar crime. One problem with our definition of white-collar crime is that it does not make clear what "respectable" actually means. This term usually is interpreted to mean that the individual offender is held in high social regard, but some have taken it to mean that the white-collar offender has no previous convictions for conventional crimes or that the offender does not think of himself or herself as a criminal. Finally, white-collar criminals are of relatively high social standing, although Sutherland and other criminologists have some-

TABLE 2.3   Major Types of White-Collar Crime

Crimes by businesses	Crimes by employees against businesses
deceptive advertising	embezzlement and employee theft
antitrust violations	expense account fraud
securities violations	
tax fraud	*Crimes by government employees*
bribery of political officials	police brutality
unsafe workplace conditions	bribe-taking by police officers and
production of dangerous products	political officials
environmental law violations	embezzlement by political officials

times treated as white-collar offenses certain crimes committed by people of relatively low status, such as bank tellers and people who repair cars.

Table 2.3 shows some of the many forms that white-collar crime takes. It may involve corporations that engage in deceptive advertising (fraud) or in collusion to fix prices or divide a market. Stock and securities fraud and theft, which may involve corporate executives, brokerage houses, and even organized crime figures, fit the definition of white-collar crime. Embezzlement of the funds with which an employee is entrusted is a white-collar crime against a firm, rather than by a company. Tax fraud by companies or businesspeople in the course of their business activities can be seen as a kind of white-collar crime. Companies also commit white-collar offenses when they violate government regulations that establish ceiling prices and that ration goods, if these offenses carry criminal penalties. White-collar crime may thus involve losses to the public, to stockholders, and to competitors, or it can involve losses to companies at the hands of their employees. Al Capone once referred to white-collar offenses collectively as "the legitimate rackets."

White-collar crime usually involves elaborate planning. A price-fixing conspiracy among electrical equipment manufacturers that resulted in the conviction of companies and executives in 1961 involved detailed planning. One conspirator described the techniques used by the offenders as follows: "It was considered discreet to not be too obvious and to minimize telephone calls, to use plain envelopes in mailing material to each other, not to be seen together on traveling, and so forth . . . not to leave wastepaper, of which there was a lot, strewn around a room when leaving" (cited in Geis, 1967: 143). Further evidence that these executives knew they were breaking the law is that they "hid behind a camouflage of fictitious names and conspiratorial codes," called their meeting roster the "Christmas card list," and referred to their gatherings as "choir practice" (Geis, 1967: 143). To ensure their anonymity, they used only public telephones and met at trade association meetings and at remote sites.

Most of the crimes that criminologists study as white-collar crime occur in the business world, but government corruption and police brutality also fit our definition of white-collar crime. Government officials (including police officers) who take bribes have committed crimes in the course of their legitimate occupations. Embezzlement of funds by public officials is also a white-collar crime.

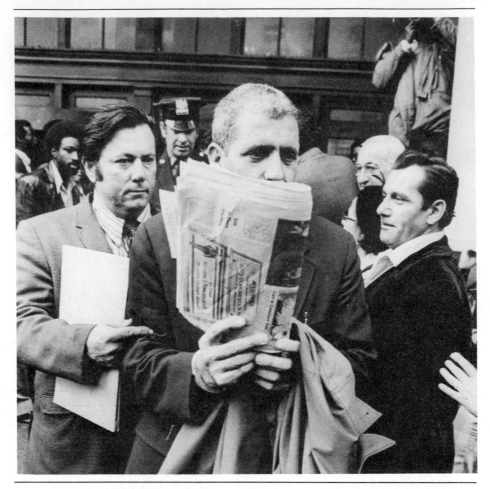

Here a New York City police detective covers his face on the way to being arraigned in a bribery case.   *Source: J. P. Laffont/Sygma*

Although police officers technically do not wear white collars, we can treat brutality and corruption on the police force as fitting our definition of white-collar crime, though it might be argued that police officers are of middle rather than high social status.

Organized Crime

Organized crime is criminal activity by a formal organization developed and devoted primarily to the pursuit of profits through illegal means. In the United States, organized crime traditionally has been equated with the Mafia or La Cosa Nostra. However, in recent years criminologists and a presidential commission

Using Criminology: RICO and Organized Crime

For years, sociologists have argued that the legal system is too oriented toward individuals and their crimes, and too little concerned with the way that criminal activity is organized. Rather than develop typologies that include only the individual offenses of loan sharking, drug smuggling, and illegal gambling, sociologists have usually included the category of "organized crime" in their typologies. What distinguishes this type from others is the structured nature of the group that engages in a series of offenses over time and is dedicated to the criminal pursuit of profits.

In 1970, the federal government responded to the criticism that its laws were insufficiently concerned with organized criminal activity by passing the Racketeer Influenced and Corrupt Organizations act, commonly known as RICO. This law prohibits the operation of an enterprise by a pattern of racketeering and allows for the prosecution of all members of a criminal organization if any member commits two or more crimes as a part of that organization's work. Membership in such an organization is thus defined as a crime. This allows prosecutors to show in court how organized crime families are structured and how they go about their daily business.

RICO was not used much against organized crime until 1981, when the U.S. Supreme Court ruled that the law need not be restricted to cases of organized crime infiltration of legitimate businesses, but could be used against any criminal racketeering scheme. RICO defines racketeering in broad terms and provides for the forfeiture of assets and for a twenty-year prison term.

The law has been successfully used to prosecute organized crime leaders in New York, Boston, Los Angeles, New Orleans, and Cleveland. Attorneys for organized crime figures have complained that the broad nature of RICO allows for the prosecution of many defendants for the crimes committed by a few, and they have argued that charges brought under RICO are difficult to defend against. Business executives have criticized RICO for being too broadly written, with the result that RICO has been used to bring civil actions against legitimate corporations in fraud cases. These executives argue that such cases were not the original intent of RICO and that the law should be limited to cases of traditional forms of racketeering such as loan sharking and illegal gambling.

SOURCE: Based on William F. Doherty, "RICO—A Broad Tool for Prosecutors," *The Boston Globe,* February 28, 1986, p. 9.

have redefined organized crime to include criminal enterprises run by Chinese, Jamaicans, Colombians, Thais, Pakistanis, Indians, Afghans, Nigerians, Ghanaians, and Israelis, as well as by Italian-Americans.

Organized crime has the characteristics of a formal organization: a division of labor, coordination of activities through rules and codes, and an allocation of tasks in order to achieve certain goals (Cressey, 1969, 1972). The organization seeks profits from crime and tries to preserve itself in the face of external and internal threats.

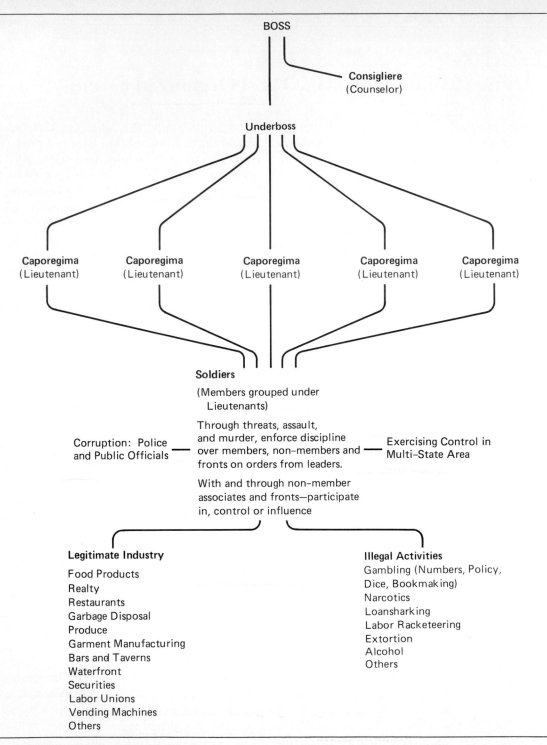

FIGURE 2.1 An Organized Crime Family *Source: The President's Commission on Law Enforcement and Administration of Justice, Organized Crime. Washington, D.C.: U.S. Government Printing Office, 1967, p. 9.*

Figure 2.1 shows the hierarchy of a Mafia organized crime "family." The family is headed by a boss with absolute authority over the members. Below the boss in the hierarchy is an underboss who acts as chief deputy and assistant, a staff of counselors or advisors, a series of lieutenants who act as buffers between the higher echelons and lower-level workers, and soldiers who operate illegal and sometimes legitimate activities for the family. According to sociologist Donald Cressey (1972: 36, 38), for this organization to function there must be an enforcer who "makes arrangements for killing and injuring (physically, financially, or psychologically) members, and occasionally nonmembers"; a corrupter who "bribes, buys, intimidates, threatens, negotiates, and sweet-talks himself into a relationship with police, public officials, and anyone else who might help 'family' members secure and maintain immunity from arrest, prosecution, and punishment"; and a corruptee who is a public official, usually not a member of the organized crime family, and who can wield influence on behalf of the organization's interests. According to economist Peter Reuter (1983), organized crime is less able today than in the past to ensure its protection from law enforcement, because there has been a decline in "localized, unitary law enforcement," which could be corrupted relatively easily, and an increase in enforcement efforts by a multitude of less easily corrupted authorities at the local, state, and federal levels.

A National Confederation?

There has long been a debate about whether organized crime is organized at the national level or only at the local level. This is not a trivial issue, for the question of how organized crime is structured determines how law enforcement can best combat it.

What is clear is that some American cities have Mafia "families," with one estimate being that there are about 1,700 active members of these predominantly Italian-American organized gangs and about ten times that number involved as associates (Werner, 1983). Most law-enforcement officials believe the twenty-five or twenty-six Mafia families in the country are knit together in a well-organized national confederation led by a commission of powerful bosses. In New York City in 1986, eight defendants were convicted of operating a national commission that ruled the Mafia throughout the country. This commission purportedly decided what illegal enterprises to pursue, determined which families would control different criminal activities in particular geographic areas, and settled disputes among families.

Some criminologists have made a strong case that organized crime is not highly organized at the national level. They have found many internal inconsistencies in the testimony that gangsters have offered as proof for such a national organization (Hawkins, 1969). An observational study of a New York City crime family found no evidence of links to a national organization, though no evidence was found that such ties did not exist (Ianni, 1972). Another study of the Mafia in New York City, where it is probably stronger than anywhere else in the nation, concluded that it "may be a paper tiger, reaping the returns from its reputation while no longer maintaining the forces that generated the reputation" (Reuter, 1983: xi). A study in Seattle concluded that organized crime was not run by a national commission, and that its local activities were not primarily even under the control of private citizens. This study found that organized crime was "a coalition of politicians, law-enforcement people, businessmen, union leaders, and (in some ways least important of all) racketeers. Who dominates the coalition varies from city to city and from time to time" (Chambliss, 1978: 9).

What can we conclude from these differing opinions about the national organization of criminal enterprises? Organized crime families do exist at the local level in some cities. Some loose ties exist among Mafia families throughout the country, but there is little solid evidence of a highly structured bureaucracy led by a commission of bosses. Powerful and well-respected family bosses may step in to resolve conflicts between families, but it seems unlikely that there is a commission that oversees criminal enterprises across the nation on a day-to-day basis. Even this loose coordination among Mafia families seems to have weakened in recent years, as law enforcement has successfully prosecuted and imprisoned many leaders, as the corruption of public officials has become more difficult, and as a variety of new criminal organizations involving ethnic groups other than Italian-Americans have taken control of certain criminal activities.

Sources of Illegal Profits

Organized crime reaps most of its illegal profits from supplying members of the public with goods and services that are in great demand but prohibited by law. A major source of profits is illegal drugs, especially heroin and cocaine. The importation and distribution of such drugs requires an elaborate network and produces great profits for those willing to assume the risk of arrest and punishment. These profits are often loaned at usurious and illegally high rates of interest to people who cannot get loans through banks. Money is also invested in legitimate businesses to enhance profits and to show the Internal Revenue Service an honest source of income. Organized crime has also proved adept at moving into other highly profitable criminal activities, including illegal gambling, bankruptcy fraud, extortion, the illegal disposal of toxic wastes, and the distribution of pornography.

Victimless Crimes

A *victimless crime* is an offense that is consensual and lacks a complaining participant (Schur, 1965). It might be more accurate to refer to victimless crimes as crimes without complainants, because some observers question the idea that there is no victim of crimes such as drug use, gambling, prostitution, and pornography. What is important is that these offenses usually involve willing participants in activities that violate the law. Because no one complains to the police about being victimized, the task of law enforcement in making arrests and prosecuting suspects is a difficult one.

Drug Use

Although we might consider drug users to be the victims of the drugs they use, drug use is a victimless crime in the sense that neither the drug seller nor the drug user is likely to report the crime to the police. Drugs do have ill effects on users, from physical deterioration to overdose deaths, but some sociologists see these effects more as the consequence of society's laws against drugs than as the result of the drugs themselves. If the drugs were legally available, these sociologists argue, they would be much less expensive and the negative effects on users would be minimized. When drugs are illegal, they are expensive, and users need to spend much of their money on drugs. This, in turn, causes drug users to neglect food, shelter, and clothing, and such neglect leads to their physical deterioration.

Because of the high cost of illegal drugs, users often turn to other crimes to support their habits. They may commit robberies, burglaries, thefts, or other property crimes to support their drug use. In this sense, drug use has secondary effects in victimizing others in these property crimes, even if the drug use itself can be seen as a victimless crime. In addition, the high cost of illegal drugs may lead some users to deal drugs, drawing into drug use some people who would not otherwise have engaged in such behavior.

Gambling

One argument for viewing illegal gambling as a victimless crime is that many states now permit certain forms of legal gambling, such as on-track betting, off-track betting, and lotteries. If these forms of gambling are not defined as crimes, why then should gambling with a bookie on sporting events and playing the numbers be treated as crimes? The great variation from state to state in defining what kind of gambling is legal and what kind is illegal makes it clear that there is no national consensus on treating gambling as a crime. The argument that gamblers may victimize members of their families if they gamble compulsively and may drive their families into poverty is correct, but so too can people who gamble legally victimize their families in this way. Nevertheless, laws in the United States still define certain forms of gambling as crimes.

Prostitution

The consensual transactions between prostitutes and their clients typically do not produce complainants, though clients who are also robbed by prostitutes or their pimps, and prostitutes who are beaten by clients, may turn to the police. In many cities, prostitution was once controlled by organized crime, but that is no longer the case. Individual prostitutes may be seen as engaging in a crime that has no victim, even though prostitution does pose risks to both the prostitute and the client, such as the high likelihood of contracting venereal diseases or

AIDS. Prostitutes who work for pimps may be the victims of physical abuse to "keep them in line," but the criminal offense of prostitution itself does not involve participants who define themselves as victims of a crime.

Pornography

The distribution and sale of pornography is a criminal offense in certain jurisdictions and under certain circumstances, though the law is vague in defining such offenses. Usually, neither sellers nor purchasers of pornographic books, magazines, or movies define themselves as victims of a crime.

There have been some efforts in recent years to define pornography as a crime because the participants in the making of the pornography—the photographic models or the actors in a film—are victims. Federal law now defines as a crime any making or selling of pornography that involves a minor, on the assumption that younger people are coerced into the making of such pornography and can thus be seen as victims. For pornography that involves adults, however, there is usually no clear victim and no one to complain to the police, even though the sale and distribution of such material sometimes violate the law.

Using the Typology of Crimes

This chapter has introduced a simple typology of crimes. Throughout the rest of the book, we look at additional material on each type of crime. We do this by discussing concepts and theories, and by looking at the way that those concepts and theories help us understand different kinds of crime. For instance, in examining the way that social and economic conditions give rise to crime, we explore the socioeconomic sources of white-collar crime, organized crime, and conventional crimes. Table 2.4 makes it clear where each type of crime discussed in this

TABLE 2.4 Location in the Textbook of Further Examinations of the Types of Crime

Chapter	Conventional Crime	White-Collar Crime	Organized Crime	Victimless Crime
3. Measuring Crime	X			
4. The Costs of Crime	X	X	X	X
5. Dimensions of Crime	X			
6. Biological and Psychological Explanations of Crime	X			
7. Socioeconomic Sources of Crime	X	X	X	
8. Social Control and Commitment to the Law	X	X		
9. Learning to Commit Crime	X	X		X
10. Opportunities and Facilitating Factors	X			X
11. Criminal Careers	X			
17. Solving the Crime Problem	X	X	X	X

chapter is examined later in the book, and the Subject Index at the end of the book gives exact page references for each type of crime. Table 2.4 shows that not every type of crime is discussed in every chapter. That would have required a book perhaps twice as long as this one. However, it would be possible to deal with each type of crime in each chapter, and a useful exercise for the reader would be to consider how this might be done. For instance, you might think about how the learning theories discussed in Chapter 9 could be applied to organized crime members, or consider the kinds of criminal careers that white-collar criminals have (Chapter 11). The conceptual approach of this book could also be applied fruitfully to offenses that receive relatively little attention in this book, such as political terrorism or confidence games.

Summary

The typology in this chapter distinguishes among four major kinds of crime: conventional crimes (both crimes of violence and property crimes), white-collar crime, organized crime, and victimless crimes.

Conventional crimes of violence include murder, forcible rape, robbery, and assault. Murder often occurs between an offender and a victim who were previously acquainted. Forcible rape, which has increasingly been defined in sex-neutral terms, occurs between total strangers about half of the time, and between a victim and an offender well known to each other relatively infrequently. Robbery involves force or threat of force to steal property, and typically involves strangers. Many robberies are not planned much in advance, but some involve organized gangs. Many assaults involve a victim and an offender who are known to each other, and assaults between people who are intimately associated are probably underreported to the police.

Conventional property offenses include burglary, larceny, motor vehicle theft, fraud, arson, and vandalism. Burglaries, which often are planned to some degree, involve unlawful entry of a building to commit a serious crime, usually a theft. Larceny or simple theft involves many varieties of behavior, including shoplifting and pickpocketing. Motor vehicle theft may involve professionals who sell the stolen car or its parts, or amateur "joy riders" who do not intend to deprive the owner of the car on a permanent basis. Fraud, or obtaining money or property by false pretenses, takes many forms. Arson, the deliberate burning of property, and vandalism, the willful destruction of property, are also property crimes.

White-collar crime is an illegal act, punishable under the criminal law, that is committed in the course of a legitimate occupation or pursuit by a corporation or otherwise respectable individual of high social standing. Many of the various kinds of white-collar crime involve elaborate planning. For our purposes, government corruption and police abuses of authority can also be treated as white-collar crimes, in addition to offenses that occur in the world of business.

Organized crime is activity by a formal organization developed and devoted primarily to the pursuit of profits through illegal means. The application of the

RICO law shows the importance of conceptualizing organized crime as something basically different from a series of individual crimes. There is much disagreement about the extent to which the Mafia is organized at the national level. In recent years, other ethnic groups have taken over criminal enterprises that the predominantly Italian-American Mafia has controlled in the past.

Victimless crimes are consensual offenses that lack complaining witnesses. They include drug use, gambling, prostitution, and pornography. Drug use might be seen as harming users, or as hurting the victims of theft by users who steal to buy drugs, but sociologists often argue that it is the law's definition of drugs as illegal, more than the drugs themselves, that produce such negative consequences. Gambling is legal in some forms in certain states, and illegal in other forms in different states, leading many to question whether illegal gambling can be said to have a victim. Prostitutes may be victimized by pimps and clients, but their transactions with clients are usually offenses that involve no complainant. Federal law now defines pornography as a crime with a victim if it involves a minor, though most forms of pornography do not involve complaining participants and are rarely prosecuted as crimes.

The various types of crime are examined throughout the book, with concepts and theories being used to understand these crimes in greater depth.

Important Terms

aggravated assault
arson
assault
burglary
forcible rape
fraud
larceny
mass murder
motor vehicle theft

murder and nonnegligent
   manslaughter
organized crime
robbery
serial murder
simple assault
vandalism
victimless crime
white-collar crime

Suggested Readings

HOWARD ABADINSKY. *Organized Crime,* 2nd ed. Chicago: Nelson-Hall, 1985. An introductory textbook on criminal enterprises in the United States.

JAMES W. COLEMAN. *The Criminal Elite: The Sociology of White-Collar Crime.* New York: St. Martin's Press, 1985. A comprehensive introduction to the various forms of white-collar crime.

EDWIN M. SCHUR. *Crimes without Victims: Deviant Behavior and Public Policy.* Englewood Cliffs, N.J.: Prentice-Hall, 1965. A sociological study that introduced the concept of victimless crime.

PART II

The Extent and Nature of Crime

In Chapter 3 we look at the development of modern criminology. We then examine three measures of crime. Official crime statistics provide us with information about crimes reported to the police and suspects arrested by the police. Victimization data gathered in surveys show that much crime is not reported to the police; these data can be used to construct a more complete picture. Crime is also measured by self-reports, which are questionnaires filled out by people who admit to their own violations of the law.

The costs of crime are examined in Chapter 4. We look at the financial costs, including the exorbitant cost of white-collar crime, the expense of maintaining the criminal justice system, and losses to the victims of conventional property crimes. We investigate the physical harm caused by crimes of violence and by white-collar crimes. Finally, we examine the social costs, including the corrosive effects of white-collar crime and government corruption and the reactions of people to the threat of conventional crime.

Chapter 5 explores some of the variations in crime rates that theories of crime must explain. Cross-national and regional variations in crime rates are investigated, as are variations in rates by size of community. Temporal variations in crime rates, such as changes over the years, are explored. We examine male-female differences in both juvenile delinquency and adult crime, and the way that female involvement in crime and delinquency has changed in recent years. We investigate variations in crime rates by age and by racial group. The complex relationship between class and both adult crime and juvenile delinquency is also examined.

CHAPTER 3

Measuring Crime

Source: Courtesy American Correctional Association

The scientific study of criminal behavior originated in Europe in the nineteenth century. Until then, there had been much speculation about crime, but it was abstract and not based on empirical research. Early ideas about the causes of crime have generally proved inaccurate or incomplete, but the history of these ideas is important for understanding the emergence of modern criminology.

The Emergence of Modern Criminology

From 1500 until about 1750, philosophers who investigated the problem of crime usually proposed that people freely chose how to act. This assumption of "free will" implies that people are responsible for the consequences of their behavior. Another implication is that people can be controlled through fear, especially the fear of pain. Punishment by the state, an institution based on a "social contract" among its citizens to live together in peace, thus becomes the primary means to instill fear and prevent criminal behavior.

Classical Criminology

These ideas were the basis of the *classical school* of criminology. This approach developed during the Enlightenment, an eighteenth-century movement in European thought that emphasized progress, individualism, the use of reason, the questioning of tradition, and the use of empirical data to test abstract ideas.

The major proponent of the classical approach was an Italian, Cesare Beccaria (1738–1794), who sharply criticized the criminal justice system, especially judges who imposed arbitrary and harsh punishments. Along with earlier philosophers, Beccaria believed that punishment was needed to prevent people from violating the law. He thought that people were motivated by pain and pleasure, that they exercised free will, and that rationality and responsibility characterized human action. According to Beccaria, fear of punishment would lead people to conform to the law.

Beccaria claimed that punishment should be based on the harm that the criminal act did to society, rather than on the harm incurred by the victim. Harm was to be judged by the consequences of the act rather than by the intentions of the offender. Marxist critics have argued that this approach contains a basic flaw: In capitalist societies, social harm will inevitably be defined in a way that protects the interests of capitalists from interference by other classes (Taylor, Walton, and Young, 1973: 3).

Beccaria hoped that making punishment proportional to social harm would limit the arbitrary punishment meted out by judges. Implicit in his theory is the notion that similar crimes should be punished similarly, an idea violated by the judges of his time as well as those of today. This idea, basic to the theory of retribution or "just deserts," suggests that an offender's characteristics and the circumstances of the crime should not be taken into account in meting out punishment.

Beccaria's ideas were the basis of the 1791 criminal code of France, but problems arose in implementing that code. The code ignored differences among offenders and differences in the circumstances of crimes. It treated first offenders and repeat offenders alike when they were convicted of similar offenses, and it gave no special attention to offenders who were minors, insane, or retarded.

The revised French criminal code of 1819 provided for somewhat more judicial discretion, allowing judges to consider the circumstances of the crime but not the offender's intent. The underlying assumption was that the idea of free will was valid, but that individual responsibility could be influenced by pathology, incompetence, or insanity. The notion of premeditation—the consideration of one's behavior prior to acting—developed as a measure of free will (Vold and Bernard, 1986). Age, mental capacity, and the circumstances of the crime were accepted as factors that could mitigate punishment, for these factors were thought to reduce personal responsibility. This led to the use of testimony by experts to help the courts decide on the extent to which defendants could be held responsible and punished for their actions.

The idea implicit in the 1819 code was that sentences had different effects on different kinds of offenders. This was the beginning of the rehabilitation rationale for punishment, the idea that the goal of punishment is to change offenders so they will not commit crime again. Individual choice of behavior was the basis of the 1819 code, but choice was increasingly seen as influenced by social and psychological factors (Taylor, Walton, and Young, 1973: 9)

Cartography

Some European nations had been gathering official data on crime since the sixteenth century, but it was not until the nineteenth century that scholars began to use these statistics to understand crime. Their approach has been called *cartography,* because it involves the use of data to map or chart patterns of crime.

Important studies using this approach were published in 1833 by Guerry, a French lawyer, and in 1838 by Quetelet, a Belgian mathematician. These two cartographers worked independently, but they came to similar conclusions from their studies of national crime data. Both found that the annual total of crime recorded in a country remains fairly constant over time, and that each kind of crime remains about the same proportion of the total over time. They concluded that officially recorded crime is "a regular feature of social activity" that is better explained by social conditions than by individual predispositions (Taylor, Walton, and Young, 1973: 37; Beirne, 1987).

The cartographic approach was used to great advantage in a ground-breaking study of suicide by Emile Durkheim (1858–1917), one of the founders of sociology. In his writings on crime, Durkheim (1895, 1938) shared with Guerry and Quetelet the idea that crime is a normal feature of social life. He did not mean that crime was good or to be encouraged, but rather that crime exists in all societies and therefore must be studied in its relationship to the social structure.

Durkheim did suggest that crime has some positive functions, or consequences, for society: It delineates what behavior is acceptable to the members of society, it draws official attention to the social conditions that cause crime, and it can create social solidarity in opposition to people who violate important social standards.

Positivism

Modern scientific criminology grew out of the work of three Italian students of crime — Cesare Lombroso, Enrico Ferri, and Raffaele Garofalo. They saw the proper course of criminology as "the systematic elimination of the free will 'metaphysics' of the classical school" (Taylor, Walton, and Young, 1973: 10). Rather than try to reduce crime by relying on the criminal justice system, as did the classical criminologists, they sought to learn the causes of crime and then eliminate the conditions that produce it. Modern criminology has been dominated by this perspective, but the criminal justice system has been dominated by classical thinking during the twentieth century.

This perspective, which is called *positivism,* relies on the scientific method, quantifying and measuring behavior and the social conditions associated with that behavior. Positivists claim that scientific neutrality is possible in the study of crime, and that criminologists should focus on criminal behavior rather than on the criminal law. Positivists see themselves as relatively objective in their work, but critics allege that a positivist approach implicitly supports the existing legal system by adopting the state's definition of crime. However, positivists do have a legitimate claim to objectivity, for compared with the work done by scholars who argue that scientific neutrality is impossible, positivists have generally produced more reliable results — that is, results that different scholars would also get if they applied the same scientific methods to the same data.

Positivists claim that human behavior is subject to causal laws. This assertion that behavior is determined, or at least influenced, by forces outside the control of individuals contradicts the classical position that people are rational beings who exercise free will and determine their own behavior. Positivism sometimes goes too far in denying individual freedom to choose how to behave, but it lends itself well to the study of social, psychological, economic, political, and biological influences. Research by positivists can thus generate recommendations for policies to reduce crime — for instance, by strengthening the family or by cutting poverty.

CESARE LOMBROSO   Cesare Lombroso (1835–1909) was the first influential proponent of the positivist approach to criminology. He has been called the "father of criminology" because he was able to direct the study of crime away from questions of free will and personal responsibility to a more scientific basis. Although Lombroso's ideas about the biological origins of crime have proved erroneous, and sometimes even ludicrous, his work did mark an important turning point in criminology. By stressing measurable characteristics, even if they were the wrong ones, Lombroso made it possible to determine which factors actually are related to criminal behavior. In the early editions of his textbook on the criminal offender, Lombroso attributed crime primarily to biological factors, but his research led him to downplay the significance of these factors and give greater emphasis to insanity, poor education, and social background in later editions of his book. This change in his views on crime causation is testimony to the positivist method, for by focusing on measurable factors Lombroso was able to test his ideas about the causes of crime and then modify his theory in light of new evidence.

BEYOND LOMBROSO   Enrico Ferri (1856–1929) and Raffaele Garofalo (1852–1934) were two positivists who went beyond Lombroso in the study of the causes of crime. Ferri focused on causes such as climate, age, race, sex, psychology, population density, and political and economic conditions. His work has been criticized for failing to specify the relative importance of each factor in the causation of crime. Garofalo shared some of Lombroso's ideas on crime causation, but his work focused on psychological factors such as the lack of compassion among offenders. Positivism is not necessarily associated with any particular theory of crime, but is instead a method that can be used to assess the influence of many different factors on criminal behavior.

By 1900 the seeds of modern criminology had been sown. The emphasis on measurement, scientific neutrality, and the testing of hypotheses with empirical data was a major advance over the speculative work of the classical school. Even if the early positivists' explanations were often inaccurate or incomplete, they did provide criminologists with the methods to determine whether explanations are right or wrong. The positivist approach offers the possibility that ultimately a theory of crime supported by research will be developed. Positivists generate theories to explain their research findings and then test those theories with more research, modifying their explanations to fit new evidence. Before a theory supported by research can be developed, however, it is necessary to collect data on the dimensions of crime that must be explained by a theory. In the rest of this chapter we look at several methods for gathering data on crime.

Official Crime Statistics

Criminologists often use measures of crime produced by law-enforcement agencies to study criminal behavior and offenders. Because students of crime frequently use statistics they do not collect, they must have a thorough knowledge of how those statistics are produced (Black, 1970). Changes in law-enforcement practices over time may alter the way that crime statistics are gathered; when this happens, a change in crime rates may reflect a change in enforcement activity rather than a real increase or decrease in the amount of criminal activity (see, e.g., Tobias, 1967).

History of Crime Statistics in the United States

Before 1870, little attention was paid to the measurement of crime in the United States. In that year, a federal law was passed that required the attorney general to report annually to Congress on the amount of crime in the country; this law was largely ignored. In the following year, an organization that was the forerunner of today's International Association of Chiefs of Police (IACP) called for the collection of national crime data, but a committee to deal with that task was not formed until 1927. Two years later a manual for reporting crime statistics was distributed to police departments around the country and the collection of data

The FBI, which began collecting crime statistics about sixty years ago, publishes an annual report that includes data on arrested suspects. *Source: Warshaw Collection / Archive Center of the Smithsonian Institution*

began. There was some disagreement over whether the Federal Bureau of Investigation (FBI) or the Bureau of the Census should gather the data and issue a report. In 1930, the FBI began compiling crime statistics, and later that year Congress passed a law authorizing the FBI to continue collecting crime data (Maltz, 1977; Inciardi, 1980a). These statistics are now published in an annual volume, *Crime in the United States: Uniform Crime Reports.*

In 1931, Thorsten Sellin stated that "the value of a crime for index purposes decreases as the distance from the crime itself in terms of procedure increases" (p. 346). This view was widely shared and led the FBI to focus on crimes reported to and recorded by the police, rather than on data on arrested suspects, defendants in court, or prison inmates. The farther we move from the report of the crime, the more likely we are to get a distorted picture of it. For example, research shows that systematic distortion in the arresting of drug suspects does not allow us to measure trends in drug offenses with arrest data (DeFleur, 1975). This is because changes in arrests over time are related to changes in the perceived seriousness of drug law violations and changes in patterns of law enforcement.

Ideally, national crime statistics would include police data on reported crimes and arrested suspects. Suspects would then be followed through the criminal justice system, and information would be recorded on the disposition of cases and the sentences meted out to convicted offenders. Maintaining such records would be costly and difficult, but it would give us a more complete picture of crime than we now have. In 1981, the Bureau of Justice Statistics in the U.S. Department of Justice, with the assistance of seven states, began to collect data on arrested suspects and the criminal justice system's processing of them. Three states dropped out of this study because of budgetary constraints and other problems, but four states provided some preliminary offender-based transaction statistics (OBTS) (Bureau of Justice Statistics, November 1983b).

FBI Crime Statistics

The FBI has achieved nearly complete coverage of the country in its collection of data from the police. It now gathers statistics from nearly 16,000 city, county, and state law-enforcement agencies, which cover 96 percent of the country's population. Coverage is best for major metropolitan areas, where 98 percent of the population is covered, and worst for rural areas, where 89 percent of the population is covered. In 1987, forty-one states had crime-reporting programs that gathered statistics from local police departments and forwarded them to the FBI; the FBI collects data directly from local police departments in the other states. What the FBI misses, however, are crimes reported to agencies and institutions other than the police. For instance, statistics on crimes recorded by campus police forces often fail to get into the FBI's annual crime reports.

The FBI presents detailed data on eight crimes, the Part I offenses that together constitute the *crime index.* The FBI presents much less information on twenty-one Part II crimes. Table 3.1 defines the eight Part I and the twenty-one

Offenses in the FBI's Uniform Crime Reporting System

Part I (Index) Offenses

Murder and nonnegligent manslaughter: the willful killing of one human being by another.

Forcible rape: carnal knowledge of a female forcibly and against her will, including attempts.

Robbery: taking or attempting to take anything of value from another person by force or threat of force.

Aggravated assault: unlawful attack by one person upon another for the purpose of inflicting severe or aggravated bodily injury, usually accompanied by the use of a weapon.

Burglary—breaking or entering: unlawful entry of a structure to commit a felony or a theft.

Larceny—theft: unlawful taking, carrying, leading, or riding away of property from the possession of another; excluding motor vehicle theft, embezzlement, con games, and forgery.

Motor vehicle theft: theft or attempted theft of a motor vehicle.

Arson: willful or malicious burning, or attempt to burn, with or without intent to defraud, of a house, public building, motor vehicle or aircraft, or personal property of another.

Part II Offenses

Other assaults (simple): assaults and attempted assaults where no weapon is used and that do not result in serious injury to the victim.

Forgery and counterfeiting: making, altering, uttering, or possessing, with intent to defraud, anything false that is made to appear true.

Fraud: fraudulent conversion and obtaining money or property by false pretenses.

Embezzlement: misappropriation or misapplication of money or property entrusted to one's care, custody, or control.

Stolen property: buying, receiving, possessing: buying, receiving, and possessing stolen property, including attempts.

Vandalism: willful or malicious destruction, injury, disfigurement, or defacement of any public or private property, real or personal, without consent of the owner or persons having custody or control.

Weapons: carrying, possessing, etc.: all violations of regulations or statutes controlling the carrying, using, possessing, furnishing, and manufacturing of deadly weapons or silencers.

Prostitution and commercialized vice: sex offenses of a commercialized nature, such as prostitution, keeping a bawdy house, procuring, or transporting women for immoral purposes.

Sex offenses (except forcible rape, prostitution and commercialized vice): statutory rape and offenses against chastity, common decency, morals, and the like.

Drug abuse violations: state and local offenses relating to narcotic drugs, such as unlawful possession, sale, use, growing, and manufacturing of narcotic drugs.

Gambling: promoting, permitting, or engaging in illegal gambling.

Offenses against the family and children: nonsupport, neglect, desertion, or abuse of family and children.

Driving under the influence: driving or operating any vehicle or common carrier while drunk or under the influence of liquor or narcotics.

Liquor laws: state or local liquor law violations, except drunkenness and driving under the influence; federal violations are excluded.

Drunkenness: drunkenness or intoxication, excluding driving under the influence.

Disorderly conduct: breach of the peace.

Vagrancy: vagabondage, begging, loitering, etc.

All other offenses: all violations of state or local laws, except the preceding offenses and traffic offenses.

Suspicion: no specific offense; suspect released without formal charges being placed.

Curfew and loitering laws: offenses relating to violations of local curfew or loitering ordinances where such laws exist.

Runaways: limited to juveniles taken into protective custody under provisions of local statutes.

SOURCE: Adapted from Federal Bureau of Investigation, *Crime in the United States, 1986: Uniform Crime Reports.* Washington, D.C.: U.S. Government Printing Office, 1987, pp. 331–332.

Part II crimes. The FBI justifies its presentation of more detail on the Part I offenses by claiming that these crimes

- are regarded by the public as very serious,
- are relatively frequent in occurrence, and
- often come to the attention of the police.

CRITICISMS OF FBI STATISTICS Critics claim that the public may regard Part I offenses as serious because the FBI gives them the most attention. In other words, the FBI's choice of what to include in Part I conveys to the public a particular image of "the crime problem," one that for the most part consists of crimes against persons and property by people who have low incomes or who are members of minority groups (Reiman, 1984).

The FBI's crime report pays little attention to white-collar crime. Of the eight Part I offenses, only arson is sometimes a white-collar crime. White-collar crimes such as price fixing and government corruption fit the FBI's criterion of being relatively frequent, but no mention is made of those offenses in its crime report. Some of the Part II crimes, such as embezzlement and fraud, are white-collar offenses. However, the FBI does not indicate that white-collar crimes inflict much greater financial losses on the American public than do all the crimes in Part I of the report (see Chapter 4). Local law-enforcement agencies rarely learn of white-collar crimes because of their complexity, because the public thinks that the police will not deal with such offenses, and because corporate victims of white-collar crime keep some of those offenses secret so as not to harm their public image. As a result, FBI crime reports convey the impression that white-collar crime is of little consequence in American society.

FBI reports are also deficient in failing to indicate the pervasive involvement of organized crime in criminal activities in the United States. Data on arrests for narcotics violations and gambling appear in the FBI's reports, but these statistics do not show gangsters' involvement in these offenses, nor are any data presented on loan sharking (usury), a major source of revenue for organized crime.

Crime Rates

The FBI Uniform Crime Report (UCR) gives the absolute number of crimes and the crime rates for the index offenses, except for arson for which data are incomplete. The FBI calculates national *crime rates* by dividing the number of reported crimes by the number of people in the country, and then expressing the result as a rate of crimes per 100,000 people. For instance, in 1986 there were 20,613 recorded cases of murder and nonnegligent manslaughter in the United States. The estimate of the nation's population in 1986 was 241,077,000. The murder rate per 100,000 is thus calculated as follows:

$$\frac{20,613}{241,077,000} \times 100,000 = 8.6 \text{ per } 100,000$$

Expressing the crime rate in this way makes more sense than simply stating how many homicides occurred in 1986. For example, if the United States had 20,613 murders in a year in the past when its population was exactly half as large as its 1986 population, the murder rate in that earlier year would have been twice as high as it was in 1986, or 17.2 per 100,000 people.

Crime rates, rather than the absolute number of crimes, are the appropriate measure for comparing countries, states, or cities. In the following excerpt from an advice column in *The Boston Globe*, the letter writer asks a question about crime rates in the correct way, but the newspaper provides an inappropriate response:

> **Q.** I have to make a job choice between New York City and Houston. Can you tell me how the crime rates for these cities compare — V.P., Burlington [Mass.]
>
> **A.** The latest available annual (1977) FBI major crime statistics for New York City and Houston are as follows: New York — 1,553 murders, 3,899 rapes, 74,404 robberies; 42,056 assaults; 178,907 burglaries; 214,838 larcenies; and 94,420 motor vehicle thefts. Houston — 376 murders; 965 rapes; 6,153 robberies; 1,810 assaults; 33,419 burglaries; 60,839 larcenies; and 13,726 motor vehicle thefts. (*The Boston Globe,* May 7, 1980, p. 86)

Here the newspaper gives the total number of crimes in each city, making it impossible for the letter writer to compare the crime rates of the cities without looking up their populations. The letter writer wanted to compare risks of victimization in the two cities, and crime rates are needed to do that. FBI reports do not give city-by-city crime rates, but these rates can be calculated by using census data on the populations of the cities and FBI data on numbers of crimes in the cities. Let us see what happens when we calculate murder rates for New York City and Houston:

	Number of Murders (1977)	Population (1977)	Murder Rate per 100,000 People
New York City	1,553	7,298,000	21.3
Houston	376	1,555,000	24.2

New York City had many more murders than Houston in 1977, but it also had a much larger population. When we calculate murder rates per 100,000 people —a measure of the risk that a person such as the letter writer will be killed in a given year— we find that the homicide rate per 100,000 people was actually higher in Houston, by 24.2 to 21.3. Based on the faulty answer by *The Boston Globe,* the letter writer would have moved to Houston, even though the risk of being murdered there was greater than in New York City.

Sociological criminology often focuses on crime rates. Rather than examining and explaining each and every criminal act, it makes more sense to look at rates of crime and seek explanations for variations in crime rates among different social groups. For instance, if poor people have a higher murder rate than well-to-do people, we might focus on blocked opportunities and frustrated ambitions as causes of murder. We might also suggest that policies that increase available jobs and reduce economic inequality could reduce the rate at which people kill others.

CRIMES OF VIOLENCE Calculating crime rates in terms of number of offenses per 100,000 people makes sense for murder, robbery, and aggravated assault because in these crimes of violence it is individuals who are at risk. The FBI rates for these and other index offenses are shown in Table 3.2.

According to the FBI's definition, forcible rape can only involve female victims. Because the FBI presents forcible rape statistics only for sexual assaults that involve women as victims, it makes no sense for it to present rates of forcible rape per 100,000 people in the country, because nearly half of the people in the denominator used to calculate the rate are men. For instance, in 1986 the FBI reported that there were 37.5 recorded rapes and attempted rapes per 100,000 people (men and women). The rate of rape would be better expressed by dividing the number of incidents (90,434) by the number of women in the country (123,776,000), a rate of 73.1 per 100,000 women. This rate gives us a better idea of the risk of rape faced by women, although calculating the rate in this way means that it cannot be compared with rates of murder, assault, or robbery which are calculated per 100,000 people (both men and women).

PROPERTY CRIMES Burglary, larceny, motor vehicle theft, and arson are crimes against property, even though it is people who own the stolen or burned property. The FBI calculates crime rates for these offenses by dividing the

TABLE 3.2   Rates of Crime per 100,000 People, United States, 1986

Crime	Rate Per 100,000 People
Murder and nonnegligent manslaughter	8.6
Forcible rape	37.5
Robbery	225.1
Aggravated assault	346.1
Burglary	1,344.6
Larceny—theft	3,010.3
Motor vehicle theft	507.8
Arson	*
Crime index total	5,479.9

*Sufficient data are not available to estimate the crime rate.
SOURCE: Adapted from Federal Bureau of Investigation, *Crime in the United States, 1986: Uniform Crime Reports.* Washington, D.C.: U.S. Government Printing Office, 1987, p. 42.

number of incidents by the number of people in the country, and expressing the rates as offenses per 100,000 people. Rates calculated in terms of number of offenses per amount of property available to be stolen or burned would provide more useful information. For instance, rates of larceny might best be calculated in terms of dollars of property stolen as a proportion of the total gross national product (GNP) that is available to be stolen each year, rather than as the number of larceny incidents per 100,000 people. Rates of property crime per 100,000 people grow dramatically during economic development and increasing affluence, because the amount of property available to be stolen is growing (Clinard and Abbott, 1973; Shelley, 1981a).

Rates of auto theft that are calculated in terms of thefts per 100,000 people conceal more information than they provide. For instance, in 1886 the rate of motor vehicle theft was of course 0 per 100,000 people, for the simple reason that there were no cars to be stolen; the first reported auto theft was not until 1905. In 1986 the rate of car theft was 507.8 per 100,000 people. Comparing this rate with the rate a century earlier means little unless we know how many cars were available to be stolen in each year. Thus, the rate of auto thefts per number of cars in the country would make more sense than the rate of auto thefts per 100,000 people that the FBI presents. Some of the increase in car thefts in recent years is attributable to the fact that the number of cars in the country has grown faster than the number of people, and there are thus more cars to be stolen. We need to remove the effects of changes in the opportunities available for this crime to see the real meaning of changes in crime rates (Sparks, 1980a).

THE FBI CRIME INDEX   In calculating an overall rate of Part I crimes, the FBI adds the reported number of seven crimes (omitting arson because of incomplete data) and divides by the number of people in the country to get a rate of index crimes per 100,000 people. In 1986 the crime index rate was 5,479.9 per 100,000 people.

The FBI does not attempt to weight the index crimes by their relative seriousness. Obviously a homicide is more serious than the theft of a quarter, but the FBI treats both the same in calculating the crime index rate. The FBI also treats all motor vehicle thefts as index crimes, even though most auto thefts are for "joy riding" rather than for resale of the car or its parts. A theft in which the car is shipped out of the country for resale would seem to be more serious than a theft in which teenagers abandon a car unharmed after it runs out of gasoline.

If the FBI systematically applied a measure of the relative seriousness of various crimes to police crime reports, the informational value of the crime index rate would be improved. However, a seriousness scale might magnify some of the problems with FBI statistics. Thus, weighting crimes would mean that robberies would count more than simple larcenies, but white-collar crimes would still be omitted from the overall crime rate. Nevertheless, some consideration of the relative seriousness of the different index crimes would provide better information than is now available from the crime index rate (Wolfgang, 1968: 281). For instance, the overall crime index rate might remain the same for two consecutive years, even if a decline of 10,000 murders were offset by an increase of 10,000 larcenies from one year to the next. Clearly crime in the second year would be less serious because of the reduction in murders, but the FBI crime index rate would not reveal that change in the composition of the crime rate.

Gathering Crime Statistics

To ensure uniformity in the reporting of crime by local police departments and state reporting programs, the FBI circulates a *Uniform Crime Reporting Handbook* to tell the police how to record crimes. Still, crimes may be counted somewhat differently by local police departments. For instance, some departments may record an auto theft the instant a car is reported missing, and other departments may put such a report aside for a few hours to make sure the owner does not call back to say that someone in the family had just borrowed the car. The FBI is aware of such differences among police departments and cautions readers of its reports "against comparing statistical data of individual reporting units," in part because of different "administrative and investigative emphases of law enforcement" (Federal Bureau of Investigation, 1987: v). However, if we cannot compare the crime rates of various communities, then we cannot add the crime rates of those different communities to get a national crime rate, and the FBI does that every year.

Sometimes multiple offenses are committed during the same crime incident. Thus, if an offender threatens a couple with a knife, forces them into their car, tells them to drive him somewhere, and then steals their money before riding off in their car, he has committed two simple assaults, two kidnappings, one auto theft, and one robbery. In this case, the FBI says to count only the most serious offense, or one robbery. Some might consider kidnapping a more serious crime than robbery, but the FBI does not treat kidnapping as an index offense, probably because it occurs relatively infrequently. Information is lost because the FBI ignores some offenses and records only the most serious crime in a series of offenses, but recording each different violation of the law would overstate the extent of crime.

CRIME REPORTING Because the police can cover only a limited territory and do not have easy access to private places, they learn of many crimes from citizens, usually victims or witnesses. Sometimes people call the police switchboard to report a crime, and other times they report crimes directly to officers on the street or in patrol cars.

Some citizen complaints to the police are not officially recorded as crimes. One study found that only two-thirds of all complaints to the police produced an official crime report (Black, 1970). Another study found that most robberies that citizens report to interviewers in a survey are not reported to the police and recorded by the police as "founded" (or verified) crime incidents (Block and Block, 1980).

In contrast to *reactive police work* in which officers respond to a citizen's report of a crime, some police work is *proactive,* or the result of efforts by the police to discover and deal with crime on their own initiative (Reiss and Bordua, 1968; Reiss, 1971). Arrests for prostitution and narcotics offenses rarely result from complaints by the public but are typically the result of efforts by the police, especially the vice or narcotics squad. In crimes such as these, the number of recorded violations may tell us more about the size of the vice or narcotics squad than about the frequency with which the offenses occur. External pressure from political officials, the FBI, or crime commissions can also affect the level of proactive police work. Because the rate of arrests for "vice" offenses fluctuates wildly with changes in the social climate and changes in law-enforcement practices, the FBI does not include them in Part I of its Uniform Crime Report.

Reasons for Nonreporting. People fail to report crimes to the police for many reasons, the most significant of which have to do with the nature of the crime incident itself. Victims are least likely to report

- offenses that are attempted rather than completed,
- offenses in which there is little or no financial loss or physical injury,
- offenses that do not threaten their sense of personal security,
- offenses that do not seem serious to them, and
- offenses in which no firearm is used (Hindelang, 1976; Skogan, 1976b, 1984; Block and Block, 1980).

The effect of loss of property and extent of injury can be seen in the results of a survey which found that only 24 percent of robberies involving no loss and no injury were reported to the police, but 72 percent of robberies with some loss of property and some injury were reported (Bureau of Justice Statistics, December 1985).

Many victims who do not report crimes to the police say they think there is little or nothing the police can do to catch the offender or retrieve the lost property. This view is supported by police statistics, which show that the police indeed are least likely to arrest suspects in those crimes that the public feels the police can do little about (Skogan, 1976a: 547–549).

Some victims do not report crimes to the police because they believe the offense is not very important. This may occur, for instance, when an inexpensive item is stolen, or when no real harm is done in an assault. The increased ownership of theft insurance — including automobile insurance — leads many victims to report crimes to the police even when they have little hope that their property will be recovered, for insurance companies often require notification of the police as proof that a theft occurred.

Some crimes are not reported because the victim is afraid of what the police might discover if they investigate the crime. Thus, a drug dealer who is robbed by another dealer may not report the crime. Other victims do not report crimes because they do not want to cause trouble for the offender. A related reason is the fear that the offender might take reprisals against the victim for reporting the crime, especially if the victim and offender are known to each other.

Victims are often unwilling to report crimes to the police because they see the offense as a private or personal matter. Rape victims may avoid the police because they feel stigmatized by the sexual attack. Assault victims may not report the crime because the attack was by a spouse or a parent. Police statistics in developing countries probably undercount assaults to a great extent, because there is often a tradition in local villages of dealing with crime — especially assaults between people who know each other — in an informal way, rather than by bringing in the police (Clinard and Abbott, 1973: 219–228).

Some victims do not report crime to the police because they think calling the police is too much trouble, especially if a suspect is arrested and they have to testify in court. Witnesses, as well as victims, may not report crimes because of inconvenience. A study in which "shoplifters" — who were actually participants in an experiment — tried to gain the attention of other shoppers in order to determine how many shoppers would report their thefts found that only 28 percent of all shoppers even said they had seen the "crime." Of those who admitted to seeing the shoplifting, only 28 percent reported it to store personnel. Many of the witnesses said that reporting the crime would have been inconvenient or troublesome (Gelfand et al., 1973).

Cross-national surveys have found that crime reporting is not closely associated with attitudes toward the police; in other words, people who are hostile toward the police seem to be as likely to report crime as people who are friendly toward the police. In addition, demographic variables such as race and income do not seem to be closely related to whether a victim will report a crime. Females are slightly more likely than men to report crimes, according to cross-national surveys, and the elderly are more likely than younger people to report crimes (Skogan, 1984). For the most part, however, it seems to be the seriousness of the incident and the type of the offense, rather than social characteristics or attitudes toward the police, that determine whether a victim or a witness will report a crime (Gove, Hughes, and Geerken, 1985).

POLICE RECORDING PRACTICES   Aside from being incomplete because of nonreporting, police crime statistics have other problems (Lejins, 1966; Chilton, 1968; Wolfgang, 1968; Weis, 1983). Because politicians and the public sometimes attribute rising crime rates to police ineffectiveness, the police may not record all of the crimes about which they learn.

The organization and guiding philosophy of a police department can influence the accuracy of its crime statistics (Kitsuse and Cicourel, 1963). A legalistic department may see the failure to arrest a suspect as a weakness of the officer, but a service-oriented department may stress the solution of problems without formal arrest; the first department would probably record more interpersonal conflicts as crimes and produce more arrests (Wilson, 1968: 172–226). If a department assigns the collection of crime statistics to precinct captains and rewards them for low crime rates in their precincts, the captains will have an incentive to omit crimes from their official reports. With centralized crime reporting through a switchboard in headquarters, with greater professionalism, and with greater departmental resources, a police department will probably record crime more accurately and more completely, and thereby provide a more valid picture of the crime problem, even though this may mean a higher official crime rate than if some crimes were omitted from the department's reports (Skogan, 1976b: 110–114; McCleary, Nienstedt, and Erven, 1982).

Sometimes the police record a crime that is reported to them but classify it as a less serious crime than it really is. This will reduce the rate of serious crimes but inflate the rate of minor offenses. Because most public attention is focused on the index offenses, this will make the police look better to outsiders. For instance, forcible rape may be classified as simple assault, and thefts in which force is used may be called larcenies rather than robberies.

POLITICAL USE OF CRIME STATISTICS   Crime statistics have been used for political purposes at both the local and national levels (Seidman and Couzens, 1974; Cronin, Cronin, and Milakovich, 1981). Rising crime rates have been used to justify higher police salaries and increases in police personnel, although police chiefs often acknowledge that police efficiency cannot be evaluated by crime data or arrest statistics. J. Edgar Hoover was a master at using rising crime rates to argue for increased FBI appropriations from Congress. However, he also argued for more funds when crime rates dropped, claiming that the crime problem was finally being solved and that it was no time to reduce support for the fight against crime.

Politicians sometimes use rising crime rates to attack their opponents as "soft on crime." They may claim that reductions in the crime rate during their own time in office show that they have successfully battled crime, even if they cannot demonstrate exactly how they did so. An interesting twist on this argument was heard during Richard M. Nixon's administration, when he asserted that even though he had not actually reduced the crime rate during his first term in office, he had managed to reduce the rate at which crime rates were increasing. Public opinion polls after both the 1968 and 1972 elections showed that the crime issue was a major reason traditional Democrats "crossed over" and voted for the Republican Nixon.

CLEARANCE AND ARREST STATISTICS   When the police are satisfied that they know who committed a crime, they classify the crime as "cleared" or solved. Most but not all cleared crimes lead to an arrest, and when someone is arrested the police provide information on the suspect to the FBI. In 1986, 20.7 percent of all index offenses were cleared by arrest; 46.3 percent of all violent crimes (murder, forcible rape, robbery, and aggravated assault) were cleared, but only 17.5 percent of all property crimes (burglary, larceny, auto theft, and arson) were cleared.

A 1984 study by the Police Foundation (Lawrence W. Sherman and Barry D. Glick, cited in Burnham, 1984) found that police departments define arrest in different ways, in spite of the FBI's efforts to standardize the definition. As a result, the probability that a citizen will end up with an arrest record depends on the jurisdiction in which an arrest is made. Because of improper and inconsistent recording practices, the use of arrest data to evaluate police departments or to assess the characteristics of offenders is risky.

The FBI's National Crime Information Center (NCIC) has developed a system of centralized and computerized records of arrested suspects (Bureau of Justice Statistics, November 1986). Supporters justify this program in the name of more efficient crime fighting, but critics say that it threatens the privacy of Americans (Laudon, 1986). Perhaps 30 percent of the American work force, and maybe 90 percent of young black males living in ghettoes, have arrest records (Radzinowicz and King, 1977: 314). Audits of the FBI's arrest files have found that as many as three-fourths of their records are "inaccurate, incomplete, or ambiguous" (Laudon, cited in Gelbspan, 1986: 99), and that each day the FBI transmits at least 12,000 invalid or inaccurate reports on suspects wanted for arrest (Burnham, 1985a). Inaccurate records of this sort may keep people from getting jobs or securing government benefits and might push some people deeper into a life of crime (Schwartz and Skolnick, 1962; Erickson and Goodstadt, 1979). Erroneous information may also make for less efficient law enforcement and may put police officers at risk from people they are unaware are wanted for crimes elsewhere. Some critics claim that the FBI's national criminal history file has little effect on crime rates, because "well over 90 percent of violent street crime is committed by local criminals who are already known to cities' and states' computerized systems" (Laudon, 1981: A27). In spite of these criticisms, a federal advisory panel recommended in 1987 that the national computer file be expanded to include information on people suspected of crimes but not yet charged.

Using FBI Data for Criminological Research

FBI crime data are of limited usefulness for criminologists, even though those data provide an indicator of the level of police activity in the nation. These statistics have also been used to get a reading on how crime rates change over time, but rising crime rates can result from more complete reporting and recording of crime as well as from increases in the actual amount of crime.

The way that the FBI gathers its statistics does not allow criminologists to do much additional analysis of the data. If the FBI collected information on each crime incident recorded by the police, criminologists could use those data to explore certain aspects of crime, such as the relationship between the age of the offender and the use of firearms. However, the FBI gathers only summaries of the number of crimes recorded by local police departments and then adds the figures from those summary reports to produce the tables in its annual report.

This report thus tells us how many murders occur each year; how many murders occur in each region of the country; and the sex, race, and age of arrested murder suspects. There is no way, however, to analyze the FBI data beyond the tables presented in the report. For instance, there is no way to determine how many whites and blacks are arrested for murder in the South in comparison to how many whites and blacks are arrested for murder in the Northeast.

A 1985 report by a consulting firm suggested changes in FBI practices that would make UCR crime statistics more useful to criminologists. In addition to calling for more thorough auditing of crime statistics to ensure their accuracy and completeness, the report suggested that local police agencies submit short accounts of each crime incident to the national office, which would then calculate crime rates. The consulting firm also recommended the collection from a sample of agencies of more detailed crime reports, both for index crimes and for other offenses such as kidnapping, extortion, and bribery. Criminologists could then analyze these reports to provide a better understanding of patterns of crime (Burnham, 1985b).

Measuring Criminal Victimization

Crime rates can be calculated in several ways, and each kind of rate has both merits and drawbacks (Erickson, Gibbs, and Jensen, 1977). Using official crime statistics, we can look at rates of recorded crime per 100,000 people, rates of recorded crime per number of available crime targets, rates of arrests for each kind of crime, and other rates based on crimes or suspects known to the police. Because many crimes are not reported to the police, or are not recorded by the police if they do learn of them, the rate at which people are victimized is likely to be greater than the rate of crime reported to the police.

History of Victimization Surveys

Apparently the first effort to measure crime by surveying members of households was carried out in 1720 in Denmark (Clinard, 1978: 222). However, the first large-scale, systematic effort to measure victimization by interviewing a cross section of a population was not conducted until 1966 in the United States (Ennis, 1967). This study of 10,000 American households by the National Opinion Research Center sought to determine how often people are victimized by crime. Since 1972, the federal government has done *victimization surveys* similar to the one carried out in 1966. These National Crime Surveys (NCS) question national samples representing 135,000 Americans from 60,000 households to measure both personal and household victimization rates. These surveys are perhaps the most costly effort to gather crime data ever undertaken (Inciardi, 1980a; Sparks, 1982). The Cross-Cultural Perspective shows that victimization surveys have also been carried out in other countries.

A Cross-Cultural Perspective: A Victimization Survey in Switzerland

Victimization surveys have been used to measure crime all over the world: in Great Britain, Canada, Australia, West Germany, the Netherlands, the Scandinavian countries, Japan, the Ivory Coast, and other nations. One comparison of crime rates in different countries that used victimization surveys was Marshall Clinard's comparison of Zürich, Switzerland; Stuttgart, West Germany; and Denver (Colorado) and Portland (Oregon) in the United States. All of these cities had populations between 383,000 and 630,000.

The Zürich survey used a representative sample of 248 households and questioned about 940 people aged fourteen and over. The survey was patterned after the one used by the NCS program to measure victimization in the United States and was administered by a large Swiss public opinion polling organization.

Because Swiss households are more closely knit than the average American household, it is likely that interviews with the head of the household in Switzerland provided more complete reporting of crimes suffered by members of the household than would be the case in the United States. Moreover, the relative infrequency of crime in Switzerland might make offenses more salient to respondents and therefore make people more likely to remember those crimes than if the crime rate were high.

The Zürich victimization survey found that neither household nor personal crime was widespread. The rate of burglaries or attempted burglaries in Zürich was about half as great as in Denver and Portland, and slightly lower than the rate in Stuttgart. The rate of larceny from the household and the rate of motor vehicle theft were also significantly lower in Zürich than in the three other cities. The rate of robbery from the person was about half as high in Zürich as in Denver, Portland, and Stuttgart. Larceny from the person was about half as common in Zürich as in Stuttgart, and much less than half as common as in the two American cities. The rate of assault was slightly more than half as high in Zürich as in Denver and Portland, but the rate of assault was somewhat greater in Zürich than in Stuttgart.

The victimization survey in Zürich confirmed the results of a cross-national comparison of official crime statistics: Switzerland has a relatively low rate of household and personal crime. For several reasons, the results of the Zürich victimization survey could not be compared with the official crime statistics for that city to determine how much crime that actually occurred there was not reported to and recorded by the police.

SOURCE: Based on Marshall B. Clinard, *Cities with Little Crime: The Case of Switzerland.* Cambridge, Eng.: Cambridge University Press, 1978, pp. 61–72.

Comparing NCS and FBI Data

The NCS program measures crime in a somewhat different way than does the FBI's Uniform Crime Reports (UCR) data collection program. Consequently, the results of these two efforts to measure crime are not strictly comparable.

The NCS measures the offenses of rape, robbery from the person, aggravated and simple assault, household burglary, larceny from the person, larceny from the household, and motor vehicle theft. It does not measure murder and kidnapping, and for reasons of economy it stopped collecting data on commercial burglary and commercial robbery in 1977. As a result, we cannot compare NCS data on burglary and robbery with the FBI's UCR data on burglary and robbery, for the latter include burglaries and robberies of commercial establishments as well as of private households and individuals.

TABLE 3.3   A Comparison of FBI Uniform Crime Reports and National Crime Surveys

	FBI's Uniform Crime Reports (UCR)	National Crime Survey (NCS)
Offenses measured:	Homicide Rape Robbery (personal and commercial) Assault (aggravated) Burglary (commercial and household) Larceny (commercial and household) Motor vehicle theft Arson	Rape Robbery (personal) Assault (aggravated and simple) Household burglary Larceny (personal and household) Motor vehicle theft
Scope:	Crimes reported to the police in most jurisdictions; considerable flexibility in developing small-area data	Crimes both reported and not reported to police; all data are for the nation as a whole; some data are available for a few large geographic areas
Collection method:	Police department reports to FBI	Survey interviews; periodically measures the total number of crimes committed by asking a national sample of 60,000 households representing 135,000 persons over the age of 12 about their experiences as victims of crime during a specified period
Kinds of information:	In addition to offense counts, provides information on crime clearances, persons arrested, persons charged, law-enforcement officers killed and assaulted, and characteristics of homicide victims	Provides details about victims (such as age, race, sex, education, income, and whether the victim and offender were related to each other) and about crimes (such as time and place of occurrence, whether or not reported to police, use of weapons, occurrence of injury, and economic consequences)
Sponsor:	Department of Justice Federal Bureau of Investigation	Department of Justice Bureau of Justice Statistics

SOURCE: Bureau of Justice Statistics, *Report to the Nation on Crime and Justice: The Data.* Washington, D.C.: U.S. Department of Justice, October 1983, p. 6.

In recording crimes against the household, the NCS and the FBI methods are the same; for instance, each counts one incident or one victimization for every burglary that is reported. However, the NCS and FBI methods of dealing with crimes against the person differ somewhat. If a robbery has two victims, the FBI counts only one robbery incident, but the NCS records two victimizations. NCS data are oriented to victimizations and to individuals, whereas FBI data are oriented to crime incidents and to both organizational and individual victims (Reiss, 1981). Table 3.3 outlines some of the differences and similarities of the two methods of collecting crime statistics.

The Dark Figure

Victimization surveys have uncovered a substantial *dark figure,* the number of crimes that actually occur but are not recorded by the police. The dark figure exists for many reasons, especially the failure of victims to report crimes and the failure of the police to record all reported crimes. Figure 3.1, a hypothetical example that graphically depicts the dark figure, shows an actual total crime rate that is constant over time, as represented by the horizontal line parallel to the time axis. At time 1 (t_1), some of this total amount of crime is reported (the solid vertical line) and some of it is unreported (the dotted vertical line, which is the dark figure). By time 2 (t_2), the rate of reported crime has increased and the amount of unreported crime has decreased, but the actual total crime rate remains the same as at time 1. By time 3 (t_3), in this hypothetical case, the official crime rate and the actual total crime rate are the same; in other words, at time 3, all crime that occurs is reported to and recorded by the police. Figure 3.1 shows how the official crime rate (the slanted line) might increase over time without any increase in the actual total crime rate (the horizontal line). This would happen if people began to report crime that previously had not been reported or

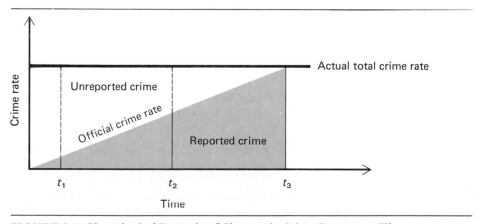

FIGURE 3.1   Hypothetical Example of Changes in Crime Rates over Time

if the police began to record more of the crime reported to them. If this happens, official crime rates could rise without any increase in the actual total crime rate.

The dark figure has several important consequences. One is to keep cases, usually the least serious ones, out of the criminal justice system. As we have seen, victims are not as likely to report less serious crimes, and so those offenses that come to the attention of the police are likely to be completed crimes, to involve larger losses of property and greater personal injury, and to be committed with firearms (Skogan, 1984). Offenders who commit crimes that are not reported to the police cannot be brought to trial, reducing the deterrent effect of punishment. Police and court resources are sometimes allocated on the basis of how much crime is recorded in a community, and thus differences in crime reporting from one area to another could lead to a misallocation of resources. Victim compensation programs and insurance programs may also be affected by the failure to report and record crime, for benefits and premiums may be based on a distorted picture of how much crime occurs. FBI estimates of the financial costs of crime must also be inflated to account for crimes that are not reported or recorded.

Methodological Problems with Victimization Surveys

Victimization surveys are subject to several methodological problems. One problem is the issue of validity, or how well the surveys actually measure the amount of crime in a society (Booth, Johnson, and Choldin, 1977). Forgetting can lead to underestimation of the amount of crime that has actually occurred, and it makes it difficult for subjects to tell interviewers exactly when they were victimized. Respondents may also refuse to tell interviewers about crimes for similar reasons to those that keep them from calling the police: the stigma of being victimized, unwillingness to confide in a stranger, and reluctance to take the time to give details of the crime.

Another problem is that victimization surveys may overestimate the amount of crime that occurs. Respondents may incorrectly interpret some experiences —such as the loss of a wallet—and report them as crimes. Overestimation of crime rates can also occur if people report crimes that occurred prior to the period about which they are being questioned as having occurred during that period. This problem of "telescoping" may result from a faulty memory or from the respondent's wish to have something to talk about with the interviewer. This problem of telescoping may inflate victimization rates by as much as 20 percent, leading to estimates of crime rates that are higher than actual rates (Brantingham and Brantingham, 1984). Overreporting can also be encouraged by interviewers who prod respondents to remember crimes, both to keep the interview interesting and to ferret out the "hidden crime" on which the victimization survey is predicated (Levine, 1976, 1978; Singer, 1978).

Because of these and other methodological problems, the results of victimization surveys should not be regarded as "true" measures of crime. These surveys do measure some of the crime that is not reported to and recorded by the police. However, a recent comparison of victimization survey results and FBI UCR statistics concluded that "if one defines crime as criminal acts serious enough to be reacted to by both citizens and the police, then [the evidence indicates that] the UCR are at least as valid and probably more valid than the data from victimization surveys" (Gove, Hughes, and Geerken, 1985: 491).

Even if they provided a valid measure of certain kinds of crime, victimization surveys have not given us a complete and balanced picture of crime. They have not been used to measure white-collar crime, organized crime, or victimless crimes (Johnson and Wasielewski, 1982). Victimization surveys provide little or no information on offenders, as do FBI data on arrested suspects. To develop a full picture of crime, the surveys must be supplemented with other kinds of data.

Another shortcoming of victimization surveys is that they have been used primarily to look at the amount and distribution of crime rather than to test or develop theories of criminal behavior (Johnson and Wasielewski, 1982). Victimization surveys have repeatedly shown that much crime is not reported and recorded, but they have contributed less to our understanding of the social processes that generate crime; as a result, they have contributed relatively little to the development of policies to reduce crime.

Measuring Crime by Self-Reports

Crime can be measured by police statistics or by questioning participants in the incident through a survey. Victimization surveys ask a cross section of the population about its experiences as victims of crime during a specific period, often six months. Another way to measure crime is to interview a cross section of the population, or a more limited sample such as high school students, about their involvement in crime and delinquency as offenders. *Self-report studies* reveal that much crime that respondents will admit to in confidential interviews or on self-administered questionnaires never makes its way into police statistics.

History of Self-Report Studies

The first use of survey methods to gather self-reported information about involvement in crime and delinquency was Austin L. Porterfield's (1946) research that used this "self-disclosure" method to compare college students with delinquents who had been through the juvenile court. Porterfield found that both groups had been involved in delinquency in similar ways during their adolescence. In 1947, a self-report survey of adults discovered that 99 percent of a sample of "law-abiding" middle-class people admitted to at least one crime (Wallerstein and Wyle, 1947). These early studies showed that much self-reported crime is never detected by the police.

In 1957, James F. Short, Jr., and F. Ivan Nye (1957) developed a checklist of delinquent activities to be filled out anonymously by respondents. They found

Using Criminology: How Many Children Are Missing?

Estimates of the number of missing children vary extensively. Incredibly, we do not know precisely how many children are abducted, how many run away, or how many are homeless. Even the most conservative estimates suggest that several hundred thousand children are missing within the course of a year.

Difficulties in making estimates

One of the major difficulties in estimating the number of missing children is that we lack a nationally based data collection system that accurately measures the size of the missing-child problem. The counting mechanisms we do have are confounded by overlapping definitions, confusion about the distinctions among the various types of missing children, and multiple criteria for defining a runaway child.

In addition, most runaways return without the intervention of a recordkeeping agency, and there is no way of counting the number of missing children who are recovered each year. Jurisdictional definitions of a missing child vary: in some jurisdictions the child must be missing twenty-four hours before being classified as missing, in other jurisdictions seventy-two hours, and so forth.

If a child is abducted and molested, or abducted and then murdered, the crime is often reported as a murder or molestation without referring to the fact than an abduction took place or that the child was missing, even for a short time. Consequently, the wide disparity in estimates of nonfamily or stranger abductions may, in part, be a reflection of the variety of definitions one can choose in formally reporting a missing child.

A recent magazine report summarized the dilemma of estimating the number of missing children as follows:

> At the center of the storm is the dispute over just how many children are missing. In 1983, the U.S. Department of Health and Human Services put the number at 1.5 million a year —a figure that has been widely circulated by private organizations. But experts say roughly 95 percent of those are runaways— many of whom return home within days and are counted repeatedly if they run away more than once a year. The vast majority of the rest are taken by estranged parents in custody battles. Only a tiny fraction fall into the category parents fear most—abductions by strangers —and even that figure is in dispute.
>
> *Newsweek,* "How Many Missing Kids?"
> October 7, 1985

We know that the vast majority of children reported missing each year are runaways and throwaways, not abducted children. Most return home unscathed on their own. In the foreword of its annual report to the Congress for fiscal year 1984, the Department of Health and Human Services estimated that the "number of runaway children in the Nation, ages ten to seventeen, is more than one million."

Despite the difficulty in obtaining consistent figures, we know that there are thousands, if not hundreds of thousands, of homeless, runaway, and throwaway children roaming the streets of our major cities. As many as one-fourth have left their hometowns. A 1983 study of the Runaway and Homeless Youth Program of the Department of Health and Human Services estimates that 16 percent of homeless children who come in contact with the Runaway and Homeless Youth Program are from out of the state, 11 percent are from out of the county, and 73 percent are from their local area.

We know that most abducted children are taken by a parent, grandparent, or other relative, frequently during a custody dispute. In a review of current literature, the National Center for Missing and Exploited Children found that the estimates of family abduction range from 25,000 to 500,000, indicating the difficulty of making precise estimates.

Children who are victims of nonfamily abduction are statistically the smallest group of missing children; however, this category is the most highly publicized and certainly the one families fear most.

National incidence study

Congress has mandated that the Office of Juvenile Justice and Delinquency Prevention (OJJDP) of the Department of Justice conduct a national study of the incidence of missing children. OJJDP has already met with researchers from various fields who have designed, funded, or conducted studies with similarly complex definitional and methodological problems to lay the groundwork for this study.

The national incidence study . . . will provide a comprehensive, verifiable assessment of the missing-children phenomenon. For each major category — runaways, throwaways, nonfamily abduction, and family abduction — the study will determine for a given year the actual number of children who are reported missing.

It is anticipated that the study will reveal important data on both the numbers and characteristics of all incidents involving missing children. It will thus provide valuable knowledge on the circumstances and duration of the absences, the child's experience while away from home, and the level of assistance provided to the child and his or her family.

If future public policy is to be grounded in fact, the actual numbers and types of children who are out of parental custody are needed. The national incidence study will greatly enhance our capacity to make informed and responsible decisions about responding to the problems of missing and abducted children.

The Uniform Crime Reporting (UCR) program, which is administered by the FBI in cooperation with state and local law-enforcement agencies, will be another important source of information. The UCR program gathers general statistical information about crimes in the United States, but little statistical data is collected concerning crimes against children. If recommendations made by an FBI study group are adopted, the UCR program will collect information about abducted and exploited children that will describe the nature of the criminal incident, including victim and offender characteristics, victim-offender relationship, the use of force, the nature and extent of injury, and the type of location.

SOURCE: U.S. Attorney General's Advisory Board on Missing Children, *America's Missing & Exploited Children: Their Safety and Their Future*. Washington, D.C.: U.S. Department of Justice, March 1986, pp. 11–13.

that delinquency was more evenly spread across social classes than was indicated by official crime statistics, which showed much more delinquency among the lower classes. Since this pioneering work, many researchers have used self-reports to test and refine theories of crime and delinquency and to provide a more complete picture of violation of the law than is given by official statistics (Weis, 1983). Table 3.4 shows six questions used by Travis Hirschi (1969) to gather self-report data on delinquency among California students and to test the control theory of delinquency.

Self-report studies have also been conducted with groups of offenders other than those who engage in conventional crimes and delinquent acts. For instance,

---

TABLE 3.4   Survey Questions Measuring Self-Reported Delinquency

1. Have you ever taken little things (worth less than $2) that did not belong to you?
   A. No, never
   B. More than a year ago
   C. During the last year
   D. During the last year *and* more than a year ago
2. Have you ever taken things of some value (between $2 and $50) that did not belong to you?
   A. No, never
   B. More than a year ago
   C. During the last year
   D. During the last year *and* more than a year ago
3. Have you ever taken things of large value (worth over $50) that did not belong to you?
   A. No, never
   B. More than a year ago
   C. During the last year
   D. During the last year *and* more than a year ago
4. Have you ever taken a car for a ride without the owner's permission?
   A. No, never
   B. More than a year ago
   C. During the last year
   D. During the last year *and* more than a year ago
5. Have you ever banged up something that did not belong to you on purpose?
   A. No, never
   B. More than a year ago
   C. During the last year
   D. During the last year *and* more than a year ago
6. Not counting fights you may have had with a brother or sister, have you ever beaten up on anyone or hurt anyone on purpose?
   A. No, never
   B. More than a year ago
   C. During the last year
   D. During the last year *and* more than a year ago

SOURCE: Adapted from Travis Hirschi, *Causes of Delinquency*. Berkeley, Calif.: University of California Press, 1969, p. 256.

in 1976 the Internal Revenue Service (IRS) mailed questionnaires to 1,200 corporations to ask about their use of illegal bribes and "slush funds." Three hundred four corporations did not respond, but among those that did, the IRS found 481 potentially illegal slush funds and seventy-one cases of apparent criminal fraud (Egan, 1978).

The Dark Figure

Self-report studies confirm the conclusion of victimization surveys that the dark figure, or hidden amount of crime, is large. For instance, a study that asked 180 boys, most of whom had been in trouble with the law, about their involvement in twenty-two crimes and delinquent acts found that the boys admitted to an average of 680 offenses (Erickson and Empey, 1963). A study of male heroin users that employed self-report questionnaires found that the drug users confessed to an average of 337 crimes per year (Inciardi, 1979). Research on forty-nine incarcerated robbers found that they admitted to a total of 10,505 offenses during their careers, an average of 214 crimes per offender (Petersilia, Greenwood, and Lavin, 1977). These and many other studies dramatically demonstrate that official crime statistics undercount the amount of crime.

Another conclusion from self-report studies is that nearly everyone in the general population has broken the law at some time, even though most of the violations are petty. The general population falls on a continuum from highly criminal to completely noncriminal; it is not composed of two discrete groups of criminals and noncriminals. Researchers who compare a sample of convicted offenders with a "noncriminal" sample drawn from the general population usually fail to consider that many of these "noncriminals" have in fact engaged in crimes themselves. Large numbers of people commit a few, often trivial, crimes; some commit a large number; others commit quite a few crimes, including some serious ones; and a small proportion of the population commits many crimes, including large numbers of serious ones (Elmhorn, 1965). Researchers have found that the more often a person violates the law, the more likely that person is to commit a relatively serious crime.

Methodological Problems with Self-Report Studies

Self-report studies have several methodological shortcomings that account for their failure to provide an ideal measure of crime (Reiss, 1975; Brantingham and Brantingham, 1984; Nettler, 1984). The questionnaires used in these studies sometimes lack validity; that is, they do not accurately measure the amount of crime that respondents have committed. Subjects may fabricate behavior to impress interviewers, or they may fail to mention some offenses out of fear that the information will be passed on to the police, in spite of guarantees of anonymity. At least two studies show that some kind of external control over lying is needed to ensure the validity of self-report instruments (Clark and Tifft, 1966; Farrington, 1973).

Self-report studies have been criticized for using school or neighborhood samples that fail to include officially labeled, chronic delinquents. Critics question the assumption of many self-report researchers that "official delinquents are no different from adolescents located at various other points along the delinquency continuum" (Cernkovich, Giordano, and Pugh, 1985: 731). These critics urge researchers to locate and study more official delinquents, because data indicate that the factors explaining relatively minor transgressions are not necessarily the same factors accounting for the actions of chronic delinquent offenders.

Another problem with self-report studies is the way they have been carried out. The use of many different self-report questionnaires by researchers means that their results are often not comparable. Self-report studies would be much more useful if the same questionnaire were administered over time to national samples. This would allow us to generalize about the amount of crime in the population as a whole, and to look at changes in the amount of crime over time (Brantingham and Brantingham, 1984). We have accumulated some data of this sort on victimization experiences, but we do not yet have such information on self-reported violations of the law. In fact, we know relatively little about self-reported crime by adults, for the vast majority of self-report studies have been carried out on samples of juveniles.

Self-report studies are also flawed in that they ignore certain kinds of behavior. They rarely include questions that add to our knowledge of white-collar crime or organized crime. The way questionnaires are written usually makes it difficult to compare the results of self-report studies with official crime statistics or with NCS data. This is partly a result of the use of self-report questionnaires with juvenile samples, for this means that respondents are asked about acts that would be crimes if they were adults as well as about juvenile status offenses such as truancy and underage drinking.

Some self-report studies classify juveniles as delinquents if they admit to one or more delinquent acts. Questionnaires that ask about large numbers of acts are more likely to classify a high proportion of respondents as delinquents, even though many of them might be only minimally involved in trivial acts of delinquency (Reiss, 1975; Hindelang, Hirschi, and Weis, 1979). Self-report studies should emphasize the frequency of delinquency and crime and the seriousness of the acts, rather than whether an individual has ever engaged in any act that violates the law.

Because of their methodological shortcomings, self-report studies cannot be employed to assess the efficiency of official crime statistics, even though these studies do confirm that there is a large dark figure of crime (Brantingham and Brantingham, 1984). They have proved useful, however, in telling us about the characteristics of people who violate different kinds of laws with various degrees of frequency. This information can be compared with official data on arrests, convictions, and sentences to assess the fairness with which the criminal justice system treats different kinds of people (Brantingham and Brantingham, 1984).

Because of the methodological problems with each of the three major measures of crime, none provides us with a perfect measure of the "true" amount of crime. When all three measures agree on the extent and distribution of crime, we can have some confidence in the conclusions. When the three measures disagree, as they sometimes do, it is difficult to know which one to use.

Summary

The classical school of criminology that developed in the eighteenth century assumed free will and individual responsibility, sought to deter offenders from crime by the threat of punishment, and emphasized punishment in proportion to the social harm caused by the criminal act. During the nineteenth century, cartographers such as Guerry and Quetelet looked for patterns of crime that appeared in official crime statistics. Positivists, reacting to the classical school's emphasis on free will, began late in the nineteenth century to use the scientific method to search for the causes of crime. Cesare Lombroso was the first to use empirical evidence to test hypotheses about why people violated the law, an approach that laid the groundwork for modern criminology.

Today criminologists use several statistical measures to study crime. Sometimes they use official statistics gathered by the police, the courts, or the prisons. The FBI began to issue Uniform Crime Reports more than fifty years ago, and these reports now provide statistics on crimes known to the police throughout the United States. The FBI provides detailed data on eight Part I crimes that together constitute the crime index, and less detailed information on twenty-one Part II offenses. The FBI's reports pay little attention to white-collar crime or organized crime and thus present a distorted picture of the crime problem that emphasizes crimes committed by young males who are often poor and members of minority groups.

Official statistics are used to calculate crime rates, usually in terms of number of offenses per 100,000 people. This kind of rate makes sense for crimes in which people are victimized, but it makes less sense when property is the target. Careful thought should be given to the way crime rates are calculated and to the exact meaning of those rates.

Crimes come to the attention of the police when victims and witnesses report offenses and the police react, and when the police uncover crime on their own initiative through proactive work. Crimes are not reported to the police for many reasons: a sense that nothing can be done, a feeling that the offense is unimportant, a belief that the police do not want to be bothered, fear of reprisals, or definition of the crime as a private matter. The police may fail to record crimes, sometimes to keep crime rates down and make themselves look more effective. Official crime statistics have been used for political purposes, at both the local and national levels. These statistics are of limited use for criminological research because of the summary form in which the FBI collects data.

A second important measure of crime is the victimization survey. A cross section of a population is questioned in detail about their experiences as victims of crime during a given period. This method was first used on a large-scale basis in the United States in 1966, and today it is employed as part of an ongoing federal effort to measure crime. Because the methods of these NCS surveys differ from those used by the FBI to collect data, the two kinds of statistics cannot be compared easily. Victimization surveys have found a large dark figure, the amount of crime that occurs but does not make its way into police records. Because victimization surveys have methodological problems, they are not a "true" measure of how much crime there is, but they are important sources of information.

A third measure of crime is the self-report survey, a questionnaire administered anonymously to get respondents to tell about crimes they have committed. Self-report surveys were first used in the United States in 1946, and since then they have been used to measure the extent of crime and delinquency and to test theories of crime and delinquency. Self-report studies find a large dark figure, and sometimes they reach conclusions about who violates the law that differ from research based on official arrest data. Self-report studies have some problems: Most have been done with adolescents, many have asked about involvement in trivial offenses, and there are some questions about how validly they measure crime and delinquency. When self-report studies agree with official statistics and victimization surveys about the nature and extent of crime, we can have confidence in the results, but when the three measures disagree, it is not clear which is the best indicator.

Important Terms

cartography	positivism
classical school	proactive police work
crime index	reactive police work
crime rate	self-report study
dark figure	victimization survey

Suggested Readings

PAUL BRANTINGHAM AND PATRICIA BRANTINGHAM. *Patterns in Crime.* New York: Macmillan, 1984. Chapters 3 and 4 contain useful discussions of official crime statistics, victimization surveys, and self-report studies.

FEDERAL BUREAU OF INVESTIGATION. *Crime in the United States, 1986: Uniform Crime Reports.* Washington, D.C.: U.S. Government Printing Office, 1987. This annual report presents statistics gathered from local police departments on crimes known to the police, cleared offenses, arrested persons, and law-enforcement personnel.

ROBERT M. O'BRIEN. *Crime and Victimization Data.* Beverly Hills, Calif.: Sage Publications, 1985. A comprehensive and critical look at the three major sources of crime statistics examined in this chapter.

RICHARD F. SPARKS. *Research on Victims of Crime: Accomplishments, Issues, and New Directions.* Washington, D.C.: U.S. Government Printing Office, 1982. A comprehensive examination of the use of survey methods to measure criminal victimization, including methodological problems with victimization surveys and what can be learned from this method of measuring crime.

IAN TAYLOR, PAUL WALTON, AND JOCK YOUNG. *The New Criminology: For a Social Theory of Deviance.* London: Routledge and Kegan Paul, 1973. An important Marxist critique of early, as well as contemporary, theories of criminology.

GEORGE B. VOLD AND THOMAS J. BERNARD. *Theoretical Criminology,* 3rd ed. New York: Oxford University Press, 1986. A useful textbook on theories of criminal behavior and the development of modern criminology.

CHAPTER 4

The Costs of Crime

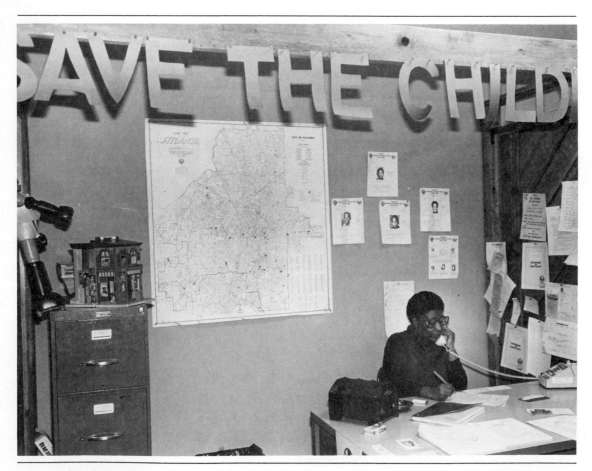

Source: Alain Keller/Sygma

The costs of crime are exorbitant. People are injured and killed, and they lose money and property. They fear strangers as potential thieves and assailants, stay home rather than venture onto unsafe streets, and criticize the police for being unable to control crime. Dishonesty by elected officials undermines faith in the political system and keeps voters home on election day. Corporate crime reduces public support for the economic system.

In this chapter we look at three kinds of costs of crime. First we examine the financial costs. Next we look at the physical harm that crime causes. Finally, we explore the indirect social costs to people who fear victimization. It is difficult to assess these costs of crime exactly, but we can make some estimates.

Financial Costs of Crime

Estimates of the financial costs of crime often appear to be more precise than they really are. Estimates can be made only if certain assumptions and guesses are made about how much crime actually occurs in the country, a problem we considered in Chapter 3. Even if we could measure exactly how much crime occurs, it would still be difficult to estimate the cost of each offense. For instance, if a robber beats up a person and steals $25, the victim loses the money but the robber has the use of that money. Placing a monetary figure on the physical and psychological harm to the victim is nearly impossible. If the robber uses the $25 to buy heroin, we might count this expenditure as another cost of crime, even though counting both the initial theft of $25 and the use of that money for heroin might be seen as double counting. If the robber is then arrested, some part of the police budget should be allocated to the crime. The arraignment and trial also cost money, and if the offender is convicted and imprisoned there would be the additional costs of incarceration. The robber's family might have to receive welfare benefits during his or her imprisonment. The absent parent might create a family environment in which the children are more likely to get involved in delinquency. We can see that the initial loss of $25 in the robbery might be quite a small amount when compared with all of the other costs associated with the crime.

Different Costs of Crime

One cost of crime is the *direct loss* of property. For example, arson destroys buildings, and vandalism ruins property. Both offenses reduce the stock of useful things in the world. We can also speak of direct losses from murder, although placing a monetary figure on lost lives is difficult.

A second kind of cost of crime is the *transfer of property*. The theft of a radio in a burglary and the theft of cash in a robbery transfer property from the rightful owner to the thief, and perhaps eventually to a fence and then to a new owner. The victim of the theft regards himself or herself as having lost the property, but from a societal perspective the property has been transferred from one person to another rather than made useless.

A third financial cost of crime arises from crimes of violence in which a victim is physically hurt. These *costs related to criminal violence* include the loss of productivity by incapacitated victims, unemployment compensation paid to victims, fees paid for physical and psychological therapy for victims, and social security payments and funeral expenses associated with homicides.

Yet another type of cost of crime is the expenditure of money on illegal goods and services such as narcotics, prostitution, and gambling. *Illegal expenditures* can be considered a cost of crime because they divert money from the legitimate economy and represent a loss of potential revenue for people who produce and supply legal goods and services. However, from another point of view, we might regard illegal expenditures as entertainment expenses, which are often paid for with income earned at a legitimate job. Some of these illegal expenditures do not victimize anyone; no direct and obvious harm to another person necessarily results from spending money on narcotics, prostitution, or gambling. Indeed, expenditures on legal goods such as cigarettes and alcohol may produce more obvious harm than do expenditures on some illegal goods and services.

Enforcement costs, a fifth kind of financial cost of crime, include the money spent by various criminal justice agencies. Employees of these agencies regard their salaries as legitimate payments for services, but from another perspective crime diverts this money from other purposes. If enforcement costs are treated as a financial cost of crime, it follows that redefining some behavior that is now criminal as noncriminal would reduce the cost of crime.

A sixth financial cost of crime involves *prevention and protection costs.* This includes the millions of dollars that people spend for alarm systems, spotlights, locks, bars, and other "target-hardening" devices, as well as the money they spend on insurance premiums to cover their losses through theft.

The Costs of Crime in the United States

Because the financial costs of crime are calculated in various ways, there is no real way to arrive at a total figure for all of the costs involved. Adding the amount of property destroyed in arson to the amount spent on illegal drugs and the total cost of police salaries is much like adding apples, oranges, and peaches. We can, however, assess the costs of certain kinds of crime, the costs of the criminal justice system, and other costs associated with crime.

TABLE 4.1   Kinds of Financial Costs of Crime

1. Direct loss
2. Transfer of property
3. Costs related to criminal violence
4. Illegal expenditures
5. Enforcement costs
6. Prevention and protection costs

WHITE-COLLAR CRIME   The most expensive crime in financial terms is white-collar crime, but estimating its cost is not easy. Not only do we have to calculate direct losses to victims, but we also must determine how much prices rise as a result of the passing on of the companies' losses to consumers. The ramifications of a single white-collar crime are often complex and difficult to assess. For instance, when a bribe is paid by a business executive to accomplish a particular objective, neither the bribe giver nor the recipient may feel that any loss has been incurred. However, there is a loss to the public from such transactions. Thus, the cost of a bribe paid by a construction firm to a city inspector may be passed on to the individual who has contracted to have the building erected, and the cost of the bribe might then be passed on to the building's tenants in higher rents. The fact that the tenants never learn of their losses does not make the bribe any less of a financial loss to them.

Even though it is difficult to place an exact dollar figure on the financial cost of all white-collar crime, we can state with some certainty that the cost of all such offenses far exceeds the cost of all conventional property crimes that constitute what is widely regarded as "the crime problem." The financial cost of crimes such as robbery, larceny, burglary, and motor vehicle theft does not approach the losses from bribery, kickbacks, stock fraud, embezzlement, computer crime, price fixing, and other white-collar crimes. The Joint Economic Committee of Congress estimated that in 1976 one-third of all financial costs of crime in the United States could be attributed to white-collar crime; $44 billion was lost in that kind of crime. The cost of white-collar crime may now be twice that estimate, but we lack good data on current costs.

About half of the losses from white-collar crime are due to consumer fraud, illegal competition, and deceptive sales practices. Consumer fraud includes the sale of defective merchandise, the misrepresentation of interest terms, and the sale of unneeded or faulty home and auto repairs. Illegal competition costs billions of dollars each year, and introducing competition where it has been absent can save consumers much money. For instance, an antitrust action against the manufacturer of the drug tetracycline reduced the price of that drug by 75 percent.

One costly white-collar crime that involves deceptive sales practices is the sale of counterfeit merchandise. A 1984 study by the Federal Trade Commission (FTC) concluded that each year fake merchandise costs American workers 131,000 jobs and causes between $6 billion and $8 billion of lost sales for American companies. The FTC report states the following:

> The quality difference between the real and the counterfeit products can be of particular importance in some industries to the health and safety of the consumer, as is the case for defective auto parts, ineffective or nonsterile drugs and pharmaceuticals, and ineffective agricultural chemicals. (cited in Farnsworth, 1984: 4)

Forty-three nations, including the United States, were mentioned by the FTC as sources of counterfeit goods that companies try to pass off as brand-name products, but the greatest problem seemed to be in East Asia. Taiwan and Hong Kong, for instance, have produced inexpensive counterfeits of Apple computers that outsell the original product by ten to one in East Asia. In the United States, cassettes of record albums and films have been counterfeited. Estimates of annual losses to the film industry from such piracy range from $100 million to $500 million (Harmetz, 1983). Counterfeiting has also caused substantial losses for couturier houses that produce designer clothing, purses, and cosmetics. Fake goods, which often carry the symbol of the designer firm and may be made from materials similar to those used by the manufacturer of the original, are often shoddily made. This may cause customers who are dissatisfied with the counterfeit product, but who think it is an original, to avoid purchasing the original in the future. In addition to lost sales, designer firms incur the expense of legal action for copyright infringement against the manufacturers of counterfeit goods.

Another business crime that is very expensive, indeed probably as expensive as all conventional property crime, is stock fraud and securities theft. Securities are sometimes stolen by brokerage house employees, who may deliver the securities to members of organized crime in return for cancellation of the employees' debts that arose from gambling or borrowing from loan sharks. The gangsters then transport the securities out of the country and use them as collateral for loans from foreign banks.

One costly crime that occurs in the commercial sector is employee theft and embezzlement. In 1984, retailers lost an estimated $1.9 billion from "inventory shrinkage," which includes employee theft (43 percent of the total), shoplifting (30 percent), shoddy paperwork (23 percent), and vendor theft (4 percent) (Lin, 1985). In some urban stores, the percentage of merchandise lost through such inventory shrinkage equals or exceeds profits. Crimes of this sort are costly for victimized companies; between 15 and 30 percent of all business failures are due to losses of this sort. Theft by employees and fraud by customers cost banks four to five times as much each year as do bank robberies. As a consequence, in the late 1970s the FBI began to focus its attention on bank frauds netting at least $100,000, and it turned over the investigation of bank robberies to state and local police agencies.

An increasingly important kind of theft is computer crime. Between 1980 and 1983, the following large-scale computer-related crimes occurred: a bank embezzlement that netted $21 million, a securities fraud that involved the loss of $53 million, a commodities fraud that produced a loss of $50 million, and an inventory fraud of $67 million. Losses from computer crimes and other forms of internal theft are often passed on to customers and clients in higher prices and fees, rather than deducted from profits or from dividends paid to stockholders.

TAX FRAUD   Cheating on income taxes is not generally regarded as a white-collar crime, for it is not committed during the course of a legitimate job, even though it is work-related. In addition, people of all classes can engage in tax fraud, whereas white-collar crime is limited to middle- and upper-class people.

However, tax cheating may be white-collar crime if it involves corporations in the intentional underpayment of taxes.

The General Accounting Office estimates that income tax cheating cost the federal government $110 billion in 1986, an increase from $29 billion in 1973, the first year for which statistics are available. Studies based on anonymous questionnaires have found that about one taxpayer in five cheats to some extent (cited in *The Boston Globe,* March 25, 1985). Some underpayment results from the "tax protester" movement, in which people file returns but omit the payment of taxes in protest of government policies. Failure to pay taxes may also result from elaborate schemes to cheat the government out of revenue; in 1985, one financial promoter pleaded guilty to carrying out a tax shelter scheme that defrauded the government of $445 million.

Compliance by taxpayers, whether individual or corporate, seems to have declined. Some simply do not report earned income, and others overstate deductions and credits. This change is probably due to a declining risk of being caught, or at least the perception that the risk has declined. Noncompliance is greatest for income about which taxpayers feel the IRS will remain ignorant. The number of IRS investigators declined in the early 1980s, even though $6 can be recovered for every $1 spent on such enforcement. In spite of widespread noncompliance with the payment of taxes in the United States, the problem is not nearly as bad here as it is in Italy, as we see in the Cross-Cultural Perspective.

CREDIT CARD FRAUD   An important part of the American economy is the credit card. About 70 percent of all families have at least one card; there are about 600 million cards in the hands of American consumers. About 30 percent of all retail sales involve the use of credit cards, and that figure has been increasing in recent years (Molotsky, 1984).

The criminal abuse of these cards has also been growing. In 1982, Mastercard International Inc. and Visa U.S.A. Inc. reported combined losses from fraud of about $125 million, and losses exceeded $200 million in 1986 (Berg, 1986). About $30 million of that was due to counterfeit cards, which have been curbed but not eliminated through the use of anticounterfeiting measures such as holograms. Credit card abuse also involves the use of stolen, lost, or altered cards; fraud in applying for cards; and telemarketing fraud in which the caller announces the winning of a prize and asks for the "winner's" credit card number to verify the "winner's" identity, and then uses that number for fraudulent purchases.

INSURANCE FRAUD   When people who face a risk insure themselves against financial loss, an opportunity for fraud exists. The American Insurance Association estimates that 15 to 20 percent of all insurance claims in 1982 were fraudulent, up from 5 or 6 percent a decade earlier. The $11 billion a year that is lost through insurance fraud is a result of claims for nonexistent or staged accidents, padded doctors' bills, overpayment of claims for burglary losses, and arson-for-profit schemes (Landis, 1982). Some people pad their claims because they as-

A Cross-Cultural Perspective: Tax Cheating in Italy

Italy has perennially had a difficult time getting its citizens to pay taxes. One widely heard explanation is that Italians are antagonistic toward taxation because for centuries foreign invaders had imposed taxes on them. In recent years, the government has taken measures to increase compliance with the tax law.

In 1972, only 2 million tax returns were filed by Italians. The introduction of a full payroll deduction system in 1974 improved the situation, and 21.5 million returns were filed in 1981. The failure to file a return was greatly reduced by the 1974 measure, but there is still much underpayment of taxes.

Returns filed in 1981 showed that the average reported income was slightly less than the earnings of an average blue-collar worker, whose income is toward the bottom of the income scale. This indicates that many, perhaps most, taxpayers underreport their incomes. Cheating is especially common among the self-employed, who are not subject to the payroll deduction system.

There is much evidence of wealth in Italy — exclusive shops in large cities, many expensive cars, and enormous ransoms paid in kidnappings. However, in 1981 only 16,000 out of 24.5 million taxpayers reported incomes in excess of the American equivalent of $62,000. Many of the wealthy either underreport their incomes or simply do not file returns.

Political leaders hope that new measures introduced in the 1980s will reduce tax cheating and thereby strengthen the government's fiscal position.

SOURCE: Based on Sari Gilbert, "Tax Cheating a Way of Life for the Italian," *The Boston Globe,* April 19, 1984, p. 54.

sume the insurance company will pay them less than they have lost. Some claims are even more blatantly fraudulent than padded claims, as we can see from the following two examples:

There was a traveling salesman who started off his fraud career by claiming he had gotten sick after finding a fly in a candy bar. This was rapidly followed by a fly in a bottle of soda. Then he took to chipping the same two teeth on half a dozen candy bars. Most of these claims were denied, so the salesman began slipping and falling around his sales territory. After breaking the same pair of glasses in nine separate men's room accidents, he made the mistake of taking his forged optometrist's bill to the same agent who had paid him for breaking the glasses before.

One body shop in New York City . . . let car owners deliver their cars to the shop in the morning, and by noon the cars would be stripped of their parts. The auto bodies were rolled out on the street to be found by the police. The owners could then report their cars stolen and collect from their insurance companies. The body shop would then roll the cars back into the shop, replace the parts, and have the cars ready for delivery the same day. (Landis, 1982: D2)

Arson-for-profit schemes are a major source of insurance fraud. Building owners who find their neighborhoods deteriorating and taxes and repair costs rising may burn down buildings. In some cases, a building is overinsured or even insured more than once, and then the insurance claim may exceed the real value of the building. Insurance companies contribute to the problem of fraud by not inspecting buildings before writing policies, by settling with arsonists if the cost of investigating the fire is too great compared with the size of the claim, and by ignoring their option of forcing the owner to rebuild rather than collect the money. One sociologist claims that arson and arson-for-profit schemes are so intrinsically a part of the capitalist economy of the United States and so closely linked to routine business decisions that they are probably beyond the control of the criminal justice system (Brady, 1982).

ORGANIZED CRIME   In 1986, the President's Commission on Organized Crime, in its final report, concluded as follows:

> The effects of organized crime on the legitimate economy show up in higher prices for consumers when competition is suppressed, lower wages for workers when labor unions are controlled, and less safety when corners are cut on construction projects or toxic waste is not disposed of properly. (cited in Ostrow, 1986: 8)

The Commission also stated that the taxes citizens pay

> must be higher by the amount of taxes not paid by these criminals to provide the government with needed revenue. Conversely, if taxes were paid on all income earned by the individuals associated with organized crime, the taxes paid by ordinary citizens could be reduced by this amount. (cited in Ostrow, 1986: 8)

Relying for its estimates on a study conducted by Wharton Econometric Forecasting Associates of Philadelphia, the Commission claimed that organized crime reduces the nation's economic output by $18.2 billion per year, cuts employment by 414,000 jobs, raises consumer prices by 0.3 percent, and reduces per capita income by $77.

CONVENTIONAL CRIMES   Although less costly than white-collar crime and organized crime, conventional crimes involve substantial losses that the general public may be even more concerned about, because such offenses touch them directly.

Crimes of Violence.   Crimes of violence such as murder, rape, robbery, and assault produce financial losses in the form of unpaid wages, hospitalization expenses, and the costs of therapeutic services. Based on victimization survey data for 1981, the Bureau of Justice Statistics (April 1984) estimated that the median medical expense to victims of rape, robbery, and assault was $120, with one-fourth of the victims incurring expenses of $375 or more. About two-thirds of all medical expenses resulting from these three types of violent crimes could be attributed to assaults.

The financial costs of murder have been calculated by adding up the total wages the victim would have earned if he or she had lived until the expected age, the cost of welfare or social security payments to the victim's survivors, and the cost of the funeral. Based on calculations of loss of economic contribution to society, one economist estimated that the financial cost of a homicide in Phoenix, Arizona, in 1976 was $121,000 (McPheters, 1979).

Another kind of cost related to criminal violence is the money spent by state compensation boards to repay victims or survivors for losses suffered during a crime.

Property Crimes. Robbery, burglary, larceny, motor vehicle theft, arson, and vandalism also involve significant financial costs. The FBI estimates that in 1986 the total reported loss from robberies was $323 million. Reported burglaries accounted for $3.1 billion in losses in that year, and larcenies produced an additional $2.9 billion in losses. Car thefts accounted for $6 billion, although most cars were recovered and even those that were damaged by the thieves had some market value. The FBI estimates that the monetary value of property lost or damaged in reported cases of arson in 1986 was $1.2 billion. No good estimate of the cost of crimes of vandalism is available. Overall, the total loss from crimes of robbery, burglary, larceny, motor vehicle theft, and arson in 1986 was $13.5 billion, much less than estimated losses from white-collar crime or from organized crime.

VICTIMLESS CRIMES   Estimates of the financial costs of victimless crimes are usually based on a calculation of the amount of money that is spent on goods and services such as narcotics, prostitution, or gambling. The assumption underlying these estimates is that if this money were not spent on illegal goods and services, it would be spent on legitimate goods and services.

Drug Use. The illegal use of narcotics entails several kinds of costs: the money paid for illegal drugs, the revenue lost to the government because required taxes are not paid on those drugs, and the cost of the secondary crimes committed by drug users to get the money to pay for drugs. Secondary crimes cost society money when shoplifting, burglary, robbery, and other property offenses are committed to support expensive drug habits. The cost of these secondary crimes is included in the cost of property crimes, but it can also be seen as a by-product of narcotics offenses.

Narcotics are more expensive when they are illegal than when they are legal, and the high price of illegal narcotics leads to crime to support drug use. One unintended consequence of drug enforcement efforts can be to drive the price of drugs up by cutting the supply. Users may then commit more crime to support their habits, although they may also switch to other, less-expensive drugs. Thus drug enforcement can increase the cost of crime in three ways. First, enforcement itself costs money; second, the transfer cost of crimes against property may increase to pay for drugs that have been made more expensive because of enforcement efforts; and third, illegal expenditures increase as the cost of drugs rises.

Prostitution. In estimating the costs of prostitution, as in estimating the costs of narcotics, some have assumed that money spent on illegal services is money that otherwise might have been spent on legitimate goods and services and so is lost to the economy. However, from another perspective, it is difficult to see how money spent for sex with a prostitute is any more of a financial loss than money spent to attend a movie or a baseball game.

Gambling. It may be easier to make a case for an economic loss from illegal gambling than to make such a case for prostitution and narcotics use. Gambling with a bookie produces a loss for the economy in those states that have lotteries or other forms of legalized gambling, if people who might bet legally use their money to bet in illegal ways. Funds are diverted from the state, which would have used that money for education or other social services. This could cause taxes to be higher, or services to be fewer, than would have been the case if the money had been gambled legally.

Another cost of illegal gambling may be that money bet with a bookie who has links to organized crime is used by gangsters to finance the importation of drugs or to engage in loan sharking. However, there is some evidence that many, perhaps most, bookies are not members of organized crime and that much money spent on illegal gambling does not make its way into the hands of gangsters (Reuter and Rubinstein, 1978; Reuter, 1983).

MAINTAINING THE CRIMINAL JUSTICE SYSTEM   Another financial cost of crime is the expense of maintaining the criminal justice system — the police, the courts, jails and prisons, and related legal services.

The costs of the criminal justice system are not direct losses to victims of crime, but rather costs that result from societal decisions about how to respond to crime. Some critics claim that these decisions are not really societal at all, but are instead made by a powerful and self-perpetuating "crime industry" that consists of vested interests in the criminal justice system who ask for and receive ever-increasing resources (Blumberg, 1974: 31). Increases in the expenditures of the criminal justice system — such as raises for police officers — escalate the cost of crime in one sense, but they do not necessarily reflect greater direct losses to victims.

In 1985, there were 1,437,000 employees of civil and criminal justice agencies throughout the country. Over half were police officers, and police departments accounted for the largest amount of expenditures of any part of the civil and criminal justice systems, as we can see from the following breakdown of the $45.6 billion spent on civil and criminal justice in fiscal year 1985 (Bureau of Justice Statistics, March 1987):

Police protection	$22.0 billion
Judicial and legal services	10.1 billion
Corrections	13.0 billion
Other justice activities	.5 billion

Most expenditures on criminal justice are at the local rather than state or federal level. In 1985, $25.4 billion was spent by local (city, town, or county) agencies, $16 billion was spent by state agencies, and $5.8 billion was spent by the federal government (Bureau of Justice Statistics, March 1987). The federal role in criminal justice was greater from 1968 to 1982 than it has been since 1982, when the Law Enforcement Assistance Administration (LEAA), an agency of the Department of Justice, was eliminated. While it was in existence, LEAA spent about $8 billion trying to reduce crime and improve the criminal justice system. LEAA may have improved the functioning of the criminal justice system, especially by encouraging planning and communication among agencies, but there is no evidence that it reduced crime, and for this reason — as well as for its cumbersomeness and wastefulness — it was disbanded in 1982.

The high cost of the criminal justice system is attributable in part to the high crime rate of the United States in comparison to other Western industrial nations. Over the last century, there has also been an increase in the proportion of all Americans who are in prison at any given time, and today's rate of imprisonment is higher than that of any other industrial nation for which we have data (Cahalan, 1979, 1986). The high cost of corrections is also explained by the fact that it costs at least $60,000 to build a new prison cell and costs about $15,000 to maintain an inmate in prison for a year.

At the end of 1985, there were 503,315 men and women in state and federal prisons, and another 254,094 in local jails. A total of 1,870,132 men and women were on probation — or under court-imposed supervision — and 277,438 were on parole — or under supervised release from jail or prison (Bureau of Justice Statistics, January 1987). The high costs of imprisonment have led some critics of the criminal justice system to argue for even more use of probation and parole, which are much less costly than incarceration, but others believe that more prison cells should be built.

The costliness of a crime is different if one considers the expenses attributable to reactions to it by the criminal justice system, rather than direct financial losses to victims. For instance, conventional property crimes account for a large proportion of police, court, and correctional costs, even though losses to victims of those property crimes are small compared with losses from white-collar crimes, which account for relatively little of the cost of maintaining the criminal justice system. In other words, the offenses on which the criminal justice system focuses its resources do not seem to be those that cost victims the most.

Physical Harm From Crime

Many crimes cause physical harm to their victims. People are murdered or raped, suffer injuries in assaults, are poisoned by contaminated food, and are hurt by defective products. Physical harm also occurs in more subtle ways. For example, by promising medical miracles, a quack doctor may prevent patients with curable diseases from seeking competent medical care until it is too late to be treated successfully.

White-Collar Crime

Many people assume that white-collar crime does not harm its victims physically. However, some victims of white-collar crimes are hurt, even though such harm is more often a result of negligence than of intent.

Physical harm from white-collar crime takes many forms. Air pollution, which sometimes involves criminal acts, causes respiratory ailments. Hazardous and often illegal working conditions result in many deaths and injuries each year. In 1985, three executives were found guilty, fined $10,000, and sentenced to twenty-five years in prison for murder in the cyanide poisoning death of an employee whose job involved the use of that chemical to recover silver from photographic film. Some of the 20 million serious injuries that occur each year as a result of the use of consumer products, including some of the 110,000 cases of permanent disability and some of the 30,000 deaths, can be attributed to criminal negligence or deceptive advertising by manufacturers (Schrager and Short, 1978: 415). The Ford Motor Company was charged with reckless homicide for the deaths of three young women in Indiana in 1978; however, a jury acquitted Ford, finding that it had marketed a defective car but had not been reckless in its recall efforts (Kramer, 1982; Cullen, Maakestad, and Cavender, 1984, 1987).

In some cases, white-collar crime even involves the intentional taking of lives. For instance, in 1976, Don Bolles, a journalist who was investigating white-collar and organized crime in Phoenix, Arizona, was apparently killed by a "hit man" hired to keep illegal activities secret.

Conventional Crimes

Conventional crimes of violence produce injury and even death. The extent of this physical harm to victims can be estimated by looking at FBI crime reports and NCS victimization studies.

MURDER Probably the most easily measured physical harm is the number of lives lost in murders. In 1986, 20,613 murders were reported to the FBI by local police departments. Because murders are usually reported to the police and because the FBI gathers data from most police departments in the country, the FBI figure is a good estimate of the number of people actually murdered (Gove, Hughes, and Geerken, 1985).

To get some perspective on the meaning of the number of murders that occur each year in the United States, it is instructive to compare the total with deaths that occur in other ways. In 1985, the FBI reported 18,976 murders. In that same year, the National Center for Health Statistics estimates that 29,453 people committed suicide, though the actual number of suicides may have been twice that number. In 1985, 45,901 people died in traffic accidents, about half of them in crashes in which alcohol was present. Thus, more people commit suicide and more people die in car accidents than are murdered each year,

Using Criminology: The Risk of Victimization

In 1985, the Bureau of Justice Statistics of the U.S. Department of Justice began to use the results of its NCS victimization surveys to calculate the risk of being the victim of a violent crime during a given year. The Bureau's Crime Risk Index can be used to compare the risks faced by different subgroups of the population (e.g., whites and blacks, men and women, the young and the old, high- and low-income groups). It can also be used to compare the risk of being the victim of a violent crime with the risk of being in a fatal car accident or contracting a certain disease.

The initial application of the Crime Risk Index found that each year 3 percent of Americans are victims of violent crime (defined as rape, robbery, and assault). The risk of victimization in a violent crime is higher for males than for females, higher for blacks than for whites, higher for those aged sixteen to twenty-four than for other age groups, and higher for low-income groups than for high-income groups.

In 1987, the Bureau of Justice Statistics began to use the NCS data to calculate the risk of being the victim of a violent crime or a theft at some time during one's lifetime. This measure may provide a better indicator of the costs of crime to individuals than do annual crime statistics, which an analyst at the Bureau said "provide a false sense of security." He added, "People are worried about the possibility that *at some time* in their lives they will be robbed or raped or assaulted, or their homes will be burglarized" (Koppel, p.1).

The Bureau estimated that one in every 133 Americans will have his or her life ended by a murder. The percentage of peo-

although the death toll from murder is high, especially compared with other industrial societies.

FORCIBLE RAPE In 1986, there were 90,434 cases of forcible rape and attempted rape reported to local police departments in the United States, but there were perhaps twice that many actual incidents, according to NCS victimization studies (Bureau of Justice Statistics, October 1987).

Rape always involves psychological damage to the victim, because by definition it does not involve consent. Rape often involves physical harm as well. A study of 646 reported rapes in Philadelphia found that 85 percent involved some physical force by the offender. In 29 percent of the cases there was roughness by the rapist; in 25 percent the rapist beat the woman "in a nonbrutal fashion"; in 20 percent the offender beat the victim brutally; in 11 percent the offender choked the victim; and in only 15 percent of the rapes was no physical force used (Amir, 1971: 155). Another study found that 48 percent of rape victims were injured and 19 percent injured seriously enough to require medical attention (Hindelang, Gottfredson, and Garofalo, 1978). According to FBI figures, in 1986 about 300 murders also involved a sex offense; many of those were rapes in which the victim was murdered.

ple who will be victimized once or more during their lifetimes (starting at age twelve) are:

Rape and attempted rape	8%
Robbery and attempted robbery	30%
Assault and attempted assault	74%
Robbery or assault, resulting in injury	40%
Personal theft, including attempts	99%

Further analysis of the NCS data allows even more refined calculations of risks. Thus, 11 percent of black women and 8 percent of white women will suffer a rape or an attempt during their lifetimes. Fifty-one percent of blacks but only 27 percent of whites will be the victim of a robbery or an attempt; 37 percent of males but only 22 percent of females will be the victim of such a crime. Males are also more likely than females to be the victim of an assault or an attempt, by 82 percent to 62 percent. Virtually everyone, regardless of sex or race, will be the victim of a personal theft or an attempt. During a twenty-year period, three-fourths of households will have a burglary, and one-fifth will have a car stolen.

These figures, based on victimization survey data from 1975 to 1984, must be updated regularly, for if crime rates change, then people's lifetime risks will also change. This new method of using the results of the NCS surveys can help people make more accurate assessments of the risks that they will be a crime victim than they can by using annual police statistics, and it thus provides a better measure of the costs of crime to individuals.

SOURCES. Based on Bureau of Justice Statistics, *The Risk of Violent Crime.* Washington, D.C.: U.S. Department of Justice, May 1985; Herbert Koppel, *Lifetime Likelihood of Victimization.* Washington, D.C.: U.S. Department of Justice, March 1987.

AGGRAVATED ASSAULT In 1986, there were 834,322 cases of aggravated assault reported to local police departments. Many victims of this crime are permanently incapacitated. Others suffer injuries from which they eventually recover, but they may lose wages or jobs as a result of being victimized. An eight-city study found that 35 percent of aggravated assault victims were injured and 18 percent injured seriously enough to need medical attention (Hindelang, Gottfredson, and Garofalo, 1978).

ROBBERY The FBI reported 542,775 cases of robbery in 1986, but it provided no information on the amount of harm suffered by robbery victims. However, an NCS study using data from 1973 to 1984 found that one-third of robbery victims were injured, and 15 percent were injured seriously enough to require medical care (Harlow, 1987).

Research indicates that physical injuries during robberies are least common when an offender has a firearm, somewhat more common when a knife is used, and most likely when the offender uses no weapon at all (Conklin, 1972; Hindelang, Gottfredson, and Garofalo, 1978; Cook, 1987). Victims confronted by armed robbers are probably least likely to resist and are thus least likely to be injured. Victims who believe they can overpower an unarmed robber are more likely to be injured while resisting.

Robberies sometimes lead to murders; these offenses would be classified as murders rather than robberies. The FBI estimates that in 1986 there were 1,830 murders that had robbery as the motive. Thus, about one murder in ten begins as a robbery. However, only about one robbery in every 300 results in a murder.

Victimless Crimes

Even though victimless crimes do not include a participant who complains to the police, physical harm sometimes results from involvement in such offenses.

DRUG USE Heroin addiction has harmful effects. Addicts' health often deteriorates because they spend their money on drugs rather than on food, shelter, and clothing. The harmful consequences for addicts' health seem to be more a result of the high price of heroin, which in turn is due to its being illegal, rather than a result of the pharmacological effects of the drug itself.

Many heroin addicts are admitted to emergency rooms for drug overdoses or for the effects of the interaction of heroin with other drugs they have used. In the United States in 1982 there were 11,538 emergency room admissions related to heroin use and 771 heroin-related deaths (Kessler, 1983). Many of the estimated 500,000 heroin addicts and 3.5 million occasional users of heroin in the country suffer physically from their use of the drug (Kihss, 1982).

PROSTITUTION Where prostitution is illegal, and therefore left unregulated, those who engage in it may suffer physically. Prostitutes are especially susceptible to venereal diseases, and there is some evidence that they run a relatively high risk of contracting AIDS. They are also frequently physically abused by their pimps, who use force to get them to work harder or remain loyal to them.

Social Costs of Crime

Crime has a much greater impact on society than can be measured by the financial loss and physical harm that it causes. The social costs of crime are indirect: fear felt by citizens, suspicion of strangers, skepticism of voters at election time, and wariness of investors in the stock market. Fear of victimization by conventional or white-collar crime affects the attitudes and behavior of people in important ways that may even contribute to the crime problem.

White-Collar Crime

White-collar crime has major social costs in addition to the enormous financial losses it inflicts on the public. The President's Commission on Law Enforcement and Administration of Justice (1967a: 5) called white-collar offenses "the most threatening of all — not just because they are so expensive, but because of their

corrosive effect on the moral standards by which American business is conducted." However, less than 1 percent of the material published by this commission dealt with white-collar crime. Edwin H. Sutherland (1949, 1983), who
first used the term "white-collar crime" in 1939, also believed that a major cost
of this kind of crime was its harmful effect on public attitudes, especially on the
public's confidence in the economy. White-collar crime may reduce the public's
willingness to invest in the stock market and engage in commercial transactions,
and a capitalist economy that relies on public investment is thus weakened.

Illegal campaign contributions by large corporations can lead to public cynicism toward business and government. Voters may believe that business is the
"power behind the throne" and that politicians are corrupt. Bribes paid to
officials of other nations can weaken foreign relations and diminish national
prestige abroad. A company's interest in protecting its foreign investments may
even lead to the rigging of elections or to the overthrow of a democratically
elected regime that is seen as hostile to American business.

Business crime may also set an example of disobedience for the general public.
Citizens who rarely see white-collar offenders prosecuted and sent to prison may
become cynical about the criminal justice system. A sense of injustice may
develop when they or their friends are given long sentences for crimes that cost
society much less than offenses committed by wealthy corporate executives or
large multinational firms.

Police corruption and brutality can also undermine the legitimacy of the
government. If those who enforce the law also violate it, citizens may feel that
they do not need to abide by the law either. Exposés of police corruption and
brutality create hostility toward law enforcers and the government they serve, as
we can see in the following exchange between a young black man and a police
chief:

"Okay man, you pretty smart. If I smack my buddy here upside the head and he
files a complaint, what you gonna do?"

"Arrest you," the chief replied.

"Cool. Now let's say one of your ugly cops smacks *me* upside the head and I file a
complaint—what you gonna do?"

"Investigate the complaint," the chief said. If it were true, the police would
"take action" and "probably suspend" the officer.

"Well," the black rejoined, "how come we get arrested and *you* only get investigated?" (Wilson, 1983: 108–109)

Organized Crime

The activities of organized crime also have social costs. One essential element of
organized crime is the corruption of public officials and police officers who
allow gangsters to operate without interference (Cressey, 1969, 1972; Conklin,
1973). Reports of corruption can undermine faith in local, state, and even

federal government. People may be unwilling to discuss political matters openly for fear that all officials are linked to organized crime (Chambliss, 1971). The influence of organized crime with elected officials can lead to public resignation and the belief that young people would be better off pursuing careers other than politics.

Conventional Crimes

Conventional crimes also have social costs in addition to financial costs and physical harm. Indeed, the effects on daily life of robbery, rape, and burglary are probably greater than the social effects of white-collar crime and organized crime, even though the financial costs of white-collar crime and organized crime greatly exceed the monetary losses from conventional crime. Victims and witnesses may be traumatized by conventional crimes, live in fear of retaliation, or spend hours testifying in court (Conklin, 1975; Sheleff and Shichor, 1980).

FEAR OF CRIME   The public seems most afraid of unprovoked attacks in public places by strangers. Robbery is a prototype of the kind of crime most feared by the public: It usually involves theft with violence or the threat of violence by a person with whom the victim has had no previous contact, and it is usually unprovoked and unpredictable. The public most fears those crimes that occur least frequently, namely, murder, rape, and robbery; "fear of crimes of violence is not a simple fear of injury or death or even of all crimes of violence, but, at bottom, a fear of strangers" (The President's Commission on Law Enforcement and Administration of Justice, 1967a: 52). This is true even though the chance of being killed by a stranger is much less than the chance of dying in a car accident or the chance of dying in an accidental fall (Silberman, 1978: 6). Many crimes of violence, particularly murder and aggravated assault, are committed by people with whom the victim is acquainted or related, rather than by strangers.

Fear of victimization seems to be greatest among people who have been directly victimized (Biderman, 1981; Skogan and Maxfield, 1981; Baker et al., 1983). However, a relatively small percentage of adults, perhaps only 3 percent, are injured in crimes of violence during any given year. Individual property crimes have modest effects on fear, but they may have a large cumulative effect because they are relatively common (Skogan and Maxfield, 1981).

The threat of crime seems to cause fear even in the absence of actual victimization (Skogan, 1981). Sometimes people's fear is much greater than seems warranted by the actual risk of victimization they face. For instance, women are the victims of crime less often than men, but they fear crime more, perhaps because of the threat of sexual assault. Likewise, many studies find a relatively low rate of victimization for the elderly, but much fear of crime among them. This may be due to their belief that they are physically vulnerable and will not recover if injured (Skogan, 1981; Skogan and Maxfield, 1981). Fear of crime among the elderly is also closely associated with their lower degree of confidence in the police (Baker et al., 1983), their greater dissatisfaction with the neighborhood in which they live, and their lower overall morale (Yin, 1982). Some research suggests that fear of crime among the elderly may have a realistic basis, because the elderly may be more susceptible to crime if we look at the amount of time they are at risk. Elderly people are probably on the streets less often than younger people, and this may mean that the number of crimes per number of hours that the elderly are actually at risk may be quite high (Lundquist and Duke, 1982; Stafford and Galle, 1984).

CONSEQUENCES OF THE FEAR OF CRIME   Fear of crime has many socially harmful consequences. Fear of crime in the schools destroys the atmosphere necessary for learning, leads students to avoid dangerous places such as restrooms, and can increase truancy. This may produce financial losses for schools if federal and state reimbursements are based on the number of students in attendance.

Fear of street crimes, particularly robberies, causes people to stay home rather than venture outdoors. People lock their doors and windows, install expensive alarm systems or bright lighting, and buy watchdogs. A 1984 survey found that 25 percent of American families had engraved valuables with an identification number, 7 percent had a burglar alarm, and 7 percent participated in a Neighborhood Watch program; 33 percent had taken at least one of these measures (Bureau of Justice Statistics, March 1986). Among men, those who are more fearful of crime are more likely to own firearms for protection (Hill, Howell, and Driver, 1985). The purchase of various protective measures might even escalate to the point that the costs of protection against crime could become greater than the losses from the crimes those measures are designed to prevent.

When people go out, they may do so only during the daylight hours or may travel only in groups. At night, they may use their cars to travel short distances or may take cabs to avoid walking on unlit streets. People who are afraid may avoid certain neighborhoods, which in turn become even more deserted and dangerous. People may give up visiting the library, attending meetings, and using local parks. They may forfeit income from overtime work that would require them to return home after dark.

A few people even respond to their fear of crime by moving to communities that seem safer. A 1980 Gallup poll found that crime was the leading reason given for dissatisfaction with cities: 24 percent of those who wanted to move from the city in which they lived cited crime as the reason, compared with 16 percent who mentioned overcrowding and 12 percent who mentioned the absence of job opportunities (Herbers, 1981). What is not clear is how many people actually move because of their fear of crime. For instance, one study found that flight to the suburbs was due more to the attractiveness of suburban living — part of which, of course, may be a safer environment — than to an effort to escape central-city neighborhoods (Skogan and Maxfield, 1981).

Fear of rape restricts women's freedom of movement. Children and adolescents who are raped often stay out of school for some time, and they may even transfer schools to avoid questions and social discomfort. Adult rape victims often need outside help in homemaking and parenting, because of either physical injury or psychological distress. Some adult victims quit their jobs or stay away from work for a time in order to avoid having to talk about the rape (Burgess and Holmstrom, 1976).

The fear of crime often becomes generalized to a fear of the streets, especially in communities that have high crime rates. As Jane Jacobs (1961: 30) says, "When people say that a city, or part of it, is dangerous or is a jungle what they mean primarily is that they do not feel safe on the sidewalks." The public nature of the streets and sidewalks evokes a fear of strangers who are encountered there. As one observer notes: "The street is public, and the public display of tabooed behavior threatens to make it part of daily life. Openness gives such behavior an actuality and carries the threat of public acceptance and approval" (Rhodes, 1972: 36).

Fear and Trust. Social life, especially in large cities, requires a faith that others will abide by the law. Crime can reduce that trust under certain circumstances, although some research finds that fear of crime is not strongly associated with mistrust and suspicion (Skogan, 1981). Even the crime of burglary, a relatively common nonviolent offense, can create mistrust. Imagine how the couple in the following incident felt:

> It was in Briarcliffe, N.Y., where a young couple went to dinner one evening at a local restaurant, and returned to find their car apparently stolen. After reporting it to the local police, they returned to their home and the next morning were surprised to see the car in the driveway, with an envelope on the windshield.
>
> "There was an emergency and we had to borrow the car," the note read. "Please excuse the inconvenience, but perhaps these two theater tickets will make up for it." The couple, surprised but pleased, told the police that their car had been returned, and the next Saturday used the theater tickets.
>
> When they returned that night, they found that their house had been completely looted. (Andelman, 1972: 49)

The burglars used the trust most people feel to their advantage; the effect on the couple probably was to make them less trusting of strangers and maybe even of their neighbors. This crime was not a violent one; the impact on interpersonal trust might well be even greater for victims of rape, robbery, or assault.

A dramatic example of the harmful effects of the fear of crime occurred in Atlanta, Georgia, several years ago. Between May 1979 and July 1981, twenty-nine young blacks disappeared; all but one were later found murdered. During this time, young blacks in the city were traumatized by their fear that they would be the next victim. Tests showed that children became less verbal and more withdrawn, a change that was greatest in neighborhoods where the murder victims had lived. Children became more mistrustful of strangers, and even interviewers had a difficult time approaching them. The children also suffered a decline in self-esteem and self-confidence. They became more hostile toward others, fought more at school, and even carried weapons to defend themselves. Nightmares became more common. Fear of the dark, fear of school, fear of being left alone, and fear of being outdoors all increased. Participation in sports and organized youth programs declined. Parents sometimes exacerbated these fears by being overprotective, an understandable response (Prugh, 1981; Rawls, 1981; Stuart, 1981). When Wayne B. Williams was arrested for some of the murders and eventually convicted of two of them, the murders stopped and tensions abated. Whether the reactions to the murders are having long-term effects on Atlanta's children can only be determined by follow-up studies.

One crime that did have long-term effects on the victims was a bizarre kidnapping in Chowchilla, California, in 1976. A school bus with twenty-six children was hijacked, and the children were buried underground in a truck trailer for sixteen hours; eventually, they dug their way out. Nearly five years later, these children, who were between five and fourteen when the kidnapping occurred, still showed effects. They experienced nightmares, feared ordinary things such as cars and dogs, and manifested an "on guard" mistrust of everyone. Some blamed themselves for their own victimization. They had a distorted sense of time, thought, and perception. Adults experiencing stress of this sort often use denial as a defense mechanism, but the children did not. They faced the reality of the event and the threat that it posed for them. Most of them continued to fear another kidnapping, even five years later (Timnick, 1981).

Fear and Community Ties. The French sociologist Emile Durkheim claimed in 1895 that crime enhances social solidarity within a community by bringing people together in opposition to an act that violates the law. A more recent study of reactions to crime concluded that

> collectivities will unite and react to crime if there is a community able to identify itself as insiders and if an opposing group of outsiders (in a sociological rather than geographical sense) can be identified. [This perspective] does not argue that solidarity will be increased within a geographical area where there are few crosscutting ties and where individuals feel no sense of community. (Podolefsky and DuBow, 1981: 10)

The heterogeneity of many American communities, particularly in urban centers where crime rates are the highest, and the high rate of geographic mobility of Americans mean that the conditions necessary for a unified response to crime will not exist in many communities.

Fear of crime can have severe consequences for a community, including

1. physical and psychological withdrawal from community life;
2. a weakening of the informal social control processes that inhibit crime and disorder;
3. a decline in the organizational life and mobilization capacity of the neighborhood;
4. deteriorating business conditions;

Using Criminology: Reducing the Fear of Crime

Because of the many harmful consequences of the fear of crime, policy makers have tried to develop programs to reduce it. In 1982, the National Institute of Justice awarded a grant to the Police Foundation to evaluate fear-reduction programs implemented by the police in Newark, New Jersey, and Houston, Texas. The police in those cities thought that by reducing fear they might prevent crime, and crime prevention was one of their primary tasks.

Careful evaluation of Newark's efforts to reduce fear found that the Coordinated Community Policing program was effective in reducing fear. The first component of this program was a storefront police community center that provided, among its services, the following:

- walk-in reporting of crimes
- distribution of crime prevention and Operation I.D. information
- recruitment for and holding of meetings of block watch groups and other community organizations
- coordination of the door-to-door activities of beat patrol officers.

The second component of this program was a directed police-citizen contact program, which assigned officers to visit residents in order to

- elicit information about their fears, and ways to fight those fears
- provide follow-up assistance, information, and referral advice
- encourage citizen involvement in block watch and neighborhood organizations
- distribute crime-prevention information.

This Coordinated Community Policing program significantly reduced fear of personal victimization, reduced worry about property crime in the area, reduced perceived problems of social disorder in the community, reduced the perceived amount of property crime in the area, and increased satisfaction with the neighborhood. The program allowed the police to learn about citizens' fears and suggestions for responding to local problems, and in the process created a sense among residents that they could improve things and increased police officers' sense that they were effectively serving the public.

5. the importation and domestic production of delinquency and deviance; and
6. further dramatic changes in the composition of the population. (Skogan, 1986: 215)

These changes can, in turn, lead to even higher rates of crime in the community.

Although a high crime rate is often a primary source of the fear of crime, that fear is often greater than is warranted by the objective risk of victimization. Fear of crime also seems to be a function of weak ties to the community among residents, a sense among those residents that they cannot control what is happening in their neighborhood, a lack of powerful local organizations, the absence of knowledge about effective ways to prevent crime, and a perception of incivility ("signs of crime") in the area. Incivility in the community includes

In Houston, three aspects of a fear-reduction program had similar effects. A Citizen Contact Patrol was designed to give residents the feeling that the police were present and involved in the community. Officers on routine car patrols stopped to meet people at their homes and in their businesses. The officers got acquainted and tried to elicit citizens' help in defining local problems. This program lowered the level of fear of personal victimization, reduced perceptions of the amount of crime in the area, decreased perceptions of social disorder in the community, and increased satisfaction with the neighborhood as a place to live.

A second component of Houston's fear-reduction program was a Police Community Station, a storefront office to which citizens could come for information or to report crimes. It was designed to increase citizens' interaction with the police and to enhance a sense of community among the residents, which was done through holding monthly meetings on topics of local interest. The presence of this Station reduced fear of personal victimization, lowered perceptions of the amount of crime in the area, and decreased perceptions of the amount of social disorder that existed locally.

The third component of Houston's program was a Community Organizing Response Team (CORT), which worked to develop a community organization. Officers identified local residents who would host block meetings and who would meet with the police to discuss problems in the community. These organizations, which eventually were taken over by local residents, mounted such programs as a neighborhood clean-up campaign, identification of "safe houses" for helping children, a drug information meeting, and an effort to get people to mark their household property with identification numbers. This CORT program did not reduce fear of crime among residents, but it did lower the amount of social disorder and crime they perceived in the community.

Both Newark and Houston have continued some of these programs beyond the experimental stage, and other cities have emulated their efforts to get citizens and the police to cooperate in reducing the public's fear of crime.

SOURCES: Based on Hubert Williams and Antony M. Pate, "Returning to First Principles: Reducing the Fear of Crime in Newark," *Crime and Delinquency* 33 (January 1987), 53–70; Lee P. Brown and Mary Ann Wycoff, "Policing Houston: Reducing Fear and Improving Service," *Crime and Delinquency* 33 (January 1987), 71–89.

gangs of teenagers hanging out on street corners, drug addicts and prostitutes in doorways, abandoned and burned-out buildings, and signs of vandalism such as graffiti and broken windows (Skogan and Maxfield, 1981; Lewis and Salem, 1986; Skogan, 1986; Taylor and Hale, 1986; Williams and Pate, 1986).

Fear of crime can generate suspicion and mistrust in homogeneous small towns as well as in heterogeneous urban communities. For example, in his book *In Cold Blood,* Truman Capote (1965) reports that a common reaction to the brutal murder of a family of four in Holcomb, Kansas, was suspicion of longtime friends and neighbors. The woman who owned the local café remarked:

One old man sitting here that Sunday, he put his finger right on it, the reason nobody can sleep; he said, "All we've got out here are our friends. There isn't

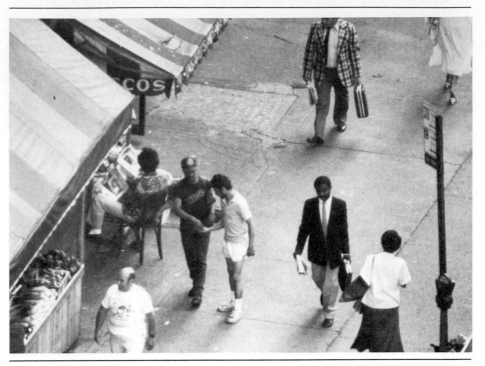

A primary source of the fear of crime is the perception of incivility, which includes drug dealers and drug users in public places. Here the police have photographed a purchase of crack on a New York City sidewalk.   *Source: Hugh Patrick Brown / Gamma-Liaison*

anything else.'' In a way, that's the worst part of the crime. What a terrible thing when neighbors can't look at each other without kind of wondering! Yes, it's a hard fact to live with, but if they ever do find out who done it, I'm sure it'll be a bigger surprise than the murders themselves. (cited in Capote, 1965: 70)

Others in the town concurred; for instance, the brother of one of the victims said, ''When this is cleared up, I'll wager whoever did it was someone within ten miles of where we now stand'' (cited in Capote, 1965: 88). When two outsiders to the community were apprehended, ''the majority of Holcomb's population, having lived for seven weeks amid unwholesome rumors, general mistrust, and suspicion, appeared to feel disappointed at being told that the murderer was not someone among themselves'' (Capote, 1965: 231). Many refused to believe that the two strangers had committed the murders. The café owner said, ''Maybe they did it, these fellows. But there's more to it than that. Wait. Some day they'll get to the bottom, and when they do they'll find the one behind it. The one who wanted Clutter out of the way. The *brains*'' (cited in Capote, 1965: 231; emphasis in the original).

These reactions do not suggest that people will always unite in response to crime, even in homogeneous and closely knit communities where the offenders are outsiders. Instead, dramatic crimes and persistently high crime rates seem to be more likely to breed mistrust, insecurity, and a weakened attachment to the community. In some neighborhoods, this can reduce human traffic on the streets, which weakens informal social control over potential offenders. Fewer people on the street also means less patronage of local businesses, which may cause shopkeepers to close early or move their businesses to other neighborhoods. The threat of crime in a community may also lead corporate decision makers to locate a new plant in a different neighborhood; this could speed the deterioration of the community by raising the local unemployment rate.

Conventional crime is a major source of fear. Fear itself is a social cost of crime, one that is enhanced when the media sensationalize bizarre crimes. Reactions to the fear of crime are also social costs. People respond to their fear of crime by staying home and avoiding strangers, mistrusting neighbors, and even moving from their community. These reactions can diminish social solidarity in a community, and this in turn can create conditions that are conducive to even higher crime rates.

Summary

Crime has several kinds of financial costs. Property can be directly lost through crime, or it may be transferred from the owner to the thief. The victims of criminal violence suffer lost wages and hospital expenses. Expenditures on illegal goods and services are often considered a cost of crime because they divert money from the legitimate economy. There is also the cost of enforcing the law and the money people spend for prevention and protection.

White-collar crime is today the most financially costly of all crimes to the American public; illegal competition, deceptive advertising, product counterfeiting, stock fraud, and price fixing are some of the crimes by "respectable" people that cost Americans billions of dollars each year. Fraud—including tax fraud, credit card fraud, and insurance fraud—probably accounts for losses even greater than the amount lost due to white-collar crimes. Conventional property crime, though very expensive in absolute terms, costs the American public much less than white-collar crime and fraud. The financial costs of crimes of violence are also significant. Narcotics crimes, prostitution, and gambling, none of which usually results in complaints to the police, divert money from legitimate economic expenditures. The cost of maintaining the criminal justice system is high, but this is more a result of decisions about how to respond to crime than a direct cost of crime to victims.

Another way to measure the costs of crime is in terms of physical harm. White-collar crime causes physical harm through environmental pollution, unsafe working conditions, and defective consumer products. Often this harm is due to negligence, but sometimes it is deliberate. Physical harm from crimes of violence can be measured by the number of victims or by the actual harm suffered by victims. Narcotics use, especially heroin use in societies where it is illegal, is associated with physical harm to users and addicts, including drug overdose deaths.

Crime affects society in ways other than financial loss and physical harm; it is detrimental to social well-being in many ways. White-collar crime and organized crime undermine faith in the economic system and the government. The fear that results from conventional crime is also costly, sometimes leading people to act in ways that actually increase the crime rate.

Important Terms

costs related to criminal violence
direct loss
enforcement costs

illegal expenditures
prevention and protection costs
transfer of property

Suggested Readings

JOHN E. CONKLIN. *The Impact of Crime.* New York: Macmillan, 1975. A detailed look at the effects of conventional crime on community life.

CHARLES M. GRAY, ED. *The Costs of Crime.* Beverly Hills, Calif.: Sage Publications, 1979. A collection of essays by economists, dealing with the costs of crime and the costs of public and private responses to crime.

DARYL A. HELLMAN. *The Economics of Crime.* New York: St. Martin's Press, 1980. An introduction to the way economists look at the financial costs of crime.

DAN A. LEWIS AND GRETA SALEM. *Fear of Crime: Incivility and the Production of a Social Problem.* New Brunswick, N.J.: Transaction Books, 1986. A study of ten neighborhoods that links fear of crime to the social organization and political environment of communities.

WESLEY G. SKOGAN AND MICHAEL G. MAXFIELD. *Coping with Crime: Individual and Neighborhood Reactions.* Beverly Hills, Calif.: Sage Publications, 1981. A report on research that examines the social consequences of crime for community life.

CHAPTER 5

Dimensions of Crime

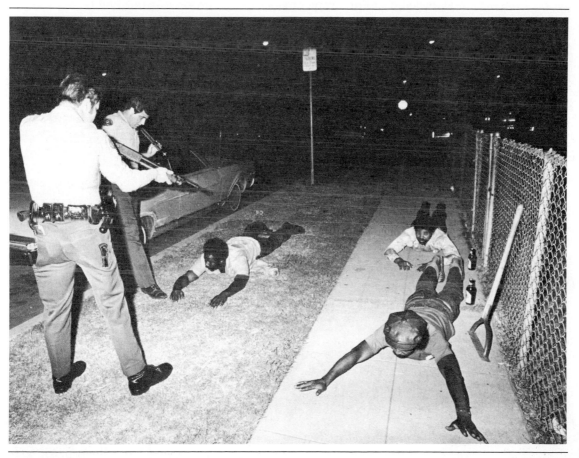

Source: Patrice Chauvel / Sygma

In 1983 the new chief of public security for China said that his country had "quite a problem" with crime. This "problem" was a rate of 71 reported crimes per 100,000 people in 1982, which compared with a rate of 5,553 index crimes per 100,000 people in the United States in the same year. There are differences in the collection of crime statistics in the two countries that make it difficult to compare crime rates, but China does seem to have a much less serious crime problem than the United States.

In this chapter, we look at differences among nations in crime rates. We also look at variations by region and by size of the community, over time, and by sex, age, race, and class. Each of the measures of crime that we use in this chapter — the FBI's UCR data, the NCS victimization data, and self-report data — has flaws. These drawbacks should be kept in mind as we look at the various dimensions of crime.

Knowledge of how crime rates vary from group to group and from society to society can point the way to a theory of crime causation. Statistical variations in crime rates are facts that criminologists' theories must explain, but these variations are not, by themselves, theories of crime. For instance, knowing that men commit more murder than women does not tell us why this difference exists, but it does tell us that a theory of crime should account for this difference.

Cross-National Variations in Crime Rates

In the criminologist's ideal world, all nations would define crime and gather statistics in the same way. We could then compare the crime rates of different countries, facilitating the development of a general theory of crime causation. Unfortunately, this situation does not exist, nor is it ever likely to. There are significant cross-national variations in laws, and the law-enforcement process and the collection of crime data also differ from society to society. Fewer than a dozen countries now have complete and reliable systems of crime statistics.

In recent years, crime rates have increased dramatically in most industrialized and developing nations. With economic development, rates of property crime have usually increased faster than rates of violent crime. However, social change is not inextricably linked to rising crime rates, as we can see from Japan's experience.

Japan

Japan is one nation that has apparently avoided a long-term increase in crime rates as it has industrialized and urbanized. In 1948, 1.6 million penal code offenses were recorded in Japan, but by 1973 that figure had dropped to 1.2 million, a decline of 25 percent. Between 1963 and 1972, Tokyo had a 13 percent decline in crime and Osaka a 37 percent decline. During the same period, the crime rate in New York City nearly tripled, the rate in West Berlin more than doubled, and the rates in London and Los Angeles increased by about 60 percent (Clifford, 1976: 1–4). In 1986, 1.6 million crimes were recorded, an increase over the 1973 figure but the same as the number of offenses reported in 1948, despite a growth in population over that time.

In 1983, the Japanese police were talking of a "crime wave," but statistics indicated that crime was still an insignificant problem compared with other industrial societies, particularly the United States. For instance, in Japan there were nearly twice as many "wanton murders"—or senseless street killings by strangers—in 1982 as there were in 1981, but the total number for 1982 was only thirteen. This is about the same number in Japan—a nation of 118 million people—as New York City with its population of 7.5 million sometimes has on a holiday weekend. Japan's rate of 1.5 murders per 100,000 people in 1982 was dwarfed by the rate of 9.1 for the United States in that year. Japan has recently experienced some increase in narcotics use, juvenile offenses, computer crime, credit card fraud, and the counterfeiting of designer products, but these crimes are not yet occurring at the same rate that they do in other industrial societies (Haberman, 1983).

Japan's experience since the end of World War II shows that social change is not always accompanied by rising crime rates. Why social change produces higher crime rates in some nations, but not in others, is explored later when we look at theories of crime causation. What is important here is that cross-national differences exist and need to be explained.

Canada

Canada has a significantly lower crime rate than the United States. For instance, metropolitan Toronto has only one-eighth as much murder and one-fifth as much forcible rape as metropolitan Dallas – Fort Worth, even though both cities are of similar size. Canada's crime rates have increased somewhat in the last few years, but they still remain below rates in the United States.

Explanations for this difference vary from one criminologist to another. One theory is that Canada has a law-abiding tradition that dates back to the settlement of the country in the eighteenth century by people from the thirteen colonies who were loyal to the King of England and unwilling to rebel against authority. The Canadian West was not as lawless as the West in the United States, for the Royal Canadian Mounted Police established order on the frontier. Some criminologists discount the importance of these historical factors and look instead at differences between the countries today. For instance, Canada does not have as large a population of minority groups that are frustrated by blocked opportunities to enter the middle class. Canada's gun-control laws are much stricter than those in most states, and this might also account in part for the lower level of violence (Meisler, 1981).

Cross-National Comparisons of Murder Rates

One offense for which some cross-national data exist is murder. Even for this crime, however, there are some significant variations from one society to another in the definition of the offense. For instance, laws differ in the role assigned to premeditation and responsibility (e.g., see Seidman, 1965). In addition, whether acts of war, civil insurrection, and political terrorism that result in death are recorded as murder or are treated as political acts differs from society to society and depends in part on who has the power to define criminal behavior. These and other problems make even murder difficult to examine cross-nationally.

Until 1975, the United Nations gathered world-wide data on murder under the general category of "all other external causes of death," a broad classification that also included wartime deaths and deaths from political violence. In 1975, the United Nations revised its list of causes of death to include one that more accurately measures murder: "homicide and injury purposely inflicted by other persons." It is this category that we use in Table 5.1, where the rates per 100,000 people are given for nations reporting to the United Nations in 1983 and 1984. Latin American nations that report their homicide rates have some of the highest rates in the world, but deaths from political violence may be counted as homicides and there are serious problems with the validity of the information reported by those countries (Salas and Wilbanks, 1981). Table 5.1 does not include data from the Soviet Union, from African nations, or from most Asian countries. What seems clear, though, is that the homicide rate in the United States is quite high compared with other industrial societies.

TABLE 5.1 Homicide and Injury Purposely Inflicted by Others as a Cause of Death. Rates per 100,000 People, 1983 and 1984

Country	Rate per 100,000	Year	Country	Rate per 100,000	Year
El Salvador	40.4	1984	Portugal	1.7	1984
Puerto Rico	13.3	1983	Hong Kong	1.7	1984
United States*	7.9	1984	Belgium	1.7	1984
Costa Rica	3.9	1983	New Zealand	1.6	1983
Bulgaria	2.9	1983	Czechoslovakia	1.4	1983
Hungary	2.6	1984	France	1.3	1983
Canada	2.3	1984	German Federal Republic	1.2	1984
Israel	2.0	1983	Japan	0.9	1984
Australia	1.9	1983	Netherlands	0.9	1984
Austria	1.8	1984	Greece	0.8	1983
Poland	1.8	1984	England/Wales	0.6	1983

*This is the FBI Uniform Crime Reports rate for murder and nonnegligent manslaughter and is not reported in the United Nations statistics. It is provided here for comparative purposes.

SOURCE: United Nations, *Demographic Yearbook 1985.* New York: United Nations, 1987, pp. 749–792.

Regional Variations in Crime Rates within the United States

The comparatively high murder rate of the United States leads us to ask what causes the differences between this country and other industrial societies. We can begin to zero in on an answer to this question by looking at variations in crime rates within the United States. One such variation is by region of the country.

In 1986, the rate of murder and nonnegligent manslaughter for the United States was 8.6 per 100,000. However, there were significant variations in the rate for different regions. The rate for the Northeast was 6.8, the rate for the Midwest was 6.6, the rate for the West was 9.2, and rate for the South was 10.6 (Federal Bureau of Investigation, 1987: 44–51). The homicide rate for the South had been about twice the rate for the rest of the nation until recently, when murder rates have become more similar for the different regions. Still, the murder rate in the South is now 41 percent higher than the rate for the rest of the country.

Several explanations have been offered for the South's high murder rate. Because both poverty and minority-group status are linked to murder, some have suggested that the South's high murder rate is a product of the relatively large amount of poverty and the relatively large proportion of blacks in that region. Regional differences have also been explained by a "subculture of violence," a set of norms that allow violence to be an appropriate response to certain situations (Wolfgang and Ferracuti, 1967, 1982). Some claim that these norms are more widespread in the South than elsewhere. Attempts to explain regional variations in murder rates by this subculture-of-violence theory are explored later in the book, but what is important here is the existence of regional differences that a theory of crime causation must explain.

Although the South has a high rate of murder, its rates of forcible rape and aggravated assault are only slightly higher than the national rates, and its robbery rate is somewhat lower than the national rate. Thus any theoretical explanation of the South's high murder rate would have to be specific to lethal violence rather than be a general theory of all violent crime.

Turning to regional variations in rates of property crime, the most notable differences are in the extraordinarily high rates of burglary and larceny in the West. These differences are difficult to explain. Regional variations in the professionalization of the police might exist, with the police in western states perhaps being more likely to record burglaries and larcenies efficiently than are the police in other regions. The more recent settlement of the West might mean that informal community control of crime is weaker there than it is in more settled areas of the country, but we would then expect the rates for all index crimes to be higher in the West. Another possible explanation is that the relatively casual life style in the West and Southwest might be conducive to theft. Warmer weather there might mean that people are away from their homes more often and leave their property unguarded, and this could inflate property crime rates by creating more opportunities for theft. The weather is also warm in the South, but the lower per capita income there may provide potential thieves with fewer opportunities for theft. We can speculate about the reasons for these regional variations in crime rates, but theories of crime causation should make sense of those variations. This assumes, of course, that the data that show such variations are valid measures of the actual distribution of crime.

Variations in Crime Rates by Community

FBI data for 1986 show that crime rates per 100,000 people increase with the size of the community, with few exceptions. For some reason, larceny rates are slightly higher in cities with populations between 100,000 and 250,000 than they are in even larger cities. In addition, rates of murder and forcible rape are higher in rural areas than they are in small towns. With these exceptions, there is an increase in FBI rates from the smallest communities to the largest.

NCS victimization data for 1983 indicate that both violent crime and property crime occur at higher rates in central cities than in suburban areas, and at higher rates in suburban areas than in nonmetropolitan areas (Dodge, December 1985). Victimization rates increase with size of the community for robbery, assault, larceny from the person, burglary, household larceny, and motor vehicle theft. Rape does not show a clear pattern of variation by size of the community (Bureau of Justice Statistics, May 1984). In general, both official crime statistics and victimization surveys point in the same direction: Conventional crime occurs at higher rates in large communities, at least within the United States.

The growth in the size of cities does not always lead to higher crime rates, even though certain social processes associated with large communities — such as the anonymity of the individual and the disruption of traditional social ties — may be associated with more crime. Since the end of World War II, Japan has become more heavily urbanized, but its crime rate has not increased (Clifford, 1976). Switzerland was also able to keep its crime rate low while urbanizing. Apparently its slow rate of urban growth made it possible to maintain social stability and avoid the disruption of traditional social ties that often accompanies urbanization (Clinard, 1978). Thus the association between size of community and crime rates in the United States should direct our attention to social processes that have occurred with urban growth in this country, rather than lead us to assume that urbanization inevitably and by itself generates crime.

Crime within Metropolitan Areas

The first systematic examination of the distribution of crime within metropolitan areas was carried out in the 1920s in Chicago by Clifford R. Shaw and Henry

D. McKay (1942, 1969). They followed Ernest W. Burgess in describing the metropolitan area as a series of identifiable concentric rings, depicted in Figure 5.1. In this *concentric-zone model* of the urban community, industry develops near the center of the city to be at the crossroads of transportation and communication. This may not be true of cities that developed after the mass ownership of cars and telephones, and in the future, cities may be located at the crossroads of electronic communications rather than at the crossroads of transportation. In Shaw and McKay's model, the central business district is at the center of the metropolis and is immediately surrounded by an area that is changing from a run-down residential area to one occupied by expanding business and industry. Beyond this are residential areas of increasing desirability and respectability.

This model of the metropolis fits some American cities quite well, but it does not describe others very accurately. In some cities, industry has developed on the outskirts, and in others there are multiple centers of business and commerce rather than the single one described by Shaw and McKay. In some nations, government-planned urban development has upset this concentric-zone pat-

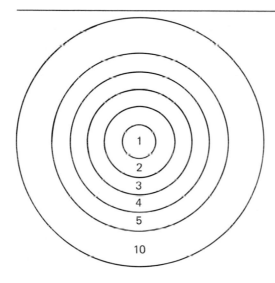

District
1. Central business district
2. Wholesale light manufacturing
3. Low-class residential
4. Medium-class residential
5. High-class residential
10. Commuter's zone

FIGURE 5.1 Shaw and McKay's Concentric-Zone Model of the City *Source: Reprinted from "The Nature of Cities" by Chauncy D. Harris and Edward L. Ullman in volume no. 242 of The Annals of The American Academy of Political and Social Science. © 1945 by The American Academy of Political and Social Science. All rights reserved.*

Using Criminology: The Chicago Area Project

Research on the distribution of delinquency in Chicago led Clifford Shaw and Henry McKay to conclude the following:

> The consistency with which certain communities produce large numbers of delinquents, over a long period of time, focuses attention on the community as the basic unit for programs aimed at an understanding of the offender, treatment, or the prevention of violative behavior. Surely the processes of the community must be understood before programs, based on this understanding, can be brought into operation. Full recognition of the implications of the fact that a large proportion of young offenders come from a few areas should lead to further concentration on the neighborhood or the community as the appropriate units for social action. (p. 387)

To encourage efforts by residents of low-income areas to prevent delinquency and rehabilitate offenders, in 1932 the Institute for Juvenile Research and the Behavior Research Fund began the work of what came to be known as the Chicago Area Project.

This was a private corporation that had a board of directors composed of prominent citizens who sought to prevent delinquency. Funds and personnel for programs were provided by foundations, public and private agencies, and local residents and institutions.

The Chicago Area Project treated the neighborhood as the basic unit of operation. Activities and programs were developed in urban neighborhoods with populations from 10,000 to 50,000. The neighborhood orientation of the Chicago Area Project reflected Shaw and McKay's assumption that delinquency was the product of community conditions and therefore had to be dealt with as a local problem with local solutions.

Programs in each community were planned and implemented by a committee of local citizens, including members of churches, unions, business groups, athletic clubs, and other local organizations. This approach contrasts with the traditional practice of outsiders to the community running local programs. Though the funds for

tern; one example is Great Britain (Baldwin, 1979). As long ago as the Victorian period, the government built roads through "rookeries," or urban areas inhabited by criminals, in order to disperse offenders throughout the metropolitan region (McIntosh, 1975: 22–23).

Shaw and McKay found that rates of arrest for delinquency—as well as rates of adult crime, truancy, tuberculosis, infant mortality, and mental disorder— were highest in the center of the city and declined with increasing distance. Since Shaw and McKay completed their research, others have done work that supports their conclusion about the distribution of crime and delinquency in metropolitan areas (see, e.g., Short, 1969: xxv–liv). Rates of crime and delinquency are usually highest in areas characterized by low incomes, dilapidated and overcrowded housing, transiency, unemployment, broken families, and minority groups. These areas are most commonly in the center of large cities (Chilton, 1964; Turner, 1969; Miller, 1974). Evidence that the highest rates of the Chicago Area Project's programs might come from outside the community, the local committee assumed full leadership of the activities. This created a sense of self-reliance in working toward common goals.

To the extent possible, the staff to carry out these programs was recruited from the neighborhood. Local workers had close ties to local organizations and residents, and these ties helped promote social action programs. These local people were also more aware than outsiders of the special strategies that were needed to make programs work in the community. Professional workers from outside the community who worked with the local committee had to learn to translate their expertise into actions that would be effective in the community.

The programs developed by the local committees of the Chicago Area Project were designed to improve the community, and especially to enhance the well-being of local children. Activities included recreation, summer camping, scouting, handicrafts, and field trips. There were also programs designed to improve housing, sanitation, and the physical appearance of the neighborhood. Parent-teacher organizations were developed to improve local schools, and to some degree there were efforts to increase job opportunities for local youths.

No systematic evaluation of the Chicago Area Project's impact on delinquency rates has been conducted. Annual committee reports document participation in the programs, tell of cases in which programs seemed to succeed in rehabilitating offenders, and show success in achieving goals such as building a new facility or gaining a concession from city government. Systematic evaluation of the Chicago Area Project is difficult because of the philosophy of trying to respond to local needs, an approach that created great variety among the programs implemented in different communities. The Chicago Area Project did succeed in increasing local participation in programs designed to solve local problems, and it forced outsiders to consider local needs before offering assistance in solving neighborhood problems.

SOURCE: Based on Clifford R. Shaw and Henry D. McKay, *Juvenile Delinquency and Urban Areas*, rev. ed., with a new intro. by James F. Short, Jr. Chicago: University of Chicago Press, 1942, 1969.

crime and delinquency occur in the center of cities also comes from research carried out in Canada, Great Britain, Venezuela, Puerto Rico, Uganda, the Soviet Union, and other countries (Wallis and Maliphant, 1967; Grillo, 1970; Clinard and Abbott, 1973; Edwards, 1973; Jarvis and Messinger, 1974; Ferracuti, Dinitz, and Acosta, 1975; Shelley, 1981a, 1981b).

Looking at data from Chicago from 1900 to 1966, Shaw and McKay found that the delinquency rate for the members of any given racial or ethnic group was higher for members of the group who lived near the center of the city and lower for members who lived in neighborhoods more distant. For instance, people of German ancestry who lived in the inner city had higher rates of arrest for delinquency than did German-Americans who lived in the suburbs. This suggests that it is certain values and norms that are transmitted from generation to generation in an urban neighborhood, rather than the values and norms of any particular racial or ethnic group, that are conducive to violation of the law.

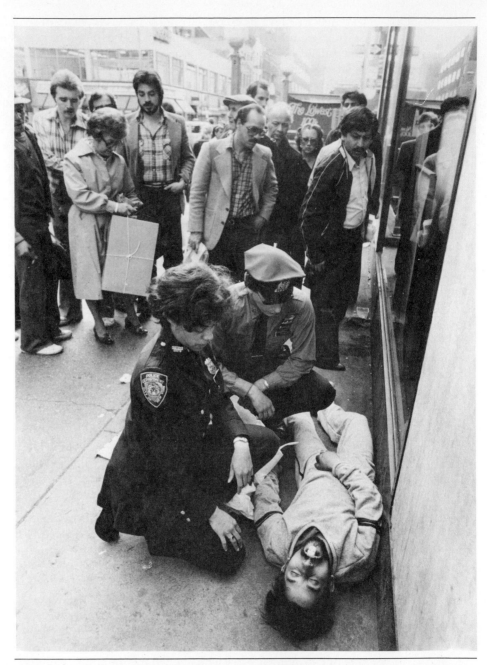

Rates of crime, including drug violations, are highest in the center of the city. Here the police try to help a young man found on the sidewalk, apparently the victim of a drug overdose. *Source: Sygma*

This conclusion is supported by Shaw and McKay's finding that the same urban neighborhoods generally had the highest rates of delinquency over the years, even when there was considerable change in the racial and ethnic composition of those communities. Areas with high delinquency rates were usually marked by rapid population turnover, socialization into patterns of crime and delinquency, and a lack of good jobs. However, a more recent study of the distribution of delinquency in Chicago found that the conclusion that rates remained the same despite racial and ethnic turnover only fit the data for 1940 and 1950. From 1950 to 1970, changes in the racial and ethnic composition of a neighborhood were often accompanied by changes in delinquency rates. Rates of delinquency remained about the same when a neighborhood was able to maintain its stability in the face of a changing racial and ethnic composition, but in many neighborhoods racial and ethnic succession destabilized the community and led to an increased rate of delinquency (Bursik and Webb, 1982).

The major value of Shaw and McKay's work is their systematic documentation of the distribution of crime and delinquency in urban areas, rather than their attempt to develop a theory to explain that distribution. They provide evidence that a theory of crime causation must explain: variations in rates of crime and delinquency within metropolitan areas.

THE GEOGRAPHY OF CRIME   Geographers have provided a picture of crime in metropolitan areas by mapping the location of crimes, the residences of those who commit crimes, and the residences of victims (Georges-Abeyie and Harries, 1980; Brantingham and Brantingham, 1984). Often they use computer graphics to show the distribution of these elements in a metropolitan area.

Crimes of violence are often depicted as a triad of elements: the residences of the offender and of the victim, and the place where the crime occurs. However, many crimes of violence — especially homicide and aggravated assault — occur within the home, where much interaction takes place. As a result, sometimes the triad is a single point, with the residence of the victim and the offender also being the location of the crime.

Crimes against property are usually depicted as a dyad of elements: the residence of the offender and the place where the property is stolen (although larceny from a person may add the third element of the victim's residence). Most property offenses, as well as most crimes of violence, occur fairly close to the offender's home, with the number of crimes decreasing with greater distance from the criminal's place of residence. People are familiar with their own neighborhoods and so can find targets there; they also know what risks they must avoid near home, even though they may run a greater risk of identification near home. Consequently, criminals' "journeys" or "trips" to the places where they commit their crimes are often short (P. Phillips, 1980; Brantingham and Brantingham, 1984). However, the dyads and triads of crime vary with the kind of offense committed and with the age and sex of the criminal.

Geographers have not mapped dyads and triads for white-collar crime. If they did, they would probably discover that the distance from the home of the offender to the location of the crime, which is usually the place of work, is considerably greater than is the case for most index crimes. Moreover, the places of residence of the victims of white-collar crimes are probably widely dispersed throughout the metropolitan area, and often throughout the nation or the world.

Migration and Crime

Migration might contribute to higher crime rates because of the disruption to the lives of people who move from small towns and rural areas to large cities, or from one country to another. However, research on the relationship between migration and crime has produced mixed results.

Studies carried out in Uganda, Kuwait, and several African and South American countries have found that migration is associated with high crime rates (Clinard and Abbott, 1973; Al-Thakeb, 1978; Shelley, 1981b). Migrants to Soviet cities have higher crime rates than long-term residents of the same cities (Shelley, 1981b). Immigrants to England from Ireland have a higher crime rate than the native-born English, a difference attributed to the disruption of traditional controls by family and church, a high unemployment rate, and residence in high-crime areas (Radzinowicz and King, 1977: 26). Data from Japan show that the high crime rate of young immigrants to Tokyo from the surrounding countryside is about one and half times as high as the rate for Tokyo residents who grew up there (Clifford, 1976: 114–115).

Research done in several European countries has yielded somewhat different conclusions. In some of those studies, the crime rates of natives and immigrants are similar, and in others the immigrants have somewhat lower rates than the natives. A study in West Germany concluded that aliens between fourteen and twenty-one had higher crime rates than their native-born counterparts, but the crime rate for all adult migrants was actually lower than the rate for native-born German adults (Albrecht, Pfeiffer, and Zapka, 1978). Other research from Europe, Australia, Canada, and the United States suggests that recent immigrants — whether permanent residents or "guest workers" — sometimes have crime rates lower than those of the native-born population (Savitz, 1960; Clinard, 1978; Shelley, 1981a).

During the first few decades of the twentieth century, there was a widespread feeling among native-born Americans that high crime rates were due to recent immigrants. In *Culture Conflict and Crime*, one of the first studies of the relationship between migration and crime, Thorsten Sellin (1938) showed that immigrants did not have crime rates higher than native-born Americans. In fact, for many crimes and for many nationalities, the immigrants' crime rates were lower. However, the rates for the offspring of the immigrants often approached the native-born rate. In other words, the crime rates of successive generations of the children of immigrants became more like the crime rates of the native-born. This indicates that crime is a learned behavior, and that socialization into the

A Cross-Cultural Perspective: Migration and Crime in the Soviet Union

Urban growth and the movement of people are controlled in the Soviet Union by population policies, an internal passport system, and registration regulations. Because the major cities—such as Moscow, Leningrad, and Kiev—are considered by Soviet planners to be large enough already, people are not permitted to move in an unrestricted way from rural areas, small towns, and the suburbs into those cities. Marriage to a resident or a job offer in the city does give a person the right to move there.

Population movement within the Soviet Union is controlled by a passport system that states a person's permanent residence and limits his or her travel within the country. This system was introduced in 1932 and applies to all citizens after their sixteenth birthday. The internal passport system makes it difficult for criminals wanted by the police to escape, for they must show their passports regularly.

One consequence of Soviet migration policies is that the major cities have not grown much in recent years, but small and medium-sized cities have grown because it is relatively

easy to secure a permit to live there. Many people have moved from collective farms to these smaller cities, where frequently they have experienced problems of adjustment to urban life that have led to higher crime rates in those cities.

In addition to curbing the crime rate by restricting migration from rural areas and small towns, the largest Soviet cities have also avoided a crime problem by applying a policy that has been used since the 1920s: Offenders who have been in prison for at least five years, and sometimes less, lose the right to return to their homes in large cities or in surrounding areas after they are released from prison. Consequently, there are fewer offenders in major cities than there would be without state restrictions on migration and place of residence. Many offenders thus move to small and medium-sized cities, causing the crime rates there to increase.

SOURCE: Based on Louise I. Shelley, "Urbanization and Crime: The Soviet Case in Cross Cultural Perspective," in Louise I. Shelley, ed., *Readings in Comparative Criminology.* Carbondale: Southern Illinois University Press, 1981, pp. 141–152.

dominant American culture is likely to be associated with rising crime rates for immigrant groups that had lower rates when they came to the country.

In 1980, about 125,000 refugees entered the United States from Cuba. Because some of these "Marielitos" had served time in Cuban prisons, the American press gave much attention to the crime they committed. Law-enforcement officials in many of the cities in which these Cuban refugees live have reported that they commit disproportionately large amounts of crime. However, a study of homicide in Dade County, Florida, found that the murder rate of these Cuban immigrants was no higher than the rate for blacks who were native to the county (Wilbanks, 1984: 26).

The fact that immigrants sometimes have crime rates no higher than the rate for the native-born population is surprising, for there are several reasons to think the immigrants would have higher rates. Migrants are most often young males, a group particularly prone to crime in all societies. Moving often disrupts ties to family, friends, and community, and this may weaken traditional controls over deviant behavior (Crutchfield, Geerken, and Gove, 1982). The hostility and discrimination sometimes encountered by immigrants might also push them into crime. In addition, there is usually more affluence in the place to which a migrant moves than in the place from which that person came, and this both provides more opportunities for crime and creates a sense of material deprivation conducive to crime. The relationship between migration and crime seems to depend on several factors, including the crime rate of the migrants prior to moving, the crime rate of the native-born population, and the problems of adjustment encountered by the immigrants in their new home.

In both industrialized and developing capitalist societies, migration is usually uncontrolled. However, in some socialist societies, migration is controlled. For instance, both China and the Soviet Union have developed policies to minimize the disruption that can occur with internal migration from rural areas and small towns to large cities. In the Cross-Cultural Perspective, we see how this policy has worked in the Soviet Union.

Temporal Variations in Crime Rates

So far we have seen that crime rates vary by country, by region within a country, and by size of the community. In this section, we will see that crime rates also vary over time.

Seasonal Variations in Crime Rates

Victimization data show that some crimes fluctuate with the seasons. A study that used NCS data for 1973 to 1977 found that household larceny and unlawful-entry burglary peaked in the summer months and reached a low point in the winter. Similar but relatively weak seasonal fluctuations were uncovered for personal larceny of more than $50, forcible-entry burglary, assault, and motor vehicle theft. Rates of robbery from the person did not differ by season. Personal larceny under $50 showed an unusual pattern: Rates peaked in October and reached a low point during the summer. Apparently this is because petty theft from the person is a common offense in school. As a result, rates are highest during the months that schools are open, and are especially high early in the school year when there are more new things to steal (Bureau of Justice Statistics, May 1980). More recent NCS data show that "almost all types of personal and household crimes are more likely to occur during the warmer months of the year," with the exception of robbery from the person (Bureau of Justice Statistics, October 1983b: 11). These temporal variations are relatively small, but they must be explained by theories of crime.

Annual Trends in Crime Rates

Figures 5.2 and 5.3 show fluctuations in rates of the FBI index crimes since 1933. Between 1933 and 1960, rates were relatively stable, but they began to increase significantly around 1963. Since the mid-1970s, rates have declined in

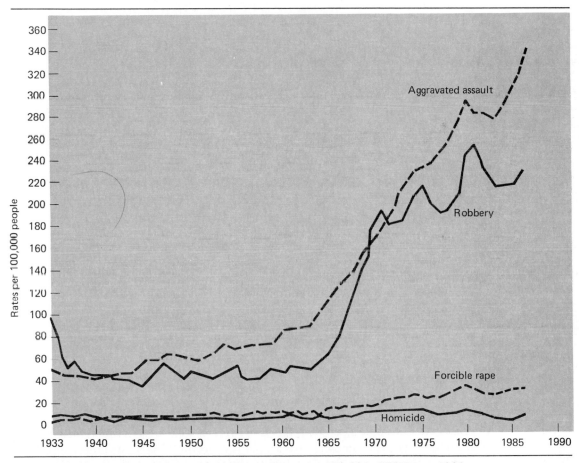

FIGURE 5.2 Trends in Crimes of Violence, Rates per 100,000, FBI Data, 1933–1986 *Source: Data from FBI Uniform Crime Reports for 1966–1986 to bring up to date the figure presented in the President's Commission on Law Enforcement and Administration of Justice, The Challenge of Crime in a Free Society. Washington, D.C.: U.S. Government Printing Office, 1967, p. 23.*

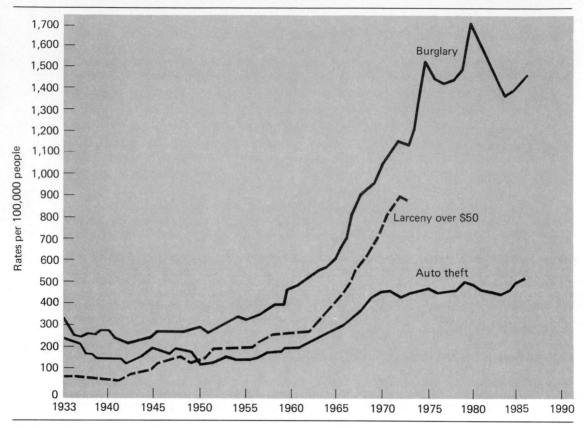

FIGURE 5.3   Trends in Crimes against Property, Rates per 100,000 People, FBI Data,
1933–1986   *Source: Data from FBI Uniform Crime Reports for 1966–1986 to bring up to
date the figure presented in the President's Commission on Law Enforcement and Administration
of Justice,* The Challenge of Crime in a Free Society. *Washington, D.C.: U.S. Government
Printing Office, 1967, p. 23.*

some years and seem to be showing signs of stabilizing or even declining. These
FBI data must be interpreted cautiously, for better crime reporting and recording could have accounted for some of the change in rates.

Figures 5.4 and 5.5 show that NCS victimization rates changed little during
the 1970s, but they declined somewhat during the 1980s. In some years, NCS
victimization rates declined while FBI rates increased. In general, both types of
data suggest a stability or decline in crime rates in recent years.

A theory of crime causation should be able to tell us why crime rates rise and
fall over the years. However, few theories have tried to explain long-term trends
in crime rates.

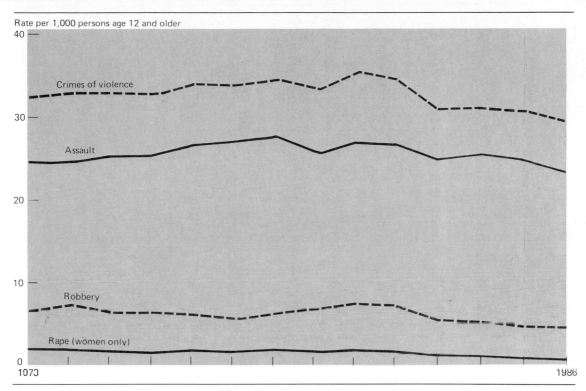

FIGURE 5.4   Trends in Victimization Rates for Crimes of Violence, NCS Data, 1973–
1986 *Source: Bureau of Justice Statistics, Criminal Victimization 1986. Washington, D.C.:
U.S. Department of Justice, October 1987, p. 3.*

Variations in Crime Rates by Sex

Not everyone is equally likely to commit a crime, or to be the victim of one.
Offense rates and victimization rates vary with social characteristics such as sex,
age, race, and class.

Perhaps the best predictor of whether an individual will violate the law is sex:
Men commit much more crime than women in every society for which we have
data. Even though male-female differences in crime rates vary from one society
to another, over time, and from one offense to another, sex is a primary factor
differentiating criminals from noncriminals. This could be partly a result of
biological differences that make men more aggressive than women, but it is
more likely the result of differences in the socialization of males and females.
Boys and girls, and men and women, are taught to behave differently and play

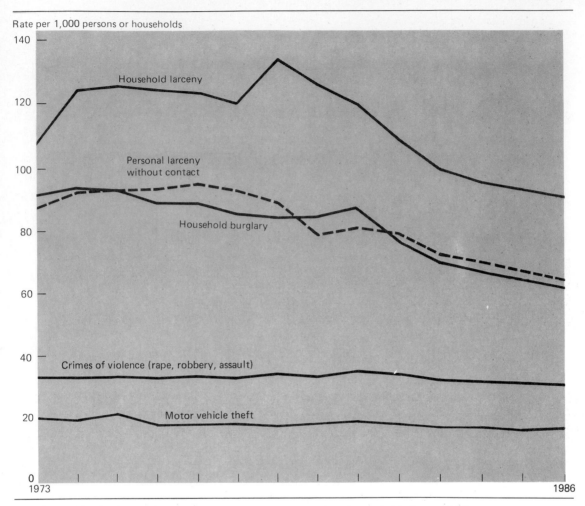

FIGURE 5.5   Trends in Victimization Rates for Selected Crimes, NCS Data, 1973–
1986   *Source: Bureau of Justice Statistics,* Criminal Victimization 1986. *Washington, D.C.:
U.S. Department of Justice, October 1987, p. 1.*

different roles. This socialization process, in combination with a social structure
that assigns statuses to people on the basis of sex, leads to differences in personality and behavior that are linked to the large difference in crime rates between
males and females.

Sex and Juvenile Delinquency

To examine male-female differences most fruitfully, we must look at juvenile
delinquency and adult crime separately. Delinquency includes acts that are

crimes when committed by adults, but it also includes juvenile status offenses (such as running away from home) that are prohibited only for those below a certain age. Because delinquency is defined so broadly, differences in expected behavior for boys and girls influence the way that each sex is treated by the juvenile justice system.

In 1986, the five offenses for which boys under the age of eighteen were most often arrested were larceny, burglary, liquor law violations, vandalism, and disorderly conduct. For girls under eighteen, the top five offenses were larceny, running away from home, liquor law violations, simple assaults, and curfew and loitering law violations. For all offenses except running away, more boys than girls were arrested. The ratio of male to female arrests varies with the offense. Boys were arrested about three times as often as girls for larceny, but boys were arrested twelve times as often for burglary. For all Part I and Part II offenses, there were three and a half times as many boys as girls arrested.

In recent years, the delinquency rate for girls has increased faster than the rate for boys, but boys still greatly outnumber girls in arrests for delinquent acts (Office of Youth Development, 1974; Canter, 1982; Federal Bureau of Investigation, 1987). Females do not seem to be catching up with their male counterparts in serious violent crimes or in gang-related delinquency, but they have become more like males in the rate at which they commit larceny, run away from home, and violate liquor laws. The failure to catch up in the more serious crimes may be attributable to the absence among girls of a youth subculture, which acts as a source of recruitment into serious crime (Steffensmeier and Steffensmeier, 1980).

Self-report studies indicate that when a girl commits an act that would be a crime if committed by an adult, she is less likely than a boy to be reported to the police or to be dealt with in court (Clark and Haurek, 1966; Gold, 1970; Chesney-Lind, 1973). Boys who engage in conventional crimes are more likely to be arrested by the police and brought before a juvenile court, partly because of the widely held opinion that girls are not as "bad" as boys or that girls who violate the law are led into crime by "bad" male accomplices.

Some research reveals that for certain juvenile status offenses, girls are as likely as—or even more likely than—boys to be arrested by the police and brought into court (Clark and Haurek, 1966; Wise, 1967; Gold, 1970; Chesney-Lind, 1973). A girl who runs away from home, drinks alcoholic beverages, or has sexual relations is more likely to become involved with the legal system than is a boy who does the same things, even though self-report studies indicate that female involvement in these acts is often no greater than male involvement (Canter, 1982). This difference in treatment by the juvenile justice system is probably related to norms about appropriate gender-role behavior: Boys are expected to "raise hell" but girls are expected to be "well behaved." These expectations lead to more surveillance and control of adolescent girls than of adolescent boys, and they result in more arrests and court appearances for girls than would be expected on the basis of sex differences in self-reported delinquency.

Sex and Adult Crime

In addition to the male-female differential in juvenile arrests, there is a significant difference between the sexes in arrests of adults. In 1986, for instance, there were 5.1 men eighteen and over arrested for every woman that age who was arrested. This is a higher ratio than for juveniles; in other words, adult crime is even more of a male phenomenon than is juvenile delinquency.

Table 5.2 shows the sex of suspects, both adult and juvenile, who were arrested for each of the index crimes in 1963 and 1986. For each offense, significantly more men than women were arrested. The only crime for which more than 14 percent of the suspects were female in 1986 was larceny.

TRENDS IN FEMALE CRIME Crime by women has received much attention since the early 1970s, mainly because of the feminist movement. Some of this attention has exaggerated the extent of female involvement in crime (e.g., see *Newsweek,* January 6, 1975).

Larceny is the one offense for which there seems to have been a significant change in female involvement between 1963 (the first year for which total arrest data are available) and 1986. For other index offenses, the percentages of all arrested suspects who were women fluctuated by only a few percentage points. In 1963, only 19.0 percent of all arrests for larceny were of females, but in 1986

TABLE 5.2   Male and Female Arrests for Index Crimes, 1963 and 1986

| | All Arrests | | | |
| | Percentage Male | | Percentage Female | |
Crime	1963	1986	1963	1986
Murder	81.9	87.7	18.1	12.3
Forcible rape*	100.0	98.9	0.0	1.1
Robbery	95.1	92.2	4.9	7.8
Aggravated assault	86.0	86.8	14.0	13.2
Burglary	96.7	92.1	3.3	7.9
Larceny	81.0	69.3	19.0	30.7
Motor vehicle theft	96.3	90.5	3.7	9.5
Arson**	—	86.3	—	13.7
Total index offenses	88.3	78.9	11.7	21.1

*A woman may be arrested for forcible rape if she acts as an accomplice to the man who perpetrates the actual rape.

**No arrest data on arson are available for 1963.

SOURCES: J. Edgar Hoover, *Crime in the United States, 1963: Uniform Crime Reports.* Washington, D.C.: U.S. Government Printing Office, 1964, p. 109; Federal Bureau of Investigation, *Crime in the United States, 1986: Uniform Crime Reports.* Washington, D.C.: U.S. Government Printing Office, 1987, p. 181.

that figure had increased to 30.7 percent. This increase accounted for much of the increase in the total number of arrests of women for index crimes over this period, because larceny is by far the most common index crime for which arrests are made. Without self-report data for women for 1963 and 1986, we cannot determine if there was an actual increase in theft by women over that time. Perhaps the arrest practices of store detectives and the police changed during that period. One response to the large increase in FBI crime rates over this time may have been a decision to arrest people in 1986 who might have been warned and released in 1963.

A systematic review of official statistics, victimization survey data, and self-report studies concludes that the relationship between sex and crime

> is strong and . . . is likely to remain so into the near future, at least in an absolute sense. On the other hand, in a relative sense, there is evidence that women are becoming more like men in their levels of involvement in crime, with this being particularly true of younger women and in the area of property crime. The areas of female criminality that are changing fastest are those that have been traditionally female, including petty forms of theft and fraud. (Nagel and Hagan, 1983: 108)

FEMINISM, WORK, AND CRIME   Some observers have suggested that crime by women has increased in recent years as a result of the feminist movement. One problem with this argument is that arrest data do not show a clear increase in all crimes by women. Another problem is that some of the increase in female crime that has occurred actually preceded the emergence of the feminist movement. Some of the increase in crime by women did come after the development of the feminist movement, but this does not prove the movement itself was the cause of the increase.

We need to ask how the feminist movement might have led to an increase in crime by women, an increase that is not large except for larceny arrests. It does not seem that women who are most active in the feminist movement are arrested very often for index crimes. Some research on female delinquency finds that violation of the law is not associated with feminist attitudes (Giordano, 1978), and some research has even shown that feminist attitudes can inhibit property offenses and violent crimes (James and Thornton, 1980).

Since the end of World War II there has been a large increase in the proportion of women holding jobs outside the home. Some, but probably not most, of this increased involvement by women in the labor force is attributable to the feminist movement and the changes in gender roles that it has produced. Other social forces that have led more women to take jobs include rising rates of divorce and illegitimacy, a delay in the age at first marriage, and the perception that inflation has so eroded the family's buying power that two incomes are needed. Whatever the reasons for increased labor-force participation by women, those women who do hold jobs outside the home may have more opportunities to commit crimes such as larceny and embezzlement. However, FBI data indicate that most female arrests are not occupationally related. Arrests of women are more common for passing bad checks, credit card or welfare fraud, and shoplifting, rather than for employee theft or embezzlement. One analysis of female crime concludes that increased theft by women is due less to the feminist movement or increased labor-force participation than it is due to changes in merchandising — such as more self-service stores or more buying on credit — that make theft or fraud easier for shoppers, a traditional female role (Steffensmeier and Cobb, 1981).

In one study of employee theft in a large retail organization, data gathered from personnel records, from files kept by the company's security force, and from interviews conducted with the firm's officials revealed that male employees committed more thefts and took more when they did steal than was true of female employees. Of 447 known dishonest workers, 56 percent were men, even though only 40 percent of the company's work force was male (Franklin, 1979). This study suggests that given similar on-the-job opportunities for theft, men may commit crime more often than women, even though we would expect female crime to increase somewhat as women gain more opportunities to steal on the job (Figueira-McDonough and Selo, 1980).

The higher rate of labor-force participation by women may have had a more subtle effect on the female crime rate. It may have increased a sense of relative deprivation or entitlement among women who are not working outside the home, or among those who are being paid less than their male colleagues for the same work. If there is a widespread perception — accurate or not — among some women that other women are doing well financially and being fulfilled by their jobs, then women who are not working may feel that they deserve more than they have. This same sense of deprivation can develop if women, whether in the labor force or not, compare their own position unfavorably with that of men. Feminism may have raised expectations faster than reality has changed, and this might have produced frustration that has led to crime by some women. This explanation is consistent with the evidence in Table 5.2 that the relative proportion of all arrested suspects who were women increased from 1963 to 1986 for crimes of theft, but decreased for murder and aggravated assault.

SEX AND CRIME IN OTHER SOCIETIES   When women took over some traditionally male roles in Germany during World War II, female crime rates rose to nearly the same levels as male rates. When women returned to traditionally female roles after the war, their crime rates dropped to prewar levels (Radzinowicz and King, 1977: 14–15). This suggests that increasing equality of gender roles might cause male and female crime rates to become more similar. For example, since the end of World War II, the contribution of Japanese women to their nation's crime rate has increased as they have entered the labor market, married later, and become more like men in the roles they play (Clifford, 1976: 125–132).

Sex and Victimization

Victimization surveys find that men are much more likely than women to be the victims of robbery and assault, and somewhat more likely to be victims of nonviolent crimes of theft. Women are most apt to be the victims of forcible rape, a crime that is often defined to include only female victims (Bureau of Justice Statistics, November 1983a). The NCS victimization survey collects no data on homicide, but the FBI's UCR data for 1986 show that men are the victims of homicide about three times as often as women.

Variations in Crime Rates by Age

Most crimes are committed by relatively young people. In 1986, FBI data showed that 29.6 percent of people arrested for index crimes were under the age of eighteen and 60.1 percent were under the age of twenty-five (Federal Bureau of Investigation, 1987: 174–175). In that year, half of the population of the country was under the age of 31.7, and half was over that age.

One of the offenses for which young people are most often arrested is running away from home. *Source: Mary Ellen Mark / Archive Pictures, Inc.*

Age-Specific Arrest Rates

The rate at which people commit crime varies with age. Arrest data do not provide a perfect picture of how involvement in crime varies with age, because young offenders may be more or less likely than older offenders to be arrested for any given crime. However, we can reach some tentative conclusions from Table 5.3, which gives the *age-specific arrest rates*—or number of arrests per 100,000 people in each age category—for the crime of robbery in 1970 and 1980, two census years. We can see that in each year there is considerable variation in arrest rates among age groups. In 1970, the arrest rates rose to a peak at age eighteen and then declined with age. In 1980, a similar pattern occurred, except that the peak age for arrests was seventeen. In both years, there was a precipitous decline in age-specific arrest rates after the mid-twenties.

Another important aspect of Table 5.3 is that the age-specific arrest rate for each group was considerably higher in 1980 than in 1970. This suggests more involvement in robbery by people of every age. The increase cannot be attributed to increasing rates of arrest by the police, for their clearance rate for robbery declined from 29.1 percent in 1970 to only 23.8 percent in 1980. In other words, by 1980 a smaller proportion of all people who committed robbery was being arrested, but still the age-specific arrest rate increased for every age group.

Peak ages and age-specific arrest rates vary considerably from one offense to another. For all index crimes, 29.6 percent of the suspects arrested in 1986 were

TABLE 5.3   Robbery Arrests per 100,000 People for Age Groups, 1970 and 1980

Age Group	Number of Robbery Arrests per 100,000 People 1970	1980	Age Group	Number of Robbery Arrests per 100,000 People 1970	1980
Under 15	16.7	19.4	24	122.0	140.2
15	139.4	211.9	25–29	75.8	99.0
16	172.9	265.5	30–34	40.4	55.5
17	189.7	292.5	35–39	21.9	30.0
18	197.5	281.2	40–44	11.6	17.1
19	194.9	242.7	45–49	6.2	9.7
20	172.2	210.6	50 and over	1.5	2.2
21	165.1	196.0			
22	142.1	166.2	Total	43.1	61.6
23	121.8	155.3			

SOURCES: Rates calculated from data in U.S. Department of Commerce, Bureau of the Census, *General Population Characteristics: United States Summary, 1970.* Washington, D.C.: U.S. Government Printing Office, 1972; J. Edgar Hoover, *Crime in the United States, 1970: Uniform Crime Reports.* Washington, D.C.: U.S. Government Printing Office, 1971; U.S. Department of Commerce, Bureau of the Census, *General Population Characteristics: United States Summary, 1980.* Washington, D.C.: U.S. Government Printing Office, 1983; and William H. Webster, *Crime in the United States, 1980: Uniform Crime Reports.* Washington, D.C.: U.S. Government Printing Office, 1981.

under eighteen, and their median age was twenty-two. For the four violent crimes, only 15.4 percent were under eighteen, and their median age was twenty-five. Suspects in property crimes were generally younger than suspects in violent crimes, with 33.5 percent of them being under eighteen and their median age being twenty-one.

Age Distribution and Crime Rates

Because arrest rates differ by age group and because this seems to reflect a difference among age groups in actual involvement in criminal activity, a society can experience an increase or a decrease in its crime rate if the age distribution of its population changes. In other words, if the young have an especially high crime rate, a society with a large proportion of young people in its population at one time will have a higher overall crime rate than it would have at a different time when a smaller proportion of its population is young.

The post-World War II "baby boom" produced a significant increase in the proportion of the American population in the high crime rate years from fifteen to twenty-four in the 1960s; between 1960 and 1975, the size of that age group increased about six times as fast as the rest of the population. The dramatic increase in official crime rates during the 1960s seems to have been due in part to the increased proportion of the population in this high crime rate age group (The President's Commission on Law Enforcement and Administration of Justice, 1967a: 27–28).

Although changing age distribution explains some of the increase in index crime rates in the United States during the 1960s and the 1970s, it does not explain most of it. Instead, there was an increase in the rate at which people of every age committed crime, as we can see in Table 5.3 for the crime of robbery. Looking at changes in the rate of violent index crimes from 1960 to 1970, for instance, we find that changes in the age distribution would have led us to expect a 40 to 50 percent increase in the rate of those offenses, but instead there was a 200 percent increase (Silberman, 1978: 31). The important theoretical question thus becomes what social changes, in addition to the change in the age distribution of the population, produced the increase in the crime rate.

Just as an increasingly youthful population can be expected to have rising crime rates, so too should an increasingly older population have declining crime rates. Recent research indicates that the decline in property crime rates from 1980 to 1984 can be attributed largely to a change in the age structure of the population, with reductions in larceny and motor vehicle theft rates being the most influenced by the aging of the population (Cohen and Land, 1987; Steffensmeier and Harer, 1987). One study found that changes in violent crime rates were not explained by the changing age structure of the population (Steffensmeier and Harer, 1987), but another study concluded that the decline in homicide rates during the early 1980s did reflect changes in the age structure over that period (Cohen and Land, 1987). If criminal opportunities do not increase, crime rates can be expected to decline until the end of the century, except for short-term fluctuations due to the business cycle and due to variations in crime reporting rates (Cohen and Land, 1987). This decline will be more significant for property crimes than for violent crimes (Steffensmeier and Harer, 1987).

Age and Victimization

Young people generally have higher rates of victimization than older people. In 1986, FBI data showed that two-thirds of all murder victims were between fifteen and thirty-nine (Federal Bureau of Investigation, 1987: 9). NCS victimization data show that rates of other violent crimes are also highest among the young. Excluding the rates for victims under twenty, victimization rates for rape, robbery, and assault decline with increasing age. Crimes of theft also show lower victimization rates for older people (Bureau of Justice Statistics, November 1983a).

An NCS report on crime against the elderly in twenty-six cities found that people over sixty-five had the lowest rates of victimization for rape, robbery, and assault. The elderly were the least likely of all age groups to be attacked or injured, and serious injury among them was rare. In part, this was because the elderly were unlikely to resist or to try to protect themselves from criminals (Hochstedler, 1981). However, as we saw in Chapter 4, there may be a sense in which the elderly have a high rate of victimization. They may be at risk less often than younger people because generally they do not go to work, they often live in age-segregated housing (including nursing homes), and they frequently stay indoors out of fear or infirmity. If victimization rates are calculated in terms of time at risk, the elderly's victimization rate may actually be as high as or even higher than that of younger people (Lundquist and Duke, 1982; Stafford and Galle, 1984).

Variations in Crime Rates by Race

Variations in crime rates by racial and ethnic group reflect social, cultural, and economic differences among groups. In the past, some have suggested that such variations in crime rates are due to biological differences among racial and ethnic groups, but it is now well established that any biological differences among racial and ethnic groups are unimportant in explaining differences in crime rates. For instance, the crime rates of black Africans are considerably lower than the crime rates of black Americans, even though black Americans have racially intermixed with whites over the centuries, and whites have crime rates lower than black Americans (Bohannan, 1960). Such variations in crime rates need to be explained by sociological theories of crime causation.

Race, Arrest Statistics, and Self-Report Studies

The FBI presents arrest data for whites, blacks, American Indian or Alaskan Natives, and Asian or Pacific Islanders; it also provides data for Hispanic and non-Hispanic suspects. FBI data do not allow us to analyze differences in arrest rates for white ethnic groups such as Irish-Americans, Italian-Americans, Eastern Europeans, or Jews. However, sociological research has found the crime rates for Jews, Japanese-Americans, and Chinese-Americans are lower than rates for the total population, and crime rates for blacks and Mexican-Americans are higher than rates for the total population (Voss, 1963; Wolfgang, Figlio, and Sellin, 1972; Tracy, Wolfgang, and Figlio, 1985). Here we examine differences in arrest rates of blacks and whites, because these two groups account for almost all of the arrests for FBI index crimes; in 1986, for instance, 98.2 percent of all arrests for index crimes were of blacks or whites.

In 1986 blacks constituted 12 percent of the population of the United States, but they accounted for 33.7 percent of arrests for index crimes. Blacks comprised 46.5 percent of arrests for crimes of violence and 30.2 percent of arrests for property crimes. For each index crime, blacks are arrested out of proportion to their numbers in the population. According to one estimate, the chance of ever being arrested for an index crime for blacks living in cities of more than 250,000 people is 51 out of 100, compared with a rate of only 14 out of 100 for whites (Blumstein and Graddy, 1981–82). In Table 5.4 the rates of arrest per 100,000 people of the same race are given for whites and for blacks; the third column shows the ratios of blacks' arrest rates to whites' arrest rates. We can see that the likelihood of a black's being arrested for an index crime is much greater than the chance of a white's being arrested. Blacks are arrested between 4.7 and 11.6 times as often as whites for violent crimes, and between 2.2 and 3.8 times as often as whites for property crimes. Overall, blacks have an arrest rate for index crimes that is 3.6 times as great as the arrest rate for whites.

We must be wary of using FBI arrest data, for they may distort actual involvement in index crimes by blacks and whites if the police are more likely to arrest black suspects than they are to arrest white suspects. However, most criminologists agree that arrest statistics for blacks and whites reflect a real difference

TABLE 5.4   Rates of Arrest per 100,000 People, 1986

Crime	White Rate of Arrest per 100,000 People	Black Rate of Arrest per 100,000 People	Ratio of Black Rate to White Rate
Murder	3.9	26.0	6.7
Forcible rape	7.8	48.8	6.3
Robbery	22.4	260.6	11.6
Aggravated assault	84.1	396.6	4.7
Burglary	126.2	375.4	3.0
Larceny	390.8	1,204.6	3.1
Motor vehicle theft	39.7	150.6	3.8
Arson	5.7	12.4	2.2
Total index crimes	680.6	2,475.0	3.6

SOURCES: Arrest rates are calculated using Bureau of the Census data for 1986 on the number of whites (204,671,000) and blacks (29,427,000), and arrest data from Federal Bureau of Investigation, *Crime in the United States, 1986: Uniform Crime Reports*. Washington, D.C.: U.S. Government Printing Office, 1987, p. 182.

between the groups in their rates of committing crimes, and that the difference in arrests between the racial groups is not primarily a result of racial discrimination by the police. Later in the book, we examine racial discrimination by the police, the courts, and the prisons.

Some self-report research finds a higher frequency of all delinquent acts by blacks (Elliott and Ageton, 1980), but other studies find that blacks and whites report similar involvement in all delinquent acts (Williams and Gold, 1972). Blacks and whites seem to be more similar in their self-reported involvement in relatively trivial delinquent acts, but blacks do seem to report serious offenses more often than whites (Williams and Gold, 1972; Hindelang, Hirschi, and Weis, 1979; Elliott and Ageton, 1980).

Race, Crime, and Background Variables

Differences in crime rates among racial and ethnic groups are a function of group differences in age, income, occupation, education, family background, and other social characteristics, as well as a function of differences in opportunities to commit crime. This would suggest that if blacks and whites of similar social backgrounds are compared, differences in crime rates between the groups will be reduced or eliminated. However, to suggest that people of different races but similar backgrounds will have the same crime rate is tantamount to suggesting that there are no cultural differences between the groups that result in different crime rates. More specifically, to argue that blacks and whites of similar backgrounds will have the same crime rate is to argue that centuries of discrimination have had no long-term effects on blacks that are conducive to criminal behavior.

Evidence suggests that blacks have higher crime rates than whites, even when individuals of similar backgrounds are compared, but that differences between the groups are reduced in comparisons of people of similar backgrounds. A study of murder in Philadelphia found that when blacks and whites with similar occupations were compared, blacks still committed homicide more often than whites (Wolfgang, 1958: 39). A study of rape in the same city found that blacks committed rape about four times as often as whites when people with similar occupations were compared (Amir, 1971: 69–72). Wolfgang, Figlio, and Sellin's (1972) cohort study revealed that 29 percent of the whites had had police contacts as juveniles, compared with 50 percent of the blacks. Even when blacks and whites of similar class backgrounds were compared, blacks were more likely to have had police contacts. Thus, 53 percent of lower-class blacks had had police contacts as juveniles, compared with only 36 percent of lower-class whites; and 36 percent of higher-class blacks had had police contacts, compared with only 26 percent of higher-class whites. From these figures, we can see that blacks of the higher class were actually as likely as whites of the lower class to have had contact with the police. Blacks thus seem to have higher rates of crime and delinquency than whites of similar background, although research indicates that black-white differences are reduced when people of similar backgrounds are compared (Green, 1970; Wolfgang, Figlio, and Sellin, 1972).

Race and Victimization

Blacks are disproportionately likely to be the victims of crime. In 1986, 44.2 percent of all homicide victims were black, although only 12 percent of the population was black. Black males who live in cities have about a 5 percent chance of being murdered, and black males between fifteen and twenty-four are murdered at a rate seven times as high as the rate for the rest of the population. In fact, murder is the primary cause of death for young black males. Some health officials have argued recently that murder among young black males should be considered a public health issue in much the same way that diseases are (Minsky, 1984; Foreman, 1987).

NCS data show that blacks have higher victimization rates than whites for rape, robbery, and assault. These victimization survey data also show that even though blacks, as a group, have a lower average income than whites, they are more likely than whites to be the victims of most property crimes. Blacks have higher victimization rates than whites for personal larceny with contact, household burglary, household larceny, and motor vehicle theft. Whites have slightly higher victimization rates for personal larceny without contact.

Victim-Offender Relationships and Race

Researchers have found that violent crime typically involves a victim and an offender of the same race. A disproportionately high number of all murders involve a black offender and a black victim, and most of the rest of murders involve a white offender and a white victim. Fewer than 10 percent of murders cross racial lines, and those that do usually involve a black murderer and a white victim. Similarly, the great majority of forcible rapes involve an offender and a victim of the same race, with most cross-racial rapes that are recorded by the police involving a black rapist and a white victim (Wolfgang, 1958; Amir, 1971; Curtis, 1974; Federal Bureau of Investigation, 1987; O'Brien, 1987).

Variations in Crime Rates by Class

When criminologists examine the relationship between *class*—which is defined as social standing based on economic resources, occupational prestige, political power, or life style—and crime, they usually look at conventional crimes such as murder, rape, robbery, and larceny. However, the most expensive crimes are white-collar crimes, and because these offenses are committed by middle- and upper-class people, we can conclude that the cost of crime is attributable primarily to violation of the law by the middle and upper classes, even though "the crime problem" defined by the FBI, the mass media, and the public usually refers to violations of the law most often committed by the lower and working classes.

Popular wisdom is that the lower and working classes engage in more crime, or at least more of the most serious conventional crime, than does the middle class. This view has existed for centuries and characterizes societies other than the United States (see, e.g., Chevalier, 1973). People act on their assumption that there is a relationship between crime and class; they avoid slums after dark, leave the doors of their suburban homes unlocked, and expect to be safer when they move from the city to the suburbs.

FBI statistics include no information on the class of arrested suspects, nor do victimization surveys provide us with that information, because victims could not be expected to judge in a reliable way the class of the offender. There is, however, much research that has examined the relationship of class to crime and delinquency. Unfortunately, that research does not lead to a simple conclusion.

Class and Adult Crime

When we look at official measures of crime produced by the police, the courts, or the prisons, we find "a small but consistent inverse correlation of social class with street crime" for adults (Hindelang, 1983: 180). For instance, one review of forty-six studies that used arrest data found consistently higher crime rates for lower-class adults (Braithwaite, 1979, 1981).

In the few studies that have been done of adult criminality using self-report questionnaires, researchers have found that the class-crime link is less strong in self-report data than in official data. These self-report studies either conclude that the lower class has a higher crime rate than other classes or that there are no significant differences by class; no self-report study of adults has found that the middle class has a higher crime rate than the lower class (Braithwaite, 1979).

Some have attributed the difference between the relatively strong association between class and adult crime found in official statistics and the weak or nonexistent association found in self-report studies to class bias by the police and the courts. In other words, if the police are more likely to arrest a lower-class suspect than a middle-class suspect, arrest data would show that the lower class is more involved in crime, even though self-report studies might show little or no difference among the classes in criminal activity. However, a review of studies of adults that have used arrest data or self-report questionnaires concluded that class bias by the criminal justice system could not explain away the strong relationship between class and crime found in studies using official statistics. The author concludes that "[l]ower-class adults commit those types of crime which are handled by the police at a higher rate than middle-class adults" (Braithwaite, 1979: 62).

Class and Juvenile Delinquency

One review of studies that have examined the link between class and juvenile delinquency found that in forty-four of fifty-three studies that used official statistics, lower-class juveniles had higher rates of delinquency than middle-class juveniles (Braithwaite, 1979). Another review of the research found a "small but consistent inverse correlation of social class with street crime" by juveniles when official data were used (Hindelang, 1983: 180).

When self-report studies rather than official data are used to look at the link between class and juvenile delinquency, the results are not clear. One review of the research found that self-report studies provide less support for a class-delinquency link than do arrest data, but that many self-report studies show higher delinquency rates for the lower class and that none finds higher rates for the middle class (Braithwaite, 1979). Another review of self-report studies of delinquency concluded as follows: "About half of the American studies support the hypothesis of an even smaller inverse relationship between various social-class indicators and reported illegal behavior [than is found in studies using official data], and half provide no support for the hypothesis" (Hindelang, 1983: 180). The class-delinquency relationship may be weaker in self-report studies than in research based on official data because the police are more likely to stop or to arrest lower-class adolescents than they are to stop or to arrest middle-class adolescents in the same circumstances.

Self-report studies seem to indicate that class differences in delinquency are most pronounced for the most serious crimes, and smallest for the most trivial offenses. Serious and repetitive violations of the law seem to be most common among the lower classes (Short and Nye, 1958; Reiss and Rhodes, 1961; McDonald, 1969; Gold, 1970; Belson, 1975; Clelland and Carter, 1980; Elliott and Ageton, 1980; Braithwaite, 1981; Elliott and Huizinga, 1983).

Self-report studies that have looked at a broader range of delinquent acts, rather than only the most serious ones, have sometimes concluded that there is little or no association between class and delinquency. One review of the research found a weak to moderate relationship between class and official data on violations of the law, but almost no relationship between class and self-reported violations of the law (Tittle, Villemez, and Smith, 1978). Other self-report studies have also found no relationship between class and delinquency (Nye, Short, and Olson, 1958; Short and Nye, 1958; Dentler and Monroe, 1961; Akers, 1964; Hirschi, 1969; Krohn et al., 1980). Several self-report studies of juvenile delinquency have even concluded that there is no relationship between class and serious, repetitive violations of the law (Karacki and Toby, 1962; Empey and Erickson, 1966; Shanley, 1967; Williams and Gold, 1972; Cernkovich, 1978a; Johnson, 1980; Krohn et al., 1980).

Contradictory evidence on the association between class and self-reported delinquency also comes from the few studies that have compared the delinquency of people from the lowest class with that of all people of higher social standing. One self-report study that found no overall relationship between class and delinquency did find that boys from the lowest class were the most prone to delinquency. Of those boys whose fathers had been without a job and had received welfare assistance, 62 percent reported at least one delinquent act, compared with only 40 percent of the boys whose fathers had not been unemployed or on welfare (Hirschi, 1969: 72). However, another study found no significantly greater amount of self-reported delinquency—measured only by acts that would be crimes if committed by adults—among the underclass—a class that is below the poverty level, uneducated, often on welfare, and unemployed or working at low-prestige jobs (Johnson, 1980).

One researcher has suggested that there might be stronger evidence for a link between class and juvenile delinquency in economically developing societies where people are categorized at birth into social groups with different perspectives on the world, where access to education is limited, and where social mobility is minimal. This view was supported by the author's research in South Korea. Using both official statistics and self-report data, he found that criminal behavior was confined largely to the lower class, and that the relationship between class and delinquency was strongest for the most serious offenses. The researcher concluded that in developing societies, "class remains an important factor in the explanation of crime and delinquency when educational opportunity is lacking" (Axenroth, 1983: 176).

Methodological Problems

Several methodological problems account for some of the inconsistency in the conclusions of the research that has examined the class-delinquency relationship. One problem is how to measure the social class of adolescents. Rather than ask adolescents about the class of their parents, as most researchers have done, it might make more sense to try to tap adolescents' job aspirations or expectations of future earnings (Stark, 1979; Thornberry and Farnworth, 1982). Another problem is that by gathering data from students who are in school on the day the survey is done, researchers miss truants and school dropouts, who may be especially prone to delinquency. In addition, because self-report surveys often ask about many relatively trivial acts, the number of respondents who are classified as delinquent is increased (Reiss, 1975; Hindelang, Hirschi, and Weis, 1979).

In spite of these methodological problems, many self-report studies find higher rates of serious and repetitive delinquency among the lower classes, and none of those studies finds higher rates of serious and repetitive delinquency among the middle class. Official arrest data show even more consistent evidence for a class-delinquency link. Moreover, for adults, arrests show a strong class-crime association, and data from the few existing self-report studies of adults reveal an association between class and crime, although a somewhat weaker one than is found in studies using official data.

We will see later that many sociological theories of crime and delinquency are based on class, even though the relationship between class and violation of the law is still somewhat unclear. These theories rarely consider that involvement in crime and delinquency can *affect* an individual's class standing by reducing job opportunities or making upward social mobility difficult; unlike sex, age, and race, the variable of class may be both a cause and an effect of crime and delinquency (Thornberry and Christenson, 1984). One review of eight theories of crime and delinquency concludes that none of them provides an adequate rationale for predicting an inverse or negative relationship between class and crime without bringing in untested or unsupported assumptions about what the lower class is like (Tittle, 1983). Perhaps sociologists would be on firmer ground in looking for general social processes — such as ways of neutralizing the constraints of the law — that are sometimes correlated with class, rather than treating class itself as a cause of crime and delinquency.

Class and Victimization

The National Crime Survey does not use a single measure of class, but it does gather data on indicators of class such as annual family income, education, employment status, and employment sector. Here we use annual family income as a measure of the class of both individual victims and households.

Victimization rates for three crimes of violence — rape, robbery, and assault — decline with increasing income levels; this pattern is least pronounced for assault. Crimes of theft from individuals show no clear variation by income. Personal larceny with contact declines with increasing income, but personal larceny without contact — the most frequent theft crime from individuals — shows a curvilinear relationship with income: The rate is highest for the lowest and the highest income categories. Victimization rates for burglary decline with increasing income, except for the highest income category. Rates of household larceny are about the same for all income levels. Rates of motor vehicle theft rise with income and reach a peak for families with incomes between $10,000 and $14,999 and then decline somewhat at higher income levels (Bureau of Justice Statistics, November 1983a).

Overall, patterns of theft from individuals and from households do not reveal a strong and consistent tendency to rise or fall with income, but crimes of violence do decline noticeably with rising levels of annual family income.

Summary

Rates of crime vary from one country to another; by region within a country; by size of a community; from one time to another; and by sex, age, race, and class. Theories of crime causation should help us make sense of these variations.

Cross-national comparison of crime rates are difficult because of differences among countries in their laws and their crime statistics. Three countries that seem to have crime rates lower than the United States are China, Japan, and Canada. The United States has an extraordinarily high homicide rate compared with other industrial nations that report crime data to the United Nations.

Within the United States, one regional variation in crime rates that has received attention is the South's high homicide rate. The West has the highest rates of burglary and larceny.

Both FBI data and NCS victimization studies show that rates of index crimes are generally higher in larger communities. Shaw and McKay found that crime and delinquency are most common in neighborhoods closest to the center of the city. Geographers have mapped the residences of offenders and victims and the places where crimes occur, finding that most offenders commit crimes close to home. Immigrants frequently have crime rates no higher than, and sometimes lower than, the native-born population, in spite of perceptions by the native-born that the new arrivals are especially prone to crime.

NCS studies show there are some seasonal fluctuations in crime rates that require explanation. FBI data show a large increase in crime rates beginning in the 1960s, with rates stabilizing or even declining in recent years. NCS data show either stability or a decline in crime rates since 1973.

In recent years, some kinds of juvenile delinquency have become more common among girls, but boys still outnumber girls in arrests. There is differential treatment of the sexes in the juvenile justice system, with girls less likely than boys to be processed formally if they commit acts that would be crimes when committed by adults, and girls more likely than boys to be processed formally if they commit status offenses such as running away from home.

Since 1963, there have been some small changes in the relative proportion of males and females arrested for index crimes, but only for larceny has the proportion of female suspects increased significantly. This may be because store detectives and the police have become more likely to treat female thieves formally rather than to release them with a warning, or because merchandising changes have made theft easier for women who shop, or because women have actually become more likely to steal. Feminism has not had a demonstrable impact on crime by women, and increased participation in the labor force by women seems to have had less of an effect on crime rates than we might expect. Males are victimized more than females by violent crime (except for rape) and by personal larceny without contact.

In the United States, most people who commit index offenses are relatively young. Changes in the age distribution of a population over time can increase a society's overall crime rate. In general, victimization rates are higher for younger people than they are for older people, but the elderly may have a high victimization rate if we take into account their limited exposure to the risk of victimization.

Black Americans are arrested in numbers disproportionate to their numbers in the population, and this is more true for violent crimes than for property crimes. Arrest data seem to reflect a real difference between blacks and whites in their perpetration of index offenses, rather than police bias in the arrest of suspects of different racial groups. Self-report data also indicate that blacks are more likely than whites to commit serious offenses, but some self-report studies find that blacks and whites differ less in the rates at which they commit less serious crimes. Comparing blacks and whites of similar social backgrounds often reduces the difference in their crime rates, but several studies have found that blacks have higher rates of involvement in crime even when people of the same backgrounds are compared. Blacks are more likely than whites to be the victims of violent crimes; blacks are also more likely to be the victims of most property crimes, even though they have a lower average income than whites. Violent crime most often occurs between an offender and a victim of the same race.

The relationship between class and violation of the law is complex. In general, official arrest statistics show that lower-class adults commit more crimes than middle-class adults; the few self-report studies of adults find a similar but weaker association between class and crime. Most studies of juvenile delinquency find an inverse relationship between official measures of delinquency and class, but in some studies the relationship is not strong. Self-report studies of delinquency are mixed in their conclusions: Some show an inverse relationship between class and delinquency, and others find no relationship. Methodological problems with self-report studies make it difficult to unravel the exact relationship between class and violation of the law, especially among adolescents. There are mixed relationships between family income and victimization rates for property crimes, but crimes of violence are least common among people with higher incomes.

Important Terms

age-specific arrest rate   concentric-zone model
class

Suggested Readings

DANE ARCHER AND ROSEMARY GARTNER. *Violence and Crime in Cross-National Perspective.* New Haven, Conn.: Yale University Press, 1984. A series of studies that use data from 110 nations, including a cross-national comparison of homicide rates.

JOHN BRAITHWAITE. *Inequality, Crime, and Public Policy.* London: Routledge and Kegan Paul, 1979. An examination of the relationship among crime, class, and slums that considers the possible impact of policies to redistribute wealth and power and policies to reduce the residential segregation of classes.

ROLAND CHILTON AND JIM GALVIN, EDS. "Special Issue: Race, Crime, and Criminal Justice," *Crime and Delinquency* 31 (January 1985). A collection that includes several papers on race and violent crime.

WILLIAM CLIFFORD. *Crime Control in Japan.* Lexington, Mass.: D. C. Heath, 1976. A detailed examination of why rates of crime and delinquency in Japan have remained low and even declined since World War II.

JOANN GENNARO GORA. *The New Female Criminal: Empirical Reality or Social Myth?* New York: Praeger, 1982. A study of changing female crime rates and the impact of the women's movement on them, with a consideration of the implications of the findings for criminological theories.

CLIFFORD R. SHAW AND HENRY D. MCKAY. *Juvenile Delinquency and Urban Areas,* rev. ed. Chicago: University of Chicago Press, 1942, 1969. An updated version of the classic study of patterns of delinquency in metropolitan areas.

PART III

The Causes of Criminal Behavior

Chapter 6 examines biological and psychological explanations of criminal behavior. We look at recent biological research on twins, adopted children, chromosomal abnormalities, and brain functioning that suggests that inherited factors may interact with psychological and social factors to cause crime. We also investigate research by psychologists on the link between intelligence and crime, the personality traits associated with criminal behavior, the psychoanalytic perspective, and conditioning theory. Rules determining criminal responsibility, including the recent debate over revision of the insanity defense, are also discussed.

Chapter 7 focuses on the socioeconomic sources of crime. Aspects of the economy and characteristics of corporations that are conducive to white-collar crime are investigated. Sources of income for organized crime are examined. In looking at conventional crime, we consider the impact of modernization, the relationship between unemployment and crime, and the way that a sense of being deprived can motivate people to violate the law. We look at several theories of delinquency: anomie, differential opportunity, reaction-formation, and lower-class culture as a generating milieu of delinquency. We also consider the subculture-of-violence theory.

The ways that offenders neutralize the law and are free to violate it because of their weak attachments to conventional institutions are considered in Chapter 8. Techniques that people use to neutralize the hold that the law has over them are considered for embezzlement, crime by blacks, murder, and juvenile delinquency. Control theory is discussed, and evidence for this theory is assessed by looking at research on the family, the school, the peer group, religion, and migration.

Chapter 9 focuses on sources of learning to commit crime: the community, delinquent gangs and peer groups, the general culture, the mass media, sports, pornography, and correctional institutions. This chapter presents differential association theory, and considers evidence for that theory. This chapter also considers the labeling perspective, which proposes that crime and delinquency are the result of the effects of labeling on self-concepts, social opportunities and relationships, and membership in subcultures. Operant conditioning theory and the economist's model of criminal behavior are also examined, with attention given to the way that offenders consider the rewards and risks of crime.

In Chapter 10 we explore opportunities to commit crime and factors that facilitate criminal activity. We look at the way crime is linked to the routine activities in which people engage, and at the way offenders choose their targets. We also examine the way alcohol, drugs, and firearms facilitate criminal behavior.

The cumulation of acts of crime into criminal careers is the subject of Chapter 11. Here we consider delinquent careers and the career patterns of adult offenders. We also look at the way career criminals eventually leave a life of crime for a conventional life.

CHAPTER 6

Biological and Psychological Explanations of Crime

Source: UPI/Bettmann Newsphotos

Modern criminology began with the positivist approach of an Italian physician, Cesare Lombroso. His theories of crime causation have since been found deficient, but his emphasis on the collection of data to test hypotheses about criminals became the basis of modern criminology. Much criminological research is now conducted by sociologists, but biological and psychological approaches to the study of crime causation have been important in the past and continue to be so today.

Biological Explanations of Crime

Biological explanations of crime propose that offenders differ from nonoffenders in some physiological or anatomical way. The idea of a biologically unique criminal minimizes the role in crime causation of social conditions such as poverty and unemployment, and instead attributes crime to individual differences. One example of a biological explanation of criminal behavior can be seen in the movie *Frankenstein*, in which the monster apparently becomes destructive because Dr. Frankenstein's assistant stole an "abnormal" brain rather than a "normal" one to transplant into a corpse.

Over the past two centuries, deviance in general and crime in particular have been seen increasingly in medical terms, being redefined over time as "sick" rather than "bad" behavior (Conrad and Schneider, 1980). This "medicalization" of deviance has given rise to an emphasis on rehabilitation and has led to a search for individual traits rather than social factors that will explain rule-breaking behavior. Some deviance — for instance, hyperactivity in children — has been explained in terms of biological factors, but the influence of the medical establishment has operated primarily through psychiatry, a branch of medicine that more often emphasizes psychological process than biological factors. The medicalization of deviance in modern society means we must look carefully at biological and psychological theories of crime, for those theories have played an important part in determining how the criminal justice system responds to criminals.

History of the Biological Perspective on Crime

The biological perspective can be traced to about 1750, but this viewpoint was most dominant at the end of the nineteenth century and the beginning of the twentieth. With the rise of modern psychology and psychiatry in the early twentieth century, the biological perspective lost influence in criminology, although important work continues to be done by biological researchers.

PHYSIOGNOMISTS AND PHRENOLOGISTS   Between 1750 and 1850, physiognomists and phrenologists tried to show links between criminal behavior and biological factors. Physiognomists studied facial features and tried to show a correlation between criminal behavior and characteristics such as the shape of the ears or the eyes. Phrenologists stressed the relationship between the external shape of the skull and an individual's propensity to engage in crime. They thought that studying the shape of the skull would allow them to tell which areas of a person's brain would dominate behavior and possibly lead to crime. Modern research indicates that certain areas of the brain do control particular types of behavior, and that stimulating certain parts of the brain can incite violence, which in turn may be socially defined as crime. However, phrenologists failed to understand the complexity of the brain and did not demonstrate any relationship between skull shape, behavioral control centers in the brain, and criminal behavior. Both phrenologists and physiognomists failed to test their theories in a methodologically sound way, but they did draw attention to the possibility that offenders and nonoffenders might differ in measurable ways.

LOMBROSO'S THEORY OF THE ATAVISM   Cesare Lombroso explored what he thought were the physically distinct features of criminals. After examining the skull of a notorious Italian criminal, he observed:

> At the sight of that skull, I seemed to see all of a sudden, lighted up as a vast plain under a flaming sky, the problem of the nature of the criminal—an atavistic being who reproduces in his person the ferocious instincts of primitive humanity and the inferior animals. Thus were explained anatomically the enormous jaws, high cheek bones, prominent superciliary arches, solitary lines in the palms, extreme size of the orbits, handle-shaped or sensile ears found in criminals, savages and apes, insensibility to pain, extremely acute sight, tattooing, excessive idleness, love of orgies, and the irresistible craving of evil for its own sake, the desire not only to extinguish life in the victim, but to mutilate the corpse, tear its flesh and drink its blood. (cited in Taylor, Walton, and Young, 1973: 41)

Lombroso theorized that criminals were *atavisms*, people "born out of time" who were similar to primitive people or lower animals in their biological makeup. This theory owed much to the influence of Darwinism at the end of the nineteenth century, but the idea that people could revert to an earlier stage of evolutionary development was not widely accepted even then.

Lombroso also erred in his ideas about what features could be inherited. For example, the tattoos he said were characteristic of criminals were obviously not inherited. Some of the features he thought were typical of offenders may have been the product of both inheritance and diet, with the latter being a function of income, education, and other social factors.

Lombroso made several important mistakes in testing his theory. He failed to select in a careful way a control group from the general population with which to compare criminals. In addition, many of the differences between criminals and noncriminals that he documented were small enough to have occurred by chance.

Lombroso's most important contributions to modern criminology were the application of measurement and the testing of hypotheses. As a result of this positivist method, his ideas on crime causation underwent revision, and he increasingly took social and environmental factors into account. In the final edition of his textbook on the criminal offender, Lombroso suggested that born criminals might account for as few as one-third of all offenders. Other types were insane criminals and occasional offenders who were the products of a poor social environment. Nevertheless, the born offender remained at the center of Lombroso's work, and he never did systematic research on the social causes of criminal behavior.

POST-LOMBROSIAN RESEARCHERS: GORING AND HOOTON   Several researchers built on Lombroso's ideas. The Englishman Charles Goring (1870– 1919) sought to test Lombroso's theory that offenders had certain physical defects or anomalies. Goring found no significant differences between offenders and groups from the general population in skull shape, eye color, hair color, or various other physical traits. He did find what he thought was a real difference in height and weight, with offenders being shorter and lighter than nonoffenders. Still, Goring (1913: 173) concluded that "there is no such thing as a physical criminal type."

Earnest Hooton, an American anthropologist who worked on crime causation during the 1930s, criticized Goring's research. Hooton (1939) contended that criminals were the products of environmental influences on organically inferior people. However, he failed to provide a clear meaning for the idea of physical inferiority or the way it might lead to criminal behavior. He offered no satisfactory evidence that "physical inferiority" was inherited rather than acquired. Moreover, Hooton's research contained important methodological problems; for instance, he did not compare offenders with a carefully chosen and random sample of nonoffenders.

SHELDON'S THEORY OF SOMATOTYPES   One biological theory that relies on psychological traits is William Sheldon's theory of *somatotypes* or body types. This theory focuses on differences among individuals in embryonic development and claims that people with different body types have different temperaments that affect their propensity to engage in crime and delinquency.

Sheldon, an American psychologist and physician, developed a rating scheme to classify bodies as one of three basic types. One study found that endomorphs, who are slow, "soft," and comfort-loving, exhibited no particular tendency to be delinquent, nor did ectomorphs, who are described as lean and fragile. However, mesomorphs, described as muscular, active, and aggressive, were twice as common among delinquents as they were among the general population (Glueck and Glueck, 1950, 1956). Nevertheless, a review of biological theories of crime concluded that "empirical research has revealed little evidence for the unique temperamental traits that Sheldon ascribed to the three somatotypes" (Pollock, Mednick, and Gabrielli, 1983: 309). There is no strong support for Sheldon's contention that specific combinations of body types and temperaments determine whether people will violate the law.

This drawing from Earnest Hooton's *Crime and the Man* (1939) ranks various "racial types" by their rates of murder and assault. *Source: From Hooton,* Crime and the Man. © *1939 by the President and Fellows of Harvard College. Reprinted with the permission of Harvard University Press.*

Modern Biological Research on Crime

Since the end of World War II, biologists have used various strategies to test for the possible impact on crime and delinquency of physical traits and inherited characteristics. Some of this research points to explanations of crime and delinquency that might fit with learning theories developed by psychologists and sociologists.

TWIN STUDIES One potentially rewarding approach to the study of biological influences on criminal behavior is the study of twins. Identical twins develop from a single female egg and have no hereditary differences. Fraternal twins develop from two eggs and do have hereditary differences. Researchers can thus look at the relative impact on crime of heredity and environment by comparing the criminality of identical twins with the criminality of fraternal twins of the same sex. Evidence for genetic factors would take the form of a higher *concordance rate*, or similarity of criminal behavior, between identical twins than between fraternal twins.

The results of twin studies done in the United States, Japan, and Europe between 1929 and 1962 are consistent with the idea that inherited factors influence criminal behavior. The concordance rates for identical twins were between 60 and 70 percent in these studies, but the concordance rates for fraternal twins were only 15 to 20 percent. However, because of methodological problems with these studies, they exaggerated the importance of genetics (Pollock, Mednick, and Gabrielli, 1983).

In what is perhaps the best twin study to date, Karl O. Christiansen (1974, 1977) examined all 3,586 twin pairs born in one area of Denmark between 1881 and 1910. He found that if one identical twin had a criminal conviction, the other twin also had a conviction in 35 percent of the cases. The rate of concordance was only 12 percent for fraternal twins. Similar results were produced from a study of twins in Norway (Dalgaard and Kringlen, 1976). In a study in Ohio, a researcher found that concordance rates for self-reported delinquency were higher for identical twins than for fraternal twins (Rowe, 1983). In general, these studies yielded smaller differences in rates of concordance between identical twins and fraternal twins than early researchers had found; this was probably due to the poor methodology of the older studies. Still, the recent research provides some evidence that is consistent with the role of inherited traits in the causation of crime.

Even this recent research does not prove beyond any doubt that genetic factors play an important role in the causation of crime. Identical twins are more alike biologically than fraternal twins, and recent researchers acknowledge that because identical twins look more like each other, they are probably more apt than fraternal twins to have similar environments when young and to receive similar treatment by parents, relatives, peers, and teachers. As a result, we would expect identical twins to be socialized in ways that are more alike than is true of fraternal twins.

ADOPTION STUDIES   An ideal method to test the relative importance of biological and environmental influences on crime would be to study identical and fraternal twins who are separated at birth and who never have contact again, and then compare their crime rates as adults. Because this situation is too rare to provide sizeable samples for study, researchers have turned to other approaches. One that is promising is the study of adopted children, who are usually separated from their biological parents at a young age and often never see them again. Researchers have compared the criminality of adoptees with that of their biological parents and their adoptive parents.

A study of all 14,427 adoptions that occurred in Denmark from 1924 to 1947 found that children who had biological parents with criminal convictions had a greater chance of themselves being involved in repetitive property crimes, but they had no greater propensity to engage in violent crimes. Among sons raised by adoptive parents, only 13.5 percent had a criminal conviction if neither their biological parents nor their adoptive parents had a criminal conviction. If their adoptive parents had been convicted of a crime but their biological parents had not, the proportion of the sons convicted of crime rose slightly to 14.7 percent. However, if at least one of the biological parents had been convicted of a crime and the adoptive parents had not been, 20 percent of the sons had a conviction. If both the biological and the adoptive parents had criminal convictions, then 24.5 percent of the sons also had criminal convictions. Similar results were found for female adoptees. These data are consistent with the idea of a biological influence on criminal behavior, but the researchers did not claim the data proved that inherited traits cause crime. Instead, they cautiously concluded that inherited traits might lead some people who are raised in certain ways and who live in certain circumstances to become criminal more often than people in the same situation who lack the inherited traits (Mednick and Volavka, 1980; Ellis, 1982; Mednick et al., 1982; Pollock, Mednick, and Gabrielli, 1983).

According to one review of adoption studies, the evidence on genetic involvement in crime causation is even stronger than these researchers assert. This review states that the evidence provided by adoption studies approaches the limits of certainty in demonstrating a genetic influence on crime causation, with an adopted person's chance of being convicted of a serious crime more accurately predicted from knowledge of the criminal record of that person's biological parents than from knowledge of the criminal record of that person's adoptive parents. According to this observer,

> to the degree that causal statements can ever be made with finality in science, the adoption studies carried out in the decade just past seem to be making the following, cautiously worded pronouncement about the involvement of genetics in criminal behavior possible: Significant amounts of the observed variation in human tendencies to behave criminally appear to be the result of some genetic factors, presumably operating on the functioning of the nervous system (at least for the variations observed in criminal behavior other than describable as victimless and status offenses). (Ellis, 1982: 57)

THE XYY CHROMOSOME   The possibility that abnormalities in the sex-determining chromosome could account for crime received much attention during the 1960s. There are twenty-three pairs of chromosomes in humans, one of which is the sex chromosome pair. The female usually has an XX pair, and the male normally has an XY pair. Beginning with the discovery of an *XYY chromosome* complement in some men in 1961, several unusual combinations have been found. During the 1960s there was speculation in the press and by some criminologists that men with the XYY pair might be especially prone to aggressive and violent crime. This idea apparently reflected the assumption that if the Y chromosome in the sex-determining pair makes a person a male, an extra Y should make that person a "supermale," hence a more violent person than the average male.

A cohort study in Denmark tested 4,139 tall men from a cohort of 31,436 men born in Copenhagen from 1944 to 1947 (Witkin et al., 1976). The reason that only tall men were studied is that earlier research had shown that XYY men are taller than average. This study found only twelve men with an XYY combination. The infrequency of this chromosome complement suggests that even if it is associated with criminal behavior, it could account for relatively little of the crime that is committed. This Danish study found that 42 percent of the twelve XYY men had been convicted of at least one crime, compared with only 9 percent of the XY group. In spite of the small number of men with the XYY combination, this difference was statistically significant; that is, the difference was very unlikely to have occurred by chance. However, the crimes for which the XYY men were convicted were not violent ones; there was no meaningful difference between the XYYs and the XYs in convictions for violent offenses.

The XYY men showed significantly lower levels of intelligence than did the XY men, but both groups had attained similar educational levels. Comparing XYY men with XY men of similar intelligence, educational attainment, height, and social status, the researchers found that the XYY group was still more likely to have a criminal record. The researchers concluded that the XYY chromosome combination does not seem to predispose men to violent crime, but it may be tied to a higher-than-average likelihood of being detected for other kinds of crime (Witkin et al., 1976).

A follow-up to this study that used the same data found that differences in intelligence could not fully explain the excess criminality of the XYYs over the XYs. The XYYs were found to have different electroencephalogram (EEG) readings of brain activity, and lower galvanic skin resistance (GSR) readings that measured arousability by noxious stimuli and rate of recovery after arousal (Volavka et al., 1977). In other words, the XYY combination may be linked to nonviolent crime through factors that are associated with brain functioning and the autonomic nervous system.

SEX DIFFERENCES   Earlier we examined differences in crime rates between males and females. The fact that male and female crime rates differ to varying degrees from one society to another suggests that much of the sex difference in crime rates is due to social and cultural factors. However, the fact that men commit more crime than women in all societies suggests that some of the difference could be the result of biological differences between the sexes.

One review of sex differences in aggressiveness cites developmental studies that show that children under six do not seem to imitate the behavior of same-sexed adults (Maccoby and Jacklin, 1980; Mednick et al., 1982). However, most studies of children under six also reveal that boys are significantly more aggressive than girls; none of those studies shows more aggressiveness among girls. The data thus "suggest strongly that greater male aggressiveness is present in children before social learning can explain it. It is a likely hypothesis that greater aggressiveness in males is related to their higher levels of male sex hormones" (Mednick et al., 1982: 30). There is, however, little direct proof that male-female differences in aggressiveness are caused primarily by differences in sex hormones. Moreover, an association between sex hormones and aggressiveness would not constitute proof that sex hormones cause crime and delinquency, for aggressiveness can take many forms other than violation of the law.

There is some evidence that levels of the male sex hormone testosterone may be associated with differences in aggressiveness, and even assaultive crime, among men. Some data indicate that plasma testosterone levels are correlated with self-reported physical and verbal aggression. Some research shows that plasma testosterone levels are higher among offenders imprisoned for violent crimes than among those incarcerated for nonviolent crimes. Another study found that rapists who are more violent have higher plasma testosterone levels than less violent rapists. Experiments that have administered psychological tests, which supposedly measure aggressivity or hostility, to prisoners and to nonprisoner control subjects have reached contradictory conclusions about whether testosterone levels are associated with aggressiveness or hostility (Mednick and Volavka, 1980: 134–135; Mednick et al., 1982: 30–31).

There are a few studies that suggest that crime committed by women is more likely to occur in the four premenstrual days and the four days of menstruation than it is to occur at other times during the menstrual cycle (Shah and Roth, 1974). In recent years, attention has been paid to *premenstrual syndrome(PMS)*, a set of symptoms that include tension, nervousness, irritability, fatigue, headaches, cramps, and depressed moods. PMS does not manifest itself in the same way in all women who suffer from it, and some doubt it is a single condition. Even though PMS has been introduced in British courts as a factor to mitigate the sentences of some female offenders, as we see in the Cross-Cultural Perspective, the evidence for its association with crime is still unclear. Women experiencing PMS may simply be more likely to be arrested for crimes they commit during their premenstrual and menstrual days, perhaps because their reaction time is slower then or because they are more fatigued. Moreover, the changes associated with menstruation do not cause most women to commit crime, and women who do violate the law commit crimes at other times during their menstrual cycles (Shah and Roth, 1974).

BRAIN DYSFUNCTIONS AND LEARNING DISABILITIES There is growing evidence that brain dysfunctions and neurological defects are more common among excessively violent people than among the general population (Schmeck, 1985; Fishbein and Thatcher, 1986). Many violent offenders seem to have defects in the frontal and temporal lobes of the brain that are associated with impaired self-control. The rate of epilepsy seems to be higher among delinquents than among nondelinquents, even though most epileptics never commit crime. In spite of such evidence, researchers have been cautious in concluding that such abnormalities cause criminal behavior. One reason is that some evi-

A Cross-Cultural Perspective: Premenstrual Syndrome and Criminal Behavior in England

In 1981, Sandie Smith, a twenty-nine-year-old English barmaid, was sentenced to three years on probation for threatening to murder a police officer with a knife. Previously, she had been convicted of almost thirty other offenses, including arson and assault, and she was already on probation for killing a woman when she threatened the police officer.

Also in 1981, Christine English, a thirty-seven-year-old English woman, was conditionally discharged for one year after pleading guilty to "manslaughter by reason of diminished responsibility." Originally, she had been charged with murder for killing her lover with her car after an argument.

In each of these cases, the defendant's punishment was reduced because she successfully claimed that premenstrual syndrome (PMS) had caused her to commit the crime. According to Ms. Smith's defense attorney, all of her crimes coincided with her premenstrual phases, which caused her to become "a raging animal" every month unless she received hormone treatments. Ms. English's lawyer claimed that at the time she ran her lover down with her car, she was experiencing "an extremely aggravated form of premenstrual physical condition" that she had suffered from for years.

British judges have thus used PMS as a mitigating factor in sentencing women, and some observers believe PMS may even become grounds for acquittal in the future.

However, there has been much debate in England about the use of PMS as a legal defense. The syndrome is difficult to define precisely. There is doubt about how accurately the hormonal changes that accompany the menstrual cycle have been measured in cases that have come before the courts. Moreover, it is often difficult or impossible to separate the effects of hormonal change from the effects of individual personality or social circumstances. One doctor who has studied the association between premenstrual symptoms and mental health in more than five hundred women doubts that PMS is a cause of aggressive behavior. Another physician who has treated women for PMS for years has claimed in court that some women become seriously mentally disturbed prior to menstruation, and that this problem can be treated with hormones.

SOURCE. Based on "British Legal Debate: Premenstrual Tension and Criminal Behavior," *The New York Times*, December 29, 1981, p. C3.

dence, such as that on the link between epilepsy and crime, is contradictory (Pollock, Mednick, and Gabrielli, 1983). Another reason is that the cause-effect relationship is not clear. For example, physical abuse of a child may cause severe head injuries, including brain damage that can lead to violent outbursts; but children who are victims of such abuse may also learn to be violent by observing their parents' behavior.

Delinquents seem to be more likely than nondelinquents to have neurological problems (Fishbein and Thatcher, 1986). There is also some evidence that the parents of violent delinquents have more neurological problems than do the parents of nonviolent delinquents, suggesting the possibility of a genetic factor associated with adolescent violence. Violent delinquency is not inherited behavior, but children may inherit a susceptibility to stress that could lead them to engage in violence in certain situations (Adams, 1979).

Some research shows that some delinquents and criminals produce abnormal EEG readings of brain activity (Strasburg, 1978; Mednick and Volovka, 1980; Mednick et al., 1981, 1982; Pollock, Mednick, and Gabrielli, 1983; Fishbein and Thatcher, 1986). One review of the research literature suggests that the EEGs of criminals may be similar to those of normal people at younger ages, suggesting that antisocial behavior may be associated with, though not necessarily caused by, "brain immaturity" (Mednick et al., 1981, 1982).

There is good evidence that delinquency is associated with *learning disabilities*, which are "impairments in sensory and motor functioning which lead to deviant classroom performance, and are the product of some abnormal physical condition" (Holzman, 1979: 78). The causes of learning disabilities are not well understood, but they seem at least partly rooted in neurological dysfunction (Fishbein and Thatcher, 1986). One learning disability is dyslexia, the failure to attain language skills commensurate with intellectual abilities. Another is aphasia, a problem of communicating verbally or understanding others' speech. A third learning disability is hyperactivity, or excessive inattentiveness and restlessness. One study found that hyperactive children were twenty times as likely to become seriously delinquent during adolescence as were children without that disorder, and that upper-class children who were hyperactive were as likely to be arrested as lower-class children who were hyperactive (James H. Satterfield, cited in *The Boston Globe*, November 26, 1982).

Some people may be more biologically predisposed than others to crime and delinquency, although many people who are predisposed that way still learn to conform to the law. Brain disorders and learning disabilities can predispose individuals to crime and delinquency, but these problems can also lead to rejection and stigmatization of people who seem unintelligent or unable to function socially. This rejection by itself may be conducive to violation of the law. Brain disorders and learning disabilities may also be reflected in poor academic performance and rejection by teachers, both of which may be conducive to delinquency. Thus brain disorders and learning disabilities may directly lead to delinquency and crime, or they may increase the likelihood of delinquency and crime indirectly by leading to social rejection or academic failure.

Biology and Modern Criminology

There are several reasons that many modern criminologists have paid little attention to biological explanations of crime and delinquency. One is that relatively little research on crime and delinquency has been done by biologists and medical researchers. Another reason is that the poor quality of much early

FIGURE 6.1   Possible Links of Brain Disorders and Learning Disabilities to
Crime and Delinquency

research and the political abuse of the biological approach in Nazi Germany
have made biological perspectives on crime suspect in the eyes of many criminologists. As a result, many criminologists have prematurely dismissed biological
theories of crime.

Many criminologists seem to react hostilely to the biological perspective on
crime because that perspective is viewed as a threat to the ideology of welfare
liberalism and social change to which they adhere. Heredity appears unchange-
able, and thus a theory that stresses biological causes of crime seems to imply that
efforts to reduce crime through social change are misguided.

Another reason criminologists have paid little attention to biological research
in recent years is that this work does not seem to explain geographic, temporal,
and social variations in crime rates. Biological explanations do not help us
understand why crime rates vary from one nation to another, from one region
to another, or among communities of different sizes. Likewise, biological
theories do not seem to explain changes in crime rates over time, for there is no
evidence that increases and decreases in crime rates are associated with changes
in biological factors. Biological factors might account for some of the difference
between the sexes in crimes of violence, but they do not seem to explain differences in property crimes. Biological research has not yet offered a good explanation of why crime rates peak in the late teens and earlier twenties, and then
decline with age. There is no evidence that biological differences among racial
groups explain differences in crime rates among those groups; racial groups are
socially defined categories rather than biologically distinguishable groupings.
Finally, there seems to be no way for biological explanations to account for class
differences in crime rates, for the factors on which biological researchers have
focused are not associated with class standing in any obvious way.

to look at research on the li
skepticism.

Another reason for some
some of these studies employ
IQ tests to prisoners and the
from the general populatio
mentally retarded people –
stituted between 9 and 30 pe
an overall percentage closer
this would be about three ti
the general population (*The*

Research that compares i
encounters several methodo
ily representative of all peop
be the least competent of all
prisoners with the general po
Second, the "general popula
bly includes many people wh
at the time of the study. As a
offenders who are imprisone
in prison but includes some o
to say much about what dis
approach would be to admin
the nation's population (incl
involvement in crime from of
and then examine the relatio
self-reported crime.

Evidence on IQ and Crim
to study the relationship betw
boys of the same class are con
nondelinquents. In other wo
than a lower-class nondelinqu
lower IQ than a middle-clas
study also found that lower-
middle-class boys of the san
quency (whether measured b
measured by standardized IQ

Wolfgang, Figlio, and Sell
delinquency. The researcher
stopped by the police was 10
had not been stopped. Table
delinquents and nondelinque
the largest IQ differences are
delinquency status; differenc
differences by class range fro

Modern biological researchers do not dismiss nonbiological explanations of crime and delinquency, nor do they claim that all criminals and delinquents have physiological or anatomical disorders that cause them to violate the law. Indeed, biological criminologists often go only so far as to say that some physical factors are associated with a propensity to crime and delinquency, not that such factors cause people to violate the law. Thus, genetic factors are usually seen as interacting with the familial and social environment to increase the probability that a person will violate the law, rather than seen as operating alone to cause crime and delinquency (Mednick and Volavka, 1980; Rowe and Osgood, 1984).

One criticism of biological work on crime is that inherited traits are specific in nature, but crime is a very broad concept. Thus, for biological researchers to make progress in their search for the causes of crime, they must focus on links between specific inheritable traits and specific kinds of criminal behavior. In a sense, there cannot be an inherited predisposition to violate a socially created law, but it is possible that certain inherited predispositions may be linked to behavior such as violence that is likely to be defined as crime.

Inherited traits can create a "range of potential" for behavior, even if they do not determine behavior; in other words, biological factors may limit the kind of behavior a person will engage in, even if the constraints are very broad. Often biological factors interact with social and environmental influences to make certain behavior more likely, as we can see from the following example from research on monkeys:

> It has been demonstrated that aggressive behavior can be evoked in free-ranging monkeys by stimulation of implanted intracerebral electrodes. However, such stimulation produces differing results depending upon the hierarchical structure of the monkey colony. Monkeys exhibit aggressive behavior with this stimulation when a submissive monkey is present as a target, but such responses are inhibited (despite the brain stimulation) in the presence of a dominant animal. (Shah and Roth, 1974: 106)

Research on humans suggests that the hierarchical structure of social relationships may influence an individual's propensity to homicide, but this research did not look at biological predispositions that might interact with the social context to produce violent behavior (Henry and Short, 1954).

A few criminologists have worked to develop an interdisciplinary approach to the study of crime and delinquency (Jeffery, 1979; Mednick and Volavka, 1980; Ellis, 1982), but more work on the interaction of biological, psychological, and social factors is needed. One effort to link genetic and environmental factors in the study of crime causation proposes the model in Figure 6.2. This approach suggests that only neurochemical factors control behavior directly, and that they are influenced both by genetics and by environment. Behavior then affects the environment in which the individual lives, and this in turn influences behavior in a feedback loop, within certain genetic constraints (Ellis, 1982).

Environment

Genetic factors

FIGURE 6.2 A Model of (
Behavior: Evidence through the
by permission of the American

Psychological Explanati

The once-popular view t
placed during the twentie
psychologically abnormal
anced" underlies the philo
offenders by psychiatrists
approach is that because
must distinguish them fro

Mental Deficiency Theo

The mental deficiency th
the intelligence to apprec
violates it, or is unable to
Nonoffenders are seen as
their actions.

IQ AND CRIME Intellig
quotient) tests, has been
Sometimes they claim t
searchers do not claim th

IQ tests have repeated
efforts to develop unbias
higher scores on IQ test
biases of the whites who
claim that IQ tests me
(Gartner, Greer, and Rei

TABLE 6.1 IQ, Class, and Race of a
Cohort of Boys

| | Average IQ Score | |
	Lower Class	Higher Class
White nondelinquents	107	111
Black nondelinquents	97	100
White delinquents	102	107
Black delinquents	94	97

SOURCE: Marvin E. Wolfgang, Robert M. Figlio, and
Thorsten Sellin, *Delinquency in a Birth Cohort.* Chicago:
University of Chicago Press, 1972, p. 62. Reprinted by
permission of The University of Chicago Press. © 1972
by The University of Chicago. All rights reserved.

five points lower for delinquents than for nondelinquents of the same race and
class. There is thus a small but consistent tendency for IQ and delinquency to be
associated with each other.

An English cohort study confirmed Wolfgang, Figlio, and Sellin's results. In
the English study, boys who were to become delinquent as teenagers scored an
average of 95 on IQ tests at ages eight and ten, and boys who did not become
delinquent during their teen years scored an average of 101 at ages eight and
ten. This difference of six points showed that performance on IQ tests at a
young age is a good predictor of future delinquency (West, 1982).

Hirschi and Hindelang (1977) reach similar conclusions about the relationship between IQ and delinquency from their systematic review of the research
literature. They claim that sociologists regularly deny individual differences
between criminals and noncriminals because "kinds of people" theories are seen
as nonsociological. They show that criminology textbooks either ignore or
argue against the role of intelligence in the genesis of crime and delinquency.
They go on to document a small but consistent and reliable difference of about
nine points between the IQs of delinquents and the IQs of nondelinquents.
Evidence for this difference comes from studies carried out in diverse settings
using different IQ tests and controlling for race and class. Hirschi and Hindelang conclude that IQ is an important correlate of delinquency that seems to be
as closely linked to delinquency as race and class. Wolfgang, Figlio, and Sellin's
cohort study, on the other hand, found race to be a more important correlate of
delinquency than intelligence.

Intelligence is related to delinquency, whether delinquency is measured by
self-reports or official statistics. However, the relationship of intelligence and
delinquency is weaker in self-report studies than it is in studies that use police or
court records, possibly because offenders with lower IQs are arrested more
often than offenders with higher intelligence levels. Hirschi and Hindelang
report that they know of no recent research that refutes the relationship of IQ

test scores and delinquency, a relationship they claim is not the result of class or cultural biases in IQ tests, the methodological inadequacy of those tests, or the instability of IQ scores over time.

Hirschi and Hindelang state that differences in IQ between delinquents and nondelinquents are consistent with some sociological theories of crime causation. For instance, if intelligence affects school performance and attitudes toward the school and its teachers, lower intelligence may be associated with a lower "stake in conformity," which can increase the chance that an adolescent will engage in delinquent behavior.

Interpreting Research on IQ and Crime. One criticism of the conclusion that delinquency and crime are related to intelligence is that IQ test scores, which supposedly measure native intelligence, are significantly influenced by the social environment. By changing social conditions, IQ test scores can be raised by even more than the nine-point difference that Hirschi and Hindelang found between delinquents and nondelinquents.

Another criticism of the conclusion that intelligence is linked to delinquency and crime is that instead of low intelligence producing trouble in school and thus generating delinquency, it may be that lower-class status is associated with both delinquency and trouble in school, and trouble in school may lead to a failure to learn. This failure to learn might then be reflected in lower IQ scores, which would produce correlations between class, IQ scores, and delinquency. Lack of motivation to do well in school might also show up in the results of IQ tests, which can be seen as a measure of academic performance rather than of basic intelligence.

A structuralist critique of the evidence linking IQ and delinquency is that this association exists only because of specific responses by institutions such as the school to low levels of intelligence, low IQ test scores, and poor academic performance. Thus,

> the absence of access to desirable social roles plus premature and/or inappropriate negative labeling mutually reinforce one another and lead to alienation, a rejection of the rejectors. Alienation, in turn, leads to delinquent behavior. The behavior generated by institutional structures through opportunity and labeling may then feed back into the institutional structure, generating responses which reinforce that behavior. (Menard and Morse, 1984: 1349)

An empirical test of this theory with self-report data revealed that structural variables—access to desirable social roles, negative labeling, alienation, and delinquent peer-group association—explained significant amounts of both serious and nonserious delinquency, and that IQ, academic aptitude, and school performance added very little to the explanation of delinquency. The researchers concluded that IQ is not causally linked to delinquency, but is instead an individual characteristic that institutions may or may not reward. Consequently, it is "the institutional pattern of behavior that (a) is causally related to delinquent behavior and (b) must be altered if the frequency or type of aggregate delinquent behavior is to be reduced or changed" (Menard and Morse, 1984: 1374).

Another problem with determining the relationship between intelligence and violation of the law is that intelligence probably varies considerably among different types of offenders. Embezzlers may well have higher IQ levels than the general population, because they can embezzle funds only if they have attained a position of trust in the business world, and intelligence may play a role in achieving such a position. On the other hand, sex offenders such as child molesters seem to have lower-than-average IQ levels. Intelligence may influence an individual's social position and thus affect the opportunities that are available for crime. For instance, a retarded person is unlikely to gain access to the economic power necessary to engage in price fixing or false advertising.

Personality Characteristics

Many studies have tried to determine if any personality traits are more common among criminals than among the general population. A 1953 survey of 113 studies concluded that no personality traits were consistently and systematically linked to criminality (Schuessler and Cressey, 1953). Forty-two percent of the studies that were reviewed showed that the personality traits of offenders differed from those of the general population, but the differences were usually small, of questionable validity, and inconsistent with the results of other research. Studies of this sort might be more likely to reveal personality trait differences if specific types of offenders were compared with the general population. Thus a comparison of embezzlers with the general population might show embezzlers to have certain personality traits, and a comparison of bank robbers with the general population might show that bank robbers differ from the general population in personality traits, and probably differ from embezzlers as well.

Another review of studies of personality traits and criminality found that 81 percent of the ninety-four studies examined showed a statistically significant difference in personality traits between offenders and control groups (Waldo and Dinitz, 1967). However, the differences were small, even though they were greater than would have occurred by chance fluctuations in sampling. This review concluded that the role of personality in the genesis of criminal behavior remains unclear.

THE CRIMINAL MIND   Researchers have not yet found a "criminal personality," but some psychologists and psychiatrists persist in the search for personalities or personality traits that distinguish criminals from noncriminals. This was the thrust of a study by Samuel Yochelson and Stanton E. Samenow (1976, 1977; Samenow, 1984). In a recent book, Samenow (1984: 5; emphasis added here) declares current thinking about the causes of crime "dead wrong" and makes the following claim:

I shall expose the myths about why criminals commit crimes, and I shall draw a picture for you of *the personality of the criminal* just as the police artist draws a picture of his face from a description. I shall describe how criminals think, how they defend their crimes to others, and how they exploit programs that are developed to help them.

It seems unlikely that all criminals—from the corporate price fixer to the sadistic rapist, from the professional burglar to the desperate addict, and from the organized crime leader to the juvenile shoplifter—would have the same personality, but that is the basis of Yochelson and Samenow's work.

In *The Criminal Personality*, Yochelson and Samenow (1976, 1977) report that in working with criminals they initally found that traditional psychiatric concepts and techniques were ineffective, and so they began a search for evidence on the psychology of the criminal in order to develop a workable treatment program. Their evidence comes from interviews with 255 offenders, many institutionalized in St. Elizabeths Hospital in Washington, D.C., and the rest from referrals by the police or the correctional system. They did not use a control group with which to compare these criminals, and the criminals were not in any sense a representative sample of all offenders, so Yochelson and Samenow's conclusions are based on a methodologically flawed research design.

Yochelson and Samenow claim to have identified "thought patterns" that exist among all offenders, whether blacks from the ghetto or whites from the suburbs, whether grade-school dropouts or college graduates. As a result, they argue that the criminal personality is not the product of socioeconomic or other environmental factors. They identify fifty-two "errors of criminal thinking" that form the criminal personality, including:

• chronic lying,
• a view that other people's property is their own,
• unrelenting optimism,
• great energy,
• fear of injury or being insulted,
• intense anger,
• manipulativeness, and
• an inflexibly high self-image.

Without a control group, however, there is no way to show that these personality traits are more common among criminals than among the general population.

Treating the Criminal Personality. Yochelson and Samenow then sought a way to treat people with this criminal personality. Traditional therapy seemed ineffective because the offenders were manipulative, mimicked psychiatric jargon, and faked insight into their problems. Job training did not work either, according to Samenow, who has said "I'm all for job training, but if that's all you do, you'll simply have a criminal with job skills. And he'll use those skills to gain entry into new avenues of crime" (cited in Krost, 1982: 8). Yochelson and

Samenow developed a technique of confronting offenders with their flaws, subjecting their thoughts and actions to detailed examination, and forcing them to accept responsibility for their behavior. Much like the technique used by Alcoholics Anonymous, their approach was rigid in demanding full conformity to the rules and in being most effective for offenders who had hit "rock bottom" and saw their only options as prison, suicide, or change. By eliminating "criminal thinking" through this "exercise in self-disgust," Yochelson and Samenow hoped to create a morally responsible person.

Did their approach work? Samenow reports that of the 255 interviewed offenders, only thirty completed the 500 hours of therapy that the program required. Of the thirty, twenty showed improvement, although precise measures of their improvement are not provided. The kind of evidence offered by Yochelson and Samenow cannot tell us whether their method works. The twenty offenders who completed treatment might have changed even without the program. They are only a small part of the initial group of offenders, and may not even be representative of that group, much less of all criminals in society. Even a success rate of 67 percent (twenty out of thirty) may be no better than would have been produced by an untreated control group over the same period.

THE PERSONALITIES OF RAPISTS   One problem with studying the personality of the criminal is that different kinds of crime may be committed by people with very different personalities. Moreover, the same crime may be committed by people with several types of personalities. For instance, one clinical study of rapists concluded that there were three psychodynamic patterns among rapists. The most common type was the "power rapist," who wanted to possess the victim sexually rather than harm her, and who used sexuality to express mastery and control. Next most common was the "anger rapist," who discharged his contempt and hostility toward all women through the act of rape; this type often harmed and degraded his victim. The third and least common type was the "sadistic rapist," who eroticized aggression toward the victim and took gratification in her anguish and suffering (Groth, 1979).

Another study, based on observations of 800 convicted rapists, categorized them as follows:

1. *Exploitative rapists* (about 50 percent of all rapists): For them, rape is an impulsive and predatory act, with the victim seen only as an object for sexual gratification. The rape is often spur-of-the-moment, and it arises out of a social situation such as a casual date. These rapists tend to see active resistance by the victim as a sexual maneuver, and this often heightens their arousal.
2. *Compensatory rapists* (about 25 percent): They are obsessed with sexual fantasies and feel very inadequate. They have fantasies that their victims will enjoy the rape, and perhaps even fall in love with them, but they also think that no woman would want to have sex with them.

3. *Angry rapists* (about 20 percent): Rape expresses their displaced anger and rage. The victim represents to them a hated woman in their life, such as a mother or wife. Sex is a way of humiliating the victim, and physical resistance often increases the offender's anger.
4. *Sadistic rapists* (5 percent): Sexual feelings are linked to aggression for this type; he becomes more violent as he becomes more aroused. Often his crimes are premeditated, and they may involve a compulsive and ritualized fantasy (Robert Prentky and Ann Burgess study, cited in Goleman, 1985b).

Knowing that the perpetrators of a single crime such as rape have very different personalities can be important in developing policies to treat criminals and counsel victims. Different kinds of rapists pose different threats to society, and they may respond to different kinds of treatment. Victims who are raped by different kinds of offenders may have quite different experiences, and counseling them may thus have to take different forms. In addition, advice to women about how to react to a rapist at the time of the crime — for instance, "resist at all costs" or "comply with the offender's demands" — often assumes a single kind of rapist, and knowledge of the different personalities of rapists should make advice givers more cautious.

AGGRESSIVENESS AND CRIME One personality trait sometimes associated with crime and delinquency is the inability to tolerate frustrating situations without resorting to aggression and violence. Frustration that arises from not being able to achieve a goal may lead to aggression that sometimes takes the form of crime, either against the frustrating object or against another object (displaced aggression). There is some evidence that children who are the most assertive, daring, prone to fight, quick to anger, and resistant to discipline are also the most likely to violate the law later in life (Radzinowicz and King, 1977: 89). One study that found a link between childhood aggressiveness and adult crime discovered that eight-year-old boys who were rated highly aggressive by their parents and friends had committed much more crime than their peers by the age of thirty. Aggressive girls did not develop into adult criminals any more often than non-aggressive girls did (Leonard Eron, cited in *The Boston Globe*, August 28, 1983).

Few psychologists today believe that aggression follows directly and simply from frustration, and even when frustrated people become aggressive they may channel their aggression into acceptable activities such as athletic or academic competition rather than engage in crime. Most behavioral scientists consider a host of variables that are conducive to aggressive acts (Goldstein, 1986). One psychologist (Megargee, 1982) identifies the following determinants of whether an individual will respond aggressively to a situation:

1. *Instigation to aggresssion*: the total of all internal factors motivating the person to commit an aggressive or violent act;
2. *Habit strength*: learned preferences for the use of aggressive behavior in a particular situation;

3. *Inhibitions against aggression*: learned preferences to avoid aggression against a certain target;
4. *Stimulus factors*: environmental influences facilitating or impeding aggressive behavior; and
5. *Competition*: making a choice among several responses to the situation so the individual's needs are met in the best way.

Even a model as complex as this does not incorporate influences on aggressive behavior such as genetic predisposition, endochrinological balance, the availability of weapons, differences in political power and economic resources, and many situational factors. Psychologists, biologists, and social scientists who have studied aggression in recent years have recognized that the causes of aggression and violence are very complex, as we can see from research on women and children who commit murder.

Women Who Kill. Recent research by John Kirkpatrick and John Humphrey (cited in Collins, 1986) on seventy-six imprisoned female murderers has illuminated the psychology and social background of women who kill. Most of the victims of these women were males, whom they often murdered after long-term provocation. For women to kill, they must usually see their situation as life-threatening, as affecting their physical or emotional well-being. Men who kill, on the other hand, more often seem to be "on the edge of violence" and easily provoked, even by relatively trivial insults. Nearly all of the women murderers in this study "came from very violent upbringings, and experienced high levels of domestic violence — seeing their mothers and fathers fighting, often with weapons" (Kirkpatrick, cited in Collins, 1986: C18). Many of the women had been beaten or tortured by their brothers, and a third of them said they had been sexually abused as children. These women thus learned early in life to deal with conflict by resorting to violence.

Women murderers also typically have experienced a loss of someone close to them. More than half of those in Kirkpatrick and Humphrey's study had lost a loved one during childhood, and a sixth reported the death of a child. Loss by itself causes stress, and it can also lead to other kinds of stress as well, such as the breakup of a household or dropping out of school when a parent dies. Their losses led these women to feel an overpowering sense of aloneness and a resentment of others for the wrongs they had suffered. They often felt isolated and that the world was conspiring against them, leading them to further withdrawal from social contacts and rejection of help that others offered. In such circumstances, women who had been abused by a husband or lover for a long time might strike out with lethal violence.

Children Who Kill. In recent years, the rate of referrals to juvenile court for ten- to thirteen-year-olds has increased faster than for older juveniles. According to one official in Florida, "Not only is the age dropping at which kids are getting involved in crime, but violent crimes are being committed by younger and younger kids" (cited in Applebome, 1987: A16). Researchers have begun to explore the origins of violence in children fifteen and under, focusing particularly on children who kill (Collins, 1982; Nelson, 1983; Gardiner, 1985).

One study of homicidal behavior by children between three and twelve included a three-year-old who held a knife to his mother's neck as she slept and a ten-year-old who twice tried to kill his mother. The psychiatrist who did this study found that compared with nonhomicidal children who were also psychiatric patients, the homicidal children were more likely to

- have a history of psychomotor seizures,
- have attempted suicide,
- have fathers who had been violent to their mothers,
- have fathers who had been homicidal, and
- have mothers who had been hospitalized for psychiatric reasons (cited in Collins, 1982).

Other research has found that violent children between thirteen and nineteen typically have psychiatric symptoms and neurological problems; many have been physcially abused by their parents, and that is often a cause of their neurological problems.

One study found two kinds of murderers under the age of sixteen. One was the "nonempathic murderer" who did not have the ability to put himself or herself in another person's place. These children had histories of assaultive behavior, did not cope well with stress, and had spent their first year of life with little affection, either in an institution or with a mother who was not nurturing. One fifteen-year-old boy who killed a six-year-old girl said, "I don't know the girl so why should I have any feelings about what happened to her?" (cited in Nelson, 1983: C8). The second type of child killer was the "sexual-identity conflict murderer." These were boys who carried weapons because they lacked physical confidence, often as a result of being taunted as effeminate. Their mothers were dominant, and their fathers absent or passive. Sometimes their parents actually encouraged them to commit crime. One thirteen-year-old boy who had his face rubbed in the mud by another boy was told by his parents to do whatever was necessary to defend himself. The boy got a large knife and stabbed his tormentor in the heart as his father watched (Nelson, 1983).

Most of these children who commit murder have experienced severe rejection by one or both parents while young, and often they have no role model in the home from whom they can learn empathic behavior. The physical abuse that many of these child murderers have suffered may produce brain dysfunctions and neurological problems that are associated with violent behavior.

THE PSYCHOPATHIC PERSONALITY The psychopathic personality is a hypothesized cluster of personality traits thought to lead to criminal behavior. A *psychopath* (or sociopath) is an asocial, aggressive, highly impulsive person who feels little or no guilt for antisocial activity and who cannot form lasting bonds of affection with others. Psychopaths are asocial in the same way as infants: They have not learned to control their desires and impulses. Psychopaths show poor judgment, do not learn easily from experience, are uncooperative, and are not easily influenced by social demands. They are narcissistic and interested only in the gratification of their immediate impulses. They seek pleasure, variety, and excitement rather than security and stability. Because of their impulsiveness, psychopaths' crimes seem purposeless to others. Because they are present-oriented, they rarely plan their crimes in much detail. When frustrated, they become furious and aggressive, and are unable to sublimate or rechannel their impulses. They feel little anxiety or remorse after hurting other people. Psychoanalysts have described psychopaths as loners with a warped capacity for love, and as cold and compassionless people who treat others as a means to their goal of personal pleasure (Cleckley, 1964; McCord and McCord, 1964; McCord, 1983).

Experts estimate that 2 to 5 percent of the noncriminal population can be described as psychopaths, and that about 10 to 25 percent of convicted offenders fit this category. However, the term "psychopath" has been given many definitions, and studies often disagree on the incidence of this personality type (McCord, 1983).

There is some evidence that psychopaths and normal people respond similarly in learning tasks that are positively rewarded, but that normal people learn well and psychopaths learn poorly those tasks that are negatively reinforced. Psychopaths

> show signs of slower autonomic nervous system responses to punishment, and they differ significantly in pulse and heart rates. In general, research indicates that psychopaths are less fearful of punishment, are less anxious, respond more efficiently to stress, are less mature neurologically (that is, less able to learn from punishment), are more eager for excitement, and have a greater propensity for violence than nonpsychopaths. (McCord, 1983: 1315)

Some research indicates that psychopaths are physiologically insensitive, compared with nonpsychopaths. Psychopaths seem less able to learn from physical punishment, and they are less responsive to skin-conductivity stimuli. This may be a result of inherited traits, such as an adrenal gland deficiency in producing or releasing the hormone epinephrine. However, this relative insensitivity to pain could also result from socialization experiences while young or from being abused as a child (Glaser, 1979; McCord, 1983). There is also evidence that psychopaths are especially likely to have brain dysfunctions and neurophysiological dysfunctions, but whether these problems are caused by heredity, accidents, physical abuse, childhood diseases, or environmental factors is unclear (McCord, 1983).

Most psychopaths have a childhood history of rejection, often severe rejection, by at least one parent. Many were institutionalized while young, and their parents frequently had a criminal record or a history of alcoholism, desertion, or neglect. One review of studies on the origins of the psychopathic personality concludes that

> (1) rejection, in combination with damage to such areas of the brain as the hypothalamus, results in psychopathy; and that (2) rejection, in the absence of neural disorder, can result in psychopathy if other influences in the environment (such as

a criminal role model, differential association with criminals, or complete neglect) help direct the person in a criminal direction. (McCord, 1983: 1316)

A Critique of the Concept of the Psychopath. Some social scientists have criticized the use of the concept of the psychopathic personality to explain criminal behavior. One critic states that the psychopath is "in fact, *par excellence*, and without shame or qualification, the model of the circular process by which mental abnormality is inferred from anti-social behavior while anti-social behavior is explained by mental abnormality" (Wootton, 1959: 250). For instance, let us take an individual who commits a "senseless" mass murder. Because the press and psychologists quoted in the press often have a difficult time explaining the murder, they may say the killer has a psychopathic personality. They assume this because the murder makes little sense. In other words, they assume that anyone who would do such a thing must be asocial, impulsive, aggressive, and compassionless—characteristics of the psychopathic personality. The murderer might well be a psychopath, but the problem is that this term may be used even if there is no information available about the offender's actual personality. Information that is independent of the act of murder is needed to assess the killer's personality; personality cannot be assumed from the act itself. This does not mean the concept of the psychopath is useless, but only that the term is sometimes used without direct evidence to label an offender.

Another problem with the concept of the psychopathic personality is that different psychiatrists and psychologists often give quite different meanings to the term. This may be one reason that anywhere from 10 to 25 percent of different samples of inmates have been classified as psychopaths. This variation might be a result of differences in the characteristics of the inmates of various correctional facilities, but it could also reflect differences among psychiatrists and psychologists in the meaning they give to the term "psychopath." The label might tell us more about the psychiatrist or psychologist classifying the inmate than it does about the inmate who is being classified.

PERSONALITY INVENTORIES   The Minnesota Multiphasic Personality Inventory (MMPI) is a personality test of 556 true-false items that have been carefully selected to distinguish average people from those who are suffering from certain forms of psychopathology. The MMPI includes ten clinical scales, three of which seem to be especially important in distinguishing criminals and delinquents from the general population:

Psychopathic deviate scale: conflict with authority and shallow personal attachments
Schizophrenia scale: bizarre thought and affect, and withdrawal from personal contact
Hypomania scale: unproductive hyperactivity.

Delinquents, especially those involved in the most serious offenses, score high on these three scales when compared with the general population, and so do

Using Criminology: The FBI's Profiles of Violent Offenders

In 1977, Robert Ressler and John Douglas of the Federal Bureau of Investigation began a survey of violent criminals, eventually gathering data from more than fifty well-known prisoners, including Charles Manson, John Gacy, Sirhan Sirhan, David Berkowitz, and Richard Speck. They gathered information on what caused these offenders to kill, what occurred during the crime incident, what the murderers did after the crime, and other aspects of their behavior. Today the results of their study, along with data collected subsequently, have been computerized by the FBI's National Center for the Analysis of Violent Crime.

Ressler and Douglas's work led them to classify violent offenders into two categories: organized and disorganized. This distinction is not absolute, as some violent offenders are of a mixed type, but the distinction seems to describe well two common types of offenders.

Organized violent offenders are above average in intelligence, are sexually and socially competent, do skilled work, were born into their families early, had fathers who had a stable work history, were inconsistently disciplined as children, were in control during the crime but got panicky if they lost control, use alcohol, often live with a woman, have a car that is in good condition, and are interested in crime news. The organized offender typically plans his crime, attacks a stranger (although one that fits a type, if multiple offenses are committed), personalizes the victim and holds a controlled conversation with the victim, seems to be in control as judged by the crime scene, often takes souvenirs of the crime, demands submission from the victim, uses restraints, engages in aggressive acts before

prisoners when compared with the general population (Hathaway and Monachesi, 1953; Monachesi and Hathaway, 1967; Megargee and Bohn, 1979). In other words, delinquents and prisoners can be characterized as having personalities that include conflict with authority, shallow personal attachments, bizarre thought and affect, withdrawal from personal contact, and unproductive hyperactivity.

To James Q. Wilson and Richard J. Herrnstein (1985: 190), who have reviewed research on the MMPI and crime, these results illustrate "vividly that institutionalized offenders have atypical personalities as compared to the general population" and that these three scales of the MMPI are "the major personality correlates of crime for adult criminals as well as juvenile delinquents." However, a closer look at what these scales are measuring makes this claim seem somewhat extravagant. "Conflict with authority" and "unproductive hyperactivity" can be taken as definitions of crime and delinquency rather than personality traits that lead to crime and delinquency; these phrases seem to describe actual behavior rather than personality traits. "Shallow personal attachments" and "withdrawal from personal contact" seem to describe social interaction murdering the victim, hides the body, and takes the weapon and any other evidence from the scene of the crime. Often the organized offender's crime follows a stressful event in his life.

Disorganized offenders have the opposite personality and background traits. They are often overtly inadequate, being loners who typically engage in solo sex. During the crime, they engage in minimal conversation with the victim, depersonalize the victim, leave a messy crime scene, use violence against the victim suddenly, engage in sexual acts after the killing, do not use restraints, and often leave the weapon at the scene and the body in view.

The FBI's profiles of violent offenders do not identify actual offenders, but they indicate certain patterns of behavior and psychological traits that may help the police eliminate some suspects from consideration, focus their attention on other possible suspects, and better understand patterns of behavior that may be repeated. For instance, serial murderers, who kill a number of victims over a period of time, seem to

develop a more refined method of murder with subsequent offenses; their behavior seems to evolve over time.

Local police agencies that seek help from the FBI in solving serial killings, sexually oriented murders, and apparently random killings submit a sixteen-page crime analysis report that includes 188 questions about the offender, the victim, and the crime scene. The FBI analyzes the information submitted by the agency, compares it with the information in its own files, and returns to the agency a report that is often of "startling clarity and detail" (Michaud, p. 40). Two internal FBI studies of the Center have concluded that it contributes significant aid in four-fifths of the more than 600 cases it accepts for analysis each year from other police agencies.

SOURCES. Based on Stephen G. Michaud, "The FBI's New Psyche Squad," *The New York Times Magazine*, October 26, 1986, pp. 40–77; Richard J. Connolly, "A New Tool for Fighting Crime," *The Boston Globe*, November 9, 1986, p. A27.

with others, and to fit well with a sociological theory of crime and delinquency called control theory, which we examine in Chapter 8. Only the "bizarre affect and thoughts" of the Schizophrenia scale seems to be a psychological construct, and we might ask, " 'Bizarre' from whose perspective? Those making and enforcing the law?"

In looking at research on crime that has used a second personality test, the California Psychological Inventory, Wilson and Herrnstein conclude that important parts of the "typical criminogenic personality" are lack of "conformity," lack of "value orientation," and lack of "social adjustment." Again, this does not seem to tell us much about the kind of personality apt to violate the law, for these "traits" are little more than ways of saying that an individual has engaged in behavior that violates social norms.

The Psychoanalytic Perspective

Another psychological approach to crime causation is the *psychoanalytic perspective* developed by Sigmund Freud (1930, 1962; 1933) and August Aichhorn

(1935, 1951). Freud proposed three aspects to the personality. The "id" is composed of instincts and drives that need immediate gratification; it characterizes unsocialized and unrestrained individuals. The "superego" is social authority or conscience; it represents parental authority expressed in the individual as a continuing acceptance of cultural norms and values. The "ego" is the mediating force that tries to adjust the id drives with the demands of the superego by rechanneling and sublimating those drives. A state of "balanced conflict" exists among the three elements in healthy and integrated personalities.

The psychoanalytic approach sees people as antisocial by nature. Thus, a newborn baby needs to be socialized to avoid becoming a criminal (Aichhorn, 1935, 1951). All people are thought antisocial by nature, in contrast to Lombroso's view that some people are born criminals and others are born noncriminals. Lombroso, especially in his early work, focused on heredity as a cause of crime in some people, implying that external circumstances had a limited impact on behavior. By contrast, the psychoanalytic position is that external circumstances lead to the socialization of most people, and that those who become criminals do so because of inadequate socialization.

The id-ego-superego framework allows for the possibility of a "socialized criminal" (Aichhorn, 1935, 1951). If the social environment tolerates, supports, or even requires criminal behavior, a person may be socialized into a life of crime (Jenkins, 1955; Russell and Harper, 1973). Psychoanalysts imply that the superego is society's conscience, but in fact various social demands are placed on people. Individuals who are isolated from law-abiding influences and exposed to crime-generating ones may learn to conform to social demands that are contrary to the law.

Part of the socialization process involves the repression of instinctual drives by pushing them back into the unconscious. When these repressed instincts break through, crime may result. In these cases, offenders may not know why they have committed a crime. Some psychoanalysts claim that certain people commit crimes because of guilt developed in childhood. Crime then becomes a way to get the punishment they feel they deserve in order to atone for forbidden desires. This might be true of offenders who commit crimes carelessly and are easily arrested, but if this theory were generally true, we would expect offenders to be arrested far more often than they now are. Most offenders try to avoid arrest, and some who seem to be careless are probably incompetent or distracted rather than trying to atone for forbidden desires.

NEUROSES AND CRIME A neurosis is a functional disorder in which a person has some difficulty in coping with everyday life. Neurotics usually seem nervous, inhibited, and overconforming rather than aggressive, and so their disorders are probably not closely linked to crime (Radzinowicz and King, 1977: 86). Neurosis has also been seen as an alternative to juvenile delinquency rather than a cause of it.

One neurosis that some people have associated with crime is the obsessive-compulsive neurosis, which can lead to certain nonaggressive crimes and to sexual perversions such as exhibitionism and fetishism. This neurosis has also been linked to kleptomania, a compulsive form of stealing sometimes thought to be caused by a desire for sexual excitement rather than financial gain. However, kleptomania seems to be a label that is applied to middle- and upper-class thieves who can afford a psychiatrist. The same behavior by a poor person would probably be labeled larceny. There is little evidence that kleptomania exists as a functional disease that can explain theft. For instance, one study of fifty-six shoplifters found almost no relationship between law-violating behavior and any neurosis or psychosis (Cameron, 1964). Shoplifters were understandably upset about being arrested, but there was no evidence of an obsessive-compulsive neurosis that led to theft. The fact that most shoplifters do not repeat the behavior after being caught once and the fact that shoplifting increases just before Christmas suggest that this form of theft is usually a way to stretch a budget and provide for material needs, rather than a form of behavior not under the shoplifter's conscious control (Robin, 1963).

PSYCHOSES AND CRIME   A psychosis is a disorder characterized by a lack of contact with reality. Sometimes psychoses involve hallucinations that lead to irrational violence, but not all psychotics are dangerous. Definitions of psychoses are sometimes vague, but probably no more than 5 percent of all prison and jail inmates are psychotic (Strasburg, 1978: 68). It is not clear what proportion of the general population is psychotic, but if it does not differ much from the proportion of inmates who are psychotic, then psychosis is not associated with crime. Moreover, many prisoners may be psychotic without their particular problem having caused them to violate the law. It is also possible that some prisoners become psychotic as a result of their prison experiences, and so their problem might not have existed prior to their violation of the law.

The psychosis that has most often been linked to criminal behavior is *schizophrenia*, which involves disordered thought patterns characterized by fantasy, delusion, and incoherence. Paranoid schizophrenics have delusions of persecution; they are nervous and sensitive to interpersonal cues, act and speak primarily with reference to themselves, demand much of loved ones but criticize them for their lack of appreciation, and feel unfairly rejected by others. Schizophrenia is sometimes associated with acts of violence, including homicide, particularly against people who are thought to be threatening to the schizophrenic. One study of ninety-seven boys in a correctional school found that 81.8 percent of those who had engaged in serious violence such as murder or rape exhibited symptoms of paranoia, and only 16.7 percent of the less violent boys (who had engaged in fist fights, set fires, or threatened others) showed symptoms of paranoia. The violent boys also exhibited more neurological disorders and were more likely to have been physically abused by their parents (Adams, 1979).

PSYCHOANALYTIC EXPLANATIONS OF ASSASSINATIONS   Psychoanalytic explanations have been offered for political assassinations in the United States. Unlike political murders elsewhere, American assassinations rarely have been motivated by a political goal or have been associated with a political group. The one exception among presidential assassinations was the 1950 attempt on the life of President Harry Truman by two Puerto Rican nationalists. Otherwise, American assassins have been motivated primarily by personal needs, and this has led to psychological explanations for their actions.

One psychiatrist observes that most assassins in the United States have been younger children in their families, and usually they have had older brothers. This situation can lead to rebellion and resentment because of low status in the family. Hatred of a powerful father can become murderous, leading to an attack on the president as an authority figure who symbolizes the father. American assassins thus seem to be striking more at a symbol of authority than at a particular individual who holds certain political views. One psychiatrist sees assassins as paranoics who have lost touch with reality, developed delusions of grandeur and persecution, and hated authority (Donald Hastings, cited in Brody, 1981). Other psychiatrists believe that assassins are characterized by depression and despair over their self-worth; these assassins try to counteract those feelings by creating a new self-image that is worthy of respect and attention through the dramatic act of political murder (Freedman, 1981).

A CRITIQUE OF THE PSYCHOANALTYIC PERSPECTIVE   Psychiatrists sometimes disagree about how to classify specific offenders in psychoanalytic terms, in part because those terms are not always precisely defined. Because many of the concepts of the psychoanalytic perspective are difficult to measure, hypotheses about the causes of crime are not easily tested. As a result, there is little systematic research that shows that neuroses and psychoses lead to specific kinds of crime.

Psychoanalytic work on crime often takes the form of case studies of offenders. In these studies, psychiatrists are usually aware that a crime has been committed before they begin to study the patient. Through a process of "biographic reconstruction," psychiatrists "demonstrate" that certain traits and aspects of the patient's background led to the crime. These case studies do not constitute evidence for the psychoanalytic explanation of crime, because psychiatrists might well find a "dormant capacity for delinquency in any normal individual" (Rettig, Torres, and Garrett, 1977: 234).

A study of 257 indicted male defendants found that psychiatrists classified 154 of them as dangerous. There was little difference between the defendants classified as dangerous and those classified as nondangerous in class, past criminal behavior, or past hospitalization in a mental institution. The most important characteristic distinguishing the two groups was the current charge against the defendant, which was known to the psychiatrist before the defendant was questioned. Defendants charged with the most serious crimes were the most likely to be found dangerous by the psychiatrists, although few of the examining psychiatrists gave the current charge against the defendant as the reason for classifying the individual as dangerous. In other words, the psychiatrists seemed to take the crime with which the defendant was charged, classify the defendant as dangerous if it was a serious crime, and then construct an explanation of why that defendant was dangerous (Cocozza and Steadman, 1978).

Until we have evidence on the psychological characteristics of the general population, we cannot know whether criminals differ psychologically from other people. Proponents of the psychoanalytic perspective rarely gather evidence on the psychological state of the general population, because they are usually concerned with doing therapy rather than with testing theories. As a result, many of the ideas of the psychoanalytic perspective on crime remain untested.

Conditioning Theory

According to the British psychologist Hans Eysenck (1977), people acquire behavior in two ways. One way is through rational learning that involves the central nervous system. People learn to engage in behavior that is pleasurable and rewarding, and they try to avoid behavior that is painful and unrewarding. The sooner the pain or pleasure results from their actions, the more effect the pain or pleasure will have on their future behavior. Thus, if much time elapses between a crime and its punishment, the sanction will have relatively little effect on the offender's future behavior, because the rewards of the crime (such as stolen property) are gained when the crime is committed.

The second way behavior is acquired is through conditioning, which works by the contiguity of stimuli rather than by reinforcement (the mechanism by which the first kind of learning occurs). This second type, often called *classical conditioning*, is exemplified by Pavlov's famous experiment with dogs that salivated at the sound of a bell; the bell elicited that behavior because it was associated with other stimuli (food). Eysenck argues that it is this classical conditioning that forms the basis of what we call conscience, the internalized force that leads us to conform to norms and laws. Criminals are people whose consciences do not restrain them from violating the law. Their inadequate conditioning may stem from their "low conditionability," something that may be linked to a deficient autonomic nervous system that makes it more difficult to acquire law-abiding behavior.

The effectiveness of conditioning depends on the sensitivity of the autonomic nervous system a person has inherited (a biological influence) and on the quality of conditioning a person receives during childhood (a social environmental influence). Some people seem to have physical makeups that allow them to ignore pain and punishment with relative ease (Shah and Roth, 1974; Glaser, 1979; Mednick and Volavka, 1980; McCord, 1983). These individuals seem to recover more slowly when aroused by noxious stimuli and seem to be aroused less easily by such stimulation. Minimal brain dysfunction can also reduce a person's ability to learn from experience (Shah and Roth, 1974). Biological and psychological predispositions can affect the ability to learn from experience, and the inability to be conditioned can lead to crime and delinquency.

CHAPTER 7

Socioeconomic Sources of Crime

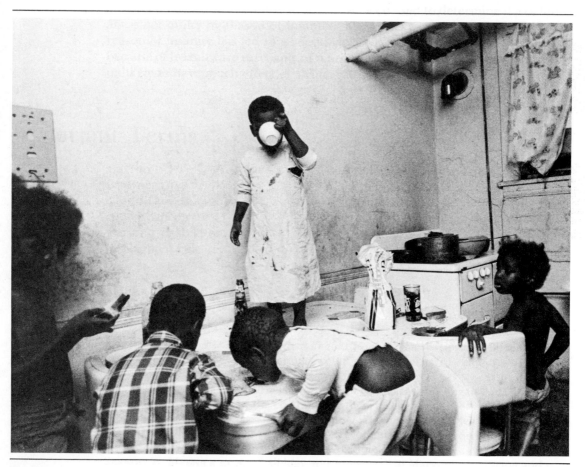

Source: *Burk Uzzle / Archive Pictures*

Until recently, a common way of dealing with arson was to focus on the individual who sets fires. Seeing the arsonist as a deviant — perhaps a "pyromaniac" with severe psychological problems — led nowhere in the prevention of arson, a crime that has destroyed major parts of our cities. A much better approach, and one already bearing some fruit, focuses on the social-structural causes of arson. There is an important link between legitimate institutions — particularly banks, real-estate developers, and insurance companies — and arson-for-profit schemes by gangsters, professional arsonists, landlords, and corrupt political officials (Brady, 1983a). This approach suggests that arson can be stopped only by reforming the social structure. Better regulation of banks, real-estate developers, and insurance companies might reduce the incidence of this crime. Studies of the relationship between arson and the deterioration of neighborhoods suggest that arson might also be reduced by citizen-action groups, arson-prediction methods, better communication between the community and the police, housing revitalization, and changes in environmental design (Brady, 1982; Cook and Roehl, 1983). In sum, the crime is most effectively understood and best controlled by paying attention to the socioeconomic context within which it occurs, not by focusing on the psychology of the individual offender.

An example of using socioeconomic factors to understand crime is one study that found that most of the changes in annual rates of homicide and car theft from 1946 to 1984 could be explained by trends in the age composition of the population, opportunities to commit crime, the business cycle, and the rate of imprisonment. These macrodynamic factors were highly predictive of fluctuations in crime rates, even in the absence of information about biological, social-psychological, and cultural variables that other theories propose as explanations of crime (Cohen and Land, 1987).

In this chapter we look at the social, economic, and cultural factors that are conducive to white-collar crime, organized crime, and conventional crime (especially juvenile delinquency). In the following chapter we examine the social and psychological processes by which people neutralize or weaken their commitment to the law. Then, in Chapter 9 we explore the ways that such individuals actually learn to commit crime.

Socioeconomic Sources of White-Collar Crime

Several aspects of the social and economic system of the United States are conducive to white-collar crime. The American economy is based as much on the stimulation of new demands as on the fulfillment of existing demands. Competition in the business world creates pressure to increase consumer demand for products and pressure to capture existing markets. This results in advertising, which sometimes goes beyond "puffing one's wares" to fraud, a crime characterized by the intent to deceive. Some advertising is thus actually criminal. Advertising can also stimulate demand that leads to theft if that demand is not fulfilled. Advertising fuels consumption in the American economy, but by urging people to consume and maintain an expensive life style, it can also lead to larceny, robbery, and embezzlement.

Free Enterprise: Profits and Competition

The American ideology of free enterprise stresses two goals: the pursuit of profits and open competition among sellers. Each goal can be conducive to violation of the law by businesspeople.

THE PURSUIT OF PROFITS   The emphasis on consumption and the use of advertising help create profits for firms. Some economists have suggested that companies seek a "satisfactory profit" rather than the maximum profit, and that corporations have goals other than making a profit. However, profits are basic to the corporation, even if other considerations play some role in corporate decision making.

In a study of sixty-four retired middle managers of large corporations, the largest number of them cited the pressure to show profits and keep costs in line as the major pressure on middle management. About nine-tenths of the retired executives said that the various pressures on middle managers sometimes lead to unethical behavior; about four-fifths of these executives said that such pressures can lead to criminal acts. Pressure on executives is more likely to lead to unethical behavior than to crime, but the drive for profits is a source of pressure that sometimes leads managers to violate the law (Clinard, 1983).

Firms seem most likely to violate the law to increase profits when the economy is unstable and profits are declining. The drive for profits can lead to antitrust violations such as price fixing, which is the illegal setting of prices by firms acting in collusion rather than depending on the free market to determine prices; this is an offense that the federal government explicitly states will be prosecuted. Profit seeking can also push businesspeople into the arms of gangsters to secure capital for investment and expansion; this sometimes leads to the takeover of legitimate businesses by organized crime. Economically weak firms may try to recoup their losses by "selling out to the insurance company"; that is, they may hire a "torch" to burn down the plant in order to collect the fire insurance. Arson increases during recessions when firms are in financial difficulty. For instance, in 1986 Houston was regarded by insurance and fire officials as the worst place in the United States for arson, a result of unemployment, home foreclosures, bankruptcies, and business failures resulting from the near collapse of the gas and oil industry on which that city had depended.

One of the largest losses in any crime in history involved an attempt to create a profitable enterprise. The conspirators sought to make the Equity Funding Corporation of America "the largest, fastest growing, most successful financial institution in the world and in the process thereby to gain fame and fortune for themselves" (Parker, 1976: 122). Their fraud involved the writing of fake life insurance policies that were sold to other insurance companies at a discount, a practice known as reinsurance. What was peculiar about this massive fraud was not the extraordinarily large losses involved, but that the conspirators created a situation in which their firm would actually have lost more money every year the fraud continued. Their crime created the illusion of making money while it was in fact losing money. The crime was apparently too complex for even its perpetrators to understand.

In 1986, indictments were returned against several Wall Street financiers for violating federal laws against "insider trading," the use of material and nonpublic information about a company to trade in its stock. These investment analysts had sold or used inside information to speculate on the outcome of corporate mergers and takeovers. One of them, Ivan Boesky, was required to pay $100 million in fines and illegal profits for his use of such information, which had helped him accumulate nearly $2 billion in capital. Many of those indicted in the insider trading cases were quite young; four who pleaded guilty in one case were between twenty-three and twenty-seven. One executive of a brokerage house said that the young people coming to work on Wall Street had changed. According to him, "they all want to do things faster, more aggressively, in terms of compensation, and that is their measure of success. They get here from the business schools with all sorts of knowledge about financial instruments, but less of a sense of what's right and what's wrong" (cited in Sterngold, 1986: 36).

COMPETITION The second element of free-enterprise ideology is open competition among firms, which is theoretically beneficial to the consuming public because it reduces profits to a "fair" level. However, competition can also lead firms to try to capture a larger share of the market through illegal acts such as false advertising or bribery. Individual firms do not seek to maximize competition for themselves and reduce their own profits to a "fair" level. Instead, they seek to reduce the strength of their competitors and maximize their own profits. To do this, they may turn to price fixing to drive competitors out of business, or to efforts to get banks to charge competing firms higher rates of interest. Competition has also led to the theft of new ideas through industrial espionage.

Competition in foreign markets has involved businesses in the bribery of officials to secure contracts and establish plants. In recent years, the increased internationalization of trade, the rise of multinational corporations, and the growing interdependence of nations have generated concern about white-collar crime in the international arena. Competition among the corporations of the world sometimes leads to clearly illegal behavior such as assassinations, and sometimes into "gray" areas that involve unethical behavior that may not violate existing laws. Since the passage of the Foreign Corrupt Practices Act in 1977, firms based in the United States that pay bribes to foreign officials are in violation of American law; however, only ten cases were prosecuted under that law in the first decade of its existence. Another unethical practice—the shipping to foreign buyers of products banned in the United States, such as carcinogenic TRIS-treated infants' clothing—is not prosecuted as a crime in the

United States. Competition and the search for new and profitable markets encourage this behavior, especially when the law does not cover the situation adequately or when the criminal justice system does not punish such actions.

Market Structure and Crime

Some white-collar crimes seem to be more likely to occur in certain market structures or economic circumstances (Leonard and Weber, 1970; Kramer, 1982). For example, seller concentration—a large share of the market being controlled by a few leading producers—may be conducive to price fixing. Overall, however, research is inconclusive as to the exact relationship between an industry's level of concentration and its rate of antitrust violations (Coleman, 1985: 224–225).

A small number of buyers or a great deal of wealth in the hands of a few buyers—called buyer concentration—can give buyers the power to demand bribes and kickbacks from sellers. When goods and services are in short supply, consumers may bribe those who control scarce resources in order to meet their needs; we see an example of this in the Soviet Union in the Cross-Cultural Perspective.

Another aspect of market structure conducive to business crime is the price elasticity of demand. When demand is price-inelastic—that is, when there will be little reduction in the demand for a product if its price increases—firms may engage in price fixing to increase profits. A slow growth rate of demand in a given market is another condition that can lead to business crimes such as false advertising.

Product differentiation, which is the ability to distinguish one's product from a competitor's product, can lead to false or deceptive advertising. Sometimes the opposite situation, trying to make one's product seem as much like another product as possible, leads to crimes such as copyright or patent infringement. Consumer demand for designer clothing or designer cosmetics is conducive to the counterfeiting of those products.

Trust and Credit

Some business crimes stem from the economic system's reliance on trust and credit. Businesspeople have faith that others will fulfill their obligations honestly; when that trust is violated, crimes may occur. Robert Vesco exploited his business colleagues in Investors Overseas Services by looting about half a billion dollars from that international corporation (Hutchison, 1974). Employers sometimes violate the trust of employees and union leaders by engaging in illegal labor practices. Merchants abuse the trust of their customers when they misrepresent prices, engage in deceptive credit practices, or substitute inferior goods upon delivery. Corporate directors violate stockholders' trust when they fail to disclose information about illegal contributions to political candidates and bribes to foreign officials. The Trustee's Bankruptcy Report on the Equity

A Cross-Cultural Perspective: Bribery in the Soviet Union

Market conditions determine how well the demands of consumers will be met. When goods and services are scarce, consumers may bribe those who control economic resources. One Soviet dissident notes that "the prevalence of bribery in Russia is accentuated by the fact that many goods are in short supply and are distributed in accordance with an elaborate network of privileges. Since people cannot buy wanted items in the usual way, they have to bribe those who control the privilege system" (Chalidze, p. 156).

Another Soviet dissident, who is an attorney, describes the process of bribery in more detail:

> Entering into relations with representatives of the government, dealing with industry, commerce, and services, the Soviet citizen, readily

and without thinking about it, uses corruption to get what is necessary for him—most often what is vitally necessary. In the same automatic way, the average Soviet citizen gives a ruble to a salesman in a store to get a piece of meat, 300 rubles to an official of the Ministry of Communication to have a telephone installed in his apartment, or 3000 rubles to an official of the District Executive Committee to get a government apartment. If he does not pay these bribes his family will not have meat; he will be forced to wait five or six years before a telephone is installed; he will remain for years with his large family in a single room in a communal apartment. (Simis, p. 298)

SOURCES. Based on Valery Chalidze, *Criminal Russia: Crime in the Soviet Union.* New York: Random House, 1977; Konstantin M. Simis, *USSR: The Corrupt Society.* New York: Simon and Schuster, 1982.

Funding Corporation of America fraud concluded that EFCA had violated the trust of other members of the insurance industry, saying that

> only someone with an exceedingly skeptical bent of mind would have . . . inferred fraud. Such an inference would have been hostile to the presumption of good faith and honest-dealing which customarily prevails in American business practice. To the Trustee, that presumption, though sometimes grievously abused, is probably indispensable to a vigorous and productive economy. (cited in Parker, 1976: 166)

One trust relationship that is conducive to certain crimes is credit, which is given on the creditor's faith that the borrower will repay the money. Many of the crimes that involve the abuse of credit involve businesspeople who defraud other large businesses. Business credit fraud is sometimes planned in advance, with a new company established to defraud suppliers, or a legitimate business converted into a firm that abuses its creditors. Banks and corporations sometimes continue to extend credit to a firm even though that firm's shaky financial condition makes it unlikely that it will be able to repay its debts (Levi, 1981). One businessman who aspired to wealth through fraudulent credit practices was

Tony DeAngelis, who borrowed millions of dollars by using as collateral for his loans salad oil that he said was stored in large tanks. His creditors trusted him, but they failed to check on the existence of the salad oil. When the tanks were found to be empty, DeAngelis defaulted on the loans and his creditors lost millions of dollars (Miller, 1965).

Corporations and Crime

Much American business is conducted by large corporations. Various aspects of these organizations — such as their bureaucratic structure, their working conditions, and their use of rationality in decision making — are conducive to crime (Conklin, 1977; Clinard and Yeager, 1980)

BUREAUCRATIC STRUCTURE   Bureaucratic structure may be associated with the fragmentation of responsibility and the difficulty of pinpointing who made a particular decision. Supervisors often blame underlings for the company's violation of the law, and underlings claim that supervisors encouraged them to break the law to meet corporate goals.

The division of tasks in a large corporation may enhance bureaucratic efficiency but may also make it difficult to exercise control over business activities. The Equity Funding Corporation of America fraud resulted in part from a fragmented corporate structure, which allowed conspirators to act in relative secrecy (Dirks and Gross, 1974: 240). The decentralization of General Electric in 1950 broke that large corporation into several relatively autonomous divisions, each of which was under pressure to show a profit. The need to stabilize profits at a high level led to price fixing, an offense that was made easier by the fragmentation of the company.

Corporate crimes can result from organizational defects such as poor information flow, lack of coordination in the bureaucracy, inaccurate promotional material, failure to deal adequately with complaints after an inaccurate advertisement, or failure to tell sales representatives all of the relevant facts about a product (Hopkins, 1980; Ermann and Lundman, 1982). A study in Australia of fifteen companies that had committed white-collar crimes involving an organizational defect found that official sanctions led at least 60 percent of the companies to make significant organizational changes to reduce the chance that the problem would recur (Hopkins, 1980).

WORKING CONDITIONS   Employees of large corporations may find it easy to steal from the company if they have little loyalty to the firm. Crime against the employing firm is apparently less common in Japan, where workers traditionally remain with one company for their entire working lives, than it is in the United States, where job mobility is great and there is little tradition of loyalty to one firm (Clifford, 1976). In addition, when union-management conflict is necessary to increase wages and benefits, workers may believe that management is not concerned with their welfare and will make concessions only grudgingly. This attitude may be used to justify employees' crimes against the firm.

Dissatisfied workers who feel exploited or underpaid and executives who are frustrated by not being promoted or by an unsatisfactory salary may justify theft or embezzlement as the only way to gain deserved compensation for low pay or poor working conditions (Hollinger and Clark, 1983). Some observers believe that workers steal to increase their spendable incomes; the policy implication is that theft can be reduced by paying workers more (Jaspan, 1974). Another view is that because many jobs are dull, repetitive, lacking in prestige, or unchalleng-ing, workers steal for job enrichment or to increase their self-esteem (Zeitlin, 1971; Altheide et al., 1978). For instance, one wealthy lawyer allegedly stole $607,000 in bonds because he was "fascinated by the challenge of constructing elaborate schemes to steal money" (Carmody, 1974). Theft for challenge is also a common motive in many computer crimes (Parker, 1976). The impersonality of the work environment in large corporations and on plant assembly lines can give rise to the need to create a challenge that workers can meet, and this may take the form of crime against the company. Giving workers a vested interest in the company's success and integrating them into the firm might reduce em-ployee theft (Hollinger and Clark, 1983).

RATIONAL DECISION MAKING The rational decision making of large corpora-tions can also be conducive to business crime. Given a low risk of arrest, a small likelihood of being convicted in court, and a negligible chance of a meaningful criminal sanction, corporate executives may knowingly violate the law or enter "gray areas" where they are aware they may be violating the law. It may seem rational, if not moral or legal, for executives to break the law if their gains are great and their risks are small. Even if the company is convicted of a crime, it will probably gain more in profits than it loses in fines, and individual executives may gain more in promotion and salary than they lose from criminal sanctions (Stone, 1974: 45–46).

In the 1970s, the Ford Motor Company calculated that it would be too costly for it to modify its cars and light trucks in a way that would prevent fuel leakage that had caused serious burns and deaths. Ford estimated it would cost $137 million to make such modifications. However, those changes would save the company only $49.5 million in repairs it would be required to make and civil damages it would be forced to pay to accident victims. This $49.5 million figure was arrived at on the basis of $700 in repairs per burned vehicle, $67,000 per serious burn injury, and $200,000 per burn death. Critics allege that on the basis of such calculations, Ford decided it would be too expensive initially to fix and later to recall the Pinto, which was involved in numerous serious accidents (Cullen, Maakestad, and Cavender, 1987).

Development of New Technology

Technology develops in a cumulative fashion, and new opportunities to violate the law often accompany breakthroughs in technology. The high-tech and computer industry has provided both new opportunities for crime and new techniques to commit traditional crimes such as embezzlement.

Computer crime, which can broadly be defined as any violation of the law in which a computer is the target or the means, often involves large losses. Computer crime includes the following kinds of offenses:

- introduction of unauthorized data into a system,
- manipulation of authorized data,
- creation of unauthorized files,
- unauthorized use of passwords or accounting codes, often called "hacking,"
- theft of hardware, software, or computer time, and
- use of the computer as a weapon.

One example of the computer's being used as a weapon occurred in 1979, when someone purposely tampered with a computerized flight plan guiding a plane's automatic pilot, causing a crash in which 257 people were killed. Another computer crime is "shaving," in which someone programs a computer to round off each employee's pay check down to the nearest ten cents and then deposit the extra few pennies in the offender's account. One programmer made $300 a

Here a police detective displays electronic equipment seized during the arrest of seven juveniles who used computers illegally to exchange information such as the numbers of stolen credit cards and methods of manufacturing explosives.
Source: Allan Tannenbaum / Sygma

week with this scheme, an amount that was two and a half times his regular salary. Another computer crime involved tapping into an oil company's computer to get information that allowed the offending company to underbid the victimized company for leasing rights.

The tremendous reduction in the cost of computers in recent years means that individuals and small businesses can afford them. This has two effects. First, individual "hackers" have an instrument with which to tap into computerized files, an act that has recently become the focus of federal law enforcement. Second, the inexpensive computers owned by small businesses usually do not have good built-in security measures, and so they are vulnerable to violation.

Several aspects of computer technology are conducive to crime. It is relatively easy for a knowledgeable computer programmer to hide a program or a modification within a larger program, or to destroy records and leave no "trail" of the crime. Computer software or programs are copied relatively easily. The courts have treated this act as copyright infringement. In 1983, one company with sales of $26 million claimed to have lost between $20 million and $40 million because of illegal reproduction or piracy of its software. The chips used in computer hardware are small but expensive, and have been a target of thieves, who then sell them to companies that cannot purchase enough chips in the legitimate market. Another aspect of computer technology is that computers emit radio waves or "compromising emanations" that can be decoded with the proper equipment. The federal government calls this the "Tempest" problem and worries about electronic espionage that might reveal secret information in computerized files.

One aspect of computer technology that is of growing importance is electronic fund transfers (EFT), which include all payment systems that permit transactions or exchanges in which value is represented by electronic messages, rather than by paper such as currency or checks. *EFT crime* is thus any violation of the law that would not have occurred except for the presence of an EFT system. This includes crimes that involve automated teller machines and wire transfers from bank to bank by a company's computer. There is no good source of data on the extent of EFT crime, though efforts to collect such data have begun, but so far EFT crime seems to be a small proportion of all crimes involving financial institutions. However, EFT crime will probably become a more important problem as the number of financial transactions conducted electronically grows (Colton et al., 1982; Bureau of Justice Statistics, February 1984; Tien, Rich, and Cahn, April 1986).

Socioeconomic Sources of Organized Crime

The tendency in American society to pass legislation that prohibits the consumption of widely demanded goods and services has produced a situation conducive to vast profits for people who are willing to supply those illegal goods and services. One example is Prohibition.

Prohibition and Organized Crime

Prior to the passage of the Eighteenth Amendment, which prohibited the manufacture, sale, and transportation of alcoholic beverages, there were gangsters in many American cities, but they were not well organized.

The efforts of religious, white, native-born Americans in small towns and rural areas to protect the dominance of their cultural values led to Prohibition in 1920. The Prohibition Amendment made a widely demanded product illegal. The consequence was that those willing to supply illegal alcoholic beverages could charge higher prices than consumers had paid when those beverages were legal and in more plentiful supply. This source of great profits led to the organization of criminal gangs that distributed alcoholic beverages to meet the public demand.

The Eighteenth Amendment was repealed during the Great Depression, partly for economic reasons. People needed the jobs that the liquor industry could provide, and the government hoped to raise more tax revenue from the legal sale of alcoholic beverages (Gusfield, 1963). Repeal was also a result of the unenforceability of the law and the public's reactions to the tactics used by the Prohibition Bureau. National prohibition became a thing of the past in 1933, but gangsters had become well organized as a result of this unsuccessful experiment in the legislation of morality.

Organized Crime after Prohibition

When Prohibition ended, gangs turned to other illegal enterprises for revenue. They became involved in prostitution, though they are not much involved in it today. The major sources of revenue for organized crime today seem to be narcotics and loan sharking, and perhaps gambling. However, gangsters have shown ingenuity in making a profit from many different illegal activities, including bankruptcy fraud, the disposal of toxic wastes, and extortion.

GAMBLING   According to some scholars and most law-enforcement officers, many bookies work for or are members of organized crime "families." One sociologist with access to evidence gathered by law-enforcement agencies has suggested that 95 percent of illegal gambling in the United States is controlled by organized crime (Cressey, 1969). However, research in New York City, where the largest number of organized crime families in the country are located, indicates that organized crime does not have a firm control over gambling and that bookies operate in a competitive market rather than as agents of organized crime. Because the gambling business is unpredictable, bookies often turn to loan sharks, who do have ties to organized crime, in order to borrow money to keep their gambling operations afloat (Reuter and Rubinstein, 1978; Reuter, 1983). Bookies thus provide a source of income for organized crime not because their profits are channeled directly to gangsters, but because they pay high interest rates to loan sharks who are members of organized crime.

LOAN SHARKING Loan sharks are a major source of income for organized crime. The interest rates on their loans are illegally high and well in excess of what borrowers pay to legitimate institutions. Loan sharks thrive on the difficulties that some people encounter in getting loans from legitimate institutions. Many borrowers from loan sharks are poor credit risks who are turned down by banks and finance companies. Other borrowers need money for purposes of which legitimate institutions would disapprove, such as the repayment of gambling debts or the financing of a drug deal. Loan sharks are willing to lend money to such people with less financial information or collateral than legitimate institutions require.

Many who borrow from loan sharks have difficulty repaying their loans on time. When this happens, a loan shark may threaten violence against the borrower or the borrower's family. However, a study of loan sharking in New York City found violence and intimidation to be less common than some accounts suggest, as borrowers and lenders often have close ties. Borrowers usually repay their loans because they hope to be able to secure loans from the loan shark again (Reuter, 1983).

NARCOTICS The money lent by loan sharks who are linked to organized crime often comes from the profits made from the importation of illegal narcotics, especially heroin. Laws against the sale and possession of narcotics lead to high profits for those who are willing to take the risk of importing and distributing drugs. As a result, heroin and other drugs are far more costly to users in the United States than would be the case if those substances were legal.

The illegality of heroin generates crime in two ways. First, it creates drug crimes such as importation, sale, and possession. Then indirectly, the illegality of heroin creates secondary or drug-related crimes such as larceny, robbery, and prostitution, which addicts commit to get the money to pay for their expensive narcotics. The supply-demand balance for heroin is similar to that for illegal alcoholic beverages during Prohibition, except there is less choice involved in an addict's use of heroin. There is a relatively constant demand for heroin among addicts, and this makes it possible for gangsters to raise prices without losing much business.

Government programs to reduce drug use and drug-related crimes by curtailing the importation of narcotics can backfire. Reducing the supply of heroin entering the country may have little immediate effect on addicts' demand for the drug, but prices may rise as demand remains steady and supply declines. When this happens, addicts may commit more crime in order to get the money to pay for the more expensive drug. Thus, a government program that succeeds in reducing the amount of an addictive drug that is imported can increase street crime by addicts without reducing drug use in any significant way.

A contrary argument is made by James Q. Wilson (1983: 212–213), who claims that law enforcement can and has reduced, or at least has stabilized, the addict population by curtailing the supply of heroin. One study of addicts found that the confiscation of drugs may drive prices up, but that quality falls as a result. Addicts seem to be less sensitive to the cost of heroin than to the quality of the drugs they are using. Consequently, government seizures of heroin might push some addicts into treatment; if this happens, it will more likely be the result of lowered drug quality than the result of higher prices (Baridon, 1976).

BANKRUPTCY FRAUD   Organized crime has sometimes taken advantage of the trust inherent in credit transactions in the business world to engage in bankruptcy fraud (DeFranco, 1973). In this crime, racketeers purchase a business that has a good credit rating or establish a "front business" with a name much like one of a respected firm. They stock up on merchandise bought on credit. They demand quick delivery, pay for initial orders with cash so as to establish and maintain good credit, and buy to the limit on credit, excusing nonpayment by the rapid expansion of their business or by the busy season of the year, the Christmas season being a favorite time for this crime. The goods they buy are appealing to consumers, can be purchased in volume, and are easy to transport and hard to trace. Office equipment, television sets, and toys are examples. The racketeers sell these goods as quickly as they can through discount houses and by mail orders, and then disappear and leave their creditors with unpaid bills. The widespread use of credit in the world of commerce makes it possible for gangsters to commit this kind of crime.

DISPOSAL OF TOXIC WASTE   Organized crime has been adaptable in moving into newly profitable areas of illegal activity. For instance, the disposal of toxic waste material produced by industry has become difficult and expensive because of strict environmental protection laws. Garbage companies owned by organized crime have developed highly profitable, but dangerous and illegal, methods of waste disposal. One method involves mixing toxic materials with recycled fuel oil (Block and Scarpitti, 1985; Szasz, 1986).

EXTORTION   Organized crime has used its control of certain labor unions and the threat of violence to extort millions of dollars a year from industry. In New York City, concrete companies, some of which have links to organized crime, overcharge construction companies about $50 million a year by threatening to withhold workers or to slow down the delivery of concrete to construction companies that are working against deadlines. A U.S. Attorney estimates that such extortion has driven up construction costs in New York City by about 20 percent, an increase that is passed on to consumers in higher rents, higher taxes for public works projects, and higher prices for goods and services (Roberts, 1985).

A virtual monopoly over the waste-removal industry makes the cost of garbage collection in New York City about 50 percent higher than it would be without organized crime involvement, according to one economist (Peter Reuter, cited in Roberts, 1985). This monopoly was created and is maintained through the threat of violence against legitimate entrepreneurs seeking to enter the industry. For instance, according to an FBI official, some time ago a man . . . entered the refuse business in New York State, mortgaging his home to buy a few garbage trucks. Before long, sugar was found in the gas tanks. . . . Then someone tried to blow up a truck. One afternoon the phone rang, and a gruff voice described what the man's ten-year-old daughter was wearing that day. The voice warned that if the trucks were not sold, the girl would disappear. The business was shut down within hours. (Shenon, 1985: E4)

Organized Crime and the Economic System

The activities of organized crime are closely interwoven with the economic system. Illegal goods and services are supplied by gangsters at a high cost to consumers and at great profit to organized crime. Gangsters act as brokers who meet an unfulfilled public demand for illegal goods and services. Organized crime serves economic functions for some people; for example, loan sharks make money available to people who cannot borrow elsewhere. Gangsters in the United States, Japan, and elsewhere often adopt the economic strategies and managerial skills of legitimate business to carry out their illegal profit-making ventures.

Legitimate industries serve important functions for organized crime. For instance, banks in the United States "launder" or recirculate billions of dollars in illegal profits each year to make it seem that the money comes from legitimate investments. The Senate Permanent Investigating Subcommittee describes how this process works in the following example:

> A drug dealer gives a large amount of cash from drug sales to a "launderer" who dispatches "smurfs" to several banks to purchase money orders or cashier's checks.
>
> The money orders or checks are then deposited in accounts which are usually fronts for criminal activity. The money from the accounts is then wired to overseas banks, where confidentiality laws prevent disclosures of information about the account's ownership or transactions.
>
> The money can be sent back to the U.S. bank accounts controlled by the drug dealer, or it can be transferred to foreign bank accounts to purchase new drug shipments. (cited in *The Boston Globe,* December 30, 1986: 10)

Thus, organized crime is made possible by the actions of legitimate economic enterprises, as well as by public demands that are not fulfilled by those enterprises.

Socioeconomic Sources of Conventional Crime

Conventional crime is influenced by the economic system in many ways. Modernization affects crime rates in significant ways. Changes in the value of goods can create new opportunities for crime. Unemployment and crime are related to each other in complex ways. If a culture encourages people to strive for material success, dissatisfaction that is conducive to the committing of crime may develop among the unsuccessful. Sociologists have sought to explain the impact of these and other socioeconomic factors on crime and delinquency.

Modernization and Crime

The process of economic development has affected the amount and characteristics of crime in both capitalist and socialist societies. In general, high proportions of all of the crimes committed in economically developed societies are property crimes, because with prosperity there are many opportunities to steal. In less-developed societies, property crimes usually make up a smaller proportion of all crimes, and violent crimes are relatively more common (Clinard and Abbott, 1973; Shelley, 1981a). The overall crime rate tends to rise with economic modernization, but some of that increase seems to be due to the development of a professional police force that keeps better records. With economic development also comes an increase in the relative amount of crime by juveniles and by women. One review of the research concludes that in developing societies women rarely commit more than one-tenth of all crimes, but in economically advanced societies they are responsible for as much as one-sixth of all crimes (Shelley, 1981a: 141).

Some societies have avoided high and rising crime rates as they have modernized. High overall crime rates have been avoided where traditional group ties and cultural values have been maintained; Japan and some Middle Eastern nations are examples. Control over urbanization and migration has also reduced the rate at which crime has increased (see the Cross-Cultural Perspective in Chapter 5). Harsh treatment of criminals — including long prison sentences or capital punishment — seemed to contain the crime problem in societies such as Stalin's Soviet Union and Franco's Spain. Eastern European nations have checked the growth of crime by redistributing income and guaranteeing jobs. By contrast, crime seems to have increased in advanced economic systems such as the United States, where there is great income inequality and where everyone is urged to strive for material success (Shelley, 1981a: 142).

Opportunity and the Economy

Property crime rates increase especially dramatically with economic development because of growing opportunities for theft. Within developed economies, fluctuations in the value of certain goods can also create new opportunities for crime. For instance, the enormous increase in the market value of gold and silver during the 1970s changed the theft patterns of burglars, who began to leave behind televisions and stereos in favor of jewelry and silverware. Street criminals began to grab gold necklaces from women's necks, injuring and in a few cases even killing their victims. This increase in the theft of precious metals had several consequences: longer waiting lists for bank safe-deposit boxes; the updating of insurance policies; the establishment of refineries in the United

States to melt down stolen jewelry, coins, and silverware; and advertisements by metal dealers to buy gold and silver with "no questions asked."

Other unusual crimes have developed as the value of goods has increased. "Bee rustling" — the theft of bee hives — became a problem as the cost of a bee colony climbed from $25 to $65 between 1975 and 1982. A truckload of one hundred hives could net the thieves $6,500 for one night of work, and the placement of hives far from their owners' homes meant that there was little risk of detection. Timber theft from national forests increased from 1,050 incidents in 1971 to 6,800 cases in 1980. This change seemed due to the increased use of wood-burning stoves as natural gas and oil became more expensive. To meet the great demand for firewood, thieves operating in bands of ten to fifteen stole tens of millions of dollars of wood from national forests, causing environmental damage in the process.

Unemployment and Crime

Unemployment is related to crime and delinquency in complex ways (see, e.g., Thompson et al., 1981). Some crimes cannot occur unless a person is working; embezzlement and price fixing are examples. In such cases, higher unemployment rates might reduce crime. Other offenders mix employment and crime by "moonlighting" in crime, by using a job as a front (as with a professional fence), or by using legitimate income as a stake for a crime (as in drug deals). For moonlighters, more unemployment might increase criminal activity, but for those who use a job as a front or use their income for a stake, unemployment might reduce crime. Some people, especially youths, alternate between employment and crime, and in these cases more unemployment might increase crime. Finally, some offenders are committed to crime as a source of income. They would not work even if jobs were available, and so a higher unemployment rate would not affect their criminal activity (Sviridoff and Thompson, 1983).

There may be an important difference between people who are working or are temporarily unemployed, and people who have been out of work for a long time or who have stopped looking for jobs. The difference between having a job or not having a job at any given moment may be less significant (Votey and Phillips, 1974). Even more important than finding a job is keeping a job over time, for having a job binds people to legitimate institutions and gives them a "stake in conformity" that they do not want to jeopardize by involvement in crime (Jeffery, 1977: 167–171). Criminals tend to have poorer work records and higher rates of unemployment than nonoffenders, but some research indicates that more and better job opportunities might lead some offenders to select legitimate sources of income over illegal ones (Freeman, 1983: 106). People who hold unattractive jobs that pay poorly, are boring, and offer little room to advance may not think they stand to lose much if they are arrested (Cook, 1975; Orsagh and Witte, 1981). As a result, finding a good job to which a person can feel committed over time seems to be more important than simply holding some job.

People who are without jobs seem more likely to commit the kinds of crime that lead to imprisonment (Viscusi, 1986; Duster, 1987). In the months prior to their incarceration, inmates of state prisons and local jails are much more likely to be unemployed than people in the general population. In addition, offenders who are even slightly more successful at work seem to commit fewer crimes than offenders who are less successful in the labor force (Petersilia, Greenwood, and Lavin, 1977). Some research also indicates that unemployment rates prior to imprisonment are a strong predictor of which inmates will engage in crime at the highest rate after their release (Greenwood, 1982). An experimental study also concluded that employment in the postrelease period and the steadiness of that employment were associated with lower arrest rates (Rossi, Berk, and Lenihan, 1980).

One explanation of delinquency focuses on youth's lack of access to jobs that provide the income they need to participate in peer-group activities and to buy the clothes, records, and other things that will win them the esteem of their friends. The exclusion of young people from adult work roles, and the increased competition that youths have recently encountered from greater numbers of female workers, deprive young people of income and make them financially dependent on their parents longer (Phillips and Votey, 1981). Juvenile delinquency has thus been attributed to the "structural position of juveniles in an advanced capitalist economy" that excludes the young from well-paying jobs by child labor laws, compulsory education, and minimum wage laws (Greenberg, 1977b: 220).

Research in New York City neighborhoods shows that persistent unemployment among adults limits the development of stable households and reduces job opportunities for young people in the community. These changes, in turn, weaken informal social control in the area, contributing to higher local crime rates. If legitimate jobs are not available or if they pay poorly, young people are more likely to turn to theft, the sale of drugs, or other crimes for income (McGahey, 1986).

Recent structural changes in the economy, such as the relocation of manufacturing to suburban areas or even to Third World countries, today threaten to create a permanent "underclass" of unemployed blacks. Discrimination in hiring and in pay in the retail industry also poses a formidable barrier to upward mobility for this class and reduces their attachment to the labor force (Auletta, 1983; Duster, 1987).

Despite some persuasive evidence for a link between unemployment and crime, *aggregate* data for the nation show that fluctuations in the unemployment rate are no more than weakly related to the rate of index crimes. A review of ten studies done before 1975 found that seven revealed no significant relationship between the unemployment rate and the crime rate (Gillespie, 1975). Research since 1975 also provides "no strong support for the proposition that 'unemployment causes crime'" (Orsagh and Witte, 1981: 1059). A recent review of the evidence concludes as follows: "There is a cyclical pattern to the crime rate, with crime rising over the cycle with unemployment — but only weakly, so that changes in crime rates are dominated by other factors" (Freeman, 1983: 106). Critics question the conclusion that unemployment and crime are not strongly associated, arguing that unemployment rates are flawed, leaving out "discouraged workers" who are no longer seeking work and failing to measure the quality of the work that people are doing (Currie, 1985). Other critics point out that the national crime rate also has important methodological flaws (see Chapter 3).

Relative Deprivation and Crime

Even more important than poverty or unemployment as a cause of crime may be the way poor or unemployed people perceive their situation. Most poor and unemployed people are law-abiding, and the crime rates of the poor in many developing nations are lower than the crime rates of Americans, who have higher absolute standards of living. For instance, blacks in the United States have higher incomes, on the average, than black Africans, but black Americans also have higher crime rates than black Africans.

What seems important, then, is people's relative standard of living. Resentment of poverty is probably more common among the poor in a wealthy nation than it is among people who have an absolutely lower standard of living in a poor nation (Toby, 1967). Quetelet observed in the nineteenth century that the rural poor in Europe were generally honest, but that the urban poor who were nearer to great wealth and temptation were more prone to crime. Relative rather than absolute poverty was given as the reason for this difference. Evidence from the contemporary United States shows that crime rates are highest in cities where the difference between the income of the poor and the income of the rich is the greatest (Eberts and Schwirian, 1968; Danziger and Wheeler, 1975; Blau and Blau, 1982; Currie, 1985; Sampson, 1985, 1986). However, a comparative study of sixty-two nations found that in other societies, inequality apparently does not lead to higher rates of property crimes, as it does in the United States. In these other countries, inequality seems more closely associated with other forms of behavior, such as political action and social protest (Stack, 1984).

The discrepancy between people's expectations and their capabilities can motivate them to violate the law. Expectations are the goods and conditions of life to which people think they are rightfully entitled, and capabilities are the goods and conditions of life they believe they can attain and maintain under the current social system (Gurr, 1970). The discrepancy between the two is called *relative deprivation*. Crime is probably more likely to occur when there is much relative deprivation with regard to deeply held goals such as material success. Crime may also occur when people think they have exhausted all constructive means to reach their goals and believe that legitimate opportunities to reduce their relative deprivation are closed to them. Crime is not, however, the only reaction to a sense of relative deprivation, for relative deprivation can also lead to political action, a social movement, suicide, or alcoholism. However, those who control political power often define the actions of the relatively deprived as crime, whether those actions are larceny, political protest, or terrorism.

Relative deprivation becomes greater when expectations increase or when capabilities decrease. A sudden drop in prosperity might reduce perceived capabilities, but relative deprivation more often increases because of a growth in expectations. In developing nations, the "demonstration effect" leads to a desire for a better standard of living among people who move to large cities where a wealthy life style can be observed firsthand. Capabilities usually do not rise as fast as expectations, and thus relative deprivation increases and crime rates rise (Clinard and Abbott, 1973).

Anomie and Crime

An important effort to link crime to American cultural values was Robert Merton's 1938 paper on social structure and anomie. Merton (1968) sought to relate particular types of behavior to the social position of the people engaging in the behavior. Whereas Freud tried to explain deviance by the failure of the social structure to socialize people to control their natural impulses, Merton looked instead at social pressures that caused deviant or criminal behavior. He saw crime as rooted in the social system rather than as intrinsic to the makeup of humans. He was not interested in explaining the behavior of each and every individual, but in explaining differences in rates of behavior for different groups and categories of people.

GOALS AND MEANS   Merton's explanatory approach is based on a distinction between culturally defined goals and the norms that regulate the means to achieve those goals.

Goals are the valued purposes and interests that the culture holds out as legitimate objectives for all members of society. American culture emphasizes equal opportunity for all to attain the goals of wealth and power. Indeed, these goals are highly valued in most cultures. American culture encourages everyone to have the same high ambition and treats the failure to achieve cultural goals as an individual failing rather than as a flaw in the social system. This belief protects the social system from criticism. The culture's emphasis on the measurement of individual worth by material success produces a society with a built-in incentive to achieve. This has helped the nation attain a high overall standard of living, but it has also generated relative deprivation and crime among those who do not achieve the goals of wealth and power.

The second factor in Merton's theory can be described as the institutionalized means to reach the cultural goals. Norms, which define acceptable ways to reach cultural goals, are derived from the values or preferences of the society, rather than from the pure technical efficiency of the means in reaching goals. Thus, performing a successful bank robbery might be the most technically efficient way for an uneducated and unskilled person to attain material well-being, but social and legal norms define this as an unacceptable way to achieve wealth. Instead, norms emphasize hard work at a socially approved occupation over a lifetime, coupled with deferred gratification of the rewards of material success, as the appropriate way to achieve financial well-being.

ANOMIE Social equilibrium exists when satisfactions accrue to people who use the institutionalized means to reach the culturally approved goals. When there is a disjunction between means and goals, *anomie* or normlessness results. A disjunction may result from the socially structured incapacity of people to use the approved means to reach cultural goals. Thus, racial discrimination in education and employment makes access to the institutionalized means of achieving success difficult for blacks and other minorities. Discrimination by class is another socially structured incapacity. Success may require a good education, which is less available to the poor, and "good manners," which are defined by the preferences of those who hold wealth and power. These socially structured incapacities are experienced as low capabilities and can lead to relative deprivation that causes crime.

Socially structured incapacities might not produce anomie in a society in which success goals are not held out to everyone. The relative significance of material well-being in comparison to other goals may be the same in the United States and other nations, but the absolute strength of the drive to attain material success is probably greater in the United States than elsewhere. This has been called the American "fetishism of money" (Taylor, Walton, and Young, 1973: 94). This fetishism is spurred by the mass media, including television and magazines such as *Time, Newsweek,* and *People.* Television commercials urge consumers to spend money on goods and services that will bring them happiness. Sometimes the message to consume is more subtle. For instance, the large kitchens that are shown in television commercials for dish soap, scouring pads, and floor wax can be found in homes that only a small proportion of Americans can afford. Television viewers may vaguely sense being disadvantaged because the kitchens they see in television commercials are so much better than their own; they may even begin to hope that they will someday have enough money to afford a home with such a kitchen, which seems to them to be "just an average American kitchen."

MODES OF ADAPTATION Merton develops a paradigm of five *modes of adaptation* to the social structure. He looks at the ways that individuals who occupy different social positions adapt to cultural goals and the institutionalized means to reach those goals. Table 7.1 indicates acceptance of a goal or means by a plus sign (+), rejection of a goal or means by a minus sign (−), and rejection of a goal or means and the substitution of a new goal or means by a plus-minus (±) sign.

Conformity. The first mode of adaptation, *conformity,* is by far the most common adaptation to goals and means in a stable society. This pattern involves acceptance of cultural goals (such as material wealth), and the acceptance of the institutionalized means to reach those goals (such as a legitimate occupation).

TABLE 7.1   Merton's Five Modes of Adaptation

Modes of Adaptation	Goals	Means
I. Conformity	+	+
II. Innovation	+	−
III. Ritualism	−	+
IV. Retreatism	−	−
V. Rebellion	±	±

+ = acceptance

− = rejection

± = rejection of goals or means, and substitution of new goals or means

SOURCE: *Social Theory and Social Structure,* 1968 Enlarged Edition, by Robert K. Merton (Copyright © 1968, 1967 by Robert K. Merton. Published by The Free Press, a Division of Macmillan, Inc.).

Innovation. Innovation is the mode of adaptation most relevant to the analysis of criminal behavior. Here the goal is accepted, but means are used that society regards as unacceptable. Innovation is especially common when the goal that is sought is charged with great emotion. Thus the strong emphasis on material wealth as a sign of individual worth in the United States produces a powerful emotional investment in that goal, leading to a readiness to resort to illegal means to attain it when acceptable means are unavailable. The author of a study of shoplifting in department stores concluded that such theft is closely related to the acquisitiveness of American society and the emphasis placed on material symbols of success. She claims that theft is encouraged because department store goods are "dazzlingly arrayed before people who have been exhorted to desire them" (Cameron, 1964: 171).

Innovation occurs when businesspeople resort to embezzlement or price fixing to attain material wealth for themselves or profits for their firms. Innovation also describes crimes such as tax fraud and larceny, which occur when the desire for more money or goods leads to violation of the law. The pressure to violate the law may be greatest among the lowest classes, because they are most distant from the goal of financial security and because their access to institutionalized means to attain material success is the most limited. However, as we have seen, the relationship between class and crime is not clearcut, even though serious and repetitive index crimes seem to be most likely to be committed by people at the bottom of the stratification system. Merton's anomie theory emphasizes the disjunction between goals and means, and this approach is general enough to apply to property crimes committed by members of all classes.

The rise of many big-city political machines in the nineteenth century grew out of efforts by Irish immigrants, who found industry and wealth controlled by native-born Americans, to gain power and status for themselves. When Italians arrived in the country some time after the Irish, they found not only that wealth was controlled by the native-born and that political power was controlled by Irish-Americans, but also that society's need for unskilled labor was less than it had been in earlier years. With the stimulus of Prohibition, some Italian immigrants innovated by using criminal means to achieve material wealth and political influence (Bell, 1962). Another view attributes the rise of Italians in organized crime not to blocked opportunities to achieve wealth and power, but rather to a rational choice of crime as an easy and exciting way to get rich (Lupsha, 1981). Just as not all Irish-Americans became politicians, so not all Italian-Americans became gangsters, but in each case some of the members of an ethnic group innovated by using new means to reach societal goals. Irish-American politicians used acceptable and legal means, and Italian-American gangsters employed unacceptable and illegal means. In recent years, other racial and ethnic groups—including the Chinese, Vietnamese, Jamaicans, and Colombians—have also engaged in organized crime activities as a means to achieve material success.

Ritualism. Merton's third mode of adaptation, *ritualism,* holds little significance for the study of crime. Ritualists accept society's norms about appropriate means to reach cultural goals; for example, they hold regular jobs that produce steady incomes. However, ritualists scale down or give up cultural goals. They may keep working but realize they will never achieve material success.

Retreatism. In *retreatism,* cultural goals are abandoned and institutionalized means are also rejected. Retreatists, such as skid-row alcoholics and drug addicts, are seen as alienated dropouts from society. Their rejection of cultural goals and their unwillingness to use accepted means to reach those goals are often interpreted as a challenge to the goals most people hold. Their behavior may be regarded as immoral and criminal, even if there is no easily identified victim of their actions.

Rebellion. The final mode of adaptation is *rebellion.* Here, a person seeks to create a new social structure that will more effectively allow people to meet what the rebel considers appropriate goals. Rebels attack the value system of the ruling class and seek to replace it with an "ideal universal concept of justice" (Schafer, 1974: 30). The goals of rebels include the humanitarian treatment of all members of society; they oppose what they see as the exploitation of some groups to further the narrow interests of those who control power and wealth. Rebels have an "altruistic-communal motivation" for crime, rather than an egoistic motivation, and their offenses are directed toward nonpersonal goals. They seek to set an example for their followers and want publicity for their crimes. They pose a threat to lawmakers because they not only reject society's goals, but also propose to replace those goals with their own. Some acts of rebellion involve conventional crimes such as vandalism, burglary, arson, and murder. Other rebellious acts, such as treason and conspiracy to overthrow the government, are defined as crimes by those who control power in order to punish people who challenge the status quo (Blumberg, 1974; Schafer, 1974; Turk, 1982).

Using Criminology: Explaining Terrorism

One form of rebellion is terrorism, the use of violence to promote political change by instilling fear in innocent people. Recent studies of hundreds of terrorists around the world have cast light on the social sources and psychological makeup of terrorists. This research may eventually be useful in developing policies and treatment methods that reduce terrorism.

Terrorism often has its origin in a social and historical context in which traditional ways of life are disrupted. Often the devastating effects of war cause people to feel dislocated and anomic, leaving them open to extreme ideologies. Of those who live in such a situation, some encounter a crisis in the form of police brutality, which threatens the masculine identity of young men and embitters them. Those among this group who are best able to keep their impulses under control are especially likely to be recruited by terrorist groups. Following the commands of the terrorist group leader and developing strong ties to other members of the group are essential to carrying out terrorist acts. These aspects of the broader social structure, the historical context, and the nature of the terrorist group combine with certain childhood experiences to produce terrorists.

As children, terrorists often had a life-threatening illness, which frightened them and later led them to deny the risk of death by placing themselves in life-threatening situations, such as hijackings and commando raids. While young, these terrorists developed a sense of hopelessness mixed with a burning rage, based on their belief that nobody, not even their parents, could prevent terrible things from happening to them. Later, they became attached to an ideology that explained their feelings and presented a solution to their problems. These ideologies typically divided the world into good and evil and justified violence in the name of the good and as a way to overcome the forces of evil. In certain social and historical contexts, those with these childhood experiences were especially likely to engage in terrorist activities aimed at changing the political system.

SOURCE. Based on Daniel Goleman, "The Roots of Terrorism Are Found in Brutality of Shattered Childhood," *The New York Times,* September 4, 1986, pp. C1, C8.

CRITIQUE OF ANOMIE THEORY   Merton's anomie theory is quite general, but it has stimulated important theoretical work on the values of different groups and the availability of legitimate and illegitimate means to reach cultural goals. The theory's assumption that everyone accepts the same cultural goals and that everyone is encouraged to achieve those goals does not describe many societies very well. Even in the United States, anomie theory seems to apply primarily to the goal of financial success and to crimes against property; it does not explain crimes of violence very well. Critics also suggest that in the United States anomie theory may apply better to men than to women, because men are socialized to pursue material success as a measure of self-worth more than women are (Leonard, 1982). If this is true, then anomie theory may help us explain why men have higher crime rates than women.

Differential Opportunity and Delinquency

During the 1950s, many cities in the United States experienced juvenile gang warfare, which involved assaults and sometimes murders. Not only did gang "rumbles" provide the basis for many newspaper, radio, and television reports, but they seeped into the popular culture in plays and movies such as *West Side Story*. During this era, criminologists focused their attention on juvenile delinquency, especially gang delinquency.

The great attention to gangs during the 1950s and 1960s, and the subsequent decline in interest in gangs, seem attributable to social and political influences on what criminologists study, rather than to an increase in gang delinquency during the earlier period and a decline in more recent years. According to one perspective, gangs were of interest in the 1950s and 1960s because the dominant political ideology then was centrist and because sociological theories were interactionist and subcultural. When ideological polarization occurred during the late 1960s, criminologists began to focus either on the larger social and economic structure or on individuals, and they started to pay less attention to groups such as gangs. Gangs were largely ignored during the 1970s because of the popularity of labeling theory, which focused on status offenses and on the way that the juvenile justice system operates (Bookin-Weiner and Horowitz, 1983).

OPPORTUNITY AND GANG DELINQUENCY   One influential work on juvenile gangs is Richard Cloward and Lloyd Ohlin's *Delinquency and Opportunity: A Theory of Delinquent Gangs* (1960) Their *differential opportunity theory* combines Merton's anomie theory and Sutherland's differential association theory, a learning theory we examine in Chapter 9.

Cloward and Ohlin follow Merton in their emphasis on cultural goals and the means people use to reach those goals. Merton claims that deviance in the form of innovation occurs when people lack access to the legitimate means to reach culturally approved goals. Cloward and Ohlin add to this theory by suggesting that people's access to both legitimate and illegitimate means is socially structured. In other words, there is "differential opportunity" to reach cultural goals by legitimate means, and there is also "differential opportunity" to use illegitimate means to reach those goals.

Differential opportunity theory focuses on the discrepancy between what lower-class juveniles want and what is available to them. It assumes that the "discrepancies between aspirations and legitimate chances of achievement increase as one descends in the class structure" (Cloward and Ohlin, 1960: 86). Lower-class youths learn their goals from the larger culture and are "unable to revise their aspirations downward" (Cloward and Ohlin, 1960: 86). As a result, their lack of access to legitimate means to reach cultural goals produces intense frustration, and they search for illegitimate means to reach cultural goals. This theory is much like Merton's, except that Cloward and Ohlin go on to show how even these illegitimate means are differentially distributed in the society.

Cloward and Ohlin's theory suggests that two kinds of opportunities are differentially distributed. First, there are differences in access to "learning structures," which are the "appropriate environments for the acquisition of the values and skills associated with the performance of a particular role" (Cloward and Ohlin, 1960: 148). Sutherland's differential association theory focuses on the process by which these values and skills are learned through interaction with others; Cloward and Ohlin draw on this theory in their differential opportunity theory. Second, there are differences in access to what Cloward and Ohlin call "performance structures," the opportunity to join with others who share a similar problem of adjustment and the opportunity to gain peer approval for one's behavior. In other words, delinquents must not only learn certain values and skills, but they must also have support for the performance of delinquent behavior once they have learned those values and skills. According to differential opportunity theory, the social structure of a community determines the access that lower-class youths will have to both learning and performance structures. The way that a community is organized affects the kind of subculture, and the kind of juvenile gang, that will develop.

Criminal Gangs. *Criminal gangs* seek material gain, power, and prestige through illegitimate means such as theft. Gangs of this sort develop in communities where there are close ties between juvenile delinquents and adult criminals. Adult criminals, such as gangsters and professional thieves, transmit to young people in the neighborhood the values and skills that are important to the perpetration of crime. This is most likely to occur in stable lower-class communities where adult offenders are closely integrated with adults who hold conventional values.

Conflict Gangs. *Conflict gangs* provide a way for adolescents to achieve prestige in the eyes of their peers. When their relationships with adults in the community are weak, and when they lack access to both legitimate and illegitimate means to achieve success, juveniles may establish their own success goals (such as having a reputation for being tough) and develop their own means (such as gang fights) to achieve those goals.

Retreatist Gangs. *Retreatist gangs* are formed by juveniles who have failed to use both legitimate and illegitimate means to achieve success. These juveniles lack access to the illegitimate means used by criminal gangs, because they do not have close relationships with the adults in their community. They also lack the ability to attain prestige in a conflict gang. As a result, these juveniles abandon success goals and retreat into the use of drugs or alcohol. The drug user and the alcoholic establish life styles in which the routine of a job, commitment to convention, and self-restraint are missing. However, critics of this idea note that the daily search for heroin and the money with which to buy it involves addicts in a way of life that requires much planning, energy, and commitment (Finestone, 1964; Preble and Casey, 1972).

CRITIQUE OF DIFFERENTIAL OPPORTUNITY THEORY Cloward and Ohlin see gang delinquency as related to the goals and means of the larger society and to the organization of the local community. They suggest that the integration of people of various ages in a community influences the kind of gang delinquency in an area, but they do not explain why a single community often has several types of gangs at the same time. Critics have questioned whether the retreatist gang really exists, for addicts and alcoholics seem to be solitary more often than they are members of organized gangs.

Like Merton, Cloward and Ohlin assume that people are socialized with the desire for cultural goals but confront obstacles to reaching those goals. Cloward and Ohlin offer no evidence that lower-class gang boys are socialized to want to reach those cultural goals, and no evidence that the discrepancy between goals and legitimate means is greater for lower-class gang members than for other lower-class youths. Like Merton, Cloward and Ohlin focus on social-structural factors such as institutionalized access to opportunities, rather than on individual decisions about how to act. A better approach might be to look at the way people actually use available opportunities or seek out opportunities, as well as focus on differences in the socially structured opportunities available to different groups.

In spite of its shortcomings, Cloward and Ohlin's differential opportunity theory has been an important contribution to the study of delinquency. It has also influenced social policies, such as those of the Great Society programs of the 1960s, that have tried to reduce crime and delinquency by increasing the legitimate opportunities available to the lower classes.

Class, Values, and Delinquency

Very closely related to Merton's and to Cloward and Ohlin's social-structural theories of delinquency are social-psychological theories that emphasize class differences in values and responses to blocked opportunities. Two important theories of this sort are Albert Cohen's (1955) reaction-formation theory and Walter Miller's (1958) theory of lower-class culture.

REACTION-FORMATION THEORY In *Delinquent Boys,* Albert Cohen (1955: 25) develops a theory to explain why a juvenile delinquent subculture that he characterizes as "nonutilitarian, malicious, and negativistic" is found among working-class male adolescents. Cohen sees delinquency as a collective solution to a shared problem: blocked opportunities to achieve cultural goals. However, he is concerned only with certain kinds of delinquency: gang wars and vandalism, rather than profit-oriented theft.

Cohen describes the dominant American values in much the same way Merton does: striving for success through hard work and discipline, deferring gratification, being ambitious, maintaining hope for the future, relying on oneself rather than on others, using individual skills to get ahead, respecting property, and controlling violence and aggression. Cohen claims that working-class adolescent males pick up these values from their parents, who share middle-class values even though they are members of the working class. Adolescents also learn middle-class values from the mass media and from former members of the working class who have entered the middle class. In addition, schools are important sources of middle-class values. Teachers communicate middle-class values and often come from the middle class themselves, and schools are organized around middle-class values such as discipline and self-reliance. According to Cohen, working-class adolescents are at a disadvantage in school, for their background does not equip them for academic success in this middle-class setting. Because they are too young to form a family or to hold a job that pays well, working-class adolescents lack legitimate opportunities to achieve culturally approved goals.

Working-class male adolescents share a problem of adjustment because of the double burden of class and youth. This shared condition is conducive to the development of a group solution to their common problem. They define their predicament in similar terms and have ample opportunity to interact. Often they band together in groups that define goals that they can achieve.

Because they are emotionally attached to middle-class goals they cannot attain, these working-class boys must repudiate those goals. This produces a *reaction-formation,* a reversal of middle-class values. For instance, the middle class favors the control of aggression, so the working-class male adolescent subculture awards prestige for the use of violence. The middle class reveres property, so the working-class gang values the senseless destruction of property. This reaction-formation is a psychological defense against the failure to achieve strongly held desires. Seeking the exact opposite of what is valued by the middle class is a way to repudiate those goals and validate the goals that replace them. The new goals increase solidarity among the working-class boys by making the middle class a common enemy.

Cohen thus links a particular class (the working class) to specific values (aggressiveness and destructiveness) that, in turn, cause certain kinds of law-violating behavior (gang fights and vandalism). The type of delinquency Cohen is interested in thus originates from a repudiation of middle-class values, rather than from conformity to working-class values.

Critique of Reaction-Formation Theory. Cohen's theory, like Merton's, requires a culture that encourages everyone to strive for the same goals, especially material success. We can see in the Cross-Cultural Perspective that Argentina is one society in which Cohen's theory does not work very well; little "nonutilitarian, malicious, and negativistic" working-class delinquency occurs there, apparently because the lowest classes are not socialized to seek middle-class goals.

Cohen's reaction-formation theory does not explain middle-class delinquency very well. Neither does it explain why some delinquents turn away from violations of the law and leave gangs as they grow older, and other delinquents move on to adult crime. Cohen's emphasis on age explains why some males move out of delinquency as they gain access to other sources of prestige such as jobs and

A Cross-Cultural Perspective: Delinquency in Argentina

To test the usefulness of Albert Cohen's reaction-formation theory of delinquency, Lois DeFleur studied boys who had violated the law and appeared in court in Córdoba, Argentina, a city of 600,000 people.

Contrary to Cohen's theory that much theft by working-class adolescent males would be nonutilitarian, DeFleur found that Córdoban boys who appeared in court sold the stolen goods or personally used them in about 80 percent of their thefts. For these boys, stealing was a means to get money and goods, rather than a nonutilitarian activity as in Cohen's theory.

DeFleur found little evidence that delinquency in Argentina was malicious, the second element in Cohen's theory. "Malicious jokes or tricks, senseless vandalism, and unprovoked assaults on others" were relatively uncommon among the Argentine boys.

DeFleur also found little evidence for the third element of Cohen's reaction-formation subculture, negativism. There was no clear evidence that the Argentine boys were expressing hostility toward people who had more property. They did envy them, wanted to have their possessions, and expressed scorn for people who worked hard, but they did not show "open animosity" toward the middle or upper classes, nor did they deliberately flout authority.

In sum, DeFleur found little evidence of a reaction-formation subculture in Córdoba. At most, there were scattered indicators of such a subculture, and even these occurred infrequently.

DeFleur did find juvenile street gangs in Córdoba. Most of them engaged in the theft of property, which was usually sold to adults. There were traditional neighborhood rivalries and gang fights, but fighting was not the gang's primary reason for existence. There was little drug use by gang members, for drugs were too expensive for these poor boys. The gangs in Córdoba represented an instrumental-theft subculture; theft was a way to pursue pleasure, not an end in itself, as it was in Cohen's reaction-formation theory.

Cohen's theory did not fit the experience of the Argentine boys very well because their culture does not emphasize success and status striving for everyone. Latin countries are more often characterized by a rigid class structure that encourages people to keep to their inherited station in life. Cohen's theory, on the other hand, requires a strong commitment to achievement and upward mobility. In Argentina, status striving is a recent development, and one that has not yet filtered down to the lower classes. In other words, there is no cultural theme of equal opportunity shared by all of the classes in Argentina, and this is an essential ingredient of Cohen's theory of gang delinquency.

SOURCE. Based on Lois B. DeFleur, *Delinquency in Argentina: A Study of Córdoba's Youth*. Pullman: Washington State University Press, 1970.

families, but his emphasis on class does not tell us why most delinquents give up illegal behavior even though they remain members of the working class.

LOWER-CLASS CULTURE THEORY   Contrary to Cohen's theory that nonutilitarian, working-class male delinquency has its roots in the rejection of traditional middle-class values is the position of Walter Miller (1958). Miller proposes that gang delinquency in lower-class communities is a result of positive efforts by adolescents to achieve goals that are spelled out in lower-class *focal concerns,* or areas of interest that elicit widespread, persistent attention and emotional involvement.

The focal concern of "trouble" refers to situations that bring unwelcome or complicating involvement with official authority. Issues of staying out of trouble and getting into trouble are of daily concern to the lower class, according to Miller. The lower class avoids illegal behavior, he says, in order to keep out of trouble, rather than because it is committed to a law-abiding way of life. The lower class seeks to avoid violating the law, but at the same time may admire those who violate the law.

A second focal concern is "toughness," a concern with masculinity, physical prowess, bravery, and daring. A third is "smartness," the capacity to outwit or "con" others and avoid being duped oneself. Through clever verbal exchanges, lower-class youths can achieve prestige by demonstrating maximum use of their mental abilities and minimum use of their physical strength. There is an apparent contradiction here, for toughness can inhibit the display of smartness, and smartness can inhibit the display of toughness; both, however, are of concern to the lower class, according to Miller.

Another focal concern of lower-class culture is "excitement," the concern with thrills, risks, and the avoidance of boredom. The life of the poor may be unstimulating because of the lack of money with which to pay for leisure goods and activities, and this may be a source of the lower class's interest in exciting activities. Indeed, a study of teenage gangs earlier in this century concluded that avoidance of boredom was a major reason for gang delinquency (Thrasher, 1927, 1963). The search for excitement can also lead to gambling and to the use of alcohol and narcotics.

Another focal concern of the lower class is "fate," an interest in luck, fortune, and jinxes. The poor often feel, and with some justification, that their lives are governed by external forces over which they have little or no control. Related to this concern with external control is a sixth focal concern, "autonomy." This refers to a desire to be one's own master, which is often expressed as "no one's going to push me around."

Miller's Lower-Class Focal Concerns

1. Trouble   4. Excitement
2. Toughness   5. Fate
3. Smartness   6. Autonomy

Critique of Lower-Class Culture Theory. Miller sees the gang as a social setting within which juveniles can gain prestige by acting in accordance with the focal concerns of their class. This theory might lead us to believe that all members of the lower class, even adults, will violate the law regularly, for the theory does not distinguish between offenders and nonoffenders from the lower class in terms of their focal concerns. In addition, Miller does not explain the origins of these focal concerns. In contrast to Miller, Cohen is concerned with the sources of the values and norms of working-class male adolescents. He treats their delinquency as deviance from middle-class values, rather than as conformity to lower-class values. Cohen and Miller diverge in their explanations of delinquency, but both examine the role of values that are linked to class.

AN EVALUATION OF DELINQUENCY THEORIES James Short, Jr., and Fred Strodtbeck (1965) have tested the theories of Cloward and Ohlin, Cohen, and Miller. They gathered data from boys between sixteen and eighteen who belonged to gangs ("gang boys"), lower-class boys of the same age who did not belong to gangs ("lower-class boys"), and middle-class boys who did not belong to gangs ("middle-class boys").

Short and Strodtbeck found little empirical support for any of the theories of delinquency. The three groups of boys all evaluated middle-class values equally highly, and all three groups evaluated middle-class values more highly than "nearly all other subcultural images, especially those that are unquestionably illegitimate" (Short and Strodtbeck, 1965: 59). They also found that neither the gang boys nor the lower-class boys evaluated lower-class values significantly more highly than they did middle-class values. None of the theories would have predicted these results, suggesting that these theories are inaccurate or incomplete.

Short and Strodtbeck found that gang boys evaluated behavior in much the same way as nondelinquents of the lower class did and in much the same way as middle-class boys did. All three groups accepted what middle-class norms prescribed or recommended. There were, however, differences in their evaluation of things that middle-class values proscribed or disapproved. Goals approved by middle-class values were meaningful to all three groups of boys, but the gang boys were more tolerant of theft and violence, which were proscribed by middle-class standards. The values of the gang boys thus *allowed rather than required* delinquent behavior. Boys became delinquent because they lacked commitment to conformity, rather than because they accepted norms that forced them to violate the law (Short and Strodtbeck, 1965: 72–76; also, see Briar and Piliavin, 1965).

One way to interpret Short and Strodtbeck's conclusion that there was no difference between delinquents and nondelinquents in prescribed norms, but that there was a difference in proscribed norms, is to assume the gang boys did not condemn theft and violence because they had been improperly socialized. However, the fact that they shared many values with middle-class boys is evidence that they had been socialized in a way similar to middle-class boys. The gang boys' acceptance of behavior disapproved by middle-class values may better be seen as a difference in values rather than as a lack of values.

DELINQUENCY AND VALUES   Class by itself does not cause crime and delinquency. Instead, violation of the law is a result of factors associated with class, such as values, goals, and socially structured opportunities. We would thus expect delinquents from all classes to have certain values, goals, and opportunities in common, and also to differ from nondelinquents of all classes in those factors.

One study that looked at lower-class, middle-class, and upper-class delinquency tried to explain youthful misbehavior in terms other than class. The researcher found that commitment to values such as short-run pleasure seeking, thrills, excitement, trouble, toughness, conning, and the search for a "fast buck" was associated with self-reported involvement in delinquency, and this was true for all classes. This study also revealed less commitment to conventional value orientations such as hard work, delayed gratification, formal education, and various themes of the Protestant ethic among boys of all classes who engaged in delinquency (Cernkovich, 1978c). This research suggests that class is a less important predictor of delinquency than values, and that values are imperfectly correlated with class.

There is reason to believe that some people are able to violate the law because they can "stretch values" (Hyman, 1966). These individuals may share values with the middle class and the law-abiding, but because of weak attachments to family, school, and work, they believe they have little to lose from violating the law. They may thus be more flexible in interpreting social constraints on their behavior. For instance, one middle-class value is respect for property; the related norm is that property should not be stolen, damaged, or used without the owner's permission. This norm is adhered to by most people, but some people are able to stretch the norm by reinterpreting it to define a purse on an office desk as property that can be stolen because the owner was careless enough to leave it unattended. The stretching of norms to permit violation of the law probably occurs among members of all classes, including poor people who shoplift and wealthy executives who engage in price-fixing conspiracies.

Short and Strodtbeck (1965: 248–264) suggest a similar interpretation of their finding that all three groups of boys in their study supported prescribed middle-class values, but that gang boys held different attitudes toward acts proscribed by these values. They propose that some lower-class males may find it more practical to be deviant in certain situations. These boys may react to situational pressures in ways that allow them to neutralize norms prohibiting certain behavior. Because American society lacks rites of passage, or formal processes, by which adolescents enter adulthood, some adolescents experiment with various forms of "adult" behavior. In these circumstances, it may be rational for boys to break the law if that behavior allows them to gain prestige among their friends. Short and Strodtbeck argue that if there is a small chance of serious consequences such as arrest, and a great chance to gain prestige from fighting or theft, it makes sense for gang boys to violate the law. The payoff in social approval is immediate, but punishment is uncertain and remote in time.

Juvenile Gangs Today

Since the mid-1960s, there has been relatively little theoretical or empirical work on delinquent gangs, compared with the efforts expended on gangs during the decade from 1955 to 1965. However, gangs continue to thrive in many American cities and have even developed in many smaller communities. For instance, Walter Miller has identified 2,200 gangs with about 96,000 members in 300 communities (cited in *The Boston Globe,* July 10, 1981).

One city that has experienced major problems with gang delinquency is Los Angeles, which in 1986 had over 400 gangs with a total of about 50,000 members. In that year, there were about 200 gang-related homicides. Gangs have existed in Los Angeles since the 1920s, but they have increased significantly in number and membership in the late 1970s and early 1980s. One explanation is that Hispanic and Southeast Asian immigrants have banded together for self-defense and to provide the social ties that families traditionally have provided. Some black and Hispanic groups in Los Angeles are involved in drug dealing; they act as entrepreneurs interested in profit rather than as retreatists. Vietnamese gangs in Los Angeles specialize in the extortion of "protection money" from merchants. In the mid-1980s, participation in gangs increased among white, middle-class youths from the suburbs of Los Angeles, with some of these gangs holding white supremacist philosophies and some taking part in Satanic rituals.

Gangs traditionally have focused on protection of their "turf," an area of the city they define as theirs. Gangs often organize along militaristic lines to protect their neighborhood from "invaders"; people have been killed just for venturing into "enemy territory." In communities where arson has razed entire blocks in recent years, turf has become a less important basis for gang solidarity. One police officer has said, "There is no land to fight over. In many of the poor neighborhoods of the city, turf consists of a block full of abandoned buildings" (cited in Chambers, 1983). In the 1980s, the emphasis has shifted from protection of turf to competition for the illegal-drug market, with gangs now fighting and killing to control the sale of drugs in a community.

FEMALES IN GANGS Females who belong to juvenile gangs are outnumbered by male participants by perhaps twenty to one. Usually these females belong to predominantly male gangs, but sometimes they form all-female gangs. These young women live in a contradictory world, fighting and stealing but holding the traditional values of wanting a husband and children. These women typically come from broken homes, are members of minority groups, and live in ghettos. They join gangs for a sense of belonging and to meet men they might marry. These men treat "their" women as subordinates, but at the same time take pride in their fighting and stealing skills. The females fight to protect their turf or to defend another gang member, as is the case with males. An unwritten rule limits fights to those of the same sex. Fights involving women tend to erupt quickly and end quickly, and usually involve fingernails, teeth, and knives rather than the firearms and crowbars favored by the men (Campbell, 1984; *The New York Times,* January 2, 1986).

The Subculture of Violence

One theory of the origin of violent crime that uses norms and values as explanatory variables is the *subculture-of-violence theory* developed by Marvin Wolfgang and Franco Ferracuti (1967, 1982). They state that the norms shared by a group of people may define violence as an appropriate response to certain circumstances. They claim that these norms have a reality of their own and that they influence behavior, sometimes leading people to engage in violent crime in order to conform to others' expectations (Della Fave, 1974). Wolfgang and Ferracuti do not explore the historical and social-structural origins of these norms in detail, but they imply that the norms originate in the social conditions of certain countries, classes, and racial and ethnic groups. Because the theory is presented as a cultural explanation of violent crime, rather than as a social-structural explanation, Wolfgang and Ferracuti emphasize norms, values, and beliefs rather than the specific social conditions that give rise to a subculture of violence.

Wolfgang and Ferracuti claim that there are identifiable subcultures in which violence and aggression are regarded as a proper response to threats, insults, or the display of a weapon. A *subculture* is a patterned way of life similar in some ways to but different in others from the dominant culture of a society. It includes specific standards of behavior that are learned and transmitted from generation to generation. In a subculture of violence, these norms differ from those of the dominant culture in expectations about the use of interpersonal aggression. As a result, the more integrated into a subculture of violence an individual or a group is, the greater the likelihood that the individual or group will engage in violent crime. Violence in such a subculture is rarely accompanied by guilt, because violence is not considered wrong or deviant. Violent individuals in a subcultural setting such as this are not pathological, but instead are conformists to the values of their group.

EVIDENCE ON THE SUBCULTURE OF VIOLENCE Wolfgang's study of homicide in Philadelphia found evidence consistent with the subculture-of-violence theory. Forty-three percent of the homicide offenders had been arrested previously for crimes against the person, and about one-fourth of the homicide victims had been arrested for crimes against the person (Wolfgang, 1958: 178). Whites had a murder rate of 1.8 per 100,000, and white males between twenty and twenty-four had a rate of 8.2 per 100,000. Blacks, on the other hand, had a murder rate of 24.6 per 100,000, and black males between twenty and twenty-four had a homicide rate of 92.5 per 100,000 (Wolfgang, 1958: 33, 66). The homicide rate for young black males was thus much higher than the rate for any

other group. Wolfgang and Ferracuti later interpreted these and other data —
such as Colombia's pattern of *la violencia,* in which 280,000 people were killed
from 1946 to 1958 — as support for their theory that among certain groups and
in certain nations there exist norms favoring the use of interpersonal violence.

There is other evidence that a subculture of violence may exist among black
Americans. One study of fifty black offenders found that about 70 percent of
them carried firearms because they anticipated attacks by others; this defensive
posture could lead to crimes of violence (Schultz, 1962). There is also some
evidence that blacks are more likely than whites to engage in angry fistfights,
even though blacks do not report that they feel group support for this activity.
The value that blacks place on "staying cool" leads to more talk about fighting
than actual fighting (Erlanger, 1974). Evidence contradictory to the idea that
there is a subculture of violence among black Americans comes from a study that
found that although whites commit less homicide than blacks, whites are more
likely to report that they own firearms, are more likely to have been assaulted,
and are more tolerant of assaultive behavior (Doerner, 1978).

HOMICIDE IN THE SOUTH: TESTING FOR A SUBCULTURE OF VIOLENCE Several criminologists have tried to explain differences between the homicide rates
of southern states and the homicide rate of the rest of the country in terms of a
subculture of violence (Hackney, 1969; Gastil, 1971; Loftin and Hill, 1974;
Erlanger, 1975; O'Connor and Lizotte, 1978; Messner, 1982, 1983a, 1983b).
In Chapter 5, we saw that southern states have homicide rates higher than other
regions, even though homicide rates in different parts of the country have
become more similar in recent years. However, the South does not have especially high rates of other violent crimes.

The methodology usually employed to test the effect of cultural values on the
homicide rates of different regions is to isolate the effects of economic and social
factors on homicide rates, and then attribute the remaining variation in regional
homicide rates to cultural differences, such as the norms of the subculture of
violence. The problem with this approach is that it includes no direct measure
of regional variations in norms and values. As a result, if the measurement of economic and social factors is inadequate or incomplete, the residual
effect of cultural factors may be exaggerated. One study concluded that the
economic, educational, and racial composition of the states was relatively unimportant in explaining regional variations in homicide rates, and suggested that a
subculture of violence explained such variations (Hackney, 1969). However, a
later study that employed a more sophisticated measure of poverty found that
poverty explained much of the state-by-state variation in homicide rates (Loftin
and Hill, 1974). Thus an index that better measured poverty left a smaller
residual variation in homicide rates that could be attributed to the subculture of
violence.

One study found that the homicide rates of 204 metropolitan areas in the
United States were influenced by the region in which the city was located and by
its racial composition, even when factors such as poverty were controlled

(Messner, 1983a). In other words, the higher homicide rates in the southern cities, and also in the cities with larger black populations, could not be accounted for by low income alone. However, this study, like most previous ones, provided no direct measure of subcultural values and perspectives.

The precise role of the subculture of violence in explaining regional variations in homicide rates is still unclear. The high rate of firearms ownership and the widespread opposition to gun-control laws in the South, along with that area's military tradition, history of lynching, and aggressive defense of womanhood, suggest to some sociologists that attitudes in southern states toward the use of violence might differ from attitudes in other regions. However, the South differs little from other regions in the ownership of handguns, the weapon most often used in crime. Instead, the South's higher rate of firearms ownership is due to regional differences in the ownership of rifles and shotguns, which are rarely used to kill people (Wright, Rossi, and Daly, 1983).

Another indirect kind of evidence cited as an indication of the greater tolerance of violence in the South is the fact that all southern states now have capital punishment, and that most of the people on Death Row and most of the people who have been executed in recent years are in southern states. One sociologist has commented that "both murder and the death penalty reflect mostly the extent to which there exists a subculture in which killing is considered a morally obligatory response to a large range of rebuff or disagreement, outweighing the moral tenet that all life is sacred" (Glaser, 1971: 57).

One reason for the high homicide rate of blacks throughout the country might be that many of them, or their parents, were brought up in the South, where they learned norms and values conducive to violence. With migration from the South, those norms and values might have become diffused throughout the country (Pettigrew and Spier, 1962). There are obviously many causes of violent crime in the United States, but the diffusion of a subculture of violence that has a southern origin might be one such cause.

CRITIQUE OF THE SUBCULTURE-OF-VIOLENCE THEORY   Some groups, regions, and countries do have high rates of criminal violence, but there is as yet no strong evidence supporting a role for the subculture of violence in the genesis of violent crime. This may be because the appropriate research design to test for this relationship has not been developed or implemented. Some researchers have inferred norms and attitudes supporting the use of violence from the high rates of violent crime among certain groups, and then explained those high rates of violent crime by the inferred norms and attitudes. This tautological approach provides no independent evidence that norms and attitudes supporting violence exist among groups that have high rates of violent crime.

We also have no direct evidence that southerners hold the values of a subculture of violence (Reed, 1971; Ball-Rokeach, 1973; Curtis, 1975). More research on cultural differences among regions of the country might be done by carrying out surveys or by examining regional variations in preferences for art, literature, music, or sports (Messner, 1983a). Even if such regional variations were found, they might not explain differences in rates of violent crime, for one study concluded that violence is more an outcome of the nature of social interaction in certain groups than a result of norms and values about when violence is appropriate (Ball-Rokeach, 1973).

Socioeconomic Factors and Variations in Crime Rates

The social, economic, and cultural factors examined in this chapter help us to make sense of the variations in crime rates that we looked at in Chapter 5.

Cross-national variations in crime rates seem to be due to differences among countries in social structure, economy, and culture. For instance, some white-collar crimes are more likely to occur in certain kinds of economies; thus, price fixing occurs in the American economy as businesspeople try to enhance profits, and bribery by consumers is more common in the Soviet Union where goods and services are in short supply. The degree to which a society relies on laws to make widely desired goods and services illegal influences the development and strength of organized crime in the society. Variations in rates of conventional crime from one society to another are attributable in part to the level of economic development, the extent of relative deprivation, and the opportunities that are available to achieve culturally approved goals.

Just as cross-national variations in crime rates can be explained by differences in the social structure, economy, and culture of a country, so regional variations can also be explained by similar differences among areas within a country. The subculture-of-violence theory proposes that variations in violent crime can be explained by regional differences in norms and attitudes toward violence, but we lack strong supporting evidence for this theory.

Variations in crime rates by size of the community may also be related to the factors examined in this chapter. For example, the economic conditions characteristic of urban communities differ from the economic conditions in small towns and rural areas, and these differences may explain in part the higher crime rates of larger communities. In addition, the close proximity of people from different classes in large communities may increase relative deprivation among the poor and lead to more conventional crime than occurs in the relatively more homogeneous small towns and rural areas.

Temporal variations in crime rates can be accounted for by changes in the social structure, the economy, and the culture. Changes in market conditions can lead to an increase or a decrease in white-collar crime. Technological breakthroughs and a growing reliance on trust and credit create new opportunities for white-collar crime. The passage of laws that prohibit the consumption of widely desired goods and services results in more opportunities for organized crime; this happened during Prohibition, and again more recently with the development of strict controls on the disposal of toxic wastes. The modernization process leads to changes in rates of conventional crime, especially rates of property crime. Conventional crimes also increase or decrease as groups experience relative deprivation, anomie, and blocked opportunities.

Variations in crime rates by sex, age, race, and class are also related to the social structure, the economy, and the culture. For example, most white-collar crimes are committed by middle-aged or older white men of the middle or upper classes. The time needed to advance to the positions in which white-collar crime is committed means that white-collar offenders are usually middle-aged or older. White-collar offenders are usually white men, because discrimination by sex and race has closed many higher-level positions in corporations to women and minorities. As such discrimination is reduced, we would expect more white-collar crimes to be committed by women and minorities.

Anomie theory, differential opportunity theory, reaction-formation theory, and the theory that lower-class culture is a generating milieu of gang delinquency all account for the higher rates of serious and repetitive conventional crime among the lower and working classes. These theories help to account for the high rate of crime by young people, for these people are the most remote from the cultural goal of material success and are probably the most likely to encounter blocked opportunities. These social-structural theories also account for the high crime rates of blacks, who have had opportunities to achieve material success blocked by racial discrimination. The subculture-of-violence theory proposes that blacks' high rate of violent crime is due to a difference between their norms and attitudes toward violence and whites' norms and attitudes toward violence, but there is no strong and consistent evidence that this is so. Social-structural theories of crime and delinquency do not seem to do a good job of explaining low crime rates for females; in some cases, these theories were specifically designed to explain violations by males. We might expect that the blocked opportunities encountered by women would lead them to commit crime at a higher rate than men, but this is not the case. This may be because men more than women are socialized to pursue the cultural goal of material success and are thus more likely to turn to crime when they do not reach that goal.

We have not looked at all of the ways in which the social, economic, and cultural factors examined in this chapter can explain geographic, temporal, and social variations in rates of white-collar, organized, and conventional crime. From this brief discussion, however, we can see that social, economic, and cultural theories are useful in explaining variations in crime rates.

Summary

In this chapter we have examined the social and economic causes of white-collar crime, organized crime, and conventional crime (with an emphasis on juvenile delinquency).

American free-enterprise ideology emphasizes profit seeking and competition. The pressure to make profits sometimes leads executives and corporations to violate the law, and efforts to outperform competitors can lead to offenses such as false advertising. Certain market conditions are conducive to white-collar crime. Trust and credit may be abused, as was the case in the Equity Funding

Corporation of America fraud. Large corporations have characteristics such as bureaucratic structure, unsatisfactory working conditions, and rational decision making that are conducive to white-collar crime and employee theft. As new technology develops, opportunities are created for crime; computer crime is one example of a costly offense that has become a problem in recent years.

Prohibition provided an opportunity for gangsters to become highly organized in their pursuit of profits. Since Prohibition ended in 1933, organized crime has turned to other sources of income, including gambling (according to some accounts), loan sharking, narcotics, bankruptcy fraud, the illegal disposal of toxic wastes, and extortion.

Conventional crimes, especially property crimes, increase with economic development. Modernization also brings increased participation in crime by juveniles and by women. New opportunities for crime develop as an economy modernizes, and changes in the value of certain goods (such as precious metals) may alter patterns of crime. Employment may be more important for the social ties it provides than for the income it produces, although there is little evidence of a strong association between the unemployment rate and the crime rate. One source of criminal behavior is relative deprivation, a situation that exists when people believe they are entitled to more than they can achieve by the legitimate means available to them.

Anomic theory proposes that a disjunction between cultural goals and access to legitimate means to attain those goals can lead to certain kinds of crime. Innovation occurs among those who strongly pursue cultural goals with means that are not socially approved; examples include petty theft by the poor and price fixing by corporate executives. Retreatists and rebels are often defined as criminals by those who control power.

Differential opportunity theory emphasizes access to both legitimate and illegitimate means to reach cultural goals. The social structure of a community affects access by lower-class youth to both learning and performance structures. As a result, the kind of gang that delinquents form — criminal, conflict, or retreatist — depends on the relationship of young people to adult criminals and the relationship of adult criminals to conventional adults in a community.

Reaction-formation theory proposes that working-class male adolescents learn middle-class values but, because they are not equipped to succeed in school and at work, they reject these values and create values opposite to them. These new values support violence and the theft and destruction of property, and this leads to "nonutilitarian, malicious, and negativistic" behavior.

The theory that delinquents react against middle-class values differs from the theory that the lower class is a generating milieu for gang delinquency. In this lower-class culture theory, delinquency is seen as a kind of conformity to the values or focal concerns of the lower class: trouble, toughness, smartness, excitement, fate, and autonomy.

A study that evaluated differential opportunity theory, reaction-formation theory, and lower-class culture theory found little support for any of them. Instead, gang boys seemed to favor the goals of the middle class but did not feel bound to avoid deviance from middle-class norms. Delinquents seemed to be able to "stretch" values, and they often had more to gain in peer prestige from violating the law than they had to lose from such behavior.

The subculture-of-violence theory proposes that among certain groups and in certain areas there is a set of norms that support violent responses to certain situations. Some groups, such as urban blacks in the United States, and some regions, such as the South, do have high rates of criminal violence. However, there is no strong evidence that these groups and regions have distinctive norms and attitudes that support violence, or that such norms and attitudes lead to violent crime.

The social, economic, and cultural factors we have looked at in this chapter are helpful in explaining geographic, temporal, and social variations in different kinds of crime.

Important Terms

anomie	mode of adaptation
computer crime	reaction-formation
conflict gang	rebellion
conformity	relative deprivation
criminal gang	retreatism
differential opportunity theory	retreatist gang
EFT crime	ritualism
focal concern	subculture
innovation	subculture-of-violence theory

Suggested Readings

MARSHALL B. CLINARD AND PETER C. YEAGER. *Corporate Crime.* New York: Free Press, 1980. An analysis of antitrust offenses, false advertising, bribery, tax evasion, and the production of unsafe products by American corporations.

RICHARD A. CLOWARD AND LLOYD E. OHLIN. *Delinquency and Opportunity: A Theory of Delinquent Gangs.* New York: Free Press, 1960. An important theoretical statement of differential opportunity theory.

JAMES W. COLEMAN. *The Criminal Elite: The Sociology of White Collar Crime.* New York: St. Martin's Press, 1985. A well-written text that looks at the causes and kinds of organizational and occupational white-collar crime, paying special attention to the law and how it is enforced.

PETER REUTER. *Disorganized Crime: The Economics of the Visible Hand.* Cambridge, Mass.: MIT Press, 1983. A study that calls into question some of the conventional wisdom on the activities and power of organized crime in the United States.

MARVIN E. WOLFGANG AND FRANCO FERRACUTI. *The Subculture of Violence: Towards an Integrated Theory in Criminology.* Beverly Hills, Calif.: Sage Publications, 1967, 1982. An important theoretical statement of the subculture-of-violence theory.

CHAPTER 8

Social Control and Commitment to the Law

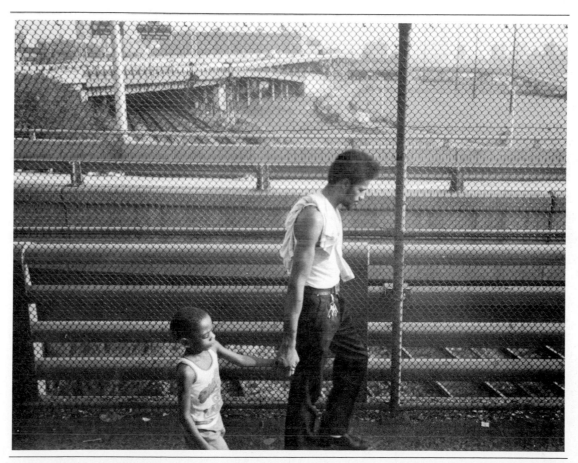

Source: Roswell Angier / Archive Pictures

Because most people learn to abide by the law, or are at least aware that the law commands widespread respect, they can engage in crime or delinquency only after they have minimized their commitment to the law. People neutralize the power of the law by justifying their offenses to themselves and to others. People who are weakly attached to conventional institutions are already relatively free to violate the law. In this chapter, we explore the ways that neutralization of the law and the absence of social control lead to crime and delinquency.

Neutralizing the Law

The theories of anomie, differential opportunity, reaction-formation, and lower-class culture that we have examined all suggest that social forces push some juveniles into delinquency. A contrasting perspective is that delinquents exercise some free will, choosing to violate the law rather than being forced to do so by the social structure. According to this view, delinquents do not hold values that are diametrically opposed to dominant values, as reaction-formation theory suggests, nor are they members of delinquent subcultures that require them to violate the law, as differential opportunity theory and reaction-formation theory imply (Matza and Sykes, 1961; Matza, 1964).

Drift

David Matza (1964) proposes that some adolescents are in a state of *drift*, a condition of limbo between a conventional life style and a criminal life style with no strong attachment to either. Juveniles drift into delinquency in an almost accidental and unpredictable way through their exercise of personal choice. Becoming delinquent involves neither a compulsion to deviate nor the complete freedom to choose how to behave. Matza does not say why juveniles continue to engage in delinquency over time, nor does he indicate why they are drawn to delinquency in the first place. In other words, he does not specify the rewards of delinquent behavior.

In describing everyday delinquency rather than explaining its causes, Matza returns to the ideas of the classical school of criminology, particularly free will. He suggests that one motive for delinquency is existential in nature: Adolescents need to "make things happen" to assure themselves of their existence and their mastery over the world. For some adolescents, delinquency involves less risk of failure, and more potential gains, than schoolwork or athletics.

Delinquent, Dominant, and Subterranean Values

Part of the attractiveness of delinquency for juveniles may be that it has much in common with the leisure activities of the dominant classes. Rather than see society as split into various strata with different norms and values—as do Cloward and Ohlin, Cohen, and Miller—Matza and Sykes (1961) examine contradictions within the dominant value system. Thus, the dominant or middle-class value system exhorts people to work hard and defer gratification, but it also encourages them to seek excitement and go on occasional sprees. The search for adventure is best regarded not as a deviant value but as a *subterranean value* in the dominant value system. In other words, the value is subordinate or below the surface in the dominant value system and is sought by most people only occasionally and in appropriate circumstances. Delinquents can then be seen as people who act in accordance with subterranean values in inappropriate circumstances. For instance, vandalism is tolerated, within limits, on Halloween, but people who destroy property at other times may be labeled delinquent. Matza and Sykes (1961: 717) see the delinquent not as alien to society, but as "a disturbing reflection or a caricature" of society's values. The delinquent's "vocabulary is different, to be sure, but kicks, big-time spending, and rep have immediate counterparts in the value system of the law-abiding" (Matza and Sykes, 1961: 717). The motivational thrust behind delinquent behavior is thus normal and derived directly from conventional morality.

Evidence that delinquents have a strong bond to dominant values is the fact that they often express respect for law-abiding citizens. If delinquents held values opposed to dominant ones, they probably would regard law-abiding behavior as incorrect or immoral. Their recognition of the moral validity of dominant values suggests an attachment to the larger culture, even if that bond is broken at times.

The fact that delinquents often are selective in choosing targets for their offenses is additional evidence that they recognize the dominant morality. Theft and violence by delinquents often are directed against people who are held in low social regard, such as prostitutes, alcoholics, or other delinquents. This suggests that delinquents can distinguish victims of whom the larger society approves from victims who would elicit negative reactions.

Techniques of Neutralization

Social norms that define expected or appropriate behavior for particular situations often lack specificity as to how and when they apply. In other words, norms have flexibility and act only as "qualified guides for action" (Sykes and Matza, 1957: 666). Thus, a norm that theft is wrong may be qualified so that theft is tolerated—or even actually encouraged—if one is hungry or needs to feed one's starving children, if theft is from another criminal, or if theft is from a large and impersonal corporation (Jones, 1941, 1964; Smigel, 1956).

Individuals can avoid moral blame and maintain self-esteem while violating the law if they tell themselves and others that they had no criminal intent or that their behavior was justified. People who have accepted the law as legitimate find it difficult to launch frontal assaults on dominant norms, and so they remove the constraints of the law by justifying their behavior in some way. These justifications, which Sykes and Matza call *techniques of neutralization*, are tangential blows against dominant norms and help to render inoperative the social controls that would otherwise check law-violating behavior, enabling but not requiring people to break the law (Minor, 1981). These justifications make it possible for people to commit crime and delinquency without serious damage to their self-image. Deviance such as this has been described as apologetic rather than oppositional deviance (Sykes and Matza, 1957: 667).

The five techniques of neutralization that Sykes and Matza look at are used prior to violation of the law to allow an offender who otherwise accepts the moral validity of the law to break it. Rationalizations may also occur after the crime, but there is less need to justify a crime that has already been committed than to neutralize the law that would have blocked the individual from committing the crime in the first place.

DENIAL OF RESPONSIBILITY   One technique of neutralization is the _denial of responsibility_, a denial by an individual of personal responsibility for his or her own actions. People may claim that a criminal or delinquent act was an accident or assert that it was caused by factors beyond their control, such as negligent parents, wayward friends, a broken home, or poverty. Those who use this technique often feel acted upon by others and by the social environment, rather than in control of their own lives. Other people may avoid crime and delinquency because they accept personal responsibility for their own behavior. When asked why he had not become a criminal, one nonoffender said: "I was given a certain amount of responsibility and learned to become responsible, and accept the fact that I was accountable for my actions" (cited in Rogers, 1977: 91).

Crime is also justified by this technique in other societies. For instance, in the Soviet Union, where the theft of socialist (state-owned) property is legally regarded as a more serious crime than the theft of private property, the public nevertheless sees the theft of socialist property as "innocent and normal behavior" (Chalidze, 1977: 190). Soviet citizens sometimes justify their theft of state property by denying responsibility, pointing to the way the failures of the state economy have forced them to steal: "If I could get it in the stores, I wouldn't steal it at work" or "There are lots of things the State fails to provide, so we have to take them for ourselves" (Chalidze, 1977: 190).

To the extent that the positivist approach to the explanation of criminal behavior has seeped into the popular culture, it may be used to deny responsibility. Sociological research that shows a link between violation of the law and factors such as poverty or minority status can be used by delinquents and criminals to argue that those factors forced them to violate the law, thereby absolving them of personal responsibility for their actions.

Walter Miller (1974) has said that the civil rights movement of the 1950s added a "justificatory vocabulary" to traditional explanations for gang activity and other kinds of juvenile delinquency. Gang behavior was not much different in the 1960s than it was in the 1950s before the civil rights movement, but in the 1960s gang members were more likely to attribute their behavior to "exploitation by the power structure, restitution for past injustices, and brutalization by

"*In extenuation, Your Honor, I would like to suggest to the court that my client was inadequately parented.*"

Source: Drawing by Lorenz; © 1983 The New Yorker Magazine, Inc.

the system" (Miller, 1974: 233). One example of this kind of justification for crime was black activist Eldridge Cleaver's "political" defense of his rape of white women:

> Rape was an insurrectionary act. It delighted me that I was defying and trampling upon the white man's law, upon his system of values, and that I was defiling his women—and this point, I believe, was the most satisfying to me because I was very resentful over the historical fact of how the white man had used the black woman. I felt I was getting revenge. (Cleaver, 1968: 14)

Professional fences also deny responsibility for their crime of receiving stolen goods. They deny responsibility by saying that they do not steal anything, claiming it is thieves who steal and the public that buys "hot" goods from fences. Fences claim that if they did not act as middlemen, others would do so. They say that because they do not commit theft or cause theft, the popular image of the thief does not fit them (Klockars, 1974: 139–150).

Denial of responsibility has also been used to justify white-collar crime and political corruption. In his final months in office, President Nixon blamed subordinates such as advisors and tax lawyers for his problems. In his resignation speech, he blamed the press that had reported the Watergate incident and Congress that had forced him to leave office. Few juvenile delinquents can maintain a noncriminal self-concept in the face of as much contrary evidence as confronted Nixon.

Rationalizations similar to Nixon's are also used by white-collar criminals. Executives may say their corporation violated the law because their subordinates misunderstood orders or took the law into their own hands; subordinates may say their supervisors told them to violate the law for the good of the company or established goals that could be met only by breaking the law. What little information we have on the denial of responsibility by white-collar criminals is usually in the form of rationalizations for offenses that have already been committed. We lack good evidence that these justifications are used prior to violation of the law to make it possible for businesspeople to reduce their commitment to the law and commit a crime.

DENIAL OF INJURY   A second technique of neutralization is the *denial of injury*, the claim by offenders that no one will be hurt by their crimes, even if they technically violate the law. Nonoffenders sometimes say they do not violate the law because of their ability to perceive injury to others and because they are concerned about inflicting harm on others. In other words, sensitivity to others may keep some people away from crime and delinquency (Rogers, 1977). Those who violate the law may be less sensitive to the effect their behavior has on victims or may regard their victims as objects or means to their own ends rather than as individuals who suffer when victimized.

An offender may say that victims who lose money or have property damaged can afford the loss, or that they can recover their losses from their insurance company. Offenders often see the losses incurred by insurance companies as unreal, even though policyholders pay higher premiums to offset the costs of claims paid by the insurance companies.

One instance of thieves' regarding their crimes as causing no real loss to anyone comes from a study of eighty-eight workers in a midwestern electronics assembly plant (Horning, 1970). Workers rationalized their theft as causing no injury by making a distinction among three kinds of property in the plant: property that belonged to the company, property that belonged to employees, and property of uncertain ownership. Property classified as being of uncertain ownership was small, plentiful, inexpensive, and expendable, and the company did not regulate its flow within the plant. The property did belong to someone or to the company, but if workers could categorize it as being of uncertain ownership, they thought they were doing no injury if they stole it. Almost all workers reported pilfering goods from the plant, but few expressed any guilt at doing so, because work-group norms supported theft when it was confined to property of uncertain ownership and limited to what was needed for personal use. The conditions under which theft was tolerated were communicated to workers through "folktales" about thefts that had occurred in the past.

Delinquents use the denial-of-injury technique to justify their violation of the law. Car thieves say they are only "temporarily borrowing" cars, rather than permanently depriving owners of their cars. Gang fights are defined as private quarrels that are no one else's business. Sometimes delinquents and adult offenders actually claim that their crimes are socially useful. They may claim to be "Robin Hoods" who steal from the rich and give to the poor. For example, professional fences sometimes justify their crimes as a way to redistribute property from wealthier neighborhoods to poorer ones (Klockars, 1974).

Criminals sometimes claim that it is appropriate to victimize certain targets, but that other targets should be avoided. The general public seems to think that theft from a large corporation is preferable to theft from the government, which in turn is better than theft from a small business (Smigel, 1956). People seem to believe that large corporations can afford the loss because they are insured, are highly profitable, can raise prices to compensate for their losses, and cheat customers anyway. Large corporations are also unpopular because they are seen as impersonal, inefficient, and unresponsive to the best interests of their customers and clients (Smigel and Ross, 1970: 4). This "rip-off mentality," which seems to have been especially widespread in the 1960s, has been used to justify theft from large corporations. One safecracker justifies his thefts in the following way:

> We [professional thieves] would never beat the average working man or anything like that. . . . When I was a young kid learning, I stole anything. But later on I became a professional and started hanging around with professionals and learned from them that you didn't steal from a home or small place of business; you only stole from a big place that could afford the loss. (King and Chambliss, 1984: 13)

Denial of injury has also been used to justify white-collar crime. Thus, a Westinghouse executive responded as follows to a question from a congressional committee about whether he knew that his meetings with other executives to fix the prices of electrical equipment were illegal: "Illegal? Yes, but not criminal. I didn't find that out until I read the indictment. . . . I assumed that criminal action meant damaging someone, and we did not do that" (cited in Geis, 1967: 144). The executive was wrong; not only did the criminal convictions and the jail sentences served by some executives show quite clearly that harm had been done, but the fact that plaintiffs recovered millions of dollars in civil damages from the offending companies also indicated that financial harm had been done.

DENIAL OF THE VICTIM   A third technique of neutralization is the *denial of the victim,* the claim that a crime is justified as rightful retaliation against the victim. Offenders see the victim as a wrongdoer, rather than seeing themselves as wrongdoers, and use that attitude toward the victim to justify the offense.

Certain targets of crime are more likely than others to be socially approved or tolerated, including prostitutes, alcoholics, and unscrupulous shopkeepers who sell shoddy merchandise or adulterated food. Offenders may appeal to widely held ideas about valued and disvalued people to justify their acts. People who are able to recognize that victims suffer, in spite of what those victims may have done to "deserve" victimization, are probably more likely to avoid criminal behavior. One nonoffender says: "If there is something I want, I work for it because I don't want to hurt anyone else by trying to obtain it by other means. I always try to remember that other people have feelings too" (cited in Rogers, 1977: 92). Offenders do not seem to share this view, but instead think it is acceptable to victimize certain people. For instance, con artists who engage in fraud and trickery justify their behavior by the complicity of their victims, who are seen as having "larceny in their hearts" (Maurer, 1974). Similarly, a rapist may justify his crime by saying that the victim "deserves" to be raped because she is sexually experienced, promiscuous, or has a bad reputation, and that such a woman is "public property" and does not have the right to reject him as a sex partner (Hills, 1980: 67).

CONDEMNATION OF THE CONDEMNERS   Another technique of neutralization is the *condemnation of the condemners*, the assertion that it is the motives and behavior of the people who are condemning the offender, rather than the motives and behavior of the offender, that should be condemned. Actions of the condemners, including police brutality and political corruption, are used to justify an offender's violation of the law. People who remain nonoffenders often can concede the imperfection of the condemners without using it to justify their own violation of the law (Rogers, 1977: 96).

Many kinds of offenders justify their actions by condemning the condemners. Murderers and bank robbers compare the harsh punishments they receive with the lack of punishment for politicians who send young men to their deaths in pointless wars. Fences point out that some of their best customers are judges and police officers (Klockars, 1974). Political criminals and terrorists use the corrupt and self-serving nature of the political system to justify crimes aimed at changing that system (Schafer, 1974). Corrupt political leaders sometimes point to the crimes of other politicians in the past to justify their own behavior.

APPEAL TO HIGHER LOYALTIES   The fifth technique of neutralization is the *appeal to higher loyalties*, an attempt to justify violation of the law by the demands of a group — such as a juvenile gang or a corporation — that is smaller than the whole society but that requires its members to conform to standards that may be incompatible with the law. Those who place loyalty to the larger social system and its laws above loyalty to individuals or a group are more likely to stay away from crime. One noncriminal expressed this as follows: "I am not a criminal . . . because I trust the system. I am willing to sacrifice for it. I believe in it" (cited in Rogers, 1977: 94).

Different types of offenders justify their violations of the law by appealing to higher loyalties. Juvenile delinquents rationalize their acts by peer pressure and the need not to let their friends down. Police officers justify graft and corruption by the need to remain loyal to fellow officers. President Nixon's appeal to national security was an effort to justify the Watergate burglary and its cover-up by demands higher than the law. In a 1977 interview, he strongly implied that whatever the President did was not a crime because the President was above the law. Another use of loyalty to demands higher than the law was by an electrical company executive involved in the price-fixing conspiracy; he said, "I thought that we were more or less working on a survival basis in order to try to make enough to keep our plant and our employees" (cited in Geis, 1967: 144).

OTHER TECHNIQUES OF NEUTRALIZATION   Other techniques of neutralization can also be used to justify crime and delinquency. A person who uses a "defense of necessity" may justify an act by saying it is required by the circumstances; this differs from the denial of responsibility in that the offender accepts responsibility for the act while claiming it was necessary. Stealing food to feed one's starving children might be justified as a necessary act for which an offender accepts full responsibility. Another technique is the "defense of the ledger," which is used by offenders who claim that the good and evil they have done balance out favorably over time (Klockars, 1974; Minor, 1981).

In his book on white-collar crime, James W. Coleman (1985: 205–212) identifies several additional techniques of neutralization. One is the claim that the law being violated is unnecessary or unjust. This argument may take the form of claiming that government interference in business affairs actually hurts the public, a kind of variation on the condemnation-of-the-condemners theme. Another technique is the claim that "everybody else is doing it too." A version of this justification is that it is not fair to condemn one offender without condemning them all. A third technique, which is sometimes used in cases of employee theft, is that the offender deserves the money or that the stolen property is a "morally justified addition to wages" or an "entitlement due from exploiting employers" (Mars, 1974: 224). Each of these techniques of neutralization can also be applied to crimes that are not white-collar offenses.

TABLE 8.1   Techniques of Neutralization

1. Denial of responsibility
2. Denial of injury
3. Denial of the victim
4. Condemnation of the condemners
5. Appeal to higher loyalties
6. Defense of necessity
7. Defense of the ledger
8. Denial of the justice or necessity of the law
9. Claim that "everybody is doing it"
10. Claim of entitlement

Evidence on Techniques of Neutralization

Several researchers have found that techniques of neutralization play an important role in the genesis of crime and delinquency, but others believe it is too early to assess the validity of neutralization theory as an explanation for violation of the law (Minor, 1981).

EMBEZZLEMENT AND THE TECHNIQUES OF NEUTRALIZATION   In his study of imprisoned trust violators or embezzlers, Donald Cressey concluded that people violate an employer's trust and embezzle funds when they face a nonshareable financial problem, become aware that they can solve that problem by turning the skills and opportunities of their job in a criminal direction, and can "apply to their own conduct in that situation verbalizations which enable them to adjust their conceptions of themselves as trusted persons with their conceptions of themselves as users of the entrusted funds or property" (Cressey, 1953, 1971: 30). These "verbalizations" are what Sykes and Matza call techniques of neutralization. They permit people to define the relationship between a nonshareable financial problem and an illegal solution to that problem in a way that makes embezzlement seem justifiable.

Cressey found that justifications were used either before or at the time of the crime; after the offense, there was no need for the verbalization. Verbalizations were often applications of general cultural values to an offender's specific situation. For instance, embezzlers said the following:

- "Some of our most respectable citizens got their start in life by using other people's money temporarily."
- "In the real estate business there is nothing wrong about using deposits before the deal is closed."
- "All people steal when they get in a tight spot." (Cressey, 1953, 1971: 96)

The vagueness of some business practices made it possible for embezzlers to say they were using the money "temporarily" and to claim that they were "only borrowing," even though they took the money without the owner's knowledge and rarely repaid it.

JUSTIFICATIONS FOR CRIME BY BLACKS   Another study that uncovered techniques of neutralization asked 150 black men between the ages of fifteen and thirty the following: "It is said that black men violate the criminal law more frequently than others. If this statement is true, are there any reasons you feel why such a higher violation rate exists?" (Davis, 1974: 74).

The men, who were approached on the street, said that the legal system lacked legitimacy for blacks and gave various reasons for a general "justification for no obligation" to the law by black men. More than four-fifths of the men thought that laws had been created by whites to control blacks, that blacks lacked equal access to participation in social institutions, and that unequal access to opportunities is unjust and indicative of hypocrisy about democratic ideals. At least two-thirds of the men said that racial discrimination had a long history and that whites had supported it over the centuries, that blacks were not obligated to obey the law because they had been forcibly brought to the country and had no choice in citizenship, and that blacks were not protected by the law in the same way that whites were.

For black men who find themselves in a state of drift and without a strong commitment to a conventional life style, these justifications may support involvement in crime. Crime by blacks may result from grievances about unjust conditions and a subsequent lowering of respect for the law and its enforcers. Illegal activity may then be accepted as a solution to those grievances. This study did not test directly for the presence of Sykes and Matza's techniques of neutralization among black criminals, but it showed that one group of streetwise black men thought that crime by blacks was a result of the ease with which blacks can neutralize the constraints of the law.

JUSTIFYING MURDER   In a study of sex-related and robbery-related murders and execution-style homicides, several justifications for these acts of lethal violence were uncovered (Dietz, 1983). Street violence was justified by the need to protect oneself or one's property, the need to control others and keep them from using violence, the need to protect a reputation from personal affronts, and the need to ward off unprovoked attacks. In sex-related and robbery-related murders, offenders sometimes forced themselves to think of the victim as an object rather than as a person with feelings. Sometimes these murderers killed to prevent the victim from reporting the crime to the police and testifying in court. In execution-style homicides, "hit men" sometimes justified their crimes by saying that the victim "deserved to die" or by claiming that the murder was a "public service."

DELINQUENCY AND TECHNIQUES OF NEUTRALIZATION   More direct evidence on the techniques of neutralization comes from a study of delinquency by Travis Hirschi (1969). Data were gathered in 1964 from interviews with California junior and senior high school students, and from school and police records. Self-reports were used to measure personal involvement in six delinquent acts: theft of property worth less than $2, theft of property worth $2 to $50, theft of property worth more than $50, auto theft, vandalism, and battery (beating someone up). The number of acts that a student admitted to formed the index of delinquency. Because few students had engaged in many delinquent acts, those who admitted to no acts were compared with those who admitted to one or more. It is questionable whether someone who has stolen only a pencil from a store should be classified as delinquent, or would be likely to be so classified by a judge, but this way of measuring delinquency was required by the data in order to explore relationships between self-reported delinquency and the acceptance of statements used to justify violation of the law.

Denial of Responsibility. Hirschi measured support for the denial-of-responsibility technique by asking students if they thought that criminals were to blame for their actions. Because few respondents—only 12 percent of the sample—said that criminals should not be held responsible for their actions, Hirschi could not use this question to measure support for this technique of neutralization.

Another indicator of support for the denial-of-responsibility technique was the following: "I can't seem to stay out of trouble no matter how hard I try." Students who agreed with this statement might be able to deny personal responsibility for their behavior and to justify violation of the law. Thus, we might expect that those who agreed most strongly with this statement would be the most likely to report involvement in delinquent acts, and those who most strongly disagreed would be the least involved in delinquency. Hirschi's data show that this was the case. Sixty-three percent of the boys who strongly agreed with the statement admitted at least one delinquent act, but only 25 percent of those who strongly disagreed with the statement admitted at least one delinquent act. Those who expressed intermediate levels of agreement with the statement showed intermediate levels of self-reported delinquency (Hirschi, 1969: 207). These findings provide tentative support for a link between denial of responsibility and juvenile delinquency.

Hirschi's study was replicated by Michael Hindelang (1973), who gathered data from boys and girls in rural New York state in 1971. This study provided similar support for an association between this denial-of-responsibility item and self-reported delinquency.

Denial of Injury. Hirschi tested for the technique of neutralization called denial of injury with the following statement: "Most things that people call 'delinquency' don't really hurt anyone." Agreement with this statement would suggest greater ease in denying harm to potential victims of delinquent acts and should thus be associated with more involvement in delinquency. This was the case: 72 percent of those who strongly agreed with this statement reported at least one delinquent act, but only 31 percent of those who strongly disagreed with the statement reported a delinquent act (Hirschi, 1969: 208). Hindelang's (1973) replication of Hirschi's study found similar support for a link between this statement and self-reported delinquency.

Denial of the Victim. The item Hirschi used to measure denial of the victim was the following: "The man who leaves the keys in his car is as much to blame for its theft as the man who steals it." This particular item was not related to self-reported delinquency; the percentages who admitted at least one delinquent act were similar for those who agreed and those who disagreed with the statement (Hirschi, 1969: 210). Hindelang (1973) did not find support for this technique of neutralization either. Hirschi suggests that had he phrased the question as "The *sucker* who leaves the keys in his car . . . ," he might have found an association between responses to this statement and self-reported delinquency. The item Hirschi did use might have said too little about the respondent's attitude toward the victim by referring to him simply as a man.

Condemnation of the Condemners. Condemnation of the condemners was measured by asking for responses to the following: "Policemen try to give all kids an even break." Agreement should be associated with low involvement in delinquency, because those who think the police are fair should be less able to justify violating the law. The evidence supports this: Thirty-five percent of the boys who strongly agreed with the statement admitted a delinquent act, but 58 percent who strongly disagreed with the statement reported a delinquent act (Hirschi, 1969: 211). Hindelang (1973) also found an association between this statement and self-reported delinquency.

Appeal to Higher Loyalties. Hirschi could not test the technique of appealing to higher loyalties with the data he collected, nor did Hindelang ask about this technique.

Conclusion. Hirschi's and Hindelang's studies tentatively support a positive association between three techniques of neutralization and self-reported involvement in delinquent acts. Their work lends some support to Sykes and Matza's theoretical ideas but does not provide a definitive test of those ideas. For instance, Hirschi's and Hindelang's data do not allow them to conclude that the techniques of neutralization were used prior to committing the delinquent acts to make it possible for the boys to neutralize the constraints of the law.

Critique of Neutralization Theory

Neutralization theory implies that people who are committed to a conventional life or who have not yet engaged in deviance will be the most likely to need to use techniques of neutralization. However, one study found that these techniques are used both by youths who disapprove of deviance and therefore need to neutralize norms, and by youths who already approve of the deviance and should therefore not need to use neutralization techniques. Moreover, the relationship between the acceptance of neutralizing excuses and subsequent deviant behavior existed only for people who had already committed that deviant act in the past, not for people who had never violated the norm before. This suggests that techniques of neutralization may only develop and be used after people commit an initial act of delinquency or crime, and that the techniques may not precede violation of the law as Sykes and Matza suggest (Minor, 1981).

The process of neutralizing the law is a social-psychological one by which potential offenders justify crime or delinquency by employing general arguments about when such violations are acceptable. Neutralization theory might be criticized for ignoring aspects of the social structure that make it easy or difficult to justify violations of the law. These social-structural aspects have been explored in control theory, which proposes that people who are the most weakly attached to social institutions are the most free to violate the law.

Control Theory

The *control theory* of delinquency developed by Travis Hirschi (1969) proposes that people who engage in delinquency are free of intimate attachments, aspirations, and moral beliefs that bind them to a conventional and law-abiding way of life. Delinquents are not forced into delinquency so much as they are free to commit delinquent acts because they lack ties to the conventional social order. Delinquency violates other people's expectations about appropriate behavior. If people do not care about the opinion of others, they are free to deviate from norms. Most people have deviant impulses from time to time, but whether they act on those impulses depends on their attachments to others.

Delinquents believe in the conventional order even as they violate its norms; the critical factor is the extent to which they believe they should obey norms. Hirschi (1969: 198) says that "delinquency is not caused by beliefs that require delinquency but is rather made possible by the absence of (effective) beliefs that forbid delinquency." This position is similar to Matza's notion of drift: The delinquent is midway between crime and convention, between deviance and conformity. It is also consistent with Short and Strodtbeck's (1965) finding that gang boys support middle-class prescriptive norms but do not support some middle-class proscriptive norms. In sum, delinquents do not hold norms that require delinquency, but rather lack norms that strongly oppose such behavior. The absence of proscriptive norms is related to the lack of attachment to social institutions, and both leave some adolescents free to violate the law.

Control theory does not make clear the motivations that give rise to violation of the law, but rather looks at the institutions that create barriers to the expression of deviant motivations (Eve, 1978). The desire to acquire material goods, the need for social approval, and association with other law violators can all push a person to violate the law. However, if a person experiencing those pressures to violate the law is also subject to social control that results from attachment to family, school, job, and friends, that control may counteract the pressure to violate the law.

The Family

One institution that is basic to all societies is the family. It socializes the young and provides surveillance over their behavior. It also controls the behavior of people of all ages who value the good opinion of other family members.

Hirschi's research shows that delinquents are much less closely attached to their parents than nondelinquents are. The critical factor is not whether the parents are always physically present to supervise the behavior of the child, but whether the parents are "psychologically present" when the child faces a temptation to violate the law. If the parents are not present in the child's mind, he or she is free to commit a delinquent act without giving any thought to how the parents might react. Nonoffenders sometimes say that they abide by the law because they take their parents' feelings into account when deciding how to act (Rogers, 1977: 37–42). Nondelinquents are also more likely to say their parents know where they are most of the time, and this acts as a check on their behavior. By contrast, delinquents are more likely to say their parents are often unaware of their whereabouts.

The closer a child's relationship with his or her parents, and the more intimate the communication with them, the less likely that child is to be delinquent. Relationships with mothers and fathers are of equal importance in controlling delinquency (Hirschi, 1969: 102). Through attachment to a parent, children learn to care about parental expectations. Attachment to parents seems to be important for children of all classes and all racial and ethnic groups. Even adolescents in groups with high crime rates are less likely to be delinquent if they have close relationships with their parents.

The School

A second important institution in controlling delinquency is the school. The most academically successful students are the least likely to be delinquent, for they are most attached to the school and its teachers. Adolescents are more likely to be delinquent if they do not care what their teachers think of them; again the expectations of "significant others" are important in controlling delinquency. As Hirschi (1969: 127) says, "Positive feelings toward controlling institutions and persons in authority are the first line of social control. Withdrawal of favorable sentiments toward such institutions and persons at the same time neutralizes their moral force."

Hirschi's research shows that students who are not much concerned with their teachers' opinions and who dislike school also have the weakest relationships with their parents. These adolescents are the most likely to report that they have committed delinquent acts.

The Peer Group

The third type of attachment that is important in control theory is relationships with the peer group. Hirschi finds that delinquents are more likely to have delinquent friends than nondelinquents are. However, the relationship between friendships and delinquency is less clearcut than the commonly assumed pattern of poor family relationships leading to attachment to peers, which then leads to delinquency. Instead, adolescents who have weak relationships with their parents tend to have weak relationships with their peers, and those closest to their parents have the greatest number of close friends. Attachment to peers does not necessarily produce attitudes conducive to delinquency, for the more adolescents respect the opinions of their friends, the less likely they are to be delinquent. Those who are more delinquent and more likely to have delinquent friends are also less likely to say their friends are worthy of respect. Contrary to the picture of the juvenile gang as a warm and supportive group similar to a family, Hirschi finds delinquents do not have warm and intimate relationships with each other, or with anyone else for that matter.

Conventional Lines of Action and Adult Activities

Thus far, the picture that control theory offers of the delinquent is of someone who lacks strong attachments to parents, teachers, or peers. Another link in the chain of circumstances leading to delinquency is an individual's aspirations to conventional lines of action, such as education and work. Adolescents who have such aspirations do not want to jeopardize their chances of success, for they risk losing their "stake in conformity" by getting into trouble with the law.

Young people who do not aspire to conventional lines of action are more involved in adult activities during adolescence. Adult privileges without adult responsibilities may compensate for a bleak outlook on the future. Delinquents are more likely than nondelinquents to see their high school years and the years immediately after as the time in their lives when they will be the happiest. They are especially likely to engage in delinquency because their lack of orientation toward the future frees them from conventional pursuits such as education and a career.

As a measure of involvement in adult activities, Hirschi uses the age at which an individual began to smoke cigarettes and the number of "adult activities" — smoking, drinking, and dating — in which the person is involved. Each indicator shows a significant relationship to self-reported delinquency. Thus, adolescents who began smoking before they were thirteen were the most likely to admit a delinquent act; those who began to smoke between thirteen and fifteen were less likely to admit a delinquent act; those who started after fifteen were even less likely to report a delinquent act; and those who did not smoke at all were the least likely to report a delinquent act (Hirschi, 1969: 167). Involvement in the three adult activities was directly associated with a higher rate of self-reported delinquency. Boys who smoked, drank, and dated reported delinquent acts three times as often as boys who engaged in none of those activities (Hirschi, 1969: 168).

In conclusion, adolescents who have fewer attachments to family, school, peers, and conventional lines of action are more likely to engage in delinquency because they do not feel society's rules are binding on them and do not fear the disapproval of others. This perception can be seen as a "master technique of neutralization" supported by the specific techniques of neutralization we have examined.

Evidence on Control Theory

Hirschi's survey provides evidence that delinquency is associated with weak attachments to conventional institutions and lines of action. Other studies, too, support control theory.

COMPARING DELINQUENTS AND NONDELINQUENTS A study of juvenile delinquency by Empey and Lubeck (1971) found some support for control theory. They used a group of boys who had been labeled delinquent in juvenile court and another group of boys who had not been so labeled. They then combined the two groups and looked at those factors that distinguished delinquents from nondelinquents.

Empey and Lubeck began their research with the theory that lower-class status reduces school achievement, which produces strain that leads to identification with peers, and this in turn draws boys into delinquency. Their analysis of the data led them to formulate a more complex explanation for delinquency. They found that lack of integration into institutions, particularly the family and the school, predicted delinquent behavior. Specifically, measures of strain—such as disharmony in the family and dropping out of school—were directly associated with peer identification, and peer identification was tied to delinquency.

The interrelationships of the critical variables related to delinquency in Empey and Lubeck's research are portrayed in Figure 8.1; a one-headed arrow means one-way causation, and a two-headed arrow means that variables have effects on each other. Hirschi's theory is diagrammed in simple terms in Figure 8.2; here four variables have direct effects on delinquency, but the four variables have no clearly specified causal relationships with each other. For instance, lack of family ties is correlated with weak ties to the school, but Hirschi does not claim that one directly causes the other. Hirschi's model can be described as follows: Lack of attachment to parents, to the school, to peers, and to conventional lines of action each increases the likelihood of delinquency.

Empey and Lubeck's model is more complicated. Low achievement in school leads directly to delinquency, but it also has an indirect effect on delinquency by producing strain in school and in the family, which in turn leads to delinquency, and by increasing peer identification, which is associated with delinquency.

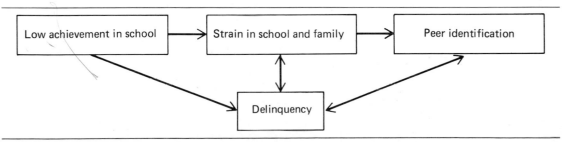

FIGURE 8.1 Empey and Lubeck's Model of Delinquency. *Source: Reprinted by permission of the publisher, from* Explaining Delinquency: Construction, Test, and Reformulation of a Sociological Theory *by LaMar T. Empey and Steven G. Lubeck, with Ronald L. LaPorte. Lexington, Mass.: Lexington Books, D. C. Heath and Company, Copyright 1971, D. C. Heath and Company. (Adapted)*

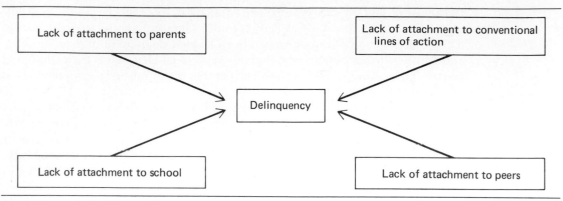

FIGURE 8.2   Hirschi's Model of Delinquency.   *Source: Based on Travis Hirschi,* Causes
of Delinquency. *Berkeley: University of California Press, 1969.*

Strain in school and in the family leads directly to delinquency and also leads
indirectly to delinquency by increasing peer identification. In addition, strain is
affected by a juvenile's involvement in delinquency; in other words, being arrested and taken to court produce problems for boys with their parents and
teachers. Peer identification leads to delinquency, and involvement in delinquency affects identification with peers, both directly and indirectly, by producing strain in school and in the family. This model is a less satisfying one than
Hirschi's model of direct, one-to-one relationships between causes and delinquency, but it is a more accurate reflection of the complex processes that lead to
delinquency.

NATIONAL SELF-REPORT SURVEYS OF DELINQUENCY AND DRUG USE   Delbert Elliott, David Huizinga, and Suzanne Ageton (1985) employed self-report
data from three National Youth Surveys conducted in 1977, 1978, and 1979 to
develop a theoretical model that would explain delinquent behavior and drug
use. This model, shown in Figure 8.3, reveals a complex pattern of interaction
among variables that have both direct and indirect effects on delinquent behavior. This model finds that delinquent behavior is directly affected by strong
bonding to delinquent peers, contrary to Hirschi's conclusion that delinquents
have weak peer ties. Delinquent behavior is also directly influenced by prior
self-reported delinquency, suggesting a continuity of behavior over time and
perhaps the impact of having been labeled delinquent in the past.

Weak conventional bonding means that individuals spend little time with
their families and on academic concerns at school, and that they express relatively little commitment to conventional norms at home and at school. This
weak conventional bonding leads to strong bonding to delinquent peers, which
in turn leads to delinquent behavior. However, weak conventional bonding
does not lead to delinquent behavior in a direct way, but only through its impact
on attachment to delinquent peers.

The arrow from prior self-reported delinquency to strong bonding to delin-

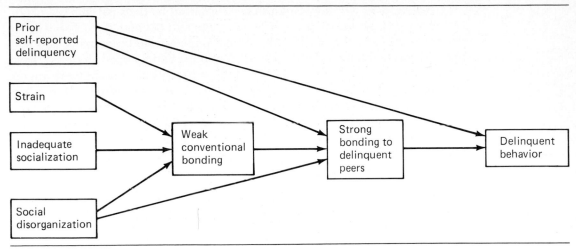

FIGURE 8.3 Elliott, Huizinga and Ageton's Model of Delinquency. *Source: Delbert S. Elliott, David Huizinga, and Suzanne S. Ageton, Explaining Delinquency and Drug Use, p. 146. Copyright © 1985 by Sage Publications, Inc. Reprinted by permission of Sage Publications, Inc.*

quent peers shows that earlier involvement in delinquency makes it more likely that an adolescent will later associate with delinquent peers, who in turn influence the adolescent to become more involved in delinquent acts. The social disorganization of the community in which the adolescent lives may also influence attachments to delinquent peers, though direct evidence of this was not offered in this study.

Weak conventional bonding to family and to school is influenced by strain, inadequate socialization, and social disorganization of the community. Strain in the family was measured by the discrepancy between the subject's goals for family life—such as getting along with parents and holding their good opinion—and the subject's perceived realization of those goals. Similarly, strain in school was measured by the perceived discrepancy between academic goals—such as high grades and teachers' good opinions of the student—and the actual realization of those goals. Strain in the family and at school does not increase delinquent behavior directly, as is suggested by control theory, but instead leads to weak conventional bonding, which then produces strong bonding to delinquent peers, which in turn leads to delinquent behavior.

This model shows that a revised version of control theory can explain delinquency, but that variables such as inadequate socialization and social disorganization that are not part of control theory are also important parts of such an explanation.

DELINQUENCY AND THE FAMILY Much research on crime and delinquency points to the crucial role of the family. This is not surprising, for the family is the primary institution in the socialization and supervision of children.

Socialization. The way children are socialized by their parents is a major factor in the causation or prevention of crime and delinquency. A study that asked students why they had not become criminals found that many said that their parents had taught them right from wrong and had been models of hard work and honesty. The students said that their parents had taught them important values, and that they abided by the law because they believed in those values rather than because they feared punishment (Rogers, 1977: 36–45). In comparison with nonoffenders, delinquents are more likely to say that their childhood experiences with their parents were unpleasant and that they rejected their parents as models while they were young (Medinnus, 1965). In general, crime seems to be more common in societies where young people have less contact and less identification with their parents during childhood (Bacon, Child, and Barry, 1963).

Socialization by parents is most likely to reduce the chance that children will violate the law if

- parents clearly define their expectations,
- there is a close relationship between parents and their children,
- parents control their reactions toward their children's rebellious behavior, and
- parents reward the learning of expected behavior and withhold rewards for the failure to learn that behavior. (Toby, 1974)

People can also be socialized to break the law. They may learn values, norms, and skills from the members of a criminal or delinquent subculture. Few parents intentionally socialize their children to violate the law, but the failure to recognize their children's crime and delinquency as deviant and the use of ineffective methods of punishment can socialize children to break the law (Hirschi, 1983).

In a longitudinal study in which records describing the family environments of boys were compared with their criminal convictions three decades later, the researcher found that six variables were predictive of adult criminality. One variable that was not associated with later criminal convictions was the absence of the father from the home. Adult criminality was more common among men whose childhoods had been characterized by parental conflict, lack of supervision, and an absence of maternal affection. Boys were also more likely to become criminals as adults if their parents were aggressive, if their fathers had engaged in deviance, and if their mothers had lacked self-confidence. Thus, the behavior and psychology of the parents, and the way they treated the boys while young, were highly predictive of whether those boys would be convicted of crimes as adults (McCord, 1979).

Discipline. Careful observation of interaction between children and their parents has led researchers at the Oregon Social Learning Center to conclude that some parents are ineffective in disciplining their children, in that they fail to make penalties contingent on their children's behavior in a systematic and predictable way. Children are most likely to break the law and violate social

Using Criminology: Making Parents Responsible for Their Children's Actions

Until 1987, parents in Detroit could be charged only with "contributing to the delinquency of a minor" if their children broke the law. In April of that year, parents were asked to sign a nonbinding pledge that they would not allow their children "to leave home for school with a gun, knife, or other weapon." After a number of shootings of children, including the killing of a high school athlete, weapons sweeps of Detroit's high schools were adopted. In May, the Detroit City council passed a Parental Responsibility Ordinance that imposes penalties on parents who fail to monitor and control their children's misbehavior.

Under this ordinance, which was passed over the mayor's veto, parents are required:

- To keep illegal firearms and drugs out of their homes and to keep legal weapons and drugs out of the reach of youngsters.
- To forbid their children from associating with "known juvenile delinquents."

- To ensure "proper" supervision for their children and to require them to attend school.

Parents who fail to obey this law may be required to undergo counseling or to attend classes in parenting skills. They may also be fined up to $500 or be sent to jail for up to ninety days. Whether this law will be effective in getting parents to educate their children about the law and to keep them from committing crimes is not clear, but some officials believe the new ordinance will be easier to enforce than the previous one which dealt with such failure to monitor and discipline children's actions as "contributing to the delinquency of a minor."

SOURCE: Based on Ruth Bayard Smith, "Detroit Law Makes Parents Responsible for Their Children's Crimes," *The Boston Globe*, May 31, 1987, p. 29.

conventions when parents care too little about their children to pay attention to their actions, when they fail to supervise their children, when they do not regard their children's misbehavior negatively, and when they fail to punish their children. The failure of parents to react consistently to deviant or criminal behavior leaves children with the belief that they cannot control what will happen to themselves by their own actions. Irritable parents who sometimes apply harsh penalties or even strike out violently at their children, but at other times "natter" at their children for similar behavior, make it seem that penalties are not linked to behavior in any predictable way (Patterson, 1980; West, 1982; Hirschi, 1983; Wilson and Herrnstein, 1985).

The most effective parental style of discipline for reducing criminal or aggressive behavior seems to be an "authoritative" approach, which combines a high degree of control over children with a great amount of support and encouragement. In contrast to this, an "authoritarian" style that combines tight control with a parental attitude that is cold and detached often leads children to withdraw from social contact. A "permissive" style that involves nurturing and encouragement, but a failure to control, often produces children who are lacking in self-control (Baumrind, 1978; Wilson and Herrnstein, 1985). This permissive style was found to be common among the parents of delinquents in a longitudinal study done in England, with the researchers concluding:

> A particularly noticeable characteristic of parents of many of the delinquents in the study was carelessness or laxness in matters of supervision. They were less concerned than other parents to watch over or to know about their children's doings, whereabouts and companions, and they failed to enforce or to formulate fixed rules about such things as punctuality, manners, bedtime, television viewing or tidying up. (West, 1982: 57)

The way in which parents discipline their children is quite likely learned from observing how they as children were disciplined by their own parents. If style of discipline is learned from one's parents and then applied to one's own children, this may explain why the children of parents with criminal records are especially likely to have criminal records themselves, for people discipline their own children in the way they were disciplined by their parents, and this style of discipline leads their children into crime just as it led them to violate the law.

Broken Homes. There has been much speculation and research on the broken home as a cause of delinquency and crime. Broken homes include those that are not structurally intact for various reasons: the death of a parent, divorce, desertion, separation, and illegitimacy (in which case the family was never completed). These broken homes could have an impact on delinquency in any of a variety of ways: by producing unstable habits and personalities in young children through inadequate socialization; by failing to provide children with ties to the conventional social order and by not controlling their behavior; by producing stress and conflict that lead children to "act out"; and by offering fewer resources and opportunities to children and thus leaving them at a disadvantage in competing with others for a good education and a desirable job (Wells and Rankin, 1986). Because families can be "broken" in so many ways and because families have so many different kinds of effects on children, it is not surprising that research on the broken family-delinquency relationship is somewhat inconclusive.

In addition, many of the studies of this problem have employed inadequate research designs. Because broken families are more common among the lower classes and among minority groups and because those groups have higher rates of officially recorded crime and delinquency, researchers need to separate the effects of class and minority-group status on crime and delinquency from the effects of family structure on crime and delinquency. For instance, some research shows that among the middle class, neither officially recorded nor self-reported delinquency is associated with coming from a broken home (Grinnell and Chambers, 1979; Richards, Berk, and Foster, 1979). Researchers need to use self-report measures to determine if there are real differences in delinquency and crime between adolescents from broken homes and those from intact homes, because adolescents from broken homes may be more likely to be arrested and found delinquent in court than are adolescents who come from intact homes (Nye, 1958; Hirschi, 1969).

The most carefully designed studies seem to find a relationship between delinquency and broken homes. That relationship is relatively weak, but delinquents are slightly more likely than nondelinquents to come from broken homes (Nye, 1958; Dentler and Monroe, 1961; Hirschi, 1969; Hennessy, Richards, and Berk, 1978). Children in families in which remarriage has occurred seem to be slightly less likely to report delinquent acts than are children in families that have only one parent, but the difference is not statistically significant (Perry and Pfuhl, 1963).

One study of broken homes and delinquency found that different family contexts influence various kinds of delinquency in different ways. Running away, truancy, and motor vehicle theft were strongly related to a specific kind of broken home, one in which both biological parents were absent. Vandalism and theft were more highly associated with school and peer contexts than with the structure of the family. In sum, certain kinds of broken families may produce particular kinds of delinquent acts (Rankin, 1983).

There is some evidence that broken homes may have greater effects on girls and preadolescent boys than on adolescent boys (Toby, 1957; Austin, 1978). Compared with girls and preadolescent boys, adolescent boys are not especially well supervised by their parents, whether they live in an intact home or in a broken one. Thus, there is little difference between the delinquency rate of adolescent boys from broken families and the delinquency rate of adolescent boys from intact homes. However, the relative lack of supervision of adolescent boys is probably a cause of their high rate of involvement in delinquency, compared with girls and preadolescent boys. The difference between coming from a broken home or an intact family is more likely to be important for girls and preadolescent boys, because these two groups are usually better supervised in intact families than in broken ones. Consequently, delinquency among girls and preadolescent boys is more common among those who come from broken homes than among those from intact homes, at least according to some research. Other research does not support this conclusion; for instance, a national survey of adolescents failed to confirm this relationship between family structure and delinquency among girls. Broken homes did increase the rate of self-reported delinquency in this study, but in comparable ways for both boys and girls (Canter, 1982). Earlier research may have found a sex differential in the impact of broken homes on delinquency because those studies used official data, which may reflect sex discrimination in the processing of adolescents by the police.

Contradictory findings about the relationship between broken families and delinquency may be due in part to the use of different kinds of samples of adolescents. One researcher tentatively concluded that the relationship between delinquency and father absence may be strongest for those groups that are the least tolerant of divorce, and that broken homes may make less difference for groups that are more accepting of divorce. If this were true, then researchers who study groups that are relatively tolerant of divorce — for instance, urban Protestants — would be likely to find less of an association between broken homes and delinquency than would researchers who use samples that are less tolerant of divorce. Future research should try to "specify the social characteristics of the chidren for whom the broken home has significant behavioral consequences" (Wilkinson, 1980: 39).

Separation of Children from Their Parents. One factor that might be related to delinquency is the early separation of children from their parents. Regular or prolonged separation from parents during the early years could make it harder for children to develop feelings for others later, and lack of empathy could be linked to delinquency and crime.

There is some evidence that delinquency is more common among the children of parents who both work outside the home (Austin, 1982). Hirschi (1969: 237 – 239) found that 37 percent of the boys whose mothers were housewives reported a delinquent act, 44 percent of the boys whose mothers worked part time outside the home reported a delinquent act, and 50 percent of those whose mothers were employed full time outside the home reported delinquency. An earlier study (Nye, 1958: 53 – 59) also found more delinquency among adolescents whose mothers worked outside the home. It is unclear whether there is a relationship between delinquency and mothers' working outside the home today, when more than two-thirds of American women with a husband present in the home and children between six and seventeen hold jobs.

Any negative effects on children of having both parents work outside the home might be attributable to a loss of supervision. However, conflict between a husband and a wife might also result from the wife's working outside the home, or the wife might take an outside job to escape from a problematic family situation, such as an alcoholic and unemployed husband. In these cases, intrafamily conflict related to working outside the home, rather than lack of supervision, might be the cause of delinquency. There is some reason to believe that interpersonal relationships in the family and the quality of care provided by parents are more important influences on delinquency than whether both parents hold jobs outside the home (Currie, 1985).

Family Cohesiveness. What seems most important in determining whether a child will become delinquent is the cohesiveness of the family, the quality of interpersonal relationships in the family, communication between parents and children, and emotional support of the children by their parents (Hirschi, 1969; Hindelang, 1973; Ferracuti, Dinitz, and Acosta, 1975; Poole and Regoli, 1979; Wiatrowski, Griswold, and Roberts, 1981). Attachment of a child to caring parents and parental supervision of that child seem to be more important factors in preventing delinquency than the simple presence of two parents in the home. For instance, there seems to be less delinquency in broken homes than there is in unhappy intact families (Nye, 1958; Belson, 1975). One study of delinquency in three cultures found less family cohesiveness, less confiding in parents, and less stable home situations among delinquents than among nondelinquents (Rosenquist and Megargee, 1969). Higher levels of hostility within the family have also been found to be associated with more deviant behavior in a study done in Mexico (Meadow et al., 1981).

The quality of family relationships may be associated in different ways with various kinds of crime. For instance, one study found that adult males who as boys had been most exposed to conflict and aggression between their parents were especially likely to commit violent crimes (such as murder, rape, and kidnapping). Men who as boys had lacked maternal affection and men whose fathers had engaged in deviance were the most likely to be arrested for property crimes (such as larceny, car theft, and burglary) (McCord, 1979).

In explaining why Switzerland has relatively low rates of juvenile delinquency, Marshall Clinard (1978) focuses on the close ties and good communication between young people and adults. He suggests that Swiss adolescents often prefer interaction in mixed-age groups to interaction in peer groups, and that people of various ages often participate together in outdoor activities. Interaction of various age groups also occurs in the large Swiss army. In addition, many Swiss continue to live with their parents after they become young adults. Clinard attributes Switzerland's relatively small problem with youth crime to the culture's emphasis on harmony and compromise, which sustain close ties between people of different ages, both within and outside the family.

The family is an especially important institution in the genesis or the prevention of delinquency and crime. The structure of the family is important, but what seems most critical is the quality of relationships among family members. Harmonious relationships between parents, and between parents and children, help to prevent delinquency and crime.

DELINQUENCY AND THE SCHOOL Crime and delinquency are more common among people who have low levels of academic achievement and who are weakly attached to their schools and teachers. School is an "apprenticeship to maturity" that eases the passage from adolescence to adulthood (Hirschi, 1969; Wiatrowski, Griswold, and Roberts, 1981). However, if academic pressure is coupled with a high likelihood of failure, adolescents may feel that school is irrelevant to their future, ungratifying, and unrewarding. They will then see their grades as unimportant and will spend less time on homework; these factors lead to lower academic achievement. Their ties to the school will then weaken, and they may drift into delinquency (Hirschi, 1969: 170–183; Hindelang, 1973; Figueira-McDonough, 1987). Poor academic performance in high school is also strongly predictive of being arrested for crime as an adult (Polk, 1980).

Nondelinquents often mention their commitment to education and their respect for their teachers' good opinions as reasons for not turning to crime. They also say that education is important to their future and that they do not want to risk their stake in conformity by violating the law (Rogers, 1977: 52–53).

Students with lower IQ levels may be more delinquent because they are less attached to the school and its teachers and less likely to experience academic success (Hirschi and Hindelang, 1977). Delinquency is correlated with poor grades, dislike of school, hostility toward teachers, and little effort at doing schoolwork (Hirschi, 1969; Empey and Lubeck, 1971).

Evidence that weakened attachment to the school is linked to delinquency was uncovered in Wolfgang, Figlio, and Sellin's (1972: 66) cohort study. Boys with more contacts with the police were more likely than boys with fewer police contacts to

- have changed schools frequently,
- have lower IQs,
- have completed fewer grades, and
- have a lower overall level of achievement.

Delinquency and Dropout. A study of delinquency and dropping out of school concluded that bonds to school could, in some circumstances, actually be conducive to delinquency (Elliott and Voss, 1974). By forcing unsuccessful students to attend school until sixteen, compulsory-education laws create a frustrating situation that stigmatizes those students as failures and reduces their self-esteem. Some students rebel by engaging in delinquency, which leads to more rejection and alienation, and thus to more delinquency. Some frustrated students drop out of school, and when they do their involvement in delinquency declines. Dropouts thus become less delinquent when they sever their bonds to the school, and delinquency is common among those who are forced to stay in school but feel alienated from it. In this sense, school is "the critical generating milieu for delinquency" (Elliott and Voss, 1974: 203).

This study directs attention to the quality of a student's ties to the school. Staying in school by itself is not an indicator that a student is concerned with the good opinion of teachers and administrators, nor that a student is afraid to jeopardize his or her future by doing poorly in school. What is important is the nature of the student's attachment to the school, the schoolwork, and the teachers. Some students who are enrolled in school do not feel a positive attachment, and so are not inhibited from engaging in delinquent behavior.

School Organization and Delinquency. Some research suggests that the organizational context of the school can influence the amount of delinquency by its students. A study in England concluded that the schools that did the best job of keeping rates of delinquency low were the ones that had a relatively high proportion of good students and the ones that combined firm but fair discipline with rewards for good academic performance. The presence of more students who found school rewarding seemed to set the tone for the whole student body in a way that kept delinquency rates down. Teachers who treated their students in the way that parents who were effective at discipline did—that is, using an "authoritative" style of discipline—also seemed most likely to suppress delinquent behavior. This kind of school required parental involvement, a strong principal, and highly motivated and experienced teachers (Rutter et al., 1979).

Research in the United States has found less truancy, class cutting, verbal abuse of teachers, and student fighting in private and parochial schools than in public schools. The private and parochial schools were more likely than the public ones to be characterized by clear goals, firm expectations, fair discipline, and rewards for work well done (Coleman, Hoffer, and Kilgore, 1982).

DELINQUENCY AND THE PEER GROUP Hirschi's conclusion that weaker peer-group ties are associated with higher rates of delinquency is challenged by other research, perhaps because Hirschi did not adequately distinguish ties to conventional peers from ties to delinquent ones. One national study found no relationship between attachment to peers and self-reported delinquency (Wiatrowski, Griswold, and Roberts, 1981), but other research has found that greater identification with peers is linked to higher rates of delinquency (Empey and Lubeck, 1971; Hindelang, 1973; Elliott and Voss, 1974; Elliott, Huizinga, and Ageton, 1985). This may be because the adolescent subculture is "oppositional" to the dominant, middle-class culture, and so closer ties to the peer group may be associated with more delinquency (Elliott and Voss, 1974).

A recent effort to assess control theory's view that delinquents' friendships are exploitative rather than supportive questioned nearly a thousand twelve- to nineteen-year-olds living in a large metropolitan area. The researchers concluded that "youths who are very different in their levels of involvement in delinquency are nevertheless quite similar in the ways in which they view their friendship relations" (Giordano, Cernkovich, and Pugh, 1986: 1191). Control theory's idea that individuals bring delinquent values to the group at the outset fits with the researchers' findings, but they also conclude that after the group forms, mutual influence further strengthens patterns of delinquent behavior. The researchers contradict control theory's assertion that delinquents lack attachments to their peers, finding that delinquents derive as many or more benefits from their friendships as other adolescents. In sum, this study suggests that the friendship patterns of adolescents, whether delinquent or not, are complex and multidimensional.

Peer Groups and Families. One study looked carefully at the effects of both parents and delinquent friends on self-reported delinquency and concluded that both had independent effects on delinquency. However, the delinquent peer group had a greater effect on delinquent behavior for adolescents who had weaker family ties than it did on the behavior of adolescents who had more family support. Adolescents who had little support from their parents were more open to the influence of their delinquent peers, and adolescents who were wary of harming their good relationships with their parents were more likely to stay away from delinquent peers (Poole and Regoli, 1979).

A study of adolescent gangs among Chinese-Canadians found that those gangs emerged as a consequence of poor family supervision and guidance. Traditionally, the Chinese family in North America has been strong and able to insulate young people from trouble with the law, but in Canada in recent years this cohesive family unit has not been as strong as it once was, and so young Chinese-Canadians have turned to gangs. In part, this may be an escape from family pressure to succeed in school, which creates problems for recent immigrants who lack the necessary language skills (Joe and Robinson, 1980).

The peer group is an important predictor of marijuana use among adolescents in both the United States and France. There is less marijuana use in France, but in both countries users are more oriented to their peer group than nonusers. Moreover, users in each country are less committed than nonusers to conventional institutions such as the school and the family (Kandel and Adler, 1982).

DELINQUENCY AND RELIGION   One bond that may prevent delinquency, but was not incorporated into control theory, is membership in organized religion or a belief in religious precepts. Studies in Great Britain and Puerto Rico have found less delinquency among boys who attend church more often and among boys who express stronger religious interests (Belson, 1975; Ferracuti, Dinitz, and Acosta, 1975).

Religion is but one of a large set of influences on delinquent behavior, and one that interacts with the influence of the family, the school, and the peer group to inhibit or cause delinquency. One study that used religious salience — the strength of a belief in the power of prayer — and religious orthodoxy as measures of religiosity found a weak to moderate relationship between religion and delinquency, but concluded that religion was not a significant predictor of delinquency when compared with other factors such as the family and the peer group (Elifson, Petersen, and Halaway, 1983).

In a review of research on the relationship between individual religiosity and criminality, Lee Ellis (1985: 511) says there is "strong support and essentially no contradiction" for the following generalizations:

1. Among church members, frequent church attenders have lower crime rates than infrequent (or non-) attenders, especially in regard to victimless crimes.
2. Among church members, Jews have lower crime rates than Christians. Among Christians, Protestants have lower crime rates than Catholics.
3. Persons who believe in an afterlife with divine punishment for sins have somewhat lower crime rates than persons who lack such beliefs.

Despite the empirical relationship between religiosity and criminality, Ellis (1985: 513) says that "no simple answer can be given to the question, do 'religious people' commit fewer crimes?" He concludes as follows:

Overall, if one means by "religious" people who hold very orthodox religious beliefs, with the exception of a belief in immortality, there appears to be little or no association. If one means by "religious" being a member of an organized religious body, the answer markedly depends upon which religious body one is considering. And if, by "religious," one means attending church services frequently, there is manifestly a strong tendency for religious people to commit fewer crimes.

MIGRATION AND THE DISRUPTION OF SOCIAL BONDS   Earlier in the book we saw that migration is sometimes associated with an increase in crime rates of the people who move. This increase in criminality seems most likely to occur when migration from one nation to another or migration within a nation disrupts social bonds and weakens the informal control of behavior by family, school, peer group, religion, and community. The social integration of groups is sometimes undercut by population turnover and the arrival of newcomers and transients; this seems to have a greater impact on intentional crimes than on impulsive offenses (Stark et al., 1983).

In developing nations, crime rates often increase as people become detached from traditional institutions through "detribalization." One study found that Ugandans who left their villages and moved to the large city of Kampala, especially to its slum shantytowns, were likely to have high rates of crime unless they established new social bonds in the city. Migration caused crime rates to increase by weakening attachments to groups that had traditionally controlled deviant behavior (Clinard and Abbott, 1973).

Migration may not be disruptive if the "receiving community" contains groups into which immigrants can be integrated or if individuals move from one place to another in groups. However, people who move alone and lack social ties in their new community are more likely to become involved in crime because there is little to control their behavior. In the study of Uganda, it seemed to be relatively unimportant for migrants to the city to maintain direct ties to their village; what was important was that they form attachments to relatives and other immigrants from their village in the city to which they had moved (Clinard and Abbott, 1973: 127).

SOCIAL BONDS IN OTHER SOCIETIES One way to examine the usefulness of control theory is to see whether it helps us understand cross-national differences in rates of crime and delinquency. If control theory is correct, we would expect the lowest rates to exist in societies characterized by close attachments to institutions. One effort to use control theory in this way suggests that it can account for the relatively low rate of delinquency in India (see the Cross-Cultural Perspective). A study of ten nations in which there is less fear of crime than in the United States found that a common characteristic of those societies was an ability to create or maintain effective social-control agencies, especially the family (Adler, 1983). Let us look briefly at the role of social bonds in several societies.

China. China is a society apparently characterized by a low rate of conventional crime, although statistics are not made publicly available. The country is also characterized by the presence of strongly integrated groups. Chinese citizens learn an ideology of attachment to the country and to a version of communist ideology; they are thus subordinated to supraindividual concerns. Moreover, the Chinese family is a strong institution that exerts control over individual tendencies to deviate from the law. Young Chinese are also tied to society through state-run recreational facilities that occupy much of their free time.

The regimentation and lack of privacy in China have been compared to life in an army barracks (Butterfield, 1982). Two institutions that maintain social control by public scrutiny of behavior are the *danwei* (or workplace) and the

A Cross-Cultural Perspective: Delinquency in India

Compared with other societies, in India juvenile delinquency is relatively uncommon and not especially serious when it does occur. This conclusion is based on both official records and self-report studies. Why is delinquency relatively rare in India?

Part of the answer is that India's economy is a peasant or agrarian one, and in such an economy young people are not superfluous as they are in advanced industrial economies. In postindustrial societies such as the United States, the absence of much need for unskilled labor means that young people must postpone their entry into the labor force. This often leads to an adolescent subculture that is sometimes supportive of delinquency. In contrast, a peasant economy makes use of unskilled labor, and children and adolescents are thus integrated into the social network of their community. In India, where many businesses are run by families, children are introduced into the economic system by their families at a young age.

Young Indians are integrated into their society to an even greater degree than their participation in the labor force would suggest. Indian society is organized in terms of role relationships that create for everyone a set of obligations to the family, the subcaste, and the community. People are expected to care for others, even distant relatives and employees. Social bonds create much interdependence. Thus, agricultural workers and landowners have mutual obligations and patterns of respect that extend beyond their relationship as worker and employer. As a result, an "employer becomes almost a surrogate parent to the worker and is obliged to look after the employee's (and the employee's family's) welfare. The worker, in turn, has obligations to the employer (or provider) that are not due simply to economic dependence, but are defined by the work role itself" (p. 78).

Because all Indians are enmeshed in a complex network of social relationships, their deviance is of concern to many other people. Informal control induces conformity. Indians learn at a young age what others expect of them and learn to conform to the expectations of those with whom they have close relationships. There is a "psychological presence" not only of the child's parents, but also of an extended family network, a subcaste, and a community. Young people thus develop a stake in the status quo, and even a degree of power to say how they will be treated.

Indian culture defines young people as a part of the social structure, not as outsiders to it. Social activities are rarely segregated by age, "hangouts" for adolescents are practically nonexistent, and there is no adolescent subculture conducive to juvenile delinquency.

SOURCE: Based on Clayton A. Hartjen and S. Priyadarsini, *Delinquency in India: A Comparative Analysis.* New Brunswick, N.J.: Rutgers University Press, 1984.

street committee. All Chinese belong to a *danwei* through the school they attend or the office or factory in which they work. The *danwei* often provides housing, schooling, and medical care. It must give permission to marry and to divorce. Ties to the *danwei* are so strong that the Chinese are more likely to be asked their *danwei* than their name if they travel to another community. The urban street committee also controls behavior, searching people's homes, recommending job assignments and housing changes, and even deciding who may have children. These and other institutions make the Chinese very sensitive to the expectations of other people and help curb delinquency and crime.

Japan. The Japanese traditionally have had strong ties to their family, to the company for which they work, and to the community in which they live. Bonds to such tightly knit groups offer security and success to individuals and ensure conformity by requiring the fulfillment of social responsibilities. The group nature of Japanese society is so strong that crime rates are low even in densely populated urban areas, where we might expect social bonds to break down and crime rates to be high (Clifford, 1976).

In Japan, individual behavior is guided by obligations to family, employer, neighborhood, and society, rather than by self-interest. The Japanese know they will benefit socially and economically by conforming to the expectations of others. Americans usually speak of their rights, but the Japanese more often think of the debts they owe to others. The social structure of Japan is similar in its group orientation to some communist nations such as China that also seem to have low crime rates, but Japan provides striking evidence that crime is more a result of the social structure of a society than a product of the society's political and economic ideology. In other words, the capitalist society of Japan and the communist society of China seem to have low crime rates because both have created or maintained social bonds that tie people to groups and institutions.

In recent years, Japan has experienced a rising rate of juvenile delinquency, even though its current rate is well below that of the United States. Much of this delinquency occurs in the schools; some has taken the form of assaults against teachers. Close to 90 percent of Japanese delinquents are middle or upper class, and they are now a younger group than they were even a few years ago. One explanation for this increase in delinquency is the breakdown of a traditional educational system that once inculcated respect for authority. Japanese leftists claim that the rising delinquency rates of the 1980s are a result of educational policies that favor the brightest students, neglect others, and create for all students "an examination-hell atmosphere from which violence is bound to erupt" (Chapman, 1983: 3). Competition for academic success has led some students to feel ignored or discriminated against by teachers, weakening their bonds to teachers and the school and freeing them to engage in delinquent behavior.

Israel. One nation that has undergone rapid social change and as a result has experienced more crime and delinquency is Israel. Until recently, Israel had a very low crime rate, but between 1975 and 1980 there was a tripling in the rate at which new criminal files were opened by the police. This has been attributed to the disruption of the social order by war and the ever-present threat of war, and to the sweeping away of traditional values by increased materialism.

Spain. Spain had a relatively low crime rate under Franco's dictatorship, but with his death in 1975 and the introduction of democracy, social control loosened and urban crime — especially by violent juvenile gangs — increased. There was a 44 percent increase in burglary and robbery in Spain in the first year after Franco's death, but the homicide rate remained low and stable over that time (Markham, 1977). It is not clear that we can attribute the growth in Spain's crime rate to political liberalization alone, but this change was accompanied by loosened social control that might have increased burglary and robbery rates. Another possibility is that crime was simply recorded more completely after Franco's death, creating the illusion of an increase in the crime rate.

Critique of Control Theory

One shortcoming of control theory is that it does not identify the social-structural sources of motivations to break the law. Attachment to the family, the school, and the peer group can keep people from violating the law even when other social forces — such as poverty — might impel them to engage in crime and delinquency. However, a complete theory of crime and delinquency needs to explain the way that social, economic, and cultural forces produce the motivation to break the law.

One criticism of control theory is that it fails to take into account possible reciprocal relationships between social bonds and delinquency, focusing instead on the way that weak attachments lead to delinquency (Agnew, 1985; Liska and Reed, 1985). One study found that parental attachment affects delinquency, but that most of the relationship between school attachment and delinquency was due to the effect of delinquency on school attachment, rather than due to the effect of school attachment on delinquency (Liska and Reed, 1985).

Attachments to different institutions probably take on varying degrees of importance at different stages of the life cycle, and control theory needs to identify more clearly the relative significance of bonds to different institutions for people of various ages. One recent study that did this found that the causal processes identified in Hirschi's control theory are most applicable to youths in midadolescence (about age fifteen), with attachments to parents and teachers and commitments to conventional lines of action being important "psychological anchors" to conformity for this age group. The influence of delinquent peers was found to be strongest for older adolescents (around age eighteen) (La-Grange and White, 1985).

The way that bonds to different institutions interact with each other needs to be more fully delineated. Some researchers have examined the relationships among bonds to family, school, and peer group (Empey and Lubeck, 1971; Liska and Reed, 1985; Patterson and Dishion, 1985), but we need much more information on problems such as how relationships with parents affect attitudes toward school and work, how bonds to teachers during adolescence influence adult work history, and how attachment to family and to job among adults is related to involvement in criminal behavior. For instance, a young father with strong bonds to a wife and children and a strong attachment to his career might experience conflict between his loyalties to family and to job; in some cases, this might cause frustration that leads to violence in the home or theft at work. In sum, control theory needs elaboration, and researchers must study the complex relationships among attachments to different institutions.

Techniques of Neutralization, Control Theory, and Variations in Crime Rates

We do not now have enough evidence on the distribution of the techniques of neutralization to know whether they can account for variations in crime rates. One country might have more crime than another because its culture includes beliefs that make it easier to neutralize the law and engage in crime and delinquency. Differences in access to techniques of neutralization might also help explain variations in crime rates by region, by size of the community, or over time; however, we have no evidence that this is so. Similarly, socialization experiences and access to criminal subcultures might account for some of the variations in crime rates by sex, age, race, and class; again we lack supporting evidence. More research on the way techniques of neutralization vary from one society to another and vary within a society by region, community, and social group might help us explain differences in crime rates.

Control theory does make sense of cross-national variations in crime rates, for nations that have lower crime rates seem to be characterized by stronger and more extensive bonds to family, peer group, school, community, and nation. We have little evidence that regional variations in crime rates in the United States can be explained by differences in the strength of attachments to institutions, but the West's high rate of property crime might be due in part to the relatively weak attachments to community of the many people who have moved there from other parts of the country. Variations in crime rates by size of the community might also be accounted for by control theory; attachment to community seems weaker in larger cities than in small towns and rural areas, and interpersonal relationships in large communities have often been described as weak and segmented. We lack good evidence that fluctuations in crime rates over time parallel changes in social bonds to institutions such as the family, the school, the peer group, the community, and organized religion; however, some scholars have attributed increased crime rates to a reduced emphasis on obligations and responsibilities to others (Davies, 1983; Wilson, 1983).

Control theory helps explain variations in crime rates by sex, age, race, and class. Adolescent boys probably have high rates of delinquency because they usually are supervised less carefully than girls and preadolescent boys, two groups that have relatively low delinquency rates. Age variations in crime rates can also be explained by control theory. Adolescents are concerned with breaking away from their parents, and this creates pressure on parents to exert less control. Adults marry, have children, take jobs, and settle down in a community; these social bonds help to account for the decline in crime rates with age. Blacks' high crime rates may be due in part to their weaker attachment to jobs, with the lack of promising jobs to which they can form strong attachments being a product of racial discrimination and the poor quality of the education available in many public schools. The higher rates of family dissolution and illegitimacy among blacks also suggest that differences in the quality of family relationships between blacks and whites might account for some of the differences in crime rates between the groups. Finally, class differences in crime rates might exist because poorer families tend to be larger, are more likely to be broken, and are more likely to experience financial strain; these factors may be associated with reduced control over deviant behavior. In addition, lower-class students may feel that they cannot win the good opinion of their middle-class teachers, or may believe that education will gain them little in improved job prospects even if they did form close attachments to their teachers.

We have little research that demonstrates that variations in crime rates among different groups, regions, and countries are directly due to variations in attachments to institutions. Control theory is, however, compatible with some of these variations in crime rates, and more research might show that this theory can account for those variations.

Summary

Most people must neutralize the hold that the law has over them before they can violate the law. People who are in a state of drift and lack strong bonds to the conventional order are free to engage in delinquency and crime, but they are not forced to do so, according to some sociologists. The values of law violators have some things in common with the dominant value system, but delinquents and criminals act on subterranean themes in the dominant value system in inappropriate situations.

Techniques of neutralization, which are used to justify delinquency and crime prior to the deviant act, include the following: denial of responsibility, denial of injury, denial of the victim, condemnation of the condemners, and the appeal to higher loyalties. These and other techniques are used by many kinds of offenders—juvenile delinquents, professional criminals, and white-collar offenders.

Evidence that these techniques of neutralization are associated with violation of the law comes from a study of embezzlers, a survey of black men interviewed on the street, a study of sex-related and robbery-related murders and contract killings, and several studies of juvenile delinquency. However, we lack good evidence that offenders use these techniques prior to violating the law, and we do not know what aspects of the social structure make it easy or difficult to justify violations of the law.

Control theory proposes that people engage in delinquency or crime when they are free of intimate attachments to the family, the school, and the peer group, and when the aspirations and moral beliefs that bind them to a conventional way of life are weak. The absence of a "psychological presence" of parents leaves adolescents free to violate the law without being afraid of how their parents will react. Close ties between adolescents and their parents inhibit delinquent behavior, as do strong ties to the school and its teachers. Adolescents who do not aspire to conventional lines of action such as school and work, but who want to engage in adult activities before assuming adult responsibilities, are also especially likely to engage in delinquency.

Comparisons of delinquents and nondelinquents generally support control theory, but the interrelationship of variables is more complex than Hirschi's initial formulation of the theory suggested. The way parents socialize their children, particularly the way they discipline them, is related to delinquency and crime. If relationships between parents and their children, and between the parents themselves, are characterized by conflict or poor communication, children are more likely to become delinquents. The relationship between broken homes and delinquency is only weak to moderate, but it is stronger for some groups than for others. In general, more cohesive families seem to help insulate their children against trouble with the law.

Delinquents have weaker ties to schools and teachers than nondelinquents do, and delinquents do less well in their academic work. Delinquency is especially common among academically poor students, but poor students who drop out of school seem to become less delinquent because they reduce the frustration they encountered as students.

The relationship between the peer group and delinquency is not entirely clear, but many studies find that delinquents usually have delinquent friends. Whether those friends led them into delinquency or whether they chose those friends after violating the law is unclear.

Some research indicates that there is less delinquency among adolescents who are more religious. Religion may also interact with the family, the peer group, and the school to curb delinquency.

Under some conditions, migration disrupts social bonds and increases criminality. This occurs when traditional social bonds are broken by moving and are not replaced by other attachments that inhibit criminality.

Control theory has several shortcomings. It does not identify the social-structural sources of motivations to violate the law. It has not yet specified the relative importance of different kinds of attachments for people of various ages. Control theory has also failed to spell out the way that attachments to different institutions interact with each other to prevent or cause crime and delinquency.

We do not yet have enough evidence on the distribution of the techniques of neutralization to account for geographic, temporal, and social variations in crime rates. Control theory does seem capable of explaining those variations, with attachments to institutions being the weakest in those countries and among those groups that have the highest crime rates.

Important Terms

appeal to higher loyalties
condemnation of the condemners
control theory
denial of injury
denial of responsibility

denial of the victim
drift
subterranean value
technique of neutralization

Suggested Readings

WILLIAM CLIFFORD. *Crime Control in Japan*. Lexington, Mass.: D. C. Heath, 1976. A fascinating exploration of a society that seems to have kept crime rates low by maintaining traditional group ties.

DONALD R. CRESSEY. *Other People's Money: A Study in the Social Psychology of Embezzlement*. Belmont, Calif.: Wadsworth, 1953, 1971. A study that shows how embezzlers neutralize the law before stealing from their employers.

TRAVIS HIRSCHI. *Causes of Delinquency*. Berkeley: University of California Press, 1969. An important statement and test of control theory.

GRESHAM M. SYKES AND DAVID MATZA. "Techniques of Neutralization: A Theory of Delinquency," *American Sociological Review* 22 (December 1957), 664–670. An important paper that shows how delinquents neutralize the law.

CHAPTER 9

Learning to Commit Crime

Source: J. P. Laffont/Sygma

Crime arises from needs that can be met by violating the law. Because most people are attached to the legal order, or at least know that the law commands widespread respect, they must justify their criminal acts and be relatively free of bonds to the legitimate social order before they can break the law. Criminals must learn techniques for neutralizing the law, and they must also learn the skills and motives that are needed to violate the law. For instance, they learn how to recognize opportunities for crime, how to break into safes, how to reduce victim resistance, and how to find outlets for the property they steal. The degree to which such skills must be learned varies from crime to crime. Thus, no particular skill is needed to steal an unattended purse, but finding a safe that contains a large amount of money, breaking into the building, and cracking the safe require considerable skill.

Sources of Learning to Commit Crime

Offenders can learn motives and techniques for violating the law from a multitude of sources. Some of the sources we will look at here include the community, the peer group, the general culture, the mass media, sports, pornography, and correctional institutions.

The Community

Opportunities to learn to commit crime are associated with the social organization of a community. Learning about crime seems to be more possible when there are close ties and frequent interaction among people of different ages within a community (Kobrin, 1951; Cloward and Ohlin, 1960). Interaction between teenagers and adult criminals, as well as between teenagers in gangs and preteens, provides an opportunity to engage in criminal activity under the supervision of more experienced offenders. An unusual instance of this was reported in 1980 in Washington, D.C., where two adults were arrested for training teenagers to rob banks. The two men recruited the teens on the street, wrote a robbery note, drove them to a bank, and instructed them to give the note to a female teller. If the youths left the bank before getting the money, they were given a "pep talk" and driven to another bank. When successful, the youths were paid $50 to $135 for the robbery.

Local criminals sometimes act as role models for young people to emulate, as we can see from the following childhood memory of one of the robbers in the 1950 Brinks holdup:

"When I was a kid, we all knew what a big-time crook was, and most of us looked up to them. I was always working to make money from the time I could walk. You wanted money because the parents were so poor. And I had all kinds of legitimate jobs, but they didn't pay nothing. But these racket guys would drive up in those big touring cars filled with pretty girls and all the money they wanted. I remember one of them giving us kids five bucks each just to stand and watch his car while he and the girl went to eat at a restaurant. Jesus, five bucks was almost as much as my father made in a week" (cited in Behn, 1977: 60).

The social climate of a community is linked to its rate of forcible rape. One study found that states in which the social climate endorses the use of violence to achieve socially acceptable ends have higher rates of rape than states with social climates less supportive of violence. In this study, rates of rape were associated with a state's "legitimate violence index," which was based on such measures as the popularity of the most violent television shows, the circulation of magazines with violent themes, the use of corporal punishment in the schools, enrollment in the National Guard, number of hunting licenses issued, the use of capital punishment, a history of lynchings, and the production of football players. Apparently, residents of states ranking highest in acceptance of physical violence as a means to legitimate ends generalized the use of force to spheres of life in which force was not socially acceptable (study by Murray Straus and Larry Baron, cited in Curwood, 1985).

The Peer Group

Learning to commit crime often occurs within delinquent gangs, but many adolescents learn not to be delinquent from their peers. Those who are concerned with their reputation and believe they have an investment in abiding by the law cite the influence of their peers as a major reason for not violating the law (Rogers, 1977: 45–49). Adolescents who do not have a stake in conformity may join gangs and learn criminal motives and skills from peers who encourage and reward violation of the law.

In the gang, adolescents come to respect older criminals, develop specific skills such as car theft, learn how to cooperate with other offenders, and become aware of fences, shady lawyers, bondsmen, and corrupt politicians and police officers (Rettig, Torres, and Garrett, 1977). One professional robber reports that he first got involved in an adult gang of robbers because as an adolescent he had a reputation as a skilled car thief. Members of the gang approached him to steal a getaway car for a robbery, and he was gradually accepted into the gang on a permanent basis (Conklin, 1972).

A study of a New York City gang shows how the integration of different age groups can generate crime. This group of young adults provided a setting where even younger delinquents gathered. The younger boys were on trial by the older boys, who occasionally took them along to "case a job." Many of the gang's exploits were planned by an adult criminal who collected information on places to burglarize, planned the crimes, and made contacts with fences for the disposal of the stolen goods. In such a highly integrated set of age groups, learning criminal motives and techniques is made easy for the gang members and for the young delinquents or "predelinquents" who interact with them (Bloch and Niederhoffer, 1958: 198–201).

The General Culture

People sometimes learn criminal motives from the general culture. For instance, the increase in violent crimes after the end of wars is particularly dramatic in nations that were actively involved in the war, were victorious, and suffered large combat losses. The best explanation of this seems to be that violence is made legitimate by war. People apparently believe that if their leaders can solve problems with violence, it is also a suitable means for them to resolve interpersonal differences (Archer and Gartner, 1976, 1984).

The techniques of neutralization that we examined earlier are part of the general culture and are used to justify violations of the law. For instance, embezzlers sometimes learn motives for their crimes from the general culture, justifying their offenses by the ambiguity that surrounds the ownership of money and property, and saying that they are only "borrowing the money temporarily" (Cressey, 1953, 1971).

Forcible rape is another crime that is closely linked to the values of the culture. Cultures that emphasize *machismo*—the demonstration of masculinity through the manipulation and exploitation of women—are likely to have more rape and other violence against women than are cultures that deemphasize differences between the sexes and provide men and women with the same opportunities (Brownmiller, 1975; Hills, 1980; Schwendinger and Schwendinger, 1983). We see an example of this in Brazil in the Cross-Cultural Perspective. One sociologist believes that rape and violence against women would be less common if "our culture considered it masculine to be gentle and sensitive, to be responsive to the needs of others, to abhor violence, domination, and exploitation, to want sex only within a meaningful relationship, to be attracted by personality and character rather than by physical appearance, to value lasting rather than casual relationships . . ." (Russell, 1975: 264–265). Conflict theorists claim that sexist values, and the economic inequality that often accompanies them, are the product of capitalism (Schwendinger and Schwendinger, 1983). However, until we have better data on the incidence of rape in noncapitalist industrial societies and until variations in rates of rape among different capitalist societies are explained, this hypothesis is unproven.

The Mass Media

Today, the average American household has a television set turned on about seven hours each day. Social scientists have done much research on the consequences of heavy television viewing, focusing especially on the large amount of violence that viewers see. Students who watch more television have poorer grades, whatever their parents' income or however much homework they do, and we have seen that low academic achievement is associated with a higher probability of delinquency.

The hypothesis that violence in the mass media has a cathartic effect and actually reduces violence by releasing tensions that might lead to violence is contradicted by nearly all research (National Institute of Mental Health, 1982:

A Cross-Cultural Perspective: Machismo and Murder in Brazil

Brazilian culture traditionally has supported the use of violence by men against women who insult their dignity. This has sometimes led men to kill their unfaithful wives and lovers, even when those men expect to have an unchallenged right to engage in sex with other women.

In a 1979 murder trial, Raul "Doca" Street, a forty-five-year-old man, shot and killed Angela Diniz, his thirty-two-year-old lover, after she ordered him to move out of her expensive villa so she could replace him with someone else. She also hit him in the face with a handbag. At Street's trial, his attorney justified the killing by calling the victim "a luxurious Babylonian prostitute" and "a lascivious woman." The attorney said that his client had suffered "a violent moral aggression" and had murdered the victim out of "legitimate defense of his honor." Women who were present inside and outside the courtroom applauded the defendant and carried signs of support for him. A jury of five men and two women convicted him of involuntary homicide, and he was given a two-year suspended sentence and allowed to go free.

According to some observers, this case caused an increase in the number of murders of women by "affronted" men, who typically were acquitted or given light sentences. One feminist described the months following Street's trial as "a hunting season on women." Brazilian women, led by a small group of militant feminists, became increasingly angry over the murder of women in defense of "masculine honor." They demanded a retrial of Street to show that women could not be killed merely for insulting a man's honor. Eventually, an appellate court, acting on an appeal from a member of the victim's family, declared that the verdict of involuntary homicide was invalid and ordered a new trial.

In the retrial, which ended in December 1981, Street was convicted and sentenced to fifteen years in prison. At the new trial, military police had to force an opening through five hundred angry feminist protesters. The atmosphere at the new trial was one of condemnation of machismo killings, rather than the supportive atmosphere of the first trial only two years earlier. Some Brazilians believe that the second verdict, and the protest over killing in defense of "masculine honor" that followed the first verdict, may have weakened this justification for murder. In three cases tried during the two weeks after the second verdict, all three men were found guilty of murdering their wives to defend their honor.

SOURCE: Based on Jim Brooke, "Feminism in Foreign Lands: Two Perspectives: Macho Killing in Brazil Spurs Protesters," *The Boston Globe*, January 3, 1982, pp. A23, A24.

40). There is evidence, on the contrary, that exposure to television violence elevates short-term aggressiveness among children, and this may lead to delinquency and crime (Bandura, Ross, and Ross, 1961; Liebert and Baron, 1972; Cater and Strickland, 1975; Muson, 1978; Garofalo, 1981). A review of 2,500 studies and reports published since 1970 concluded that there is "overwhelming" scientific evidence that watching televised violence and aggression are positively correlated in children. This review of the data concluded that "it appears that observational learning and attitude changes are the most likely explanations of television's effects on aggressive behavior" (National Institute of Mental Health, 1982: 40).

Longitudinal research suggests that children's exposure to televised violence while young even affects behavior in later years. A study that measured the viewing habits of eight-year-olds, and then studied them again ten years later, concluded that for boys "the best single predictor we had on how aggressive these people were at eighteen was the violence in the programs they viewed at age eight" (Leonard Eron, cited in Bennetts, 1981: 25). For girls, there was no relationship between the viewing of television violence at age eight and aggressive behavior at age eighteen. Perhaps only the boys were encouraged or reinforced in their expressions of violence, which they modeled after what they saw on television. In addition, what the boys watched on television when they were eighteen was not related to their aggressiveness at that age, possibly because television violence was no longer realistic to them or perhaps because the modeling effect only occurs earlier in life (Lefkowitz et al., 1977). In response to commonly heard methodological criticisms of this and similar studies, one of the researchers in this study states the following:

> Now, it could have been said that aggressive youngsters like violent programs to begin with. But because of the methodology we used to control the experiment, we were fairly certain this was a cause and effect relationship, with television viewing preceding the aggressive behavior. The highly aggressive youngsters who were watching nonviolent programs were significantly less aggressive by age eighteen than the youngsters who were not aggressive at eight but who had watched violent programs; they turned out to be more aggressive in the end. We later repeated the study, and found the same thing. Furthermore, the more violent the program, the more aggressive the children became. (Leonard Eron, cited in Bennetts, 1981: 25)

Media attention to real acts of violence may also trigger additional violence in the general population. Thus, after the assassination of President John Kennedy in 1963, there was an increase in aggravated assaults and robberies throughout the country. Similar increases occurred in 1966 after two widely reported crimes: the murder of eight nurses by Richard Speck and the killing of fourteen people by Charles Whitman from a tower at the University of Texas (Berkowitz and Macaulay, 1971). One study even found a noticeable increase in the homicide rate after heavyweight championship boxing matches, and an especially great increase after those matches that were most heavily publicized (Phillips, 1983). News stories about violence that is rewarded, such as a championship fight, seem to be followed by a short-term increase in the nation's homicide rate, but news accounts of violence that is punished, such as a murder for which the perpetrator is executed or imprisoned for life, seem to be followed by a short-term drop in the country's homicide rate. Apparently, the homicide rate is not affected by reports of violence that is neither punished nor rewarded (Phillips and Hensley, 1984).

Television networks often point to the methodological flaws of the many studies that show a link between media violence and aggressiveness and cite the smaller number of studies that fail to find such an association. However, these networks solicit billions of dollars in advertising from companies on the assumption that what people see on television does influence their behavior.

The general thrust of the research done to date is that the mass media, and their portrayal of violence, probably contribute to crime and delinquency in the larger society, but that factors other than exposure to media violence are also important in the explanation of crime and delinquency. The age of the viewer is important, with young viewers probably being the most vulnerable to the effects of media violence. More realistic violence, and violence that forms the central theme of a show, probably have the greatest impact on viewers (Seymour Feshbach, cited in Bennetts, 1981). A useful position is that of psychologist Leonard Berkowitz (cited in Bennetts, 1981: 25): "There is no one factor at work, but one of the things that happens is that people get ideas as well as inclinations, and if their inhibitions happen to be weak at the time, these ideas or inclinations can be translated into open behavior." This position can, with little modification, be fitted into control theory: People exposed to media violence may engage in violent behavior if they lack attachments to conventional institutions and lines of action, or if they have techniques available for neutralizing the constraints of the law.

Sports

There is growing evidence that sporting events can contribute to the aggressiveness of both athletes and spectators. High school and college athletes in combative sports such as football and hockey anger more easily than athletes in less combative sports such as swimming. In addition, athletes in the more combative sports tend to grow more aggressive during the course of the season and are more likely to remain more aggressive after the season ends (Goleman, 1985a).

Watching sporting events seems to make spectators more aggressive. One study found that fans at an Army-Navy football game were more hostile after the game than before it, and that hostility increased whether the fan's preferred team won or lost, or even if the fan did not care who won the game. The largest increase in hostility occurred among fans of the winning team, apparently because they had seen aggression on the field rewarded with a victory. This study also found no increase in hostility among spectators at an Army-Navy gymnastics match—a nonaggressive sport—on the same weekend (Goldstein, 1986). Another study found that aggressiveness increased among spectators at hockey and wrestling matches, but not at swim meets, again suggesting that viewing aggression increases aggressiveness among spectators (Arms, Russell, and Sandilands, 1979).

Factors other than simple imitation of athletic aggressiveness also contribute to spectator violence. The anonymity and excitement of the event may weaken normal inhibitions against aggression, and the consumption of alcoholic beverages can have a similar effect. In addition, spectator violence seems limited primarily to young males, a group especially prone to violent activity in other contexts. Other factors — such as nationalism, unemployment, general social unrest, and the cultural context — also make sports violence more likely, but it is clear that the game itself builds up aggressiveness among spectators (Goleman, 1985a).

Whether the increased aggressiveness of athletes and spectators leads to criminal behavior, and the exact conditions under which it does so, is not clear. Assaults by athletes on each other and assaults by fans against each other constitute crimes, even though they may not be prosecuted as such. In Latin America, there have been assaults by soccer fans on referees who make unpopular decisions. Following the 1971 World Series victory celebration in Pittsburgh, twelve women were raped. In 1985, thirty-nine people died when British fans at a soccer game in Belgium attacked a part of the stadium where Italian fans were sitting, resulting in the unexpected collapse of a part of the stands. It seems clear that sports can heighten aggressiveness, but the way that aggressiveness is channeled — whether into criminal assaults or into loud cheering and boisterousness — is less well understood.

Pornography

There is a widely held view that people who view or read pornography are more likely to commit sex offenses, because they learn to see such behavior as rewarding or because they are stimulated to act on their sexual fantasies. *Pornography* is material that is intended to arouse people sexually by portraying sexual matters in visual or verbal terms. *Obscene material* is material, often pornographic in nature, that has been declared illegal because it poses a threat to the state or to organized religion, violates common morality, has no redeeming social value, or appeals to the prurient or lascivious interest.

Pornographic material does arouse people sexually, although not everyone responds to it in the same way. Those who are most likely to be aroused sexually by pornography are the young, the college educated, the religiously inactive, and the sexually experienced.

Exposure to pornography rarely causes any major changes in the viewer's sexual behavior, except for short-term increases in masturbation or sexual intercourse with regular partners. No effects on sexual morality have been found, nor is there consistent evidence that nonviolent pornography causes sex crimes (The President's Commission on Obscenity and Pornography, 1970; Goldstein and Kant, 1973; Donnerstein, Linz, and Penrod, 1987). The 1986 Attorney General's Commission on Pornography concluded that most pornography "bears some causal relationship to the level of sexual violence, sexual coercion, or unwanted sexual aggression" (cited in Shenon, 1986: A1). However, critics, including two members of the Commission, said that current social science research does not support that statement, and one psychologist characterized the Commission's conclusions as "bizarre" (Edward Donnerstein, cited in Goleman, 1986: 1).

Contrary to what the Commission's conclusions would suggest, the legalization of pornography in Denmark in 1966 actually preceded a decline in arrests for sex crimes. From 1959 to 1969, there was a decline in arrests for exhibitionism, voyeurism, child molesting, and physical indecency with adult women. Rates of rape and other serious offenses against adult women seemed unaffected. Falling numbers of arrests do not necessarily prove a reduction in criminal behavior; they could simply indicate more police or public tolerance of the behavior. However, the data are consistent with the hypothesis that the legalization of pornography reduced sex crimes in Denmark. At the very least, the data suggest that the legalization of pornography did not increase sex crimes (The President's Commission on Obscenity and Pornography, 1970; Gagnon, 1974).

One study that looked at exposure to pornography among several groups — including the general population, regular users of pornography, child molesters, homosexuals, transsexuals, and rapists — found no clearcut pattern of antisocial sexual activity following arousal by pornography. Erotic material was a factor in a few offenses, but sex crimes were more likely to be associated with lowered inhibitions due to alcohol consumption, rejection by wives or lovers, and interaction with peers who suggested sex crimes. Sex offenders rarely mentioned pornography as stimulating, but some did mention being aroused by material depicting violence (Goldstein and Kant, 1973).

Several experiments have found that pornography that combines sex with explicit violence against women increases aggressiveness toward females. Nonviolent erotic material does not have the same effect (Donnerstein, Linz, and Penrod, 1987). However, these experiments used college students as subjects, and measured aggressiveness by the subjects' administration of electric shocks and by the subjects' responses to questionnaires. We cannot generalize from these studies and say that violent pornography increases actual sex offenses among the population at large. There is some evidence that men who are already angry may have their level of aggressiveness increased by exposure to hard-core pornography, but this is not the same as showing that exposure to hard-core pornography causes sex crimes among the male population at large, or even among men who are already angry (Donnerstein, Linz, and Penrod, 1987).

Exposure to pornography may weaken condemnation of rape by both men and women. One experiment found that students who were exposed to more pornographic films recommended more lenient prison sentences for convicted rapists than did people who were exposed to less pornography (cited in *The Boston Globe*, November 21, 1982). Another study found that viewers of films showing extreme violence against women, even films that were not very sexually explicit, became "more callous in the face of the films' portrayals of violence toward women and more likely to believe that a woman who was raped wanted to be" (Goleman, 1984: C1). However, other evidence suggests that exposure to violent pornography does not necessarily cause such callous attitudes, but may instead simply reinforce and strengthen attitudes that people already hold (Donnerstein, Linz, and Penrod, 1987).

Correctional Institutions

Another commonly mentioned source of learning to commit crime is the correctional institution. Prisons, jails, and juvenile detention centers have been described as "schools of crime" where relatively inexperienced offenders are thrown into daily contact with skilled criminals. Conversations in these settings often focus on crime, spreading criminal motives and techniques from more experienced offenders to less knowledgeable inmates, and possibly increasing involvement in crime by those inmates after they are released.

There are no reliable data on the extent to which this kind of learning actually takes place. Many offenders are quite skilled in crime before they are incarcerated. There seems to be no clear relationship between the length of time inmates are imprisoned and the likelihood they will return to crime when released (Von Hirsch, 1976: 113). Indeed, the longer inmates spend in prison, the less efficient and more out-of-practice they may become in the commission of crimes that require skill (Irwin, 1970: 147). Thus, any learning of criminal motives and skills by an inmate may be counterbalanced by the loss of efficiency that occurs with the passage of time.

To the extent that criminal motives and skills are learned in an institution, this seems to occur during an inmate's middle stage of confinement. Inmates are less likely to pick up skills when they are first incarcerated or when they are about to be released (Radzinowicz and King, 1977: 271–272). In addition, whether inmates learn criminal motives and skills is probably related to personal characteristics. For instance, inmates who have families and plan to "go straight" when released are probably less likely to learn criminal motives and skills than are inmates who have no family ties and are committed to a life of crime.

Incarceration can lead to crime in indirect ways. The prison experience may be conducive to the formation of motives to engage in crime. The deprivations of prison life, including lack of freedom and demeaning treatment, can cause resentment that is later used to justify crime (Sykes, 1958). Material deprivations and crowded living conditions lead to the exploitation and manipulation of inmates by one another, and sometimes to homosexual rape, assault, and even homicide (Silberman, 1978: 379–381). Because prisoners lack opportunities to make their own decisions and take responsibility for their own lives, they do not acquire the everyday skills needed to lead law-abiding lives once they are released, and this can push them back into crime after they leave prison (Kassebaum, Ward, and Wilner, 1971; Cordilia, 1983).

In addition to learning the motives and skills to commit crime from their prison experiences, and sometimes from other inmates, offenders also learn motives and skills from adults in the community, from peers, from the general culture, from the mass media, and from sports. One theory of crime causation that looks at the process by which people learn to commit crime is differential association theory.

Differential Association Theory

Edwin Sutherland introduced *differential association theory* in the 1939 edition of his criminology textbook. He modified the theory in 1947, but it has remained the same since then (Sutherland and Cressey, 1978). This theory seeks to explain why crime rates are distributed as they are among various groups and why any given individual does or does not become a criminal or a delinquent. Because the theory purports to be a theory of all crime and delinquency, it is very general in nature.

Principles of Differential Association Theory

The first principle of differential association theory is that criminal behavior is *learned*. This assertion denies the possibility that individual pathology or biological factors cause crime. It also claims that criminal behavior is not unique to or invented anew by individuals, but is instead learned from others. This is questionable, for some crimes — such as the Equity Funding Corporation of America fraud or one kidnapper's attempt to have ransom money delivered through a computerized bank terminal — seem to be unique to the offender. Many aspects of an offender's behavior may be learned from others — for example, the motives and justifications for the crime   but the criminal's specific actions may result from a combination of skills, ideas, and opportunities that are available only to that individual.

The second major statement of differential association theory is that most learning of criminal behavior takes place *in face-to-face interaction* with other people. This means that differential association theory regards the mass media as relatively unimportant in the causation of criminal behavior, even though there is some evidence that criminal motives and skills may be learned from the mass media. Differential association theory was developed before mass ownership of television; today 98 percent of all American households have television sets. This major change in the role of the mass media requires a modification of differential association theory to incorporate learning directly from the mass media.

The third principle of the theory is that people learn from others both *the techniques of crime and the direction (legal or illegal) of motives, drives, and attitudes*. However, some crimes require little or no skill. For instance, the murder of a spouse requires little skill, especially if a handgun or a knife is available, and many forms of theft require little skill. Embezzlers have to learn "verbaliza-

Using Criminology: Learning Not to Bully

Bullies, who are usually boys, torment their victims by being quick to use force in response to insults and threats, which are often imagined or exaggerated. This behavior is learned from others, especially parents, while young, but recent research suggests that bullies can be taught techniques of interacting with others in a nonaggressive way. The success of such measures can keep bullies from becoming adults who commit violent crime or abuse their wives and children.

Bullies often are the sons of parents who use severe and inconsistent discipline, and who punish the child more in response to their own moods than in response to the child's behavior. If a parent is angry, the child will be punished, often for trivial things. If the parent is feeling good, the child will not be punished, even for violent or destructive behavior. This capricious behavior by parents makes them, and other people in general, seem unpredictable and threatening to the bully. The fear of not being in control is a source of the bully's need to dominate others. The bully's parents also present him with a model of aggressiveness that he learns and applies in dealing with other children.

Most children gain self-control as they pass through kindergarten and first grade, but bullies become less self-controlled. Whereas others learn to negotiate and compromise, bullies learn to rely on force. Bullies are more likely than other children to see ambiguous situations as threatening and to blame others for causing trouble, and bullies are more likely to justify an aggressive response to a perceived provocation.

Psychologists have recently used their research to develop programs that teach bullies how to behave in different ways. These programs focus on four-to-ten-year-olds, on the assumption that waiting to change behavior until bullies become adults would require intensive therapy and be extremely difficult. These early-intervention strategies do not deal directly with personality traits produced by parental socialization, but instead involve efforts to teach bullies to get their way with other children in more peaceable ways.

One project takes groups of four or five boys identified by their teachers as bullies, and shows them how to handle situations that frustrate and anger them. The bullies are shown how to respond to perceived insults and threats in a playful way, to count to ten before reacting at all, or simply to walk away. The bullies may also participate in role-playing exercises that give them an opportunity to practice starting conversations with others or getting on school buses when other children are taunting them. The bully is shown how to find friendly responses that will preserve his self-image and sense of worth, such as telling other children that he does not like being teased or by asking others to stop provoking him. The bully is taught to play with others cooperatively and to resolve conflicts without fighting. This involves practice in spelling out to others what is bothering him and in making verbal agreements with others that will satisfy all parties.

SOURCE: Based on Daniel Goleman, "The Bully: New Research Depicts a Paranoid, Lifelong Loser," *The New York Times,* April 7, 1987, pp. C1, C4.

tions'' that allow them to use their accounting skills for illegal ends, but they do not need to learn specific techniques of embezzlement (Cressey, 1953, 1971: 147–151).

Differential association theory then proposes that *the direction of motives and drives is learned from definition of the law as favorable or unfavorable.* This assumes that people orient their actions toward the law; in other words, the law is not irrelevant to any individual in deciding how to behave. Some situations are defined as favorable to violation of the law; thus, an unattended bicycle may be seen as a chance to steal. However, the same situation may also be defined as unfavorable to violation of the law, with the unattended bicycle being viewed as a chance to alert the owner to the risk of theft or as a chance to watch the bicycle until the owner returns. Some people define the situation in one way, and others define it differently. The way the situation is defined depends on the favorable or unfavorable definitions of the law that have been learned in the past.

The primary proposition of differential association theory is that a person becomes delinquent or criminal because of *an EXCESS of definitions favorable to violation of the law OVER definitions unfavorable to violation of the law.* This principle stresses association with criminal or noncriminal definitions but does not require contact with criminal or noncriminal individuals. One can learn definitions favorable to violation of the law from law-abiding people, and one can learn definitions unfavorable to violation of the law from criminals. Parents may not violate the law but verbally approve of theft for certain purposes (such as feeding a family) or in certain situations (such as in a large store). Parental approval of this sort may convey to children a definition favorable to violation of the law. On the other hand, a professional thief may convey to young thieves the need to avoid violence against victims of theft. Some offenders even warn others away from behavior that they themselves engage in. For instance, heroin addicts often tell nonusers to stay away not only from heroin but also from marijuana, the drug with which many of them began.

Critical to differential association theory is the *ratio* of definitions favorable to violation of the law to definitions unfavorable. Any one individual holds both types of definitions. It is only when the definitions favorable to violation of the law exceed the definitions unfavorable that a person turns to crime or delinquency. There is an obvious difficulty in measuring these definitions of the law so that an exact ratio can be calculated for any given person.

Definitions of the law are a result of associations with criminal and noncriminal patterns that vary in *frequency, duration, priority, and intensity.* It is the nature of associations with criminal and noncriminal patterns, rather than the mere fact of those associations, that is important. Associations that are more frequent play a larger role in the balance between definitions favorable to violation of the law and definitions unfavorable to violation of the law. Associations that endure over the longest time are the most significant in determining criminal behavior. Associations that occur earlier in life — in childhood or in adolescence — are the most important in forming definitions of the law; this is called priority. Finally, the intensity of associations is important. This means that the prestige of the source of the definition of the law and the individual's emotional reactions to the source are significant in learning definitions of the law. Thus, a young child who learns a definition favorable to violation of the law from a parent who presents that definition frequently and over long stretches of time will be more influenced in the direction of violating the law than an adult who is exposed to a definition favorable to violation of the law by a passing acquaintance whom the adult sees infrequently and for short periods.

Critique of Differential Association Theory

The theory of differential association stresses the ratio of definitions favorable to violation of the law over definitions unfavorable to violation of the law. It may be mistaken in looking at definitions of the law in general, for individuals violate specific laws. Thus, a person might not need to hold an overall unfavorable view of the law before committing a crime; holding an unfavorable definition of one specific law may be enough.

Differential association theory examines the learning process by which people become criminals, but it does not explain why people have the associations they do. Because the theory does not tell us how the associations that expose people to different definitions of the law are distributed throughout the social structure, it does not fulfill its goal of explaining why crime rates vary among groups as they do.

Because differential association theory looks at the individual's perception of the situation, rather than at the actual situation itself, the theory is a social-psychological rather than a social-structural one. It is not, however, a purely psychological theory, because it does not consider personality traits and psychological variables to be important factors in crime causation.

One criticism of differential association theory is that it may better describe how some people initially become involved in crime and delinquency than why people continue in a criminal career. Thus, the direct rewards of crime — such as money, euphoria from illegal narcotics, or prestige among peers — may be a sufficient cause of continued violation of the law.

Because differential association theory is so general and imprecise, it is not easily tested. Even if the concepts of the theory could be defined in measurable terms, an enormous amount of data would be needed to test the theory. Consider, for example, the difficulty of measuring not only all associations with criminal definitions, but also all associations with noncriminal definitions, from the time a person is conscious of the social environment. To test the theory, it would be necessary to measure how frequent all of those associations are, how long they last, how they vary in significance because of the person's age, and how the person reacts emotionally to the various sources of definitions. Because this measurement process cannot realistically be accomplished, some sociologists have tried to test the theory by examining hypotheses derived from it. Full verification of differential association theory would require extensive research that examines many specific hypotheses generated by the theory, and this has not yet been done.

Modifications of Differential Association Theory

Because of the shortcomings of differential association theory, several modifications of the theory have been proposed. Two important ones are differential identification theory and differential association-reinforcement theory.

DIFFERENTIAL IDENTIFICATION THEORY   *Differential identification theory* stresses the way people choose models for their behavior. The choice of models does not necessarily involve interaction with others in intimate personal groups, as required by differential association theory. Instead, according to differential identification theory, "a person pursues criminal behavior to the extent that he identifies himself with real or imaginary persons from whose perspective his criminal behavior seems acceptable" (Glaser, 1956: 440). This approach has been described as follows:

> Differential identification allows for human choice, and stresses the importance of vocabularies of motives existing in the wider culture independently of direct intimate association. That is, direct, social and symbolic support for deviance need not necessarily coexist before deviant action is undertaken. . . . Once this step has been taken, differential association becomes important only to the extent that personal interaction is a considerable factor in criminality and the "excess of definitions favorable over those unfavorable" is now seen to be involved with the relative weightings purposively given to these factors by the actor. (Taylor, Walton, and Young, 1973: 129–130)

Testing differential identification theory would require the application of role theory to people who do and do not violate the law, which might be somewhat easier than testing differential association theory.

DIFFERENTIAL ASSOCIATION-REINFORCEMENT THEORY   Another important modification of differential association theory is Burgess and Akers's (1966; Akers et al., 1979; Akers, 1985) *differential association-reinforcement theory.* This social learning theory is broader than differential association theory. It states that learning occurs through operant conditioning in both nonsocial and social situations, even though most learning results from interaction with others. People learn attitudes and techniques conducive to crime from positive reinforcement (rewards) and negative reinforcement (punishments) that result from their own behavior, whether it is criminal or law-abiding. Thus, an absence of rewards from attending school or holding a menial job would make criminal behavior seem more attractive.

Evidence on Differential Association Theory

There is some research that is consistent with differential association theory. Much of this research focuses on the relationship between delinquent behavior and patterns of interaction among adolescents, demonstrating that the associates of delinquents are other delinquents and that delinquency is often a group

phenomenon. Even though this evidence is consistent with differential association theory, the absence of a time dimension in the research makes it impossible
to conclude that the learning of delinquent behavior from others precedes and
causes violation of the law.

EVIDENCE AGAINST DIFFERENTIAL ASSOCIATION THEORY Differential association theory does not explain all crimes. For instance, it is not consistent with
some evidence on rural offenders or with research on landlords who violate
rent-control regulations (Clinard, 1942; 1944; 1952, 1969). In addition, some
check forgers operate alone and apparently lack the associations with criminal
patterns required by differential association theory (Lemert, 1953). Some
crimes are evidently invented anew by offenders who do not experience the
learning process proposed in differential association theory. Unique situations
can generate or facilitate crimes without the offender's learning criminal motives or techniques from others.

Offenders who are not part of a criminal subculture or who have no ties to
criminals may lack exposure to the patterns and associations needed to learn
criminal motives and skills. One study of shoplifters found that often they had
no contact with a criminal subculture or with other criminal patterns. Few of
those who were apprehended had prior convictions, most were "respectable"
people who were employed or were housewives, many did not live in poor
neighborhoods, most took inexpensive merchandise with little resale value, and
many were ignorant of the arrest process (Cameron, 1964: 146–148). These
characteristics suggest a lack of contact with a subculture that could have provided the shoplifters with criminal motives and techniques.

PROFESSIONAL THEFT AND DIFFERENTIAL ASSOCIATION THEORY Evidence
consistent with differential association theory comes from studies of professional thieves. Members of the subculture of professional thieves teach new
recruits the skills that make expert theft possible, and immersion in the subculture isolates the thieves from noncriminal patterns (Sutherland, 1937; Maurer,
1955, 1964; 1974; Letkemann, 1973). The process of *tutelage* or instruction
provides new thieves with knowledge of how to spot opportunities for theft, how
to plan thefts, and how to carry out thefts. Thus, burglars learn specific skills
such as how to enter a building or how to blow open a safe. Robbers learn how to
interpret the body language of potential victims, how to control victims, and
how to show self-confidence and mastery during the crime. Con artists learn
how to lie convincingly, how to size up and manipulate victims, how to display a
winning personality, and how to look respectable.

Pickpockets learn to look unobtrusive in public, be cautious, and use the
opportunities with which they are presented. Manual dexterity is a source of
professional pride for pickpockets. Good pickpockets are expected to have the
skill to take money from a victim if they can figure out where the victim is
carrying his or her money. Pickpockets learn timing, speed, misdirection, con-
cealment, rhythmic movement, and dexterity. They learn to blend these skills

into a "single, almost instantaneous, and practically invisible act of theft" (Maurer, 1955, 1964: 41). Pickpockets also learn about garments and their pockets, and how to take wallets from different pockets. These skills are learned through direct interaction with skilled pickpockets: "One thief turns out another. That is, he teaches him" (Maurer, 1955, 1964: 157). Pickpockets first learn that it is possible to steal from other people. Then they learn specific skills, practice them, and are evaluated by other thieves, so that they refine their skills and eventually become accepted as professionals by other pickpockets. If thieves are arrested and imprisoned, as most eventually are, their pickpocketing skills may grow rusty because they cannot practice them in prison.

A study of professional thieves in a Canadian prison concluded that early involvement in juvenile delinquency seems to be a prerequisite for an adult career as a professional criminal (Letkemann, 1973). As juveniles, these thieves learned such things as how to avoid attention when stealing and what a typical police reaction to a certain crime might be. Their usual pattern was a gradual progression from awkward juvenile theft, to some learning from other thieves while incarcerated, to trial and error with new forms of theft, and then to learning from skilled thieves and from personal experience. These professional thieves learned mechanical skills, social skills such as the management of victims, and organizational skills such as planning and executing a crime. They learned these things from other prisoners, from members of their gang, and from thieves they met in bars. In this way, safecrackers learned about different styles of safes and how to break into them; this information had to be continually updated.

JUVENILE DELINQUENCY AND DIFFERENTIAL ASSOCIATION THEORY   Juvenile gangs reinforce and stimulate delinquency by supporting law-violating behavior and by offering protection from outsiders to gang members who break the law. A study of juvenile theft in Great Britain found that association with other adolescents who had already stolen property was very important in leading to theft by boys, especially if that association began when a boy was quite young, continued over a long time, and involved boys who stole frequently (Belson, 1975).

Research in the United States reveals that much delinquency takes place in groups, although the extent to which this is true varies with the specific offense and the sex of the offender (Erickson and Jensen, 1977; Giordano, 1978). One study concludes that juvenile shoplifters often learn attitudes and techniques from other juveniles. Because older juveniles are more likely to steal by themselves, and younger thieves are more likely to steal in groups, the researcher suggests that younger thieves learn motives and skills from others but are eventually able to steal by themselves (Cameron, 1964: 148–149).

Several studies focus on the ability of differential association theory to explain adolescent use of drugs and alcohol. One study finds that differential association theory must be modified, even though it is generally supported by the data. Peer groups seem to have a direct effect on drug and alcohol use among teens, independent of the internalized definitions of the law held by adolescents. Differential association theory in its original form suggests that peer groups affect behavior by their impact on these definitions, and the data do not support that idea. Moreover, definitions held by adults who are important in the adolescents' lives do not seem to play a role in marijuana use. Peer groups or a drug subculture, rather than adults, seem to affect the use of marijuana by teens. However, adolescents' use of alcohol is influenced by adult definitions, and this finding is compatible with differential association theory. In conclusion, this study suggests that peer groups' definitions help to generate some kinds of delinquent behavior, but that their impact varies with the kind of behavior in question (Jaquith, 1981).

SEXUAL AGGRESSION AND DIFFERENTIAL ASSOCIATION THEORY   One recent study found a strong association between sexual aggression by males and the presence of sexually aggressive friends. This study measured sexual aggression by self-reports, asking subjects the following:

> It has been noted that in the course of men's and women's sexual lives together, some men on occasion make physically forceful attempts at sexual activity which are disagreeable and offensive enough that the woman responds in an offended manner such as crying, fighting, screaming, pleading, etc. Have you ever engaged in such behavior?

The strongest predictor of such sexual aggression, which includes the crime of forcible rape as well as lesser degrees of sexual assault, was the presence of sexually aggressive friends. Subjects most likely to report sexual aggression had sexually aggressive friends, had served in Vietnam, and held attitudes legitimizing sexual aggression (Alder, 1985). Though not offering direct proof of differential association theory, this study suggests that sexually aggressive males, including rapists, may learn such behavior through interaction with peers.

WHITE-COLLAR CRIME AND DIFFERENTIAL ASSOCIATION THEORY   Differential association theory is useful in explaining crime in the business world. White-collar crime arises in part from learning cultural goals, such as material success, and then pursuing those goals through illegal means. Because there is no enforceable code of business ethics to limit the pursuit of those goals to legal means, definitions unfavorable to violation of the law may not readily be learned in the world of business.

Some business crime results from what C. Wright Mills (1956) calls "structural immorality," a characteristic of the corporate milieu that leads to a lack of personal responsibility among some businesspeople. Individuals who are most assimilated into a business organization are probably the most likely to violate the law, and those new to the world of business are less likely to do so because they are more apt to be guided by the definitions unfavorable to violation of the law that they bring with them from the outside world. A study of attitudes toward bribes and payoffs made by businesspeople to foreign officials found that experienced executives who were enrolled in business school programs were more tolerant of such bribes and payoffs than were undergraduate business students who lacked experience in the world of business (M. Jensen, 1976). This suggests that experience in business is conducive to the learning of definitions supportive of bribes and payoffs. Whether these definitions lead to actual violation of the law depends on factors such as exposure to definitions unfavorable to violation of the law and the presence of opportunities to break the law.

Learning from superiors and from peers in the company is probably a more important determinant of business crime than is the personality of the individual. A former head of the Securities and Exchange Commission's Division of Enforcement states this bluntly: "Our largest corporations have trained some of our brightest young people to be dishonest" (Stanley Sporkin, cited in Kohlmeier, 1976: 53). Social pressure to violate the law has been described as follows for the Equity Funding Corporation of America fraud: "Corporations can and do create a moral tone that powerfully influences the thinking, conduct, values, and even the personalities of the people who work for them. The tone is set by the men who run the company, and their corruption can quickly corrupt all else" (Blundell, 1976: 46).

Differential association theory fits much of what we know about white-collar crime. Businesspeople learn definitions favorable to violation of the law, such as loyalty to the corporation over loyalty to the law. This learning process includes techniques of neutralization that are conducive to violation of the law. It also involves the segregation of businesspeople from the law-abiding public, thus making them relatively immune to public criticism and limiting their exposure to definitions unfavorable to violation of the law. Ties to the law-abiding public are weakened and dependence on the corporation is strengthened by the common practice of regularly moving young executives from one region to another (Coleman, 1985).

From his study of the black market that developed when prices were regulated by the Office of Price Administration (OPA) from 1942 to 1947, Marshall Clinard (1952, 1969) concludes that definitions of the situation and justifications for black market violations were transmitted from one businessperson to another in conversations and were described in the general press and in business trade papers. He suggests that differential association theory is consistent with aspects of the black market such as the similarity of offenses, the shared attitudes of businesspeople toward government regulation, and the failure to condemn violators of the regulations. However, this evidence does not prove that businesspeople learned to commit their crimes in face-to-face interaction with people who held criminal definitions of the law. The similarity of their violations may have been due to a common response to OPA regulations, the market structure of certain industries, and available opportunities to violate the law.

Donald Cressey (1953, 1971) assesses the usefulness of differential association theory in his study of embezzlement. He finds that offenders did not learn specific techniques and skills for embezzlement through interaction with others, but rather employed regular job skills to commit their crimes. They learned rationalizations for their offenses from the general culture, but most of them could not give specific sources of their justifications for theft. Cressey concludes that the general emphasis of differential association theory is correct, in spite of his finding that the associations of embezzlers did not change prior to their thefts in a way that would have produced an excess of definitions favorable to violation of the law.

Even though research on embezzlement and black market violations indicates that differential association has its limitations, the theory seems to be consistent with two conclusions about white-collar crime. First, it is often learned from the general culture, from the ideology of business, and from peers and superiors in the firm. Second, it is frequently associated with the isolation of business offenders from norms and values that support the law.

Though there is some evidence consistent with differential association theory, there is no firm support for the theory as it is formally stated. In other words, there is no concrete evidence from studies of various kinds of offenders that they initially became criminals because of an excess of definitions favorable to violation of the law over definitions unfavorable to violation of the law. To demonstrate this would involve a measurement task that might be impossible. It would also require a comparison of offenders with a sample from the general population who did not become offenders.

The Labeling Perspective

Since Edwin Lemert's (1951) pioneering work on the labeling of deviant behavior, much attention has been directed to the effects on individuals of being treated as deviants. Labeling is a general perspective on deviance that has been applied to mental illness, homosexuality, and even stuttering. Because crime and delinquency are forms of deviant behavior, this perspective should help us understand some of the causes of law-violating behavior.

The *labeling perspective* assumes that people first violate a norm by chance or for unexplained reasons. This initial act of deviance, called *primary deviation,* sometimes elicits reactions from others. These reactions often take the form of stereotyping and rejecting the deviant. Thus, one study suggests that offenders are treated more harshly by the courts if they fit the stereotype of a "normal primitive," an image of lower-class blacks and other minorities whose limited education, lack of job skills, orientation to the present, possession of weapons, and immaturity are thought to predispose them to violence (Swigert and Farrell, 1976, 1977). Another stereotype is of lower-class delinquents, who are thought to violate the law because of blocked opportunities, poor education, or other defects of the social structure. This contrasts with the stereotype of middle-class delinquents, who are said to violate the law because of a temporary lack of commitment to adult roles and values, a view that relies on social-psychological factors and control theory (Cernkovich, 1978b). Ideas about why different types of people break the law can influence the way those people are treated by the criminal justice system.

Differences in norms about parental supervision of the sexual activity of sons and daughters can lead to the labeling of one sex but not the other as delinquent, even though the behavior of both sexes is the same. Many girls who are brought into juvenile court are there for reasons related to their "adult" sexual activity. By contrast, the males with whom they were sexually involved are rarely labeled delinquent for the same behavior.

People who engage in socially disapproved behavior are labeled as disvalued individuals. Their status as a deviant sometimes becomes a *master status;* that is, other aspects of their behavior are submerged in a social identity as a deviant. The labeling perspective directs attention away from the causes of primary deviation, or rule breaking, and focuses instead on the people and institutions that have the power to label behavior deviant (Schur, 1971, 1979). The processing of rule breakers by institutions, such as prisons and mental hospitals, keeps deviants at a distance from the rest of society. Deviant acts would occur even if there were no such institutions, but the deviant acts' "nature, distribution, social meaning, and implications and ramifications are significantly influenced by patterns of social reaction" (Schur, 1969: 115). The assumption of the labeling perspective is that a major cause of continued deviant behavior is the way that people who initially violate norms are treated by lawmakers, police officers, judges, psychiatrists, and others who have the power to affix the label "deviant." Deviant behavior that is a product of this labeling process is called *secondary deviation.*

Labeling and Self-Concepts

One way the labeling of deviant behavior leads to secondary deviation is through the effects of the label on the self-concept of the person who has been labeled. People who violate the law and are arrested by the police and tried in court may have their conceptions of themselves altered and come to think of themselves as criminals or delinquents. Court appearances have been called "status degradation ceremonies" in which people accused of violating the law are recast as unworthy persons (Garfinkel, 1956). These people may then reject other people and become hostile to society in order to maintain their self-esteem (Schrag, 1974). Being labeled criminal or delinquent in court can thus produce a self-fulfilling prophecy, so that people behave in ways consistent with their altered self-concepts. In other words, once they are labeled criminal by the police, the courts, and the prisons, people may continue to behave as criminals.

The labeling perspective would suggest that the first time youngsters engage in minor vandalism or petty theft, they might think little of it. If they are arrested, brought to court, and treated as delinquents, they may come to think that they have done something drastically wrong and that perhaps they are unworthy people. As a result, they may begin to associate with others who have also been labeled as troublemakers, and this could lead them into additional and

People who are arrested may have their conceptions of themselves altered and come to think of themselves as criminals or delinquents.   *Source: Phyllis Graber Jensen / Stock Boston*

more serious delinquency. A study of adolescent shoplifters found that those who had been exposed to the police by store officials were more likely to engage in subsequent shoplifting than were adolescent shoplifters who had not been subjected to the police (Klemke, 1978). This is consistent with the labeling perspective's assumption that processing a deviant can amplify or increase deviance.

Rather than engage in more deviance because of being labeled, some people who are labeled deviant react by trying to change their behavior to conform to social expectations. The fact that many juveniles who are arrested are apprehended only once can be interpreted to mean that the status degradation ceremony that occurs in juvenile court persuades some of them to avoid delinquency in the future. This probably is most likely to occur for first-time offenders with the following characteristics:

- They have a stake in conformity.
- They are sensitive to others' evaluations of themselves.
- They are labeled in private rather than in public.
- They are not committed to a delinquent or criminal career.
- They are able to remove the label with good behavior in the future. (Thorsell and Klemke, 1972)

SELF-CONCEPTS AND CONTAINMENT THEORY   Self-concept plays an important role in the *containment theory* of crime and delinquency (Reckless, 1973, 1978). This theory proposes that people are insulated to various degrees against pressures to commit deviant acts by "external" and "internal" factors. External containment results from attachments to family, community, and other parts of the social structure. Internal containment is composed of the following "self" components:

1. A favorable image of self in relation to other persons, groups, and institutions.
2. An awareness of being an inner directed, goal oriented person.
3. A high level of frustration tolerance.
4. Strongly internalized morals and ethics.
5. Well developed ego and superego. (Reckless, 1978: 189)

Greater strength of either internal or external containment will reduce vulnerability to crime and delinquency, but "the inner containment is the more important in the mobile, industrialized settings of modern society" (Reckless, 1978: 189).

There is some evidence that juvenile delinquents have poorer self-concepts than nondelinquents, and that delinquents are more likely to believe that they will break the law, not finish school, and be unsuccessful (Dinitz, Scarpitti, and Reckless, 1962; Jensen, 1973). Delinquency has been seen as a defense against low self-esteem caused by doing poorly in school (Mann, 1981). Delinquents seem to be less likely than nondelinquents to be committed to long-range goals, and they are more likely to strive beyond their means, be impulsive, have a short time perspective, and feel unable to control themselves (Dinitz, Scarpitti, and Reckless, 1962; Jensen, 1973; Reckless, 1973).

In contrast to delinquents and criminals, those who abide by the law tend to see themselves as accountable for their actions. They feel good about themselves and behave accordingly, taking into account the "hypothesized reactions" of others before they act. This is much like what Hirschi calls the "psychological presence" of parents and authority figures. Noncriminals see themselves as vulnerable if they deviate from the law, and they fear the loss of material rewards and the good opinion of others (Rogers, 1977: 64–68).

There is some evidence that negative self-concepts are associated with crime and delinquency, but some research suggests that the relationship between self-concept and violation of the law is not a strong one (Farrell and Nelson, 1978). One study concludes that self-esteem has a negligible impact on subsequent delinquency, but that involvement in delinquent behavior does lower subsequent self-esteem somewhat (McCarthy and Hoge, 1984). However, another study concluded that self-rejection—as measured by self-derogation, perceived lack of socially desirable attributes, and perceived rejection by parents and teachers—had a strong direct effect on junior high school students' disposition to deviance—as measured by disaffection from family, school, and the conventional community. That disposition to deviance in turn had a strong direct effect on deviant behavior, including many acts that might lead to being labeled delinquent (Kaplan, Martin, and Johnson, 1986).

REJECTING THE LABEL   An individual's self-concept is a product of many influences. It is influenced by the reactions of others, but it is also the product of choice and reflection by the individual. The label attached by the criminal justice system can affect a person's self-concept, but the individual can also reject or fight the label. Self-concepts are constructed in an active way. The opinions of others are considered and sometimes incorporated into the self-concept, but those opinions may also be rejected as inconsistent with a person's idea of himself or herself (Scimecca, 1977).

Conventional Criminals.   Conventional offenders sometimes are able to disavow the label "criminal." Professional fences see themselves as decent people who perform a socially useful function (Klockars, 1974: 151–161). Robbers claim that they are "not too dishonest" because they steal from their victims in a direct way, rather than sneaking around in a house at night to commit a burglary (Inciardi, 1975: 71–72). Apprehended shoplifters often disavow the label of criminal when first caught, but the threat of prosecution usually forces them to redefine themselves as offenders; this happens because they fear exposure and lack support for a noncriminal definition of self (Cameron, 1964: 159–170).

White-Collar Criminals.   White-collar offenders often believe that because few of them are arrested, convicted, and imprisoned, they are not "real criminals." This view is even shared by some law enforcers. The head of the Antitrust Division of the Department of Justice expressed this nicely in 1940:

> While civil penalties may be as severe in their financial effects as criminal penalties, yet they do not involve the stigma that attends indictment and conviction. Most of the defendants in antitrust cases are not criminals *in the usual sense.* There is no inherent reason why antitrust enforcement requires branding them as such. (cited in Sutherland, 1949, 1983: 54; emphasis added here)

White-collar criminals often see their offenses as "technical violations of governmental regulations" and are thus able to maintain a noncriminal self-concept, even when labeled criminal in court. A General Electric vice-president, who was on his way to jail after a conviction for price fixing, said to the press: "All of you know that next Monday, in Philadelphia, I will start serving a thirty-day jail term, along with six other *businessmen* for conduct which has been *interpreted* as being in conflict with the *complex* antitrust laws" (cited in Geis, 1974: 273; emphasis added here). Here we see a convicted criminal disavowing the label of criminal. This is easier for offenders who do not fit the stereotype of the typical criminal, who are treated with leniency by the courts, and who enjoy the support of their families, friends, and colleagues.

THE EFFECTS OF LABELING ON SELF-CONCEPTS Some research suggests that the effects of official labeling on the self-concepts of delinquents and criminals may not be as great as the labeling perspective proposes. One study found that labeling by law enforcers had no major effect on self-satisfaction, identification with other delinquents, or future commitment to delinquency (Hepburn, 1977). A longitudinal cohort study found that a single delinquent experience often had a limited effect, and that being labeled once as a delinquent did not necessarily transform a person (Polk, 1980). Delinquents often express concern with the outcome of their cases, but their appearances in court may not be obviously stigmatizing and may not have major effects on their self-esteem (Mahoney, 1974).

The effects of labeling seem to vary with the individual who is labeled. One study found that the self-concepts of lower-class white delinquents appear to be more influenced by an appearance in juvenile court than are the self-concepts of other delinquents (Ageton and Elliott, 1973). Self-concepts of delinquents may be less influenced by official sanctions than by the frequency and seriousness of the delinquent's illegal acts. In other words, a self-concept may be grounded more in actual behavior than in official reactions to that behavior, with the police and the courts validating or rubber stamping an individual's self-concept rather than applying a totally new label.

Even if official labeling affects a person's self-concept, it does not necessarily increase delinquent or criminal behavior, for there is no strong evidence that changes in self-concepts cause changes in law-violating behavior (Mahoney, 1974). Moreover, any effects that the labeling has may fade with time.

There is thus some evidence that official labeling by the criminal justice system may not have the dramatic effects suggested by the labeling perspective. However, the effects of labeling might be subtle and complex and might occur only over long periods. In addition, research on labeling, self-concepts, and violation of the law may simply not yet have uncovered all of the effects of stigmatizing people as criminals or delinquents.

Labeling and Opportunities

A second effect of labeling — in addition to its possible effects on self-concepts — is the reduction of opportunities and the harm to the social relationships of people who are labeled by the criminal or juvenile justice system. Even if self-concept does not change, a person may experience difficulty in relationships with parents, friends, teachers, or potential employers if those people react negatively to the label of delinquent or criminal.

A study of 196 adolescent boys sought to determine if juvenile court intervention had reinforced their deviance by producing "spoiled" identities or by harming their relationships with people who viewed them with mistrust and suspicion because of their official status as delinquents (Foster, Dinitz, and Reckless, 1972). In general, the boys did not believe that their contact with the law had created any major problems for them in their social relationships. They perceived no negative effects on their friends' attitudes toward them. Few of the boys thought that being in trouble with the law would cause them any special problems at school, because they would be protected by the secrecy of juvenile court records and by their ability to separate their out-of-school life from their role as student. The boys believed that their court experiences would not influence their parents' attitudes toward them, other than simply confirming attitudes their parents already held. This conclusion is consistent with other research that finds that parent-child relationships are well established before court appearances and are not substantially influenced by those appearances (Mahoney, 1974).

The boys in this study did think that their contact with the courts might have some negative effects in two areas: their relationships with the police and their relationships with future employers. About half of the boys said that the police would be more likely to keep an eye on them because they had been to court, but they thought this problem could be solved by convincing the police that they had given up delinquency. Nearly half of the boys believed that future employers might hold their court appearances against them, but many thought that this liability would be unimportant if they avoided encounters with the law in the future. The boys also counted on the passage of time and the secrecy of juvenile court records to minimize their problems with future employers.

This study concluded that the labeling perspective overemphasizes the effects on the individual of stigmatization by the juvenile courts. Such labeling may actually close legitimate opportunities or harm social relationships, but the boys in this study did not generally perceive this to be the case. However, nearly half of the boys had been involved with the juvenile justice system before, and a study of the impact of their first court appearance might have found more dramatic effects on their social relationships.

Even though somewhat more than half of the boys in this study thought that their appearance in juvenile court would not hurt them with future employers, there is some evidence that job opportunities may be closed if potential employers learn about a person's problems with the law (Erickson and Goodstadt, 1979). In fact, even the knowledge that a job applicant has been acquitted of charges seems to make some employers less willing to offer that person a job (Schwartz and Skolnick, 1962). As a result, the law in the United States now prohibits employers from asking about arrests, limiting them to questions about actual criminal convictions. The law also "seals" or keeps secret juvenile court records so that job opportunities are not denied to those who get into trouble with the law at a young age.

Labeling and Subcultures

In addition to the effects of labeling on self-concepts and social relationships, labeling can push people into subcultures in which they learn criminal motives and skills. Thus, contact with other offenders can result directly from the imposition of the label of delinquent or criminal, regardless of any change in self-concept. Once contact has been made with the members of a subculture, the learning process described by differential association theory may increase law-violating behavior. This learning process can then affect the offender's self-concept, even if labeling by the police or the courts did not have that effect. Thus, a woman convicted of prostitution may be approached by a pimp, by drug dealers, or by gangsters who see her "spoiled identity" as making her vulnerable to exploitation. By pushing an offender into a subculture, labeling can make reintegration into society difficult and increase the probability that people will repeat their crimes.

Critique of the Labeling Perspective

Figure 9.1 shows the labeling perspective in schematic form. The perspective proposes that primary deviation, or rule breaking, sometimes leads to the labeling of the rule breaker. This can affect an individual's self-concept and opportunities and drive the person into a subculture. In the subculture, the individual may undergo a change in self-concept through differential association with other deviants. In these ways, the labeling process can amplify or increase deviant behavior, leading to secondary deviation.

The labeling perspective has some shortcomings. It does not tell us why some people engage in primary deviation and why other people do not break rules or do so infrequently. The labeling perspective helps us understand what society makes of primary deviation, but it tells us little about rule breaking that is not socially labeled. The perspective fails to make clear the conditions under which labeling will alter self-concepts, restrict opportunities, hurt social relationships, and drive deviants into subcultures. It has also not made clear when a label will be accepted by a rule breaker and when a deviant will reject or disavow a label.

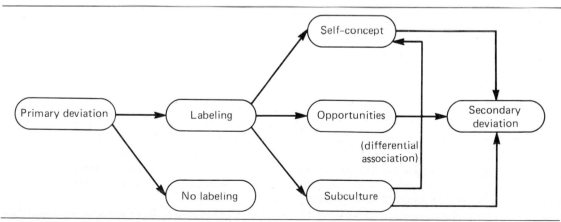

FIGURE 9.1 The Labeling Perspective

In addition, there is little empirical evidence that labeling by the criminal justice system actually increases crime or delinquency. Experiences with the criminal justice system sometimes deter potential offenders, and some offenders who are labeled and then commit more crime might have gone on to commit more crime even if they had not been labeled. The labeling perspective is useful in directing our attention to social processes that may, under some circumstances and for some kinds of people, reinforce tendencies to violate the law, but it is not yet a fully developed and empirically tested theory of crime and delinquency.

Rewards and Risks of Crime

Differential association theory suggests that people turn to crime when their attitudes become supportive of crime — that is, when their definitions favorable to violation of the law outweigh their definitions unfavorable to violation of the law. The labeling perspective suggests that being processed by the criminal justice system changes self-concepts and social relationships and pushes people into criminal subcultures. Another approach sees criminal behavior as learned and reinforced through the intrinsic rewards and risks that it offers to offenders.

Operant Conditioning and Crime

Operant conditioning theory emphasizes the interaction of the person and the environment; people's behavior affects the world around them in ways that in turn influence their future behavior. The reasons for an initial criminal act may be accidental, experimental (curiosity), or instrumental (goal seeking), but an individual is more likely to continue that behavior over time if it is found to be intrinsically rewarding. Thus, a boy who steals property — or even forgets to pay for something that he picks up in a store — will find the act rewarding if he is not caught, for he has the item and still has his money. Over time, this boy's thefts may become more frequent and more consciously planned, and may involve increasingly expensive goods. Positive reinforcement of this sort is probably most common for property crimes, but aggression against others can also escalate if it is reinforced (Berkowitz, 1974).

The Economist's Model of Criminal Behavior

The *economist's model* of criminal behavior focuses on instrumental rather than expressive offenses. An *instrumental crime* is one in which an offender gets some satisfaction from the product of the crime, and an *expressive crime* is one in which the act itself fulfills an emotional need for the offender. Instrumental crimes are commonly planned in advance, but expressive crimes are more often impulsive. Economists look at crimes purposefully chosen by offenders to achieve certain ends; they see offenders as acting in a conscious manner, making reasoned and informed choices in much the same way that intelligent consumers do. Economists admit that the criminal's rationality is "bounded," or limited, in certain ways, but they do not specify what the limitations on rationality are.

The Reward-Risk Model of Criminal Behavior

In recent years, an integrated *reward-risk model* of criminal behavior has evolved from the work of operant conditioning psychologists, economists, political scientists, and social learning theorists. This model assumes that everyone, including criminals, chooses how to behave in a rational way, and that everyone's actions are influenced by the consequences of his or her behavior.

If the rewards of crime are great and its risks small, and if the rewards from a noncriminal way of life are comparatively small and its risks relatively great, people may rationally choose to violate the law. Potential offenders thus consider the rewards (or benefits) and the risks (or costs) of criminal and noncriminal behavior before breaking the law. According to Wilson and Herrnstein (1985: 44), "The larger the ratio of net rewards of crime to the net rewards of noncrime, the greater the tendency to commit crime." Table 9.1 shows some of the many risks and rewards of criminal activity. Money is one of the rewards from property crimes, but many of the rewards from crime are noneconomic, including excitement and challenge, satisfaction in carrying out a difficult crime, prestige in the eyes of other offenders, and the chance to be one's own boss.

The impact of the rewards and risks of both crime and noncrime on the behavior of individuals is associated with several important characteristics of those rewards and risks. Rewards and risks that are more certain will influence behavior to a greater degree than rewards and risks that are less apt to be

TABLE 9.1   Rewards and Risks of Theft

Rewards (or Benefits)	Risks (or Costs)
Money earned from crime	Being caught and punished (lost freedom if imprisoned; lost money if fined)
Freedom from taxation	
Excitement of criminal activity	
Satisfaction in a crime successfully carried out	Loss of benefits from legal work (paid vacation, social security, medical insurance)
Much leisure time	
Reputation as a successful criminal	
Free room and board if caught and imprisoned	Time to learn criminal skills
	Costs of equipment to do the crime
	Risk of injury while stealing (by police or by victim)
	Work involved in casing a target and carrying out the crime
	Anxiety about punishment
	Stigma of being labeled a criminal

SOURCE: Adapted from Gwynn Nettler, *Lying, Cheating, Stealing.* Cincinnati, Ohio: Anderson Publishing Company, 1982, p. 97. Reprinted with permission.

experienced. Rewards and risks that are experienced in the present alter current behavior more than rewards and risks that will not be experienced for a long time. In addition, the more reinforcement (rewards and punishments) a person is receiving at any given time, the less impact any additional reward or punishment will have. Finally, people consider not only what they may gain from crime or noncrime, but also what others will gain from what are seen as comparable efforts. As Wilson and Herrnstein (1985: 57) state this "equity equation," "Individuals do not simply compare their gains to the gains of others; they compare the ratio of gains and contributions."

RISKS Before looking in more detail at some of the rewards of crime, we will consider some of its risks or costs. The primary risk is the threat of arrest, conviction, and imprisonment. Offenders sometimes plan their crimes to minimize these risks.

Most people who continue in crime for any significant amount of time are eventually arrested. Sometimes they are turned in by informants, sometimes they are caught because the police happen to be near the scene of the crime, and sometimes they are arrested because of efficient police investigative work. The probability of arrest for any single crime is relatively low, with the overall clearance rate for index crimes in 1986 being only 20.7 percent, but the chance of being arrested for at least one crime if a large number of crimes are committed is quite high. Even if an offender has an 80 percent chance of escaping arrest for a given offense, the chance of escaping any arrest if two such crimes are committed is only 64 percent, the chance of not being arrested at all if three offenses are perpetrated is 51 percent, the chance of not being arrested if ten offenses are committed is only 11 percent, and the chance of escaping any arrest if the offender commits twenty crimes is only 1 percent (Glaser, 1978: 86–90). In other words, the chance of not being arrested for a single crime may be quite high, but the chance of never being arrested over the course of a criminal career is quite small. Consequently, most criminal careers are eventually interrupted by arrest.

Continued criminal activity may make offenders more expert, thus minimizing their chance of being arrested, but with continued success many offenders become overconfident and careless. Moreover, chance factors play an important role, and in a real sense an offender's luck will eventually run out if he or she continues to violate the law.

REWARDS In spite of the high probability of being arrested, convicted, and imprisoned sometime during a criminal career, many offenders find that the rewards, or perceived rewards, of crime justify continued violation of the law. Some offenders believe the income they derive from crime is more certain and more substantial than the income they could earn from the legitimate jobs that are available to them (Holzman, 1982). However, even if all offenders were paid the amount they realize from their criminal activities, many of them would probably continue to violate the law because of the noneconomic rewards of crime.

One noneconomic reward of criminal behavior is the challenge of violating the law and getting away with it. This element of challenge is important in many computer crimes:

> A general characteristic of computer programmers is their fascination with challenges and desire to accept them. In fact, they face the great challenge of making computer systems do their bidding day in and day out. Telling a programmer that a computer system is safe from penetration is like waving a red flag in front of a bull. The challenge of an unauthorized act often overshadows the question of morality. (Parker, 1976: 47–48)

Another important noneconomic reward from crime is excitement. A study of "the criminal mind" concludes that "thinking about the crime is exciting. Committing the crime is exciting. Even getting caught is exciting. Trying to figure out a way to beat the rap is exciting" (Stanton Samenow, cited in Serrill, 1978: 90). For juvenile delinquents, excitement and relief from boredom are often motives to violate the law (Thrasher, 1927, 1963; Mayo, 1969; Belson, 1975; Csikszentmihalyi and Larson, 1978). A study of adolescent shoplifting found that equal numbers stole for instrumental reasons and for expressive reasons such as excitement (Klemke, 1978). One study treats middle-class delinquency as a form of play, claiming that much middle-class delinquency serves needs similar to those served by other forms of leisure: adding interest to the daily routine, providing entertainment, learning new techniques and skills, and learning social rules (Richards, Berk, and Foster, 1979).

We need to ask why violating the law is fun for some people. It may be that breaking rules set by others is satisfying, perhaps because it gives the rule breaker a feeling of autonomy. Sometimes the physical activity involved in a criminal or delinquent act is pleasing, or the consequences of the act are gratifying in some way. For instance, there may be an aesthetic element involved in vandalism, with vandals enjoying the visual, auditory, and tactile sensations resulting from their "creative conversion" of material things (Allen and Greenberger, 1978). The fun or "kicks" derived from crime may be short-lived, and this might lead to continued criminal activity. Some thieves claim that stealing is hard work with little thrill about it, and some say they are very tense while committing their crimes, but many offenders seem to be motivated by the challenge, excitement, and relief from boredom that they derive from criminal activity.

Some crime is motivated by a desire to preserve individual or collective honor. Trying to maintain one's self-image when insulted by another person can lead to homicide (Luckenbill, 1977). A study of Chicano gang violence found that preservation of the gang's collective honor and the self-esteem of its members often led to gang violence (Horowitz and Schwartz, 1974).

The Rewards and Risks of Crime

Different crimes offer different kinds of rewards and risks, and so an offender's choice of criminal activity may be influenced by the perceived benefits and costs of a particular crime. For instance, some thieves commit robberies to gain quick access to cash, even though they risk identification. Other thieves commit burglaries to avoid identification and confrontation with the victim, but they must then convert the stolen goods into cash.

CONVENTIONAL PROPERTY CRIMES   The conventional property offenses of robbery, burglary, car theft, and arson involve many risks, but they also offer rewards in addition to money and excitement. Thus, professional thieves mention satisfaction in a job well done, the leisure time between jobs, being their own boss, the nonroutine nature of theft, and the intrinsic satisfaction of stealing (Sutherland, 1937). Especially for those who lack the education and skill to get a good job, the choice of property crime as a source of income may seem rational.

Robbery. A study of "casual robbers" in the United States found that they stole to buy drugs and clothing, to maintain or enhance their standing among peers, and to create a more exciting life. Their "adventurous deviance" was more pleasurable because it was risky, but they tried to keep their risks to a "manageable level" (Lejeune, 1977: 125).

Other robbers are more systematic in their crimes. For instance, one study found that two robbers who committed nearly two hundred crimes in an eighteen-month period had decided to engage in robbery in a very calculating way. They had some money but lacked good job prospects and disliked the manual labor available to them. They wanted to make money quickly and decided on crime, which they saw as a business with risks and rewards like any other job. They spent four days in a public library doing research to find the best way to get money quickly and safely. They examined crime statistics, including the number of crimes committed, the amounts stolen, and the chances of arrest and conviction. They decided on armed robbery. They understood the risks they were taking, and picked robbery because it was direct and did not require them to convert property into cash. To reduce the risk of being injured by victims or the police, they carried firearms (Jackson, 1969: 20–21). Few offenders select their crimes this carefully, but these two robbers considered the rewards and risks of crime in a way that is consistent with the economist's model of the rational offender.

Burglary. A study of burglars found that excitement and solidarity with peers were considerations in the decision to commit crime, but that money was the primary motivating factor. Only 10 percent of the offenders said they would continue to commit burglary if all of their financial needs were met. Seventy-three percent said they would abandon burglary if their financial needs were satisfied, and 17 percent were uncertain what effect financial security would have on their criminal activity (Reppetto, 1974: 21–23). These burglars did not steal for survival; they usually spent their money on clothes, drugs, or alcohol. Few people ever think all of their financial needs are met, and so it is unlikely that many burglars would give up crime because they thought they had enough money.

Car Theft. Car theft has multiple motives. Some thieves steal cars for "joy riding" — to have a good time and enjoy prestige in the eyes of their peers. Others steal cars for short-term transportation; this results from situational pressures for rapid mobility and from the lack of other ways to get around. Some car thefts are for transportation over longer periods; these thieves keep stolen cars for personal use for some time. Cars may be stolen to commit other crimes, such as burglaries and robberies, because stolen cars cannot be traced to the offenders. Amateur thieves sometimes strip cars of their tires or batteries, and well-organized professionals steal cars, repaint them, and ship them out of state or out of the country for sale (McCaghy, Giordano, and Henson, 1977). The declining rate of recovery of stolen cars and the increasing age of arrested car thieves suggest that professionals have become more involved in car theft in recent years.

Arson. There are also multiple motives for arson. Some crimes of arson are said to be motivated by "pyromania" — a supposed psychological abnormality in which the arsonist or "firebug" derives pleasure from seeing things burn. Other motives for arson include revenge against the inhabitants or owners of a building, and desire for profit. People who seek a profit from arson have diverse motives. Landlords may burn buildings they cannot rent, maintain, or pay taxes on. Manufacturers suffering economic hardship "sell out to the insurance company" by burning a plant and collecting the insurance. Arsonists may burn buildings if others pay them to, or they may burn a building so they can steal and sell copper tubing or plumbing from the building (Nettler, 1978: 25 – 26).

WHITE-COLLAR CRIME   For white-collar offenders, the risks are relatively small. Few are convicted of a crime, and those who are usually are punished leniently. The instrumental nature of white-collar crime lends itself to a careful calculation of the costs and benefits of violating the law. For instance, we saw in Chapter 7 that in marketing the Pinto the Ford Motor Company carefully considered the costs it would incur in legal actions resulting from burn injuries and deaths and from burned vehicles. After determining that those costs were less than the cost of modifying the vehicles, Ford went ahead and produced dangerous automobiles (Cullen, Maakestaad, and Cavender, 1987).

DRUG USE   Drugs such as marijuana, cocaine, and heroin can be seen as rewarding for their physiological effects on users, and also for the profits they yield for those who import and sell drugs.

The Effects of Drugs. One study of marijuana use found that people who first try the drug by themselves often experience no pleasurable effects (Becker, 1973). Those who use marijuana for the first time in the presence of experienced users get feedback from them about the proper way to smoke, how to perceive the drug's effects, and how to enjoy those effects. People who continue to use marijuana do so because they find it personally rewarding.

Various addictive drugs are used by some physicians, especially anesthesiologists, who seek relief from the tension and exhaustion caused by their jobs. Drugs offer an escape, a way to relax, and a euphoria that allows some medical personnel to maintain a sense of competence at their jobs. Doctors and nurses have easy access to drugs and are generally aware of the positive effects of the drugs, while minimizing the potential dangers of prolonged use (Winick, 1964; Altman, 1983a, 1983b).

Many heroin users are given the drug free by friends and acquaintances the first time they use it; few first-time users have been looking for heroin on their own (Chein et al., 1964). Peer influence is a major force in initiating youths into heroin use. The idea that it is usually schoolyard pushers who lure youths into heroin use is incorrect (Hunt and Chambers, 1976).

The effects of the first use of heroin are sufficiently strong for some people that they do not need to learn from others how to enjoy the effects of the drug; one book on heroin is titled *"It's So Good, Don't Even Try It Once"* (Smith and Gay, 1972). For many users, however, it is necessary to learn to experience the effects of heroin as pleasurable. This is especially true for long-term use in a society in which the drug is illegal and therefore expensive, as it is in the United States (Goode, 1974).

Causes of Heroin Addiction. There is disagreement about the causes of heroin addiction. One long-standing theory developed by Alfred Lindesmith (1938, 1947, 1965, 1968, 1975) holds that heroin addicts become hooked when they make a connection in their minds between the administration of the drug and the alleviation of withdrawal symptoms — such as sweating, nausea, trembling, and hallucinations — that occur when the amount of heroin in the body gets too low. Addicts crave heroin. Whether this craving is psychological or physiological, or some combination of the two, is not clear, but craving does occur in people who have been addicted but are no longer using heroin.

Research by McAuliffe and Gordon (1974, 1975) with street addicts in Baltimore concludes that addicts need a drug that staves off withdrawal pain but want a drug that produces euphoria. Whereas Lindesmith discounts the importance of the desire for euphoria, McAuliffe and Gordon present strong evidence that pleasurable sensations are the primary reason addicts use heroin. They find that almost all addicts would like to get high every day, even though commitment to a conventional life style — including a family and a legitimate job — and lack of money keep some addicts from getting high more than two or three times a week.

Heroin Use and Crime. The rewards of heroin use can lead to addiction. In the United States, this inevitably leads addicts to violate the law, because the sale, possession, and use of heroin are illegal. In Great Britain, the use and possession of heroin are legal for addicts who are registered with the government and who are prescribed heroin or other addictive drugs by licensed physicians.

The use of heroin in the United States leads to crime in other ways as well. There are state and federal laws against the possession of "works," the hypodermic syringes that are used to administer the drug intravenously. Some addicts have adapted to such laws by gathering in "shooting galleries" where syringes are passed from one user to another (Howard and Borges, 1972). This allows fewer addicts to possess needles, and some addicts can thus avoid violating the law against the possession of works. Shooting heroin in the presence of others also provides group support for drug use and psychological protection against outsiders, and it gives users a chance to observe addicts who are "on the skids" and thus get a realistic but depressing view of their own future. Because heroin users know there is a good chance of contracting AIDS or hepatitis from shared needles, those who share needles are acting self-destructively. However, the rewards of needle sharing — not having to buy and carry works and the camaraderie of using heroin in a group — make this activity a favored one by some users.

Heroin addicts also engage in crimes that are secondary to their addiction. Where heroin is illegal, the cost of the drug is far above what it would be in an unrestricted market. One sociologist estimates that a heroin habit costing between $25 and $100 per day would cost no more than $1 a day if heroin were legally available (Glaser, 1978: 297). The cost of illegal heroin is so great that few addicts can support a habit on the income derived from legitimate work. McAuliffe and Gordon (1974) found that the average daily cost of a heroin habit was $40. If such a habit were supported with income from a legitimate job, the habit alone would require a net annual income of about $15,000. To have this much money left after taxes, social security payments, and other deductions would require a gross income of nearly $20,000. Fewer than half of the families in the United States earned that much money in the year McAuliffe and Gordon did their research. Because heroin addicts tend to come from less educated groups and from disadvantaged minorities, it is clear that few of them can rely on legally earned income to support their habits. As a result, most heroin addicts turn to crime. Research indicates that weekly and daily cocaine users also earn much of their income illegally (Collins, Hubbard, and Rachal, 1985).

Table 9.2 shows the sources of income for male and female street addicts in a study carried out in Miami. We can see that criminal activities were mentioned by the largest number of addicts as a source of income; only about half as many mentioned legitimate jobs as a source of income with which to buy drugs. Smaller numbers mentioned public assistance and family and friends as sources of income to support their habits. In McAuliffe and Gordon's study, 96 percent of the addicts who got high every day committed crime to support their habits. Addicts' criminal activities include drug sales, pickpocketing, shoplifting, burglary, robbery, con games, gambling, and prostitution (McAuliffe and Gordon, 1974; Inciardi, 1979; Rosenbaum, 1981, 1982; Wilson, 1983).

TABLE 9.2   Sources of Support for Drug Use
and General Economic Needs among Active
Street Addicts in Miami, Florida*

Source of Income	Males	Females
Criminal activity	97.4%	94.9%
Legitimate employment	49.4%	43.6%
Public assistance	20.0%	18.8%
Family and friends	12.5%	31.6%

*Columns add to more than 100% because addicts
mentioned several sources of income.

SOURCE: James A. Inciardi, "Heroin Use and Street
Crime," *Crime and Delinquency*, Vol. 25, No. 3 (July
1979), p. 341. Copyright © 1979 by the National
Council on Crime and Delinquency. Reprinted by
permission of Sage Publications, Inc.

Many heroin addicts engaged in some crime even before they became addicted, suggesting that people who become addicts often experienced the rewards of crime before they started to spend the proceeds of their crimes on
heroin (Greenberg and Adler, 1974; McGlothlin, Anglin, and Wilson, 1978;
Inciardi, 1979; Anglin and Hser, 1987). Studies have found that 50 to 80
percent of all addicts were arrested for crime before becoming addicted to
heroin, but that they generally increased their criminal activities greatly after
becoming addicted (Baridon, 1976; McBride and McCoy, 1981; Gropper,
1984). For instance, one study found that a sample of 237 addicts committed an
estimated total of 500,000 crimes during an eleven-year period (*The New York
Times,* March 22, 1981).

Criminal activity seems to decline when addicts enter treatment or kick their
habits. One study found that addicts' crime rates were 84 percent lower when
they were not dependent on heroin than when they were using the drug on a
regular basis (*The New York Times,* March 22, 1981). However, research also
indicates that addicts' involvement in crime remains greater after addiction
than it was before addiction (Vorenberg and Lukoff, 1973; Cushman, 1974;
Stephens and Ellis, 1975; Silberman, 1978). This suggests that the rewards of
crime may still be sought when crime is no longer necessary to support a drug
habit. Money previously spent on heroin may be used for a car or a better
apartment. At best, treatment programs seem to moderate rather than eliminate addicts' involvement in crime.

Critique of the Reward-Risk Model

The idea that crime can be explained by its intrinsic rewards and risks directs
our attention to motives for violating the law. One problem with this model is
that it suggests that people choose to commit crime in a rational way. Some
offenses, such as white-collar crime, seem to involve more careful calculation

than other crimes, such as forcible rape, and the reward-risk model thus seems to explain some crimes better than others. More research is needed on the decision-making process engaged in by offenders who commit different kinds of crimes (Clarke and Cornish, 1985).

The reward-risk model fails to tell us exactly how potential offenders weigh the various benefits and costs of criminal and noncriminal behavior. For instance, how does an offender calculate the probability of arrest, or balance a small chance of a prison sentence against a high probability of making a small financial gain from a property crime? The reward-risk model also does not examine the sources of people's methods of evaluating rewards and risks. Thus, for people who have little stake in conformity, a small financial gain may be worth risking arrest for; others who have a greater stake in conformity may think that even the possibility of a large financial gain is not worth a small risk of arrest. The reward-risk model thus fails to spell out in detail the actual process of balancing rewards against risks, the reasons people balance rewards and risks differently, and the way the social structure influences the balancing of rewards and risks.

Learning Theories and Variations in Crime Rates

The learning theories examined in this chapter suggest some ways that geographic variations in crime rates might be explained. If there are geographic differences in the definitions favorable and unfavorable to violation of the law to which people are exposed, differential association theory might help explain variations in crime rates by nation, region, and size of the community. Geographic variations might also be due to cross-national, regional, or community differences in the groups that control power and label behavior criminal. For instance, the difference between the United States and Great Britain in rates of drug addiction and secondary crimes associated with addiction has been attributed to the definition of drug addiction as a crime in the United States and as a medical problem in Great Britain (Schur, 1962, 1965; Judson, 1974). Another possible explanation of geographic variations in crime rates is that people in different places may balance rewards against risks differently. For instance, if people living in one country have a low stake in conformity, they may be willing to take more risks to gain the rewards of crime than are people elsewhere who have a greater stake in conformity. To date, however, we have little direct evidence that such cross-national, regional, or size-of-community variations in crime rates can be explained by the learning theories explored in this chapter.

Learning theories do not seem to provide very good explanations for temporal variations in crime rates. For differential association theory to explain changes in crime rates, it would have to tell us why an increasing or decreasing number of people have an excess of definitions favorable to violation of the law over definitions unfavorable to violation of the law. The theory does not make clear why that might happen and thus does not do a very good job of explaining changes in crime rates. Labeling theory would suggest that the kind of behavior defined or treated as criminal fluctuates over time as certain groups gain power or change their views about the kind of behavior that is threatening to them. However, there have been few efforts to use the labeling perspective to explain temporal variations in crime rates. Similarly, there have been few attempts to use the reward-risk model to explain changes in crime rates, although the way people evaluate and balance rewards and risks might change over time in ways that would help explain increases or decreases in crime rates.

Learning theories might help us make sense of variations in crime rates by sex, age, race, and class. Differential association theory suggests that exposure to criminal and noncriminal definitions of the law varies by social group, with males, young people, minority groups, and the lower classes being the most likely to commit crime because they are the most likely to be exposed to an excess of definitions favorable to violation of the law over definitions unfavorable to violation of the law. This explanation does not, however, tell us why differences in definitions of the law are distributed in society in this way, nor does it provide direct evidence that these groups actually differ in their exposure to definitions favorable and unfavorable to violation of the law. The labeling perspective suggests that one reason official crime rates may be higher among certain groups is that those groups lack the power to define what kind of behavior will be defined as criminal. Young people, minorities, and the lower classes may thus be especially likely to have the kind of behavior in which they engage defined and treated as crime by older people, dominant racial and ethnic groups, and the middle and upper classes. This approach would not explain the higher crime rate of males, because for the most part it has been men who have written and enforced criminal laws. The reward-risk model might suggest that people with different social characteristics evaluate the rewards and risks of criminal and noncriminal behavior differently, but there is little direct evidence that this is so.

In sum, the learning theories examined in this chapter might help us explain some of the geographic, temporal, and social variations in crime rates that we have looked at, but there have been few explicit attempts to use those theories to make sense of such variations.

Summary

People learn skills and motives to commit crime from various sources. The social structure of some communities is conducive to learning criminal and delinquent behavior. Many delinquents become involved in violation of the law by learning from peers and from older adolescents in gangs. People also learn criminal motives and techniques from the general culture. The mass media, especially television, are another source of learning to commit crime. There is some evidence that viewing or participating in sports can increase aggressiveness, which may lead to crime in some circumstances. Exposure to pornographic material does not seem to cause sex offenses, but violent pornography may have this effect on people who are otherwise predisposed to commit such crimes. There is little solid evidence that correctional institutions act as "schools of crime," but some sociologists believe that interaction among inmates in prisons and jails is an important source of criminal motives and skills.

Differential association theory proposes that crime and delinquency are learned through face-to-face interaction. Techniques and motives are learned from definitions of the law in favorable or unfavorable terms. People violate the law when definitions favorable to violation of the law exceed definitions unfavorable to violation of the law. These definitions result from associations with criminal and noncriminal patterns that differ in frequency, duration, priority, and intensity. This theory is not easily tested, but some research is consistent with it. The theory has been modified in two forms: differential identification theory, which emphasizes the emulation of role models, and differential association-reinforcement theory, which stresses social learning.

Differential association theory fits much of what we know about white-collar crime, although the theory has not been subjected to rigorous testing. Business offenders seem to be exposed to definitions favorable to violation of the law within the company, and they seem to be somewhat isolated from definitions unfavorable to violation of the law. Research on juvenile delinquency is also consistent with differential association theory. Much delinquency occurs in groups, and delinquents seem to interact frequently with other delinquents. Professional thieves often are introduced to crime through tutelage by experienced thieves.

The labeling perspective proposes that some people who engage in primary deviation, or rule breaking, are labeled delinquent or criminal by institutions such as the police and the courts. This can change an individual's self-concept, close off opportunities, alter social relationships, and push people into subcultures. This leads to secondary deviation, or repeated rule breaking by those who see themselves as criminals or delinquents. There is mixed evidence about the actual effects of labeling on self-concepts, and it is not certain that changes in self-concepts necessarily lead to more violation of the law. However, delinquents seem to have poorer self-concepts than nondelinquents. Some deviants are able to reject the label of criminal or delinquent. It is not clear that labeling closes off opportunities for all labeled deviants, but some adult offenders seem to have their job opportunities reduced. In some cases, labeling pushes delinquents and criminals into a subculture, leading to a changed self-concept and more crime as a result of differential association with other offenders.

Crime offers offenders various rewards or benefits and produces certain risks or costs for them. Operant conditioning theory focuses on the reinforcement of criminal activity. Economists look at the rational choice of instrumental behavior in terms of its rewards and risks. In recent years, an integrated reward-risk model has evolved from the work of scholars in different disciplines. The major risk that most crime poses is the possibility of arrest and punishment. Rewards vary from crime to crime. Monetary gain is a primary reward, but challenge, excitement, and autonomy are other benefits derived from criminal activity. Some offenses, such as arson and car theft, provide different kinds of rewards to different offenders. Heroin addicts seem to be motivated by a desire for euphoria, although they need a certain amount of the drug to prevent the pain of withdrawal. The reward-risk model focuses our attention on the factors that motivate offenders, but it may exaggerate the rationality of some criminal activity. This model needs to provide more details on the exact way offenders consider the rewards and risks of crime, and it needs to look at the influence of the social structure on the way people balance rewards and risks.

Differential association theory, the labeling perspective, and the reward-risk model may help us make sense of the geographic, temporal, and social variations in crime rates, but so far there have been few explicit attempts by researchers to show how these learning theories explain those variations.

Important Terms

containment theory
differential association-
  reinforcement theory
differential association theory
differential identification theory
economist's model
expressive crime
instrumental crime
labeling perspective

machismo
master status
obscene material
operant conditioning theory
pornography
primary deviation
reward-risk model
secondary deviation
tutelage

Suggested Readings

DARYL A. HELLMAN. *The Economics of Crime.* New York: St. Martin's Press, 1980. An introduction to the economist's model of criminal behavior.

BRUCE JACKSON. *A Thief's Primer.* New York: Macmillan, 1969. An examination of the rewards and risks of criminal activity, as reported by one thief.

PETER LETKEMANN. *Crime as Work.* Englewood Cliffs, N.J.: Prentice-Hall, 1973. A study of professional theft in Canada, focusing on the learning of criminal motives and techniques.

EDWIN M. SCHUR. *Interpreting Deviance: A Sociological Introduction.* New York: Harper & Row, 1979. A textbook that provides a useful introduction to the labeling perspective.

EDWIN H. SUTHERLAND AND DONALD R. CRESSEY. *Criminology,* 10th ed. Philadelphia: Lippincott, 1978. A textbook that presents and uses differential association theory.

JAMES Q. WILSON AND RICHARD J. HERRNSTEIN. *Crime & Human Nature.* New York: Simon and Schuster, 1985. A lucid presentation of the integrated reward-risk model of criminal behavior.

Opportunities and Facilitating Factors

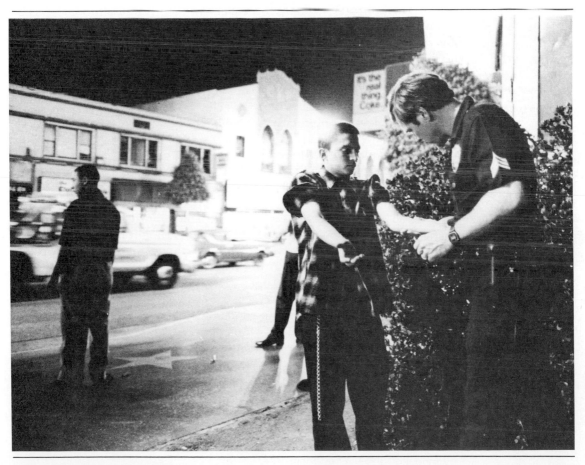

Source: Tom Zimberoff/Sygma

Crime is the product of a social structure that is conducive to violation of the law, the weakening of commitment to the law through techniques of neutralization or detachment from conventional institutions, and the learning of criminal motives and skills. However, crime cannot be committed unless there are opportunities to break the law. In the first section of this chapter, we look at the way people's everyday behavior creates opportunities for crime. Then, we examine the way offenders select their targets. In the final section, we investigate three factors that are often associated with crime, even if they do not actually cause it: alcohol, drugs, and firearms. These are facilitating factors that increase the chance that a situation will lead to crime.

The Routine Activities Approach

The *routine activities approach* sees crime as a function of people's everyday behavior. This approach includes three elements: motivated offenders, target suitability, and guardianship. In earlier chapters, we examined the factors motivating offenders to commit crime. The second element is target suitability, which refers to the form and value of property, the visibility and accessibility of targets, and the vulnerability of property and people to victimization. The third element is guardianship, the presence of people who can protect targets from victimization. The routine activities approach proposes that crime occurs when motivated offenders are present near suitable targets that are not adequately protected. This approach can help us explain crime rates, forecast trends in crime rates, and plan future needs for criminal justice services and personnel (Cohen and Felson, 1979; Cohen and Cantor, 1980, 1981; Cohen, 1981; Cohen, Kluegel, and Land, 1981; Messner and Tardiff, 1985; Felson, 1987).

The routine activities approach suggests that the presence of an abundance of goods that can be stolen will be associated with a high rate of property crime. In fact, economically developing societies do encounter rapidly rising rates of theft (Clinard and Abbott, 1973). A study of Sweden's crime rates from 1950 to 1979 found that theft increased as more goods became available. This increase in theft seemed to be better explained by changes in opportunities for theft than by changes in income inequality (Stack, 1982).

Guardianship can be measured in several ways, all of which try to gauge the extent to which people in the course of their daily behavior do, or do not, protect property and individuals from crime. Some recent changes in patterns of behavior may have reduced guardianship, and thus increased crime rates. These changes include the following:

- a large increase in the proportion of women holding jobs outside the home,
- an increase in the proportion of all households that have only one person,
- more recreational activity outside the home, and
- more frequent and longer vacations.

On the other hand, we would expect crimes such as burglary to decrease if recreational activities became more home-centered, even though this might create more opportunities for interaction among intimates that could lead to violent crime.

We can use the routine activities approach to help explain why there is a low rate of property crime in Switzerland (Clinard, 1978). Swiss cities have low rates of robbery, even though opportunities are plentiful. The Swiss carry much cash and rarely use checks. This makes them vulnerable to robbery and increases the potential gain from robberies of stores, where cash is available because customers typically do not pay with checks or credit cards. Moreover, the Swiss leave property in public places with little fear of theft; in other words, they lack a tradition of guardianship. The lack of guardianship and the presence of available targets for theft suggest that Switzerland should have a high rate of property crime, but it does not. The routine activities approach would lead us to expect that this is because there are relatively few motivated offenders in Switzerland. To understand why a country has the crime rate it does, we must examine all three elements of the routine activities approach.

A Critique of the Routine Activities Approach

Researchers who have used the routine activities approach have typically used demographic variables such as sex, age, race, and class as indicators of people's daily behavior (Cohen and Cantor, 1981). What is needed is to test the routine activities approach more fully with direct evidence about people's life styles and patterns of behavior, rather than to assume how people with different social background characteristics behave (Cohen, 1981; Messner and Tardiff, 1985). One study that measured exposure to the risk of victimization with data on the nature and quantity of people's activities outside the home found that the routine activities approach predicted variations in property crime rates better than it predicted variations in violent crime rates (Miethe, Stafford, and Long, 1987).

In the future, application of the routine activities approach will require more detailed exploration of the idea of "exposure to risk." Greater attention must also be paid to the relative importance of each of the three major components of the approach: motivated offenders, target suitability, and guardianship. Moreover, the routine activities approach must focus more on the motivation of offenders and on possible motivational differences between property criminals and violent offenders (Miethe, Stafford, and Long, 1987).

Targets of Crime

There is a nearly unlimited number of targets for crime. What is important is the way these targets are perceived by potential offenders. An offender may see a bank with both a front and a rear entrance, a nearby expressway, and weak security as an excellent opportunity for a bank holdup; law-abiding citizens will view the same bank simply as a place to deposit and withdraw funds. The crime-generating process examined in previous chapters — the social-structural pressure to commit crime, the neutralization of the law, and the acquisition of criminal motives and skills — is necessary but not sufficient for crimes such as bank holdups. Without an opportunity, there will be no crime.

The target selected by an offender depends in part on the specific skills the offender possesses. Some criminals specialize in one kind of offense, but many are quite versatile. Even experienced professional thieves usually "hustle" for opportunities for crime, rather than seek specific targets. They read newspapers, swap information with other thieves and fences, and keep their eyes open for targets for crime. Specialization would force them to pass up lucrative opportunities. Many thieves prefer certain crimes but do not limit themselves to those offenses (Gould et al., 1966; Letkemann, 1973).

Property Crimes

Thieves consider several factors in choosing targets for their crimes. The form of the property to be stolen is important, as is the value of that property. Target vulnerability and the likelihood of victim resistance are also considered by thieves.

FORM OF THE PROPERTY   The form of the property to be stolen is important. If assets are in the form of computerized data, most thieves will have to avoid computers as targets for crime because they lack the necessary skills. However, assets in this form are vulnerable to theft by computer operators who have the necessary skills. Some have suggested reducing theft by eliminating cash and replacing it with computerized assets, thereby making property inaccessible to many thieves, at least until they develop computer skills.

Most thieves steal cash or property. Stolen property either is for personal use or is converted into cash. Conversion of stolen property into cash requires access to a fence, a receiver of stolen goods who usually pays the thief one-tenth to one-third of the retail value of the stolen merchandise. Young burglars often steal goods that they dispose of among their acquaintances, but older and more experienced burglars are more likely to steal goods that they convert into cash or drugs with fences (Reppetto, 1974: 20 – 21). Amateur shoplifters ("snitches") often take small, easily concealed goods for personal use. Professional shoplifters ("boosters") usually steal more expensive items and sell them to professional fences or to jewelry stores and clothing shops that are primarily legitimate retail outlets (Cameron, 1964).

The conversion of property into cash is time-consuming, and this is an important consideration for offenders who require cash immediately, such as thieves who are heroin addicts looking for a fix. Selling stolen goods to a fence can be risky as well as inconvenient, because the police may trace stolen property back to the thief through the fence. For these reasons, some offenders prefer the direct theft of cash from victims and turn to robbery. Robbery has the important advantage over other forms of theft of providing offenders with immediately usable assets that cannot be traced back to them. Robbery also requires relatively little preparation in most cases, and there is an abundance of potential targets. Robbers often claim that burglary is more trouble than robbery because it involves entry into a house or building, a search for valuable goods, the physical labor of carrying the goods from the building, and the need to convert those goods into cash. Robbery is faster and more direct, and it provides readily usable assets, but it also involves the risk of a violent confrontation and the risk of identification by the victim.

VALUE OF THE PROPERTY   Thieves who commit robbery, burglary, and other types of theft consider from which victims they can get the most money with the least risk. Pickpockets usually select their "marks" or victims by criteria such as sex (men being thought to carry more money), age (older people being thought to carry more money), and race (whites being thought to carry more money) (Maurer, 1955, 1964). For robbers, the holdup of a commercial establishment such as a supermarket or a bank will typically net more money than the robbery of an individual on the street (Conklin, 1972). Burglars have to locate the money or valuable property once they enter a building, even if they have chosen a potentially lucrative target.

Offenders usually choose victims on the basis of general expectations about how much money or property they will get. Sometimes they are systematic in calculating their profits in advance, especially if the crime involves elaborate planning and substantial risk. One gang of jewelry store robbers regularly sent its "straightest-looking" member into a store a few days before a planned crime in order to examine the jewelry and decide whether the robbery was worth the trouble and risk it would involve. The gang would then steal only the most valuable jewelry and fence it with a receiver of stolen goods in a different state. The members of the gang had a very good idea of how much they would gain in a particular holdup. Another robber secured information about the number of employees working for a firm and the approximate amount earned by each worker; his robbery of the company on payday netted him an amount that was very close to his estimate (Conklin, 1972).

The amount of money a given target will yield is often calculated in detail by professional thieves, who seek as large a "score" as possible while keeping risks to a minimum. By contrast, opportunistic thieves look for smaller gains and are less methodical in assessing what they will get from a theft. Still, even opportunists consider what they are likely to get from potential victims. They observe how expensively potential victims are dressed and watch to see who "flashes a large wad of bills." Sometimes they try to improve their odds of a large score by stealing on paydays and on days when welfare checks are delivered.

Vulnerability of Victims

A major factor that criminals consider in choosing a target is the vulnerability of their victims. Check forgers believe some stores are more willing to accept checks from strangers and are therefore easier to victimize. For instance, supermarkets are seen as easy "marks," but men's clothing stores are thought to be relatively invulnerable to check passing (Jackson, 1969). Shoplifting is also easier in certain stores. For instance, stores that emphasize self-service seem to accept shoplifting as a cost of doing business. Managers may even think that if shoplifting is infrequent, their merchandise is not attractive enough or accessible enough to customers (Cameron, 1964: 17–19).

Opportunistic robbers—typically young, male members of minority groups who often operate in gangs—tend to choose victims who are elderly, female, and alone. In other words, they seek victims who are vulnerable because of their age, sex, or lack of company, even though these victims usually carry less money than other potential victims (Conklin, 1972: 89–91). Because these opportunists often lack experience and skill in committing crime, they place greater emphasis on victim vulnerability and the minimization of risk than they do on the size of the score. In contrast, professional robbers have a broader conception of vulnerability; for them, a vulnerable target is one from which they can steal after considerable planning. For example, the 1950 Brinks robbery was directed against a target that would be seen as invulnerable by most robbers, but careful observation and planning showed the thieves that the Brinks office lacked adequate security and was vulnerable to theft (Behn, 1977).

Certain obstacles to theft may turn offenders away from particular targets. Exact-fare requirements on buses may reduce robberies of bus drivers but may lead thieves to steal from the stores or newspaper stands that make change for bus riders. Since 1940, there has been an increase in bank security, including the installation of electronically controlled doors and cages, alarm systems, and closed circuit television. These measures have eliminated sneak theft from banks, a crime in which thieves go behind a counter, grab money from a till, and run from the bank (Inciardi, 1975: 15–19).

In a study of residential burglary, nearly one hundred convicted burglars were shown slides of buildings and asked to pick the type of target from which they usually stole (Reppetto, 1974). They were then asked why they chose a particular building. Older offenders usually selected single-family houses because of easy access and affluence, and younger offenders picked housing projects and multiple-family houses for their easy access. Overall, the burglars cited the following as reasons for their selection of particular targets:

- ease of access (44 percent of all burglars),
- appearance of affluence (41 percent),
- an inconspicuous setting (21 percent),
- isolation of the neighborhood (19 percent),
- the absence of police patrols (19 percent), and
- lack of surveillance by neighbors (12 percent).

The type of information the burglars said they wanted about a target before committing a burglary included

- whether occupants were present (70 percent),
- whether there was a burglar alarm (36 percent),
- what valuables were available (34 percent),
- where escape routes were located (20 percent),
- the location of entrances to the building (15 percent), and
- the presence of police or security patrols (14 percent).

The importance of occupancy is shown by the fact that the more hours of the day a dwelling was unoccupied, the greater the chance it would be burglarized. Offenders learned whether anyone was home primarily by observing the dwelling, but sometimes they made telephone calls, questioned neighbors, or looked for signs of nonoccupancy such as piles of newspapers or mail. They learned if there were valuables to be stolen by peeping in windows and by tips from friends and fences.

One study suggested that vulnerability to burglary might be minimized by symbolic barriers to theft, rather than by creating actual physical obstacles (Barbara Brown, cited in *The New York Times*, November 17, 1983; also, see Greer, 1986). Neatly trimmed hedges, for instance, can easily be passed through or around by a burglar, but, by showing that the residents feel a sense of protectiveness or territoriality about their homes, these hedges can indicate that potential intruders should keep out. Shrubs and trees can make a house seem well cared for and less exposed, and thereby minimize the chance of burglary. The way houses are situated on a street, or the fact that a street is a cul-de-sac, can also create a sense of territoriality that potential burglars will be reluctant to violate.

Thieves try to minimize their risk by selecting targets that are not likely to be under police or neighborhood surveillance. They prefer targets that are isolated from the view of passersby, whether the police or private citizens. Even those who rob commercial establishments try to conceal themselves from public view during the crime, picking establishments that are set back from the street or positioning themselves inside the store so as to be invisible from the street. "Lookouts" are often stationed outside the building to report any threat of intrusion.

Robbers often use nonverbal cues to asses the vulnerability of potential victims. A study that asked inmates who had been convicted of violent attacks on strangers to rate people who had been videotaped while walking on the street found that the people who were rated "easy to mug" by the inmates showed distinctive body movements that signaled that they would be good targets:

> Specifically, the most muggable people tended to take strides that were of unusual length, either too short or too long. Instead of walking heel to toe, they walked flatfooted. Instead of swinging their left arm while striding with their right foot, they moved their left arm and left foot, then right arm and right foot together.

Instead of the usual figure 8-like sway of upper body and lower body, the most muggable people seemed to move their torsos at cross purposes to the bottom half of their bodies.

And instead of moving "posturally" (letting the movement start from within the body core), potential victims seemed to move "gesturally" (moving one part of the body, an arm for instance, as though the movement started outside the body). Indeed, the most muggable people seemed to walk as though they were less in touch with their bodies. (study by Betty Grayson, described in Foreman, 1981: 21–22).

These movements were more important to offenders in choosing a victim than were age and sex. Body movement seemed to indicate something about the way people presented themselves to the world. Muggers read movement as an indicator of vulnerability, but this seemed to occur without their conscious awareness of the factors discovered by the researcher.

VICTIM PRONENESS   One measure of vulnerability is the frequency with which people are victimized repeatedly. There may be *victim proneness* among certain people because of their personal characteristics, social situation, physical location, or relationship to offenders (Wolfgang and Singer, 1978; Nelson, 1980; Sparks, 1981). In a study of robbery in Boston, twenty-three of ninety victims who were held up in 1968 were robbed again during the next two and a half years, even though the city's robbery rate suggested that only one or two of them would have been robbed again in that time if robberies were randomly distributed across the city's population (Conklin, 1972: 96–97). Whatever made these victims vulnerable to robbery in the first place continued to make them vulnerable, and whatever measures they took to reduce their vulnerability seemed to have little effect.

Multiple victimization, or victim proneness, seems to be due to several factors, including:

1. *Precipitation or provocation:* The victim does or says something that causes an offender to violate the law;
2. *Instigation or perpetration:* The victim actively encourages a crime or takes criminal action against another person;
3. *Facilitation:* The victim places himself or herself at risk by deliberation, recklessness, or negligence;
4. *Vulnerability or invitation:* Some people are unusually susceptible because of personal attributes, social status, or entry into a risk-filled situation;
5. *Cooperation:* The victim is a party to a consensual crime such as gambling or prostitution;
6. *Attractiveness:* Affluence will often attract offenders; and
7. *Impunity:* Offenders can expect that the victim will not report the crime to the police or testify in court, perhaps because the victim is also breaking the law. (Sparks, 1981, 1982)

Victim Precipitation

Victim precipitation means that the person who suffers eventual harm from a crime plays a direct role in causing the crime to be perpetrated. For instance, a homicide victim may be the first to use force. In one case encountered in this author's robbery study (Conklin, 1972), an incarcerated offender reported that he had regularly used a knife to hold up drugstores because "a knife is quieter than a gun." A few months after the interview, this offender attacked another inmate with a homemade knife. The other inmate took the knife away and stabbed the attacker to death. This is a clear case of a victim-precipitated murder.

Victims who act in particular ways with regard to potential offenders may create opportunities for crimes where none existed before. Thus, a man who enters a bar, picks an argument with another customer, and draws a knife has in a sense contributed to his own murder if the other person responds by killing him with a handgun. This may not absolve the murderer of legal responsibility, but it could mitigate the punishment.

One definition of victim precipitation suggests that we need much information to assess the role of the victim in the causation of a crime:

> Victim precipitation occurs when the offender's action in committing or beginning to commit a crime is initiated after and directly related to an action (be it physical or verbal, conscious or unconscious) on the part of the victim. The offender perceives the victim's behavior as a facilitating action (including temptation, invitation) to the commission of the crime. The action of the victim might be said to have triggered the offender's behavior. (R. A. Silverman, cited in Curtis, 1974: 96)

There is a continuum from deliberate provocation by the victim, to some involvement by the victim, to little or no victim contribution. The intent of the offender must be considered on a continuum from deliberate premeditation, to some intent, to none at all. Victim precipitation exists when offenders have little or no intent to commit a crime and victims clearly provoke them to commit a crime. Real-life situations are usually less clearcut. Information on the interaction between the offender and the victim, and the state of mind of each, is difficult to get after a crime has been committed, especially if one participant is murdered. Witnesses may describe how the crime developed, but it is often difficult to gather data on the perceptions and expectations of the participants.

MURDER   About one murder in four is victim-precipitated (Wolfgang, 1958: 254; Curtis, 1974: 82–84), although one study found that 38 percent of a sample of homicides were caused in part by the victim (Voss and Hepburn, 1968). Victims of victim-precipitated murders are especially likely to be male and black and to have prior criminal records. Female murderers are more likely than male murderers to be involved in victim-precipitated murders, because female murderers have often been provoked by their male victims.

Robert Chambers claimed that his victim Jennifer Levin had precipitated her own 1986 murder by hurting him while they were having sex. In 1988 he admitted this story was a lie, pleaded guilty to first-degree manslaughter, and was sentenced to five to fifteen years in prison.   *Source: James Hamilton / Sygma*

In a study of interaction between offenders and victims prior to murder, about half of the seventy cases were found to involve prior hostility or physical violence between the offender and the victim (Luckenbill, 1977). Homicides were not usually one-sided events in which a passive victim was attacked by the murderer. In nearly two-thirds of the murders, the victim initiated the interchange, the offender stated an intent to harm the victim, and the offender then killed the victim. The interaction among the offender, the victim, and the audience to the murder can be analyzed in the following stages:

1. The offender first feels personally injured by the victim's behavior, which can be intentional or unwitting. This may include physical or verbal insults, gestures, or refusal to comply with the offender's wishes.
2. The offender then seeks to restore "face" by retaliating, expressing anger or contempt, or casting the victim as an unworthy person.
3. The victim next reacts to the offender's behavior by defining violence as the appropriate solution to the disagreement.
4. The offender interprets the victim's behavior as intentional noncompliance with his or her wishes.
5. Commitment to violence develops and actual violence is made more likely by the presence of weapons.
6. The offender "drops" the victim and then flees, voluntarily stays at the scene, or is involuntarily held at the scene by witnesses to the murder. (Luckenbill, 1977)

Another study looked at the interaction leading to 159 incidents of homicide and assault and found similar patterns of behavior. Physical violence typically followed an "identity attack," a failure to influence the antagonist, threats, and sometimes efforts at evasive action or mediation. Offenders retaliated in an effort to reestablish a favorable identity, and the situation escalated into assault or murder. Each individual responded to the other's actions and the implications of those actions for his or her well-being and honor. Consequently, it was difficult to classify violent crime as offender-precipitated or victim-precipitated. Victims often acted aggressively, but they attacked less often and were more likely to take evasive action than were the offenders. Efforts at mediation and evasion suggested that offenders and victims may not have shared norms supporting violence as the appropriate response to an identity attack (Felson and Steadman, 1983).

FORCIBLE RAPE There is a cultural stereotype, which has been eroded somewhat by feminists, that rape victims often contribute to their own victimization (Weis and Borges, 1973). This belief reflects the mistaken idea that rape is primarily a sexual act rather than a violent crime, even though victims experience rape as violence rather than sex. The widely held view that some victims provoke rapists, and even enjoy the act, is used to defend rapists' actions as justifiable, excusable, or understandable. Violent pornography can contribute to this view (Donnerstein, Linz, and Penrod, 1987).

The idea that rape is often a victim-precipitated crime overlooks an important difference between rape and homicide. In the events leading to a homicide, the lives of both the eventual victim and the eventual murderer are usually at risk. However, in a confrontation between a rapist and a woman, only the woman is at risk. Thus, most murders are symmetrical in terms of the risk of being killed, but rapes are asymmetrical in terms of risk.

Nevertheless, the view that rape victims precipitate their own victimization persists in the minds of the public and the jurors who decide rape cases. Many people regard situations in which a woman places herself at risk — for instance, by hitchhiking or by telling dirty jokes in a bar — as a form of victim precipitation. Sociologist Barbara Reskin (cited in Brozan, 1985) interviewed 360 jurors in rape cases and concluded that their decisions frequently were based on the reputation and social life of the victim. Jurors were especially likely to acquit defendants whose victims seemed to be sexually active, led a busy social life, and drank. There are now "shield laws" to prevent defense attorneys from questioning rape victims about their sex lives, but attorneys have developed strategies to plant in jurors' minds the idea that a victim leads an unchaste and nontraditional life, and jurors seem to respond by "blaming the victim" for the crime and exonerating the defendant.

One researcher concluded from his study of rape in Philadelphia that 19 percent of the cases were victim-precipitated, in that the victim had actually agreed to have sexual relations with the offender — or had been thought to have agreed to this by the offender — but had retracted before the act, or had not reacted "strongly enough" when the suggestion of sex was first made by the offender. This researcher also categorized rapes as victim-precipitated if they were preceded by "risky situations marred with sexuality," such as a woman's using "indecent" language or gestures or behaving in a way that could be taken as an invitation to sexual relations (Amir, 1971). Application of this extremely broad definition of victim precipitation led the researcher to conclude that nearly one rape victim in five contributes to her own victimization, even though "contribution" here seems to encompass anything outside a very restricted range of puritanical behavior.

Using a different definition of victim precipitation of rape, a seventeen-city survey of violent crime found that only 4 percent of rapes were victim-precipitated, 83 percent were not, and 13 percent could not be classified easily or accurately (Curtis, 1974: 87–90). In this study, rape was defined as victim-precipitated if a female agreed to sexual relations and clearly invited them verbally or by gestures but then retracted before the act.

CRIMES AGAINST PROPERTY   Theft can be precipitated by property owners. Individuals who leave their homes vacant while on vacation, allow mail and newspapers to collect on the porch, and leave windows and doors open while away provide potential burglars with obvious signals that the dwelling is an easy target. People who leave car keys in the ignition facilitate car theft, because a thief does not even have to possess the skill to start the car without a key.

Similarly, leaving property where it can easily be stolen encourages theft. A study of crime in Uganda found that immigrants to a large city from small villages brought with them a tradition of leaving property unguarded, thus encouraging theft. In the village, thieves could be observed and recognized, so the tradition of leaving property unguarded did not lead to theft there. In the city, similar informal controls were absent and the tradition frequently led to theft (Clinard and Abbott, 1973).

Offenders who lack a strong commitment to crime as a way of life may break the law when they happen upon easy opportunities to gain something with little risk. Sometimes they are drawn into crime because of victim precipitation. Thus, marginally committed offenders may steal unattended property, enter an empty house through an open window, or attack someone who insults them.

Facilitating Factors: Alcohol, Drugs, and Firearms

Three factors that often are present when crimes are committed, but do not actually cause crime, are alcohol, drugs, and firearms. The high frequency with which these factors are present during crimes suggests that they are facilitating factors that increase the chance that a situation will lead to criminal violence or theft.

Alcohol and Crime

There is substantial evidence that alcohol use and crime are correlated with each other (Pittman, 1974; Petersilia, Greenwood, and Lavin, 1977; Collins, 1981a, 1981b). A 1979 survey of the inmates of state prisons found that nearly 30 percent of them said "they had drunk heavily just before they committed the offense for which they were convicted," and another 20 percent said they had been drinking but not heavily (Bureau of Justice Statistics, January 1983: 1). A more recent survey found that 54 percent of a sample of jail inmates convicted of violent crimes said they had been drinking before committing the offenses for which they were incarcerated (*The Boston Globe*, November 4, 1985). Such self-reports may be questioned as to their validity, because inmates may try to diminish their personal responsibility for violating the law by blaming it on the effects of alcohol.

The 1979 survey of inmates also found that alcohol use varies from one kind of offender to another. Slightly higher proportions of property offenders than of violent offenders had been drinking just prior to their offense. The same pattern held for heavy drinking in the year prior to the crime (Bureau of Justice Statistics, January 1983). Offenders incarcerated for burglary, rape, and assault were especially likely to be heavy drinkers, both just before the crime and during the year before the offense. Drug offenders were the least likely to be very heavy drinkers, but we can see from Table 10.1 that even they frequently were heavy users of alcohol.

TABLE 10.1   Alcohol Use by Type of Offense, 1979, Percentages

Current Offense	Very Heavy Drinking in the Year Prior to the Offense	Very Heavy Drinking Just Prior to the Offense
Violent	35	60
Homicide	33	56
Assault	45	62
Rape	41	65
Robbery	34	60
Other violent	36	63
Property	40	68
Burglary	43	71
Forgery or fraud	32	59
Larceny	31	61
Other property	44	68
Drugs	28	46
Public order	37	55
Total	36	62

SOURCE: Bureau of Justice Statistics, *Prisoners and Alcohol*. Washington, D.C.: Bureau of Justice Statistics, U.S. Department of Justice, January 1983.

Alcohol is present in a significant proportion of homicides and assaults, and a smaller proportion of rapes, according to studies that have used official crime statistics. Most research indicates that alcohol is present in at least one-third of murders, and half of the studies find it present in 60 percent or more of all murders (S. Greenberg, 1981).

Alcohol also seems to play a role in various sex offenses. The Philadelphia study of forcible rape found that alcohol was present only in the victim in 10 percent of the cases, only in the offender in 3 percent of the cases, and in both the offender and the victim in 21 percent of the reported rapes (Amir, 1971: 98). A common pattern for incest is an unemployed man with an absent wife and an available daughter (or, less commonly, a step-daughter), coupled with a pattern of heavy drinking by the man (Gebhard et al., 1965). Physical and social isolation of the family and tension within the marriage are also conducive to incest. These conditions are especially likely to lead to incestuous behavior if the strong norms against it are neutralized by the heavy consumption of alcohol. Other sex offenses, such as child abuse and child molestation, are also associated with alcohol use (McCaghy, 1967, 1968). Overall, most studies find that alcohol is present in 40 percent or more of sex offenses (S. Greenberg, 1981).

EXPLAINING THE ALCOHOL-CRIME RELATIONSHIP   Several explanations have been offered for the relationship between alcohol use and crime. One explanation is that alcohol may reduce inhibitions and trigger law-violating behavior in some people. The reduction of inhibitions from alcohol consumption is suggested by the results of a study of homicide in Philadelphia, which found that murders in which alcohol was present involved more violence and brutality than did murders in which neither the offender nor the victim had been drinking (Wolfgang, 1958). Another piece of evidence that is consistent with this disinhibition explanation comes from a study of robbery, which found that alcohol was present in 71 percent of the crimes that were committed on the spur of the moment, but in only 44 percent of the crimes that were planned (G. D. Wolcott, cited in Petersilia, Greenwood, and Lavin, 1977: 81).

A second explanation of why alcohol use is linked to crime is that people who are actively involved in a life of crime may rely on alcohol to reduce their anxiety or to build up their courage for crimes they have planned (Collins, 1981a, 1981b). However, the inmate survey found that heavy alcohol consumption was typical daily behavior for one inmate in five; it was not something they did just before committing a crime. Thus, many offenders seem to be heavy drinkers even when not engaging in crimes, and so they probably do not drink just to build up their courage. It is more likely that they are problem drinkers who occasionally commit crimes when their inhibitions are reduced by alcohol.

A third explanation of the association of alcohol use and crime is that groups have norms about how people who are under the influence of alcohol should behave. Among some groups, drunkenness is seen as a "time out" from conventional demands. In this situation of relaxed behavioral standards, aggressive or even criminal behavior may be tolerated or expected. There is little research on differences among groups in their norms about "drunken comportment," but if such differences exist they would help explain why alcohol use and crime are associated with each other in different ways for various groups (MacAndrew and Edgerton, 1969).

We do not yet have enough research to tell us why alcohol use is associated with crime. More studies are needed to make clear "(1) the role of alcohol in the criminal situation, (2) the prevalence of alcoholism among criminals, and (3) the criminal history of alcoholics" (S. Greenberg, 1981: 106–107; also, see Wilbanks, 1981).

Drugs and Crime

Earlier in the book, we saw that many kinds of drug use are defined as crime, and that the need to support a drug habit can lead to secondary crimes. Drugs can also facilitate crime by reducing inhibitions or clouding a user's judgment, much as alcohol may facilitate crime. The extent of drug use among offenders can be seen in a 1976 survey of 624 male felons in California prisons, which revealed that 42 percent of them had used or been addicted to drugs — usually heroin — during the three years before their current incarceration. Inmates who had used drugs reported more property crimes than did nonusers (Peterson and Braiker, 1981).

In the 1979 survey of state prison inmates, nearly a third of them reported that they had been under the influence of an illegal drug at the time of the crime for which they were incarcerated (Bureau of Justice Statistics, March 1983). Seventeen percent were under the influence of marijuana, 9 percent had been using heroin, and 5 percent had been using cocaine. Table 10.2 shows the percentage of inmates under the influence of any illegal drug when they committed the offense for which they were incarcerated at the time of the survey. Burglars, robbers, and drug offenders were the most likely to have been under the influence of a drug at the time of their crime. Homicide, rape, and public-order (often drunkenness) offenders were the least likely to have been using an illegal drug.

Table 10.2 also shows that 56 percent of all prisoners had used illegal drugs in the month prior to their offense, and that 78 percent had used illegal drugs some time in the past. Again, burglars, robbers, and drug offenders reported the most illegal drug use. Homicide, rape, and public-order offenders reported illegal drug use least often (Bureau of Justice Statistics, March 1983).

The inmate survey did not compare inmates' alcohol use with that of the general population, but it did compare inmates' drug use with use by the general population. For each illegal drug, a higher proportion of inmates than of the general population reported that they had ever used the drug. The difference was especially great for heroin; only 2 percent of the general population reported ever having used this drug, but 30 percent of the inmates had used this drug at some time. Inmates were also more likely to have used an illegal drug recently than were people in the general population.

Recent research has employed accurate urinalysis techniques to test for the presence of drugs other than marijuana and alcohol in suspects arrested for serious crimes (see Using Criminology). In March 1984 in Washington, D.C., 56 percent of arrestees tested positive for at least one drug; in September 1986, the proportion testing positive was nearly three-fourths of all arrestees. In New

TABLE 10.2   Illegal Drug Use by Type of Offense, 1979, Percentage

Current Offense	Illegal Drug Use		
	Ever	Month Prior to Offense	Under Influence at Time of Offense
Violent	75	53	30
Homicide	64	41	21
Assault	73	47	27
Rape	64	39	22
Robbery	86	66	38
Other violent	79	59	34
Property	80	58	35
Burglary	85	64	40
Forgery or fraud	69	45	25
Larceny	78	53	30
Other property	75	51	30
Drugs	92	74	47
Public order	69	42	19
Total	78	56	32

SOURCE: Bureau of Justice Statistics, *Prisoners and Drugs.* Washington, D.C.: Bureau of Justice Statistics, U.S. Department of Justice, March 1983, pp. 3–4.

Using Criminology: Drug Testing and Crime

In recent years, the courts have applied the results of research that shows that serious offenders are often users of illegal drugs, and that demonstrates that changes in the extent to which offenders use drugs are associated with corresponding changes in the frequency of their criminal activities. A program implemented in Washington, D.C., in 1984 sought to identify arrested suspects who were high-risk drug abusers and to deal with those suspects in a way that would control their drug use and reduce their threat to the community.

This program used up-to-date technology to produce accurate drug tests in a short time and then fed this information to judges to use in determining the conditions under which defendants would be released pending trial. Because drug-abusing defendants have been found by researchers to be especially likely not to show up for scheduled court appearances and also to pose a high risk to community safety, information on a defendant's drug abuse can be used to establish more restrictive conditions of release. For instance, a defendant who tests positive for any of the drugs tested — Phencyclidine (PCP), opiates (heroin), cocaine, methadone, and amphetamines — might be required to undergo regular drug testing as a condition of release. These defendants are then released under a court order not to use drugs and are required to report for a weekly drug test. Violation of these conditions of release may lead to the defendant's being held in contempt of court or being jailed for a short period.

The testing of defendants in Washington showed that the extent of drug abuse was much higher than anyone had previously thought, with almost two-thirds of arrestees testing positive for some illegal drug. Moreover, testing results showed a change from 1984 to 1986 in the kinds of drugs used. Heroin use remained steady, but cocaine — which was used less than either PCP or heroin in 1984 — became the most popular drug by 1986. Once the city government realized that cocaine and PCP were so widely used, it was able to redirect its treatment resources to deal with those forms of drug abuse. In addition, the city appropriated more funds for public education and for the treatment of drug abuse and was able to allocate those resources efficiently because of the availability of current information on patterns of drug abuse among arrestees.

One objection to drug testing is that it violates constitutional rights. However, the Washington program has withstood all legal challenges. The urine samples collected from arrestees are used only for determining the conditions of their release; positive tests for drugs cannot be used for determining guilt in court. The tests are voluntary as well. As a result, there arises no issue of self-incrimination, against which the Fifth Amendment protects. Other legal challenges to this drug testing program — such as the claim that the tests are unreliable — have also been withstood, and as of mid-1986 this program was functioning effectively in providing the courts with valuable information to use in determining the conditions under which arrestees would be released prior to trial.

SOURCE: Based on John A. Carver, "Drugs and Crime: Controlling Use and Reducing Risk through Testing," *NIJ Reports*, September/October 1986, pp. 2–7.

York City in 1984, 42 percent of a sample of arrestees tested positive for cocaine; in September-October 1986, the proportion testing positive for that drug had risen to 80 percent (Graham, 1987). Voluntary urine tests of more than 2,000 men arrested for serious crimes in 1987 in twelve cities found that 70 percent tested positive for heroin, cocaine, PCP, marijuana, or amphetamines (Kerr, 1988).

Clearly, drug use is associated with greater involvement in other criminal activities. Heroin addicts in California prisons and jails report that they commit more than ten times as many thefts, robberies, and burglaries as non-drug using inmates. Research in Baltimore shows that addicts commit four to six times as many crimes during periods of heavy drug use as they do when they are relatively drug-free. A study in New York City finds that drug users are at least as violent as their counterparts who do not use drugs (Graham, 1987).

EXPLAINING THE DRUGS-CRIME RELATIONSHIP The greater amount of drug use by offenders does not, however, tell us the reason for the association between drug use and crime. Offenders may commit crime to secure the funds with which to purchase expensive drugs. They may have their crimes facilitated by the effects of drugs. However, they might also be especially likely to be arrested because they are known by the police to be drug users, or because the drugs affect their behavior in ways that draw the attention of the police.

Firearms and Crime

Firearms are often used in crime in the United States. In 1986, 44 percent of all reported murders were committed by handguns, 7 percent by shotguns, 4 percent by rifles, and 4 percent by other or unknown kinds of firearms (Federal Bureau of Investigation, 1987: 8). Thus, more than half of all murders involve firearms.

Firearms are also used to facilitate crimes such as rape, robbery, aggravated assault, and burglary. The FBI does not report the use of firearms in rapes, but one study found that 21 percent of all rapists intimidated their victims with some weapon, although not necessarily a firearm (Amir, 1971: 150). NCS data reveal that 9.5 percent of all rape victimizations from 1973 to 1982 involved a firearm (Rand et al., 1986). These same data show that 20 percent of all robbery victimizations during this period involved a firearm. In 1986, 34 percent of all robberies reported to the police were committed with a firearm (Federal Bureau of Investigation, 1987: 18). Victimization data for 1973–1982 show that 11 percent of assaults were committed with a firearm, and FBI data for 1986 indicate that 21 percent of all reported aggravated assaults involved firearms (Rand et al., 1986; Federal Bureau of Investigation, 1987: 22). Firearms also play a role in nonviolent crimes; for example, one study found that 8 percent of burglars carried a firearm (Reppetto, 1974: 107).

EXPLAINING THE FIREARMS-CRIME RELATIONSHIP   The relationship between firearms and crime is complex. Firearms might, under some circumstances, deter potential offenders from crime. Thus, a robber might think twice about holding up a store in which the owner had shot another thief the week before. Overall, however, there is little evidence that citizen ownership of firearms directly deters crime (Green, 1987). Gun ownership might have an indirect effect on crime by making people feel more secure and affecting their behavior in ways that help keep crime rates low, for instance, by encouraging a storekeeper who feels safer to stay open at night, thereby providing informal control over nearby sidewalks and streets. On the other hand, firearms that people keep for self-protection are often stolen by burglars, who may then use them for illegal purposes (Wright, Rossi, and Daly, 1983; Kates, 1984; Wright and Rossi, 1986; Green, 1987).

Crime and firearms may also be related in another way: Fear of crime might cause people to arm themselves. However, most firearms in private hands in the United States are not for self-defense against criminals, but for other purposes such as hunting, target shooting, or collecting. One survey found that only about one gun owner in three gives self-defense as a reason for owning a firearm (DuBow, McCabe, and Kaplan, 1979: 133–134), and a more recent review of research suggests that only 10 to 20 percent of all firearms are for self-defense against other people (Wright, Rossi, and Daly, 1983). Fear of crime and victimization experiences do not seem to be directly and strongly linked to firearms ownership, although a low level of citizen confidence in the ability of the criminal justice system to control crime appears to be associated with more gun ownership (Young, McDowall, and Loftin, 1987).

Firearms may also facilitate the commission of crime. The presence of a weapon during an argument can lead to an escalation of violence, producing a murder when an assault would have occurred if no firearm had been present. Firearms may also give some robbers and rapists the courage to commit crimes that they would otherwise have avoided. Guns can act as catalysts, pushing people over the borderline between the wish to act violently and the actual commission of a violent crime. However, a recent assessment of research concludes that there is "little or no conclusive evidence to show that gun ownership among the larger population is, per se, an important cause of criminal violence" (Wright, Rossi, and Daly, 1983: 137). Switzerland, for instance, has widespread private ownership of firearms but no tradition of using guns to settle interpersonal disputes, and so it has a low rate of criminal violence with firearms (Clinard, 1978). The mere presence of weapons does not cause crime, and so restricting firearms ownership by the general population might not be an effective way to prevent criminals from getting firearms. On the other hand, such restrictions might make access to firearms by potential offenders more difficult and reduce crime to some degree. Tight restrictions on firearms ownership in Japan, for example, have often been cited as a reason for that society's low crime rate. In the Cross-Cultural Perspective, we see that Israel is a nation that has both widespread ownership of firearms and strict controls on those weapons.

A Cross-Cultural Perspective: Firearms in Israel

Israel is a nation "pervaded by guns, but . . . not excited by them." This attitude is largely due to the fact that all men and women serve in the army and are taught to use firearms carefully. An Israeli political scientist contrasts American attitudes toward firearms with attitudes in his country as follows:

> America and Israel are both immigrant societies, but immigrants to America come as individuals, whereas in Israel people immigrate as part of a people, and therefore the conceptions of security are different. The holding of a gun in Israel is interpreted as more of a commitment to collective security than as a sign of unyielding commitment to self-defense in an individual sense. In America it is much more connected to a fear of crime, and here [in Israel] much more connected with national defense, an external threat, the idea of a people's army. When we see individuals carrying guns, we see them almost as organs of the community.

Both automatic weapons and handguns are common in Israel, but firearms ownership is strictly regulated outside the military and the system of national security. Possession of a firearm without a license can lead to a seven-year prison term. Ammunition is also strictly controlled. Licensing clerks determine who will get a firearms license, and they may reject applicants because they have no need for a weapon, have been institutionalized in a mental hospital, have a police record, are under twenty years old, or are on active military duty. About one applicant in five is rejected.

Firearms are not used by criminals in Israel very often, although there has recently been some concern about the theft of firearms by criminals from licensed owners and from the military. The police estimate that there are three to four times as many unlicensed and illegal firearms in the country as there are licensed weapons, but many of the unlicensed weapons are in the hands of private collectors rather than criminals.

Overall, Israel, much like Switzerland, has a relatively low crime rate with little use of firearms by murderers, robbers, and rapists. This is true in spite of the pervasive ownership of weapons in the country, a situation tied to military and security measures for the nation as a whole.

SOURCE. Based on David K. Shipler, "To Pistol-Packing Israelis, a Gun Is a Patriotic Badge," *The New York Times*, April 13, 1981, p. A2.

FIREARMS AND MURDER   With about 120 million firearms, including 50 million handguns, in private hands in the United States, and with about half of all households having at least one firearm, there is a good chance that one will be present at the scene of a bitter argument or a fight (DuBow, McCabe, and Kaplan, 1979; Wright, Rossi, and Daly, 1983). If a firearm is used during an altercation, murder is a likely result. Thus, one study found that the increased number of handguns in Detroit between 1963 and 1971 accounted for most of the substantial increase in murders in that city over that period (Fisher, 1976). Other studies have also found a relationship between gun ownership and homicide rates (Seitz, 1972; Cook, 1983).

Assaults with firearms are much more likely to result in death than assaults with a knife or assaults without a weapon. According to one study, firearms assaults are fatal about 13 percent of the time, knife attacks are fatal about 3 percent of the time, and attacks with hands, fists, and feet are fatal only 1.7 percent of the time (Morris and Hawkins, 1970: 66). Other research finds that firearms assaults lead to death about two to five times as often as attacks with knives (Wright, Rossi, and Daly, 1983: 198). Because guns are the most deadly weapon, it would seem that their easy availability would be associated with a higher homicide rate. However, we cannot infer from these statistics that substituting knives for guns in the hands of assailants would reduce fatalities, because assailants who decide to use firearms might be more single-minded in their desire to kill victims, and they might be more intent on doing so even if they had to use a knife (Wright, Rossi, and Daly, 1983).

FIREARMS AND ROBBERY   Relatively few studies have asked offenders what role the firearm plays for them in the commission of a crime. One study of robbery did conclude that the idea that firearms serve mainly expressive purposes is probably incorrect. Rather than using weapons as psychological props to create a sense of omnipotence or masculinity, as some psychologists and psychiatrists suggest, robbers usually employ weapons primarily for instrumental purposes—to acquire money more easily and with less resistance and to ensure a safe escape from the scene of the crime (Conklin, 1972: 108–112; also, see Wright and Rossi, 1986).

Paradoxically, the use of firearms by robbers may prevent violence, because victims are less likely to resist offenders who carry guns (Conklin, 1972; Block, 1977). When victims do resist, offenders may increase the level of intimidation by cocking the pistol, holding it to the victim's head, or using it as a blunt instrument to hit the victim. Sometimes, of course, firearms are used to shoot victims, and then robberies may lead to serious injury or death. Victims who resist armed robbers are about three times as likely to be injured seriously as are victims who do not resist (Block, 1977, 1981).

We cannot say exactly how much robbery would be prevented if no firearms were available, but at least some marginally committed and opportunistic robbers would probably give up that form of theft if they could not get a gun. Some of them might turn to nonviolent crimes such as burglary, shoplifting, and larceny. Even if they continued to commit robberies without firearms, that might be preferable to robberies committed with guns.

GUN CONTROL AND CRIME RATES   There is mixed evidence as to whether crime can be reduced by controlling access to firearms. One study that compared five states with strong gun-control laws to five states with weak laws found that the states with the strong laws had lower homicide rates. In these states, a smaller proportion of the homicides that did occur were perpetrated with firearms (Criminal Division, U.S. Department of Justice, 1968). Although this study suggests that strong gun-control laws might reduce the homicide rate, the results can also be interpreted to mean that the states that were able to pass strong gun-control legislation were the states in which people were more opposed to the use of firearms to begin with or were the states in which firearms were relatively unimportant to residents. Thus, both the low murder rate and the gun-control law may have been products of a nonviolent, antiweapons attitude on the part of the state's residents. This attitude, rather than the law itself, might account for a low homicide rate.

In recent years, several states have passed laws that have attempted to reduce crime by controlling firearms. One approach is to control the possession and use of firearms by the general public. Thus, in 1975 the Bartley-Fox law was implemented in Massachusetts to require a one-year jail sentence for anyone caught carrying an unlicensed firearm. One evaluation of the impact of this law found that it seemed to have reduced the incidence of gun assaults, but it also produced a more than offsetting increase in assaults with weapons other than guns, apparently because people who avoided carrying firearms turned to other weapons to commit assaults. Gun robberies were reduced by the law, but armed robberies without firearms increased; however, the increase in robberies without firearms did not offset the decline in gun robberies. The law reduced homicides with firearms without any increase in nongun homicides. Thus, the Bartley-Fox law had some effect in reducing homicides and robberies with firearms. However, the researchers concluded that it was the publicity about the intent of the law, rather than the severity or certainty of the sanctions that were actually imposed, that produced this reduction in firearms crime; the researchers were unwilling to attribute the changes to the impact of the mandatory jail term (Pierce and Bowers, 1981). A more recent evaluation of this law concluded that

> although there is some evidence that the Massachusetts Bartley-Fox Amendment achieved at least an initial impact on gun-related crime, there is substantial reason to believe that long-range effects are not to be expected or will be considerably reduced in magnitude. In other words, there is some evidence that under some conditions gun-related crimes can be reduced through gun control legislation, but this outcome will be neither very common nor especially pronounced. (Wright, Rossi, and Daly, 1983: 308)

In 1980, New York state implemented a law similar to Bartley-Fox, except that in New York the mandatory sentence of one year was applied only to people who had been convicted of a crime in the previous five years. There is no evidence that this law has reduced street crime with firearms, and many who have been convicted under the law have not served the "mandatory" one year in jail (Basler, 1982; Barbanel, 1984).

A strategy tried by other states, including Michigan and Florida, requires judges to impose an additional prison term on offenders convicted of a serious crime in which they used a firearm. A study in Detroit found that crime rates declined after the implementation of a two-year mandatory additional penalty for the use of a firearm in a serious crime, but it concluded that the decline did not seem to be attributable to the new law. The decline began before the law was implemented, and unarmed violent crime as well as crime with firearms showed a decrease. The law's lack of impact was attributed to the fact that "offenders were not responsive to a mandatory two-year increment in sanctions for offenses which already carry maximum sentences much greater than two years" (Loftin, Heumann, and McDowall, 1983: 310). Thus, the law did not increase the perceived certainty or perceived severity of punishment in a significant way. The law would have affected rates of murder, robbery, and assault only if offenders who used weapons in those crimes placed relatively little value on the use of weapons, and this apparently was not the case. The fact that Detroit's population was heavily armed when the law was passed probably meant that offenders placed great value on being armed because of the high probability that they would encounter armed resistance from their victims (Loftin and McDowall, 1981; Loftin, Heumann, and McDowall, 1983; also, see Loftin and McDowall, 1984).

Research has not demonstrated that gun-control laws that require mandatory jail sentences for anyone carrying an unlicensed weapon or for anyone using a firearm in a serious crime can have a long-run effect on the use of firearms in crime. Sometimes "mandatory" penalties are not imposed. Either the police do not arrest everyone who carries an illegal firearm, or judges fail to impose the required sentence. Even if the criminal justice system imposed the mandatory penalty, it is not clear that felons would give up their firearms.

THE CONTINUING DEBATE OVER GUN CONTROL   In spite of the uncertain effects of gun-control laws, most Americans support stronger laws than we now have. A 1987 poll found that 60 percent of Americans favored stricter legal controls on the sale of pistols, and polls since 1975 have found a majority supporting this proposal. In 1987, 42 percent favored and 50 percent opposed a law that would ban handgun possession (Schmidt, 1987). The town of Morton Grove, Illinois, banned pistols in 1981, and a few other communities have enacted similar ordinances, but local laws of this sort are not likely to have much effect on the nation's crime rate. People can easily find firearms in nearby communities and carry them to the town where they are banned.

One reason federal gun-control laws are relatively weak is not for lack of public support for stronger laws, but rather because of the power of the National Rifle Association (NRA). This well-financed organization of about 2 million members can mobilize its supporters to write to members of Congress to oppose any gun-control legislation that is being considered. Many NRA members are "single-issue" voters who will vote against candidates who favor tougher gun-control laws. Because most voters who support tougher gun-control laws will not vote for or against candidates solely because of their stand on gun control, NRA members pose a more significant risk of lost votes to candidates, and thus many politicians vote against gun control out of fear of alienating the opponents of stronger gun-control laws.

In recent years, several lobbyist groups — such as People against Handguns, the National Coalition to Ban Handguns, and Handgun Control, Inc. — have fought for stronger gun-control laws. These organizations have been hampered by a lack of funds, by little support from "single-issue" voters, and by well-organized opposition from the NRA and the firearms industry.

The debate over gun control continues. Opponents claim a constitutional right to bear arms, even though the Constitution specifies that this right is not to be abridged because of the need to raise a national militia. The handguns involved in murders and robberies are not designed for military use, nor do their owners buy them for that purpose. Another argument against stronger gun-control laws is that criminals will find guns even if stronger laws are passed. Proponents of stronger gun-control laws claim that the laws might reduce crime, but we lack solid research data to support that argument. Further research may clarify the effects that different kinds of gun-control laws can have on various forms of crime.

Summary

In this chapter we have looked at the way offenders seek suitable targets that are not protected by owners or bystanders. Opportunities for crime are a function of people's everyday behavior, according to this routine activities approach.

Criminals consider various aspects of potential targets for crime: the form and value of property, and the vulnerability of victims. Some victims are more prone to victimization than others because they have characteristics or play roles that make them especially vulnerable.

Sometimes a victim precipitates an offense, contributing to his or her own victimization. Homicide victims are often the first to use abusive language or force in an interaction that culminates in murder. Rape victims sometimes enter risky situations, although this does not absolve rapists of legal responsibility for their crimes. Owners of property precipitate crimes by leaving their property unguarded and vulnerable to theft.

Alcohol and drugs sometimes facilitate crime. There is an association between alcohol use and crime, with many offenders being drunk or under the influence of alcohol when they violate the law. Similarly, many offenders are under the influence of illegal drugs when they engage in crime. More research is needed to determine the precise manner in which drugs and alcohol are associated with the commission of crime.

In the United States, many offenses are committed with firearms. Guns seem to facilitate crimes such as murder and robbery. Assaults with firearms are more likely to produce death than are attacks with other weapons, and so the presence of a firearm seems to make murder a more likely outcome of an altercation. However, countries such as Switzerland and Israel have relatively low crime rates even though they have widespread ownership of firearms. The effects of gun-control laws on crime rates are unclear. Mandatory penalties are often not applied, and additional penalties for the use of a firearm in a serious crime do not seem to deter most offenders. The debate over the impact of gun-control laws continues. A majority of Americans favor stronger laws, but such restrictions are opposed by the well-financed and powerful National Rifle Association.

Important Terms

routine activities approach   victim proneness
victim precipitation

Suggested Readings

JAMES J. COLLINS, JR., ED. *Drinking and Crime: Perspectives on the Relationships between Alcohol Consumption and Criminal Behavior.* New York: Guilford, 1981. A collection of eight papers that review research on the link between alcohol use and crime.

JOHN E. CONKLIN. *Robbery and the Criminal Justice System.* Philadelphia: Lippincott, 1972. A study of how robbers choose their targets, and their use of firearms, drugs, and alcohol.

ANDREW KARMEN. *Crime Victims: An Introduction to Victimology.* Monterey, Calif.: Brooks/Cole, 1984. A text that contains a good discussion of the victim's role in crime.

THOMAS A. REPPETTO. *Residential Crime.* Cambridge, Mass.: Ballinger, 1974. A study of burglars and how they select their targets.

JAMES D. WRIGHT AND PETER H. ROSSI. *Armed and Considered Dangerous: A Survey of Felons and Their Firearms.* New York: Aldine de Gruyter, 1986. A national survey of the use of firearms in the commission of serious crimes.

CHAPTER 11

Criminal Careers

$15,900 Reward *in* Gold

ROY A. A. DE AUTREMONT
Picture taken early in 1923

RAY CHARLES DE AUTREMONT
Picture taken in 1920
He now resembles closely his twin brother Roy

HUGH DE AUTREMONT
Picture taken in 1923

ROY A. A. DE AUTREMONT, alias R. A. Harris, alias R. A. Burton, age 23 in 1923; weight 135-140 pounds; height 5 feet 6 inches. Complexion medium light. Hair medium light brown. Eyes peculiar looking, narrow and squinty, light brown. Wears glasses in reading. Face broad at the cheek bones. Nervous, and a "dreamer." Likes to argue against the Bible. Long, turned up nose and prominent nostrils. Tonsils have been removed. Head round. Wears No. 6 shoe. Boastful and egotistical. Clips his words. Forward and presuming with women. First upper right molar tooth has amalgam filling, as have both first right and left lower molars.

RAY DE AUTREMONT, alias R. C. Burton, alias William Elliott, alias Chas. R. Joseph, age 23 in 1923. Height 5 feet 6 inches. Weight 135-140 pounds. Complexion light. Hair medium light brown. Broad face. Prominent nostrils. Short cut neck. Eyes, peculiar looking, light brown, small and squinty. Wears glasses when reading. Big toe nail on left foot turned up. Cut scar at tip of left forefinger inner, and at back of second joint right middle finger, also round cut scar back of head. Gold foil in upper left cuspid, mesial surface. Amalgam filling, upper left first molar, occlusal surface. Gold inlay, upper right cuspid, mesial and incisive angle.

HUGH DE AUTREMONT, alias E. E. James, alias Hugh DeKay, alias Hugh De Lerious, alias Hugh DeCoy. Age 19 in 1923, looks older. Height 5 feet 7 inches. Weight about 135 pounds. Complexion fair, eyes blue. Nose slightly pug. Hair medium light, slightly sandy and curly. Amalgam filling right and left molars, and same in first right upper molar. Likes to argue and is good debater. Fond of sports, particularly boxing and running. Expressed desire for traveling, and has boasted of trips he has made by riding freight trains. He is bright and alert and has a high school education. Little fingers turn outward at first joint.

REWARDS totaling $15,900 (*$5,300 FOR EACH MAN*) are offered for information leading to the arrest and conviction of these men, who are wanted for the holdup of train near Siskiyou, Oregon, and the murder of the railway postal clerk and three trainmen on October 11, 1923

▼

*COMMUNICATE INFORMATION TO YOUR POSTMASTER,
TO PEACE OFFICIALS, AND TO—*

C. RIDDIFORD,
Post Office Inspector in Charge
Spokane, Wash.

D. O'CONNELL,
Chief Special Agent, Southern Pacific
Company, San Francisco, Calif.

Source: Warshaw Collection / Archive Center, Smithsonian Institution

A career is a "sequence of movements from one position to another in an occupational system made by an individual who works in the system"(Becker, 1973: 24). A *criminal career* is not an "occupation" as we commonly understand that term, but a sequence of crimes over time can be analyzed much like a career in a legitimate occupation, for both involve skills, tasks, and commitment (Letkemann, 1973; Gibbs and Shelly, 1982). As long ago as 1893 it was recognized that "correct statistics of offenders can be developed only by a study of the total life histories of individuals" (Otto Kobner, cited in Petersilia, Greenwood, and Lavin, 1977: 2–3). Another student of crime noted in 1917 that the proper study of crime requires an examination of "the manner in which criminality develops in the course of a human lifetime" (Georg Von Mayr, cited in Petersilia, Greenwood, and Lavin, 1977: 3).

Even though criminal careers are similar to legitimate careers in some ways, we must be alert to differences between them. Legitimate careers develop in stable contexts, such as within a corporation or a law firm. Criminal careers usually develop in less formal contexts; for instance, robbers' and burglars' careers develop outside a stable organizational context, even though gangsters have careers within the relatively stable setting of an organized crime "family." In addition, criminal careers often lack the well-defined sequence of stages and the pattern of upward mobility that frequently are characteristic of legitimate careers. Although some legitimate workers do not experience these changes during their careers, and some offenders do gain in status over their lifetimes, there is probably less upward mobility in deviant careers than in legitimate ones. Careers in crime are also less structured and perhaps more dependent on individual initiative in seeking out rewards than are legitimate careers. Moreover, criminal careers develop in secrecy from established authorities, whereas legitimate occupations often have the support of social institutions (Luckenbill and Best, 1981).

We can study criminal careers by examining the autobiographies of individual offenders. These accounts reveal much about the subjective states and actual experiences of certain offenders, although they may not be representative of all criminals. Another approach is to develop conceptual typologies, or categorizations, of criminal careers. Arrest statistics have also been used to study the careers of offenders, but because relatively few crimes lead to arrest, these data seem to tell us more about contacts with the criminal justice system than about actual involvement in criminal behavior (Petersilia, Greenwood, and Lavin, 1977).

Knowledge of criminal careers has practical value. If we know why offenders get involved in a life of crime, we may be able to implement policies that prevent criminal careers from developing. If we know why some career offenders "retire" from crime, we may be able to create programs that hasten their departure from crime. There is evidence that relatively few career criminals account for a large proportion of all of the crime that occurs. This suggests that the punishment and treatment of career offenders might have a significant impact on the crime rate. As we will see later, career criminal programs have been developed to concentrate the criminal justice system's resources on offenders who repeatedly commit serious crimes.

Analyzing Criminal Careers

The analysis of criminal careers requires attention to the social conditions that influence the development of patterned criminal activity. Labeling by the criminal justice system can affect an individual's life chances and thus make criminal behavior more or less likely. Criminal careers can be analyzed by looking at an individual's alternation between legitimate work and criminal activities. We also need to examine the way people are recruited into criminal careers, and especially the way involvement in juvenile delinquency is linked to adult criminal careers.

Career Contingencies

Criminal careers depend on various *contingencies,* or factors that determine movement from one criminal role to another, or from one crime to another (Becker, 1973). For instance, organized and professional crime primarily involves males, even though sex segregation in the underworld varies from one crime group to another. Women are at a disadvantage in being recruited into crime groups, in the criminal career paths available to them, and in their access to opportunities for learning criminal skills and gaining the rewards of crime. Gender-role socialization and patterns of parental surveillance of boys and girls also limit females' access to certain criminal careers (Hoffman-Bustamante, 1973; Steffensmeier, 1983).

Career contingencies include apprehension for violating the law. People who break the law, are arrested by the police, and are convicted in court may later engage in crime because of the social contacts they make while incarcerated. Experience with the criminal justice system may contribute to a criminal career by causing bitterness or by closing off job opportunities. However, offenders may also commit more crime if they are not arrested and convicted, because successful crimes can reinforce their law-violating behavior by providing them with rewards. Short-run rewards of peer prestige and money can create a "mobility trap" for juvenile delinquents, who gain immediate prestige and property at the cost of long-term upward mobility if they are expelled from school, are socially stigmatized, or become known to the police as offenders (Wiley, 1967).

The Labeling Perspective

The labeling perspective focuses on the development of deviant careers, including careers in crime. People who break rules repeatedly and are labeled deviant by others may organize their lives around deviant behavior. What begins as casual experimentation with rule breaking can become a deviant career, or "a whole sequential process in identity formation" (Rettig, Torres, and Garrett, 1977: 192).

Most people who break the law repeatedly are eventually arrested and convicted. As criminals say, "If you want to play, you have to pay," or "If you can't do the time, don't do the crime." As we saw earlier in the book, the chance of avoiding arrest for any given crime is good, but the chance of never being arrested if one commits many crimes is small. Offenders who are more skilled may go longer without an arrest, but eventually they "take a fall."

The response by the criminal justice system to people who break the law creates a set of contingencies that can push some individuals into criminal careers. The criminal justice system seems to deal more harshly with some people than with others. For instance, the police react to suspects on the basis of the seriousness of the offense, the individual's demeanor, the complainant's preferences, and the requirements of the police department (Piliavin and Briar, 1964; Black, 1980). The arrest, conviction, and imprisonment of an individual may be more likely if he or she is seen as a member of a criminal subculture who is likely to continue to commit serious crimes, rather than perceived as someone who violated the law because of poor judgment or situational pressures (Cloward and Ohlin, 1960: 12). Reactions to defendants by the criminal justice system may be based on valid assumptions about the likelihood that different kinds of people will continue in a life of crime, but these reactions can also elicit patterned and persistent behavior. In other words, the label "criminal" can structure other people's responses to the offender; some people, for example, will refuse to hire an ex-convict. Responses of this sort can then act as contingencies that influence the development of a criminal career.

The "Zigzag Path": Criminal Careers and Legitimate Pursuits

Criminal careers vary considerably. One study of thieves found that most followed a "zigzag path" back and forth between criminal and noncriminal pursuits (Glaser, 1974). Offenders would commit crimes, go to prison, try to get a job when released, and often return to crime later. Contacts with other criminals and the difficulty of finding a good job often made a return to crime the "path of least resistance" (Rettig, Torres, and Garrett, 1977: 4). The effects of situational factors such as peer influence and financial need were mediated in part by the ex-convict's commitment to a criminal career or commitment to a legitimate career, but tempting situations sometimes drew even those who were committed to a conventional way of life back into crime. However, people who are committed to a conventional way of life apparently engage in less crime than people who are committed to a criminal career, even if they do not stay away from crime altogether (McAuliffe and Gordon, 1974).

Success at crime can lead to continued criminal activities, and success in legitimate pursuits can lead to a continuation of those activities. Once people have engaged in crime and escaped arrest, they may think the risk of negative consequences from crime is small and the rewards are great. Even if they are caught the first time, they may receive only a "slap on the wrist" in court and believe the chance of a harsh sanction is small. Serious failure in either criminal activities or legitimate pursuits can lead people to shift to the other form of behavior. Thus, losing a job might push a person into crime, and being arrested might lead someone else to look for a legitimate job (Glaser, 1974).

Recruitment into a Criminal Career

Recruitment into a criminal career often begins during adolescence, with early delinquency often being a prerequisite for an adult career in theft and violence. While still in their teens, future career criminals learn skills and motives, what a criminal way of life involves, and how the police react to different crimes (Letkemann, 1973). Access to criminal careers seems to be greater in communities where there are close ties between adolescents and adult criminals who can act as role models and communicate to the adolescents the values and skills necessary to crime. Access to criminal careers is also greater where there are stable relationships between people with conventional values and people with criminal values (Cloward and Ohlin, 1960). In such communities, a delinquent subculture is more likely to develop, and involvement in this subculture increases the likelihood of entry into adult criminal careers.

Adult offenders must also learn criminal skills and motives. For instance, to move from various forms of hustling into a specialty as a professional fence, one career criminal had to acquire considerable knowledge about merchandise, including what he should pay for it and how much he could sell it for. This fence also needed "ability, energy, ingenuity, and certain persuasive skills," as well as a willingness to deceive both the buying public and the thieves who sold to him (Klockars, 1974: 177). To become a buyer of stolen goods required a modest amount of capital, skills about to how to purchase goods, opportunities to buy goods for less than their retail price, a regular source of supply, a predictable demand for goods, and the ability to avoid arrest and imprisonment. The fence also needed a convincing front that would keep the police away but still attract customers looking for low prices.

Career criminals are recruited from various settings. Sutherland (1937) found that professional thieves had rarely been amateur thieves in slum areas, but instead came from legitimate occupations and severed their ties to the legitimate world after a period of unemployment. They spent time in bars and hotels where professional thieves gathered. Bartenders, taxi drivers, bellhops, waiters, and prostitutes who worked in the social world of the professional thief sometimes entered a life of crime by taking tangential roles in the commission of crime (Inciardi, 1975). Often they began by playing a small part in one crime and were called on later for more important roles in other offenses, gradually acquiring the skills and status of a professional thief. Others became career criminals by applying specific job skills to crime; for example, a printer might become a counterfeiter, or a locksmith might become a safecracker.

Typologies of Criminal Careers

One way to analyze criminal careers is to construct a typology of offenders and their patterns of criminal activity. Such a typology is developed from criteria that a criminologist thinks are important in distinguishing one criminal career from another. This kind of typology assumes there is some specialization among offenders in the sorts of crime they commit.

GIBBONS'S TYPOLOGY OF CRIMINAL ROLE CAREERS   Don Gibbons (1987) has developed an influential typology of "criminal role careers," which are patterns or sequences of criminal behavior and related social situations. He suggests that a good typology will describe real offenders accurately and will be comprehensive. With such a typology, criminologists can develop specific theories that explain each criminal role career. A typology can also be used to develop treatment methods for various kinds of offenders.

Gibbons's typology is not a logically exhaustive set of criminal career types. Instead, he selects several dimensions he thinks are important aspects of criminal careers and then describes a set of criminal role careers in terms of those characteristics. The dimensions he examines are the offense itself, the interactional setting of the behavior (alone or with others), the offender's self-concept and attitudes, and the pattern of crime over the offender's lifetime. Gibbons also looks at the offender's class background, family background, peer-group associations, and contacts with law-enforcement agencies. From these dimensions, he derives the following types of criminal role careers:

1. Professional thieves
2. Professional "heavy" criminals
3. Semiprofessional property offenders
4. Naive check forgers
5. Automobile thieves—"joyriders"
6. Property offenders, "one-time losers"
7. Embezzlers
8. White-collar criminals
9. Professional "fringe violators"
10. Personal offenders, "one-time losers"
11. Psychopathic assaultists
12. Statutory rapists
13. Aggressive rapists
14. Violent sex offenders
15. Nonviolent sex offenders
16. Incest offenders
17. Male homosexuals
18. Opiate addicts
19. Skid Row alcoholics
20. Amateur shoplifters. (Gibbons, 1987: 212)

Critique of Gibbons's Typology. This typology has several problems. Gibbons does not indicate why he selected these career types and not others. For instance, there is empirical evidence for distinguishing between two types of opiate addicts: "hard-core addicts" who get high on heroin nearly every day and usually commit crime to support their habits, and "weekenders" who get high on heroin only a few times a week (although they use heroin daily) and are less often involved in crime (other than the offenses of purchasing and possessing heroin) (McAuliffe and Gordon, 1974). Gibbons's typology would be more accurate if he replaced his "opiate addict" career criminal with those two kinds of addicts.

Gibbons's decisions about what constitutes a criminal role career sometimes seem to be based more on intuition than on empirical evidence. For example, research indicates that some offenders consciously choose between robbery and burglary as specialties but that other thieves switch back and forth between these offenses (Conklin, 1972: 87–88). Gibbons includes robbers and burglars in the professional heavy criminal category and also in the semiprofessional property criminal group; it might be more accurate to create six distinct types: professional and semiprofessional robbers, professional and semiprofessional burglars, and professional and semiprofessional thieves who engage in various property offenses. Any typology will include certain assumptions about what factors are critical in distinguishing one criminal career from another, but those assumptions should be as consistent with the empirical evidence as possible.

Gibbons's typology is not really a typology of criminal careers, if the term "career" means the development of criminal behavior over time in a patterned way. He does not stress the cumulative nature of criminal behavior, offenders' deepening involvement in crime, or the way that experiences at one time lead to later career developments. In other words, his typology has a static quality, whereas criminal careers by definition evolve dynamically over time.

Another problem with Gibbons's typology is that some of the criminal role careers he identifies are careers in only the most limited sense of the term. There is a problem in speaking of an embezzler role career, because few embezzlers are involved in crime over time. Likewise, statutory rape — sexual intercourse with a female under the legal age of consent — is probably not the basis of a criminal role career very often; few men seem to have a long-term commitment to engaging in intercourse with young women. Incest is probably not the basis of a criminal career very often either; it may be a repeated offense, but it is usually with the same partner and is likely to cease after the offender is caught.

Gibbons states that comprehensiveness is a criterion of a good typology, but he also acknowledges that many offenders cannot be categorized easily. A study by Hartjen and Gibbons (1969) assessed the usefulness of an earlier version of Gibbons's typology by trying to classify 655 offenders who were on probation. Using three probation officers to classify the offenders, Hartjen and Gibbons concluded that only 48 percent of the probationers could be fitted into one of the twenty-six career types they used. In only 22 percent of the cases did all three probation officers agree on how to classify offenders. Of the 312 offenders who were assigned to a career type by either two or three of the probation officers, three-fifths of them fell into four categories and all of them fell into seventeen of the career types. Hartjen and Gibbons concluded that the typology they used included some dramatic but relatively rare criminal career types. They suggested a revision of the typology to include more mundane offenses, such as nonsupport of dependents and traffic violations.

Typologies of criminal careers can be useful, but they must be based on empirical evidence on patterns or sequences of crimes. There is evidence that many offenders are versatile in their selection of crimes, and typologies usually emphasize specialization. The proportion of all crimes that can be accounted for by career criminals who specialize in one kind of offense is thus smaller than is implied by typologies such as Gibbons's. As Gibbons (1987: 219) himself has concluded after a review of the evidence, "Considerable pessimism is in order concerning classification systems which assign criminal offenders to a relatively small number of distinct types."

CHAIKEN AND CHAIKEN'S TYPOLOGY OF OFFENDER TYPES Another potentially fruitful approach to the development of typologies is to categorize people by the specific combinations of offenses they commit over time. A survey of nearly 2,200 adult male inmates in three states identified ten types of offenders by the combination of offenses they had committed. Chaiken and Chaiken (1982a, 1982b, 1983, 1984) found that these ten types differed in their rates of committing crime, their persistence in crime, and their personal characteristics. Table 11.1 shows these ten offender types and the kinds of crimes they committed.

Chaiken and Chaiken gave the most attention to the first type of offender, the violent predatory offender. This offender engages in robbery, assault, and drug dealing, and sometimes in burglary and other kinds of theft. The violent predatory offender commits a disproportionate amount of all of the crime committed by inmates, is usually quite young, has been arrested frequently, began to commit crime at an early age, rarely has any family obligations, and has an irregular employment record. Violent predatory offenders are difficult to identify from official records, because they are young and the juvenile records that would indicate their heavy involvement in criminal activity generally are unavailable for use by researchers, probation officers, prosecutors, and judges.

Delinquent Careers

One way to examine criminal careers is to look at lifetime patterns of delinquency and crime for a sample of individuals born in the same year. A cohort study of this sort was conducted by Wolfgang, Figlio, and Sellin (1972) in a project described in Chapter 1. They used school records, police and court records, and draft board records to study 9,945 males who were born in 1945 and lived in Philadelphia from their tenth through their eighteenth birthdays.

TABLE 11.1   Ten Offender Types by Combinations of Offenses Committed

Group	Robbery	Assault[a]	Burglary	Theft,[b] Fraud, Forgery, Credit Card Crimes	Drug Deals	Percent of Study Sample[c]
Violent predators (robber-assaulter-dealers)	+	+	?	?	+	15
Robber-assaulters	+	+	?	?	0	8
Robber-dealers	+	0	?	?	+	9
Low-level robbers	+	0	?	?	0	12
Mere assaulters	0	+	0	0	0	5
Burglar-dealers	0	??	+	?	+	10
Low-level burglars	0	0	+	?	0	8
Property and drug offenders	0	??	0	+	+	6
Low-level property offenders	0	0	0	+	0	8
Drug dealers	0	0	0	0	+	6

Note: + = Group member commits this crime, by definition.
          0 = Group member does not commit this crime, by definition.
          ? = Group member may or may not commit this crime. Analysis shows that nearly all members of the group do.
          ?? = Group member may or may not commit this crime. Most don't.

[a]Assault includes homicide arising out of assault or robbery.

[b]Theft includes auto theft.

[c]Percentages add to 87%. The remaining 13% did not report committing any of the crimes studied. Some serious crimes (e.g., rape, kidnap) were not included in the self-report survey. Respondents with missing data (150 out of 2,190) were excluded in calculation of percentages.

SOURCE: Marcia R. Chaiken and Jan M. Chaiken, "Offender Types and Public Policy," *Crime and Delinquency,* Vol. 30, No. 2 (April 1984), p. 198. Copyright © 1984 by Sage Publications, Inc. Reprinted by permission of Sage Publications, Inc.

Tracy, Wolfgang, and Figlio (1985) later replicated this study, using the same methods to study a cohort of 27,160 males and females who were born in 1958 and lived in Philadelphia from their tenth through their eighteenth birthdays. These Cohort I and II studies made it possible to examine past contacts with the juvenile justice system but did not allow the researchers to question individuals and administer self-report questionnaires to learn about offenses that never came to the attention of the police and the courts.

Chronic Offenders

Wolfgang, Figlio, and Sellin found that a relatively small proportion of the boys in Cohort I accounted for a large proportion of all of the cohort's contacts with the police that resulted in written reports. Table 11.2 shows the proportion of Cohort I that had no contact with the police (nondelinquents), the proportion that had one contact (one-time offenders), the proportion with two to four contacts (nonchronic offenders), and the proportion with five or more contacts (chronic offenders). Only 6.3 percent of the 9,945 boys were chronic offenders, but this group accounted for 51.9 percent of all of the cohort's contacts with the

TABLE 11.2   Police Contacts among Members of Cohort I

Type of Offender	Percentage of Cohort	Percentage of All of Cohort's Police Contacts
Nondelinquents	65.1	0
One-time offenders	16.2	15.8
Nonchronic offenders	12.4	32.3
Chronic offenders	6.3	51.9

SOURCE: Marvin E. Wolfgang, Robert M. Figlio, and Thorsten Sellin, *Delinquency in a Birth Cohort.* Chicago: University of Chicago Press, 1972, p. 89. Reprinted by permission of The University of Chicago Press. © 1972 by The University of Chicago. All rights reserved. (Adapted)

police. The nonchronic group accounted for 12.4 percent of the cohort, but 32.3 percent of all police contacts. If the nonchronic and chronic groups are combined into a category of "career delinquents"—that is, those with more than one police contact as a juvenile—we find that the 18.7 percent of Cohort I classified as career delinquents accounted for 84.2 percent of all police contacts for the cohort. There is thus a high concentration of police contacts among a relatively small proportion of the cohort.

Tracy, Wolfgang, and Figlio's Cohort II study confirmed the findings of the Cohort I study with regard to the concentration of police contacts among a small proportion of the total cohort. The 7.5 percent of Cohort II classified as chronic offenders (five or more police contacts) accounted for 61 percent of all contacts with the police for the cohort. These chronic offenders accounted for 68 percent of all police contacts for FBI index offenses, including 73 percent of the cohort's robberies and 75 percent of the cohort's rapes.

A cohort study in Racine, Wisconsin, looked at the police contacts of both juveniles and young adults and found a similar concentration of police contacts among a small percentage of three different cohorts. Between 5 and 7 percent of the people in each cohort accounted for more than half of all nontraffic contacts with the police, and about 20 percent of each cohort accounted for 80 percent of all nontraffic police contacts in the cohort. Moreover, 8 to 14 percent of each cohort accounted for all of the felony arrests in the cohort (Shannon, 1982: 3).

A cohort study in London found that 132 of 396 boys were convicted of an offense before the age of twenty-five. Of the 132, twenty-three were chronic offenders with six or more convictions. This group of chronic offenders accounted for about half of all of the convictions that were recorded for those youths who had ever been convicted of an offense. These chronic offenders differed from the nonchronic offenders in that they "tended to be convicted at any early age, to come from low-income families, to be rated troublesome in their primary schools, to have low IQ and attainment, to be clumsy on psychomotor tests, and to have convicted older siblings" (Blumstein, Farrington, and Moitra, 1985: 196).

Patterns of Delinquent Careers

Wolfgang, Figlio, and Sellin examined several issues related to delinquent careers. They discovered that boys who had one contact with the police and then had no more contacts usually had engaged in relatively trivial offenses the first time. However, boys with at least two police contacts were more likely to have been stopped the first time for a relatively serious offense that involved injury, theft, or damage.

Of the boys in Cohort I with at least one police contact, 53.6 percent were stopped a second time. Of those stopped a second time, 65.1 percent went on to a third contact with the police, and of those with three or more contacts, the chances of being stopped an additional time ranged from 70 to 80 percent. In other words, the likelihood of never again being stopped by the police for delinquency is greatest after the first contact with the police; after a second contact, the chance of continuing in a delinquent career is greater. Another study found even higher "transition probabilities" among a sample of 1,591 adults arrested for violent crimes; the chance of being arrested again after any given arrest was about 80 percent, whatever the individual's prior arrest history (Miller, Dinitz, and Conrad, 1982).

Juveniles who are first stopped by the police at a very young age are more likely to have another police contact than are juveniles whose first contact with the police comes at a later age. Early age at first contact also seems to be associated with a long career in crime and delinquency, a rapid development of that career, and involvement in serious offenses (Wolfgang, Figlio, and Sellin, 1972; Peterson and Braiker, 1981; Miller, Dinitz, and Conrad, 1982; Tracy, Wolfgang, and Figlio, 1985). Early contact with the police may indicate a serious behavioral problem that is conducive to a criminal career, or early contact with the police may subject individuals to a labeling experience in juvenile court that closes off legitimate opportunities, breaks conventional bonds, and pushes people into lives of crime.

Neither Philadelphia cohort study found a relationship between the type of offense for which a juvenile was stopped by the police and the number of contacts the juvenile had with the police, contrary to an expectation that offenders would specialize over their delinquent careers. If police contacts reflect actual behavior, it seems that delinquents begin anew each time they commit a delinquent act. An additional cohort study also found no clear offense patterns among delinquent youths (Lab, 1984), and a study of status offenders that used both official data and self-reports found no patterns of escalation in the seriousness of offenses as careers developed (Datesman and Aickin, 1984; also, see Tracy, Wolfgang, and Figlio, 1985). A study in Columbus, Ohio, of 1,222 boys and girls arrested at least once for a violent crime concluded that even violent juvenile offenders do not tend to specialize in the kinds of crime they commit, and that they do not progress from less serious crimes to more serious offenses during their criminal careers (Hamparian et al., 1985). In sum, several studies point to the conclusion that juvenile delinquents tend not to specialize in one type of crime, and that when they continue to break the law they do not engage in increasingly serious offenses.

The Philadelphia Cohort I study found that the time between police contacts became compressed over the course of an individual's delinquent career. The average time from first contact to second contact was sixteen to eighteen months. However, the average time from second contact to third contact was only ten months, and the average time from the third to the fourth contact was only eight months. The interval continued to decrease with additional police contacts, so that the average time between contacts after the twelfth one was only about three months. A similar compression of arrests as the criminal record lengthens has been found for adult offenders (Miller, Dinitz, and Conrad, 1982). It is unclear whether this compression results from increased criminal or delinquent activity once a career begins, or whether it occurs because the police are more likely to arrest people they consider to be troublemakers because of their past contacts with the police.

Juvenile Delinquency and Adult Criminal Careers

Wolfgang and his colleagues (1974) have recorded police contacts up to the age of twenty-six for a sample of 567 members of the original Philadelphia cohort of boys. The probability of being stopped by the police before eighteen was .35; that is, thirty-five of every one hundred males in Cohort I had contact with the police as a juvenile. The probability of any police contact from age ten to age twenty-six was .43. Twenty-three percent of the adults in the sample of 567 had a police contact between eighteen and twenty-six.

The likelihood of police contact as an adult for a person who had been stopped by the police as a juvenile was .44, but the probability of contact as an adult if a person had not been stopped as a juvenile was only .12. Thus, a male with a juvenile record was nearly four times as likely as a male without a juvenile record to have a police contact as an adult. Even though males who had been stopped by the police as juveniles were much more likely to have trouble with the police as adults than were males who had not been stopped as juveniles, it is also true that many people who had had contact with the police as juveniles did not go on to have trouble with the police as adults.

The study of the Columbus, Ohio, cohort of 1,222 juveniles arrested for violent offenses found that 59 percent of them were arrested at least once for an adult felony by the time they reached their mid-twenties. The youthful violent offenders who were most likely to be arrested for a felony as an adult were male, had been arrested for an index violent offense as a youth, had first been arrested at age twelve or less, and had been committed to a state juvenile correctional facility (Hamparian et al., 1985). However, about two-fifths of this cohort of youthful violent offenders did not go on to be arrested for serious crimes as adults, although many may have committed offenses for which they were not arrested.

It is not too surprising that many juvenile offenders do not go on to commit crimes as adults, because often their delinquent acts would not be crimes if committed by adults. There is no reason to expect that a fifteen-year-old boy apprehended for underage drinking or skipping school will commit robbery or burglary as an adult, or even as an adolescent. Researchers have found weak or nonexistent relationships between such status offenses and serious acts of delinquency (LeBlanc and Biron, 1980; Rojek and Erickson, 1981–82, 1982; Kelley, 1983). Because juvenile delinquency includes status offenses as well as acts that would be crimes if committed by adults, juvenile delinquents cannot be seen simply as criminals who happen to be under the age at which people are legally treated as adults.

Even juvenile delinquents who do commit serious crimes often realize that when they become adults, the chance of a harsh punishment increases greatly. They may be aware that their juvenile record is secret and that they start with a clean slate when they reach adulthood. These considerations lead some juvenile offenders to avoid breaking the law when they become adults. Other juvenile offenders settle down when they become adults, taking full-time jobs, getting married, and having children. These changes take them away from the street life and gangs that are conducive to criminal activities and reduce their motivation to engage in crime.

There is, nevertheless, a relationship between juvenile delinquency and adult criminal careers, both in the United States and in England (see the Cross-Cultural Perspective). Some attribute this relationship less to the continuity of behavior over time than to the effects of the juvenile and criminal justice systems on young people (Wolfgang, Figlio, and Sellin, 1972; Shannon, 1982). This view focuses on the labeling of juveniles as an important factor in the development of adult criminal careers and often leads to support for a strategy of *radical nonintervention* (Schur, 1973; Shannon, 1982). A radical nonintervention policy would minimize official reaction to delinquency in an effort to prevent the labeling of adolescents that could drive them into criminal careers. Another view is that adolescent offenders who represent the most serious threats to society are the most likely to be labeled delinquent, and it is they who would be the most likely to go on to engage in crime as adults even without official intervention when they are young. To date, researchers have not provided persuasive evidence of whether the relationship between juvenile delinquency and adult criminal careers is a result of labeling, a result of continuity of behavior over time, or some combination of the two.

Adult Criminal Careers

One way to look at criminal careers is to examine the lifetime criminal and noncriminal experiences of one kind of offender. Petersilia, Greenwood, and Lavin (1977) used this approach to study forty-nine men who were serving sentences in a California prison for armed robbery and who had been in prison

A Cross-Cultural Perspective: Juvenile Delinquency and Adult Crime in England

An English cohort study that examined delinquent and criminal careers began with 411 boys who were eight and nine years old in 1961.

Each of the following factors enhanced the likelihood that a boy would be arrested and convicted: low family income, large family size, criminal parents, poor child rearing, and low IQ level. Parents who had been convicted of crimes tended to have children who were also convicted of criminal and delinquent acts, but there was no evidence that the parents taught their children to violate the law or encouraged them to do so. Instead, criminal parents seemed to be poor at supervising their children, sometimes because of their own imprisonment, and therefore they were less likely to be "psychologically present" when their children found themselves in situations in which they were tempted to violate the law. There may also have been some police bias against children whose parents were known criminals, with the police being more likely to arrest rather

than to warn those children if they were caught violating the law.

Sixty-one percent of the boys who were convicted of delinquent acts were eventually convicted of crimes as adults, but only 13 percent of the boys who were not found delinquent went on to be convicted as adults. Some adult criminals had avoided any contact with the law as adolescents; in fact, nearly one-fourth of the adults who had two or more convictions had never been found delinquent. Boys who were convicted of delinquent acts at the earliest ages were the most likely to become persistent adult offenders. There was little specialization by type of offense by the age of twenty-one, although there was some continuity in aggressive behavior over time.

SOURCE. Based on David P. Farrington, "Longitudinal Research on Crime and Delinquency," in Norval Morris and Michael Tonry, eds., *Crime and Justice. An Annual Review of Research*, Vol. 1. Chicago: University of Chicago Press, 1979, pp. 289–348.

at least once before. They used self-reports of criminal activity as well as official data on arrests and convictions to trace the careers of these habitual offenders.

Career Patterns

The armed robbers had been incarcerated an average of half of their criminal careers, and they averaged about twenty years from first self-reported offense until current incarceration. Collectively, the forty-nine robbers reported 10,505 offenses over their careers, an average of 214 per offender. They had moved from crimes such as auto theft and burglary when they were juveniles to more serious offenses such as robbery when they became adults. The average age at first arrest was fifteen, but 29 percent had begun significant criminal activity by twelve, 75 percent had started by fifteen, and 90 percent had started by eighteen. Over their careers, the average amount stolen in a crime was about $250, and their average annual income from crime was only a few thousand dollars.

There was no strong tendency toward crime specialization among these offenders; they often switched from one offense to another. They would continue one kind of crime as long as it proved successful and as long as they could find opportunities. Other studies support this finding of little specialization by type of crime (Gould et al., 1966; Shover, 1973; Blumstein and Cohen, 1980; Petersilia, 1980; Peterson and Braiker, 1981; Rojek and Erickson, 1982; Kempf, 1987). One study of thieves involved in commercial burglary and truck hijacking found considerable versatility in the choice of crimes (Gibbs and Shelly, 1982). A study of 1,591 offenders chosen because they had been arrested for a serious violent crime found that 93 percent of them showed "no discernible pattern of violence" in their arrest histories; few habitually violent offenders were found in the sample (Miller, Dinitz, and Conrad, 1982: 59).

The armed robbers were more likely to be arrested for any given crime as adults than they were as juveniles; arrest rates were calculated in terms of number of arrests per self-reported crime. Why they became less successful in avoiding arrest as their criminal careers progressed is not clear. Few of them believed they were watched more carefully by the police because of their prior record. They may have become more careless over time, perhaps because their long experience in crime had made them overly confident.

These armed robbers continued to commit crimes after their earlier releases from prison because they had difficulty getting good jobs, lacked financial resources, and continued to interact with other offenders. A criminal record can be an impediment to securing a good job, but even more important may be an offender's lack of job skills and experience. The jobs these career criminals found were often low-paying, menial jobs with little or no opportunity for advancement. The ex-convicts who managed to get good jobs had lower offense rates than the ex-convicts who found poor-paying jobs or no jobs at all.

Planning Crimes

Relatively few of the armed robbers did much planning of their crimes. One-fourth did no planning or preparation at all, about half did very little planning, and one-fourth planned their crimes to some extent. Planning was more common when the offenders were young adults or adults than when they were juveniles, but even planning of crimes by adults was quite limited. Offenders typically included in what plans they did make the location of the crime, the presence of police patrols, when money would be present, whether there was an alarm on the premises, where a getaway car would be stolen, what disguise (if any) to wear, and how to escape from the scene of the crime.

As the habitual armed robbers got older, they increasingly operated by themselves. This allowed them to keep the profits of their crimes for themselves and reduced the risk that a partner would be arrested and cooperate with the police.

Some offenders used fences or drug dealers to meet certain needs, but in general there was a decline in reliance on others over time.

Use of the Stolen Money

While the armed robbers were juveniles, their crimes tended to fulfill expressive needs, such as peer approval, revenge, hostility, excitement, and a sense of being grown up. Over the course of their criminal careers, financial needs became relatively more important (Petersilia, 1980). The increased importance of financial needs suggests that economic assistance or a job that pays well might draw some older criminals away from crime and into a conventional way of life.

In a survey of 624 male California inmates who were serving time for felonies, researchers discovered that 47 percent reported that economic distress was an important reason for their crimes; offenders who cited this reason reported fewer violent offenses than inmates who said they had other motivations for their crimes (Peterson and Braiker, 1981). Thirty-five percent of the felons reported that their desire for high living and high times motivated them to commit crime; these offenders reported the most frequent commission of offenses. Finally, 14 percent of the inmates reported that temper was an important reason for their crimes, which were frequently violent. These three motivations for crime — economic distress, a desire for high living and high times, and temper — were found to be statistically unrelated to each other.

Intensive and Intermittent Career Criminals

Petersilia, Greenwood, and Lavin's research on armed robbers led them to distinguish between two kinds of career criminals: intensives and intermittents. *Intensive offenders* engage in criminal activity that begins at an early age and is sustained over time, consciously planned, persistent, skilled, and frequent. In contrast, *intermittent offenders* engage in irregular and opportunistic crimes with low payoffs and great risks and do not think of themselves as professional criminals. Intensive criminals see themselves as career criminals, have a specific goal for their crimes (such as supporting high living or a drug habit), and try to avoid arrest but do little planning of their crimes. Compared with the intermittent offender, the intensive criminal steals more money in each crime and is more likely to injure the victim. Intensives commit relatively serious crimes and engage in crime often, admitting to an average of fifty-one crimes per year, compared with an average of only five self-reported offenses per year for intermittent offenders (Petersilia, Greenwood, and Lavin, 1977).

The survey of 624 male felons in California prisons estimated that the average incoming prisoner had committed about fourteen serious crimes per year during the three years prior to his incarceration. However, this average conceals the fact that most inmates had committed few offenses, and a small number had committed many. More than half of the inmates had committed fewer than three offenses per year while on the street, but the most criminally active of the inmates accounted for more than sixty serious offenses per year (Peterson and Braiker, 1981). Another study that showed the disproportionately large number of crimes accounted for by intensive offenders found that 6 percent of all suspects arrested in Manhattan for robbery, assault, burglary, and rape in 1979 were responsible for nearly one-third of all crimes of that sort reported in that year. These intensive offenders averaged thirteen prior arrests and committed an average of thirty-four crimes per year (*The New York Times,* April 9, 1981). In Chapter 14, we will see that this high rate of crime by intensive offenders has been the basis of programs that focus the criminal justice system's resources on the apprehension, conviction, and imprisonment of career criminals.

Leaving a Life of Crime

In Chapter 5, we saw that the rate of arrest for index offenses declines with age; for instance, in 1986, only 9.2 percent of all suspects arrested for index crimes were over the age of forty. We will see later that there is considerable evidence that programs to rehabilitate offenders have been, for the most part, ineffective. If rehabilitation programs cannot account for the small number of arrests of older people, what does? One possibility is that criminals "exit" or "retire" from criminal careers as they get older for reasons that have little to do with treatment programs.

The idea that criminals "burn out" or "mature out" of crime comes from studies of narcotics addicts. Heroin addicts are often young, and samples of addicts rarely include many older addicts. The absence of older heroin addicts cannot be accounted for solely by overdose deaths. Some addicts apparently stop using opiates, either on their own or as a result of an effective drug treatment program. Addicts who join such programs may already be "burned out" physically and mentally by the burdens of maintaining a habit and may thus be ready to stop using addictive drugs.

Exiting is the successful disengagement from a previous pattern of criminal behavior. If a criminal career is seen as a "zigzag path" or alternation between criminal and noncriminal activities, we then need to ask what conditions or contingencies promote the change from criminal activities to noncriminal pursuits.

A Model of the Exiting Process

Neal Shover (1983, 1985) studied this exiting process through interviews with fifty ordinary property offenders. Most of these men had a high degree of identification with crime as a means of livelihood but had been unsuccessful at this pursuit, either making little money from their crimes or spending much time in prison. Figure 11.1 shows the theoretical model of the exiting process that Shover derived from his research.

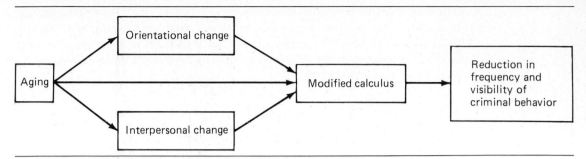

FIGURE 11.1   Shover's Model of the Exiting Process   *Source: Neal Shover,* Aging Crimi-
*nals, p. 118. Copyright © 1985 by Sage Publications, Inc. Reprinted by permission of Sage
Publications, Inc.*

As offenders get older, they experience both orientational change and interpersonal change. Change in orientation involves four elements:

1. *A new perspective on the self.* Offenders become more critical of their past
   behavior and more detached in evaluating how they behaved when younger.
2. *A growing awareness of time.* Offenders see time as a diminishing resource,
   viewing life in terms of the number of years they have left rather than in
   terms of how many years they have been alive. Offenders begin to plan how
   to use the rest of their lives. Sometimes this change is related to a fear of dying
   in prison.
3. *Changing aspirations and goals.* Offenders reduce their expectations of material well-being and assign greater priority to good relationships with others, a
   peaceful life, and a legitimate job.
4. *A growing sense of tiredness.* Offenders come to fear injury or death to a greater
   degree and may become more wary of betrayal by crime partners. They may
   feel they have slowed down relative to other offenders and inmates and must
   be careful of being victimized by them. Offenders may also grow weary of
   fighting the more powerful criminal justice system.

In Shover's model, change in interpersonal relations is also important to the
exiting process, with this change involving two components:

1. *Ties to another person.* Offenders seek mutually satisfying relationships with
   members of the opposite sex or with members of their family.
2. *Ties to a line of activity.* This typically involves finding a satisfying job, which
   provides direct rewards to offenders and also reinforces their noncriminal
   identity. A job occupies their time, leaving little time for criminal activity.

According to Shover, these orientational and interpersonal changes lead to a
"modified calculus," an alteration in the offender's balancing of the rewards

and risks of criminal behavior. Rewards are seen as less satisfying or less predictable, and the risks of crime are given greater importance in the offender's mind. This changed calculus then leads either to a reduction in the frequency and visibility of criminal activity so as to keep risks to a minimum or to exiting from a criminal career altogether.

Reasons for Leaving a Career as a Professional Thief

Evidence from biographical and autobiographical accounts of professional thieves suggests various motives for leaving a life of crime. Thieves may give up crime if they violate the code of the criminal subculture and are ostracized by other thieves; if they become inefficient as a result of fear, narcotics, alcohol, or increasing age; if they can no longer find other thieves to work with them; if they cannot guarantee themselves immunity from conviction and incarceration because they have lost the trust of a fixer or the police; or in rare cases if they make a "big score" (Sutherland, 1937: 24–25). Thieves may also leave a criminal career if a long prison term shocks them into reforming, if they take a legitimate job, or if they marry into the legitimate world (Inciardi, 1975: 73–74; Shover, 1983, 1985). Over time, thieves may see that the financial rewards of a legitimate job actually outweigh the financial rewards of crime, for few thieves ever make much money from crime (Krohm, 1973; Petersilia, Greenwood, and Lavin, 1977: 71; Silberman, 1978: 68).

Whatever their reasons for retiring from crime, professional thieves who do so of their own volition and who still retain their skills at theft may be seen as "retired" professional thieves rather than as new members of the conventional world (Sutherland, 1937). Thieves who leave criminal careers may not regret their past behavior and may reflect with nostalgia on the excitement and the scores of the past. They may retain a "latent criminal identity," an affinity for others who are involved in crime (Irwin, 1970: 202). They may never fully break their bonds with criminals and may never become fully integrated into the conventional world. In a sense, exiting or retiring from crime can be seen as a change in criminal identity from a manifest to a latent form.

Reasons for Leaving a Career as a Drug Dealer or Smuggler

An in-depth study of upper-level drug dealers and smugglers, most of whom trafficked in marijuana and cocaine, found that about 90 percent of those who were observed and interviewed had decided to get out of the business (Adler and Adler, 1983; Adler, 1985). Early in their criminal careers, they had seen their drug dealing as temporary. As they grew aware of the restrictions and sacrifices imposed by a deviant career, and as they tired of life as a fugitive, they decided to abandon this career. What had once been a novel form of activity had become routine, exhausting, dangerous, and isolating.

However, these drug dealers and smugglers were bound to their careers by the rewards of money, drugs, and sex; by their commitment to a deviant career;

and by the difficulty of finding another way to earn a good income. As a consequence, they oscillated between a deviant career and a legitimate way of life, often for years after they had decided to leave the deviant career. They moved out of dealing and smuggling temporarily, and then back into the drug business, a process described as "phaseout and re-entries" (Adler and Adler, 1983: 201). They found it hard to stay out of the drug underworld because they were unable or unwilling to reduce their drug use and change their extravagant life style, and so their "exits" were usually temporary rather than permanent.

Exiting and Theories of Crime Causation

The theories of crime causation we examined in earlier chapters suggest why some offenders may leave a life of crime. A complete theory of criminal behavior should be able to explain why some people break the law and others do not, and also why some people who engage in crime eventually disengage from a criminal career (Frazier, 1976). Here we will look at some of the implications of different criminological theories for the process of exiting

DIFFERENTIAL ASSOCIATION THEORY Differential association theory would explain exiting by a change in a career criminal's ratio of definitions favorable to violation of the law over definitions unfavorable to violation of the law. In other words, just before leaving a criminal career, an offender should interact more with others who provide definitions that are not favorable to continued criminal activity or should interact less with people who are sources of definitions favorable to violation of the law.

There is no research that directly supports or refutes this explanation of exiting. However, this explanation is questionable, because many offenders probably decide to leave a criminal career while in prison, where their exposure to definitions favorable to violation of the law is great and where they are isolated from definitions unfavorable to violation of the law. Some inmates might decide to exit because they are exposed to law-abiding values held by a correctional officer, a social worker, a visiting family member, or even another inmate who decides to go straight.

Another problem with using differential association theory to explain exiting is that Sutherland proposed that associations are more important if they occur early in life (the priority factor). This would suggest that an older career criminal would require very intense and frequent exposure to definitions unfavorable to violation of the law to change the ratio of definitions in a way that would lead to exiting. In a few cases, this might occur through religious conversion.

THE LABELING PERSPECTIVE The labeling perspective offers a better explanation of why career criminals continue to commit crime than of why some of them abandon a life of crime. As criminal careers develop, the label "criminal" or "ex-convict" is more firmly affixed by the criminal justice system and the public. A criminal record, sometimes even an acquittal, signifies to the rest of the world a continuing intention to do social harm (Schwartz and Skolnick, 1962; Stebbins, 1971). There is little reason to change that label as long as an individual is involved in crime, and thus we would not expect a change in the label to precede the abandonment of a criminal career. Even an offender who decides to terminate a life of crime faces continued labeling as an ex-convict and must deal with closed-off job opportunities and social contacts. More positive support from the criminal justice system and from people with whom the ex-convict interacts would make exiting easier.

Exiting sometimes involves deviance-disavowal by an offender or the relabeling of an offender by others (Frazier, 1976). Relabeling may take the form of *certification,* the social verification by the criminal justice system or by conventional people that an offender is rehabilitated. Certification can ease the transition from a criminal career to membership in the conventional social world (Meisenhelder, 1977).

ANOMIE AND DIFFERENTIAL OPPORTUNITY THEORY   Theories that focus on anomie and differential opportunity would suggest that exiting is caused either by increased access to legitimate means to reach socially approved goals or by reduced aspirations. There is some evidence that changes in aspirations are associated with the decision to abandon a criminal career (Shover, 1983, 1985). Research indicates that securing a job that holds promise for career advancement may be important to exiting, but this evidence fits better with control theory than it does with anomie or differential opportunity theory, because it seems that the bond to the conventional order offered by a job is more important than the income produced by the job (Meisenhelder, 1977; Shover, 1983, 1985).

CONTROL THEORY   Control theory would propose that a career criminal "retires" when he or she forms bonds or attachments to conventional people and institutions. Just as adolescents who lack ties to family, school, peers, or a job are the most likely to become delinquents, so older offenders may be more likely to move out of crime when they form such attachments.

Control theory probably offers the most convincing explanation of the process of exiting. Exiting usually seems to require the acquisition of meaningful bonds to the conventional social order, the opposite process to the one that control theory describes as giving rise to delinquency. Thieves leave a life of crime as they form attachments to a life of conformity and develop a reluctance to give up those new bonds by risking further imprisonment. One important tie to the conventional order is a job that seems to have the potential for advancement and that is seen as meaningful and economically rewarding . A good job shifts a criminal's attention from the present to the future, and it provides a solid basis for the construction of a noncriminal identity. It also alters an individual's daily routine in ways that make crime less likely (Meisenhelder, 1977; Shover, 1983, 1985).

The correctional system does not play a major role in the exiting process, but an inmate's attachment to a correctional officer or counselor may hasten exiting. Correctional officers and counselors can also help an offender leave a criminal career by certifying the offender to be rehabilitated.   *Source: Photo by Dennis Brack/Black Star, Courtesy U.S. Department of Health and Human Services*

Good personal relationships with conventional people such as a spouse, a lover, children, or peers create bonds to the social order than an individual wants to protect. These people may then be "psychologically present" if the individual faces situations that offer a temptation to violate the law. Family members and lovers also provide a place of residence, food, and help in the development of everyday skills such as paying bills and scheduling time (Irwin,

Using Criminology: Encouraging Exiting — The TARP Experiment

About the only sure knowledge we have of the recidivism problem is that aging and employment are effective antidotes. Older men and ex-felons who find jobs and retain them are less likely to be returned to prison. There is little that any social policy can do about the aging process, but there is much that can be attempted to help ex-felons enter the employed sector of the economy. (p. 6)

This idea was the basis of the Transitional Aid Research Project (TARP), an experiment begun in 1976 by the U.S. Department of Labor. TARP sought to provide offenders who had completed prison sentences with financial support so they could become reintegrated into the conventional social world. The project aimed to encourage the ex-convicts to leave a life of crime.

Ex-felons are "among the least employable groups in our society" (p. 6). Because many of them have spent much of their adult life in prison, they have had little opportunity to develop marketable job skills and have had little work experience. Their educational attainment is low; the TARP subjects averaged a ninth-grade education, but they had a functional grade equivalent of sixth grade. Some jobs are barred to ex-convicts. At the very least, ex-convicts must explain to potential employers where they have been and what they have been doing in

recent years. As a consequence of these problems, the only jobs open to most ex-felons are unattractive, poorly paid, and unpleasant, and offer little opportunity for advancement. These jobs do not bind the ex-convict to conventional society and thus create little incentive to exit a career in crime.

In addition to having difficulty finding a good job upon release from prison, ex-convicts reenter the civilian world with few resources. They receive only a small sum of money, if anything, upon release, and they are ignored by welfare and social insurance systems. Typically, these new releasees turn to their families for help, but this often strains their families' limited resources. New releasees are under pressure to take the first job available, often one that does little to attach them to the social order, even if it provides an income sufficient to pay for food and shelter. Lack of attachment to the conventional order and a low income from a legitimate job can then contribute to the ex-convict's motivation to turn once again to property crime as a source of funds.

In the TARP experiment, about 2,000 ex-felons in Georgia and the same number in Texas were randomly assigned either to control groups that received no transitional aid payments or to one of several experimental groups. The experimental subjects

1970). Other bonds that may lead people away from crime include involvement in organized religion and in extravocational and extradomestic activities, such as sports and hobbies (Irwin, 1970: 203). However, attachments of this sort are usually less important in the exiting process than are ties to jobs and to other people (Meisenhelder, 1977; Shover, 1983, 1985).

received payments that were much like unemployment compensation. For some subjects, payments were reduced by a dollar for each dollar they earned at a legitimate job, but for others the benefits were reduced by only twenty-five cents for each dollar earned.

The hope of the TARP experiment was that experimental subjects would be more likely than control subjects to exit a life of crime. However, the results were mixed. Overall, experimental subjects and control subjects were similar in number of arrests for property crimes during the year after their release from prison. However, those who received payments found jobs that paid more and that seemed to have better working conditions. Moreover, a comparison of experimental subjects and control subjects who had similar levels of employment during the year found that those who received TARP payments were arrested less often. This suggests that the TARP payments did reduce property crime, but that the reduction was offset by a counterbalancing effect.

This counterbalancing effect was due to the work-disincentive provided by the TARP payments. In other words, ex-felons who received payments were less likely to work because the payments provided a source of income. To be eligible for the TARP payments, the experimental subjects had to be unemployed, and unfortunately those who could keep three-fourths of their benefits if they also earned income at a legitimate job were not fully informed about this aspect of the experiment. As a result, those receiving payments were often unemployed, and their unemployment increased their arrest rate above what it would have been had they been working, thus wiping out the arrest-reducing effect of the TARP payments. To sum up, "The TARP payments did reduce recidivism but . . . such effects were masked by an increase in unemployment that in turn increased arrests" (p. 16).

Overall, the TARP experiment showed that payments are useful in reducing recidivism, that payments are a cost-effective way to reduce crime, and that programs that stress employment as a way of getting ex-convicts to abandon criminal careers can be beneficial. However, for programs such as TARP to be fully effective, the work-disincentive effect of the payments needs to be eliminated or reduced. One way to do that is to offer financial incentives to ex-convicts to find jobs, such as letting them keep most of their benefits as well as their legitimate earnings, and to inform them fully that they can do this. Future research can test this and other modifications of the TARP program to create programs that offer ex-convicts an incentive to leave careers in crime for legitimate work.

SOURCE: Based on Peter H. Rossi, Richard A. Berk, and Kenneth J. Lenihan, *Money, Work, and Crime: Experimental Evidence.* New York: Academic Press, 1980.

Exiting and the Correctional System

Correctional treatment programs are designed to rehabilitate offenders. In other words, administrators see prisons as places where inmates should learn to "go straight." However, some researchers suggest that the conditions necessary for exiting are largely outside the control of the correctional system (Meisen-helder, 1977; Petersilia, 1980).

Some critics of the correctional system even claim that it impedes the process of exiting. In prison, inmates often learn a way of life directly opposed to what they need to leave a criminal career. They depend on the prison administration for their material needs, but after release they must rely on themselves to meet those needs. In prison their time is structured for them, and much of the time they are idle; after release, they must learn how to structure their time to keep themselves from drifting back into crime. Prison life is easier for inmates who do not spend much time thinking about their future, but outside prison they must construct goals for themselves. In sum, changes produced by prison often hinder offenders who might otherwise leave a life of crime (Cordilia, 1983).

In order to leave a life of crime, the released inmate must "keep out of the old bag," a way of life that involves the commission of felonies and a high likelihood of arrest and conviction (Irwin, 1970). The "old bag" offers excitement and glamour, but also physical danger and the risk of a return to prison. Some observers believe the only way to leave a criminal career is to stay away from all criminal behavior; this opinion is similar to the claim of Alcoholics Anonymous that alcoholics cannot drink at all without risking a relapse.

An ex-convict's first few weeks on the street after release are especially criti-cal. During that time, the individual must become reaccustomed to the outside world, which has a faster pace and less routinization than life in prison. Often a released offender feels like a foreign traveler during the first few weeks on the street (Irwin, 1970).

As the ex-convict develops bonds and as time passes, the motivation to stay away from crime increases. The longer the individual stays away from crime, the less the chance that he or she will return to crime. Conversely, the greater a person's past involvement in crime and the longer a person's criminal career, the less the chance of abandoning a life of crime (Kitchener, Schmidt, and Glaser, 1977; Glaser, 1979).

The successful termination of a criminal career seems to require detachment from other offenders and from a criminal subculture, and attachment to a conventional way of life that usually involves a family, law-abiding friends, and a job that holds promise for the future. The process by which offenders detach themselves from one way of life and become attached to another is not yet fully understood, but more research on this process may reveal as much about the causes of crime as do studies that focus on the way that people become involved in crime in the first place.

Summary

Individual acts of law breaking may cumulate over time into a criminal career, which is similar in some ways to a legitimate career but which also differs in important ways.

Certain contingencies influence the development of a criminal career. An individual's sex can close off access to illegitimate occupations. Another important contingency is contact with the criminal justice system, which can influence the course of a criminal career through the labeling process. Offenders often alternate in a "zigzag path" between criminal activities and legitimate pursuits. They often are recruited into criminal careers through a delinquent subculture or from occupations close to the underworld.

Typologies can be useful in developing theories to explain different patterns of criminal behavior and in establishing effective treatment methods. One potentially fruitful approach is to develop typologies that categorize offenders by specific combinations of crimes they commit over time.

Studies of delinquent careers find that a small number of offenders account for a very large proportion of all contacts with the police in any cohort. The chance of being stopped again by the police increases as the number of police contacts increases. People who have contact with the police while very young are especially likely to have further contacts and to go on to commit crimes as adults. Delinquents show little inclination to specialize in one type of crime; this is true of adult career criminals as well. The time between police contacts becomes compressed as a delinquent career lengthens, indicating either increased delinquent activity or more attention to known offenders by the police. People who have police contacts as juveniles have a much greater chance of being stopped by the police as adults than do people who have no police contacts as juveniles. This may be because of the labeling effects on young offenders, or it may be because of a continuity of law-violating behavior over time.

Most adult offenders do not plan their crimes in much detail. As they grow older, they increasingly spend the money from their crimes for instrumental rather than expressive purposes. Intensive career criminals commit many more crimes than intermittent offenders do. These intensive offenders also engage in more planning and are more skilled and persistent in their criminal activity. As a result, they account for a disproportionately high percentage of all serious crimes.

Career criminals exit or retire from a life of crime for many reasons, but the exiting process usually involves a growing detachment from other offenders and a criminal subculture, and a growing attachment to a conventional way of life that includes a family and a job. Different theories of crime causation would explain exiting in different ways, but control theory seems to make the most sense of the data we now have on the exiting process. The correctional system seems to play a relatively minor role in the process of exiting.

Important Terms

certification   intensive offender
contingency   intermittent offender
criminal career   radical nonintervention
exiting

Suggested Readings

ALFRED BLUMSTEIN ET AL., EDS. *Criminal Careers and "Career Criminals"*, Vols. 1 and 2. Washington, D.C.: National Academy Press, 1986. A comprehensive, technical summary of previous research on criminal careers (Vol. 1), and a series of original papers on issues relating to the study of criminal careers (Vol. 2).

JAN M. CHAIKEN AND MARCIA R. CHAIKEN, WITH JOYCE E. PETERSON. *Varieties of Criminal Behavior: Summary and Policy Implications.* Santa Monica, Calif.: Rand, 1982. A summary of a research project that produced a typology based on the combinations of crimes that offenders commit over time.

CARL B. KLOCKARS. *The Professional Fence.* New York: Free Press, 1974. A fascinating autobiographical account of the development of one kind of criminal career.

JOAN PETERSILIA, PETER W. GREENWOOD, AND MARVIN LAVIN. *Criminal Careers of Habitual Felons.* Santa Monica, Calif.: Rand, 1977. A detailed examination of the criminal careers of forty-nine armed robbers.

RICHARD P. RETTIG, MANUAL J. TORRES, AND GERALD R. GARRETT. *Manny: A Criminal-Addict's Story.* Boston: Houghton Mifflin, 1977. An interesting account of one offender's life, illustrating the various contingencies that lead to different kinds of criminal behavior.

NEAL SHOVER. *Aging Criminals.* Beverly Hills, Calif.: Sage Publications, 1985. An innovative study of the exiting process, based on interviews with fifty men previously incarcerated for ordinary property crimes.

PART IV

Reactions to Crime

Chapter 12 deals with community reactions to crime. We look at the informal social control of criminal behavior, including the way that architectural design may foster control and thereby curb crime. Bystander responses to crime, and collective reactions such as urban patrol groups, are explored.

Chapter 13 provides an overview of the criminal justice system. We look at the history and organization of the police and the way officers do their job. We examine aspects of the courts, including bail, preventive detention, and plea bargaining. We look at prosecutors, defense attorneys, judges, and juries. Disparities in sentences by race and by sex are investigated. Prison conditions and parole are also examined. Finally, we explore the changing role of the victim in the criminal justice system.

Deterrence and incapacitation are the topics of Chapter 14. We consider the idea that the threat of punishment can keep people from violating the law and look at research that has tested this idea. We explore aspects of the criminal act and the sanctioning process that influence the deterrent effect of penalties. We also examine the way the deterrence perspective affects the operation of the criminal justice system. Finally, we look at incapacitation, the idea that crime can be prevented simply by locking up offenders.

In Chapter 15 we look at retribution or "just deserts," the idea that punishment should inflict suffering on offenders commensurate with the harm they have inflicted on others. We examine the way this idea has influenced the operation of the police, the courts, the prisons, and the use of capital punishment.

Rehabilitation is explored in Chapter 16. We look at the effect on the criminal justice system of the idea that offenders should be treated in ways that will reform them and keep them away from crime in the future. We also examine evaluations of treatment programs to see whether they are effective in changing offenders.

Chapter 17 looks at the conservative, liberal, and radical approaches to the crime problem. It investigates crime and politics in the United States since the 1960s and then explores three major strategies of reducing crime: reforming the criminal justice system, situational crime prevention, and dealing with the causes of crime.

CHAPTER 12

Community Reactions to Crime

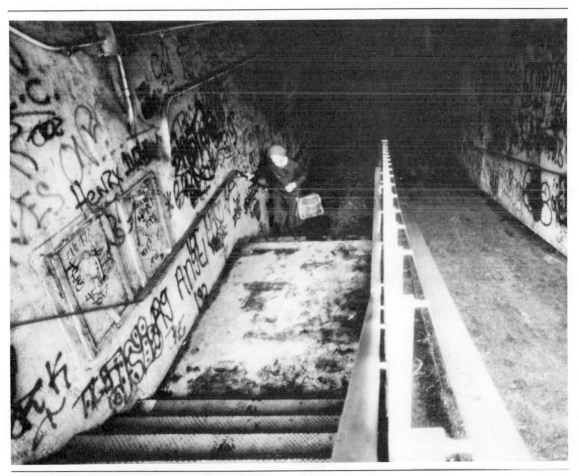

Source: Geoffrey Clifford / Wheeler Pictures

Toward the end of the last century, the French sociologist Emile Durkheim (1895, 1933: 73) defined crime as behavior that shocks the sentiments found in all "healthy" consciences. According to Durkheim, these sentiments are intensely held and specific to particular situations, and commonly form the basis of criminal codes. Crime is thus behavior that offends a shared sense of what is valued and worth pursuing, and punishment is a reaction to that behavior.

Societal reactions to crime often lead to *social control,* a process that brings about conformity to society's norms and laws. One kind of reaction to crime is *formal social control,* the effort to bring about conformity to the law by agents of the criminal justice system such as the police, the courts, and correctional institutions. We examine these agents of formal social control later in Chapter 13.

Informal social control, or the reactions of individuals and groups that bring about conformity to norms and laws, includes peer and community pressure, bystander intervention in a crime, and collective responses such as citizen patrol groups. There is some reason to believe that the amount of formal social control varies inversely with the amount of informal social control; that is, the agents of the criminal justice system will exercise more control when informal social control is weaker (Black, 1976: 107–111).

One sociologist has even treated some criminal behavior as a kind of informal social control, arguing that violent and property crimes are sometimes the results of efforts to engage in self-help, correct injustice, and pursue justice against perceived wrongdoers (Black, 1983). Murders in which people kill because they feel insulted by their victims, vandalism in which youths destroy school property because of hostility toward teachers who have hurt their self-esteem, and theft from stores that overcharge customers can be seen as efforts to correct serious wrongs perpetrated by others—that is, as efforts to exercise informal social control over unjust actions. Sometimes informal efforts to control crime actually violate the law; for instance, vigilante groups that lynch suspected offenders violate due process rights and may break federal laws by denying others their civil rights.

Informal Control of Crime

Because only 1 or 2 percent of all serious crimes are reported to the police and lead to arrest, conviction, and imprisonment, the formal sanctions of the criminal justice system may be less important in controlling criminal behavior than are informal sanctions such as group censure and bystander intervention. Loss of esteem in the eyes of relatives and peers may be a more significant cost for an offender than a court's judgment that a crime has been committed. For instance, white-collar offenders seem to be affected more by accusation and indictment than by a criminal conviction. Concern for the good opinion of friends, relatives, and neighbors is also a strong force controlling deviant behavior in Japan, where an internal "social policeman" seems to induce conformity out of fear of losing face (Clifford, 1976).

Community and Informal Social Control

By creating fear, mistrust, and suspicion, crime can reduce interaction among the residents of a community (Conklin, 1975). As social solidarity in a community weakens, informal control over behavior dissipates. This can increase crime rates because interpersonal pressures on potential offenders to abide by the law are attenuated. One indicator of the effectiveness of a community's standards in controlling deviance is the proportion of all crimes in the community that are committed by local residents. In a study of crime in Honolulu, Andrew Lind (1930: 218) concluded: "An area capable of maintaining the strength of its prohibitions is likely also to discourage its wayward residents from attempting the violation of taboos within the boundaries of the district, although it may not succeed in entirely repressing the behavior." Similarly, another study found that riot activity during the 1960s was more common where there was no "extensive informal social interaction," and thus little informal control over potential rioters (Warren, 1969).

MECHANICAL AND ORGANIC SOLIDARITY   Simple preindustrial societies, such as tribal groups, are characterized by more intimate relationships and more social integration than are modern industrial societies. In simple societies, primary groups such as the family and the peer group are relatively stronger than they are in complex societies. These simple societies are held together by what Durkheim (1895, 1933) called *mechanical solidarity,* a unity based on shared values and norms and on the similarity of functions performed by all members of the society. Children in these simple societies learn shared values and norms through face-to-face interaction, and this socialization process perpetuates the collective conscience over the generations.

In larger and more complex societies, primary groups diminish in relative strength, and secondary groups such as corporations, labor unions, and schools become more important. Interpersonal relationships become less intimate, and people carry out very different tasks in their daily lives. Complex societies are integrated by *organic solidarity,* a unity based on an interdependence of functions, much as in a complex biological organism. In modern industrial societies, the collective conscience is less strong than it is in simple societies, and so legal institutions develop to control behavior. Sanctions are designed to restore disrupted social situations. The overall severity of formal sanctions seems to decrease in complex societies, as normative diversity increases and some acts that are violations of the collective conscience in simpler societies are redefined as private matters (Durkheim, 1895, 1933; Green and Allen, 1981–82). However, legal sanctions are still invoked against people who violate intensely held values and norms.

SMALL TOWNS AND LARGE CITIES   Related to the idea that informal social control is stronger in simpler societies is the notion that informal control is greater in small towns than in larger cities. If informal social control is indeed stronger in small towns than in large cities, this would help explain a fact that we examined earlier in the book: Crime rates, in general, are lower in smaller communities.

Evidence on the real nature of informal social control in small towns is mixed. A study of the Massachusetts Bay Colony in the seventeenth century found that the small size and cultural homogeneity of the community helped control deviant behavior by pressuring potential deviants to conform (Erikson, 1966: 169–170). Informal controls operate most effectively where people know each other well and interact on a regular basis, and small and homogeneous communities may be best suited to this kind of interaction.

In general, there is probably less informal social control in large cities than in small towns. The large size of the city means that residents may have a difficult time distinguishing strangers from residents, and the heterogeneity of the city means that many neighborhoods will include a variety of values and norms. Urban residents encounter many people on a day-to-day basis and have to screen out some of the input they receive in order to prevent "informational overload" (Milgram, 1970: 1462). A multitude of demands on city dwellers may generate "norms of noninvolvement" that lead to mistrust of strangers, a desire for privacy, and withdrawal from social interaction (Milgram, 1970: 1463). Urban residents are more likely than the residents of small towns to deal with others in terms of the roles they play rather than on a personal basis. Thus, urban residents will probably be concerned only with paying for their groceries at a supermarket checkout counter, but small-town residents may ask the local grocer how his sick wife is feeling or how his children are doing in school.

A study of reactions to crime in cities, suburbs, small towns, and rural areas in Missouri found that large-city residents were the most likely to think that crime would occur in their community. These people were also the most likely to say that their neighbors would not call the police about a burglary they observed. A majority of the residents of all communities believed their own community was safe, but city dwellers were the least likely to feel that way. When asked what made their own community safe, more residents of rural areas and small towns than residents of suburban and urban areas mentioned informal controls, such as a social network in the community that would lead bystanders to intervene in a crime. In comparison to the residents of small towns and rural areas, people in the suburbs and cities were more likely to say that crime in their community was kept in check by formal agents of control such as the police. Urban residents were thus the most likely to expect crime, and they relied more on formal than on informal means to control crime in their community (Boggs, 1971).

One study examined formal and informal social control in two Israeli communities (Schwartz, 1954, 1976). One community was a collective in which there was no formal mechanism to resolve legal disputes. The other community was a semiprivate settlement that had a judicial committee to handle legal disputes. According to the researcher, the collective did not require a legal committee because behavior was informally controlled through intense and frequent face-to-face interaction. On the other hand, the semiprivate settlement had considerably less interaction and less consensus; much everyday behavior was not visible to the members of the community. Consequently, informal control was less effective, and formal control was needed. This evidence suggests that the structure of interpersonal relations may be more important than size alone in determining the degree of informal control in a community. Intense and regular interaction, normative consensus, and surveillance of behavior all seem to be conducive to the informal control of behavior.

DIFFERENCES AMONG URBAN COMMUNITIES   In developing nations, the process of migration from tribal villages to large cities sometimes reduces informal control over deviant behavior. For instance, in Liberia

> the effectiveness of tribe and family as agents of social control has always depended upon the cohesiveness of the particular unit. In the urban areas, this cohesiveness increasingly gives way to individualism and the vacuum created by the decline in family and tribal authority has only been filled by the impersonal sanctions of the law. (Zarr, 1969: 194)

A comparison of two communities in the city of Kampala, Uganda, found that the area with less crime had greater social solidarity, more interaction among neighbors, more participation in local organizations, less geographic mobility, and more stable family relationships (Clinard and Abbott, 1973: 149). There was also greater cultural homogeneity and more emphasis on tribal and kinship ties in the community with the lower crime rate; these conditions seemed to alleviate the anonymity that recent migrants to the city might otherwise have felt. Crime in the community with the lower rate was prevented in part by strong primary group ties among residents, which made strangers to the area conspicuous.

A study of two neighborhoods in Cambridge, Massachusetts, supports these conclusions. Although residents of the two communities were similar in several ways, the community with the higher delinquency rate was less socially integrated. Residents of the community that had the higher delinquency rate were more heterogeneous in religion and ethnicity, knew fewer neighbors by name, thought they had less in common with their neighbors, and liked the community less. They were no more tolerant of deviance than were adults in the community that had less delinquency, but the residents of the high-rate area were less likely to do something about delinquency if they observed it. More adults in the area with the high delinquency rate said that people ought to mind their own business and not interfere when the children of their neighbors committed delinquent acts. This unwillingness to do something about observed violations of the law creates "an atmosphere in which delinquency can grow more easily. . . . [T]he lack of social integration appears to have certain direct effects in a lowered level of social control of delinquent and pre-delinquent activities" (Maccoby, Johnson, and Church, 1958: 49, 51). Here we see that the informal control of crime and delinquency is greater in some urban neighborhoods than in others. The

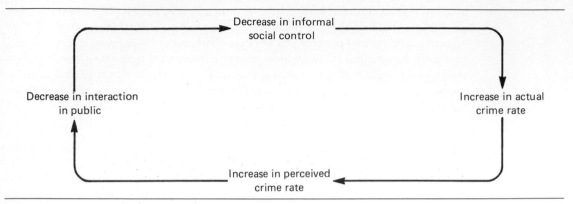

FIGURE 12.1:   The Crime Cycle

degree of informal control seems to be related to the social structure and the nature of social relationships in a community, rather than to the absolute size of the community.

Feeling unsafe in an urban neighborhood usually means not having a sense of security when in public places such as streets, sidewalks, and parks (Jacobs, 1961). Fear of venturing out-of-doors at night means that the streets may become deserted. Informal controls that would check crime if people were there are absent. The presence of people on the street creates surveillance of public places and attracts the attention of others to the streets, thereby reducing opportunities for crime. A study of slum neighborhoods in Chicago found "impersonal domains" that were deserted and seen as dangerous at night, even though informal control over deviance was maintained in those areas during the day by businesspersons and their customers (Suttles, 1968: 36–37).

In Figure 12.1, we diagram a "crime cycle" in which responses to crime can change behavior in ways that actually increase the crime rate. Less interaction in public places may decrease informal social control, leading to an increase in both the actual and the perceived crime rate, which can then decrease interaction in public and begin the cycle anew.

Architecture and Informal Social Control

Informal control of criminal behavior can be enhanced through architectural design. Oscar Newman (1972, 1973) is an architect who claims that citizen involvement in crime prevention is needed and that it is possible to construct residential complexes that deter crime by creating *defensible space*. Defensible space involves the subdivision and design of housing to allow residents to distinguish stranger from neighbor. The design of housing can reinforce or create opportunities for surveillance of a building and its surrounding grounds by eliciting from residents a feeling of territoriality and a sense of proprietary interest in the protection of the community.

A survey of residents of New York City housing projects found that more than half felt unsafe. Newman (1973: 92) claimed that this sense of insecurity had important consequences: "Fear, in itself, can increase the risk of victimization through isolating neighbor from neighbor, witness from victim, making remote the possibility of mutual help and assuring the criminal a ready opportunity to operate unhampered and unimpeded." Project residents were less threatened by crime if they knew more of their neighbors, and they were more likely to know their neighbors in housing projects where architectural design facilitated interaction.

Housing design can enhance interaction and foster interest in nearby areas, thereby creating informal control over behavior. Crime may be reduced by making the interior spaces of large buildings visible to people outside the building. Design can define private and semiprivate space near and within buildings. For instance, the area enclosed by an L-shaped building often becomes the focus of surveillance and informal control by residents of the apartments that face the enclosed area, especially if the building is only a few stories high. Apartment clusters also create zones of influence by residents if shared areas are defined as private and are carefully watched. When children play in hallways or on playgrounds near a building, parents often watch those areas to protect their children from strangers. Filling the space around housing projects with play equipment, benches, or athletic facilities can attract people and attention, and keep children near home where they will be under surveillance by parents and neighbors.

Newman (1973: 59) states that residents of housing projects will feel safer if they can "see and be seen, hear and be heard, by day and night." Surveillance deters crime, and it also reduces anxiety by creating an image of a safe environment. People who feel less anxious will spend more time in public places, thereby increasing surveillance and the informal control of behavior. Surveillance must be backed up with a willingness to intervene in a crime, either personally or by alerting the police, or mere observation will have little effect. If potential offenders believe that they will be seen committing a crime but will not be interfered with or reported to the police by the witness, they will not be affected much by surveillance. Only a real risk of apprehension can deter offenders (Merry, 1981; Murray, 1983).

EVIDENCE ON DEFENSIBLE SPACE AND CRIME   There is some evidence on the impact of architectural design on crime rates. For instance, research supports a revised version of the defensible space model, showing that building height and accessibility had the anticipated effects on the attitudes and behavior of housing project residents, and that these effects in turn had the predicted impact on levels of crime (Newman and Franck, 1980, 1982).

Because much of the research on defensible space has been done in public housing projects, we do not know if this concept can be applied to other kinds of living environments (Taylor, Gottfredson, and Brower, 1980). One researcher concludes that the defensible space concept can be used to prevent vandalism and burglary in the indoor public areas of apartment buildings, but that it may not apply to other crimes and to other areas. Even for indoor areas and for vandalism and burglary, the impact of defensible space design on crime seems to be small, although consistent (Booth, 1981). A review of research on defensible space and crime carried out in Great Britain finds that the concept may have some "limited relevance to levels of delinquency (particularly vandalism) in English housing areas" (Baldwin, 1979: 55).

Overall, the idea that defensible space design can dramatically reduce crime lacks strong empirical support. Some of Newman's ideas on defensible space are difficult to test, either because they are unclear or because they are difficult to define in operational terms (Baldwin, 1979). Researchers testing the idea of defensible space often fail to account for the possible displacement of crime from well-designed housing projects to nearby targets. Thus, crime may be shifted to other locations rather than prevented when the defensible space concept is implemented.

CRITIQUE OF THE DEFENSIBLE SPACE MODEL   A major flaw in Newman's defensible space model is that it pays attention to physical design features but slights or ignores social variables. For instance, the model ignores the demographic characteristics of the people who live in a housing area. Thus, a project that includes many teenagers and many elderly people probably will have a higher crime rate than a project limited to the elderly, whatever the defensible space design of each project. The model also pays little or no attention to other social aspects of the area, such as neighborhood stability, residential mobility, employment rate, and racial integration. According to some critics, then, defensible space is a concept that lacks social reality (Taylor, Gottfredson, and Brower, 1980; Booth, 1981).

Another problem with the model is that the built environment can affect the crime rate either by encouraging residents to take action against potential offenders who violate the defensible space or by reducing opportunities for crime through controlled access or "target hardening " (for example, locks and bars on doors and windows). To test the idea of defensible space, it is necessary to separate these two processes. The defensible space model claims that crime is controlled by environmental influences on residents' behavior, but so far there is more evidence that the built environment reduces crime by limiting opportunities to break the law (Heinzelman, 1981).

Sometimes the design of the built environment impedes informal social control, as in areas with high-density housing. However, those areas may attract more police officers, which might enhance formal control of crime there (Gillis and Hagan, 1982). In other words, the characteristics of the physical environment may be associated with both formal and informal social control, rather than just with informal control as the defensible space model implies.

One critique concludes that we need a revised defensible space model that takes into account recent advances in the study of human territoriality. This revised model would pay more attention to barriers that deter access by unwanted outsiders, territorial markers that show that an area is cared for, and signs of incivility that indicate the disintegration of civil order in an area. This revised model would look at the way sociocultural characteristics affect territorial behavior; for instance, culturally homogeneous neighborhoods probably exert more territorial control than do heterogeneous neighborhoods. A revised model would look not only at physical design, but also at the traits of people who might exercise territorial control and the ways that social networks are formed and affect territorial control. In addition, a revised model should incorporate evidence on the way features of the physical environment affect the perceptions and behavior of offenders (Taylor, Gottfredson, and Brower, 1980, 1984; Taylor and Gottfredson, 1986).

Individual Response to Crime

Informal control of crime depends not only on the surveillance of public places by the residents of a community, but also on the willingness of those people to take action if they see a crime in progress. The combination of cooperative surveillance and willingness to intervene has been called *protective neighboring* (Schneider and Schneider, 1978). Protective neighboring seems to be more common among people with higher incomes, among long-term residents of a community, and among homeowners. Just as crime and delinquency are less common among people who have a stake in conformity, so it seems that efforts to control crime and delinquency are also more common among people who have a stake in conformity.

The most common action people take in response to a crime is to call the police to report it. Sometimes victims respond directly by taking action against offenders. A controversial case involving the right of victims to use deadly force against offenders occurred in New York City, where Bernhard Goetz, a white man, shot four black youths on a subway, because he feared he was about to be robbed when one of the youths asked him for five dollars. This incident occurred in December 1984; in June 1987, Goetz was cleared of all attempted murder and assault charges, but he was convicted of the felony of illegal possession of a firearm. Supporters of this verdict applauded the jury's apparent willingness to allow potential crime victims to defend themselves against their attackers. Critics of the verdict said that it opened the way for vigilante justice and posed a threat to young black men from whites who are afraid of crime.

Occasionally, bystanders respond to a crime in progress by intervening. This response is probably least likely where fear of crime leads people to withdraw from social contacts, stay home at night, and avoid strangers. These reactions minimize the likelihood that anyone will be around to observe a crime, and they cause those people who are on the street to adopt a self-protective stance and avoid intervening personally in a crime.

Using Criminology: Preventing Theft from Stores

In recent years, some stores have adopted new strategies to combat robbery and to reduce "inventory shrinkage" through shoplifting and employee theft. Rather than rely exclusively on expensive security guards and closed-circuit television, these stores are now applying the insight that crime may be effectively curtailed through the process of informal social control.

To prevent robbery and shoplifting, the 7-Eleven chain of convenience stores developed a security system that relied in part on informal controls. Cashiers were told to look their customers in the eye when waiting on them, thus giving potential thieves the idea that they might be identified to the police by the cashier. Lighting was improved outside the stores, and display racks were lowered so that thieves would not get the idea that they were hidden from passersby on the street and from other customers. These and other changes — such as a special cash register that made it impossible to steal large sums of money — were responsible for a 26 percent reduction in robbery in 7-Eleven stores between 1976 and 1982, as well as for a decline in the average amount of money stolen in each crime.

Other stores have paid bounties to their employees for turning in shoplifters or dishonest fellow workers. In 1986, Marshall Field paid $114,000 to more than 700 of its workers. They were given $100 for reporting a shoplifter to a store detective and $500 for reporting a theft by a fellow employee. One result of this policy of greater reliance on informal surveillance by store clerks was a 25 percent reduction in the store's full-time security force between 1984 and 1987.

Stores have also tried to enlist their workers in the fight against theft by increasing their stake in conformity. One chain of stores has developed an "S.T.O.P." program, an acronym for "Shortages Threaten Our Paychecks." A handbook distributed to employees emphasizes the relationship between losses from shoplifting and the company's ability to provide increased wages and benefits.

SOURCES: Based on "The 7-Elevens' Battle to Curb Crime," *The New York Times,* May 7, 1982, p. D4; Gary Taylor, "When Everyone Is a Store Detective," *The New York Times,* September 13, 1987, p. F19.

Bystander Responses to Crime

The issue of bystander response to emergencies such as crime has been called the *Good Samaritan problem* (Ratcliffe, 1966). The crime that most dramatically brought this problem to public attention was the 1964 murder of Kitty Genovese in Queens, New York. This crime occurred in a middle-class neighborhood that had a relatively low crime rate. A man attacked Kitty Genovese at about three o'clock in the morning when she was returning from work. She screamed, and lights went on in nearby apartments. People looked out and one witness

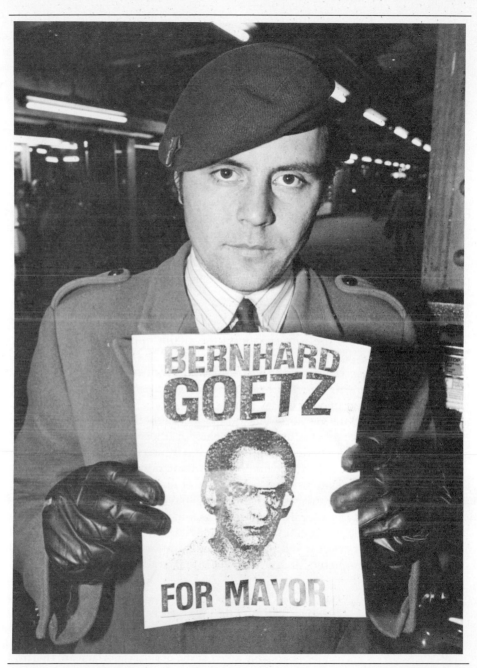

Here Curtis Sliwa, founder of the Guardian Angels patrol group, holds a poster supporting Bernhard Goetz's shooting of four youths he thought were about to rob him.   *Source: Allen Tannenbaum / Sygma*

shouted at the assailant to leave the woman alone. The assailant left but soon returned. Again lights went on and again the assailant left. When he returned a third time, he killed Miss Genovese. The three attacks took place over a period of about thirty-five minutes, and at least thirty-eight witnesses knew of the violence. When the witnesses were later asked about their failure to take action, some said they had been too tired to do anything and others said they had not wanted to get involved.

At first, social scientists were unable to provide a convincing explanation of the bystanders' failure to help the victim. Letters to the newspapers suggested printing the names of the nonresponsive witnesses. Others blamed the police, saying that New Yorkers were afraid of the police and were therefore unwilling to call them in an emergency. What was puzzling was that no help was forthcoming from a group as large as thirty-eight; had only one or two people observed the crime, it might have been possible to point the finger at a few heartless individuals. Many commentators concluded that something must be wrong with society as a whole; several gave apathy as the cause of the problem, concluding that people just no longer cared about their fellow citizens.

THE LAW AND THE GOOD SAMARITAN PROBLEM Anglo-American law does not generally require witnesses to emergencies such as crimes to help victims, unless the witness caused the victim's plight. Only a few states have laws that require intervention in emergencies. In contrast, most European countries have laws that punish "Bad Samaritans" with criminal sanctions. For instance, a few dozen citizens of France are punished each year for failure to help the victims of emergencies (Geis, 1981).

There is some question as to whether laws that require bystander assistance have much effect on the behavior of people who witness emergencies. There is limited evidence suggesting that if such laws exist, people will know about them and will be more likely to condemn nonresponsive bystanders. However, there is no evidence that knowledge of such laws increases the chance that people will actually intervene in an emergency (Zeisel, 1966). One reason is that bystanders may fear legal action by the victim or by the victim's surviving dependents if the rescue attempt fails. Bystanders may also fear being attacked by the offender if the crime is in progress, or being the target of reprisals later if the crime has been completed. As one observer points out,

> the original Good Samaritan extolled by St. Luke was fortunate in not arriving on the scene until after the thieves had set upon the traveler, robbed him, and beaten him half to death. The Samaritan cared for him and showed him great kindness, but he did not put himself in any peril by doing so. Perhaps this is about as much as can be reasonably asked of the ordinary mortal man. (Barth, 1966: 163)

REACTIONS TO EMERGENCIES How then do people respond when faced with a crime or other emergency that requires action? Lawrence Zelic Freedman (1966) suggests that the initial response is fear of being hurt and fear of reprisals. Often witnesses cannot fit the unusual event into any familiar category of past experience. Thus, the failure of the witnesses to the Genovese murder may be attributed in part to the crime's seeming "totally incongruous in a respectable neighborhood"; this "created a sense of unreality which inhibited rational action" (Milgram and Hollander, 1970: 208).

Before witnesses take action, they must clearly define the situation as an emergency that requires personal intervention. Emergency situations are often ambiguous to witnesses; for example, several witnesses to the Genovese murder interpreted it as a "lovers' quarrel." Witnesses often fail to respond appropriately; they deny to themselves that anything so unusual could be happening in their presence. What appears to be apathy may in fact be massive inhibition or paralysis of consciousness resulting from internal conflict. Freedman (1966: 175) claims that in response to emergencies,

> apathy and indifference are the least likely primary psychic vectors. . . . The sequence as I see it is, first, the intense emotional shock—characterized predominantly, but not exclusively, by anxiety; second, the cognitive perception and awareness of what has happened; third, an inertial paralysis of reaction, which as a non-act becomes in fact an act; and fourth, the self-awareness of one's own shock anxiety, non-involvement which is followed by a sense of guilt and intra psychic and social self justification.
>
> I do not assume that these things happen in such neat sequence. For all practical purposes they seem to occur simultaneously.

Witnesses may justify their inaction by claiming that the victim and the offender must know each other, which may be the case. Research indicates that bystanders are much more likely to intervene in assaults between strangers than to offer help when it seems that the assault involves a married couple (Dowd, 1984). Witnesses are probably more likely to intervene if they believe the victim is totally innocent and if they can identify in some way with the victim. Similarly, witnesses find it easier to tolerate the victimization of people who occupy disvalued social statuses, such as prostitutes or skid-row alcoholics. If a witness's identification with a victim is slight, the chance that the witness will assist the victim is probably low (Sorokin, 1930; Shils, 1967; Blumenthal et al., 1972).

Experimental Studies of Bystander Response. Social-psychological experiments have cast light on the reasons that witnesses to emergencies help under some conditions but not others. Bibb Latané and John Darley (1970), who conducted several of these studies, claim that neither public apathy nor the absence of norms that require emergency assistance can explain bystander nonresponse. In a series of experiments, they clarify the characteristics of situations that are conducive to bystander intervention. Personality traits that might plausibly influence helping behavior did not bear any relationship to such action. Situational determinants of bystander assistance are so strong that differences among the personalities of witnesses pale in significance as determinants of their behavior.

Before bystanders will intervene, they must make a series of decisions. A negative decision at any point means they will not help the victim. They must notice the situation and define it as an emergency. Then they must determine that they have a personal responsibility to do something; if they think the situation is none of their business, they will not help. Bystanders must also decide what kind of aid to offer — personal intervention, or calling the police or an ambulance. Finally, bystanders must decide how to implement the course of action on which they have decided (Latané and Darley, 1970). The social context within which this decision-making process occurs will influence the outcome.

One reason for the public's condemnation of the nonresponsive bystanders in the Genovese murder was the failure of a large number of witnesses to help. The commonsense assumption is that if there are more people around, the chance that at least one will help should be greater. However, social-psychological research demonstrates that the presence of others at the scene of a crime or an emergency actually inhibits helping behavior. People might be embarrassed to help for fear their assistance will turn out to be unwanted or unneeded. When no witness in a group of bystanders immediately offers help, others may assume their interpretation of the situation as one requiring aid is wrong; if help were needed, would not someone already have offered it? People in groups takes cues from others, and if no one helps they may reinterpret the event. This has been referred to as *pluralistic ignorance:* Witnesses in a group fail to help because they interpret the failure of other witnesses to help as a sign that no help is needed (Latané and Darley, 1970).

Witnesses who are alone when they observe a crime or an accident are more likely to help than are witnesses who are in groups of two or more. Lone witnesses are more likely to seek information about the situation, to help the victim by their own efforts, and to report the situation to someone else who can provide assistance. A witness who is with another person is more likely to help the victim if that witness is personally acquainted with the other witness than if the other witness is a stranger; this is probably because personal knowledge breaks down pluralistic ignorance by making communication between witnesses more likely. However, pairs of witnesses who know each other are less likely to help victims than are witnesses who are alone. One reason for this is that there is no *diffusion of responsibility* when there is only one witness present (Latané and Darley, 1970). Diffusion of responsibility occurs in groups of witnesses because people can say to themselves that someone should act but that it need not be themselves, because other potential helpers are present. Especially when a victim's cries for help are not directed toward a specific bystander, people who witness an emergency can soothe their consciences by claiming that someone else should help or that others are equally responsible if no one helps. Indeed, the larger the group of bystanders, the more responsibility is diffused and the less likely it is that help will be offered.

One experiment that suggests that bystander intervention is more likely when responsibility is focused on a particular bystander was conducted on Jones Beach, Long Island. A "victim" placed a blanket near another bather, turned on a radio, and a short time later said to the bystander, "Excuse me, I'm going up to the boardwalk for a few minutes. Would you watch my things?" This committed the bystander to watch the radio. Other bystanders were only asked for a match and were thus not committed to watching the radio. In a few minutes, a "thief" —who was actually part of the experiment—picked up the radio, which was playing loudly, and walked away with it. Another participant in the experiment observed the reactions of bystanders. Of twenty uncommitted witnesses who later said they had noticed the theft, only four tried to stop the thief. However, of twenty committed bystanders, nineteen made some effort to stop the thief. Prior contact between the victim and the bystander had focused responsibility on the committed bystanders to take some action when the theft occurred (Thomas Moriarity, cited in Horn, 1973).

Other aspects of the situation also affect the likelihood of bystander assistance to the victim. Familiarity with the location is important; help is probably more likely to be given if witnesses are in their own neighborhood than if they are in a strange neighborhood. Bystanders also consider the risks of providing help; they may be less willing to help if a weapon is present or if there are several offenders rather than one. Offering help may be a function of other activities in which the witness is engaged at the time, for instance, help is probably more likely to be given if a witness is standing on the street doing nothing than if a witness is rushing to a doctor's appointment or a job interview (Darley and Batson, 1973).

Bystanders who are self-assured, feel good about themselves, or have specialized training in first aid, life saving, or medical and police techniques seem to be especially likely to help others. People who seek training in such skills may be more inclined to help to begin with, or they may learn an ethic of helping behavior as they learn those skills (Geis, 1981).

A study of thirty-two people who had intervened in actual crimes of violence or theft found that all but one were men, and that they tended to be above average in height and weight and were usually larger than the offenders they confronted (Geis, 1981). Perhaps size and sense of competence led more men than women to risk taking action when faced with a crime in progress. However, an experimental study at the University of Virginia staged a theft and found that three-fourths of the women but only half of the men tried to stop the theft (Austin, 1979). This experiment, which elicited a promise from the bystander to watch the "victim's" goods, led the researcher to conclude that women might be more unwilling than men to break a promise, or that women perhaps feel more empathy for victims than men do. These explanations would not, however, tell us why nearly all of the bystanders who intervened in actual crimes in the first study were men.

Collective Response to Crime

People sometimes band together in a collective response to crime. They may work for a political candidate who promises "law and order," meet to plan a crime-prevention program, or even unite in a civilian patrol group to perform tasks that they think the police are not doing adequately. Group action of this sort has been both condemned as a mob taking the law into its own hands and praised as citizen involvement in crime prevention.

A Historical and Comparative Perspective

Collective response to crime has a long history. Ancient Roman plebeians engaged in community self-help when they threw alleged offenders from the Tarpeian rock. Early Germans raised a hue and cry, took up arms, blew horns, chased suspects, and occasionally lynched them (Pound, 1921). More recently, "people's police" have sometimes had to be restrained from attacking innocent people in the Soviet Union. In China, people informally police their communities, and Africans in tribal villages sometimes impose harsh punishment on suspected criminals (Radzinowicz and King, 1977: 181). In the Cross-Cultural Perspective, we see an example of citizen self-help in dealing with the crime problem in urban Brazil.

The history of vigilante activity in the United States covers more than two centuries. The first recorded movement was in the 1760s in South Carolina, where a group called the Regulators sought to bring order to communities in the Back Country (Brown, 1963). The Regulators apparently reduced crime, but they violated the due process rights of suspects. They elicited much hostility and eventually were disbanded when they began to mete out severe punishment, select victims rashly, and even supervise the morals and family life of law-abiding citizens.

Vigilante groups on the American frontier developed in response to a perceived lack of social order, rather than in response to specific crimes. Because the new frontier communities often lacked the resources to hire law-enforcement officials, because they were usually far from towns that could provide those officials, and because they were near open spaces to which suspects could flee, frontier vigilante groups sometimes developed as a way to establish social control over crime and bring stability to the community.

The leaders of many vigilante movements in the West were young men from the East who sought power and prestige and wanted to establish an orderly community in which they could pursue their ambitions. The rank-and-file members of these vigilante movements were often drawn from the middle classes, and the lower classes provided most of the targets of these movements.

Vigilante organizations in the West ranged in size from a dozen to as many as 8,000 participants; usually they had a few hundred members. Most groups lasted only a few weeks, but some endured for over a year. In nearly half of the recorded vigilante movements, there was at least one execution of an alleged offender, usually after a brief and formal — but extralegal — "trial."

Vigilantes traditionally espoused popular sovereignty, the right of the people to wield power in their own best interests (Brown, 1969). They also supported the idea that people had the right to revolt against established authority if it failed to maintain order. Vigilante groups sought to preserve and protect the life, liberty, and property of their members and the other residents of the

A Cross-Cultural Perspective: Lynchings in Brazil

Rising crime rates in the Brazilian cities of Rio de Janeiro and São Paulo have elicited a variety of public responses. A majority of the public favors restoration of the death penalty. People have moved from houses to apartment complexes that are protected by armed guards. Residents of some neighborhoods have hired guards to stand watch on street corners. More Brazilians are carrying weapons. In some communities, crime is controlled by "death squads" of off-duty police officers who beat and kill "known offenders."

Perhaps the most dramatic response to Brazil's crime problem is citizen involvement in the lynching of suspected offenders. A public opinion poll in December 1983 found that 26 percent of a sample of the residents of Brazil's two largest cities approved of lynchings, and an additional 33 percent favored such action "depending on the crime." These lynchings seem to be a response to the perception that the criminal justice system has been ineffective in controlling crime. One lynching is described as follows:

Osvaldo Otávio Pires was brought handcuffed into Elio's Bar in the Jardim Guanhambu slum on the outskirts of São Paulo at about 8 A.M. on April 2. Over 100 men, women and children had gathered in the small wooden building to await his arrival.

Mr. Pires, 33 years old, was thrust onto a bench facing the crowd and the handcuffs were removed. He was allowed to smoke a cigarette and drink a glass of rough liquor, but no one moved when he asked to see his two small children. Witnesses recalled that his hands were trembling.

Mr. Pires, long feared in Jardim Guanhambu, then heard an array of charges of armed assault brought by people filling the bar. After 20 minutes, participants in the meeting later told reporters, a voice was heard to say, "All those in favor of death raise their hands." Dozens of arms were lifted; apparently no one objected.

Mr. Pires was pushed out of Elio's Bar and the crowd fell on him with sticks, poles and stones. Once he lay dead in the dusty street, the police were called. When they arrived, they took the names and addresses of 43 people who said they had joined in the lynching. No arrests were made.

SOURCE: Based on Alan Riding, "Brazilians Turn to Lynchings to Fight Soaring Crime Rate," *The New York Times*, April 15, 1984, pp. 1, 12. Also, see Alan Riding, "A Crime Rise Spurs Brazil Lynch Mobs," *The New York Times*, January 21, 1987, p. A10; Alan Riding, "In Rio Slums, Some Cheers for Death Squads," *The New York Times*, May 31, 1987, p. 13.

community, and in this sense their extralegal efforts to preserve civil order were conservative (Little and Sheffield, 1983).

Some vigilante movements were socially constructive, dealing with specific problems of disorder and then disbanding; these movements usually represented the consensus of the community. By contrast, socially destructive vigilante movements encountered stiff opposition and produced community strife. Movements became socially destructive when they failed to exercise control over violent or sadistic members. The possibility that vigilante movements, including civilian patrol groups in today's cities, may become battlegrounds for

personal and group conflicts rather than represent genuine community consensus is one reason to distrust such movements. Such consensus is difficult to
establish in large and heterogeneous cities.

Urban Patrol Groups and Neighborhood Watches

Vigilante groups on the American frontier developed to provide social control
of deviant behavior. Just as the western frontier was in transition from wilderness to settled territory, so can the transition from a small preindustrial city to a
heavily industrialized urban center be understood as a kind of frontier. In Great
Britain in the eighteenth and nineteenth centuries, urbanization and industrialization created a kind of frontier, a transition between social forms, that left
growing cities without effective law enforcement. Just as vigilante groups
emerged in the American West, so did private "prosecution societies" develop
in these English cities. These prosecution societies sought to make the criminal
justice system more accessible and more effective. They supported the rule of
law and rarely meted out sentences on their own (Little and Sheffield, 1983).

Today, about 5 million Americans belong to crime-stopping groups such as
Neighborhood or Block Watches, which are sponsored by law-enforcement
officials in about 2,500 communities. These groups "share information about
local crime problems, exchange crime prevention tips, and make plans for
engaging in surveillance ('watching') of the neighborhood and crime-reporting
activities" (Rosenbaum, 1987: 104). Surveillance involves communicating directly with the local police about crimes and problems observed in the community. In general, Neighborhood Watches and similar groups seek to supplement
the police rather than to replace them. They differ from frontier vigilantes
because they operate in a context in which there is already a fully developed
system of law enforcement.

In 1984, about one-fifth of American families lived in a community with a
Neighborhood Watch program; 38 percent of households in areas that had such
a program participated in it (Bureau of Justice Statistics, March 1986). These
figures lead us to ask whether participation in such programs can be expanded,
setting in motion increased informal social control that will reduce the crime
rate. One expert questions whether this can happen. Dennis Rosenbaum (1987)
suggests that there is some evidence that people who live in high-crime areas
would not participate in such programs even if they had the opportunity to do
so. He also suggests that the interaction of citizens at Neighborhood Watch
meetings sometimes increases rather than decreases fear of crime. He suggests
there is little direct evidence that such meetings cause residents to engage in
actual neighborhood surveillance and bystander intervention, which are
needed to strengthen informal control and reduce crime. Rosenbaum does not
condemn Neighborhood Watch programs, but instead suggests that much more
research is needed on their actual impact. He also questions whether collective
citizen action and the informal social control it may activate can be implanted in
communities where they do not already exist.

A study of twenty-eight civilian patrol groups in American cities found that seventeen of them could be classified as supplemental groups that sought to assist the police rather than to oppose them. Seven groups were adversarial, in that they thought people had to defend themselves against the police as well as against criminals. The four other groups were mixed in their attitudes toward the police (Marx and Archer, 1971, 1972, 1973). The police usually regard adversarial patrol groups as spies on their activities or as challengers to their authority. Patrol groups that are adversarial to the police and opposed by the police are the kind of group most likely to engage in violence, as well as the type most likely to be the target of police violence. In general, there is more community support for supplemental patrol groups than for adversarial ones; the latter are less likely to represent community consensus and may create or exacerbate intergroup conflict in the community.

One patrol group that has received much attention is the Guardian Angels. This organization, which now has branches in many large cities, is made up primarily of young Hispanics and blacks who patrol subway stations and subway cars in groups, wearing red berets and Angel T-shirts in order to deter robbery and assault. Guardian Angels are trained in karate, resuscitation methods, and the legal requirements for citizen arrests. In some cities, this group is supported by the police, but in other cities officials have been silent or critical of the Angels. The effectiveness of the Angels in preventing crime is unclear; they may simply displace crime to other locations or to a time when they are not around. One study in New York City found that Guardian Angel patrols apparently did not affect either the amount of crime on the subways or the level of fear felt by riders, nor did they change passengers' willingness to assist one another (Kenney, 1987).

OBSTACLES TO URBAN PATROL GROUPS Patrol groups face several problems (Marx and Archer, 1971, 1972). To sustain the interest of their members and the support of the community, they need to make the crisis to which they are responding continuously felt. Patrol groups need a charismatic leader to inspire confidence in their members and in the residents of the community. Patrol groups need to be formally organized, and they require financial support. They have a better chance of survival if they have an ideology that states positive, specific goals; vague targets such as crime and disorder do not seem to sustain patrol groups for long. These groups are most effective in limited and well-defined settings, such as housing projects and rock concerts, where there are homogeneous populations separated from other people by clear boundaries. Even if all of these conditions are met, patrol groups face difficulties:

> Self-defense groups often lack a clear mandate from the groups they wish to serve and their legal position regarding the use of force and citizen arrests is ambiguous. They may have trouble defining their task. The tendency of the groups to lack the resources for recruiting, screening, and training appropriate manpower and for sustaining motivation beyond that which stems from a deeply felt crisis (along with the degree of autonomy some groups have) may contribute to ineffectiveness and abuses. And even if internal problems are solved, the groups may face harassment from the police. (Marx and Archer, 1971: 68)

Overall, the police made 100,739 felony arrests, of which 75,661 proceeded to some disposition by the criminal justice system. Only 42,129 of the felony arrests, or 56 percent of the arrests disposed of by the criminal justice system, produced a conviction on some charge. Twenty-seven percent of the arrests, or 20,503 cases, led to a jail or prison sentence. However, only 5 percent of the arrested suspects, or 3,811 defendants, were sentenced to "felony time," or more than one year in jail or prison (Vera Institute of Justice, 1981).

In 1973 the Comprehensive Data Systems program developed a Computerized Criminal Histories/Offender-Based Transaction Statistics (CCH/OBTS) system to gather information on defendants' prior criminal behavior and responses to that behavior by the criminal justice system. The Federal Bureau of Justice Statistics did not direct states' attention to that program until 1981, and its initial report in November 1983 provided data for only four states, which asked to remain anonymous because their data had not been fully verified (Bureau of Justice Statistics, November 1983b). If this CCH/OBTS system is refined and implemented by all states, it would provide important information on the operation of the criminal justice system, including case attrition, and on the role that the police, the courts, and the prisons play in the careers of criminals.

The Police

The police are the first formal line of defense against crime, for only if the police arrest suspects will the rest of the criminal justice system come into play in trying, convicting, and punishing offenders.

History of the Police

For centuries, societies have had some kind of a police force, an armed group of specialists who keep order and deal with violations of the law. The first modern police force was organized in London in 1829 by Sir Robert Peel, with officers nicknamed "bobbies" after their founder. This police force differed from earlier law-enforcement units in being full time, paid, uniformed, and organized for the city as a whole. Standards of literacy and character were established, and recruits were trained to perform their duties (Bayley, 1983).

Public police forces have existed in the United States since early in the seventeenth century, but it was only in Boston in 1837 that the first modern police force was organized, along the same lines as London's department. By the 1870s nearly all large American cities had their own police force, which provided all citizens, rather than just wealthy ones, with the services of criminal investigation. Urbanization had weakened the informal social control provided by families and neighbors, and the police were needed as a formal means of controlling deviance. Another important factor in the rise of American police forces was the threat to the social order posed by mob violence in nineteenth-century cities (Bayley, 1983).

Marxist criminologists regard the police in capitalist society as a tool used by the bourgeoisie to maintain a social order that is profitable to themselves and that exploits laborers (Harring, 1981, 1983; Spitzer, 1981). Marxists have shown how capitalists historically have used the police to quell collective action by organized labor. However, one study using data from 1950 to 1980 found no relationship between inequality in the distribution of a city's income and the strength of a city's police force, a finding inconsistent with conflict theory (Greenberg, Kessler, and Loftin, 1985).

Marxist criminologists point to the unequal treatment by the police of suspects from disadvantaged classes and racial and ethnic groups. However, there is evidence that members of all classes agree on the need to punish those crimes to which the police devote most of their attention: murder, rape, assault, and theft. Moreover, these crimes are the subject of police activity in socialist and communist societies as well as in capitalist ones. In addition, the criminal law is probably not the most important mechanism for maintaining the social order, nor is it a very effective tool for the dominant class to use in controlling all members of society (Sparks, 1980b).

There is, however, some evidence that the criminal justice system responds to threats to the social order. For instance, one study found that a city's expenditures on its police force can be predicted by the racial composition of the city's population and by the level of black mobilization activity in the city. Cities with larger black populations spend more on salaries, operations, and capital expenditures for the police than do cities with proportionally fewer blacks. In addition, cities with more political activity by blacks have higher rates of police capital expenditures. One explanation of this is that police expenditures are increased when minorities are seen as a threat to the dominant racial group (Jackson and Carroll, 1981). A more recent study, using data from 1950 to 1980, found a moderate to strong relationship between a city's racial composition and the strength of its police force only for the South prior to 1970. This relationship was weak outside the South, except for the period from 1960 to 1970 (Greenberg, Kessler, and Loftin, 1985).

Organization of the Police

The police in the United States are organized at four levels. The first to develop were county sheriffs' departments, followed by municipal police departments. Next there were established state police departments, first in Texas and then in Massachusetts. Federal marshalls, established in 1789, were the first federal police agency. Over time, the national government has expanded its policing activities, with the Bureau of Investigation — renamed the Federal Bureau of Investigation in 1935 — being established in the Department of Justice in 1908 (Bayley, 1983).

Municipal police departments are organized hierarchically, with a police chief or superintendent at the top. Detectives and specialized investigative units — robbery, vice, and homicide, for instance — focus on solving crimes. One important aspect of police departments is that the individual at the lowest level of the hierarchy — the patrol officer on the street — has the most contact with the public and with criminal suspects, and also has a great deal of autonomy because superiors have difficulty directly supervising the officer's activities. Within police departments, conflict and competition often develop between administrators concerned with efficiency and productivity, and officers on the street who must deal with the public and with suspects (Reuss-Ianni, 1983).

For the police, fighting crime is but a small part of their job. In cities of more than 50,000 people, only forty-five of every one hundred officers on duty at any time are actually on patrol. The police spend only about 15 percent of their time dealing with crime; they spend the rest filing reports, providing ambulance service, or managing traffic (*U.S. News & World Report,* November 1, 1982). Much police effort is also expended in maintaining social order. For instance, to keep peace on skid row — a run-down area of the city frequented by the homeless, the unemployed, the alcoholic, and those without families — the police must cultivate personal relationships to gain knowledge about the people who live there (Bittner, 1967).

In their efforts to maintain order and enforce the law, the police in a democratic society are required to act in accordance with the legal rights of citizens and certain constraints on official behavior, which have been spelled out in the Constitution, legislative enactments, and judicial decisions. As part of a bureaucracy, however, the police have an ideology that emphasizes order, efficiency, and initiative. These values are sometimes in tension with the value of legality. Thus, " 'law' and 'order' are frequently found to be in opposition, because law implies rational restraint upon the rules and procedures utilized to achieve order. Order under law, therefore, subordinates the ideal of conformity to the ideal of legality" (Skolnick, 1975: 9).

Police Abuses of Authority

The conflicting demands under which the police operate sometimes lead them to abuse their authority. For instance, departmental pressure on officers to use their initiative and to be efficient in solving cases may lead to violations of due process rights, such as illegal seizure of evidence or coercion of a confession. Laws that define victimless crimes such as gambling, possession of drugs, or prostitution require the police to make arrests for consensual crimes in which the participants do not define themselves as victims; in such cases, the police may find it easy to justify taking a bribe not to make an arrest. Stressful work conditions may increase police sensitivity to challenges to their authority and make brutality against citizens more likely. The camaraderie of the police subculture may encourage retaliation against those who assault or kill fellow officers. For the most part, police abuses of their authority seem to be structurally induced, rather than the product of personality flaws in individual officers. Sometimes, entire departments engage in systematic violations of the law, as we see in the Cross-Cultural Perspective.

Periodically, police corruption scandals occur, often before elections and frequently with an activist press involved. A commission may be established to

A Cross-Cultural Perspective: Police Corruption in Mexico

In Mexico, the police "have become symbols of corruption, abuse of power and in some cases outright criminality." A newspaper editorial claims that Mexicans see the police officer as "a hot-tempered individual, capable of extreme cruelty and easily corruptible." One lecturer and author writes: "Society has come to fear the police more than it fears criminals." Indeed, the distinction between police officer and criminal is often unclear, as Mexicans were reminded when a former officer was shot to death while resisting arrest after kidnapping and murdering an eleven-year-old boy.

When it was revealed that an illegal detective corps in Mexico City had run secret jails where people were beaten until ransoms were paid, Mexico's new president dismantled the unit. However, this unit was so feared by Mexicans that some were afraid of the consequences of letting its officers loose on the public. One newspaper remarked: "They are too dangerous to be cast into the ranks of the unemployed."

Widespread corruption from the bottom to the top of the Mexican police force has led to public cynicism toward the government. When the police march in parades, they are heckled. A major source of this hostility is the "mordidas," or bribes, that the police demand from drivers they accuse of violating traffic laws. These bribes are distributed upward throughout the police organization. Officers justify the taking of bribes by the fact that they had to "buy" their jobs

or by their low salaries. A $5,000 per month payoff from a drug smuggler can be tempting to an officer earning only $200 per month in pay. This corruption pervades not only the police, but also district attorneys' offices and the court system. As one official notes, "With defenders of the law acting outside the law, the citizen doesn't stand a chance."

President Miguel de la Madrid, elected in 1982, promised a "moral renovation" of the criminal justice system. In his first three years in office, he dismissed 2,500 police officers for corruption or brutality. He also introduced a training program for new recruits to the police force to try to reduce their abuse of power.

Nevertheless, critics charge that the Mexican police still collect mordidas and continue to torture both common criminals and political prisoners. The government admits that the problem has not been solved, but asserts that bribery and torture are aberrations in an improving criminal justice system. Others claim, however, that these problems are endemic to the system and that recent reforms have not gone far enough to eradicate police corruption and brutality.

SOURCES: Based on Alan Riding, "Criminals in Mexico: How Many Are Policemen?" *The New York Times,* February 13, 1983, p. 12 (source of all quotations); and Julia Preston, "Police Torture Becomes Political Issue in Mexico," *The Boston Globe,* December 8, 1985, p. 3.

document police corruption and bring charges against officers; action against those who pay bribes is less common. For a time, the department may be "cleaned up," as officers become wary of accepting bribes. Eventually, matters usually get back to "normal," with at least small favors for the police becoming common again. An exception to this pattern seems to be the New York City Police Department, which has been able to sustain an effort to control corruption. In 1972, the Knapp Commission was established to investigate charges by officer Frank Serpico that corruption was rampant in the department. The commission found that a majority of officers were engaged in some corrupt practices, and distinguished between "grass eaters," who did not pursue payoffs actively but did accept them, and "meat eaters," who expended much effort in soliciting bribes and payoffs (*The Knapp Commission Report on Police Corruption,* 1972). A 1982 report found that departmental pressure to avoid corrupt practices was still strong, and that officers continued to fear indictment and punishment. Reorganization of the department, intensive supervision, and the internal investigation of corruption—including systematic informing on dishonest officers by others who were assigned to report to the Internal Affairs Division—have kept corrupt practices at a lower level than before the Knapp Commission (Farber, 1982b).

The Working Personality of the Officer

Police officers develop a *working personality,* a distinctive approach to situations and events they encounter in their jobs (Skolnick, 1975). This working personality develops in response to the danger of the job, the authority vested in the police officer, and the need to appear efficient in the performance of assigned duties. The police learn to respond to "symbolic assailants," whose crimes threaten community standards and the police themselves. Officers learn how to do their jobs from the police subculture, which shares values such as conformity and authority with the larger culture, but which also includes specific values of its own such as suspiciousness and the need to maintain respect for the police at all costs. New recruits quickly learn the values and norms of this subculture. For instance, one study found that officers soon agreed that they sometimes had to use force to gain citizen compliance and that respect in tough areas depended on their willingness to use force (McNamara, 1967).

SUSPICIOUSNESS   Suspiciousness is a key element of the police officer's working personality. Officers learn to suspect that a crime is being committed or is about to be committed in situations to which other people would not give a second thought. What is not clear, even after many judicial decisions, is exactly when an officer's suspiciousness is a legal basis for making an arrest.

DISCRETION   A second important aspect of the working personality of the police officer is the exercise of *discretion,* the use of judgment to decide what action to take. The police are clearly given delegated discretion, such as the power to decide when to give a traffic ticket. Unauthorized discretion is that which the police exercise but for which they may not have authority, such as making decisions on the basis of a suspect's race or sex (Skolnick, 1975).

The way the police exercise discretion helps define the outer limits of permissible behavior. They may regard some offenses as mere nuisances, and decide to warn an individual rather than make an arrest. In general, the police are most likely to exercise discretion in dealing with minor offenses. In serious crimes, they have less freedom in deciding how to treat suspects and usually make arrests.

One decision that is difficult for the police to make is when to use force against a citizen. The police are legally justified in shooting people under certain circumstances, such as when an officer or another person is attacked by an armed offender or when a fleeing suspect poses a threat of serious harm to an officer or other people. The decision to shoot must be made quickly and under stressful conditions, and it is not always clear what action is called for. As a result, legal constraints on police use of force combine with dangerous situations on the street to make it difficult for officers to decide whether to shoot suspected offenders.

Another situation in which the police must exercise discretion is the "domestic dispute." The police traditionally have dealt with arguments or assaults between people who live together by making a judgment about the possible consequences of either arresting someone or trying to settle a dispute by mediating between the parties, even though few officers have been trained in crisis-intervention techniques (Oppenlander, 1982). An officer may judge that an arrest in a domestic disturbance will heighten conflict in the household over the long run, or believe that the complainant will not press charges in court. In these cases, the officer may decide not to make an arrest. Officers may choose to make an arrest if they think the conflict will flare up again as soon as they leave. Feminist organizations have protested this use of police discretion, claiming that many wives are abused repeatedly by their husbands because the police are reluctant to make arrests. This is true, but so is the officer's contention that many women refuse to help in prosecuting their husbands, often out of fear, and that arrests can exacerbate tensions in the household. A recent Police Foundation study, which we examine in the following chapter, found that arrest deters future domestic violence more effectively than does the mediation of disputes. This study has been used as the basis for recent changes in police practices and state laws.

The decision to arrest a suspect is often based on the nature of the interaction between the officer and the suspect. In dealing with juvenile suspects, officers consider the youth's prior record, but they also assess the suspect's character by his or her group affiliations, age, race, hair style, dress, and demeanor. Demeanor includes how contrite the suspect is about the offense, how much respect the adolescent shows the officer, and how afraid of possible sanctions the juvenile seems to be (Piliavin and Briar, 1964; Black, 1980). Fitting the image of a dangerous delinquent by being a member of a male delinquent gang can also increase a suspect's chances of being arrested (Morash, 1984).

One study found than an officer's decision to take a suspect into custody was influenced by

- the dispositional preferences of the victim,
- the race and demeanor of the suspect,

- the presence of bystanders, and
- the seriousness of the offense.

Males and females were equally likely to be arrested, and antagonistic behavior by suspects of either sex increased the chance of arrest. Bystanders increased the probability of arrest, because the police thought they needed to show others that they were in control of the situation. In addition, arrest was less likely if the victim and the suspect knew each other, because this indicated that the victim would be less likely to help in prosecuting the suspect (Smith and Visher, 1981).

Police discretion is, ideally, based on an officer's best judgment about the future course of a suspect's behavior and the likely effects of an arrest or a warning, but this judgment must be made within legal constraints. For instance, if an officer judges that one suspect is more likely than another one to commit more crime if not arrested and thus arrests the first suspect and only warns the second one, this decision involves illegal discrimination rather than delegated discretion if the only basis for the officer's decision is that the first suspect is black and the second one white.

Discretion and Racial Discrimination. There is mixed evidence on whether the police discriminate against minority groups. The complexity of this issue can be seen in a study based on data collected in 1965 and 1966 in Boston, Chicago, and Washington, D.C., by observers who rode in police cars and systematically observed police behavior (Black and Reiss, 1970; Black, 1980). The researchers found that the police were much more likely to arrest a black juvenile suspect than a white juvenile suspect. However, two factors other than racial discrimination seemed to explain this difference. One was that more of the black juveniles were stopped for serious crimes, and the police acted on the legal basis of seriousness of the offense in arresting more of the black suspects. Second, most complaints about black juveniles came from black adults, and they were more likely than white adults who complained to the police about white juveniles to demand that the police make an arrest, rather than merely warn the juvenile. In making arrest decisions, the police thus seemed to respond to the seriousness of the crime and the preferences of the complainant, rather than to the race of the suspect.

Much research, especially that done outside the South in recent years, finds that the race of the suspect is a less important influence on the police arrest decision than are factors such as the seriousness of the offense, prior criminal record, demeanor, and the socioeconomic status of the neighborhood in which a police encounter occurs. However, even when these other variables are taken into account, some studies find that race remains as a factor that influences the disposition of a case. For instance, one study found that there was more evidence of racial bias by the police in deciding to send juvenile suspects to court than there was of racial bias in court decisions. This racial bias by the police increased the chance that a youth from a minority group would have a record, which could then contribute to a criminal career by affecting police actions and court decisions in the future (Dannefer and Schutt, 1982).

If the police discriminate by race, we would expect that black offenders would stand a greater chance of being arrested than would white offenders who committed the same offense. We can test this for the crime of robbery, which involves a face-to-face confrontation between offender and victim. If the police "overarrest" black robbers, we would expect the proportion of all arrested suspects who are blacks to be higher than the proportion of all robbers that victims report to be blacks. We can see, however, from Table 13.1 that in a study of robbery in Boston the police actually "underarrested" black robbers in comparison to white robbers. In the first six months of 1964, 55 percent of all robbers were blacks, according to victims, but only 44 percent of all suspects arrested for robbery were blacks; this suggests that black robbers had a smaller chance than white ones of being arrested for their crimes. The data for 1968 show a similar pattern (Conklin, 1972). A study of robbery in 1974 in Milwaukee, Wisconsin, found that the percentage of all arrested robbery suspects who were blacks was about the same as the percentage of all robbers identified as blacks by victims (Pruitt and Wilson, 1983). Neither of these studies supports the contention that the police are more likely to arrest black suspects than white suspects, at least for the crime of robbery. A study that used victimization survey data and FBI arrest data concluded that there was "virtually no criminal justice selection bias for either rape or robbery but there [was] such bias for assault, especially aggravated assault" (Hindelang, 1978: 101).

The observational study of the police carried out in Boston, Chicago, and Washington, D.C., in the mid-1960s uncovered a significant amount of prejudice among the police, with about three-fourths of the officers classified as very prejudiced or considerably prejudiced against blacks on the basis of spontaneous comments and behavior. This study found that prejudice, an attitude, was not necessarily associated with discrimination, which is behavior. The observers saw forty-four cases of police assault on citizens during seven weeks of around-the-clock observation; in many of these assaults no suspect was arrested. They found a higher rate of undue force used against whites than against blacks. Black and white officers used violence with about the same frequency, and usually against members of their own race, something that seemed to reflect the areas to which the officers were assigned. The police may have been less likely to use violence against blacks during this period because of the threat of an urban riot,

TABLE 13.1   Percentage of All Robbers Who Are Blacks

Percentage Who Are Blacks	*1964**	*1968**
By victim identifications	55%	66%
By arrest data	44%	53%

* Data are for the first six months of each year.

SOURCE: Adapted from John E. Conklin, *Robbery and the Criminal Justice System.* Philadelphia: J. B. Lippincott Company, 1972, p. 33.

for riots occurred in many cities from 1965 to 1968. The gains of blacks in the area of civil rights may also have convinced some officers that police abuses would be reported and lead to trouble for them. In addition, officers may have adjusted their behavior in the presence of observers to avoid the appearance of discrimination, although they apparently did not adjust their verbal comments to avoid the impression of racial prejudice (Reiss, 1968, 1971).

One area in which the police may discriminate by race is in the shooting of civilians. A study of police shootings in Chicago between 1974 and 1978 found that if rates of being shot by the police were calculated for blacks, Hispanics, and whites by dividing the number of shooting victims of each group by the number of people of that group arrested for "forcible felonies"—defined as murders, rapes, robberies, assaults, and burglaries—then whites were somewhat more likely to be shot than blacks and Hispanics, although differences among the groups were relatively small. Rates were calculated in this way to account for group differences in involvement in serious crimes, the situations that most often led to police shootings. This study suggests that the police are about equally likely to shoot whites, blacks, and Hispanics; that is, the police do not seem to discriminate by racial or ethnic group (Geller and Karales, 1981).

A study of police shootings in Memphis, Tennessee, found that the police were more likely to shoot blacks than whites, even if differences between the groups in involvement in criminal activity were taken into account (Fyfe, 1981). This suggests that police discrimination against minorities in the use of force may exist in some cities but not in others. Differences in the relative power of minorities, the organization of the municipal police department, and the department's administrative directives may account for such city-to-city variations in the use of force by the police against minorities (Fyfe, 1981; Waegel, 1984).

Between 1971 and 1984, in cities with populations over 250,000, there was a 51 percent decline in police killings of civilians, a decline that reflected a national trend toward more restrictive policies on firing weapons, more progressive police administrators, the financial incentive of avoiding civil suits, and the increased political influence of blacks (Sherman et al., 1986).

Discretion and Sex Discrimination. There is evidence that the police respond differently to male and female defendants. One study in a midwestern city found that from 1948 to 1976, police disposition of males and females became more similar for juvenile and adult misdemeanors and for adult felonies, but that males and females continued to be treated differently for juvenile status offenses and juvenile felonies. Overall, treatment of the sexes became more alike over time, but sex discrimination had not disappeared by the mid-1970s. Female status offenders were treated more leniently and paternalistically even in the 1970s (Krohn, Curry, and Nelson-Kilger, 1983).

A study that covered the period from 1934 to 1979 found that sex differentials in arrests had diminished in most offense categories, with the largest changes occurring in the 1960s and 1970s. Women showed the most significant increases in arrests for petty property crimes—such as larceny, fraud, and forgery—and for vagrancy and disorderly conduct, which were often related to prostitution. The researchers concluded that the narrowing of the sex differential had not yet produced a convergence of male and female arrests. This narrowing seemed to be due to changes in law-enforcement practices and changes in FBI statistical coverage of a larger part of the nation, as much as or even more than it was due to changes in actual behavior by men and women (Steffensmeier and Cobb, 1981). The following changes seemed to have produced increased arrests of females:

1. A decline in chivalry and sympathy for female defendants;
2. A possible increase in the surveillance of women because of growing attention to crime by women;
3. Increased social and legal pressure to administer the law in a nondiscriminatory way;
4. Professionalization and bureaucratization of the police;
5. Improvements in police recording practices, including a greater likelihood of recording a suspect's sex; and
6. Changes in welfare agencies, which have led to more prosecution of crimes such as fraud and larceny. (Steffensmeier and Cobb, 1981)

The Clearance Rate

To measure their effectiveness in dealing with crime, the police use the *clearance rate*, or proportion of offenses that they solve to their satisfaction (Skolnick, 1975). Many cleared cases lead to arrest, prosecution, and conviction, but the police also classify as cleared some cases that do not produce an arrest. Sometimes an offender cannot be arrested because he or she is deceased, out of the country, or in prison in another state. Thus, a man who kills his wife and then commits suicide would leave the police with no one to arrest for the murder, but the police would still call the homicide cleared. In other cases, the police strongly believe they know who committed a crime but lack the evidence to make an arrest; often these crimes are classified as cleared.

There are some problems with relying on clearance rates to measure the effectiveness of the police. Because the police themselves decide when a case is cleared, they can classify cases as cleared to make themselves look good. This might mean that the actual offender in a crime that is erroneously marked cleared will no longer be hunted by the police; such "false clearances" could reduce the deterrent effect of the law. Another difficulty with clearance rates is that a crime committed by several offenders may be marked cleared with the arrest of a single suspect; this action exaggerates the police's effectiveness in apprehending criminals. Departmental pressure to clear cases can lead the police into illegal actions to draw people into behavior for which they can be arrested. Critics see this as illegal entrapment, but supporters justify it by saying that only people predisposed to crime would be drawn into it.

In the Boston robbery study, close attention was paid to the way the police cleared cases. The clearance rate for all robberies recorded by the police in the first six months of 1968 was 35.8 percent. Thirty-eight percent of all of the clearances resulted from an arrest at or near the scene of the crime, with the police interrupting the robbery or finding a suspect nearby. One-fifth of the clearances resulted directly from information supplied by the victim or a witness; this included giving the police the name or address of the robber or identifying a "mugshot." Nearly as many robberies were cleared by victim identification of a suspect in another case; 18 percent of the clearances resulted from victims' saying they were robbed by someone whose photograph was shown to them by the police or by an offender they picked out of a lineup. Another 18 percent of the clearances resulted from what we might call "multiple clearance by confession." This method, which did not use the victim as a check, involved suspects who confessed to similar offenses about which the police asked them. In cases of this sort, suspects know the police will not charge them with the additional crimes to which they confess, and may even be more lenient on the offense for which they were arrested, if the suspect cooperates and helps the police clear their books. These multiple clearances by confession are used to make the department look more efficient at solving crimes. The final method by which robbery cases were solved was by a detective's investigation; this method accounted for only 6 percent of all clearances (Conklin, 1972).

THE ROLE OF THE DETECTIVE IN CLEARING CASES   There are several reasons that detectives solve relatively few robberies. One is that if robbers escape from the scene of the crime, there is usually little that detectives can do to find them. There is rarely any physical evidence, such as fingerprints, and victims' descriptions are often vague and unreliable. Those few cases that detectives do solve may well be the most serious robberies, such as bank robberies and grocery store holdups.

One study of the role of detectives in solving crimes concludes that their efforts are as important as the investigative work of patrol officers in solving robberies and burglaries. Robbery and burglary cases were divided into three categories within the department:

1. Cases that could not be solved with a reasonable amount of effort;
2. Cases that are solved by circumstances, requiring only the arrest of a suspect and the development of the case for prosecution; and
3. Cases that could be solved with a reasonable amount of effort.

Many robberies and burglaries were not even assigned to detectives for investigation because there were few or no leads or because the case was solved by circumstances, but of those cases that were assigned to detectives, many were solved by investigation. This investigation process included interviews with witnesses and informants, discussions with other police officers, and an examination of the department's files. Interviews with victims led to few arrests (Eck, 1984).

A detective's decision to investigate a victim's complaint about the theft of property is affected by the characteristics of the victim and the crime. Detectives are more likely to spend time in a follow-up investigation if there is some evidence that might help them solve the crime. In burglary cases, victims living in relatively well-to-do communities seem to receive more attention from police investigators than victims who live in poor communities. Minority-group members who are burglary victims seem to be only slightly less likely than white victims to receive favorable treatment by police investigators. Police activity in the follow-up investigation of violent crimes is influenced to some degree by the willingness of the victim to aid in the prosecution of the case (Bynum, Cordner, and Greene, 1982; also, see Sanders, 1977).

A study of responses to reported burglaries found that a southern sheriff's department was more likely to use evidence technicians to dust for fingerprints when entry into the building involved force or when the property that had been stolen was "a marker of the self." Jewelry, silver, and firearms were items that recalled the past or had special personal significance for victims, and the sheriff was more likely to make special investigative efforts when such property had been taken. Dusting for fingerprints rarely led to an arrest, but it did help foster good public relations and restore the victim's peace of mind after a serious breach of the home "as a private place and as a territory of the self" (Stenross, 1984: 400).

The police are especially likely to investigate complaints about crimes that have certain characteristics. These crimes are serious, provide evidence, occur in relatively well-to-do neighborhoods, have a victim who is willing to prosecute, and involve the loss of property with personal significance. We can see that not every crime is equally likely to produce an arrest. The nature of police work thus introduces several contingencies into an offender's career, with offenders who commit certain kinds of crime being especially likely to be arrested and processed by the courts.

Criminal Courts

In the United States, suspects are presumed to be innocent from the time they are arrested by the police until they are found guilty or innocent in court. As a consequence, they have a right to gain their release pending the disposition of charges against them. Usually after some delay, a prosecutor brings charges against the suspect, a defense attorney helps the defendant get acquitted or secure the most lenient sentence possible, and a judge or a jury decides guilt or innocence. Often a defendant pleads guilty in return for an agreed-on sentence that is less than the one that might result from a trial. When judges sentence the guilty, they sometimes give very different penalties to offenders who have similar criminal records and have been convicted of similar offenses.

Bail

The Eighth Amendment states that "excessive bail shall not be required" of criminal defendants, even though the practice has developed of denying bail to defendants in crimes that carry the death penalty. *Bail* is a system designed to ensure that defendants will show up to face charges against them when their trial is scheduled, while allowing them to remain free until the trial takes place. To do this, an amount of money is set that must be deposited with the court before the defendant can be released. Because bail requires suspects to pay money, it discriminates against those with low incomes who cannot afford their release. As a result, jails that hold suspects awaiting trial are usually filled with poor defendants (Shenon, 1983).

A study conducted in Philadelphia concluded that defendants who were detained on bail — either because bail was denied or because they could not afford bail — differed from the average defendant entering the criminal justice system. Those who were detained on bail were more likely to be charged with serious crimes, more likely to have many prior arrests and convictions, more likely not to have shown up for trials in the past, and more likely to have been arrested when out on bail in the past. Thus, defendants held on bail seemed to be especially likely to commit new crimes ("bail crimes") if released, and especially likely to "default," or not show up for trial, if released. However, a significant number of the detained defendants, 13 percent of the total, were classified as "low risks" who might have been released with little threat of bail crime or default. If these low-risk detainees had been released, jail overcrowding would have been alleviated (Goldkamp, 1983).

Defendants are released in several ways. Some are released on their own recognizance, a promise to appear for trial. Others gain their release by placing with the court an amount of cash equal to the bail set by the judge, or by giving the court security equal in value to the amount of bail, such as a savings account pass book or a deed to real estate. Because most defendants have little money or property, a system of bail bondsmen has developed in the United States to help defendants gain their release.

Bail bondsmen write a bail bond, a kind of insurance policy, that guarantees the court that they will pay the full amount of the bail if the defendant fails to appear for trial as scheduled. In return for this guarantee, the bondsman charges the defendant 5 to 10 percent of the total amount of the bail to write the bond. This fee is like an insurance premium; the defendant does not get it back if he or she appears for trial, because the bondsman assumes a risk for that money. Bondsmen make it easier for defendants to gain their release, but they do not seem to increase the chance that defendants will show up for trial and they cost defendants much money. They have also frequently been involved in corrupt practices. As a result, two states, Illinois and Kentucky, have replaced bondsmen with a system that allows defendants to place 10 percent of the amount of the bail with the court as a deposit, which is returned when their case is disposed of, even if they are found guilty.

Preventive Detention

Long delays from arrest until trial provide opportunities for defendants who are released on bail to commit crimes. Concern with such "bail crimes" has led critics of the criminal justice system to call for *preventive detention,* a system that holds some defendants without bail. Washington, D.C., has a little-used preventive detention system that has been in effect since 1971, and preventive detention was authorized for the federal court system in 1984. In about half of the states, judges are allowed to consider whether a defendant is dangerous to others in making a decision to release the defendant prior to trial. Even where preventive detention is not specifically authorized, judges often set very high bails for defendants they believe will endanger the safety of others or commit bail crimes. These defendants are held in jail when they cannot afford to make bail.

Most European nations have preventive detention systems that allow judges to hold defendants in jail without bail. For instance, French law allows judges to deny pretrial release to suspects if a judge believes it is the only way to protect evidence, prevent the coercion of witnesses, or avoid unlawful concertation between the defendant and accomplices. French law also permits judges to hold suspects without bail if they believe it is required in order to prevent a repetition of the crime, to protect the accused, or to guarantee the appearance of the suspect in court. Informally, French judges also deny bail when they believe a defendant needs a "taste of prison" to be rehabilitated or when they think it would be psychologically harmful to release a suspect who will eventually be imprisoned; these reasons for denying bail are not stipulated in French law (Gerety, 1980).

In the United States, numerous objections to a system of preventive detention have been raised (Ervin, 1971). Critics claim that it may be unconstitutional, because setting no bail seems to violate the Eighth Amendment's requirement of setting a reasonable bail. However, in 1987 the U.S. Supreme Court rejected that argument, declaring preventive detention legal if a prosecutor could show that freeing a defendant would endanger the community. Another objection to preventive detention is that it imprisons people for acts they *might* commit if they were released, and accurately predicting the behavior of pretrial releasees is difficult (Angel et al., 1971; Floud and Young, 1981; *British Journal of Criminology,* July 1982). Even the best predictors of what released suspects will do before they are tried make many errors, especially the error of incarcerating defendants who would not actually have engaged in any crimes if they had been released.

Preventive detention might contribute to criminal careers, for defendants who are held in jail awaiting trial are less able to consult with their attorneys and contact witnesses to help in their defense, and they may make a worse impression on judges or jurors in court. Preventive detention may thus set in motion a cycle in which suspects thought to be dangerous are denied bail, are then more likely to be convicted as a result of being held in jail, and thus have a worse criminal record that is used to hold them without bail again in the future. In addition, the denial of bail can cause defendants to lose their jobs, force their families to go on welfare, sever their bonds to the conventional order, and even make criminal behavior by their children more likely.

Prosecutors

Prosecutors, or district attorneys, are lawyers who are elected officials. Often they see themselves as independent of public control, while still serving the public, and regard themselves as lawyers whose behavior should reflect the standards of the legal profession (Neubauer, 1974). They work on behalf of the public to bring charges against defendants and to ensure that justice is done. Prosecutors are concerned with all aspects of the criminal case. They interact with police officers, defense attorneys, judges, jurors, witnesses, victims, and defendants.

Prosecutors measure their success by a conviction rate, just as the police measure their effectiveness by a clearance rate. Some prosccutors blame the police when they are unable to get convictions, claiming that the police are more concerned with clearing cases than with presenting cases that can produce convictions. The police, on the other hand, often accuse prosecutors of being too willing to reduce charges from felonies to misdemeanors just to secure convictions, rather than using the resources of the prosecutor's office to convict suspects on more serious charges. Prosecutors do screen cases brought by the police to find the ones that are the most likely to produce convictions. Once defendants are convicted, prosecutors are not necessarily concerned with getting judges to mete out the harshest possible sentences (Neubauer, 1974; Stanko, 1981–82). Prosecutors are concerned with fairness, rather than with getting the longest possible prison sentence or with getting a conviction in a case in which the evidence does not warrant it.

Defense Attorneys

The American criminal justice system is based on an adversary model or "fight theory" that assumes the correct verdict will emerge if the prosecutor presents the best case against the defendant and the defense attorney presents the strongest case for the defendant. Later we will see that many more criminal cases are settled by guilty pleas by defendants than are settled by trials that use this adversary model. The expertise of defense attorneys is important in helping defendants get the best possible sentence in exchange for a guilty plea. When cases are tried before a judge or a jury, defense attorneys can help defendants get acquitted, convicted on the least serious charge, or sentenced as leniently as possible.

The Supreme Court decisions in *Gideon* v. *Wainwright* (1963) and *Argersinger* v. *Hamlin* (1972) guaranteed free counsel to any indigent defendant facing the threat of incarceration in a felony or misdemeanor case. Poor defendants are provided with legal counsel through public defender organizations or through the assignment of lawyers by the court. Within the legal profession, attorneys who specialize in criminal law are often held in low regard, because of the social standing of their clients and because they tend to have relatively low incomes. As a consequence, criminal law usually attracts the less expert lawyers, and so defendants often are not very well served in court.

In a study of the criminal justice system in a small Illinois city, the defense attorneys acted as counselors who tried to keep defendants out of court and do the best for them. Defense attorneys interpreted the law for their clients and tried to get them the "normal" penalty or "going rate" for the offense with which they were charged. At the arraignment, judges informed defendants of the maximum penalty for the crime with which they were charged. The threat of a very long sentence — which few defendants actually received — made them more than willing to seek the advice of defense attorneys (Neubauer, 1974).

Defense attorneys are an integral part of the court system. They interact cordially with prosecutors and judges, rather than behave in an adversary manner, for good relationships with other court personnel make plea bargaining easier and help defense attorneys get trial dates postponed when necessary. The close relationship of defense attorneys with other court personnel dilutes the adversary nature of the American criminal justice system, a system that seems designed to produce the most expeditious processing of cases (Blumberg, 1979).

Judges

In lower criminal courts, where most criminal cases are first heard, one of the judge's primary functions is to ratify agreements between defense attorneys and prosecutors about the sentences that defendants will receive for pleading guilty. When cases go to trial, judges act as decision makers, or as supervisors of the proceedings when cases are tried before juries. Perhaps the most important function for the judge is the sentencing of convicted offenders.

Judges are supposed to sentence convicted offenders on the basis of legal criteria: the nature of the crimes for which they have been convicted, and perhaps their criminal records. Criminologists have been concerned that judges may sentence offenders on the basis of extralegal criteria such as race, age, or sex. As we will see, most research indicates that sentences are based primarily on legal criteria, although sentences are sometimes influenced by personal characteristics of defendants that are supposed to be irrelevant to punishment.

Juries

The jury has been criticized as a group of amateurs who lack the legal training to make decisions that have major effects on defendants' lives. Others have defended the jury as important to a democracy, because it involves the average citizen in the process of defining and meting out justice. However, no more than 5 percent of all felony cases that are prosecuted involve jury trials, as guilty pleas account for most convictions (Baldwin and McConville, 1980).

An important study of the American jury asked judges to fill out questionnaires about the jury trials over which they had presided. In about four-fifths of the cases on which data were collected, judges agreed that jurors had reached the same verdict that they themselves would have reached. In the remaining cases, juries were much more likely to acquit defendants when judges said they would have convicted them, rather than to convict defendants whom the judges would have acquitted. The jurors seemed to require more proof to find guilt beyond a reasonable doubt than did the judges, and so we might say that juries are "defendant-friendly." The judges thought the juries performed quite well, considering the evidence carefully and taking longer to reach verdicts in cases the judges thought were the most difficult from a legal point of view (Kalven and Zeisel, 1966).

In contrast to this study's conclusion that juries are somewhat more lenient toward defendants than are judges, a more recent study found that juries were significantly more likely than judges who tried cases to convict defendants (Levine, 1983). This study of more than 58,000 felony trials concluded that since the 1950s there has been a growth in public conservatism toward crime that supports harsher treatment of defendants, and this change underlies a shift toward more convictions by juries. This researcher's methods differed from those of the earlier study, and so we must be cautious in attributing differences between the conclusions of the two studies to actual changes in jury behavior over time.

Plea Bargaining

Over 85 percent of all felony convictions in American courts are the result of guilty pleas (Smith, 1986). *Plea bargaining* is an informal but structured process of negotiation in which the prosecutor and the defense attorney agree about a guilty plea and the sentence that the prosecutor will recommend to the judge. Because defendants can request trials or delays, which are costly and time-consuming for the court, prosecutors are often willing to agree to a reduced charge or a light sentence in exchange for a guilty plea. Because prosecutors have the power to go to trial and ask for a severe sentence, defendants are frequently willing to plead guilty and accept a penalty less than the one they might receive if convicted in a trial (Rosett and Cressey, 1976; Maynard, 1984).

One study found that judges sentenced defendants to longer terms if they asked for trials than if they pleaded guilty. Judges seemed to adopt the position that if a defendant took some of the court's time to have a trial, which is of course the defendant's legal right, then the judge would take some of the defendant's time by meting out a longer prison sentence (Uhlman and Walker, 1980). Another study that compared cases of similar severity that involved the same sort of evidence and offenders who had similar characteristics found that even when these factors were controlled for, defendants who were convicted after trials received harsher sentences than defendants who pleaded guilty (LaFree, 1985). However, another study concluded that although more defendants convicted after trials were incarcerated than was true for defendants who pleaded guilty, this difference was not evidence that plea bargaining was coercive. Instead, the difference in incarceration rates for the two groups was attributable to two factors: (1) some of the defendants who pleaded guilty would not have been convicted if they had gone to trial, and (2) cases in which pleas were negotiated had characteristics different from cases in which convictions followed trials (Smith, 1986: 966).

Plea bargaining has both critics and supporters. Critics claim that it may induce innocent defendants to acquiesce to a guilty plea in order to get a more lenient sentence than they would if they demanded a trial and were found guilty by a judge or a jury. Critics also complain that plea bargaining goes on behind closed doors, and that this keeps the legal process from public view and makes abuses more likely. Including defendants in the plea negotiation conference might minimize the routine way that defendants are treated by the courts. In addition, claim some critics, defendants cannot be sure that judges will mete out agreed-on sentences after the defendants plead guilty in court. Sentences given out as a result of plea bargaining usually fall far short of maximum sentences so as to induce defendants to plead guilty, and critics argue that this means that the penalties resulting from plea bargaining are invariably less than justice demands. These relatively lenient penalties may also undermine the deterrent and incapacitative effects of punishment.

Supporters of plea bargaining argue that the criminal courts could not function if every defendant asked for a trial. Resources of the courts would have to be multiplied many times to process all of the cases if plea bargaining were not used to resolve most charges. Supporters claim that plea bargaining provides just sentences — that is, penalties proportional to the harm caused by offenders — even if those penalties fall short of the legal maximum. They point out that the actual penalties meted out are much longer in the United States than in other Western democracies, and that plea bargaining keeps punishment from being even more severe than it already is (Rosett and Cressey, 1976).

Probation

One penalty that judges sometimes impose on convicted offenders is *probation,* a form of supervised release. Probation originated in the work of a Boston shoemaker named John Augustus, who began to supervise offenders and report on them to the court in 1841. In 1878 Massachusetts became the first state to pass a probation law; today all states and the federal government provide probation for at least some kinds of offenders.

Probation is designed to offer convicted offenders treatment outside prison where they can maintain their ties to conventional society. Judges, with the help of probation officers who present them with presentence reports, try to select for probation those offenders who seem to be the best risks to stay away from crime. In addition to providing probationers with services, this system aims to control behavior through surveillance by probation officers to whom offenders have to report regularly (Gottfredson, 1983). However, many probation officers are so overburdened with cases that they have little time to supervise their clients or provide them with services. Probation is less expensive than incarceration, which is one reason that two and a half times as many offenders were on probation as were in the nation's jails and prisons in 1985 (Bureau of Justice Statistics, January 1987).

Sentence Disparity

A major problem with American courts is *sentence disparity,* the difference in the criminal sanctions that are meted out to people who are convicted of similar offenses and who have similar criminal records. For instance, there is significant variation in sentences from one state to another, from one city to another, and from one judge to another in the same city. Later in the book, we examine sentence disparity in terms of the principle of retribution, but here we consider the influence that a defendant's characteristics — particularly race and sex — have on the kind or length of sentence that a judge metes out.

RACE AND SENTENCING   The fact that blacks constitute a disproportionately high percentage of all inmates in American jails and prisons — close to half of all prisoners — while being only 12 percent of the population has led some critics of the criminal justice system to blame the imprisonment of so many blacks on racial discrimination by the judges who sentence offenders.

Much research has been done on racial discrimination in the sentencing of offenders, particularly for capital offenses, but the results are not conclusive. In noncapital crimes, the research seems to indicate that race plays a less important role in sentencing than do legal factors such as the offense and the defendant's prior criminal record (Kleck, 1981; LaFree, 1981; Hagan and Bumiller, 1983; Pruitt and Wilson, 1983; Peterson and Hagan, 1984). When these and other legally relevant criteria are taken into account, race either disappears as a factor influencing sentencing or, more often, diminishes significantly in importance. However, some research finds that race does affect sentencing (Thornberry, 1979; Christianson, 1981). One study even concludes that both severity and leniency may exist toward black defendants, with the social context and nature of the crime determining the meaning that is given to race by the criminal justice system (Peterson and Hagan, 1984). Thus, one study found that blacks convicted of sexual assaults against white victims received especially severe penalties, but that blacks convicted of sexual assaults against black victims were treated particularly leniently, a form of racial discrimination based on the race of the victim (Walsh, 1987).

A useful distinction is between "direct" discrimination — in which race or ethnicity plays a part in the sentencing decision, even after taking into account seriousness of the crime and prior criminal record — and "organizational" discrimination—in which economically disadvantaged people are more likely to be convicted or to get a long prison term because they cannot afford to be released on bail or pay for a private attorney. Organizational or economic discrimination may not be based directly on race, but it affects the way blacks are treated by the criminal justice system, because they have lower incomes, on the average, than whites and are thus more affected by organizational discrimination (Unnever, 1982). Thus, some of what seems to be racial discrimination may actually be due to disadvantages suffered by blacks, such as poverty, lack of job skills, unemployment, low levels of education, and residence in blighted urban areas.

The relationship between direct discrimination and organizational discrimination is complex and has important consequences for social policy. Evidence of direct racial discrimination would require civil rights remedies, but evidence of organizational discrimination would point to the need for policies to alleviate the burden of poverty for people of all races. Most recent research finds that race plays some part in sentencing, but that its role seems to be diminishing and that its effects are compounded by the higher poverty rate of blacks.

A study in a large northeastern city found that sentence severity was not affected by race, once the seriousness of the charge and prior criminal record were taken into account. Blacks did receive harsher sentences than whites, but this was because blacks were charged with more serious crimes and had more prior arrests for serious crimes. There was also a tendency for blacks to be sent to prison more often than whites, and for whites to be put on probation more often; this tendency persisted even when legal and extralegal variables were taken into account. This study also found organizational or economic discrimination, with harsher penalties given to defendants who could not afford pretrial release or a private attorney. This economic discrimination fell most harshly on blacks, who tended to be poorer than whites (Spohn, Gruhl, and Welch, 1981–82).

Research conducted in California, Texas, and Michigan found that blacks and Hispanics received harsher sentences than whites in felony cases, even when they were charged with the same offenses and had similar criminal records. Minorities were more likely than whites to be released after arrest; but whites were more likely to be placed on probation, to be sent to a local jail rather than to a state prison, to get shorter sentences, and to serve less time in prison. There were no differences between whites and minorities in being considered for treatment programs in prison. In Michigan, but not in California or Texas, the parole board equalized sentences somewhat by releasing minority inmates earlier to compensate for their longer court-imposed sentences. The researcher did not attribute her findings to deliberate racial discrimination, but rather to the beliefs of many judges that minority offenders had characteristics—such as coming from broken homes or having poor employment records—that made them likely to return to crime if they were given short sentences. However, there was no evidence in this study that minority offenders had higher rates of returning to crime after release. The lighter sentences for whites seemed to be partly due to the fact that they were more likely than blacks and Hispanics to engage in plea bargaining, which led to convictions but also produced relatively lenient sentences. Blacks and Hispanics, on the other hand, were more likely to have jury trials, which could produce an acquittal but led to longer sentences when defendants were convicted (Petersilia, 1983).

Discrimination against racial and ethnic minorities sometimes takes subtle forms. For instance, a study of sentencing in California found that being white, black, or Hispanic did not directly affect sentences, but that these groups were treated differently because judges emphasized different factors, such as type of offense and prior record, in determining sentences for members of each group. Thus, judges used the prior records of Hispanic defendants to justify longer sentences for them but were less likely to use the prior records of white and black defendants to justify longer sentences for them (Zatz, 1984, 1987).

Procedures adopted by the courts — such as release prior to trial, the assignment of defense attorneys to indigent defendants, and the use of information about job history and family stability — seem to result in longer sentences for minority-group members than for whites, even when direct racial discrimination does not occur. Changes in court procedures could reduce the impact of race and ethnicity on sentencing. For instance, a study in Milwaukee, Wisconsin, found that between 1967 and 1977 judges became more "race neutral" in their sentencing of convicted robbers and burglars and came to rely more heavily on legal factors such as type of offense and prior record. Growth in the caseloads of the courts forced the development of a more bureaucratic system of criminal justice, and this led to more reliance on formal rules that punished offenders on the basis of legal criteria rather than individual characteristics. In addition, the diminishing impact of race on sentencing was a result of an increasingly liberal judiciary and more professionalized prosecutors and defense attorneys (Pruitt and Wilson, 1983).

One review of the research on racial discrimination in sentencing concludes that in noncapital cases, the evidence is largely against general or widespread overt discrimination against blacks, even though there is discrimination in some jurisdictions and for some offenses (Kleck, 1981). However, in cases involving the death penalty, there have been several recent studies that indicate that race plays a role in sentencing.

Race and Capital Punishment. The major reason that the Supreme Court declared the states' death penalty laws unconstitutional in the 1972 case of *Furman* v. *Georgia* was that the application of those laws had shown an excessive degree of arbitrariness, especially in the more frequent use of capital punishment for black defendants. Since 1972, three-fourths of the states have enacted new death penalty laws to satisfy the criteria established by the Supreme Court, but these new laws have not eliminated racial discrimination in the use of the death penalty (Bowers and Pierce, 1980a; Bowers, 1984). For instance, a study using data from Florida for 1973 to 1977 found that the race of both the defendant and the victim influenced the classification of homicides by the police and by prosecutors in a way that increased the likelihood that the death penalty would be imposed on blacks (Radelet and Pierce, 1985).

Recent studies have found that the race of the victim is an important predictor

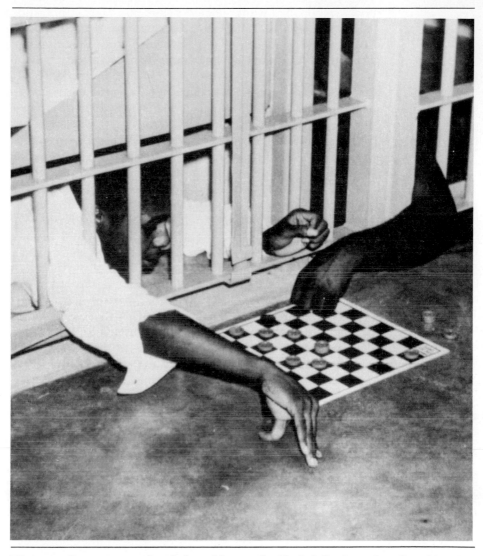

The more frequent use of capital punishment for black defendants than for white ones led to the 1972 Supreme Court decision in *Furman* v. *Georgia*. Here two black inmates await execution in Texas.   *Source: Courtesy American Correctional Association*

of which homicides will result in the death penalty (Bowers and Pierce, 1980a; Zeisel, 1981; Bowers, 1983, 1984; Paternoster, 1983; Gross and Mauro, 1984). For instance, a study of homicide in Florida in 1976 and 1977 found that people charged with killing white strangers were more likely to be indicted for first-degree murder (a capital offense) than were people accused of killing black strangers. Differences by race at the stage of bringing formal charges (indictment) thus accounted for the more frequent imposition of the death penalty on people who killed white strangers (Radelet, 1981). In a study of homicides in eight states from 1976 to 1980, defendants in homicide cases were much more likely to receive the death penalty if their victims were white than if their victims were black. This suggests that the courts place greater value on the lives of whites than on the lives of blacks (Gross and Mauro, 1984). In the 1987 case of *McCleskey* v. *Kemp,* the U.S. Supreme Court upheld the constitutionality of the death penalty despite evidence that killers of whites are given the death penalty more often than killers of blacks.

Until 1977 forcible rape was a capital offense in some states, but in that year the Supreme Court ruled in *Coker* v. *Georgia* that the death penalty could not be imposed for rape. Before that decision, there was much racial discrimination in the administration of the death penalty for rape, particularly in the South for black males convicted of raping white females (Kleck, 1981). One study finds that black men accused of raping white women still receive harsher penalties than either white men who rape white women or black men who rape black women; rapes of black women by white men seem relatively rare. It thus appears to be the race of the victim, or a combination of the race of the victim and the race of the offender — rather than the race of the offender by itself — that is most important in determining sentences for convicted rapists (LaFree, 1980).

Much of the research on the death penalty that has found past discrimination in rape cases, and past and current discrimination in homicide cases, relies on data from the South. In part this is because all southern states, but only some nonsouthern states, now have the death penalty; and in part it is because southern states have meted out capital punishment much more often than those nonsouthern states that have death penalty laws. Between 1977, when executions were resumed after a ten-year hiatus, and 1987, about 95 percent of the executions that were carried out occurred in southern states. One study has found that outside the South, black homicide defendants actually seem less likely than white ones to be sentenced to death or to be executed (Kleck, 1981).

SEX AND SENTENCING   One review of the research on the differential treatment of men and women in the criminal justice system concluded that women were more likely than men to be released on their own recognizance (without bail), but that when bail was set there seemed to be no difference by sex in the amount at which it was set. Sex did not seem to make a difference in the decision to prosecute a defendant, nor were there differences by sex in the use of plea bargaining or in the likelihood of being convicted. At the sentencing stage, there was a small but consistent differential leniency toward female defendants, even when variables such as prior criminal history and the nature of the offense were taken into account (Nagel and Hagan, 1983). These findings of no differences by sex in prosecution, plea bargaining, or conviction, but a difference by sex in the sentencing of convicted offenders, were confirmed by a study in Dade County, Florida (Curran, 1983).

Although the juvenile courts seem to treat girls more harshly than boys for certain offenses (e.g., see Chesney-Lind, 1973), the criminal courts seem to sentence women more leniently than men. However, women are less likely to have a prior criminal record and are more likely to commit less serious crimes, and so we must compare the fate of male and female defendants who have similar histories of criminal activity and who face similar charges. When this is done, somewhat contradictory conclusions are reached. Some studies find that men and women with the same records and facing the same charges are sentenced similarly by the courts, and other studies find that women are treated more leniently (Parisi, 1982).

The differential leniency toward female defendants has sometimes been attributed to "chivalry." Some claim that women who exhibit behavior that is socially defined as appropriate for women are the most likely to be treated leniently. Thus, older white women who are apologetic and submissive are less apt to be treated severely by the criminal justice system than are women who are black, young, and hostile toward authorities. Similarly, women who are more economically dependent on their husbands may be treated more leniently than women who are economically independent, perhaps because judges think the courts need to exert less formal social control over women who are controlled by the men on whom they are economically dependent (Kruttschnitt, 1982).

Greater leniency by judges toward female defendants is also due to factors other than chivalry. Judges may think it impractical to incarcerate women who have young children. They may believe that women are only led into crime by men and are unlikely to violate the law on their own. Women may also seem less dangerous or more easily rehabilitated than male offenders (Steffensmeier, 1980).

In spite of continuing leniency toward women, recent years have seen an increase in the number of women in prison. Between 1980 and 1987, the number of women incarcerated in state and federal prisons increased by 111 percent, compared with a 71 percent increase in male prisoners. However, in 1987 only 5 percent of all inmates were women.

The Prisons

Probably no more than 1 or 2 percent of all serious crimes leads to the imprisonment of an offender, but most people who commit many crimes eventually end up in jail or prison. Prison sentences probably deter some people from crime, even though the certainty of punishment is relatively low in the United States today.

History of Prisons

For centuries, jails and prisons were places to hold people before they were punished for their crimes, rather than places of punishment for convicted offenders. People were locked up until they could be executed, pilloried, or subjected to other forms of suffering. Jails, which are institutions run by cities or counties, serve much the same purpose today, holding defendants until they can be tried in court. Defendants who are found guilty in court are given a criminal sentence such as a fine, time on probation, a sentence to a state prison or local correctional institution, or the death penalty.

In the late eighteenth century, the Quakers in Philadelphia developed a use for prisons different from the earlier practice of holding people until they were punished. The Quakers believed that even the worst offenders could be saved, and they sought to do this by requiring offenders to serve long periods in total silence in prison, hoping this would lead prisoners to reflect on their mistakes and see the correct way to behave. These institutions were called penitentiaries, because the Quakers thought that inmates would grow penitent about their crimes while reflecting on their lives. However, inmates often died in prison, and those who were released often had become mentally ill while incarcerated.

In the nineteenth century, prison reformers developed an institution at Auburn, New York, that used a different philosophy of punishment: Put prisoners to work and teach them to become law-abiding by instilling in them the work ethic. Since then, inmates have often been put to work, although usually only for part of each day and often at menial and poorly paid tasks.

In contrast to the view that prisons originally had a humanitarian impulse behind them, a more recent view is that they were and continue to be weapons of class conflict, a tool used by the powerful and the wealthy to control the "dangerous classes" (Rothman, 1971; Foucault, 1978; Ignatieff, 1978).

Prisoners Today

At the end of 1986, the number of prisoners under the jurisdiction of state and federal correctional authorities was 546,659, the largest number in the history of the United States (see Figure 13.2). Of this number, one in twenty was a female. Slightly less than half of the inmates were black (Bureau of Justice Statistics, February 1987, May 1987).

A survey of 126,839 new admissions to state prisons in 1983 (Beck and Hester, 1986: 3) found that the most serious offense for which the inmates were being sent to prison were as follows:

burglary	26.3%
robbery	14.3%
larceny	11.3%
drug offenses	8.3%
public order offenses	7.6%
assault	7.0%
murder or manslaughter	5.7%
forgery or fraud	5.7%
rape or other sexual assault	5.0%
auto theft	2.2%
other offenses	6.6%

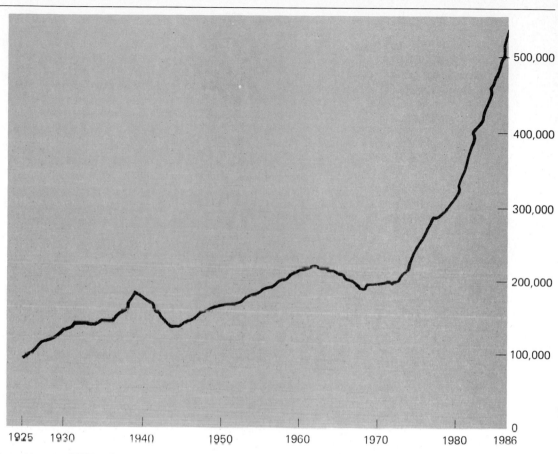

Note: Prior to 1977, prisoner reports were based on the custody population.
Beginning in 1977, focus is on the jurisdiction population.

FIGURE 13.2 Number of Sentenced State and Federal Prisoners, Year-End 1925–
1986. *Source: Bureau of Justice Statistics,* State and Federal Prisoners, 1925–85. *Washington, D.C.: U.S. Department of Justice, October 1986, p. 1. Updated to 1986 from Bureau of Justice Statistics,* Prisoners in 1986. *Washington, D.C.: U.S. Department of Justice, May 1987.*

Overall, 48.6 percent of new admissions were being sent to prison for property offenses, 34.2 percent for violent crimes, 8.3 percent for drug offenses, 7.6 percent for public order offenses, and 1.3 percent for other crimes. The median sentence for these inmates was thirty-six months. The median time actually served by inmates who were released in 1983 was nineteen months.

Prison Crowding

A 1983 survey of 1,400 criminal justice officials identified crowded jails and prisons as the most serious problem confronting the criminal justice system (Hall, 1987). The dimensions of this problem are described as follows by the Director of the U.S. Department of Justice's Bureau of Justice Statistics:

> This was the state of affairs at the end of 1985: Prison systems were operating at 106 percent to 121 percent of capacity. (Incidentally, the American Correctional Association recommends that a facility never operate at more than 90 percent of capacity. Prison officials always need some room for maneuvering.) More than two percent of the prison population was backed up in local jails. . . . And 19 states reported releasing a total of more than 18,600 inmates ahead of schedule specifically for the purpose of relieving crowded conditions. (Schlesinger, 1987: 1)

One inmate in Ohio notes that state veterinary services standards recommend forty-three square feet of space for a calf that is more than five weeks old, and that he only has thirty-two square feet of living space in his cell. Overcrowding creates unpleasant living conditions for inmates: lack of privacy, arguments and fights over the use of limited space, and the threat of sexual assaults (Gaes, 1985).

What are the sources of prison crowding? One source is a long-term increase in crime rates, arrests, and commitments to prison. From 1957 to 1984, serious crime (murder, rape, robbery, and burglary) rose by 414 percent and arrests for serious crime increased by 385 percent. However, over this same period, the state prison population grew by only 165 percent, and state prison capacity increased by only 79 percent (Schlesinger, 1987). Thus, the growth in prison capacity did not keep pace with the increase in the number of offenders sentenced to prison, resulting in more crowded conditions. Moreover, the failure of prison capacity to increase faster may have led judges not to sentence to prison some offenders whom they would have sentenced to prison had there been greater capacity, and this may have resulted in a decrease in the deterrent and incapacitative effects of punishment.

Some of the increase in prison crowding in recent years is due to an especially large age cohort of men in their twenties, the group with the highest imprisonment rate in the population. Other reasons for the increase include mandatory minimum sentences, laws that give judges less discretion in sentencing, tightened parole release, and a national campaign against illegal drugs (Blumstein, 1983).

Steps have been taken to alleviate crowded jail and prison conditions. The courts have found four-fifths of the states to be operating institutions under conditions that violate the Constitution. In response, the states have built new prisons and expanded existing ones. From 1979 to 1984, there was a 29 percent increase in total available prison space. However, over this same period the prison population grew by 45 percent. It is expensive to construct new cells, each one costing about $60,000 to $90,000. In some cases, taxpayers have been unwilling to support expensive proposals to expand prison space, but national surveys indicate that many Americans are willing to pay higher taxes to increase the capacity of penal institutions (Krajick, 1982).

Some critics of prison crowding oppose the construction of new facilities, claiming that the new prisons would be filled to capacity in short order as judges send more people to prison and parole boards keep inmates behind bars longer. These critics call for shorter prison terms, or no prison sentences at all for less serious offenders, as the way to reduce crowding. Research is inconclusive on the issue of whether building more prison cells will result in a larger prison population rather than alleviate crowding (Abt Associates, Inc., 1980; Blumstein, Cohen, and Gooding, 1983).

An increasingly popular solution to the problem of prison crowding is the punishment of offenders outside prison walls. Southern states, which have higher incarceration rates than the rest of the nation, have turned to such programs as confining convicts to their homes, allowing them out only to work at jobs or to perform community service; community work centers, which house inmates who work for no pay at city or county jobs; and intensive probation supervision, in which offenders see probation workers five times a week (Clendinen, 1985). Foundations, labor unions, and other private groups have begun to get more involved in developing these and similar programs for punishing and treating offenders outside prisons. If sanctions can be devised that ensure the public's safety, satisfy a sense of justice, and are inexpensive, prison crowding might be alleviated.

Prison Riots

Prison crowding sometimes sets the stage for an inmate uprising. Other causes of prison riots include ineffectual prison administrators, real or imagined grievances by inmates, and racial discrimination by administrators and correctional officers (McKay, 1983).

One of the most dramatic prison riots occurred at Attica (New York) State Prison in 1971. Prisoners took control of part of the prison and held officers hostage. The state acceded to many of the inmates' demands but refused to grant them amnesty for offenses committed during the uprising. An assault by the state police enabled the state to regain control of the prison, but during the assault the police killed twenty-nine prisoners and ten correctional employees who were being held hostage.

Another major riot occurred in 1980 at the New Mexico State Prison at Santa Fe. Gangs of convicts held control of the prison for a day and a half, taking a dozen guards hostage and torturing and sexually assaulting them. Armed prisoners tortured and mutilated other inmates, and thirty-three inmates were killed by other prisoners before the uprising was subdued. One sociologist has attributed this riot to changes by the prison administration toward a more coercive system of control, rather than to crowding, poor food and services,

Using Criminology: Felons on Probation

As prisons have become more crowded, judges have increasingly sentenced serious adult offenders to probation. In the past, most probationers had committed less serious kinds of crime, but today many probationers are convicted felons. These felony probationers pose a possible threat to public safety.

In an effort to assess the extent of that threat, researchers at the Rand Corporation carried out a study of 1,672 felony probationers in Los Angeles and Alameda counties in California. The researchers followed the felony probationers for forty months after their sentencing and concluded that they "present a serious threat to public safety" (p. 381). During this follow-up period,

65% were arrested again;
51% were convicted of a new crime;
18% were reconvicted of a serious violent crime; and
34% were reincarcerated.

In addition, more than three-fourths of the new charges filed against the felony probationers involved the kinds of crimes most threatening to the community: burglary, theft, robbery, and other violent offenses.

The researchers concluded that this poor performance of the felony probationers shows the need for a new type of punishment that is intermediate between probation (which offers offenders their freedom) and imprisonment (which takes away their freedom). The sanction they propose is an intensive surveillance program (ISP), which is already in use in some jurisdictions. This sanction would involve "intensive monitoring and supervision; real constraints on movement and action; employment; added requirements of community service, education, counseling, and therapy programs; and mechanisms for immediately punishing probationers who commit infractions" (p. 384). The researchers claim that this kind of punishment "will be one of the most significant criminal justice experiments in the next decade," and that if it proves successful it can "restore probation's credibility and reduce imprisonment rates without increasing crime" (p. 385). This kind of penalty "would force offenders to be gainfully employed, functioning members of a community, and this might help them break old habits and establish new and more positive lifestyles" (p. 386).

SOURCE: Based on Joan Petersilia et al., "Executive Summary of Rand's Study, 'Granting Felons Probation: Public Risks and Alternatives,'" *Crime and Delinquency* 31 (July 1985), 379–392.

lapses in security, conspiracies by administrators, or a "new breed" of inmate who was more prone to violence. The administration's shift from a policy of accommodating inmate power to a policy of trying to maintain order by using force and restrictions on inmates set the stage for the riot (Colvin, 1982). Another sociologist saw the riot in terms of the breakdown of social organization among the inmates, arguing that the integrating activities of employment opportunities and recreational activities provided by the administration from

1970 to 1975 were curtailed sharply after 1975, leading to social disorganization and feelings of deprivation that eventually produced the riot (Useem, 1985).

The Prisoners' Rights Movement

One response to crowding, guard brutality, poor food, lack of access to lawyers, and other deprivations of prison life is the *prisoners' rights movement,* which has been led by ex-convicts and attorneys on behalf of people still in prison. Since the late 1960s, this movement has successfully brought cases to the courts, particularly the federal courts. These cases have led to judicial rulings that treatment must be provided for inmates, that minimum standards of shelter and food must be met, and that inmates' constitutional rights cannot be abridged. One summary of the accomplishments of the prisoners' rights movement of the late 1960s and the 1970s concludes that it established the following principles:

> (1) prisoners retain certain constitutional rights in spite of conviction and incarceration; (2) [pretrial] detainees retain even greater constitutional protections; (3) many existing practices and conditions within prisons and jails abridge those retained rights and protections; (4) correctional officials carry the burden of justifying the restriction of constitutional rights; and (5) the Civil Rights Act is an appropriate tool for protecting and enforcing the constitutional rights of prisoners and detainees. (Krantz, 1983: 1192)

Prisons and Race

The fact that nearly half of all federal and state prisoners are blacks has led some people to claim that the criminal justice system discriminates by race. Blacks have about seven times as high a per capita rate of imprisonment as whites, and during the 1970s the imprisonment rate for blacks increased faster than the rate for whites (Christianson, 1981; Blumstein, 1982). We have seen that most sentences are meted out according to legally relevant criteria, but race plays some role in sentencing in certain jurisdictions.

Even if all racial discrimination in sentencing were eliminated, the prisons would still include a disproportionately high number of blacks, because blacks, to a much greater degree than whites, commit those crimes defined by the law and regarded by the public as the most serious ones, and those crimes therefore carry the longest sentences. Because more blacks than whites are convicted of serious crimes, in proportion to their numbers in the population, and because the crimes that blacks are most likely to be convicted of when compared with whites are the most heavily punished offenses, more blacks go to prison and stay there a long time. By one estimate, differences in arrest rates, which do not seem to exaggerate blacks' actual involvement in crime, account for about 80 percent of the difference in incarceration rates between blacks and whites (Blumstein, 1982). Another study also concluded that the high proportion of blacks in state prisons in attributable more to the greater involvement of blacks in crime than it is to racial discrimination by the criminal justice system (Langan, 1985). However, there is some research that indicates that racial discrimination accounts for at least some of the higher incarceration rate of blacks (Carroll and Mondrick, 1976; Thornberry, 1979; Christianson, 1981).

Racial discrimination in prison is an important part of inmates' lives. The Attica Prison riot and other uprisings have been attributed, at least in part, to racial antagonisms between guards (who are typically white) and inmates (many of whom are black). A study of a medium-security prison in the South sought to determine if blacks and whites were treated differently by guards. Using self-report questionnaires, the researchers found that black and white inmates engaged in equal amounts of rule-breaking behavior, but that blacks were more likely to be disciplined formally for their violations. Part of this differential treatment was directly due to racial discrimination. Some of it was due to the fact that blacks were more likely than whites to have prior criminal records, and guards were likely to see any inmate with a prior record as dangerous and in need of discipline when the inmate violated prison rules. Taking formal disciplinary action against an inmate can cause hostility that may lead to further violation of the rules (Poole and Regoli, 1980).

Parole

Prison crowding and the high cost of incarceration can be alleviated by releasing inmates before they complete their full sentences. They can then be supervised on the street and sent back to prison if they violate the conditions of their release. This system is called *parole*.

A state parole board meets regularly to review an inmate's progress toward rehabilitation, and to determine whether the inmate can be safely released if certain conditions are met. Parole board decisions cause anxiety and bitterness in prisoners, who often see these decisions as arbitrary and in violation of their due process rights (Irwin, 1970). One study found that the most annoying thing to inmates about serving time in prison was never knowing when they would be released: Fifty-two percent mentioned this problem, and only 12 percent mentioned the next most commonly voiced complaint, being treated like a child by the prison staff (Kassebaum, Ward, and Wilner, 1971: 31).

If the parole board decides to release an inmate, it specifies the conditions of release, which typically include a steady job, staying away from known offenders, and avoiding the use of alcohol and illegal drugs. The parolee is required to meet regularly, perhaps once or twice a month, with a parole officer to discuss problems of adjustment and signs of progress. Parole officers frequently know of violations of parole conditions but usually do not send inmates back to prison for minor infractions. Instead, parole officers "save" these infractions so that if a major one occurs, such as arrest for a new crime, their decision to revoke parole and send the parolee back to prison can be justified with a list of infractions.

Not all inmates who leave prison are paroled. Some choose to "wrap up" their sentence, that is, to complete the full sentence in prison. The use of parole has been restricted in response to criticisms that the granting of parole is arbitrary and perhaps in violation of due process rights and that the behavior of parolees is difficult to predict and to monitor (Von Hirsch and Hanrahan, 1978). The federal prison system and a few states have abolished parole altogether, and other states have limited its use through sentencing reforms. Even where parole is widely employed, inmates usually must serve a minimum part of their sentence before they are eligible.

The Victim in the Criminal Justice System

The American criminal justice includes many defendants' procedural rights to protect them against the power of the state. Some people complain that this emphasis on defendants' rights neglects "victims' rights," or what those who are victimized are entitled to. It may seen unfair that fines paid by criminals go into the state's coffers rather than back to the victims. Critics also complain about the slowness of the legal process, which costs victims and witnesses time and money to sit in court hallways awaiting trials.

In recent years, more attention has been paid to victims. State systems of compensation and restitution have been developed to repay victims for their losses. District attorneys have come to realize that cases cannot be prosecuted successfully without cooperative victims and witnesses. Judges have increasingly considered the impact of crimes on victims before sentencing offenders, and parole boards sometimes listen to victims before releasing inmates.

Compensation

Compensation is a system in which the state repays victims for their financial losses or physical injuries. Under this system, it is not necessary to arrest and convict an offender for a victim to be compensated, nor does a convicted offender have to be financially solvent for the victim to be repaid for his or her losses. Three-fourths of the states have laws that provide compensation for victims, even though many of these programs are not well-funded or well-publicized.

Compensation has been justified in several ways. Some say that the state has an obligation to protect the welfare and safety of its citizens, and that when it fails to prevent crime, it should pay victims for their losses. Another rationale for compensation is that it may prevent victims from becoming angry at the criminal justice system and alienated from the political system (Schafer, 1968; Stookey, 1981). Even though compensation programs are sometimes aimed at improving public attitudes toward the criminal justice system and the government, research indicates that many victims who have sought compensation are disenchanted with the criminal justice system. Indeed, administrative obstacles to securing compensation and the inadequate rewards provided to victims seem to engender more discontent toward the legal system among applicants for compensation than exists among people who do not apply for compensation (Elias, 1983, 1984).

Compensation programs must deal with the problem of the victim's contribution to the crime. Earlier in the book, we saw that victims sometimes precipitate a crime or contribute to their own victimization, and in such cases the state might choose not to compensate the victim. For instance, someone who first uses force against another person and then ends up badly injured in a fight might not be compensated if the state compensation board found that the crime would not have occurred without the victim's initiating actions. In Great Britain, compensation is limited to "deserving cases," and this is determined in part by the degree to which the victim is to blame for his or her own victimization (Schafer, 1968).

Restitution

A system of *restitution* requires offenders to make monetary payments or provide services, either to the victim or to the community at large. Relatively few criminal courts have used restitution extensively, but growing concern for victims' rights has led some judges to require offenders to repay victims for their losses.

Some claim that restitution makes offenders take responsibility for their behavior and thus helps rehabilitate them (Deming, 1976). Others claim that offenders who repay their victims may not feel guilty for their crimes if they believe they have corrected their wrongs, and that this may make it more likely that they will continue to commit crime. Restitution might improve crime reporting if victims thought they would be repaid for their losses. Moreover, by easing public hostility toward offenders, restitution might reduce the isolation of offenders from conventional society and make it easier to reintegrate them into society after they are released from prison. Restitution would also lighten the burden on taxpayers if it replaced a system of state compensation (Barnett, 1977; Bridges, Gandy, and Jorgenson, 1979).

The Changing Role of the Victim

Many states have implemented programs to help the victims of crime, including compensating them for their losses and requiring offenders to make restitution. Victims have been given a greater voice in the sentencing of offenders, although defendants are usually allowed to respond to victims' statements. In some jurisdictions, victims must be notified of hearings and trials and be informed when an inmate is being considered for parole or escapes from prison.

District attorneys have started to pay more attention to the role of the victim in the criminal justice system. They can help to deal with a victim's fear of retaliation by the offender, frustration with delays in court, and intimidation by a defense attorney's cross examination. District attorneys can also impress on victims and witnesses the importance of testifying in court. In some jurisdictions, victims have even been included in plea bargaining conferences with the district attorney, the defense attorney, and the defendant (Heinz and Kerstetter, 1981). One study found that victim-witness programs in prosecutors' offices contributed in an important way to keeping victims informed about the progress and outcome of cases, and that crime victims expressed more satisfaction with the criminal justice system when they knew the outcome of a case and thought they had influenced that outcome (Forst and Hernon, 1985).

Few judges learn directly from victims about the impact crime has had on their psychological well-being, physical condition, and financial situation. Usually, judges learn about this only from presentence reports prepared by probation officers, who draw on secondhand information from police reports, medical records, or victim discussions with prosecutors. As a result, some courts have introduced *victim impact statements,* detailed written reports based on interviews with victims about the effects of crime on them (Forst and Hernon, 1985). One study of sexual assault cases found that these victim impact statements had little influence on the sentences that judges imposed, beyond the effects one would expect from legally relevant variables (e.g., seriousness of the crime and prior criminal record). However, this study suggested that there was often agreement, nevertheless, between the sentences recommended by victims and the actual sentences. This might produce a "placebo" effect in which victims are satisfied with the outcome of a case because they believe they have influenced the sentence, even if the sentence would have been the same without their recommendation (Walsh, 1986). In 1987, the U.S. Supreme Court ruled that such victim impact statements could not be used in hearings on the imposition of the death penalty, arguing that those hearings should focus on the defendant's "moral blameworthiness" rather than on the impact of the crime on the family of the victim.

In 1987, forty-three states permitted victims to appear at parole board hearings or to file written statements with parole boards, in order to make known their wishes about whether a prisoner should be released. This reform was introduced to the federal prison system in 1984. Many victims do not take this opportunity to make their wishes known, either fearing retaliation or not wanting to dredge up unpleasant memories of past crimes.

Those who oppose the use of victim testimony to parole boards and victim impact statements in court fear that those reforms might introduce public pressure or vengeance into proceedings that should be more dispassionate. They claim that poor and uneducated offenders might be punished more severely if they are confronted with articulate victims who demand long sentences. These critics assert that sentencing and parole should be based on an individual's threat to society and behavior while in prison, not on a victim's wishes.

Supporters of these reforms argue that they draw the victim into the criminal justice system in a direct way, thereby providing a new perspective to criminal justice administrators. They also point to the greater degree of satisfaction with the criminal justice system among victims who believe their wishes have been taken into consideration in meting out punishment, arguing that a satisfied victim is more likely to report crime and aid in the prosecution of defendants in the future, and that this may help deter crime.

Summary

The criminal justice system aims to mete out justice and reduce the crime rate. In doing so, it also influences the development of criminal careers. This system has been described as a funnel or sieve that sorts out cases as they pass from the police through the courts and to the prisons.

The police were first formally organized at the municipal level in the nineteenth century. They are organized so that the most important contacts with the public and with suspects are by patrol officers, who are not easily supervised by administrators. The working personality of a police officer includes a demand for respect, suspiciousness, and the exercise of delegated and unauthorized discretion. The exercise of discretion is influenced by what an officer sees as the likely consequences of an arrest or a warning, by the community in which an offense occurs, by a suspect's demeanor, and sometimes by race and sex. Much research indicates that the police do not discriminate in dealing with black and white suspects, but there is some evidence that they are less likely to arrest females than males for certain offenses.

The police measure their effectiveness with clearance rates, which are indicators of the proportion of offenses they solve to their satisfaction. They sometimes inflate clearance rates by encouraging suspects to confess to multiple offenses. Relatively few robberies and burglaries are solved by police detectives.

Suspects who are arrested by the police have the right to have bail set at a reasonable level. The bail system discriminates against the poor. Preventive detention has been proposed as a way to reduce "bail crimes," those offenses that are committed between the time of pretrial release and the trial.

Prosecutors, who bring criminal charges against defendants on behalf of the state, measure their effectiveness by conviction rates. Defense attorneys try to get their clients acquitted, or at least get them the lightest possible sentences. Because many defendants are poor, defense attorneys are often appointed by and paid for by the state. Prosecutors and defense attorneys theoretically engage in a "fight" or adversary process, out of which the truth is supposed to emerge. In practice, they often engage in plea bargaining over guilt and an appropriate sentence in order to save the time and resources of the court. Judges then ratify the negotiated plea and sentence, treating defendants more leniently for speeding up the processing of cases. Judges preside over trials, but their most important function is probably the sentencing of convicted offenders. Juries also try cases, but no more than 5 percent of all felony cases are tried before a jury. In general, juries seem to perform quite well, in spite of their lack of legal expertise. Convicted offenders are sentenced in various ways, one of which is probation, a form of supervised release.

One problem with the courts is sentence disparity. Legal criteria are usually the basis of judges' sentences, but race sometimes plays a role in the sentencing of offenders. This may be due to direct racial discrimination, but often it is a result of organizational or economic discrimination that affects minorities more because of their lower incomes. Criminal justice procedures rather than direct racial discrimination seem to account for most of the disparity in sentences among racial and ethnic groups. However, in capital cases, murderers who kill blacks are punished less severely than murderers who kill whites. The sex of a defendant makes some difference in the sentencing of convicted offenders, with women being treated somewhat more leniently than men.

Prisons in the United States are crowded, but there is some evidence that demographic changes and prison reforms are beginning to alleviate this problem. Not everyone agrees that building more prisons is the best solution to this problem, because judges might simply imprison more offenders if there were more cells. Crowding, ineffectual prison administrators, coercive control strategies, inmate grievances, and racial discrimination sometimes lead to prison riots. Another response to these problems has been the prisoners' rights movement, which has achieved important gains through the courts since the late 1960s. Prisoners are sometimes released on parole prior to the expiration of their sentence and are then supervised on the street to help them become rehabilitated.

Recently, victims have come to play a more important role in the criminal justice system. Compensation programs and penalties of restitution are designed to repay victims for their financial losses and physical suffering. In some states, victims can testify before a judge about the sentence they believe is appropriate for an offender, and in some places they can appear before a parole board to say whether they think an offender should be released. The criminal justice system would probably function more efficiently if it counseled victims and witnesses and tried to incorporate them more into the processing of defendants.

Important Terms

bail	preventive detention
case attrition	prisoners' rights movement
clearance rate	probation
compensation	restitution
discretion	sentence disparity
parole	victim impact statement
plea bargaining	working personality

Suggested Readings

JOHN IRWIN. *The Felon.* Englewood Cliffs, N.J.: Prentice-Hall, 1970. An important examination of prison from the inmate's perspective, written by a former prisoner who is now a sociologist.

ANDREW KARMEN. *Crime Victims: An Introduction to Victimology.* Monterey, Calif.: Brooks/Cole, 1984. A useful text that includes chapters on the victim and the criminal justice system, restitution, and compensation.

DAVID W. NEUBAUER. *Criminal Justice in Middle America.* Morristown, N.J.: General Learning Press, 1974. An empirical study of the components of the criminal justice system in a small American city.

ARTHUR ROSETT AND DONALD R. CRESSEY. *Justice by Consent: Plea Bargains in the American Courthouse.* Philadelphia: Lippincott, 1976. An examination of the pros and cons of plea bargaining, including a detailed look at one case from the perspective of the defendant, the prosecutor, the defense attorney, and the judge.

JEROME H. SKOLNICK. *Justice without Trial: Law Enforcement in a Democratic Society,* 2nd ed. New York: John Wiley, 1975. A fine account of how police officers do their job, based on first-hand observations.

CHAPTER 14

Deterrence and Incapacitation

Source: Library of Congress

One justification for punishment is *deterrence,* the inhibition of criminal activity by state-imposed penalties. This rationale is a utilitarian one — that is, it is based on the idea that punishment should help a society prevent crime. Deterrence is a philosophy of punishment, but it raises empirical issues that social scientists have explored through research. For instance, research indicates that the deterrent effect of sanctions is related to the nature of the act to be prevented and to the severity, certainty, and promptness with which punishment is applied.

The Deterrence Model

Deterrence is based on assumptions about why criminals violate the law and how the law can affect their behavior. Many of these assumptions are centuries old, but recently empirical data have been collected to test their accuracy.

History of the Idea of Deterrence

Philosophers such as Cesare Beccaria (1738–1794) and Jeremy Bentham (1748–1832) argued that the punishment of criminal acts can deter potential offenders by making the negative consequences of crime greater than its rewards. Writing in the eighteenth century, Beccaria (1764, 1963: 42) stated that the goal of crime prevention should be pursued with punishments "which will make the strongest and most lasting impression on the minds of men, and inflict the least torment on the body of the criminal." He believed that punishment should be as certain as possible and as harsh as necessary to deter potential offenders, but that "all beyond this is superfluous and for that reason tyrannical" (Beccaria, 1764, 1963: 43). For Beccaria, punishment should be consistent with the principle of retribution or just deserts, a principle we examine in the next chapter.

For much of the twentieth century, the notion of deterrence was ignored or held in disrepute by social scientists, because positivists focused attention on individual and social pathologies as causes of crime. The idea of rehabilitation thus dominated the field of corrections. However, beginning with an influential paper published by the Norwegian law professor Johannes Andenaes in 1952, there has been a rebirth of interest in deterrence. Since the mid-1960s, much research has been done on the deterrent effects of punishment.

Assumptions about Behavior

The deterrence model assumes that people engage in an act only after carefully and rationally considering its costs (or risks) and benefits (or rewards). People who comply with the law seek the rewards of conformity and try to avoid the costs of deviance. Punishment supposedly induces compliance, because people fear punishment and do not want to risk their stake in conformity. In the deterrence model, the rationale for punishment is to affect future behavior, rather than to inflict pain that offenders supposedly deserve because of their past actions; the latter is the retribution or just deserts rationale for punishment.

The deterrence model assumes a degree of free will or voluntarism; it suggests that people choose how to behave, even if they are limited in their choice by social, psychological, and biological factors. However, not all behavior is governed by a careful consideration of costs and benefits, for much behavior is unplanned or habitual. Moreover, internalized values and beliefs, sometimes referred to as "conscience," often guide behavior. Other behavior may be avoided because people lack the skill or the opportunity needed to commit an act.

As we have seen in earlier chapters, rational choice is involved in some criminal behavior. Some offenders consider risks carefully and try to minimize them by planning their crimes. They consider possible gains from the crime and pick targets accordingly. However, even these offenders often lack good information on the real risks of arrest and conviction, and on the rewards to be gained from a particular crime. More importantly, many offenders do not consider risks and rewards as rationally as is assumed by the deterrence model. Many act on impulse; murderers who kill "in the heat of passion" are one example.

Deterrence and Other Effects of Penalties

In the deterrence model, a criminal penalty acts as a negative inducement or cost to discourage people from engaging in behavior that violates the law. However, deterrence is not the only effect of punishment. The very existence of a criminal penalty for an act indicates moral condemnation of the behavior and a corresponding support for certain values; people learn these attitudes through socialization and formal education. The law has an "eye-opener effect," in that it directs attention to punished acts and invites reflection on the reasons those acts are condemned (Andenaes, 1974). The actual punishment of offenders makes credible the threat of a sanction and helps convince people that the government's effort to deter crime is a serious one. Punishment also keeps some people in line by convincing them that those who violate the law gain no advantage over those who abide by the law (Zimring and Hawkins, 1973).

One analysis of the factors that inhibit criminal behavior suggests that three forces operate independently and have additive effects on keeping crime in check:

1. Moral commitment, or internalized legal norms;
2. Social disapproval, or fear of informal sanctions by peers; and
3. Threat of legal punishment, or fear of physical and material deprivation from legally imposed sanctions. (Grasmick and Green, 1980)

Usually, only the third of these factors is called deterrence. All three inhibiting forces are associated with criminal behavior, but much of the variation in criminal behavior among people cannot be explained by any of the three, because

FIGURE 14.1 A Model of Crime-Inhibiting Factors

these inhibiting effects apply only to people who are motivated to violate the law (Grasmick and Green, 1980).

One criticism of this approach to the inhibition of criminal behavior suggests that data collected at only one point in time cannot lead to firm conclusions about the effect of these inhibiting factors on criminal behavior. Subjective appraisals of social disapproval and of the threat of punishment may influence criminal activity, but involvement in crime can also alter perceptions of social disapproval and the threat of punishment. Criminal activity may show an offender that the consequences of breaking the law are not serious, lead the offender to make a moral reassessment of norms, or provide the opportunity for an offender to learn an accomplice's values (D. Greenberg, 1981). Testing the effects of the three inhibiting factors thus requires a model like the one depicted in Figure 14.1.

One study that tried to test a model like this one found that internalized normative constraints, or moral commitment, was the best predictor of later delinquency by junior and senior high school students. Perceptions of the threat of both informal and formal sanctions added significantly to the model's ability to explain subsequent delinquency. There was also some evidence that the threat of sanctions might compensate for weak internalized constraints in inhibiting delinquency (Bishop, 1984).

Some research that has tried to disentangle the relationships shown in Figure 14.1 has found a difference between "deterrent effects" — which are measured by perceived sanctions a year before a self-report questionnaire is used to measure criminal behavior — and "experiential effects" — which are measured by perceived sanctions at the time the self-report questionnaire is filled out. Experiential effects are due to the influence of past criminal behavior on current perceptions of the risk of punishment. In other words, deterrence cannot be measured accurately by questions asked at the same time that a person reports his or her criminal activity, because current perceptions of risk reflect the individual's earlier experiences with the law. Some studies indicate that the deterrent effect — measured by the association between perceived threat a year before and current self-reported crime — is much weaker than researchers had thought it to be, and that the experiential effect is substantially stronger than once thought (Minor and Harry, 1982; Saltzman et al., 1982; Paternoster et al., 1983).

Specific and General Deterrence

Deterrence can be analyzed in terms of specific deterrence or general deterrence. *Specific deterrence* means that individuals who are punished for a particular crime will not commit that crime again because their risk-reward calculations have been altered by the punishment. They have learned that the risk is greater than they thought, and so the rewards become relatively less attractive, leading them to avoid crime in the future. Specific deterrence has not been explored much, partly because when offenders are punished, many things happen before they have the opportunity to commit another crime. Thus, upon release from prison, convicted robbers may refrain from robbery (1) because they fear further incarceration (specific deterrence), (2) because they have learned that robbery is wrong (a socializing effect), (3) because they have been changed by prison treatment programs (rehabilitation), or (4) because they are older than when they entered prison and are ready to retire from a criminal career (the exiting or maturing-out effect). Researchers have not yet succeeded in separating the specific deterrence effect from these other consequences of punishment.

General deterrence is the inhibition of the desire to engage in crime among the general population through the punishment of certain offenders. Most research focuses on the general deterrence effects of punishment rather than on specific deterrence. One report on deterrence even defines it only in terms of the inhibiting effects of sanctions on the criminal activity of people other than the punished offender (Blumstein, Cohen, and Nagin, 1978: 3).

Absolute, Restrictive, and Marginal Deterrence

The effects of punishment in deterring people from crime are rarely absolute. *Absolute deterrence* means that people refrain entirely from committing crime because of the perceived threat of a penalty. If a person never commits a crime, it is not necessarily due to absolute deterrence. For several reasons, that individual might never have committed a crime, even if the act were not punished at all, and thus the person cannot be said to have been deterred from the crime (Gibbs, 1975).

Restrictive deterrence means that people limit their violation of the law in order to minimize the risk of punishment. They may continue to violate the law, but they do so less frequently or less openly, in the belief that regular and overt

The pillory was widely used in the eighteenth century to try to deter the general public from committing crime.   *Source: Trustees of the British Museum*

violation of the law increases the chance of apprehension and punishment. People who engage in crime are not absolutely deterred by the threat of punishment, but the extent to which the threat of punishment leads them to restrict their criminal activity is not known (Gibbs, 1975).

The *marginal deterrent effect* of punishment means the extent to which crime rates respond to incremental changes in the threat of sanctions (Nagin, 1978). Increasing the rate at which the police arrest offenders from 0 to 100 percent would undoubtedly deter more criminals, but increasing the arrest rate from 20 to 22 percent would probably have little or no impact on crime rates. Similarly, most research indicates that murder is not deterred by executing offenders rather than imprisoning them for life.

Deterrence and the Criminal Act

Some criminal behavior is apparently more easily deterred than other criminal behavior, either because of the nature of the offense itself or because of the way that certain crimes are planned.

A Typology of Crime Deterrence

William Chambliss (1969: 360–372) has developed a useful typology of the kinds of crimes that are more or less easily deterred by criminal sanctions.

One dimension of the offense that Chambliss says is related to the ease with which a crime can be deterred is whether it is an instrumental or an expressive act. Instrumental or goal-oriented behavior, such as theft, is more easily deterred than expressive behavior that results from the inner needs of an offender, such as a violent outburst that leads to murder. This distinction between instrumental and expressive acts is not always easy to make. For instance, a juvenile gang member may steal in order to feel a sense of mastery over others (an expressive need), rather than to acquire property (an instrumental goal). Another difficulty with the instrumental-expressive distinction is that there is some evidence that expressive acts, such as homicide, can be deterred by increasing the risk of imprisonment, the length of prison sentences, and the penalty for carrying a firearm (Gibbs, 1968; Knight, 1979).

Chambliss also links the deterrence of crime to an offender's commitment to a life of crime. Offenders who are highly committed to a life of crime are more difficult to deter than offenders who are marginally committed to crime or not committed at all to crime as a way of life. Marginal offenders are those who are committed neither to a life of crime nor to a law-abiding way of life; they are perhaps the most easily influenced by the threat of punishment. People who are not committed to crime at all do not need to be deterred by the threat of punishment (Blumstein, Cohen, and Nagin, 1978).

Table 14.1 presents Chambliss's typology of crime deterrence in terms of the expressive or instrumental nature of the act and the offender's degree of com-

TABLE 14.1   Chambliss's Typology of Crime Deterrence

Commitment to Crime as a Way of Life	Type of Criminal Act	
	Instrumental	Expressive
High	Professional thief	Most drug addicts
	Booster[a]	Some murderers
	Some check forgers	Some sex offenders
	Some murderers	
Low	Snitch[b]	Most murderers
	Parking-law violator	Some drug addicts
	White-collar criminal	Most sex offenders
	Some murderers	

[a]A booster is a professional shoplifter.

[b]A snitch is an amateur shoplifter.

SOURCE: From *Crime and the Legal Process* by William J. Chambliss. Copyright © 1969 McGraw-Hill Book Company. Used with the permission of McGraw-Hill Book Company.

mitment to a life of crime. The type of offender who is least apt to be deterred is one with a high commitment to crime as a way of life and whose offenses result from expressive needs. Thus, most addicts and some murderers and sex offenders are not easily deterred. The expressive, high-commitment nature of drug addiction makes this crime difficult to deter; heroin addicts have relapse rates that range from 50 to 97 percent after they are withdrawn from the drug.

Instrumental crimes by offenders who are not highly committed to a life of crime are probably the easiest to deter because those offenders are likely to reflect on the possible rewards and risks of committing a crime. If the costs of the crime outweigh its benefits, the offender may not commit the crime or may select a different kind of crime. A potential criminal is more likely to make such a decision if he or she has a low commitment to crime as a way of life.

Deterrence and Conventional Crime

Deterrence theory overlooks the fact that some conventional offenders, such as robbers and burglars, commit crime without carefully assessing the risks. Indeed, as we saw earlier in the book, risk may even make violation of the law exciting and thus rewarding to an offender. In addition, offenders may assess risks in quite a different way from the way that the general population does. For instance, one offender has described his feelings prior to his first mugging as follows: "I was scared, but it was exciting. You see, the whole thing, I was scared and excited. And I knew, you know, I had *a fifty-fifty chance* of either getting away or getting caught. But I figured *that was the chance I was going to take.* I wanted to get the money" (cited in Lejeune, 1977: 129; emphasis added here). This robber clearly overestimated the chance that he would be caught, for only about one-fourth of all reported robberies are solved by the police, and perhaps half of all robberies are not even reported, meaning that a mugger's real risk of being arrested is more like one in eight than one in two. Most people would probably not commit a robbery if they thought the chance that they would be arrested was one in two, but some robbers are willing to run such a risk.

Relatively few researchers have asked offenders what role the risk of arrest plays in their planning of particular crimes. Many offenders do not seem to consider the possible consequences of their crimes, because to do so would reduce their confidence in being able to perpetrate the crime or because they might not commit the crime if they seriously thought about the possibility of arrest (Conklin, 1972; Letkemann, 1973; Petersilia, Greenwood, and Lavin, 1977; Erez, 1980). Some offenders deliberately repress any thoughts of arrest before a crime; and others use alcohol or drugs to help them avoid thinking about the risks they are taking.

Conventional criminals sometimes think about the risks and rewards of their crimes. When they do, they probably tend to underestimate the risks more than do members of the general public, and they may place a greater emphasis on the rewards they expect from their crimes. This situation might result from the lack of educational and work opportunities, which makes crime seem relatively more rewarding than it would if there were alternative courses of action open to them. Offenders sometimes consider the following factors: the risk of being caught in one community rather than in another, the probability that the residents of one area rather than another will call the police, the emphasis that the police place on solving different kinds of crimes, and differences in penalties for various offenses. However, we have little systematic research that offenders weigh all of these factors before committing a crime, or that they plan their offenses in great detail in order to avoid arrest.

Deterrence and White-Collar Crime

White-collar crime usually involves instrumental acts by people with a low commitment to crime as a way of life, and thus this kind of offense is probably relatively easy to deter (Conklin, 1977; Braithwaite and Geis, 1982).

A realistic threat of detection and punishment can deter white-collar crime. Prison sentences for executives and stiff fines for corporations based on their assets or based on their illegal gains might force decision makers to consider the risk of punishment more seriously. The executives convicted of price fixing in the electrical equipment case in 1961 felt stigmatized and refused to allow their families or friends to visit them in prison. Lawyers who worked on that case believed that the prosecution, conviction, and incarceration of executives did deter price fixing:

> No one in direct contact with the living reality of business conduct in the United States is unaware of the effect the imprisonment of seven high officials in the electrical machinery industry . . . had on conspiratorial price fixing in many areas of our economy; similar sentences in a few cases each decade would almost

completely cleanse our economy of the cancer of collusive price fixing, and the mere threat of such sentences is itself the strongest available deterrent to such activity. (Spivack, 1963: 382)

One convicted executive said that the jail sentences in this case made other people in business reexamine their moral values. Some corporations established programs to reduce the chance of antitrust violations in the future, but the effectiveness of these programs was never evaluated (Whiting, 1962).

When substantial sentences were handed out to violators of the Office of Price Administration's (OPA) regulations during and after World War II, compliance with the regulations seemed to increase (Clinard, 1952, 1969). This compliance apparently resulted from the threat of punishment and the fear of injury to one's reputation.

A study of sixty-four retired middle-level executives found that several cited the threat of government sanctions as a major deterrent to illegal corporate behavior, singling out the effects of legal action against antitrust violators (Clinard, 1983). In one case, when the government filed a complaint for price fixing against bakery companies for colluding on prices, and when civil suits for treble damages were threatened, price fixing stopped and the price of bread dropped, even though no executives were actually convicted or sentenced to prison (Block, Nold, and Sidak, 1981).

In addition to imprisonment and fines, other sanctions might also deter white-collar crime. Convicted offenders might be suspended from a job or from a particular industry as a condition of probation or parole. They might be required to work at jobs that would increase their sympathy for the victims of their crimes; for instance, executives could be required to work in plants for which they had provided inadequate safety measures (Geis, 1974). One strategy to reduce corporate crime is to give adverse publicity to firms that violate the law (Fisse and Braithwaite, 1983). This might take the form of requiring corporations convicted of fraud or false advertising to spend their own money to inform the public of their violations. Firms that are repeatedly convicted of serious crimes might even be punished with a "corporate death penalty" by being forced into involuntary bankruptcy (Braithwaite and Geis, 1982).

Deterrence and Tax Evasion

Another offense that can apparently be deterred is tax evasion. The former head of the United States Bureau of Prisons has said, "The doctrine of deterrence, while it hasn't worked very well for some types of crime and offenders, has had a most benign effect on those who do not like to pay taxes" (Bennett, cited in Geis, 1974: 278). The effectiveness of the threat of detection is suggested by the response to the federal government's requirement that banks and corporations report to the Internal Revenue Service (IRS) all interest and dividends paid to individuals, beginning in 1964. This change led to a 45 percent increase in the amount of interest reported on individual tax returns, and to a 28 percent increase in the taxes paid on that income (The President's Commission on Law Enforcement and Administration of Justice, 1967b: 103).

In the mid-1970s the IRS in Idaho sought to get delinquents to pay their taxes through public embarrassment. Offices were padlocked and cars were chained to telephone poles. A 1973 memorandum stated the following:

> A proven method of preventing delinquency has been through embarrassment to certain taxpayers. It has been my experience that seizures which result in "sensationalism" tend to remain fixed in the public's mind and are a great deterrent to delinquency. (cited in *The New York Times,* November 24, 1980, p. A24)

This policy was abandoned in 1977.

In recent years, tax cheating has become less risky for offenders, and therefore more common. The number of IRS agents has declined, whereas the number of tax returns filed has increased. Even though computer audits are being used, the probability that any given tax return will be examined has fallen somewhat, down to 1.1 percent in 1986. Each IRS agent recovers six or seven times his or her salary in unpaid taxes, but efforts to reduce the size of the government bureaucracy have led to cutbacks in the IRS's staff since the mid-1970s. The reduction in deterrence from these cutbacks can be seen in the estimated increase in unpaid taxes from $29 billion in 1973 to $110 billion in 1986. In 1983, the IRS began to use computerized information on the neighborhoods in which taxpayers live, the property they own, the cars they drive, the credit card purchases they make, and the size of their telephone bills in order to identify people whose expenditures suggest that their incomes are higher than indicated by the taxes that they pay.

Deterrence and the Sanctioning Process

People have imperfect knowledge of the maximum penalties for various crimes, but they usually have some awareness of how the criminal justice system would punish them for committing a crime. People's perceptions of the severity of sanctions, the certainty with which they will be administered, and the promptness of punishment influence their choice of behavior.

Severity of Punishment

Lawmakers seem to assume that the severity of penalties has the greatest impact on behavior, for when confronted with a crime problem, they often increase penalties. In fact, such changes in penalties seem to have little effect on crime rates. Stated in another way, the marginal deterrent effect of harsher penalties seems limited, at least within the range of penalties used in any society at a given time. In some circumstances, harsh penalties can even backfire. For example, in early nineteenth-century Great Britain where over two hundred crimes could be punished with the death penalty, juries often acquitted defendants rather than send them to the gallows for relatively trivial offenses (Kalven and Zeisel, 1966).

The harshness of penalties clearly has some effect on behavior, but the limited range of penalties used for most offenses does not permit us to examine exactly how offenders react to increases or decreases in the severity of sanctions. For instance, a $100 fine for an expired parking meter would probably deter more drivers from overtime parking than would a $5 fine, and a fine less than the amount that had to be put in the meter would deter very few people. In a different context, one safecracker comments that "a law was passed which made using nitroglycerin on a safe a forty year prison term automatically. So everybody quit using it" (cited in King and Chambliss, 1984: 13–14). Alternative methods for breaking into safes were developed, but the harsher penalty did affect criminal behavior.

We do not have enough information on marginal deterrence effects to know how much crime will be deterred by a particular change in sanctions. There does seem to be a diminishing return from increased punishment at certain levels. Thus a twenty-year prison term probably deters more crime than a $10 fine, but it is not at all clear that a twenty-five-year sentence deters more crime than a twenty-year sentence.

A study in Chicago found that juvenile delinquents who were punished more harshly were arrested less often after they were punished. The "suppression effect"—that is, the drop in arrest rates after punishment—was greatest for juveniles who were treated most severely. For instance, offenders who were removed from their community and incarcerated for an indefinite time on an involuntary basis and with custodial supervision showed a greater drop in their rate of arrest after release than did juveniles who were removed from their community for a specified period and placed in a noncustodial and voluntary program. Moreover, the least harsh forms of treatment—supervision and probation—did not significantly reduce the rate at which juvenile offenders were rearrested. The researchers tentatively concluded that the juveniles reduced their involvement in delinquency because harsh punishment had altered the risk-reward ratio and deterred them from a continued high level of law-violating activity, even though their misbehavior did not cease altogether (Murray and Cox, 1979).

Certainty of Punishment

Probably more important than the maximum statutory penalty for a crime or the length of the sentences actually meted out by the courts is the certainty of some punishment for the crime. This was recognized two centuries ago by Cesare Beccaria (1764, 1963: 58), who stated the following: "The certainty of a punishment, even if it be moderate, will always make a stronger impression than the fear of another which is more terrible but combined with the hope of impunity." Thus, a 100 percent chance of a one-year prison term may well deter more crime than a 5 percent chance of a twenty-year sentence.

Increased certainty of punishment will probably have a greater effect in reducing crime rates than will increased maximum penalties, but the exact trade-off between certainty and severity is not known. A certain sentence of a $10 fine or one day in jail will probably deter few robbers, because they will think that "crime pays" if the costs are that low. Similarly, the low certainty of any punishment for white-collar crime probably limits the deterrent effect of even those laws that allow for harsh penalties. A convicted antitrust violator is, according to one estimate, less likely to be sentenced to prison than a violator of a migratory bird law (Yoder, 1978). However, a 5 percent chance of being executed would probably deter instrumental crimes by people who have little commitment to crime as a way of life; in these cases, the effect of a very severe penalty might offset the low certainty of punishment.

We have relatively little research on the exact combination of certainty and severity that maximizes the deterrence of particular crimes by various kinds of offenders. One study of felonies found an inverse relationship between certainty and severity; the greater the certainty of punishment, the less was its severity, and vice versa. Very severe penalties seemed to reduce the certainty of a conviction. At any given level of certainty, the severity of a penalty had only a weak-to-moderate relationship with the rate at which most felonies were committed. Perceived certainty of punishment had to be very high before increments in the severity of punishment would have a deterrent effect (Grasmick and McLaughlin, 1978).

One study found that juveniles' perceptions of the certainty of punishment for particular crimes reflected the actual likelihood of punishment for those offenses. However, the relationship between their perceptions of the certainty of punishment and their involvement in self-reported crime was only moderate. Objective certainty of punishment was associated with perceived certainty, but perceived certainty did not seem to be linked to self-reported crime in a direct way. The researchers concluded that for the ten offenses and for the juveniles they studied, the deterrent effect of punishment was limited (Erickson and Gibbs, 1978).

One effort to deter drug sales and drug use was a New York state law that was implemented in 1973. This law increased the severity of penalties, especially for major drug dealers, who were to be sentenced to a minimum of fifteen years and a maximum of life in prison. An evaluation of this law found that it did not reduce heroin traffic in New York City and did not reduce property crimes associated with heroin addiction (Joint Committee on New York Drug Law Evaluation, 1978). The problem with the law was that although it increased the severity of sanctions, it left several ways for defendants to avoid these penalties. As a result, certainty of punishment after passage of the law was no greater than before, and many defendants avoided severe sanctions through plea bargaining. Indeed, the more severe penalties led those who were unable to plea bargain to their satisfaction to demand trials, causing a backlog in the courts that delayed punishment (another factor that may reduce the deterrent effect of punishment) (Wilson, 1983).

It is not clear that certainty of punishment can easily be increased. Doing so would require better citizen reporting of crime, more complete recording of offenses by the police, higher arrest rates, higher rates of prosecution, or higher conviction rates. These changes cannot be made without greater expenditures, reorganization of law-enforcement agencies, or infringement on defendants' constitutional rights.

Promptness of Punishment

In addition to severity and certainty of punishment, the promptness with which sanctions are administered also seems to affect criminal behavior. However, there is little research on the impact that promptness of punishment has on violations of the law. If an offender is punished soon after committing a crime, operant conditioning theory and learning theory suggest that both the specific deterrence of that individual from additional crime and the general deterrence of the public that knows of the punishment are likely to be greater than if the offender is punished years later. The closer in time a negative reinforcement (or legal sanction) is to the crime, the more likely it is that the behavior that elicited the negative reinforcement will be avoided. Punishment in the distant future may not be associated in people's minds with the offense that elicited the sanction. This was recognized years ago by Beccaria (1764, 1963: 56), who said that

> the promptness of punishments is more useful because when the length of time that passes between the punishment and the misdeed is less, so much the stronger and more lasting in the human mind is the association of these two ideas, *crime and punishment;* they then come insensibly to be considered, one as the cause, the other as the necessary inevitable effect.

Types of Punishment

One aspect of punishment that has received relatively little attention from deterrence theorists and researchers is the type of punishment meted out to offenders. Little is known about the relative deterrent effects of imprisonment, restitution, fines, probation, and other sanctions. Marginal deterrence is often examined by focusing on the reduction of crime that results from using more of one type of penalty, rather than from using a different kind of penalty.

An experiment sponsored by the Police Foundation in Minneapolis in 1981 and 1982 tested the impact of different sanctions on men accused of domestic violence. The sanctions included arrest, mediation or advice, and ordering the violent men to leave the home for eight hours. Officers used one of these methods, chosen at random, to deal with "moderate" domestic violence, a simple assault that did not produce severe or life-threatening injury. Suspects were followed up for six months to determine if violence recurred; both official data and victims' reports were used. The results showed that arrests seemed to deter domestic assaults by male offenders. Only 10 percent of the arrested men were involved in a new official report of domestic violence within six months. By contrast, 16 percent of those receiving mediation or advice were involved in official reports of new incidents within that time, and 22 percent of those who had been ordered from the home for eight hours were involved in a new domestic dispute within six months. Using victim self-reports, 35 percent of cases in which no arrest was made led to new violence in the home within six months, but only 19 percent of the victims of men who had been arrested reported new violence within six months. This experiment involved men and women who were married or living together in low-income areas in the center of the city. The stigma of arrest for middle- or upper-class men might be even more effective in deterring domestic violence (Sherman and Berk, 1984; also, see Berk and Newton, 1985).

Parents who fail to pay child support as ordered by the court have traditionally been forced to pay only when their former spouses persist in bringing them into court and demanding payment; even then compliance is erratic. Michigan sought to change this situation by charging the courts with initiating action against delinquent parents and by sentencing to jail those parents who continued not to pay. The proactive approach by the courts and the use of jail sentences for noncompliance significantly increased the overall rate of compliance with child support agreements (Lempert, 1981–82).

Penalties different from those that have traditionally been used might increase the deterrent effect of punishment by increasing severity, certainty, or promptness. The exact combination of severity, certainty, promptness, and type of sanction that will maximize deterrence for different kinds of crimes is not yet known, but these factors strongly influence the effectiveness of punishment as a means of reducing crime.

Deterrence and the Criminal Justice System

Until recently, most deterrence theorists and researchers focused on the circumstances under which the threat of punishment deters criminal behavior. Economists who have studied crime over the last few years have raised the problem of *simultaneity:* Sanctions may reduce crime, but the crime rate also affects the sanctions that are meted out by the criminal justice system. Thus an inverse relationship between crime rates and the severity or certainty of punishment — for example, higher crime rates when punishment is less certain, and lower crime rates when punishment is more certain — may exist because the threat of sanctions reduces crime, but this inverse relationship might also exist because a high crime rate reduces the certainty or severity of sanctions. For

Using Criminology: Dealing with Domestic Violence

In the mid-1980s, city police departments and state legislatures developed policies to deal with violence between spouses as a crime, rather than as a problem to be solved within the family. This change in policy was attributable to several factors. First, feminist groups that had long been demanding that domestic violence be treated as a crime finally convinced the police and lawmakers to change their approach to the problem. Second, the growing emphasis on the victim by the criminal justice system led to greater attention to those who suffered spousal abuse. Third, the police were concerned with violence done to them when they investigated reports of domestic violence, with spouses sometimes turning on officers. Fourth, civil court damage awards led the police and city governments to change their policy toward domestic violence. For instance, one woman won a $2 million judgment against the City of New York because the police failed to protect her, despite repeated calls to them about her husband's attacks on her. Finally, research dramatically demonstrated that the police could deter domestic violence with arrests.

Criminological research was instrumental in spurring changes in police practice and state law. The Minneapolis study showed that arrest was more effective than either mediation or ordering the abusive spouse from the home for eight hours. A study by the Bureau of Justice Statistics that used National Crime Survey victimization data found that nearly half of all women who told interviewers they had been abused by their husbands did not report it to the police. Of those who did not call the police, 41 percent were assaulted again within six months, but of those who did report the domestic violence to the police, only 19 percent were abused in the subsequent six months. Both of these studies showed a strong deterrent effect of arrest on abusing spouses.

Responding to this research, as well as to the other influences discussed above, many police departments issued new guidelines for dealing with domestic violence. In 1984, the Commissioner of the New York City Police Department ordered officers to stop mediating disputes and start arresting offenders, leading to a doubling in arrests for domestic violence in one year. The new guidelines required officers to arrest suspects in all felony assaults, and to make arrests in misdemeanor assaults if the victim wanted an arrest made or if the crime was committed in view of the officer. When the assault occurred in the officer's presence, he or she was required to make an arrest, even if he or she preferred to mediate the dispute and even if the victim did not want an arrest made. Other police departments also issued new guidelines for police practice. For instance, the Seattle police were told that if a firearm or knife was involved in a domestic dispute, they should consider it a felony and make an arrest.

In 1986, Connecticut became the seventh state to require the police to make arrests in domestic disputes, regardless of whether the victim wished to prosecute. The Connecticut law required a court hearing the

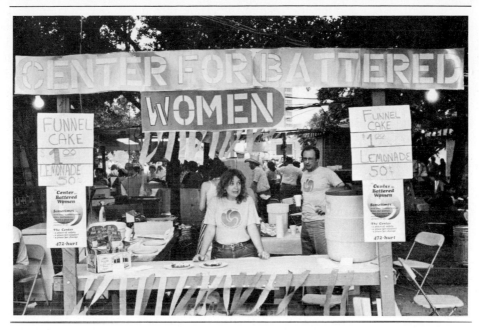

One factor leading to recent changes in the law's treatment of domestic violence has been efforts by feminist groups to increase the public's awareness of the problem. Here a group raises money to support a shelter for the victims of domestic assaults.   *Source: David E. Kennedy/TexaStock*

day after the assault, established advocates appointed by the court to help victims, required an investigation into previous abuse in the family, provided training for criminal justice personnel in dealing with domestic violence, and limited the liability of police officers who make arrests in these cases. First-time misdemeanor offenders could be fined $250 and required to participate in classes on the causes and control of rage. Their convictions would be erased if there were no more incidents within a year.

The U.S. Department of Justice, in July 1986, called on the local police to focus more on domestic violence and to deal with it as they deal with violence by strangers.

Citing estimates that more than 2 million people each year are beaten by their spouses, the Justice Department offered detailed advice to criminal justice administrators about how to deal with domestic violence. This report may encourage even more change by police departments and state legislatures to treat domestic violence as a serious crime. Research suggests that such changes will be effective in deterring violence in the family.

SOURCES: Based on "Calling Police Protects Abused Wives, Report Says," *The New York Times,* August 18, 1986, p. A9; "Justice Dept. Study Asks Tougher Policy on Domestic Violence," *The Boston Globe,* July 7, 1986, p. 34.

instance, a sudden increase in the crime rate might overburden the criminal justice system, reducing the ability of the police to arrest suspects or reducing the capacity of the prisons to incarcerate serious offenders. This would decrease the certainty and severity of punishment. Thus, the crime rate may affect the certainty and severity of penalties as much as the certainty and severity of penalties affect the crime rate (Blumstein, Cohen, Nagin, 1978). We need to be aware of this simultaneity of causation in looking at the role of the criminal justice system in deterring crime.

Deterrence and the Police

The question of simultaneity between crime rates and risk of apprehension by the police "remains unresolved at this time" (Blumstein, Cohen, and Nagin, 1978: 35). Increasing the resources of the police might increase the arrest rate and thus deter crime. However, a rising crime rate might lead to the appropriation of more resources for the police, which might increase the arrest rate and deter crime.

DETERRENCE AND SIZE OF THE POLICE FORCE   This is little evidence that increasing the resources or the numbers of the police will significantly alter crime rates. The President's Commission on Law Enforcement and Administration of Justice (1967a: 96, 106) found that for cities with populations over 500,000, there was no apparent correlation between the city's crime rate and the number of police officers per 1,000 residents of the city. At least within the range of police per 1,000 people that exists in the United States, increasing or decreasing the number of officers will probably have no significant marginal deterrent effect on crime rates (Greenberg, Kessler, and Loftin, 1983). For instance, a study of Detroit found no systematic relationship between the level of that city's crime index and the size of its police force from 1926 to 1977 (Loftin and McDowall, 1982).

It does seem that large variations in the number of police officers may affect crime rates. For instance, a ratio of one officer to every private citizen would clearly have some deterrent effect. Police saturation of certain areas sometimes occurs for a short time, and it can reduce crime, but this policy is not feasible over the long run (Sherman, 1986). At the other end of the spectrum, the presence of very few or no police officers would probably cause crime rates to rise. Several American cities have experienced widespread looting during blackouts, a time when the resources of the police are overtaxed. Montreal had disorder during a police strike in 1959, and in 1977 that city had a significant increase in crime during a police "slowdown." When the Nazis arrested the Danish police in 1944, rates of robbery, burglary, and larceny rose dramatically in spite of harsher penalties for people who were caught and convicted of crimes (Andenaes, 1974). In contrast to these impressions about the impact of reduced police presence is the conclusion of a study of eleven cities that have had police strikes (Pfuhl, 1983). This study found very limited support for the idea that such strikes have any significant or systematic effect on rates of reported crime. This conclusion is consistent with the findings of other research that police presence has a minimal deterrent effect. Of course, during a police strike it may be difficult to get an accurate count of crimes, because there are fewer officers available to take citizen reports.

One problem with studies that look at the relationship between the number of police per capita in a city and that city's crime rate is that more crimes may be recorded if there are more police officers. One study that tried to avoid this problem correlated the number of officers per capita in twenty-six cities with the NCS victimization rates for those cities. Higher numbers of police per capita were associated with lower victimization rates for household burglary, household larceny, personal larceny without contact, aggravated assault, simple assault, and rape; associated with higher victimization rates for robbery without injury and personal larceny with contact; and not significantly associated with rates of motor vehicle theft and robbery with injury (Decker, Shichor, and O'Brien, 1982).

DETERRENCE AND RISK OF ARREST   The police may deter crime by increasing the risk of arrest. Even if the police are ineffective in arresting suspects, they may deter crime if people perceive the risk of arrest to be high. Some research has found an inverse relationship between clearance rates and crime rates; in other words, the more crimes the police solve, the fewer crimes of that sort there are (Phillips and Votey, 1972; Tittle and Rowe, 1974; Logan, 1975; McPheters, 1976). A study that used victimization rates, rather than official crimes, also found that crime rates were inversely related to arrest rates (Wilson and Boland, 1976). However, a study that used data from 1964 to 1970 for ninety-eight American cities found no consistent support for the idea that higher clearance rates cause lower crime rates (Greenberg and Kessler, 1982).

The police, legislators, politicians, and the public commonly assume that the police deter crime through arrest or the threat of arrest, even though the rate at which the police solve crimes is quite low. Table 14.2 shows the percentage of index crimes cleared by arrest in 1986. These figures overestimate the chance that an offender will be arrested for any given crime, because many crimes are not reported to or recorded by the police.

Table 14.2 shows that crimes of violence are solved more easily than property crimes. This is because the offender and the victim in violent crimes are often acquainted with each other, and because face-to-face confrontations in violent crimes allow victims to identify offenders. Even though arrest rates are higher for violent crimes, these offenses are probably less easy to deter than property crimes. Violent offenses are often expressive in nature and often occur in private settings to which the police have little access (Stinchcombe, 1963; Mawby, 1981). Crimes against property seem to involve planning and consideration of risks and rewards more often than crimes of violence, but property crimes are solved infrequently and so may not easily be deterred.

TABLE 14.2   Clearance Rates of FBI Index
Crimes, 1986

Offense	Percentage Cleared by Arrest
Murder	70.2
Forcible rape	52.3
Robbery	24.7
Aggravated assault	59.4
Burglary	13.6
Larceny	19.7
Motor vehicle theft	14.8
Arson	15.3
Total index crimes	20.7

SOURCE: Federal Bureau of Investigation, *Crime in the United States, 1986: Uniform Crime Reports.* Washington, D.C.: U.S. Government Printing Office, 1987, p. 156.

DETERRENCE AND POLICE PATROL TACTICS   Police patrol cars increase the area that the police can cover, and increased mobility enhances the likelihood that officers will be at or near the scene of a crime when it occurs. However, patrol cars can isolate the police from the public and thus cut off a source of information that can be used to maintain order, prevent crime, and arrest suspects (Bittner, 1967).

There have been a few experimental studies to determine whether police patrol has a deterrent effect. Perhaps the best of these studies was conducted in Kansas City, Missouri, in 1972 and 1973 (Kelling et al., 1974). In this experiment, the number of patrol cars was doubled in five areas of the city, the number remained the same in five areas, and in five additional areas all patrol cars were taken off duty and reassigned to other areas (although they did answer calls for help). The fifteen areas were matched with each other by crime rate, characteristics of residents, and number of calls to the police. This study has been criticized because the areas that supposedly had no preventive police patrol did in fact have cars riding on the perimeter of the area, crossing the area to get to other parts of the city, and responding to calls (Larson, 1975; Pate, Kelling, and Brown, 1975). Thus the areas with no assigned patrol cars were not really entirely free of police presence.

The Kansas City experiment showed that changes in police patrol practices in the fifteen areas had "little value in preventing crime or making citizens feel safe" (McNamara, 1974: iii). There were no significant differences among the areas in the following measures of crime: rates of offenses reported to the police, rates of crime reported in victimization surveys, citizen fear of crime, and citizen satisfaction with the police.

The Kansas City experiment found no evidence of a *displacement effect,* a change in the pattern of crime without a reduction in the total amount of crime as a result of criminals' efforts to avoid punishment. Crime can be displaced from one target to another, from one area to another, or from one kind of offense to another (for instance, a burglary instead of a robbery). Displacement also refers to changes in a criminal's tactics or *modus operandi,* and to changes in the times at which crimes are committed (Hakim and Rengert, 1981a, 1981b). Visible police patrols might simply change patterns of crime by displacing crime rather than preventing it, but the Kansas City experiment found no evidence of such displacement as a result of variations in police patrol tactics.

There is, however, evidence from other studies that the police sometimes displace crime from one area to another where there are fewer officers or cars, or from a time when there are more officers and cars around to a time when the police are less likely to be present (Reppetto, 1974: 87–88). In a report on crime-reduction efforts in New York City, precinct captains and headquarters commanders claimed a drop in robbery rates as a result of police efforts, but officers on the street were more likely to believe that patrol tactics had merely displaced robbery. One community relations officer said, "As long as there are haves and have nots, we're never going to deter crime. We're just going to push it from one area to another" (cited in Farber, 1982a: B6). Displacement showed itself

> in the prostitutes whom the police have thrown off the north side of 86th Street but who parade, each night, along the south side; in the drug dealers and gamblers who renew their operations in one store or on one corner almost as quickly as they are shut down on another, and in the youths who, with their beer and their blaring radios, annoy residents of one block after they have been chased from the last. (Farber, 1982a: B6)

Even if an increase in the number of police officers could reduce the crime rate, we would have to weigh the cost of the additional officers against the number of crimes they prevent. For instance, a study of police patrols in subways found that it cost an estimated $35,000 for each felony that was prevented by increased patrol activity (Chaiken, Lawless, and Stevenson, 1974). Many people would think that such a program is too expensive, even if it does reduce crime.

Most research on the deterrent effects of the police has looked at the amount of money allocated to police departments, the number of officers on patrol, and clearance rates. Even more important than these factors may be what the police do while on patrol. An experiment in San Diego found that crimes such as robbery, burglary, theft, auto theft, assault, sex crimes, malicious mischief, and disturbances were reduced by an aggressive patrol strategy that included field interrogations or "street stops" (Boydstun, 1975; also, see Wilson and Boland, 1978, 1981–82; Jacob and Rich, 1981–82). These street stops apparently changed perceived risks of apprehension, even though they had no significant impact on the actual number of arrests made by the police.

Japanese experience is consistent with the idea that methods of police patrol can reduce the crime rate. The ratio of the police to the population is lower in Japan than in the United States, but the Japanese police patrol the streets in a way that apparently keeps the crime rate low. They spend much time getting acquainted with local residents, calling on them in their homes, and asking about suspicious persons and occurrences in the neighborhood. Cooperation between the police and the citizenry in Japan produces intensive surveillance of behavior. Such surveillance might be seen as oppressive by Americans, but it seems to contribute to Japan's low crime rate (Bayley, 1976a; Clifford, 1976).

Deterrence and the Courts

Research on crime rates and the risk of conviction indicates that there is an inverse relationship between the two; lower crime rates are associated with higher conviction rates (Blumstein, Cohen, and Nagin, 1978). Again the issue of simultaneity arises. A greater risk of conviction may deter offenders, but a lower crime rate may make convictions more likely. A high crime rate might reduce the risk of conviction if prosecutors drop cases because they lack the resources to bring all suspects to trial or if they lose cases because of hasty preparation. A high crime rate might also increase pressure for plea bargaining in order to ease the court's workload, and this might result in more guilty pleas but fewer convictions on the original, more serious charges. Because of the problem of simultaneity, one report found that "no conclusion on the evidence of a deterrent effect of the conviction risk is yet warranted" (Blumstein, Cohen, and Nagin, 1978: 44).

One study that minimized the problem of simultaneity in looking at the relationship between certainty of conviction and draft evasion offenses compared the experiences of the various states, holding constant social characteristics and public opinion toward the Vietnam War. The researchers found that a higher certainty of punishment was linked to a lower rate of draft evasion. Draft evasion cases were a small part of the caseload of the federal courts, and these cases were given high priority by prosecutors. Consequently, the association between certainty of punishment and the rate of draft evasion did not seem to be due to a high rate of draft evasion causing an overload on the criminal justice system, which might then have reduced the certainty of punishment. Instead, the research seemed to point to a deterrent effect of sanctions on draft evaders (Blumstein and Nagin, 1977).

A study of England and Wales from 1894 to 1967 suggests that changes in the certainty of punishment may cause changes in crime rates. Data of this sort are difficult to interpret, because other historical changes could have caused crime rates to rise and fall. However, the researcher provides several reasons to think that the association between certainty of punishment and crime rates was due to the deterrent effect of arrest, conviction, and punishment, rather than simply due to an overburdening of the criminal justice system (Wolpin, 1978).

One factor that often undermines the deterrent effect of conviction is the lack of promptness of punishment. The parties to criminal cases often want delay or have no particular interest in obtaining a speedy verdict. Defendants who are actually guilty seek delays so that witnesses will grow weary and refuse to come to court. Attorneys seek delays because they have taken on too many cases or because they require more time to prepare for a trial. Prosecutors go along with requests for delays because they assume that a defendant who is languishing in jail will feel pressured into pleading guilty, thus saving the court the inconvenience and expense of a trial and ensuring a conviction. Judges usually acquiesce to requests for postponements, because their refusal to grant delays could lead to the overturning of cases on appeal if the defense had inadequate time to prepare for trial (Fleming, 1973). These factors cause delay, which may reduce the deterrent effect of convictions.

Deterrence and the Prisons

Researchers have generally found an inverse relationship between crime rates and the risk of imprisonment, but some of their studies have not found an inverse association between crime rates and the actual amount of time served in prison (Blumstein, Cohen, and Nagin, 1978). One study found that higher crime rates seemed to reduce the risk of imprisonment, but it did not find that a greater risk of imprisonment reduced crime rates (Nagin, 1978). However, another study found that higher rates of incarceration did seem to lead to lower crime rates, and that lower crime rates also led to lower rates of incarceration (McGuire and Sheehan, 1983). Another study found an inconsistent relationship between crime rates and imprisonment rates from 1941 to 1978 and concluded that evidence was lacking that crime could be reduced by the imprisonment of more offenders (Bowker, 1981). One review of the research on this problem concluded that "no sound, empirically based conclusions can be drawn" about the existence of a deterrent effect of imprisonment on criminal behavior (Blumstein, Cohen, and Nagin, 1978: 42).

One strategy that has been tried as a deterrent to delinquency is a "shock sentence," with offenders being given "a taste of the bars" to keep them from further wrongdoing. For a time, the Massachusetts Department of Youth Services sentenced some juvenile offenders to thirty to sixty days of confinement, in the hope that their experience with "hard time" would break their pattern of delinquent activity. This probably would only work for people who have not already been incarcerated, and even for them it is not clear that it would be effective. For instance, one study found that a shock sentence and then probation had no apparent marginal deterrent effect over regular probation, if offenders with similar prior records were compared (Parisi, 1981).

A program similar to the shock sentence is the "Scared Straight" program. This program brings young people into prison to listen to a group of inmates talk about the unpleasantness of prison life; violence and homosexual rape are described in graphic terms to "scare straight" these young people. This program, called the Juvenile Awareness Project, was initiated at Rahway State Prison in New Jersey in 1976 and was the basis of a television documentary broadcast nationally in 1979 and shown again with a follow-up report in 1987. The show claimed that the program kept more than 80 percent of its participants from getting into trouble with the law again. However, a more systematic evaluation that used a six-month follow-up of delinquents who had and had not gone through the program found that those who had participated were actually arrested more often than those who had not (Finckenauer, 1979, 1982). This study had some methodological flaws, such as lack of random assignment of the juveniles to the treatment and control groups, but the researcher reanalyzed his data in response to methodological criticisms and still concluded that the Juvenile Awareness Project seemed more likely to set in motion a process by which those exposed to it became more rather than less delinquent. Another evaluation of the "Scared Straight" program reached a more optimistic conclusion, following up for twenty-two months a group of young men who had been arrested at least once. This study found that involvement in delinquent behavior by those who had participated in the Juvenile Awareness Project remained relatively constant after participation, but that the delinquent behavior of those who had not participated in the program increased significantly. This suggests that the program may keep delinquents from becoming more delinquent, which would have been their fate had they not been exposed to the program (Langer, 1979). This study too has been criticized for its methodology. In addition, though the participants in the Juvenile Awareness Project did better than the control group, still 85 percent of those participants engaged in delinquent acts after exposure to the program.

Deterrence and Capital Punishment

Much research has been done on the deterrent effect of capital punishment. One strategy has been to compare the homicide rates of states that have the death penalty with the homicide rates of states that do not have the death penalty. Some researchers have studied the homicide rates in a state before and after its abolition of capital punishment to determine if that change affected murder rates. Another method has been to look at murder rates in an area just before and just after executions to see if those executions affected the homicide rate. These and other studies have consistently produced no evidence that either death penalty laws or actual executions deter homicide. One cross-national study even found that the abolition of the death penalty in a country was followed by a decline in the homicide rate more often than by the increase that deterrence theory would predict (Archer, Gartner, and Beittel, 1983). However, a review of the research on the death penalty concluded that although few studies have found a deterrent effect, "the current evidence on the deterrent effect of capital punishment is inadequate for drawing any substantive conclusions" (Blumstein, Cohen, and Nagin, 1978: 62).

A frequently cited study that used econometric methods did find a deterrent effect of the death penalty (Ehrlich, 1975). However, the methodological shortcomings of this study are such as to invalidate its conclusions (Blumstein, Cohen, and Nagin, 1978; Knorr, 1979). Another study that looked at twenty-two well-publicized executions in London from 1858 to 1921 found a 35.7 percent drop in murders below the expected number in the two weeks after an offender was put to death. However, there was an increased number of murders a short time later, and by five weeks after the execution there was no net reduction in homicides (Phillips, 1980). One critic of this study says that it found a "delay effect" rather than a deterrent effect, ignored the important question of whether the death penalty has a marginal deterrent effect over life imprisonment, and used too much discretion in the choice of cases to study (Zeisel, 1982). A study of executions in the United States from 1950 to 1980 found that there was an average of thirty fewer homicides nationally in the month of highly publicized executions. Little-publicized executions were not associated with a reduction in homicides. Once executions become relatively commonplace, any deterrent effect they have apparently diminishes, because they are then considered less newsworthy and thus affect public perceptions of risk less (Stack, 1987). In contrast to these studies, an investigation of the short-term effects of four American executions failed to find a pattern of deterrence (McFarland, 1983).

There is some evidence that the administration of the death penalty may actually increase rather than decrease the homicide rate. One study found that an average of two additional homicides more than the normal number occurred in the month after an execution (Bowers and Pierce, 1980b; Bowers, 1984). This *"brutalization effect"* seems to be due to the failure of most sane and rational citizens to identify with the kind of people who are executed, whereas unstable people who already have a victim, weapon, and motive in mind may be spurred to murder by seeing the state use lethal violence to take an offender's life. Evidence that contradicts the brutalization hypothesis comes from a study that examined actual executions and concluded that states that do not execute murderers do not have lower homicide rates than states that do (Lempert, 1983). One argument against the brutalization effect of executions is that people are able to distinguish between the state's use of force against serious criminals and their own use of violence in interpersonal disputes. Moreover, the ten-year moratorium on executions beginning in 1967 should have reduced the nation's homicide rate, according to the brutalization thesis; however, over that decade, the homicide rate increased by 44 percent (Yunker, 1982). Perhaps executions encourage some people to commit murder (the brutalization effect) and dissuade others from lethal violence (the deterrent effect), but researchers have not yet been able to separate and measure these two effects (Bailey, 1983).

Most research is consistent with the conclusion that capital punishment does not deter those crimes for which it has been used in the United States — forcible rape (until 1977) and homicide. There are several reasons to expect no deterrent effect from capital punishment for these crimes. Murderers and rapists usually do not reflect much on the future consequences of their behavior. Murder often occurs between people who are intimately associated with each other. Such relationships are often charged with emotion, and this may interfere with a careful assessment of the risks of violating the law. Moreover, before an execution takes place, years may elapse while the case is appealed. This lack of

Number

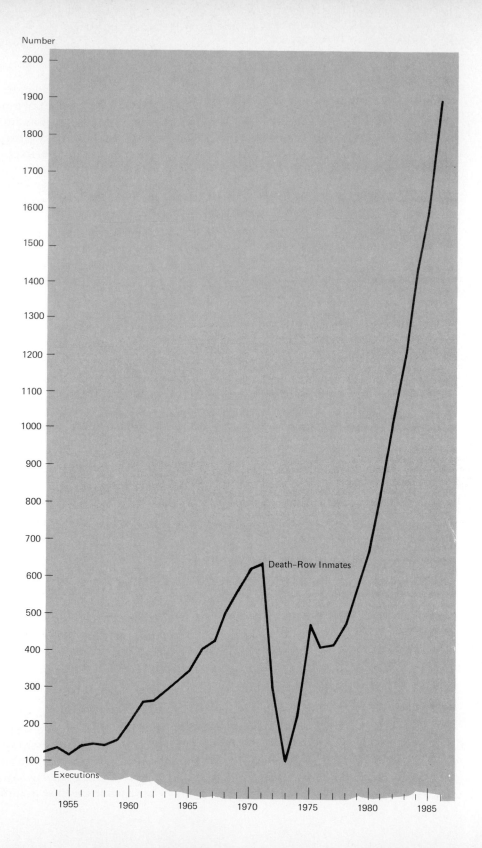

2000
1900
1800
1700
1600
1500
1400
1300
1200
1100
1000
900
800
700
600
500
400
300
200
100

Death-Row Inmates

Executions

1955   1960   1965   1970   1975   1980   1985

promptness of punishment may reduce any general deterrent effect the death penalty would have. Many capital punishment statutes apply only to specific kinds of murder, such as premeditated murders, extremely brutal slayings, the killing of police or correctional officers, or assassinations. As a result, we would not expect these laws to have a general deterrent effect on all murders.

In addition, capital punishment in the United States lacks certainty. Thus, in 1985 there were 18,976 cases of murder and manslaughter reported to the police, 273 inmates admitted to prisons under sentence of death, and eighteen prisoners executed (Bureau of Justice Statistics, October 1986). Most murderers are not sentenced to death, and most of those who are given the death penalty are never executed (see Figure 14.2).

PUBLIC OPINION, THE DEATH PENALTY, AND DETERRENCE   When the Supreme Court declared the states' death penalty statutes unconstitutional in 1972, no one had been put to death for five years. However, the public reacted to the Court's decision by demanding that the death penalty be put back on the law books. Some of this outcry may have resulted from the large increase in official crime rates from 1963 to 1972. Today there is substantial public support for the death penalty; in 1985, three-fourths of Americans favored it, according to the Gallup poll.

Most people who support the death penalty believe that it deters crime, but many say they would support it even if it had no deterrent effect. Some have argued that the public's support for the death penalty is based more on expressive or symbolic grounds than on instrumental (deterrent) grounds, and that support for the death penalty is a value position learned through socialization (Tyler and Weber, 1982). There is a direct association between support for the death penalty and the belief that it is a deterrent, but it is not clear that people support the death penalty because they believe it deters crime (Vidmar and Miller, 1980). A study of northern Californians found that most based their support for or opposition to the death penalty on symbolic or ideological grounds, rather than on a set of reasoned beliefs. Nearly all of the 58.8 percent of the sample who supported the death penalty believed it was a better deterrent than life imprisonment, but two-thirds of those supporters said they would favor capital punishment even if it had no deterrent effect. Nearly all of the 30.8 percent of the sample who opposed the death penalty believed it had no marginal deterrent effect over life imprisonment, but about three-fourths of them would continue to oppose the death penalty even if it proved to be a much better deterrent than life imprisonment (Ellsworth and Ross, 1983).

FIGURE 14.2   Number of Death-Row Inmates and Number of Executions at Year-End, 1953–1986   *Source: Bureau of Justice Statistics,* Capital Punishment 1982. *Washington, D.C.: U.S. Department of Justice, August 1984, cover page. (Updated with data for 1983 to 1986.)*

A Cross-Cultural Perspective: Capital Punishment in China

Beginning a crackdown on crime in August 1983, the Chinese government started to execute criminals at an unprecedented rate. By unofficial estimates, as many as 20,000 offenders had been put to death by January 1986. There were even rumors that the government had set quotas for the number of criminals to be executed.

Offenders facing execution often appeared at public "sentencing rallies," where they carried banners telling of their crimes. They were paraded through the streets in trucks on their way to their executions, which were carried out by a bullet in the back of the head. These public displays were designed to create a general fear of punishment and thus deter crime.

Chinese law was changed at the beginning of this crackdown on crime. Public trials were suspended, and judicial review of death sentences for violent crimes was discontinued. The expansion of capital punishment to crimes other than murder can be seen in the offenses for which fifty-one people were put to death in Peking in mid-October 1983: fifteen for murder, fourteen for "hooliganism," six for rape, eight for burglary or robbery, four for kidnapping and selling girls or women, and four for other offenses. Chinese offenders were also put to death for embezzlement; for instance, two accountants who had stolen funds to pay their gambling debts were executed.

The use of the death penalty is rooted in Chinese values that emphasize society's survival over the survival of the individual. There is a strong belief in the deterrent effect of capital punishment, and so there was no public opposition to the increase in executions. One intellectual remarked, "If you don't execute someone who committed murder, other criminals will take a lesson from him." To instill widespread fear of the death penalty, the Chinese government even executed criminals who were descendants of national heroes and who had been Communist party leaders, and women as well as men were put to death for their crimes.

In 1985, the Justice Ministry reported to a United Nations conference that the crackdown had reduced crime in China by 36 percent, though crime statistics for China are not routinely made available to the public and thus cannot be used to verify this claim.

SOURCES: Based on Christopher S. Wren, "Crime and Capital Punishment in China," *The New York Times*, November 20, 1983, p. E9; Jeff Sommer, "Chinese Execute 5000 since Start of Crime Crackdown," *The Boston Globe*, November 24, 1983, p. A42; John F. Burns, "When Peking Fights Crime, News Is on the Wall," *The New York Times*, January 28, 1986, p. A2.

Research by social scientists has focused on the deterrent effects of capital punishment, and the results of their work are consistent with the idea that executions do not deter crime, even though this proposition cannot be said to be proved. Still, people in the United States continue to support the death penalty, as do people in other societies such as China (see the Cross-Cultural Perspective). Public attitudes toward the death penalty seem to be based as much on ideas of retribution or just deserts as on ideas of deterrence. Issues such as the value of human life, the moral justification for the state's taking the life of a convicted offender, and public outrage at certain criminals would exist even if there were definitive proof that the death penalty does or does not deter crime. We examine some of these issues in the next chapter.

Incapacitation

Incapacitation is the custodial control of convicted offenders so that they cannot commit crimes that affect the general public (Van Dine, Conrad, and Dinitz, 1979: 125). Incapacitation must be separated from specific and general deterrence and from rehabilitation as ways to reduce the crime rate. Incapacitation is based on the idea that offenders will commit a certain number of crimes if they remain in society, and that those crimes can be prevented by placing the offenders in prison for some time. Whether they reform during that time is not the issue; what is important is that they do not commit more crimes while in prison. The incapacitation rationale for punishment was succinctly stated by a Catholic priest as follows: "I am concerned that people who assault human lives should be safely contained like nuclear waste so their destruction in our midst will stop" (Byrne, 1979: A23).

According to James Q. Wilson (1983), incapacitation would work if three assumptions were correct:

1. Some offenders are repeaters.
2. Offenders who are taken off the street are not immediately and completely replaced by other offenders.
3. Prison does not increase crime by changing inmates in ways that offset the reduction in crime from incapacitation.

Wilson suggests that the first assumption is clearly correct. The second one is plausible for certain offenses. Replacement occurs in organized crime families, and probably among prostitutes, drug dealers, and white-collar offenders to some degree. Replacement is probably unimportant for crimes of family violence and for conventional crimes. Wilson acknowledges that the third assumption is debatable, but he suggests that the "schooling" effect of prison probably does not outweigh its incapacitative effect.

Estimating the effect of incapacitation on crime rates is difficult. Because we lack good data on criminal careers—specifically on how many offenses different criminals will commit in a given period—it is difficult to determine how much crime is prevented by locking up offenders for a time. Offenders who are at the end of a criminal career might have stopped committing crime even if they had not been imprisoned, and so for them there would be little or no incapacitative effect.

Types of Incapacitation

Several approaches to the development of a policy of incapacitation have been proposed, with each approach differing in how to determine which offenders should be held in prison for longer terms. Three approaches are collective incapacitation, selective incapacitation, and criminal career incapacitation (Greenberg, 1975; Cohen, 1983a, 1983b).

COLLECTIVE INCAPACITATION   One approach to incapacitating offenders is *collective incapacitation,* a policy of giving the same prison sentence to everyone convicted of a particular offense (Cohen, 1983a, 1983b). Estimates of how much a policy of collective incapacitation would reduce crime vary, depending on assumptions about how many crimes the average offender commits during a year on the street. Collective incapacitation might reduce crime by about 10 to 20 percent, a smaller effect than supporters of this policy sometimes claim. Even this much of a reduction would require a substantial increase in the prison population, and a corresponding investment of tax revenue to construct new prisons. It is not clear how much support there would be for higher taxes to build new prisons if people knew that to achieve a 10 percent reduction in the crime rate would require a doubling, a tripling, or even more of an increase in the prison population (Cohen, 1983a, 1983b; Blumstein et al., 1986).

SELECTIVE INCAPACITATION   A more refined notion than collective incapacitation is predictive restraint or *selective incapacitation.* Instead of holding all offenders of a particular type in prison, only those who are the most likely to commit more crime if released would be held. This approach tries to separate high-risk offenders from low-risk offenders, and hold only those who are the most likely to be dangerous if released.

An important study of selective incapacitation by Peter Greenwood (1982, 1983, 1984) proposes a system that would help criminal justice practitioners decide which offenders should get long, "incapacitating" prison sentences and which ones might be released or placed in alternative programs. In this way, the limited amount of prison space might be allocated more efficiently and crime rates reduced. Greenwood claims that his plan could reduce robberies by adults in California by 20 percent with only a 2.5 percent increase in the prison population. A reanalysis of the data concluded that Greenwood's estimate of the expected reduction in the robbery rate was too high, and that the most favorable effect would be a 13 percent reduction (Visher, 1986).

Using interviews with incarcerated robbers and burglars, Greenwood (1982, 1984) found that the offenders who perpetrated the most crimes in a given period had four or more of the following characteristics:

1. An earlier conviction for the same offense;
2. Imprisonment for more than half of the two years prior to the current arrest;
3. A conviction before the age of sixteen;

4. Previous commitment to a juvenile institution;
5. Use of heroin or barbiturates during the previous two years;
6. Use of heroin or barbiturates as a juvenile; and
7. Unemployment for half or more of the preceding two years.

Among imprisoned robbers, those who fit four or more of these criteria committed an average of thirty-one robberies per year while on the street, compared with an average of only two robberies per year for those who fit one or none of the criteria.

Critique of Selective Incapacitation. Greenwood's study of selective incapacitation has been subjected to criticism, some of it on methodological grounds. For instance, there is a problem in extrapolating from data gathered from a sample of incarcerated robbers and burglars to robbers and burglars who are still on the street. Offenders who are not locked up might commit less crime, or more crime, than inmates; not knowing which is the case makes it impossible to predict what impact a policy of selective incapacitation would have on offenders who are still at large.

Greenwood's study relies on self-reported information, and this information would probably not be available at a hearing in which a judge decides how to sentence an offender. Moreover, some of the criteria listed by Greenwood to predict behavior would not be available to the judge; for instance, juvenile records are often confidential. There is also some reluctance to use certain criteria — such as employment history — as a basis for incarcerating offenders for long periods.

Critics claim that the statistical association between the predictive criteria and subsequent criminal behavior might be good by some standards, but that it is weak enough that many errors of prediction would be made if the scale were used to predict behavior. Specifically, there is much concern with the high rate of "false positives," offenders who would be predicted to be likely to repeat their crimes and thus be incapacitated, even though they would in fact not have returned to crime if they had been released (Blackmore and Welsh, 1983; Cohen, 1983a, 1983b; Von Hirsch, 1984a, 1984b; Decker and Salert, 1986).

One response to these criticisms is that judges and parole boards now decide on sentences and release dates on the basis of their guesses about future behavior, and a selective incapacitation policy would simply allow them to use available data in the most efficient way possible to make their decisions. Statistical predictions may err, but even more mistakes are probably made when criminal justice practitioners operate on hunches about offenders' future behavior (Greenwood, 1982, 1984).

In addition to the methodological criticisms of selective incapacitation, there are also some moral objections. One is that offenders should get the punishment they deserve, based on the seriousness of the crime and their own blameworthiness; this is the policy of retribution or just deserts that we examine in the following chapter. Some of Greenwood's criteria fit a just deserts approach to punishment; indeed, a good case could be made that the only criterion that may not be an indicator of an offender's blameworthiness is unemployment for more than half of the preceding two years. However, critics argue that prior criminal history should play a less important role in determining a just penalty than does the harmfulness of the offense itself, and that none of Greenwood's predictive criteria base punishment on the amount of harm done (Von Hirsch, 1984a, 1984b). On the other hand, Greenwood's approach would seem to be compatible with those just deserts models that make use of the blameworthiness of the offender as well as the harmfulness of the crime.

Most researchers, including both Greenwood and his critics, object to the use of predictive criteria over which offenders have no control, even if those criteria are associated with future criminal conduct. Thus, race, class, sex, and perhaps unemployment record might be excluded from predictive schemes. Only unemployment is on Greenwood's list of criteria, and it might be argued that unemployment to some extent reflects voluntary behavior by the offender. One researcher found that home atmosphere when young and parental attitudes and behavior predicted later convictions of males for index crimes, but she concluded that people could not be punished on the basis of such predictors because they were not responsible for those factors in the same way that they were responsible for their own criminal activity (McCord, 1981). Making predictions of future behavior is difficult, but not making predictions creates problems too, for it means that all offenders would be sentenced to the same term even though research shows that they are not equally dangerous (Greenwood, 1984).

CRIMINAL CAREER INCAPACITATION   In addition to collective and selective incapacitation, a third approach is *criminal career incapacitation* (Cohen, 1983a, 1983b). This approach would identify classes of criminals who seem to be the most likely to remain active in crime, and then incarcerate them. For instance, a study in Washington, D.C., found that convicted robbery and burglary defendants committed crimes at high rates during relatively short criminal careers. Short prison sentences might significantly reduce robbery and burglary rates by locking these offenders up during the most active periods in their careers. For instance, a minimum two-year sentence for all adults convicted of robbery would have produced an 8 percent drop in robberies by adults, while increasing the prison population by 7 percent (Blumstein and Cohen, 1979; Cohen, 1983a, 1983b).

This criminal career incapacitation approach would use past and present criminal records to sentence offenders, thereby avoiding some of the problems of selective incapacitation models that use personal data to predict future behavior. In addition, criminal career incapacitation would be a form of "targeted collective incapacitation" and would be applied in the same way to groups of similar offenders.

One researcher who has looked closely at criminal careers says that existing data do not permit us to identify, with confidence, who will continue in a criminal career. We know that there is a group of offenders who commit much crime over time, but identifying them accurately has proved difficult so far (Petersilia, 1980).

Career Criminal Programs. With federal support, local district attorneys' offices around the country have established units to prosecute career criminals who repeatedly commit felonies. These programs concentrate resources on those suspects who have prior records of serious crimes in an effort to incapacitate them as quickly and for as long as possible. For instance, a New York state program focused on offenders with at least one prior felony conviction who were currently charged with a major crime. More than 95 percent of these defendants were convicted, and nearly four-fifths of those who were convicted were sentenced on the highest charge they faced (Fowler, 1981).

Career criminal programs have managed to increase rates of conviction and incarceration and the length of sentences by only a small amount, although that amount is statistically meaningful (Phillips and Cartwright, 1981). These programs have achieved a slight reduction in crime rates, but their major importance seems to have been as a symbolic gesture to show the public that the criminal justice system can work effectively at times (Greenwood, 1980).

Summary

Deterrence is the utilitarian philosophy that criminal activity can be inhibited by state-imposed punishment. This model assumes that offenders rationally consider the risks and rewards of crime before acting. Sometimes this assumption is correct, but not all offenders act with deliberation. Deterrence is but one of several effects of criminal sanctions, and separating it from the other effects has proved difficult.

Specific deterrence refers to the impact of a penalty on the offender who is punished. General deterrence refers to the effect that penalties have on the behavior of the general public. Penalties rarely deter crime absolutely, but sometimes they cause offenders to restrict their criminal activity. Marginal deterrence refers to the greater impact of one penalty rather than another on criminal behavior.

Instrumental acts are probably easier to deter than expressive crimes, and offenders who are not committed to crime as a way of life are easier to deter than those with a commitment to crime. White-collar offenders are probably relatively easy to deter by the threat of punishment, because they commit instrumental crimes and have a low commitment to crime as a way of life.

Severity of punishment is probably less important in deterring crime than certainty of punishment. A high certainty of even a relatively minor penalty may reduce the amount of some kinds of crime. Punishment is probably a better deterrent if administered promptly than if delayed. In addition, the type of sanction makes a difference in determining the degree to which criminal behavior is deterred.

The impact of the police, the courts, and the prisons on crime rates is difficult to determine, because the problem of simultaneity arises; that is, crime rates affect the criminal justice system, just as the criminal justice system influences crime rates. The size of the police force does not seem to have much effect on a city's crime rate. There is little evidence that police patrol tactics have a major impact on the crime rate, although they may sometimes displace crime from one place to another or from one time to another. A higher probability of conviction can deter crime, but again the problem of simultaneity arises in interpreting the data. The same is true for the relationship between rates of imprisonment and crime rates.

There is little or no evidence that capital punishment deters the crimes for which it has been used, but research has not yet definitively established the absence of a deterrent effect. There is some evidence that executions may "brutalize" a population and increase a society's homicide rate. The low certainty of this very severe penalty and the lack of promptness in administering it suggest that capital punishment is unlikely to deter crime.

Incapacitation is the policy of locking up offenders to prevent them from committing crimes that affect the general public. Collective incapacitation is a policy of sentencing everyone convicted of a particular crime in the same way; this policy would be expensive to implement and would reduce crime less than its supporters claim. Selective incapacitation would imprison those convicted offenders who are the most likely to commit more crime if released. This form of predictive restraint would use past behavior, including criminal activity, to determine who should be incarcerated. A third policy is criminal career incapacitation, an approach that would incarcerate those kinds of criminals who seem to be the most likely to remain active in crime. Criminal career programs that concentrate the resources of district attorneys' offices on convicted felons have had only a small impact on crime rates, but they may show the public that the criminal justice system can work effectively at times.

Important Terms

absolute deterrence
"brutalization effect"
collective incapacitation
criminal career incapacitation
deterrence
displacement effect
general deterrence

incapacitation
marginal deterrent effect
restrictive deterrence
selective incapacitation
simultaneity
specific deterrence

Suggested Readings

ALFRED BLUMSTEIN, JACQUELINE COHEN, AND DANIEL NAGIN. *Deterrence and Incapacitation: Estimating the Effects of Criminal Sanctions on Crime Rates.* Washington, D.C: National Academy of Sciences, 1978. An important review of the research on deterrence and incapacitation.

JACK P. GIBBS. *Crime, Punishment, and Deterrence.* New York: Elsevier, 1975. A detailed examination of the deterrence model of punishment.

PETER W. GREENWOOD, WITH ALLAN ABRAHAMSE. *Selective Incapacitation.* Santa Monica, Calif.: Rand, 1982. A report on an important study of selective incapacitation.

MARK H. MOORE ET AL. *Dangerous Offenders: The Elusive Target of Justice.* Cambridge, Mass.: Harvard University Press, 1984. An evaluation of proposals to deal selectively with dangerous offenders.

FRANKLIN E. ZIMRING AND GORDON J. HAWKINS. *Deterrence: The Legal Threat in Crime Control.* Chicago: University of Chicago Press, 1973. Another detailed exploration of the deterrence model and its implications for the reduction of the crime rate.

CHAPTER 15

Retribution

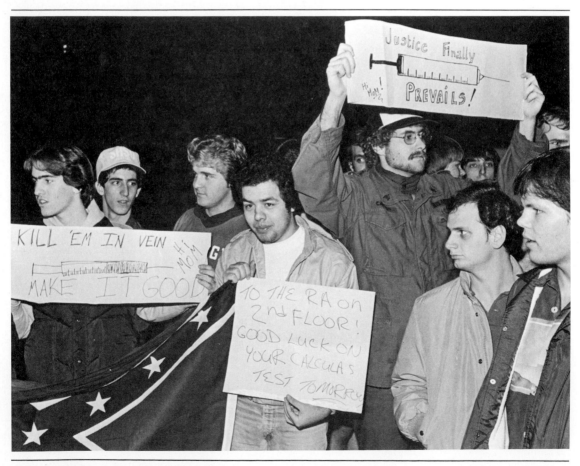

Source: Sygma

In 1981, *The New York Times* and other newspapers carried editorials that strongly opposed parole for Sirhan Sirhan, the man who assassinated Senator Robert Kennedy in 1968. The editorials argued that an early parole, which was not granted, would have provided too lenient a sentence for a crime the magnitude of Sirhan's.

In another case that had received much media attention a few months earlier, William Rummel was sentenced to life in prison for his third felony conviction. The three crimes leading to this sentence under Texas's habitual offender law cost victims a total of $229.11 and involved no violence or threat of violence. The Supreme Court ruled by 5 to 4 that this sentence was not unconstitutionally "cruel and unusual," but Rummel eventually gained his release because of procedural irregularities.

In a 1987 case, a fourteen-year-old boy in Illinois was convicted of breaking into a home to steal firearms in order to join a street gang, and then shooting five children in the home and cutting the throat of a sixth. None of the victims died. The boy, however, received a sentence of 120 years in prison and will not be eligible for parole until he is seventy-four years old.

In another case that same year, former U.S. Secretary of the Treasury Robert Anderson, who was seventy-seven years old, was convicted of evading the payment of income taxes and of operating an illegal offshore bank, which cost investors $4.4 million. He could have been imprisoned for ten years and fined $500,000, but the judge took into account his "distinguished service . . . rendered at top levels of government and the civic honors [he had] received" and sentenced him to one month in jail, five months of house arrest, five years on probation, payment of all the taxes he owed, and restitution to the victims of his banking scheme (cited in Prial, 1987: A1, A27). In court, the judge said that he meted out this sentence because the community had the right to be protected from this offender.

These cases raise the issue of how much punishment offenders deserve for their crimes. In the previous chapter, we looked at deterrence, a utilitarian rationale that requires sanctions to keep potential offenders from committing crimes in the future. The next chapter examines the rehabilitation rationale, the idea that punishment should reform or change offenders so that they do not commit crimes again. In contrast to deterrence and rehabilitation, *retribution* or *just deserts* reflects the idea that offenders should be punished because they deserve to suffer for the harm they have caused. Retribution is oriented toward behavior that the offender has already engaged in, rather than toward future conduct of the offender or other potential offenders.

The Retribution Model

The retribution or just deserts rationale for punishment asserts that people who violate the law deserve punishment because they have intentionally hurt others. If there is no harm, a retributivist would claim there should be no punishment.

Retributivists argue that offenders deserve to be punished because they have gained an advantage over others by their crimes, and they must be punished in order to restore a balance among all citizens. The theory of retribution thus sees punishment as deserved and necessary "to restore an objective order rather than to satisfy a subjective craving for revenge"(Van den Haag, 1975: 11).

Retribution and Vengeance

Retribution differs from *vengeance,* which is "private and personal" and not imposed by an established authority such as the state. In contrast, retribution requires an authority with the acknowledged right to mete out sanctions to convicted offenders (Armstrong, 1971). Whereas vengeance is typically motivated by the desire to be gratified or compensated for a loss, retribution is justified instead by the need to enforce the law and maintain social order (Van den Haag, 1975).

The retribution rationale is commonly associated with *lex talionis,* the principle of "an eye for an eye, a tooth for a tooth," which was expressed in the Code of Hammurabi in the eighteenth century B.C. To take this rule literally, a person who blinded another person would be blinded in return. Being made to pay a small fine would be an unjustly lenient sentence, and execution would be an unjustly harsh penalty. Thus, retributivists claim that offenders should be punished because they deserve to suffer harm. Moreover, offenders should be punished only in direct proportion to the harm they have caused. The idea of making punishment proportional to the seriousness of the crime makes mercy possible, "because to be merciful is to let someone off for all or part of a penalty which he is recognized as having deserved" (Armstrong, 1971: 36).

Some critics argue that the principle of just deserts or retribution is simply a way to justify harsher criminal sanctions, perhaps to shore up a faltering capitalist economy (Reiman and Headlee, 1981; Reiman, 1982). Others point out that just deserts theorists have not supported harsh penalties in recent years, and that their work has not been directed at strengthening a troubled capitalist system (Greenberg and Humphries, 1982). In response to the criticism that a just deserts model inevitably leads to severe sanctions, one lawyer writes as follows:

> If one looks at the sentencing standards actually adopted in this country, one is struck by the fact that several of the more desert-oriented schemes (those of Minnesota and Oregon, for example) are moderate in their penalty levels, whereas some of the harshest systems (e.g., the sentencing standards adopted in New Mexico and Indiana) stress goals of incapacitation and deterrence. (Von Hirsch, 1981: 778)

Retribution Compared with Deterrence and Rehabilitation

The principle of retribution suggests that people who violate the law are blameworthy and deserve moral disapproval for their acts. This reprobation is seen as the basis for punishment, even if that punishment does not serve a socially useful function such as deterring people from crime or rehabilitating offenders.

Retributivists assume that offenders are responsible and rational people who have freely chosen to violate the law. This implies that behavior is not determined by forces beyond people's conscious control, and that people are aware that punishment may result from their breaking the law. Retributivists sometimes assert that punishing people only because they deserve to suffer for having inflicted harm on others is treatment with dignity, because such an approach assumes that people who choose to break the law will pay the price in terms of punishment. This contrasts with the deterrence perspective, which has as its aim the social goal of crime control; offenders are punished so that they or other people will not commit crime in the future. The principle of retribution also differs from the rehabilitation perspective, which sees criminals as people who have made an incorrect decision to commit crime that they will not make again if they can be reformed. Some have claimed that the idea implicit in the rehabilitation perspective that offenders would not commit crime if they were the "right" kind of people undermines the dignity of those who break the law (Kittrie, 1971).

A retributive system of punishment would thus treat offenders as responsible people who have freely chosen to violate the law and who should be held accountable for their behavior. Unlike the theories of deterrence and rehabilitation, retribution does not require that punishment serve a larger social good. As one philosopher notes,

> It is too rarely noticed that retributivists in principle are fundamentally indifferent between the state of the world in which there is no crime, and the state of the world in which there is a wide variety of horrible crimes each of which is punished fully and exactly as retribution requires. Depressing the crime rate is of no concern to the retributivist; neither is avoiding recidivism; he willingly leaves these concerns to the utilitarian, thereby revealing just how narrow are his interests in the overall social problem of crime and punishment. (Bedau, 1977: 69)

If the only goal of punishment were to deter people from crime, innocent people might be punished as long as the public believed they were actually guilty. The punishment of individuals who were thought to be guilty might then deter others from criminal behavior. Similarly, a very severe penalty administered with certainty might have a strong deterrent effect; thus a thirty-year prison term for petty theft might deter stealing. The usual objection to punishing the innocent and to very harsh penalties is that those penalties are unjust. It is this idea of the "justness" of penalties that is the essence of a retribution rationale for punishment.

If rehabilitation were the only goal of punishment, people identified as potentially dangerous might be imprisoned and subjected to treatment even before they were convicted of a crime. If there were no effective treatment for a mass murderer, the rehabilitation rationale might require that such an offender not be imprisoned at all. If there were an effective treatment method that could fully reform a petty thief with a thirty-year prison sentence, such a penalty might be justified in terms of rehabilitation. The usual objection to penalties such as these is that they are fundamentally unjust. Indeed, it has been argued that if there were general agreement that a six-month prison term is a just penalty for petty theft, keeping a convicted petty thief locked up for even one month longer would be improper, even if that offender were rehabilitated by the extra month in prison and even if other people considering theft were deterred by that extra month (Von Hirsch, 1976).

Retributivists assert that deterrence and rehabilitation are secondary or derivative goals of punishment; the primary justification for punishment is that offenders deserve to be punished in proportion to the harm they have inflicted on the victim and on society. However, others suggest that deterrence and rehabilitation should play a part in determining sentences. Thus, one philosopher says that "a modified retributive theory is perfectly possible, one which only uses retributive considerations to fix some sort of upper limit to penalties and then looks to other factors to decide how much and what sort of pain shall be inflicted" (Armstrong, 1971: 38–39). A just deserts model might thus set an upper limit, a lower limit, or a range of penalties. Considerations such as deterrence, incapacitation, or rehabilitation might then play a part in determining where within those limits the actual punishment falls (Morris, 1981; Wilson, 1983). For instance, a 1979 report by the American Bar Association called for a sentencing system in which just deserts would set broad limits but selective incapacitation would determine specific punishments. Some retributivists disagree with this approach, claiming that penalties should be proportional to the seriousness of the current offense, and that other considerations should not play a role in determining punishment (Von Hirsch, 1981, 1985).

A strict retributivist might argue about the appropriateness of the penalty meted out in a 1984 case in which a sixty-six-year-old man shot and killed his twenty-seven-year-old son, who had been suicidal and who had been disfigured after dousing himself with gasoline and setting himself on fire. The judge sentenced the father to one hundred hours of community service a month for five years, saying that no punishment could be more severe than what the father had already suffered. The judge saw the crime as a mercy killing that had caused the father great anguish, and believed that a relatively light sentence would not reduce the deterrent effect of the law for others because of the unusual circumstances of the case. The judge also apparently thought the father was not in need of rehabilitation. Retributivists might claim that the harm done, the taking of a life, was worthy of harsher punishment, even though they might agree that the circumstances of the crime could be used to mitigate the father's penalty.

A System of Just Deserts

A workable system of retribution or just deserts would require the rank ordering of crimes by their relative seriousness and the rank ordering of punishments by their relative unpleasantness. Seriousness of crimes and unpleasantness of penalties are not objective facts about crime and punishment, so these rankings must be based on subjective evaluations (Erickson and Gibbs, 1979). These scales must be carefully devised; attention must be given not only to the relative rank ordering of different crimes and different punishments, but also to the intervals between points on each scale (Hospers, 1977). For instance, a twenty-year prison term may be perceived as more unpleasant than a fifteen-year term, and a fifteen-year term may be seen as more unpleasant than a ten-year term. However, it is not obvious that people will regard a twenty-year term as being as much more unpleasant than a fifteen-year term as a fifteen-year term is in comparison to a ten-year term.

After researchers develop scales of the seriousness of crimes and the severity of penalties, they then must find a way to link the two scales so that crimes of specific degrees of seriousness will be associated with penalties of certain levels of severity (Von Hirsch, 1976; Nevares-Muniz, 1984).

The Seriousness of Crimes

A scale that ranks offenses by seriousness might be based on the amount of harm caused by a crime and the blameworthiness of the offender, with harmfulness and blameworthiness being combined into a single measure of the seriousness of the crime (Bedau, 1977). There has been some research to develop a scale of the harmfulness of different crimes, and also some research on how to rank offenders by degree of blameworthiness. There has, however, been little work to develop a measure of the seriousness of crimes that combines harmfulness and blameworthiness.

BLAMEWORTHINESS OF OFFENDERS The issue of using the blameworthiness of an offender to judge the seriousness of a crime is a complex one. One form of retribution theory claims that penalties should be imposed only for the harm caused by the crime; this position would ignore the perpetrator of the offense. Another form of retribution theory holds that because offenders should be punished as they deserve, their blameworthiness must be considered in determining just sentences.

Blameworthiness can be measured in different ways. One way is to use the motivation or mental state of the offender to determine blameworthiness. There is some evidence that people's judgments of the seriousness of crimes are affected by the mental state they attribute to offenders, independently of the effect on those judgments of the harm done by offenders. When no mental state is specified, people tend to attribute intentionality to conventional criminals, and recklessness or negligence to people who commit certain white-collar offenses (Sebba, 1980, 1984).

Blameworthiness may also be judged by the circumstances of a crime. Thus, an offender who is involved in a victim-precipitated crime or who is an unwilling or peripheral participant in a crime might be treated as less blameworthy than someone who plans and perpetrates a crime alone.

Perhaps the most common way to measure blameworthiness is by the number and seriousness of an individual's prior convictions. It is assumed that an offense is more serious if it is committed by a person who has committed other crimes in the past, rather than if it is committed by a first-time offender. There are, however, some problems with using prior record as an indicator of blameworthiness. One problem is that prior record can be measured in several ways (Welch, Gruhl, and Spohn, 1984). Another problem is that the use of prior arrests or prior convictions to indicate blameworthiness might lead to "a cyclic reconfirmation of criminality" (Farrell and Swigert, 1978: 451). Because some research indicates that there is a bias in the criminal justice system against lower-class offenders—with such offenders being more likely than middle-class offenders to be arrested, convicted, and severely punished for the same crime—the use of prior records to indicate blameworthiness and determine penalties might have the effect of locking lower-class offenders into criminal careers.

HARMFULNESS OF CRIMES   More research has been done on developing a scale to measure the harmfulness of crimes than has been done on measuring the blameworthiness of offenders. Sellin and Wolfgang (1964) carried out a pioneering study of the perceived seriousness of offenses and found widespread agreement about how crimes should be ranked. They showed that various components of a crime, such as amount of injury to the victim and amount of monetary loss, could be assigned scores, and a summary score could then be derived for the offense. This permitted Sellin and Wolfgang to rank crimes by their harmfulness and to state how much more serious one crime was than another.

Table 15.1 shows the values assigned to the various elements of a crime incident. A robbery in which the victim suffered minor injuries and lost $300 when verbally threatened would have an overall score of 6. This is the sum of 1 point for minor injury, 3 for the theft of $300, and 2 for verbal intimidation in connection with a theft. A robbery in which there was no injury to the victim but a loss of $5 as a result of verbal intimidation would receive a score of 3. This is the total of 0 points for no injury, 1 point for the loss of $5, and 2 points for verbal intimidation in connection with the theft. We could thus say that the first robbery was twice as serious as the second one.

Sellin and Wolfgang's scoring system allows for a more meaningful measurement of crime than is possible by just counting the number of incidents. The difference between a bank robbery in which a guard is seriously injured by an armed offender who steals $10,000 and a schoolyard robbery in which a child gives up his lunch money because of a verbal threat would not show up in the FBI's UCR statistics, because each event would be counted as one robbery. Sellin and Wolfgang's scoring system would emphasize the difference between the incidents. The bank robbery would be scored 16. This is the sum of 4 points for the use of a weapon in connection with the theft, 7 for injury to the guard, and 5 for the theft of $10,000. The schoolyard robbery would be scored 3: 1 point for the theft of less than $10 plus 2 points for verbal intimidation connected with the theft.

A national survey conducted in 1977 asked people to rank 204 illegal acts

TABLE 15.1   Seriousness Scores for Elements
of Crimes

Element of the Crime	Score Value
Minor injury to victim	1
Victim treated and discharged	4
Victim hospitalized	7
Victim killed	26
Victim of forcible sexual intercourse	10
Intimidated by weapon, add	2
Intimidation of persons in connection with theft, etc. (Other than in connection with forcible sex acts):	
Physical or verbal only	2
By weapon	4
Forcible entry of premises	1
Value of property stolen and/or damaged	
Under $10	1
$10–$250	2
$251–$2,000	3
$2,001–$9,000	4
$9,001–$30,000	5
$30,001–$80,000	6
Over $80,000	7
Theft of motor vehicle (recovered, undamaged)	2

SOURCE: Thorsten Sellin and Marvin E. Wolfgang,
The Measurement of Delinquency. New York: John Wiley,
1964, p. 298. Copyright © John Wiley & Sons, Inc.
Reprinted with permission.

(Wolfgang et al.; 1985). Table 15.2 shows the average severity scores for some of these offenses. In general, different kinds of people agreed on the ranking of the crimes. However, victims tended to assign higher severity scores than non-victims did. In addition, blacks and other minorities generally assigned lower severity scores than did whites, and older people ranked thefts with large losses as more severe than did younger respondents. In ranking a crime, people took into account factors such as the following:

- The ability of the victim to protect him/herself
- Extent of injury and loss
- For property crimes, the type of business or organization from which the property is stolen
- The relationship of the offender to the victim. (Bureau of Justice Statistics, October 1983: 5)

Public Ranking of Severity of Crimes

Severity Score	Offense
72.1	A person plants a bomb in a public building. The bomb explodes and twenty people are killed.
52.8	A man forcibly rapes a woman. As a result of physical injuries, she dies.
43.2	A person robs a victim at gunpoint. The victim struggles and is shot to death.
39.2	A man stabs his wife. As a result, she dies.
33.8	A person runs a narcotics ring.
27.9	A woman stabs her husband. As a result, he dies.
24.9	A person intentionally sets fire to a building, causing $100,000 worth of damage.
22.9	A parent beats his young child with his fists. The child requires hospitalization.
20.6	A person sells heroin to others for resale.
19.5	A person smuggles heroin into the country.
19.5	A person kills a victim by recklessly driving an automobile.
15.9	A teenage boy beats his mother with his fists. The mother requires hospitalization.
15.5	A person breaks into a bank at night and steals $100,000.
14.1	A doctor cheats on claims he makes to a federal health insurance plan for patient services.
13.9	A legislator takes a bribe from a company to vote for a law favoring the company.
13.0	A factory knowingly gets rid of its waste in a way that pollutes the water supply of a city.
12.0	A police officer takes a bribe not to interfere with an illegal gambling operation.
11.2	A company pays a bribe to a legislator to vote for a law favoring the company.
10.3	A person operates a store where he knowingly sells stolen property.
9.7	A person breaks into a school and steals equipment worth $1,000.
9.7	A person walks into a public museum and steals a painting worth $1,000.
9.6	A person breaks into a home and steals $1,000.
9.4	A public official takes $1,000 of public money for his own use.
9.2	Several large companies illegally fix the retail prices of their products.
8.6	A person performs an illegal abortion.
8.5	A person sells marijuana to others for resale.
7.9	A teenage boy beats his father with his fists. The father requires hospitalization.
7.5	A person, armed with a lead pipe, robs a victim of $10. No physical harm occurs.
7.4	A person illegally gets monthly welfare checks.
7.3	A person breaks into a department store and steals merchandise worth $1,000.
6.9	A person steals property worth $1,000 from outside a building.
6.5	A person uses heroin.
6.4	A person gets customers for a prostitute.
6.2	An employee embezzles $1,000 from his employer.
5.4	A person has some heroin for his own use.

TABLE 15.2

Severity Score	Offense
5.3	A person loans money at an illegally high interest rate.
5.1	A man runs his hands over the body of a female victim, then runs away.
4.9	A person snatches a handbag containing $10 from a victim on the street.
4.7	A man exposes himself in public.
4.6	A person carries a gun illegally.
4.5	A person cheats on his federal income tax return.
3.7	A labor union official illegally threatens to organize a strike if an employer hires nonunion workers.
3.6	A person knowingly passes a bad check.
3.5	A person runs a place where he permits gambling to occur illegally.
2.2	A person steals $10 worth of merchandise from the counter of a department store.
2.1	A woman engages in prostitution.
1.9	A person makes an obscene phone call.
1.6	A person is a customer in a house of prostitution
1.6	A male, over sixteen years of age, has sexual relations with a willing female under sixteen.
1.3	Two persons willingly engage in a homosexual act.
1.1	A person takes bets on the numbers.
0.9	A person under sixteen years old runs away from home.
0.2	A person under sixteen years old plays hooky from school.

SOURCE: Adapted from Marvin E. Wolfgang et al., *The National Survey of Crime Severity.* Washington, D.C.: U.S. Department of Justice, June 1985, pp. vi–x.

In addition to some evidence of consensus among various groups within the United States on the relative harmfulness of different crimes, there is research that points to a cross-cultural consensus on the ranking of crimes. One study of India, Indonesia, Iran, Italy (Sardinia), Yugoslavia, and the United States found considerable agreement on the perceived harmfulness of various deviant acts and on the amount and type of punishment thought to be appropriate for each act. In this study, the effects of social-background variables on perceptions of deviance were minimal (Newman, 1976). Other research has found that the rankings of offenses are similar in the United States, Canada, Norway, Finland, Sweden, Denmark, the Netherlands, Great Britain, and Kuwait (Scott and Al-Thakeb, 1977; Kvålseth, 1980; Evans and Scott, 1984). However, not all researchers have found unanimity on how people in different societies rank crimes (Hsu, 1973).

The Unpleasantness of Penalties

A retributive system of punishment requires data on how people perceive the severity of penalties relative to each other. For example, how do people perceive the relative unpleasantness of a sentence to a state prison, a sentence to a county jail, a fine, and probation? We also need to know the perceived unpleasantness of an increment of a particular kind of penalty; for instance, do people think that a ten-year prison term is twice as severe as a five-year sentence?

There is probably general agreement on how unpleasant criminal sanctions are. Probation is seen as unpleasant because it imposes restrictions on offenders; they are required to report regularly to probation officers, and they have their mobility and privacy limited. Fines are unpleasant because they deprive offenders of property; they are a relatively lenient form of punishment because they do not disrupt ties to family and job as imprisonment does, but they do discriminate against people who cannot afford to pay. Imprisonment deprives offenders of freedom of movement and contacts with the outside world. Restraint on freedom of movement is subject to many gradations, with the amount of time and the institution in which an offender is confined indicating the severity of the penalty.

We have little research on the equivalence of different amounts of the various kinds of punishment. One study had people rate the severity of different penalties in comparison with a standard of one year in jail (Erickson and Gibbs, 1979). The researchers then developed a series of scales that allowed them to equate a particular jail sentence with a specific prison sentence, probationary period, or fine. For instance, one year in a local jail was perceived as equivalent to a six-month sentence in a state prison, 7.8 years on probation, or a fine of about $3,000. Similarly, a six-month jail sentence was equated to a three-month prison sentence, three years on probation, or a $1,000 fine. The researchers suggested that eventually it might be possible to convert different penalties into a common quantitative measure of perceived severity. Such a measure might be used to compare judges and jurisdictions in terms of the severity of penalties meted out. It might also be used to give convicted offenders a choice from a list of equivalent penalties, such as a choice of spending a year in jail, six months in prison, or eight years on probation, or paying a $3,000 fine. One controversial effort to give offenders a choice of penalties has involved several judges who have offered convicted rapists a choice between a long prison sentence and castration.

A graded scale of penalties was developed by the Committee for the Study of Incarceration (Von Hirsch, 1976). The most lenient sentence suggested by the committee was a warning with unconditional release of the offender. Next was intermittent confinement, such as on weekends and during certain nights of the week; this would be more unpleasant than a warning and release, but less onerous than full-time incarceration. Incarceration, the most unpleasant of the recommended penalties, would be used for serious offenders. Fines were excluded from this system because of the difficulty of equalizing fines for people with different incomes.

Linking Penalties to Crimes

Developing a scale that measures the seriousness of crimes or the unpleasantness of penalties is easier than determining how unpleasant a penalty should be

A Cross-Cultural Perspective:
Amputation as Punishment in the Sudan

Cultures vary in terms of the penalties that are seen as appropriate for different kinds of offenders. In most industrial societies, capital punishment is regarded as "cruel and unusual punishment," though the U.S. Supreme Court has not held that to be the case in the context of American culture. However, the Supreme Court and nearly all Americans would probably define as "cruel and unusual" a punishment often imposed on convicted thieves in the Sudan: the amputation of a hand or a foot.

Since this African nation imposed strict Islamic law in 1983, more than 300 Sudanese have had a hand or a foot amputated for stealing property worth $40 or more. Other penalties in Sudanese law include the stoning of convicted adulterers, the execution of heretics, and the whipping of those who sell or consume alcoholic beverages.

Amputations follow conviction in court for theft and are performed by law-enforcement personnel with no medical training. The amputees then have to find medical care on their own, leading some of them to turn again to crime to pay for such care. Others

resort to crime to support a drug habit brought on by the need to escape the physical pain of the amputation.

This harsh penalty stigmatizes the thieves as outsiders to society, makes employment nearly impossible, often leads to their wrongful arrest, and causes their families to ostracize them. In response to these problems, amputees have formed a self-help organization to raise the funds with which to start small businesses and pay for medical care and legal counsel.

Though most of the world would regard amputation for theft as a disproportionately severe penalty for the harm caused by a thief, most of the industrial world also sees the use of the death penalty in the United States as a cruel and unusual punishment. What any particular society defines as an appropriate penalty for a given crime depends on that society's culture.

SOURCE: Based on Sheila Rule, "Life of Shame of Amputees in the Sudan," *The New York Times*, June 16, 1986, p. A5.

administered to a person who commits an offense of a certain degree of seriousness. The Eighth Amendment to the Constitution bars "cruel and unusual" punishment, but the Supreme Court has rarely overturned penalties for being excessively harsh. In a rare case of this sort, *Solem* v. *Helm* (1983), the Court ruled 5 to 4 that a sentence of life in prison without the possibility of parole was "significantly disproportionate" to the crime, which was the passing of a bad check for $100 by a man who had six previous convictions for nonviolent crimes. The Court saw this case as different from the one of William Rummel, the Texas man who received a life sentence for three property crimes, because in *Solem* v. *Helm* the offender would never have been eligible for parole. This decision reaffirmed the retributivist position that penalties must be proportional to the seriousness of the crime. According to the Court, a disproportionately long sentence would be one that exceeded the gravity of the crime and that was harsh when compared with the sentences meted out for similar crimes in other courts in the state.

In an effort to establish standards that link crimes of differing degrees of seriousness with penalties of different magnitudes, the Committee for the Study of Incarceration recommended that a limited number of sentence levels should be used for offenders convicted of crimes of varying degrees of seriousness. The committee proposed that crimes be categorized by the harmfulness of the offense and by the number and seriousness of the offender's prior convictions. The committee suggested the following penalties:

1. *Minor offenses* should be punished least severely—by warning-and-release for the first offense, and by a light schedule of intermittent confinement (e.g., a loss of a few Saturdays) for repetitions. . . .

2. *Intermediate-level offenses* (from the slightly more than minor to the nearly serious) should be punished mainly by intermittent confinement, although warning-and-release should be used for first offenses in the lower range of this category. For offenses in the upper range, there would be stiff schedules of intermittent confinement involving substantial deprivations of offenders' leisure time. But incarceration should not be employed, since we are still speaking of crimes that do not qualify as serious. . . .

3. *Serious offenses (lower range)* might be punished by intermittent confinement for the first offense, reflecting our conception of a scaled-down penalty for first offenders. Repeated violations, however, should be punished by incarceration. . . .

4. *Serious offenses (upper range)* should receive sentences of incarceration in any event. Intentional and unprovoked crimes of violence that cause (or are extremely likely to cause) grave bodily injury to the victim fit here, as would the worst white-collar offenses such as those in which people's lives are knowingly endangered. (Von Hirsch, 1976: 137–138)

The committee recommended that penalties for lower-range serious offenses be less than eighteen months, and that sentences for upper-range serious offenses fall between eighteen months and three years. There would be no sentences over five years, except for certain murders and a few cases involving exceptional circumstances.

This proposal for a system of punishment is based on the idea of just deserts. People might disagree over which crimes to place into which categories or disagree with the recommended penalties, but the committee's approach has several benefits. It would reduce penalties for first offenders and provide alternatives to incarceration for less serious offenders. It would limit the length of prison terms and standardize sentences. This proposal would also limit the discretion of judges and thus reduce sentence disparity.

The recommendations of the Committee for the Study of Incarceration are not derived from research on people's perceptions of how particular crimes should be punished. Research that first produces a scale of severity of penalties and a scale of seriousness of offenses, and then asks people to recommend specific penalties for different offenders, would be a better basis for a system of just deserts. Efforts to link crimes and penalties in this way have encountered obstacles, but there is some evidence that people use the principle of just deserts to prescribe penalties for crimes about which they are questioned. In other words, some research finds a close match between perceived seriousness of crimes and perceived severity of penalties (Hamilton and Rytina, 1980). For instance, one recent study of California residents found significant agreement among various demographic and political groups about what was fair punishment for different crimes. Their recommended penalties did not differ much from those in the California Penal Code (Samuel and Moulds, 1986).

However, other studies have found no straightforward relationship between a scale of seriousness of crimes and a scale of punishments, with a severe penalty being perceived as relatively much worse than a severe crime; this lack of proportionality in the two scales makes it hard to fit them together in a just deserts system (Hamilton and Rotkin, 1976). One study found that people agreed on the relative severity of sentences for a group of offenses, but disagreed on the absolute magnitude of the sentences that were appropriate for each crime (Blumstein and Cohen, 1980). In other words, people may agree that a murderer should receive a harsher sentence than a rapist, but whether the murderer should be executed, get life in prison, or serve ten years in prison is a question that produces disagreement. A study that used a sample from the Boston metropolitan area discovered that whites and blacks differed in the way they made their judgments about appropriate punishments. Whites recommended punishments on the basis of the crime's seriousness, but blacks were less influenced by the crime's seriousness and more likely to consider the characteristics of the offender and the circumstances surrounding the crime (Miller, Rossi, and Simpson, 1986).

Research indicates that people view white-collar crimes as serious enough to warrant harsher sanctions than are now used, even though the criminal justice system would probably be unable to punish white-collar offenders more severely without a tremendous increase in the resources available to prosecutors (Braithwaite, 1982). A study at a southern university found that students favored lenient sentences for some white-collar criminals, but they recommended relatively harsh penalties for a bank officer who embezzled a large sum of money, a landlord whose failure to repair a building caused a tenant's death, and a stockbroker who knowingly sold fraudulent securities (Reed and Reed, 1975). A survey in San Francisco found that about as many people wanted an antitrust violator imprisoned as called for the incarceration of a car thief, and about as many asked for the imprisonment of an advertiser who misrepresented a product as thought that someone who committed an assault should be sent to prison (Gibbons, 1969). The National Survey of Crime Severity (see Table 15.2) found that some white-collar crimes are regarded by the public as being as serious as, or even more serious than, some conventional crimes (Wolfgang et al., 1985). In

Surveys indicate that there is considerable public support for harsher penalties for white-collar criminals. Here Ivan Boesky leaves court after having been sentenced to a three-year prison term for "insider trading."   *Source: Rick Maiman / Sygma*

sum, there is evidence that a just deserts model would have to treat certain white-collar crimes — especially those that involve physical harm — as being more serious, and thus deserving of more punishment, than many observers have thought them to be (Schrager and Short, 1978, 1980; Vidmar and Miller, 1980; Cullen, Link, and Polanzi, 1982; Cullen et al., 1983).

In general, people seem to call for the most severe penalties for offenders who violate laws that have the greatest social support. They are also most punitive toward offenders who appear to have committed their crimes intentionally and offenders who seem unrepentant; such offenders are thought to be more likely to repeat their crimes, because they do not acknowledge the moral validity of the law. Repeat offenders are also the targets of greater punitiveness, because continuing criminal behavior indicates a lack of commitment to the law. Offenders who show a commitment to group values are usually regarded with less punitiveness.

Retribution and the Criminal Justice System

During the twentieth century, the criminal justice system in the United States has emphasized deterrence and rehabilitation. One sociologist has noted that the principle of retribution "does not appear to tell us how the law should be enforced, except to make the general requirement that a crime must never go unpunished."He goes on to say that the retribution model of criminal justice is "reactive and inert" and that the theories of deterrence and rehabilitation "have more to say about law enforcement" (Newman, 1978: 197).

Nevertheless, considerations of retribution and just deserts play an important part in the criminal justice system, and this role has increased in recent years as research has cast doubt on the effectiveness of rehabilitation. Today, as in the past, "doing justice" and giving offenders the penalties they deserve are major goals of the criminal justice system.

Retribution and the Police

One way to determine the goals of the police is to examine how they allocate their resources. Much of the time the police are not employed in the enforcement of the law or the maintenance of public order. They are called upon for public services such as driving an injured person to the hospital, searching for lost persons, or removing a fallen tree. Even though less than half of police patrol time involves law enforcement and order maintenance, the police probably consider these crime-control functions the essence of their work.

The structure of police departments gives us some idea of the attention that the police pay to serious crimes. Departments include detectives who specialize in the investigation of the most serious offenses. There may be a homicide squad or a narcotics squad to deal with crimes thought to be especially serious. A study of how police departments use their resources to investigate crime would find that more resources are spent on crimes that rank higher on the scale of seriousness, with the exception of white-collar crimes that cause physical harm.

There is some evidence that the way the police respond to apprehended suspects may be related to retributive considerations. The police are more likely to refer an apprehended juvenile to court for formal processing than to release that juvenile if the offense is a harmful one and if he or she appears blameworthy, something that might be indicated by prior contacts with the police (Goldman, 1963; Thornberry, 1973; Black, 1980). The harmfulness of the crime and the blameworthiness of the suspect probably affect police treatment of adult suspects as well. Retributive considerations thus influence the effort that the police expend on the investigation of unsolved cases and their disposition of suspects apprehended in the course of those investigations.

Retribution and the Courts

The principle of retribution is one consideration in district attorneys' decisions about how to prosecute defendants, and it is a factor in judges' decisions about how to sentence convicted offenders.

PROSECUTORS' DECISION MAKING   Prosecutors operate on the assumption that the defendants against whom they bring charges are guilty and should "receive their due" from the criminal justice system. In order to save the court's time, they pressure defendants to plead guilty. In negotiating a plea, prosecutors consider the harmfulness of the alleged offense and the prior criminal record of the defendant. As a result, defendants are usually punished according to the principle of just deserts (Sudnow, 1965; Rosett and Cressey, 1976). A formal system called the Prosecutor's Management Information System (PROMIS) has been developed to calculate a score (based on Sellin and Wolfgang's scale) for each crime and to use information on defendants to help prosecutors assign priority to cases (Roth, 1978).

One study of prosecutors' attitudes toward different offenses produced some unexpected results. Prosecutors thought that white-collar crime was very serious, equivalent to offenses such as kidnapping and rape and more serious than the theft of a similar amount of money by a conventional offender. The amount of money stolen in a crime was not seen as an important consideration in determining the seriousness of an offense, because the amount of money available to be stolen was often a matter of chance. In addition, whether the victim of an assault died was seen as partly due to chance, and so manslaughter was viewed as only slightly more serious than aggravated assault (Roth, 1978). These considerations are not written into the criminal code, but prosecutors depend on them to determine the penalty they think is appropriate for a defendant in a particular case.

JUDGES' DECISION MAKING   Judges also consider how much punishment is deserved by defendants. Both judges and prosecutors typically assume guilt and are then faced with the problem of determining an appropriate penalty. Evidence from several studies indicates that the sentence is influenced primarily by the current charge and the prior record, when defendants of the same race, sex, or class are compared (Kleck, 1981; Spohn, Gruhl, and Welch, 1981–82; Pruitt and Wilson, 1983). However, other researchers have found that extralegal factors such as race, income, sex, and age sometimes do affect sentencing (Clarke and Koch, 1976; Cohen and Kluegel, 1978; Strasburg, 1978). One review of sentencing in the United States concluded that only 7 to 10 percent of all sentences reflected "arbitrary or idiosyncratic judicial behavior," and that the rest of the sentences could be predicted from legal factors such as harmfulness of the crime and blameworthiness of the offender (Silberman, 1978: 292). As court personnel have become more professional and the courts more bureaucratized, these legal factors have become relatively more important in the sentencing of offenders (Pruitt and Wilson, 1983).

In spite of the strong relationship between penalties and the seriousness of offenses, there has been much concern with the consequences of judicial discretion. Until the 1970s, the *indeterminate sentence* was the most widely used penalty in the United States. Under this system, state legislators established long maximum sentences for different crimes. Judges could then impose any penalty up to the maximum. Sentences were often a range of years to be served in prison, such as five to ten years. Actual release dates were then set by parole boards, based on the board's opinion that an inmate had been rehabilitated.

In recent years, concern with the leeway that the indeterminate sentence allows judges, along with evidence that rehabilitation does not seem to work, has led to sentencing reforms. The Committee for the Study of Incarceration's proposal that we examined includes a limited number of *presumptive sentences*. In other words, an offense of a certain degree of harmfulness committed by someone with a particular prior record would be presumed to carry a specified sentence, unless extraordinary circumstances justified a departure from that presumptive sentence. One way to establish such a system is to have a sentencing commission write explicit and detailed sentencing guidelines that reflect popular perceptions of appropriate sanctions for given offenses and offenders. Crimes can then be defined as fitting into a given class, which has a narrow range of prescribed prison sentences. A judge then metes out a specific sentence from within that range, and the parole board cannot release the inmate until the sentence has been served, except by giving some time off for good behavior in prison. Judges can give a sentence outside the prescribed range only if they carefully spell out in writing the reasons for the unusual sentence. Defendants can appeal sentences above the upper limit, and prosecutors can appeal sentences below the range.

In 1978, the Pennsylvania legislature created a Commission on Sentencing to establish guidelines of this sort. In the first year in which the guidelines were applied, 88 percent of all sentences meted out fell within the ranges established by the commission; nine-tenths of those sentences that departed from established ranges were less severe than the guidelines recommended. The sentencing guidelines were instrumental in reducing previous disparities in sentences by race and by urban-rural jurisdiction. Whether compliance with the guidelines and reductions in sentence disparity will be maintained over time is unclear, but sentencing reform in Pennsylvania did have the expected impact over the short run (Kramer and Lubitz, 1985).

Sentencing guidelines were implemented in federal district courts in 1987, though the constitutionality of the commission issuing those guidelines has been challenged in the courts. These guidelines aimed to reduce sentence disparity among federal judges, enhance deterrence by increasing certainty of punishment, and create greater proportionality between the seriousness of the crime and the severity of the punishment. Federal crimes are classified into forty-three categories, and the category into which an offense is classified determines the length of the sentence. For instance, level 43 crimes (e.g., first-degree murder, aircraft hijacking resulting in death, and treason) receive life in prison; level 25 offenses (e.g., production of pornography through sexual exploitation of a minor) are given sentences of fifty-seven to seventy-one months; and level 17 crimes (e.g., burglary of a residence) receive sentences of twenty-four to thirty months. Judges have to mete out sentences within the prescribed range, based on their assessment of the seriousness of the crime and the criminal record of the offender. Sentences outside the range require written statements by judges as to aggravating or mitigating circumstances. Parole is eliminated, with the time served equaling the full sentence, less time off for good behavior while in prison. These guidelines are expected to lead to the incarceration of more white-collar criminals, to lengthen terms for drug offenders, and to lead to more prison crowding. The federal prison population, 56 percent over capacity in 1987, is expected to increase by 10 percent by 1997.

JUVENILE JUSTICE   In recent years there have been efforts to introduce retributive considerations into the juvenile justice system. Some states have proposed and even passed laws that lower the age at which defendants are to be tried as adults, and all states allow some juveniles accused of serious crimes to be tried in criminal court rather than dealt with in juvenile court. These proposals and changes spring from the belief that there is a lack of proportionality between the harm caused by juvenile offenders and their degree of blameworthiness, on the one hand, and the way that they are treated by the juvenile courts, on the other hand.

One proposal to deal with juveniles would require states to pass laws that use current charge and prior record to determine which juveniles must be tried as adults in criminal court (Feld, 1983). However, there is some evidence that even in states where "dangerous" juvenile offenders are singled out for treatment as adults, the criteria adopted by legislators to identify such offenders "single out many juveniles whose records do not appear to be very serious and fail to identify many juveniles whose records are characterized by violent, frequent, and persistent delinquent activity" (Osbun and Rode, 1984: 199). Another study also concluded that there was no evidence that juveniles remanded to adult criminal court were the most dangerous and intractable delinquents, nor was there evidence that the policy of trying juveniles in criminal court enhances public safety (Bortner, 1986).

Some proposals suggest that records of juvenile offenses, which traditionally have been kept "sealed" or secret, should be used to assess the blameworthiness of either juvenile or adult offenders so as to set penalties that fit with the principle of retribution. The United States today has a "two-track" system in which juvenile records are not routinely available to judges in dealing with juveniles or in sentencing adults. Thus, frequent juvenile offenders may receive light sentences for their first few adult offenses, because they seem to be first-time offenders (Boland and Wilson, 1978). In 1981, the Attorney General's Task Force on Violent Crime recommended a "one-track" system similar to that of England, where juvenile records are regularly used in criminal court

Using Criminology: Sentencing Guidelines for Juveniles

In 1986, a panel of ten lawyers and scholars, financed by the U.S. Department of Justice's Office of Juvenile Justice and Delinquency Prevention, recommended that state legislatures adopt sentencing guidelines for juveniles who are convicted of crimes.

Current practice is for juvenile court judges to decide on sentences in consultation with social workers and psychologists, and for parole boards to determine when juvenile offenders should be released. This system has produced much disparity in the sentences meted out to juveniles.

To reduce sentence disparity, this panel recommended that the states adopt sentencing guidelines similar to those adopted for federal offenders. Under these proposed guidelines, sentences would be based on a point system tied to the harmfulness of the offense and the age, criminal record, and background of the juvenile. For instance, a thirteen-year-old boy with one previous conviction for burglary might have his sentence in a second burglary case determined as follows:

50 points for the current burglary conviction;

20 points for the previous burglary conviction; and

10 points because the previous conviction occurred within a year of the current one.

The total of 80 points would be multiplied by .5 because the boy is only thirteen, for a total of 40 points.

Under the sentencing guidelines to be used by judges in this state, 40 points might correspond to a three-month sentence in a youth detention center.

Judges might also be allowed to choose from a limited range of punishments, but they would be expected to sentence within that range unless they found a "manifest injustice" in doing so. Then, they would have to write an explanation for their departure from the established range of sentences.

Because the federal government has no jurisdiction over state juvenile courts, the panel's recommendations do not have the force of law. They are only suggested changes in policy that the states could adopt.

Critics fear that sentencing guidelines of this sort might introduce too much rigidity into the sentencing of juveniles. In other words, they favor sentence disparity as necessary for the proper treatment and punishment of juvenile offenders. Critics also assert that such guidelines might lengthen sentences for juveniles, and perhaps lead to more crowded facilities or higher taxes to build new institutions.

SOURCE: Based on Philip Shenon, "Federal Study on Youth Urges Fixed Sentences," *The New York Times*, August 29, 1987, p. A12.

proceedings involving adults (U.S. Department of Justice, 1981). One longitudinal study in England found that prior convictions as a juvenile influenced sentence severity for adults on their first conviction, independently of the harmfulness of the offense or the age of the defendant (Langan and Farrington,

1983). A study using data from Los Angeles, Seattle, and Las Vegas concluded that even in jurisdictions where juvenile records are available, they do not always affect sentencing. Prior juvenile record has little impact if there is a clear predisposition for or against incarceration, but it seems to influence the sentence when the decision is less clearcut. This study found that for some types of cases harsher sentences were meted out to those with longer juvenile records (Greenwood, 1986).

Retribution and the Prisons

State and federal correctional systems include prisons that differ in their amount of control over inmates. Maximum-, medium-, and minimum-security institutions limit inmates' freedom of movement and isolate them from the outside world to varying degrees. The blameworthiness of the offender and the harmfulness of the crime largely determine the kind of institution to which an offender is sent.

Because sentences in many states cover a range of years — for example, five to ten years for a robbery — the decision about how long an inmate actually stays in prison is made by the parole board rather than the court. Some studies indicate that parole boards may reduce sentence disparity among inmates, but this research is not yet conclusive (Gottfredson, 1979a, 1979b; Petersilia, 1983).

Decisions about when inmates are to be released from prison are predictable to a large degree from the harmfulness of the offense for which they have been imprisoned, their prior criminal record, and their conduct while in prison (Silberman, 1978). In other words, the decision about how much of a court-imposed sentence is actually served is based largely on retributive considerations, even when this decision is theoretically determined by whether an inmate has been rehabilitated.

Retribution and Capital Punishment

As we saw in the previous chapter, public support for the death penalty is based partly on the belief that it is a deterrent, but many supporters say they would favor it even if it had no deterrent effect. Rather than focusing on the utility of the death penalty, many people believe that justice requires that people who commit certain heinous crimes be deprived of their own lives. This belief is reflected in the Soviet Union's legal system, as well as in the American system, as we can see in the Cross-Cultural Perspective.

The death penalty has been both supported and opposed on religious grounds. One minister suggests that "capital punishment must stand as a silent but powerful witness to the sacredness of God-given life"; he bases this argument on "the authority of Scripture" (Vellenga, 1959: 7 – 9). Traditionally, the Roman Catholic Church has accepted the right of the state to execute people convicted of serious crimes. However, in recent years the death penalty has been redefined as inconsistent with Catholic theology because execution lacks utility and dignity, fails to contribute to the common good and the well-being of

A Cross-Cultural Perspective:
Capital Punishment in the Soviet Union

The Soviet Union has had capital punishment since 1918, the year after the Bolshevik Revolution. Since 1961, it has been used for economic crimes such as bribery, corruption, and embezzlement. The death penalty can also be administered for murder, rape, treason, sabotage, espionage, the killing of a police officer, and air hijacking.

In 1982, a former deputy minister in the Ministry of Fisheries was put to death for illegal involvement in the sale of caviar to a Western company. An article in Pravda by the public prosecutor suggested that just deserts was the basis for this harsh penalty: "Bribery is a particular social danger. This forces us to apply the most severe measures of punishment. . . . There can be no indulgence here whatsoever."

The idea that punishment should be pro-

portional to the harm caused by an offense is clear from the way that executions are usually reported in the Soviet press: "In connection with the exceptional scope of the crime, [the defendant] has been sentenced to the supreme measure of punishment, execution by shooting."

In recent years, the Soviet legal system has been inflexible in administering punishment to people who cause "irreparable suffering in the lives of individual Soviet citizens." Flexibility and humanitarian considerations are used only when dealing with minor offenders.

SOURCES: Based on Serge Schmemann, "In Soviet, No Debates Rage around Capital Punishment," *The New York Times*, August 3, 1983, pp. A1, A4; Harry Trimborn, "Soviet Official Executed," *The Boston Globe*, April 29, 1982, p. 3.

citizens who are directly affected by the punishment, and discriminates against the poor and minorities (Beristain, 1977). In 1983, Pope John Paul II asked for clemency or pardon for people under the sentence of death; this was the first time that a pope has criticized capital punishment. In recent years, Catholic bishops in the United States have also voiced opposition to the death penalty, linking their rejection of capital punishment to a "right to life" philosophy that includes opposition to abortion (Franklin, 1983). Protestant religious leaders in the United States have opposed capital punishment since 1957, denying that the state has any right to execute offenders and seeing capital punishment as "a contradiction of both the values of our Christian traditions and the principles of humane government" (cited in Franklin, 1982: 30).

Some opponents of the death penalty claim that even if certain offenders deserve to die, a civilized society should not execute them. They argue that it is immoral for the state to take a human life as a form of punishment, and that by doing so the state "cheapens the value of human life" and may even encourage others to kill.

Even people who support capital punishment do not always agree about when it is appropriate for this penalty to be administered. Thus, few Americans today would support capital punishment for thieves, but thieves were executed in eighteenth- and nineteenth-century England. However, many Americans now would favor the death penalty for someone who brutally murdered several children or someone who assassinated the president.

The Supreme Court has changed its view over time as to what crimes can appropriately be punished with death. The Eighth Amendment to the Constitution prohibits "cruel and unusual punishment," and although the Court has never ruled that capital punishment by itself is cruel and unusual, it has ruled that the death penalty is cruel and unusual punishment for some crimes — specifically, crimes of forcible rape (*Coker* v. *Georgia* [1977]).

In 1972, the Supreme Court, in *Furman* v. *Georgia*, struck down the states' death penalty statutes because they had been administered in an excessively arbitrary way. Four years later the Court approved a new kind of law that it thought would be administered more fairly. In a criminal trial, a defendant's guilt or innocence is determined, and then in a second and separate proceeding a judge or a jury considers the death penalty as a possible sentence. Looking at the harmfulness of the offense and the blameworthiness of the defendant, the judge or jury can choose the death penalty only if there are aggravating circumstances that are defined by state law, and if there are no mitigating circumstances that counteract those aggravating factors. The introduction of specified aggravating and mitigating factors was the result of an attempt to be fair to defendants while still using the principle of retribution.

Since the 1960s, a majority of Americans have supported capital punishment. It is not clear that a majority would actually favor the execution of any specific offender, or would support the immediate execution of all prisoners on Death Row, but there is at the very least considerable support for having the death penalty available for use.

Even though the American public supports capital punishment, there is not much articulate support for the death penalty in the intellectual community. Two exceptions are Walter Berns (1979) and Ernest Van den Haag (1975, 1983), both of whom have argued that the death penalty is a deserved and appropriate penalty for some crimes. They believe that justice requires capital punishment, and that this penalty is a reasonable expression of community outrage at the violation of important values. They argue that executions can reinforce the moral order. Critics of this position point out that retribution simply requires a punishment proportional to the crime, not any specific kind of penalty such as the death penalty (Bedau, 1980).

A report on the families of murder victims provides some support for Berns's and Van den Haag's argument that punishment may be functional in expressing community outrage. Some people report a sense of satisfaction after the killer of their relative has been executed and express frustration when appeals delay the execution for years and keep the memory of the murder alive. One execution that took place nine years after the murder led the brother of the victim to remark that the execution "was an extraordinary relief. I don't know how to explain it. It relieved the grief. This has been an overriding obsession for all of us" (cited in Joyce, 1984: A18).

One argument against the death penalty is that when an error is made in the criminal justice system and an innocent person is executed, there is no way to rectify the error as there is with other penalties. One study documented twenty-three cases between 1900 and 1985 in which Americans were wrongfully executed (Bedau and Radelet, 1987). Because this study did not examine every execution that occurred during this period, and because it is difficult to reconstruct cases years later, there were probably even more innocent people executed. Some abolitionists suggest that the execution of even one innocent person is reason enough to get rid of the death penalty. Proponents of the death penalty argue that only a few mistakes in the more than 7,000 executions since 1900 indicates that the criminal justice system is quite reliable. These proponents also claim that recent developments in the procedural rights of defendants have greatly reduced the chance of such errors today, but the evidence does not support that contention (Bedau and Radelet, 1987).

Support for and opposition to the death penalty are based to a large extent on considerations of just deserts. Even if we had irrefutable evidence that the death penalty does or does not deter crime, the ultimate decision about its use would probably be based on values concerning the sanctity of human life and the requirements of justice. However, evidence that many people do not see capital punishment as a much more severe penalty than life imprisonment without parole suggests that the public's sense of justice might be satisfied if the most serious offenders were incarcerated for life rather than put to death (Hamilton and Rotkin, 1976).

Summary

Most criminal justice systems use the principle of retribution or just deserts: Only the guilty should be punished, and penalties should be proportional to the harmfulness of the crime and the blameworthiness of the offender. In contrast to the theories of deterrence and rehabilitation, the principle of retribution does not try to contribute to the social good, but simply aims to do justice by punishing offenders. Retribution does not require harsher penalties than exist under other systems of punishment.

A system of just deserts that is based on empirical data would include a scale to measure the seriousness of crimes and a scale to rank the severity of punishments. The seriousness of a crime is determined both by the harmfulness of the act and the blameworthiness of the offender. There is much agreement on the ranking of crimes by seriousness, and there is some evidence that people rank penalties by degree of severity in a similar way. However, there is little research that links the two scales, and this is needed for a system of just deserts. Some white-collar crimes, especially those in which physical harm is done to victims, rank relatively high on the scale of seriousness of crimes and seem to warrant more punishment than they usually receive.

Retribution plays an important part in the criminal justice system, and its role has increased in the United States in recent years. The police show that they consider some offenses to be more serious than others in the way they allocate their resources and in the special attention they pay to crimes such as murder and rape. Prosecutors take into consideration the harmfulness of the crime and the blameworthiness of the defendant in negotiating guilty pleas, and in deciding which cases to prosecute with the greatest vigor. Judges use just deserts considerations in deciding how to sentence offenders. The exercise of judicial discretion in imposing indeterminate sentences has led to reforms in recent years, including presumptive sentencing systems that limit the discretion of judges. The idea of just deserts has been introduced into the juvenile justice system in recent years, with efforts being made to reduce the age at which people are treated as adults and to allow juveniles accused of certain kinds of crimes to be tried in adult court. Retribution also plays a part in the incarceration of inmates; length of sentence and kind of prison are determined in large part by the harmfulness of the crime and the blameworthiness of the offender.

The death penalty is often supported or opposed on grounds of just deserts. Religious beliefs have been used both to support and to oppose the death penalty. Some people do not think the state should execute anyone, and others disagree about which crimes warrant capital punishment. Only a few intellectuals support the death penalty, but three-fourths of the American public do. The Supreme Court has not yet ruled that capital punishment itself is cruel and unusual, but it has ruled that capital punishment is a cruel and unusual punishment for forcible rape.

Important Terms

indeterminate sentence   presumptive sentence
just deserts   retribution
lex talionis   vengeance

Suggested Readings

ERNEST VAN DEN HAAG AND JOHN P. CONRAD. *The Death Penalty: A Debate.* New York: Plenum, 1983. A good introduction to the arguments supporting and opposing capital punishment.

ANDREW VON HIRSCH. *Doing Justice: The Choice of Punishments.* New York: Hill and Wang, 1976. A lucid presentation of the just deserts model of punishment.

————. *Past or Future Crimes: Deservedness and Dangerousness in the Sentencing of Criminals.* New Brunswick, N.J.: Rutgers University Press, 1985. A careful consideration of just deserts and utilitarian rationales for punishment.

MARVIN E. WOLFGANG ET AL. *The National Survey of Crime Severity.* Washington, D.C.: U.S. Department of Justice, June 1985. A report on a 1977 survey in which people ranked 204 illegal acts by relative seriousness.

CHAPTER 16

Rehabilitation

Source: Courtesy, American Correctional Association

Rehabilitation is the restoration of criminals to a law-abiding way of life through treatment. More specifically, rehabilitation is the result of any planned intervention focused on the offender that reduces criminal activity, whether that reduction is achieved by changes in personality, abilities, attitudes, values, or behavior. Excluded from rehabilitation are the effects of fear and intimidation — or specific deterrence — and the maturational effects that cause older offenders to leave a life of crime (Sechrest, White, and Brown, 1979: 20–21).

The Rehabilitation Model

The rehabilitation model had its origins in the eighteenth and nineteenth centuries, but it was probably most influential in the United States between the 1920s and the 1970s. The assumptions of this model, and the policies that are derived from it, are quite different from those of the deterrence model and the retribution or just deserts model.

Historical Background

In Colonial America, punishment was not designed to rehabilitate offenders. Instead, physical pain was publicly inflicted on convicted criminals in order to humiliate them and to deter other people from crime. Imprisonment was rarely used for punishment.

During the late eighteenth century, theories of punishment began to change. The ideas of the Enlightenment and the work of European philosophers, most notably Cesare Beccaria, led Americans to see people as rational beings who could control their own behavior, rather than as sinful beings. This view led to a reevaluation of punishment and the beginning of a search for the causes of criminal behavior. Prison was increasingly seen as a way to punish offenders, but not yet as a way to rehabilitate them (Cullen and Gilbert, 1982). In 1787, Dr. Benjamin Rush urged that a prison be established to cure offenders, rather than simply to punish them. This pioneering effort relied on the work of the English prison reformer John Howard, who a few years earlier had suggested that reflection on the errors of their ways would lead inmates to repent.

The belief that offenders could be rehabilitated began to take hold in the 1820s and 1830s. Reforms were aimed at creating orderly prisons, enforcing discipline among inmates, separating offenders from criminal influences, requiring hard work, and training inmates in religion. Geographic and social mobility, urban growth, and economic development disrupted American society during this time, and many people began to see crime as a symptom of the breakdown of social order. People started to believe that offenders should be placed in "an orderly environment that would effect their reform by furnishing them with the strong moral fiber needed to resist the corrupting influences that were rampant in the wider community" (Cullen and Gilbert, 1982: 61; also, see Rothman, 1971, 1980).

During the 1820s, two approaches to rehabilitation emerged, but both shared the belief that "the purpose of the criminal justice system should be to rehabilitate offenders and not merely to subject them to the irrationality of aimless punishment" (Cullen and Gilbert, 1982: 64). The Quakers recommended silence and reflection, and the isolation of inmates in their own cells, where they worked, ate, and read the Bible by themselves. This approach was implemented in a prison established at Cherry Hill in Philadelphia in 1829. A different approach was used at the New York state prison at Auburn in the 1820s. There inmates slept alone in their cells, but they worked, ate, and worshipped together during the day, although they were to remain silent while in each other's presence.

American prisons had not succeeded in establishing rehabilitation as their primary goal by the time of the Civil War. Because offenders served sentences that were fixed by the courts, there was little to motivate them to change. Post-Civil War reformers suggested giving offenders the incentive of early release as a way to motivate them to reform, and so the indeterminate sentence was introduced. A "new penology" that was developed at the National Congress on Penitentiary and Reformatory Discipline in 1870 advocated industrial labor and training, education, religious instruction, better living conditions in prison, assistance to ex-convicts in becoming reintegrated into society, separate institutions for women and juveniles, and the training of correctional officers. Two ideas guided these recommendations: "a firm belief in the curative powers of the indeterminate sentence and a fundamental conviction that the 'supreme aim' of American criminal justice should be 'the reformation of criminals, not the infliction of vindictive suffering'" (Cullen and Gilbert, 1982: 72). These recommendations were first implemented in a reformatory at Elmira, New York. Other states followed this model, though they were more likely to use it for younger, less hardened offenders than for older career criminals.

The Progressive Era of the early twentieth century was characterized by faith in the state's ability to improve society through liberal reform. Progressives used the ideas of the new penology articulated in the 1870s as the basis of their approach to crime: rehabilitation rather than retribution. They relied on the indeterminate sentence to effect rehabilitation, advocated treatment within the community rather than in prison, favored parole boards to release offenders who seemed likely to stay away from crime, argued for probation or supervised release of convicted offenders, and suggested that probation officers examine the backgrounds of convicted offenders and provide judges with presentence reports to be used to individualize sentences (Cullen and Gilbert, 1982). The positivist approach of the newly developing behavioral sciences, especially sociology and psychology, supported this therapeutic approach by focusing on the causes of crime. These developments gave rise to a medical model that saw law breaking as a kind of disease that could be diagnosed, treated, and cured (Conrad and Schneider, 1980; Cullen and Gilbert, 1982).

The Progressives had a major impact on the American system of criminal justice. The number of states with indeterminate sentence systems increased

The loom in this nineteenth-century prison cell reflects the contemporary belief in the therapeutic value of work.   *Source: Courtesy, American Correctional Association*

from five in 1900 to thirty-seven about two decades later. By the mid-1920s, almost every state had parole, though few did in 1900. In 1897, only two states had probation, but by 1920 two-thirds of the states had it for adults and all had it for juveniles (Cullen and Gilbert, 1982). The philosophy of rehabilitation espoused by the Progressives probably had its greatest effect on the juvenile justice system. The first juvenile court was created in 1899 in Illinois as a result of the "child saving movement"; by 1920, all but three states had juvenile courts (Platt, 1977).

In spite of its important consequences for American criminal justice, the rehabilitation model was never fully implemented. Crime was never treated solely as a medical problem that could be cured. No state had sentencing that was fully indeterminate; all states set upper limits on the time to be served. Probationers and parolees never received the intensive supervision and help in becoming reintegrated into society that the Progressives had envisioned. Community corrections did not replace incarceration, and parole and probation seemed to be ways for states to expand their control over law breakers rather than ways to take inmates out of prisons and put them on the streets (Cullen and Gilbert, 1982). In spite of these shortcomings, the ideology of rehabilitation was the dominant perspective, indeed almost an unchallenged one, in the criminal justice system from the 1920s to the 1970s, when attacks on the therapeutic model led to a search for alternative ways of dealing with offenders.

Assumptions Underlying Rehabilitation

One of the best statements of the rehabilitation model of punishment is Francis Allen's (1971: 318):

> It is assumed, first, that human behavior is the product of antecedent causes. These causes can be identified as part of the physical universe, and it is the obligation of the scientist to discover and to describe them with all possible exactitude. Knowledge of the antecedents of human behavior makes possible an approach to the scientific control of human behavior. Finally, and of primary significance for the purposes at hand, it is assumed that measures employed to treat the convicted offender should serve a therapeutic function, that such measures should be designed to effect changes in the behavior of the convicted person in the interests of his own happiness, health, and satisfaction and in the interest of social defense.

This position assumes that offenders can be changed by treatment, even though prisons emphasize custody more than treatment. The principle underlying these treatment programs is to return "the offender to society not with the negative vacuum of punishment-induced fear but with the affirmative and constructive equipment—physical, mental and moral—for law-abidingness" (Wiehofen, 1971: 261).

Inmates are not required to join treatment programs, but these programs are not truly voluntary. Prisoners are deprived of their liberty while incarcerated, so they are in prison against their will. To gain their release, inmates must either serve the full sentence or convince a parole board that they are sufficiently rehabilitated to be released without posing a threat to the community. To be released by a parole board requires inmates to be relatively free of disciplinary reports while in prison and to demonstrate that they have tried to change. This usually means that inmates feel under pressure to join prison treatment programs that will help them change. Inmates may join these programs more to gain early release than to change, for they know that participation is viewed favorably by the parole board. In a sense, then, treatment programs are not really voluntary, because freedom depends on participation in those programs. Joining too few treatment programs may be taken as evidence that the inmate has not changed and does not wish to, but joining too many programs may suggest to the parole board that the inmate is trying to win over the parole board rather than to change. As a result, inmates must try to figure out how many programs to join and which programs are favored by those who have the power to release prisoners.

Court decisions have guaranteed inmates the right to have access to treatment programs that can help them. The law thus sees rehabilitation as a required function of punishment. A different view is that inmates may suffer from having treatment forced on them and should thus be guaranteed the right to refuse treatment (Kittrie, 1971). We must remember that "measures depriving persons of their liberty against their will are essentially punitive in nature no matter how well-intentioned the authorities administering those measures" (Wiehofen, 1971: 259). Treatment may be dehumanizing and destructive of human dignity. Many criminals are rational rather than ill, and to tell them they are defective and in need of treatment is degrading as well as inaccurate. The idea of rehabilitation implies not only that the behavior that led to punishment was legally wrong, but also that it was the result of personal defects. One ex-convict has reacted to this assumption as follows:

> The whole point of the psychological diagnosis is to get [the inmate] to go for the fact that he's "sick," yet the statement he's sick deprives him of his integrity as a person.
>
> Most prisoners I know would rather be thought bad than mad. They say society may have a right to punish them, but not a hunting license to remold them in its own sick image. (cited in Mitford, 1973: 104)

Offenders who consciously choose to violate the law and are willing to accept their punishment if caught resent treatment programs based on the premise that they are "sick." For example, one man imprisoned for robbery was a bookie who went badly into debt when several of his customers unexpectedly won large bets. He borrowed a large sum of money from a loan shark to get his bet-taking operation back in order. To recover more quickly, he bet this borrowed money, but lost. The loan shark then threatened to kill the bookie's wife and children unless the bookie repaid the debt immediately. At this point, the bookie robbed a bank, escaped with a large sum of money, and paid off the loan shark. He was eventually caught and given a long prison sentence for the robbery (Conklin, 1972: 66). Some might claim that this man needs rehabilitation, but it would be difficult to attribute his decision to rob the bank to deep-seated psychological problems that require intensive therapy. From his perspective, the decision to hold up the bank was rational, given the situation in which he found himself. He received a long prison sentence, but he said he would do the same thing again if faced with the same situation. He believed he had chosen wisely in trading a long prison term for the safety of his family. Many inmates see their crimes as rational and conscious efforts to solve problems confronting them at a particular time, and they often deny that they need to be rehabilitated.

Rehabilitation Compared with Retribution and Deterrence

The rehabilitation perspective is quite different from the retribution and deterrence perspectives. Retributivists claim that penalties should be specific and just, thus allowing punished offenders to retain their dignity by paying for their crimes. C. S. Lewis (1971: 306) has contrasted rehabilitation with retribution as follows:

> To be "cured" against one's will and cured of states which we may not regard as disease is to be put on a level with those who have not yet reached the age of reason or those who never will; to be classed with infants, imbeciles, and domestic animals. But to be punished, however severely, because we have deserved it, because we "ought to have known better," is to be treated as a human person made in God's image.

Retribution does not necessarily lead to more severe penalties than rehabilitation. Indeed, as we will see later in this chapter, the rehabilitation model may actually produce longer sentences, which are justified by the need to cure inmates.

The deterrence perspective sees offenders and potential offenders as rational decision makers who will stay away from crime if the threat of punishment is great enough; those who commit crime presumably think the threat of punishment is outweighed by the rewards of crime. The rehabilitation perspective, on the other hand, regards people who violate the law as defective and in need of treatment, not as rational decision makers who knowingly take risks when they break the law.

Rehabilitation and the Criminal Justice System

The rehabilitation perspective has had a significant impact on the American criminal justice system, especially in the three decades following World War II. The behavior of the police, prosecutors, judges, and especially correctional administrators has been influenced in important ways by the belief that offenders can and should be changed.

Rehabilitation and the Police

Rehabilitation is not generally considered a police function, because the police deal with people suspected, rather than convicted, of breaking the law, and it would seem to violate the legal principle that suspects are to be presumed innocent until proved guilty if the police tried to rehabilitate suspects. Nevertheless, the rehabilitation perspective does influence the way the police deal with suspects.

The police claim that they only enforce the law, but in fact they exercise considerable discretion in doing so (Skolnick, 1975). The idea of rehabilitation may influence a police officer's decision to charge a suspect with a crime or to release that suspect with a warning. An officer may think a particular suspect will avoid crime in the future if subjected to the shock of arrest and a court appearance, or believe another suspect will be most likely to stay away from crime if sent home to his or her parents. If the police do not think correctional programs work, or believe the negative effects of a court appearance will outweigh its beneficial effects, they may formally charge a suspect with crime only as a last resort.

Police officers are especially likely to consider the possibility of rehabilitation for juvenile suspects. Some cities have *police diversion* programs that allow the police to recommend to juvenile suspects that they enroll in a program that offers counseling or training. Some police departments provide treatment through an informal *police probation* program that requires juvenile troublemakers to report to the police regularly, attend school, make restitution, and maintain a neat personal appearance (Lemert, 1971). Police probation usually results from informal agreements among officers, juveniles, and the juveniles' parents or guardians. Police probation and police diversion programs may avoid the legal stigma of court appearance and institutionalization, but these programs do involve the police in the treatment of individuals who have not been proved guilty or found delinquent. Because these programs channel individuals into formal programs, they may have the unanticipated consequence of labeling young people who would not have been labeled at all had these programs not existed (Cressey and McDermott, 1973).

Rehabilitation and the Courts

The rehabilitative ideal plays an important part in the courts, both in the decision to prosecute and in the decision about how to sentence offenders.

PRETRIAL DIVERSION   Many jurisdictions have *pretrial diversion* programs that allow district attorneys to recommend to judges that a criminal proceeding be suspended while a suspect participates in a treatment program. Pretrial diversion may keep suspects from acquiring criminal records and criminal identities, although one study concluded that there was not enough evidence that court appearances had labeling effects to justify the creation of diversion programs on those grounds (Mahoney, 1974; also, see Thomas and Bishop, 1984).

Pretrial diversion programs for suspected drug offenders include halfway houses, methadone treatment, group therapy, education, and job training. Similar programs exist for people charged with other crimes. If a suspect is not arrested again while enrolled in a diversion program and seems to profit from that program, the judge at the suggestion of the district attorney may "file" the case—that is, not charge the suspect and eventually dismiss the case.

Juvenile courts have adopted pretrial diversion on the assumption that the labeling effects of a court appearance may do more harm than good. One study that looked at status offenders—juveniles charged with acts that would not be crimes if committed by adults—found no difference in the likelihood of re-arrest for those processed formally by the juvenile courts and those placed in diversion programs. The researcher concluded that the data supported neither labeling theory's contention that diversion is better nor deterrence theory's claim that court processing will keep status offenders from getting into trouble again (Rausch, 1983). Another study also concluded that the diversion of status offenders had no significant effects on their behavior or attitudes, but it found there was competition for diverted juveniles among various community-based programs and warned that this might "widen the net" of the juvenile justice system and lead to the processing of more juveniles (Rojek and Erickson, 1981–82).

Pretrial diversion is based on the idea that rehabilitation may be more likely for some suspects if they are not formally processed by the criminal justice system or the juvenile justice system. One problem with pretrial diversion is that suspects may feel pressured to enter such programs rather than face the charges against them in court. However, they are given the option of facing charges rather than participating in diversion programs.

PLEA BARGAINING   The sentences to which district attorneys and judges agree in exchange for guilty pleas from defendants may be influenced to some degree by district attorneys' and judges' ideas about what kinds of sentences are most likely to lead to rehabilitation. However, considerations of just deserts probably play a more important role in determining the kinds of penalties to which prosecutors and judges will agree. Critics of plea bargaining sometimes claim that it creates cynicism toward the criminal justice system among defendants and thereby impedes their rehabilitation. Others see plea bargaining as an essential first step in the rehabilitation process, because it forces defendants to take responsibility for their own behavior (Casper, 1978).

SENTENCING   Once a defendant is convicted, a judge's decision about the length and type of sentence may depend on the idea of rehabilitation as well as on the principle of just deserts. Judges consider the possible benefits of the various treatment programs available in the community and in correctional institutions. They may consider the rehabilitative effects of paying a fine or making restitution, or place offenders on probation if they think that this is the best method to keep them away from a life of crime (Langley, 1972). Other offenders may be sent to prisons that have treatment programs appropriate to their needs. In reality, judges usually have few sentencing alternatives from which to choose. State prisons rarely differ much in their treatment programs, and many offenders cannot be fined or placed on probation because the law prohibits it or because the judge's or the public's sense of just deserts would not permit it.

Rehabilitation and the Prisons

The major way the correctional system has been influenced by the idea of rehabilitation is in its use of the indeterminate sentence and the parole board.

THE INDETERMINATE SENTENCE Introduced at the end of the nineteenth century in the United States, the indeterminate sentence is a penalty meted out by a judge that requires an offender to serve an inexact period of time in custody. For example, an offender may receive a sentence of one year to life in prison, or a sentence of five to ten years. The offender will be released from custody when he or she is deemed rehabilitated by a parole board. The offender may serve the maximum sentence, the minimum sentence, or some time between the two, or he or she may be paroled after serving a fixed proportion of the minimum sentence. If rehabilitation programs are ineffective, offenders may be kept in prison for periods closer to the maximum than to the minimum.

The rationale for the indeterminate sentence was a humanitarian one: Inmates should be released as soon as they are cured. However, the actual impact of the indeterminate sentence has been to lengthen sentences for offenders. For instance, in 1900 the inmates at Indiana State Prison, sentenced under the recently introduced indeterminate sentence system, served an average of six months and twenty-three days longer than inmates committed to the same institution for the same crimes in 1890, when a system of definite sentences was in effect (Mitford, 1973: 84). The length of time served by inmates also increased when the California correctional system introduced the idea of rehabilitation (American Friends Service Committee, 1971: 91). Indeterminate sentences can also lead to the incarceration of more offenders, as well as to longer sentences for those who are imprisoned, because the underlying assumption of the indeterminate sentence is that people who are imprisoned are being helped. The principle of rehabilitation thus acts as a "highly efficient control mechanism," even though its original justification was humanitarian (Irwin, 1974: 975).

PAROLE Parole boards determine when an offender serving an indeterminate sentence is ready to be released. Parole boards determine how much of a sentence is to be served behind bars, and how much if any is to be served under the supervision of a parole officer on the street. In deciding when to release an inmate, the parole board considers the offense for which the offender was sent to prison, the inmate's prior criminal record, the number of disciplinary reports filed against the inmate while incarcerated, and the treatment programs in which the inmate has participated. Participation in treatment programs and number of disciplinary reports are used to indicate the extent to which an offender is rehabilitated and ready for release. The original offense and prior criminal history are retributive considerations in deciding on the length of incarceration.

The conditions the state places on paroled offenders are designed to aid in the rehabilitation process: staying away from known criminals, establishing ties to a job, supporting a family, and avoiding the use of alcohol and drugs. However, some parole conditions — such as restrictions on having a driver's license or on driving a great distance from home — can impede rehabilitation by making it more difficult to live a normal life and get a good job. Moreover, the heavy caseload of most parole officers means that ex-convicts receive little counseling that might help them avoid a return to crime. Critics have thus suggested that parole is "surveillance and control, not casework and counseling" (Kassebaum, Ward, and Wilner, 1971: 3).

Does Rehabilitation Work?

The goal of treatment programs is the rehabilitation of inmates, but it would be surprising if these programs had significant effects. Most of them are poorly funded, inadequately staffed, and available to a limited number of inmates. Even when treatment and social services are available, they are often of little use in rehabilitating offenders. Skills learned in prison industries are often inapplicable to the outside world; for example, there is little demand for the skill of manufacturing license plates, because many states manufacture all license plates in their prisons.

Measuring the Success of Treatment Programs

The effectiveness of a particular method of treatment can be assessed by the reduction in the likelihood of getting into trouble with the law again, or by various indicators of improved social functioning such as holding a job or supporting a family.

RECIDIVISM RATES   The usual way to measure whether offenders are helped by the treatment they receive in prisons, on probation, or on parole is by a *recidivism rate*. This rate is typically calculated by taking the percentage of offenders who, during a specific period after their treatment has ended, are arrested and convicted of new offenses or have their punishment made more restrictive because they have failed to meet the conditions of a less restrictive sentence. The recidivism rate of inmates released from prison is often calculated by adding the number of releasees who are arrested for new crimes and the number who are sent back to prison because their parole is revoked, and dividing that number of "failures" by the total number of released inmates. Thus, if one hundred inmates are released from prison, and within three years eighteen of them are back in prison because they have been convicted of new crimes, and another thirty-three are back in prison because their parole has been revoked for a suspected new crime or for violation of parole conditions, the recidivism rate would be 51 percent for the three-year period.

Recidivism rates vary from one study to another. In some jurisdictions, parole is revoked quickly, and so those communities have high recidivism rates. Where parole officers are more tolerant of violations of parole conditions, recidivism rates are lower. The length of the follow-up period also affects the recidivism rate; the longer the period after release, the higher is the recidivism rate. For instance, one study (Kitchener, Schmidt, and Glaser, 1977) found the following percentages of federal ex-convicts returned to prison as parole violators or for new sentences for felonies or felony-like offenses:

Years after Release	Recidivism Rate
1	15%
2	34%
5	51%
10	59%
18	63%

A more recent study that used data from fourteen states found that 14.9 percent of inmates were back in prison within a year of their release, 26.1 percent were back within two years, and 31.5 percent were back within three years. Half or more of the ex-convicts who were returned to prison were sent back for new crimes rather than because their parole had been revoked (*The Boston Globe*, December 3, 1984).

A major problem in using rearrest data to measure recidivism is that many crimes that ex-convicts commit are not reported to the police or do not lead to an arrest if they are reported. For instance, a study of eighty-three convicted rapists and fifty-four convicted child molesters found that they admitted to two to five times as many sex offenses as they had been arrested for. Because of the low visibility of sex offenses — that is, their low rate of being reported to the police and the difficulty of making arrests in such crimes — recidivism rates may be especially poor measures of the degree to which sex offenders have been rehabilitated (Groth, Longo, and McFadin, 1982).

OTHER MEASURES OF TREATMENT EFFECTIVENESS   Recidivism rates are not the only way to determine the effectiveness of treatment. Another way is to measure self-reported crime by offenders. This might produce a more accurate indicator of the rate at which inmates have returned to crime, because many crimes are not reported and recorded and many are not solved. However, it would be difficult to get valid results from such self-report studies, because inmates who have recently been paroled or released after "wrapping up" a sentence would fear that revealing undiscovered offenses might lead to rearrest or to the revocation of parole.

The effectiveness of rehabilitation programs could also be measured by changes in personality, attitude, or behavior that are produced by treatment. The impact of drug and alcohol treatment programs might be measured by the rate of relapse by inmates who have drug and alcohol problems. The outcome of treatment programs can also be measured by how released inmates function in the community, on the job, in school, and within the family (Lipton, Martinson, and Wilks, 1975: 12–14). A treatment program that improves the ability of ex-convicts to support a family or hold a legitimate job, even if those ex-convicts occasionally engage in petty crime, might be considered more successful than a program whose graduates also commit petty crimes but lack the ability to support a family or hold a job.

Rather than designate ex-convicts as "successes" or "failures" on the basis of whether they remain crime-free after release, it might be better to measure differences in criminal behavior before and after treatment. Thus, the success of a treatment program could be measured by the degree to which it reduced or suppressed the rate of arrest of its participants. A program might also be considered a partial success if it lengthened the time from release until the time ex-convicts committed new crimes. For instance, a program whose graduates were crime-free for two years but then returned to crime might be seen as more successful than a program whose graduates returned to crime within a month of their release. A reasonable goal for a rehabilitation program is to reduce the number and the seriousness of the crimes its participants commit, even if they are not kept from criminal activity altogether. Treatment programs that have such beneficial effects may eventually make it possible for offenders to leave a life of crime.

Measures of diminished criminal activity and personal adjustment are used to evaluate treatment programs less often than is the rate at which releasees return to prison. As the American Friends Service Committee (1971: 44) says:

> Surely it is ironic that although treatment ideology purports to look beyond the criminal's crime to the whole personality, and bases its claims to sweeping discretionary power on this rationale, it measures its success against the single factor of an absence of reconviction for a criminal act.

EXPERIMENTAL DESIGN AND TREATMENT EFFECTIVENESS Inmates who are released from prison may not return to crime because they are deterred by the fear of more punishment, because they have matured while in prison, or because they have been rehabilitated. The proper way to isolate the effect of treatment from the other effects of imprisonment is to assign inmates randomly to a group that receives treatment (experimental group) or to a group that does not receive treatment (control group). If the treatment is effective, inmates in the experimental group will show a lower recidivism rate (or some other kind of improvement) in comparison with the control group. The difference between the experimental and control groups in recidivism rates or some other measure of improvement can then be attributed to the effects of treatment, because chance determined the group to which an inmate was assigned, and the inmates in each group presumably had similar experiences in prison except for their exposure or lack of exposure to treatment.

Efforts to evaluate treatment programs by experimental studies often encounter problems in implementing a research design in an institutional setting. Because these studies sometimes take years to complete, results may not be available when policy makers need them to develop intervention strategies. Forces outside the prison also make it difficult to evaluate treatment programs; for instance, the effects of labeling by family, friends, and employers may vary from one ex-convict to another and make it difficult to assess the impact the treatment program itself has on its participants. Properly conducted experiments are expensive, and it may be difficult to find the funds to evaluate programs, but the failure to carry out such experiments means that treatment programs that are both expensive and ineffective will continue (Sechrest, White, and Brown, 1979).

THE AMENABILITY ISSUE   One issue that complicates research on rehabilitation is the possibility that certain kinds of offenders are amenable to treatment of a particular sort, with other kinds of offenders not gaining from exposure to the same treatment. This *amenability issue* might arise in evaluating a treatment program in which 50 percent of the participants avoided recidivism and 50 percent returned to prison. In this case, it is possible that those who were not recidivists were amenable to the treatment they received, and those who returned to prison were not amenable to that treatment. Randomization in the evaluation of treatment methods avoids some of this difficulty but still leaves unanswered the question of whether inmates with specific characteristics might be matched to particular treatment methods in ways to achieve higher rates of success. One review of evaluations of rehabilitation programs concluded that we do not yet really know anything about the suitability of certain kinds of offenders for different forms of treatment, and that more research is needed on this issue (Sechrest, White, and Brown, 1979).

Types of Treatment

Treatment programs take many forms. Some deal with individuals and others with groups. Some seek to alter personality and others only to change behavior. Some equip offenders with vocational skills or educational credentials and others try to cure drug addiction or alcoholism.

EDUCATION AND WORK PROGRAMS   Since World War II, several states have established prerelease programs such as work-release and education-release. These programs emphasize the problem of reentry into society and help inmates gain access to jobs and educational opportunities outside prison walls (Moeller, 1974). Furlough programs serve similar functions, but the release of inmates for a few hours or days during their prison term has generated public opposition and probably has little value as a method of rehabilitation.

In an effort to provide work experience for inmates to help them find jobs after they are released and also to give private firms a source of inexpensive labor, in 1979 Congress passed a law allowing products made by inmates to be sold and distributed in interstate commerce, something that had been prohibited since 1940. Since 1979, many states have also passed legislation to expand work opportunities for inmates. In seven pilot projects, inmates were hired by private firms to work within prison walls at a minimum wage, considerably more than the fifty cents to one dollar per day that inmates typically earn at prison work. There was strong opposition to this program from labor unions, who criticized businesses for hiring cheap inmate labor rather than union members who could do the same work (Gargan, 1983).

One analysis of employment and crime suggested that the only effective long-term strategy may be to provide job training and education for inmates, because there are few indications that job-placement or income-supplement programs reduce crime rates in the short run. Those who are most likely to give up crime for a legitimate job seem to be offenders who are older, married, and educated; have no major drug or alcohol problems; have shown a willingness to work; have committed crimes for monetary gain; and are of relatively low economic status (Orsagh and Witte, 1981).

METHADONE PROGRAMS   One treatment program that was introduced in the United States in the late 1960s and early 1970s is *methadone maintenance* for heroin addicts. Methadone is an addictive drug that does not produce euphoria if taken orally in regulated doses, but it does block the euphoric effects of heroin that is used. Methadone is inexpensive, and has effects that last for a full day, and its oral administration avoids the risk of contracting a disease from an infected needle.

One premise behind methadone treatment programs is that much crime that addicts commit to support their expensive habits could be eliminated if they were taken off heroin and put on methadone. Methadone maintenance programs have attracted many heroin addicts, but the majority of addicts do not try to enter such programs. Researchers have found that these programs have a limited impact on crime rates. Drug offenses become less common among those who stay in the program, but many participants continue to engage in crime even after they have stopped using heroin (Epstein, 1974). In addition, methadone programs that allow participants to take their doses home rather than come to the clinic every day have found much illegal resale of methadone on the streets and high rates of overdoses among those who buy and use methadone illegally.

BEHAVIOR MODIFICATION   One treatment program that has been tried in some prisons is *behavior modification* or behavior therapy. This approach tries to change behavior, rather than personality, by rewarding desirable actions and punishing undesirable ones. This approach sees criminal behavior as learned, and is built on the principles of classical and operant conditioning. Criminal behavior is not regarded as a symptom of underlying personality problems that must be dealt with, as it is by psychotherapists and counselors. Instead, criminal behavior is seen as a problem that must be dealt with directly.

Behavior modification is "the systematic application of proven principles of conditioning and learning in the remediation of human problems" (Milan and McKee, 1974: 746). Classical conditioning pairs an undesired behavior with an unpleasant event; for instance, alcoholism may be treated by administering electrical shocks when a person drinks alcoholic beverages. Operant conditioning allows the effects of a person's behavior on the environment to produce consequences for that individual and thus shape his or her behavior; giving money for desired behavior is one method that has been tried with juvenile offenders.

A major question regarding behavior modification is whether changes produced in inmates will persist after they are released. One review of twenty-four treatment programs of this sort concluded that virtually all of them succeeded in modifying the behavior of the offenders, who were usually juveniles, while they were institutionalized. However, only four of the programs followed offenders after their release. Three found no lasting and significant effect of the program, and one found such an effect (Ross and McKay, 1978). More evaluation of the long-term impact of behavior modification is needed, but research to date offers little reason to believe that behavior modification programs within institutions can change how offenders will act after their release.

Behavior modification methods also raise ethical issues. Some claim that such methods must be voluntary to be ethical, but as we previously suggested, no treatment program in prison is truly voluntary if inmates can be released earlier for participating in such a program.

INDIVIDUAL THERAPY   A method of treatment commonly used in prison is *individual therapy* carried out by psychiatrists, psychologists, or psychiatric social workers. This approach assumes that offenders are emotionally troubled people who need to solve the psychological problems that cause them to commit crime.

We would not expect therapy to work unless inmates did have psychological problems, and, though offenders have behavior problems, there is not much evidence that they have psychological problems (Halleck and Witte, 1977). Another reason we might not expect psychotherapy to work is that therapists manipulate and control verbal behavior rather than change overt actions directly.

One inmate claims that offenders sometimes manipulate therapists, pretending to be "crazy" in the early sessions by presenting a "good case" and then acting increasingly normal and showing "insight" as time passes. This may convince the therapist that the inmate is being helped, and the therapist may then recommend to the parole board that the inmate is ready to be released (Rettig, Torres, and Garrett, 1977: 167–168).

A major problem with psychotherapy is that it tries to deal with offenders within institutional walls, rather than in the environment in which criminal behavior actually occurs. There is thus a question about the extent to which any beneficial effects that therapy appears to have on inmates will carry over to behavior in the outside world. Moreover, very few prisons provide therapy that is intensive enough to have much impact on inmates.

Here a caseworker helps an inmate develop plans and skills to ease his transition to parole. *Source: Courtesy, American Correctional Association*

CASEWORK In many prisons, social workers provide inmates with individual counseling that is intended less to help them understand their motivations than to help them cope with specific problems they face. This *casework* approach is oriented toward getting inmates to realize their own capacities for change, advising them on how to solve problems of daily living, teaching them how to adapt to reality, and informing them of community resources that might aid them in their rehabilitation (Lipton, Martinson, and Wilks, 1975: 10).

MILIEU THERAPY *Milieu therapy* is a treatment method that introduces the idea of rehabilitation into all aspects of an institution, including relations between inmates and staff members. Milieu therapy employs casework and group counseling, stresses inmate responsibility and self-determination, and creates a warm and supportive climate for change.

GROUP COUNSELING Another treatment method is *group counseling*, which allows several inmates to be treated at the same time and at a low cost, especially

Using Criminology: Testing the Effectiveness of Group Counseling

To determine the effectiveness of a group counseling program in a medium-security California prison for men, Gene Kassebaum, David Ward, and Daniel Wilner used an experimental research design to test three hypotheses about changes such a program might produce:

1. Group counseling would lessen endorsement of the inmate code.
2. Group counseling would reduce the number of prison disciplinary reports.
3. Group counseling would reduce the rate at which inmates were returned to prison.

The groups ranged in size from ten to twelve, met for one or two hours per week, and had a correctional officer as the leader.

Because the group counseling program took place in a prison that was just being opened, the researchers were able to get the administration's permission to assign inmates randomly to experimental groups (with group counseling) and control groups (without group counseling). The experimental groups varied in size, and the leaders of some of the groups were given extra training in running groups. The inmates were followed for three years after their release to see if they were arrested for new crimes or had their parole revoked.

The researchers determined that group counseling had little impact on the inmates. It did not reduce their endorsement of the values and beliefs of the inmate code, did not influence social solidarity among inmates, and did not reduce their opposition to the prison staff. Group counseling also had no effect on an inmate's employment record while on parole, nor did it have an impact on the number of parole citations for drug or alcohol abuse.

The traditional measure of success, the recidivism rate, also did not indicate that group counseling had achieved its goals.

if correctional officers are used as group leaders. Other group counseling programs use as leaders either psychotherapists or people who have been trained in guided-group interaction.

In these groups, where inmates discuss their feelings and attitudes, the goal is to create mutual acceptance and a supportive environment. However, in a correctional system that uses parole, inmates may conceal their true feelings rather than risk having the feelings they reveal in the group be used against them later in a parole hearing.

Group counseling may emphasize either the change of an individual with the support of the group, or the change of the group as a whole. Alcoholics Anonymous has been used as a prototype for some group counseling programs. These programs seek to change an individual deviant to conform to the nondeviant values of other group members, and then to have group members reinforce

About half (51 percent) of all inmates were back in prison within three years of their release; 18 percent were convicted of new offenses and 33 percent were returned for parole violations. Experimental and control groups did not differ significantly in felony or misdemeanor arrests while on parole, nor did they differ in number of weeks spent in jail after release. In other words, "parole performance . . . was no different for the participants in group counseling than it was for the nonparticipants" (p. 242).

Neither the size of the group nor the amount of training received by the group leader made any difference in parole outcome. Similarly, there was no difference between the experimental group and the control group that was due to the initial attitudes of inmates toward the staff or toward the value of counseling. Regularity of attendance at group meetings and changes in group leaders also did not influence parole success.

Group counseling probably failed to have any significant impact on recidivism rates or other outcome measures because it took place in a context that emphasized custody rather than treatment. It also failed because

most inmates were released to the same social environment that had led them into crime in the first place. They associated with the same friends, probably had more trouble finding a good job, and encountered the same temptations and pressures to commit crime. A correctional system that pulls offenders out of their social environment, "warehouses" them for a time, and then returns them to the same social setting can be expected to have a high recidivism rate.

The social causes of crime are hardly touched by group counseling in prison, but this treatment method continues to be used throughout the nation, including at the California prison where it was found ineffective. The program does not work, but it apparently does no harm to inmates, and it is inexpensive to run. The program may help the prison administration control inmates, especially if correctional officers are used as group leaders.

SOURCE: Based on Gene Kassebaum, David A. Ward, and Daniel M. Wilner, *Prison Treatment and Parole Survival: An Empirical Assessment.* New York: Wiley, 1971.

their own commitment to nondeviant values by working to convince newer members to conform to those values.

The Effectiveness of Treatment Methods

Thousands of treatment programs have been tried in prison and in the community, but only a few hundred programs have been designed so that they can be evaluated according to the standards of social science research. Many obstacles stand in the way of people who try to evaluate rehabilitation programs. Some programs have no control group. Others fail to follow participants after they leave the program. Programs may also not be established or maintained according to their stated goals. Researchers sometimes face the problem that even programs that have been properly designed and evaluated are difficult to assess because information about those programs is not widely disseminated and not published in scholarly journals that rely on professional peer review.

EVALUATIONS OF TREATMENT EFFECTIVENESS   The most comprehensive examination of treatment programs is Lipton, Martinson, and Wilks's (1975) review of 231 programs conducted between 1945 and 1967. Each of the programs yielded data that made it possible to evaluate the effectiveness of treatment by the conventional methods used by social science researchers. In other words, each program produced an independent measure of the improvement of participants and a comparison of an experimental group of treated offenders with a control group of untreated ones. However, no more than 35 percent of these programs randomly assigned inmates to experimental and control groups (Sechrest, White, and Brown, 1979).

Martinson (1974: 25) has summarized the impact of treatment on recidivism as follows: "With few and isolated exceptions, the rehabilitative efforts that have been reported so far have had no appreciable effect on recidivism." He goes on to say that the data reviewed

> are the best available and give us very little reason to hope that we have in fact found a sure way of reducing recidivism through rehabilitation. This is not to say that we found no instances of success or partial success; it is only to say that these instances have been isolated, producing no clear pattern to indicate the efficacy of any particular method of treatment. And neither is this to say that factors *outside* the realm of rehabilitation may not be working to reduce recidivism — factors such as the tendency for recidivism to be lower in offenders over the age of 30; it is only to say that such factors seem to have little connection with any of the treatment methods now at our disposal. (Martinson, 1974: 49)

Lipton, Martinson, and Wilks uncovered little evidence that even those prison treatment programs that prepared inmates for life outside prison through education, vocational training, or the development of social skills had any appreciable impact on recidivism rates. There was little evidence that individual counseling or group counseling reduced recidivism rates, nor did Lipton, Martinson, and Wilks find any evidence that milieu therapy worked. They said that existing evidence did not permit them to conclude that the length of a sentence or the type of institution where a sentence was served affected recidivism rates. Apparently, shorter sentences would not increase recidivism rates much; they would, however, reduce the burden on convicted offenders and minimize the expense of maintaining and staffing prisons, the cost of welfare assistance to the inmates' dependents, and the loss of productivity during periods of incarceration.

Lipton, Martinson, and Wilks found that programs tried outside prison walls also seemed to have little impact on recidivism rates. Intensive supervision on probation in lieu of prison seemed to improve behavior, but this was apparently due to deterrence rather than rehabilitation. Probationers threatened by the severe sanctions that might result from intensive supervision by probation officers seemed to stay away from crime.

Several other reviews of treatment programs have reached conclusions consistent with those of Lipton, Martinson, and Wilks. An examination of one hundred programs found that the rehabilitative effects were "slight, inconsistent, and of questionable reliability" (Bailey, 1966: 157). A survey of programs a few years later also concluded that treatment programs did not have important beneficial effects (Robison and Smith, 1971). Yet another survey of evaluations of treatment programs found that "many correctional dispositions are failing to reduce recidivism" (Greenberg, 1977a: 140). The author went on to say the following:

> Much of what is now done in the name of "corrections" may serve other functions, but the prevention of return to crime is not one of them. Here and there a few favorable results alleviate the monotony, but most of these results are modest and obtained through evaluations seriously lacking in rigor. The blanket assertion that "nothing works" is an exaggeration, but not by very much. (Greenberg, 1977a: 140–141)

An updating of Lipton, Martinson, and Wilks's review of treatment programs that was carried out for the National Academy of Sciences found that the conclusion that nothing yet tried has been proved effective was still essentially correct, and that the earlier survey may even have been too generous toward treatment programs in assessing their benefits. Programs evaluated since 1967 — the cut-off date for Lipton, Martinson, and Wilks's review — provided little evidence that any form of rehabilitation works (Sechrest, White, and Brown, 1979).

Even the Swedish correctional system, one of the world's most progressive, has not succeeded in curbing recidivism. A review of treatment programs in Sweden concluded as follows: "Despite shorter terms of confinement, more open institutions, and more treatment resources given both during and after institutionalization, the Swedish correctional institutions seem to produce recidivism rates as high as the American" (Ulla Bondeson, cited in Ward, 1979: 135). One reason that has been given for Sweden's lack of success is that rejection by other Swedes makes it difficult for offenders to become reintegrated into society. Some have also suggested that the relatively good conditions in Sweden's prisons lead to "prisonization," with some parolees not being especially upset at the prospect of having to return to prison.

Why Rehabilitation Is Ineffective.   Defenders of the rehabilitation perspective sometimes claim that the apparent ineffectiveness of rehabilitation efforts is simply a result of the failure to implement treatment programs properly, but critics suggest that the rehabilitative ideal has intrinsic flaws that may make it unworkable. For instance, Martinson (1974: 49) suggests that treatment programs may not work because

> there is a . . . radical flaw in our present strategies — that education at its best, or that psychotherapy at its best, cannot overcome, or even appreciably reduce, the powerful tendency for offenders to continue in criminal behavior. Our present treatment programs are based on a theory of crime as a "disease" — that is to say,

as something foreign and abnormal in the individual which can presumably be cured. This theory may well be flawed, in that it overlooks—indeed, denies—both the normality of crime in society and the personal normality of a very large proportion of offenders, criminals who are merely responding to the facts and conditions of our society.

An effective method of rehabilitation requires an empirically supported theory of crime causation. Today's treatment methods are often based instead on vague or untested assumptions about why individuals commit crimes. One review of treatment programs makes this statement: "Where the theoretical assumptions of programs are made explicit, they tend to border on the preposterous. More often they are never made explicit, and we should be little surprised if hit-or-miss efforts fail" (Greenberg, 1977a: 141). In a similar vein, Kassebaum, Ward, and Wilner (1971: 320) say the following:

> The most fundamental requirement for further research on the effectiveness of prison and parole programs would seem to us to be a frank recognition that psychological treatment programs involve assumptions about the causes of crime, the informal and formal organization of the prison and parole, and the nature of the postrelease experience, all of *which may be quite unrealistic when applied to actual existing conditions.* (Emphasis in the original.)

Enrico Ferri (1901, 1971: 231) recognized this long ago when he said that punishment is "directed against effects, but it does not touch the causes, the roots, of the evil." Only if the causes of crime are clearly identified can effective strategies to reduce crime be devised. For instance, strengthening the conventional bonds of offenders and minimizing their ties to other criminals is a correctional strategy that can be derived from control theory and differential association theory (Glaser, 1979).

REAFFIRMING REHABILITATION Not everyone accepts the conclusion that rehabilitation is ineffective. Some criminologists reject the conventional wisdom that nothing works, pointing out that there is mixed evidence about the impact of treatment and that "treatment destruction techniques" have been used to cast doubt on the positive results that some programs have had (Palmer, 1975; Gottfredson, 1979c; Cullen and Gilbert, 1982; Greenwood and Zimring, 1985).

The effort to reaffirm the rehabilitation perspective points out that even those reviews of the research that conclude that treatment programs have not been proved effective often find that many programs do have positive results. For instance, Lipton, Martinson, and Wilks found that about half of the sixty-five programs in their sample that had used the most scientifically acceptable research designs had achieved positive results (Palmer, 1975). Other reviews of evaluations of treatment programs also have found that many had positive results (Gottfredson, 1979c). Even Martinson (1979), in a follow-up study of more recent treatment programs, concluded that some treatment programs can lower recidivism rates under certain circumstances. An analysis of 111 studies of residential programs for adjudicated delinquents determined that there was a modest reduction in recidivism from such treatment (Garrett, 1985). A review of ninety-five correctional programs carried out and evaluated between 1973 and 1978 found that some programs had beneficial results under certain conditions; family intervention strategies were found to be especially effective. Several reasons that some criminologists have concluded that "nothing works" are cited by the authors of this review:

1. Treatment programs are sometimes evaluated singly, rather than in combination with other correctional methods.
2. Evaluators often look at a single outcome measure, rather than at several measures of improvement.
3. The amenability issue has been ignored.
4. Program participants often get insufficient treatment.
5. Lack of cooperation among different agencies sometimes impedes treatment (Gendreau and Ross, 1979).

Those who seek to reaffirm the effectiveness of rehabilitation argue that critics of the rehabilitation perspective often apply especially rigorous methodological standards to their evaluation of treatment programs, and thus are led to conclude that nothing has yet been proved to be effective (Gottfredson, 1979c). One treatment destruction technique, or way of making even positive results seem questionable, is to raise possible alternative explanations for the positive findings, thereby casting doubt on the conclusion that the program itself has had a beneficial effect. Another method of attacking positive results is to show that the criterion of success is inadequate. Thus, parole revocation might be criticized as a criterion of success if one argues that the decision to revoke parole is highly arbitrary and unreliable as a measure of an ex-convict's readjustment to society. Likewise, arrest rates might be questioned as a criterion by the claim that most crimes do not lead to arrests. Another treatment destruction technique is to claim that even if a program seems to work, it may not work for everyone, or at least has not been proved to work for everyone. These methodological criticisms are valid, but those seeking to reaffirm the effectiveness of rehabilitation claim that the application of such high standards means it is unlikely that any treatment program will ever be declared an unqualified success. They argue that these methodological criticisms serve to minimize the beneficial effects some treatment programs have on certain offenders.

Another argument for the rehabilitation perspective is that even if the impact of treatment on recidivism rates is unclear, rehabilitation programs do seem to have some positive effects on adjustment in prison, attitude and personality change, educational achievement, and vocational adjustment (Cullen and Gilbert, 1982: 172). Rehabilitation has also been supported as "the only justification of criminal sanctioning that obligates the state to care for an offender's needs or welfare" (Cullen and Gilbert, 1982: 247). Thus, it is claimed, we should not abandon the rehabilitative ideal, because it contributes in an important way to the humanity of the correctional system.

"DOING LESS"   Even if treatment programs have not been proved to be effective in reducing offenders' chances of returning to crime, these programs do not seem to make offenders any worse. This has led some observers to conclude that "if we can't do more for (and to) offenders, at least we can safely do less" (Martinson, 1974: 48). Alternatives to imprisonment are less expensive; for instance, it costs about ten times as much to imprison offenders as to have them on parole or probation. Alternatives to imprisonment are also less onerous for offenders and may even benefit society. Thus, punishing convicted offenders by requiring them to work for a time — say, one eight-hour day a week for six months — for a public or charitable agency would allow them to atone for their crimes, subject them to a regular work routine, satisfy the public's demand for just deserts, provide society with a useful service, permit surveillance by probation or parole officers, and be less expensive than imprisonment (Brown, 1977).

In order to reduce prison crowding and the high cost of incarceration, some states have introduced community corrections or expanded their use of probation and parole. In the early 1970s, Massachusetts replaced its reform schools for delinquents with community-based work and educational programs, specialized foster care, and group homes. Researchers who carefully assessed this change concluded that the reforms "did not bring about a decrease in the recidivism rate, and it is equally clear that the reforms did not generate an explosive youth crime wave" (Coates, Miller, and Ohlin, 1978: 172). In the Cross-Cultural Perspective, we see how China deals with its youthful offenders.

Critics have attacked community corrections and alternative sentencing programs for failing to fulfill their promise of reducing the prison population, and for perhaps even contributing to recent increases in the prison population (Irwin, 1980; Austin and Krisberg, 1982; Hylton, 1982). These programs have also been criticized for extending the criminal justice system's control over a larger number of offenders, without effectively reducing their recidivism rate.

REINTEGRATING THE OFFENDER INTO SOCIETY   The idea that offenders need to be reintegrated into the community is at best part of the answer to the crime problem. The important issue is the kind of community into which an offender is being reintegrated. Community-based correctional institutions, work-release, and education-release may all help offenders maintain ties to a community that is characterized by crime-generating conditions as well as by more positive social conditions. What is needed are programs in the community that help offenders develop a stake in conformity and form conventional social bonds.

More attention must be given to the adjustment problems faced by ex-convicts. On leaving prison, they must support themselves financially, cope with parole restrictions, and stay away from the "old bag" (their former life of crime)

A Cross-Cultural Perspective: Dealing with Juvenile Delinquency in China

The Chinese have dealt with their rising rate of juvenile delinquency by adopting a program "aimed at restoring self-respect in the youngsters and showing them love in cases where love is lacking." Youths who commit minor infractions are placed in a situation with "a high ratio of concerned adults to each offender." Party committees organize teams of pensioners, teachers, police officers, and parents to help delinquents. When young workers break the law, they are assigned to the best worker in their factory so that they can learn appropriate attitudes toward work and society.

In China, no one under eighteen can be imprisoned, except for the most serious crimes, but there are "work-study schools" or reformatories where delinquents between fourteen and sixteen are sent for one to three years. These reform schools are run by the Ministry of Education. The day is spent on moral instruction, academic work, manual labor, and political study. The youths are taught self-discipline and how to be law-abiding citizens. They are allowed to visit home one day a week, and their parents usually visit them once a week in the reform school.

In general, the Chinese aim to rehabilitate the less serious juvenile offenders in the community, but when this fails they turn to a system much like traditional reformatories in the United States.

SOURCES. Based on James P. Sterba, "China Says Its Rising Juvenile Crime Stems from Cultural Revolution," *The New York Times*, December 26, 1979, p. A12; Tom Ashbrook, "In China, Juvenile Delinquents Are Redirected with a Soft Touch," *The Boston Globe*, April 14, 1984, p. 3.

(Irwin, 1970). Many inmates want to gratify their desires and meet certain goals when they leave prison, but lack of resources and unfamiliarity with the outside world make this difficult. Providing ex-convicts with a place to live and new clothing could ease their transition from prison to the outside world. One important aspect of this transition is finding and keeping a job that offers some hope for future advancement. One thief describes a predicament faced by many ex-convicts as follows: "During the last month [since release from prison] I have had at least forty invitations from thieves to go out stealing with them, but I have not had a single suggestion from a legitimate person about how I could make some money honestly" (cited in Sutherland, 1937: 188). Providing ex-convicts with good jobs in times of high unemployment rates can be difficult, particularly if honest, unemployed workers think that ex-convicts have an advantage over them. Sometimes it is difficult to motivate ex-convicts to search for work and keep a job, because their lack of job skills often means that only the most mundane jobs are open to them and because they may have unrealistically high expectations.

The effectiveness of programs that ease the "post-release trauma" for ex-convicts is unclear. A program in Iowa and Illinois claims a recidivism rate only one-third the national average for its clients, who are given food, shelter, clothing, counseling, education, and assistance in finding housing and medical care (*The New York Times,* October 2, 1983). However, another look at the post-release trauma concludes that its impact on ex-convicts is exaggerated. This study questions the "role discontinuity" for released inmates, suggesting that for many of them a criminal life style existed before they were imprisoned, affected their behavior while in prison, and continues to influence their actions after release. This study finds that programs that try to ease the transition from prison to the outside world have not yet been shown to be effective in reducing the recidivism rate (Minor and Courlander, 1979).

The Future of Rehabilitation

Today the rehabilitative ideal has been abandoned by some of its former advocates, while others seek to reaffirm it. Critics argue that treatment programs have not been proved effective, but defenders of those programs point to some that have had beneficial results. Critics claim that the indeterminate sentence and the ineffectiveness of treatment programs have combined to lengthen sentences and extend the criminal justice system's control over offenders. Defenders of the rehabilitative ideal claim that it has been a force for greater humanity in the correctional system.

Diminished faith in the rehabilitative ideal has led some criminologists, lawmakers, and citizens to argue that until treatment is shown to be effective, punishment should be based on the principle of just deserts (Von Hirsch, 1976). Offenders found guilty of crimes serious enough to warrant imprisonment would be incarcerated for fixed terms under humane conditions. Voluntary treatment programs might then be provided for inmates, with the clear understanding that participation would not affect the length of the sentence or the conditions of release. Because most treatment until now has been provided under a system of indeterminate sentences and because participation in programs has affected the time and terms of release, we cannot know whether treatment under such a just deserts system would be more effective than it seems to have been so far. Treatment might be more effective under such a system because programs presumably would be populated only with inmates who sincerely wanted to change (Goodstein, 1980).

In spite of efforts by some criminologists to reaffirm the rehabilitative ideal, it has become less dominant in the American criminal justice system since the mid-1970s. Lawmakers have introduced sentencing reforms that are based on the theories of just deserts, incapacitation, and deterrence, rather than on the rehabilitative ideal. For instance, parole has been restricted or eliminated, weakening inmates' motivation to participate in treatment programs. Rehabilitation efforts will continue, but they are now given relatively less attention by the correctional system than they were just a few years ago.

Summary

The idea that punishment should rehabilitate or reform offenders so they do not commit additional crimes had its origins in the ideas of the Enlightenment and in the work of prison reformers during the eighteenth and nineteenth centuries. This rehabilitation model was dominant in the American criminal justice system from the 1920s until the mid-1970s, when considerations of just deserts, incapacitation, and deterrence became relatively more important. Rehabilitation can be demeaning to offenders, who are treated as defective people in need of change, rather than as rational decision makers or as people who should pay the price for having broken the law.

The criminal justice system is influenced in many ways by the rehabilitation rationale for punishment. The police exercise their discretion in part on the basis of ideas about what kind of response is most likely to keep a suspect away from crime in the future; sometimes suspects are kept out of court and prison by police diversion or police probation programs. In court, pretrial diversion is sometimes used to prevent labeling, which might push defendants into a life of crime. Plea bargaining may be influenced by prosecutors' and judges' ideas about what kind of punishment is most likely to reform an offender. Judges are influenced by their ideas about rehabilitation when they sentence offenders. Indeterminate sentences and parole are products of the idea that offenders should be sentenced to indefinite periods and released only when they are rehabilitated. Because treatment in prison is generally secondary to the goal of custody, rehabilitation programs have not usually been given priority by prison administrators.

Efforts to measure the success of treatment programs typically employ recidivism rates, but other measures of improvement have also been used. Treatment may be considered effective if it causes ex-convicts to reduce the rate at which they commit crime or if it helps them function better in the community, in their family, or at a job. Research on rehabilitation has been complicated by the amenability issue, the idea that some kinds of offenders may be suited only to certain types of treatment.

Among the many forms of treatment are education and work programs, methadone treatment for heroin addicts, behavior modification, individual therapy, casework, milieu therapy, and group counseling. Evaluations of treatment programs that have used experimental and control groups have not proved that any kind of treatment consistently and significantly reduces involvement in criminal behavior, even though some programs seem to show positive results. Even if the impact of treatment on recidivism rates is unclear, we might do less to and for offenders than we now do without changing the crime rate significantly. Using alternatives to prison might reduce the financial cost of punishment and lessen the burden on offenders. However, critics claim that alternative sentencing programs and community corrections have not reduced the recidivism rate and may even have increased the prison population and the extent of control over offenders by the criminal justice system. Reintegration of offenders into the community is an important aspect of correctional policies, but careful attention must be paid to the kind of community into which offenders are being reintegrated. Rehabilitation will continue to be an important part of the American criminal justice system, but it is now a less influential perspective on punishment than it once was.

Important Terms

amenability issue   milieu therapy
behavior modification   police diversion
casework   police probation
group counseling   pretrial diversion
individual therapy   recidivism rate
methadone maintenance   rehabilitation

Suggested Readings

FRANCIS T. CULLEN AND KAREN E. GILBERT. *Reaffirming Rehabilitation.* Cincinnati, Ohio: Anderson, 1982. An eloquent argument for keeping the rehabilitation perspective central to the American criminal justice system; includes a thorough history of rehabilitation in the United States.

GENE KASSEBAUM, DAVID A. WARD, AND DANIEL M. WILNER. *Prison Treatment and Parole Survival: An Empirical Assessment.* New York: Wiley, 1971. A meticulous experimental study that finds a lack of impact of group counseling on prison inmates.

DOUGLAS LIPTON, ROBERT MARTINSON, AND JUDITH WILKS. *The Effectiveness of Correctional Treatment: A Survey of Treatment Evaluation Studies.* New York: Praeger, 1975. A comprehensive assessment of 231 treatment programs carried out between 1945 and 1967.

ROBERT MARTINSON. "What Works?—Questions and Answers about Prison Reform," *The Public Interest* No. 35 (Spring 1974), 22–54. A widely cited and controversial paper that summarizes the results of the study by Lipton, Martinson, and Wilks.

LEE SECHREST, SUSAN O. WHITE, AND ELIZABETH D. BROWN, EDS. *The Rehabilitation of Criminal Offenders: Problems and Prospects.* Washington, D.C.: National Academy of Sciences, 1979. An evaluation of research on treatment programs that updates the Lipton, Martinson, and Wilks study, but with much the same conclusion.

CHAPTER 17

Solving the Crime Problem

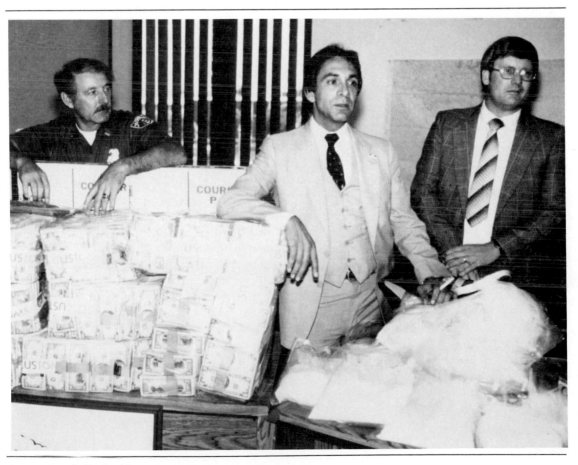

Source: Randy Taylor/Sygma

Many solutions to the crime problem have been proposed, but few have reduced crime in any significant way. As a result, there is widespread pessimism about the possibility of solving the problem. We may know too little about the causes of crime to design crime-reduction programs, or we simply may not yet have developed and implemented the correct policies. In this chapter, we look at three ideological positions and their proposals for reducing crime. We then trace the politics of crime in the United States since the mid-1960s. Finally, we look at three strategies for solving the crime problem: reforming the criminal justice system, minimizing the opportunities for crime, and dealing with the causes of crime.

Ideological Approaches to Solving the Crime Problem

Three general ideological orientations toward the crime problem can be delineated: a conservative approach, a liberal approach, and a radical approach. Each position includes a set of general beliefs and assumptions about the causes of crime and the appropriate ways to reduce it. The assumptions of each position underlie the policies proposed by its adherents, even though those assumptions may not always be made explicit (Miller, 1973; Fairchild and Webb, 1985; McGarrell and Flanagan, 1987).

The Conservative Approach

The *conservative approach* seeks to preserve the status quo from criminals, who are seen as challengers to the existing social order. Conservatives focus on the high costs of crime and the criminal justice system. They emphasize conventional crimes such as the FBI's index offenses; white-collar crime and government corruption are ignored, denied, or even justified.

Conventional crime is attributed to the lower and working classes, who are thought to be improperly socialized or irresponsible. Crime is said to be caused by the defective family structure of the poor and by the failure of those families to inculcate in children the values appropriate to a law-abiding life. Conservatives' concern with the permissiveness and immorality of groups that have high rates of conventional crime has a long history, going back at least as far as nineteenth-century Paris, where crime was attributed to the "dangerous classes," a term synonymous with the lower and working classes (Chevalier, 1973).

The conservative solution to the crime problem is to encourage "adherence to the legitimate directives of constituted authority" (Miller, 1973: 144). The means to do this include the improvement of family life, better discipline, more self-control, and harsher and more certain penalties. Because conservatives are ideologically opposed to the intrusion of the government into the home, even into homes that produce criminals, they rarely give much attention to programs to strengthen the family or to teach parents better ways to instill law-abiding values in their children. Instead, conservatives emphasize deterrence, incapacitation, and just deserts, and rely on the criminal justice system to mete out certain, severe, prompt, and just penalties. Conservatives call for a larger, more efficient, and less restrained police force; a higher conviction rate in court; and longer prison sentences. Conservatives are often willing to sacrifice or abridge the procedural rights of defendants, and indeed the rights of the entire population, in order to increase the chances of arrest, conviction, and punishment.

The Liberal Approach

The *liberal approach* holds that crime can be reduced by policies that attack its underlying causes. Liberals claim that people are the products of the social and economic system in which they live. Inequality of income and power and the lack of opportunities for certain groups increase the probability that more members of disadvantaged groups will engage in behavior defined as criminal by those who hold power.

Liberals believe society can be reformed in ways that will reduce the crime rate, but they reject the idea that a full-scale revolution is required. They tend to focus on conventional crimes, which they see as a lower-class and working-class phenomenon that results from poverty, discrimination, and oppression. As a consequence, they propose that educational and vocational training, welfare assistance, job opportunities, antidiscrimination laws, and community organization and change can reduce the crime rate. Liberals traditionally have argued that the primary function of criminal penalties should be the rehabilitation of convicted offenders, but with growing evidence that many treatment programs do not work, some liberals have shifted to a theory of punishment that stresses just deserts to a greater degree (Bayer, 1981).

The Radical Approach

A third perspective on the crime problem is the *radical approach*. This viewpoint focuses on crime by both the underprivileged and the privileged, and attributes crime by both groups to the conditions of a capitalist society. Radicals point to evidence — such as some self-report studies — that indicates that crime is more evenly distributed among the classes than is suggested by official crime statistics. Differences in crime rates among various groups are then attributed to the differential handling of groups by the criminal justice system, rather than to actual differences in their criminal behavior. The crime problem is regarded as a socially defined product of selective crime reporting and recording, media attention, and differential treatment by the criminal justice system.

The radical approach places greater emphasis on white-collar crime and political corruption than do the conservative and liberal approaches. Conventional criminals are seen as victims of a capitalist system, rather than as offenders against society. Radicals shift attention from the criminal offender to the social and economic system that defines certain behavior as criminal and pushes people into crime by failing to meet their needs. The radical perspective emphasizes justice rather than crime, and looks at the negative implications of values such as competition and material success.

The radical perspective offers few specific solutions to the crime problem, other than calling for the construction of a new and basically different social system, one that is vaguely described as communist or socialist. Whether such a society now exists anywhere or can be created in the future is open to question; radicals rarely describe in detail the alternative society that might keep crime to a minimum.

The Politics of Crime

Since the 1960s, crime has sometimes been a major issue for politicians at the national, state, and local levels. Generally, those who have made the most use of the crime issue have been "law-and-order" politicians who have adopted a conservative approach, although in the 1984 election the more liberal Democratic party developed policies to deal with the problem of crime.

The President's Commission on Law Enforcement and Administration of Justice

The rates of index crimes began to rise dramatically in the mid-1960s. One of the earliest political reactions to this increase was President Johnson's 1965 appointment of the President's Commission on Law Enforcement and Administration of Justice. President Johnson asked the Commission to "deepen our understanding of the causes of crime and of how society should respond to the challenge of the present levels of crime" (The President's Commission on Law Enforcement and Administration of Justice, 1967a: 2). The seventeen volumes published by the Commission in 1967 included many proposals to deal with crime, but little new information about the causes of crime. Because most of the Commission's members were lawyers, police administrators, judges, and correctional officials, it is not too surprising that the Commission's recommendations emphasized reform of the criminal justice system.

The conservative approach to crime reduction was stressed by the Commission. The very first sentence of the summary chapter of its final report stated that "America can *control* crime" (The President's Commission on Law Enforcement and Administration of Justice, 1967a: 279; emphasis added here). The Commission did give passing attention to the liberal approach:

> [C]rime flourishes where the conditions of life are the worst, and . . . therefore the foundation of a national strategy against crime is an unremitting national effort for social justice. Reducing poverty, discrimination, ignorance, disease and urban blight, and the anger, cynicism or despair those conditions can inspire, is one great step toward reducing crime. *It is not the task, indeed it is not within the competence, of a*

> *Commission on Law Enforcement and Administration of Justice to make detailed proposals about housing or education or civil rights, unemployment or welfare or health.* However, it is the Commission's clear and urgent duty to stress that forceful action in these fields is essential to crime prevention, and to adjure the officials of every agency of criminal justice—policemen, prosecutors, judges, correctional authorities—to associate themselves with and labor for the success of programs that will improve the quality of American life. (The President's Commission on Law Enforcement and Administration of Justice, 1967a: 279; emphasis added here)

Why the Commission thought its broad mandate from the President to devise a national policy to reduce crime allowed it to avoid detailed proposals about the social causes of crime is a puzzle.

To reduce crime in America, the Commission recommended federal support to meet eight major goals:

1. State and local planning.
2. Education and training of criminal justice personnel.
3. Surveys and advisory services concerning organization and operation of criminal justice agencies.
4. Development of coordinated national information systems.
5. Development of a limited number of demonstration programs in agencies of justice.
6. Scientific and technological research and development.
7. Institutes for research and training personnel.
8. Grants-in-aid for operational innovation. (The President's Commission on Law Enforcement and Administration of Justice, 1967a: 285)

The implementation of these proposals might have produced a more streamlined and better-funded system of criminal justice, but there is little evidence from criminological research that such changes would have reduced the crime rate.

The Law Enforcement Assistance Administration

The work of the Commission led to a 1968 law, the Omnibus Crime Control and Safe Streets Act, which established the Law Enforcement Assistance Administration (LEAA) in the United States Department of Justice. This agency funneled money appropriated by Congress to the states to fund various crime-control programs. The budget of LEAA rose dramatically from $63 million in 1968 to $880 million in 1975, but declined to $486 million in 1980. The agency was disbanded in 1982, but during its existence it spent $7.7 billion.

Some of LEAA's funds were used for controversial purposes, such as establishing a computerized file of "suspected subversives" and purchasing tanks for local police departments to use during riots. LEAA did not have an overall guiding philosophy behind its disbursement of funds; indeed, the development of such a rationale was inhibited by the requirement that most funds be given to the states in block grants that were to be used as the states wished. Over the years, LEAA funds were increasingly used for correctional programs rather than for police crime-control measures.

LEAA may have improved the efficiency and professionalism of local law-enforcement agencies, but it failed to meet its goal of reducing the crime rate. An analysis of the impact of LEAA that was based on interviews with federal officials concluded that the agency's impact was primarily negative: It helped weaken the belief that capital punishment was a deterrent; it undermined faith in rehabilitation as a solution to the crime problem; and it showed that changes in police methods — such as saturation patrolling, faster response time, and more education for officers — would not reduce the crime rate (Cronin, Cronin, and Milakovich, 1981).

The 1968 and 1972 Presidential Elections

In the 1968 presidential election, the major domestic issue was crime, with the Vietnam War being the major foreign policy issue. Two of the candidates, Richard Nixon and George Wallace, were ardent and vocal advocates of a "law-and-order" approach to crime that was based on the conservative belief that the crime rate could be reduced by strengthening the criminal justice system (Epstein, 1975). Nixon and Wallace claimed that the Democrats, incumbents for eight years, had been "soft" on street crime, ghetto rioting, and campus violence. The Democratic candidate, Hubert Humphrey, did not speak out in favor of such violence, but Nixon and Wallace were able to parlay the issue of "crime in the streets" into millions of votes in November. Many voters switched their traditionally Democratic votes to the Republican party or the American Independent party because of the crime issue.

The burglary at the Watergate complex occurred in 1972, the year of another presidential election. The power of the office of the presidency was great enough to allow President Nixon to cover up this crime until he was reelected. Ironically, surveys show that a major reason for his victory in 1972, as well as in 1968, was the "law-and-order" vote (Gallup, 1972). People who would otherwise have voted for the Democratic candidate, Senator George McGovern, voted for President Nixon because of his opposition to crime in the streets.

Crime is still a political issue, but its significance has waned since the 1972 election. One reason is that official crime rates continued to climb during the 1970s in spite of the election of law-and-order politicians, and so it became difficult for them to claim they had solved the crime problem. Another reason for the decline in crime as a political issue after 1972 was that economic issues such as inflation and unemployment began to occupy voters' attention. Finally, the fact that several law-and-order candidates were shown to be hypocritical and involved in criminal activities themselves reduced their credibility. Vice President Spiro Agnew, an outspoken advocate of harsh punishment for criminals, resigned under pressure because he had violated laws on taxation and bribery.

President Nixon resigned in 1974 after a congressional committee voted bills of impeachment against him for obstruction of justice and other illegal acts. Some claim that these and other law-and-order politicians who violated the law were no more dishonest than other politicians, but the fact that they had adopted a holier-than-thou attitude undermined their law-and-order approach to crime reduction and lessened the political impact of the crime issue. We can see in the Cross-Cultural Perspective that crime also has been a political issue in France in recent years.

The National Advisory Commission on Criminal Justice Standards and Goals

In 1971, the National Advisory Commission on Criminal Justice Standards and Goals was established to formulate policies to reduce crime. The recommendations of this commission were similar to those of the 1967 President's Commission on Law Enforcement and Administration of Justice, for they also emphasized criminal justice reforms as the way to reduce crime (The National Advisory Commission on Criminal Justice Standards and Goals, 1973). Neither commission approached the problem of crime reduction by looking for the underlying causes of crime and then proposing ways to eradicate those causes. Both assumed that the existing criminal justice system was the appropriate apparatus for dealing with crime and that this system only needed improvement to solve the crime problem.

The Crime Issue during the Reagan Administration

Crime was not the major issue in either the 1980 or the 1984 presidential election, but President Reagan made occasional use of the issue during his time in office. In a speech before the International Association of Chiefs of Police in 1981, he incorporated several recommendations made by the Attorney General's Task Force on Violent Crime in its report issued earlier in that year (U.S. Department of Justice, 1981). The Task Force focused on the criminal justice system as the solution to the crime problem, and Reagan followed suit, except that he did comment on the causes of crime. In his speech, President Reagan did not mention the Task Force's recommendation for $2 billion in federal assistance to the states for the construction of prisons. He called for the denial of bail under certain conditions for defendants who seemed likely to commit more crime if released, even though this system of preventive detention had been ineffective in Washington, D.C., during the previous decade. The President supported reform of the exclusionary rule, which disallows the use in court of evidence illegally seized by the police. Reagan also called for capital punishment, the use of the military to develop information to be used in curbing drug importation, mandatory prison terms for people convicted of using handguns during felonies, and the use of IRS records to prosecute gangsters and drug

A Cross-Cultural Perspective:
The Politics of Crime in France

In the 1970s, street crime in France began to increase steadily, and by the late 1970s public concern with crime had become an important issue that conservative politicians exploited. The rightist government of President Valéry Giscard D'Estaing blamed crime on immigrants and on lenient judges. In 1980s, Giscard D'Estaing introduced a "Security and Liberty" law that proposed harsher penalties, eliminated much judicial discretion, and allowed the police to make unlimited checks on people's identities. Judges opposed this law, but Parliament passed it in 1980. An immediate effect was a substantial increase in the size of the prison population.

In spite of these changes in the criminal justice system, crime rates continued to rise.

In May 1981, Giscard D'Estaing lost office to François Mitterand and the Socialists, who had criticized the incumbent for contributing to the public's fear of crime and for threatening civil liberties. Mitterand's minister of justice, Robert Badinter, led an assault on Giscard D'Estaing's policies. He abolished capital punishment, urged the use of alternative sentences such as restitution and community service, sought harsher penalties for white-collar crime, and made prison life less stringent.

These reforms ran into strong opposition. French judges and the "penitentiary lobby," which is composed of prison guards and administrators, attacked Badinter's prison reforms. This lobby, which is closely linked to conservative political parties, claimed that

dealers. Most of these proposals involved changes in the law, rather than any increase in federal expenditures.

This speech reflected a conservative, law-and-order approach to the crime problem. In it, the President called crime "ultimately a moral dilemma," rather than simply a question of more funds for the criminal justice system. He claimed that the "war on crime will only be won when an attitude of mind and a change of heart take place in America," and when truths such as right and wrong, individual responsibility, and swift and certain punishment for wrongdoing take hold. He criticized social scientists, social workers, and psychiatrists who assert that poverty, disadvantaged childhoods, and a bad environment lead to crime. Instead, he claimed that crime is a way of life that some people consciously choose, not usually because they are "seeking bread for their families," but because they "are driven crazy with desire for stuff they'll never be able to afford." He saw criminals as people who commit crime because it is easy and not very risky, and who believe they are entitled to what they steal. President Reagan did not propose to treat the causes of crime directly by changing people's values — for example, by restricting advertising that stimulates materialism — but instead focused on the criminal justice system to mete out penalties based on the ideas of deterrence, incapacitation, and just deserts.

the Socialists' policies contributed to the crime rate by emptying the prisons. Extreme right-wing groups, such as the National Front, criticized Mitterand's government for exacerbating the crime problem, pointing to immigrants and lax judges as the sources of that problem. Mitterand resisted pressure for a more conservative approach to crime, but even the Socialist-dominated Parliament supported some conservative measures, such as the right of the police to make identity checks, and there was little evidence among government officials of support for Badinter's efforts to liberalize the criminal justice system.

In March 1986, a conservative government led by Prime Minister Jacques Chirac took office, strongly supporting a law-and-order approach and attacking the Socialists' softness on the crime issue. The interior minister, Charles Pasqua, promised to improve the security of citizens within thirty days. Pasqua, the son of a police officer, took a number of steps to show his support for the police. However, widespread criticism of police excesses soon developed, following two police killings of suspects and an unusually high number of shootings and beatings by the police. The newspaper *Le Monde* said the government should control the police force and "remind it that its mission is to protect the citizens, not to make them anxious" (p. 18).

In 1986, the police commissioner of Paris was forced to resign after he released statistics showing that crime in that city had declined slightly, even during the Socialist administration. Interior minister Pasqua said the commissioner had no right to release crime statistics without the permission of the government.

SOURCES: Based on Daniel Cohen, "Problems of Punishment," *Atlantic Monthly* 253 (January 1984), 28–32; Ronald Koven, "In France, a Stir over 'Law and Order,'" *The Boston Globe*, August 17, 1987, p. 18

In October 1984, President Reagan signed into law the Comprehensive Crime Control Act, which he had recommended and pushed but which was also the product of bipartisan efforts in Congress. This law was wide-ranging in its reforms, but because it applied just to federal law, under which only 5 percent of all criminal defendants are tried, it has had little impact on the nation's crime problem. The law introduced preventive detention on the federal level in order to reduce bail crime. It led to the elimination of parole for federal prisoners and established a committee that in 1987 established sentencing guidelines that would limit judicial discretion and reduce sentence disparity. The law limited the insanity defense to people who were unable to appreciate the wrongfulness of their acts. It also created a victim-compensation program, expanded federal jurisdiction over credit-card fraud, made it easier for the government to seize the illegal profits of drug dealers and organized criminals, and lengthened penalties for drug dealers and repeat offenders.

In 1986, the President's Commission on Organized Crime issued its report. The Commission documented the criminal activities of many gangs run by groups other than the Mafia. It described the laundering of organized crime profits by financial institutions and urged federal legislation to curb this practice. In one of its most controversial recommendations, it asked for drug testing of American workers, a suggestion that stemmed from frustration over the failure of policies aimed at drug traffickers. In late 1986, President Reagan ordered drug testing of those of the 2.8 million federal employees who held "sensitive" jobs. This policy led to legal challenges, and by three months after the President's order thirteen of seventeen court decisions had found such drug testing unconstitutional (Kerr, 1986).

In October 1986, an important piece of legislation was passed and signed to deal with drug abuse. The Anti-Drug Abuse Act allocated $1.7 billion to fight drugs. Only 12 percent of this was to be spent on drug education. Another 22 percent was to be spent on treatment and research, with most of the remainder going to federal and state law-enforcement agencies. Three months after he signed this bill, President Reagan submitted a budget to Congress that called for sharp cuts in federal funds for drug enforcement, prevention, and treatment.

Crime and the Criminal Justice System

In this section we look at several proposals for reducing crime by reforming the criminal justice system. These proposals deal with the kinds of behavior over which the law should or should not have jurisdiction and with the operation of the police, the courts, and the prisons.

Overreach of the Criminal Law

Some critics propose that the criminal justice system might be more effective if it gave up jurisdiction over certain kinds of behavior. This claim that efficiency is hindered by the "overreach" of the criminal law is often applied to victimless crimes, those offenses that are consensual and lack a complaining participant. One argument for this change is that the principle of retribution requires that acts that harm no one should not be punished. Another argument is that the limited resources of the criminal justice system could better be applied to conventional crimes than to victimless crimes such as public drunkenness and gambling (Morris and Hawkins, 1970).

From time to time the proposal has been made to reduce the overreach of the criminal law by legalizing heroin. Because drug enforcement overburdens the police, the courts, and the prisons, one way to free resources for other criminal investigations is to make heroin legally available to addicts in clinics. Free or inexpensive heroin would reduce addicts' need to commit property crimes to support their habit, although many of them probably would continue to commit some crime anyway. Legalization might increase the number of addicts by making heroin more easily available. A counterargument is that legal heroin would have less of the mystique that now leads some people to use it. For years, Great Britain has made drugs legally available to addicts who are registered with the government and treated by a physician (Trebach, 1982). Whether this system would be effective in the United States is questionable. Indeed, there is even some question about the effectiveness of this approach in Great Britain, where the estimated number of heroin addicts quadrupled from 1980 to 1985, and where officials state that only about 12 percent of the country's addicts were registered for treatment in 1985 (*The New York Times*, April 11, 1985).

The Police

Suggested reforms in the criminal justice system often focus on how the police might combat crime more effectively, even though there is little evidence that the police make much difference in crime rates. As we saw earlier in the book, within the range that now exists for the size of police forces in American cities, the number of officers per capita makes little or no difference in crime rates, even though the public seems to believe that putting more officers on the street is a major part of the solution to the crime problem.

Even if more police officers were available, there is little reason to expect that crime would be reduced. There is a nearly unlimited number of targets for crime, and offenders have little difficulty finding targets in spite of the presence of the police. The Kansas City police patrol experiment found that the number of officers in an area did not affect the amount of crime in the area (Kelling et al., 1974). Even if the presence of the police did deter an offender from committing a crime against a particular target, the offender could easily wait until the police leave or could search out another target. Street patrols might change the type of crime that an offender commits; for instance, a criminal might avoid robbery in favor of burglary. We cannot say with certainty that the police never prevent crime, but there is little evidence that they can have a major impact on the crime rate.

If more police officers do not make any obvious difference in the crime rate, it is still possible that the kind of action that the police take will affect criminal behavior (Sherman, 1986). For instance, we saw earlier that a study of police response to domestic violence in Minneapolis showed that arrest was a more effective deterrent than police mediation of disputes, which in turn worked better than having the police tell members of the household to separate for eight hours.

A study by the Police Foundation concluded that rather than measure the productivity of officers by the number of arrests they make, police administrators would contribute more to the reduction of crime if they weighed the net impact of each arrest. Arrests of chronic criminals, who may average five or more serious offenses per week, contribute more to curbing crime than arrests of occasional offenders, and a weighted clearance rate that takes this into account would be a better way of assessing the performance of officers and focusing more attention on the apprehension of career criminals (Martin, 1986; Martin and Sherman, 1986).

Crime might also be reduced over the long run if the police established better relationships with the community and increased public trust so that more crimes were reported. Offenders might then realize that the chance their crimes would be reported was greater, and that the probability of arrest and conviction was higher. However, it is not clear that the public's reporting of crime can be increased enough so that potential offenders will realize they face a significantly greater threat of punishment.

FEDERAL LAW ENFORCEMENT The federal government has usually adopted a policy of dealing with drug use that relies on policing the borders of the country to prevent drug importation. These efforts apparently have increased the amount of drugs confiscated at the borders, but even this increased amount appears to be only a small proportion of all of the drugs importers try to get into the country. Importers may simply increase their activity to compensate for the larger amounts lost to law enforcers. Estimates of the proportion of all heroin, cocaine, and other illegal drugs seized while coming into the country range from 2 to 13 percent, but these figures are only guesses (Maitland, 1983). In 1983, the U.S. General Accounting Office said that rivalry among various federal law-enforcement agencies and the failure to prosecute many arrested suspects in drug trafficking cases had limited the impact of recent efforts to curb drug importation.

In 1967, the National Crime Information Center (NCIC) was established under the jurisdiction of the FBI. The NCIC has expanded its computerized records in recent years, in spite of concern about the accuracy of those records and their threat to privacy. After criticism about the threat to privacy, in 1984 the FBI shelved a plan to expand the NCIC to cover people considered suspicious but not wanted for crimes. In spite of problems with this system, a national clearinghouse for information on crime is an important tool for law enforcement. Local police departments can get rapid responses to their inquiries about whether a car is stolen or whether suspects they are questioning are wanted outside their state. The importance of a nationally coordinated system can be seen in the results of an FBI study that concluded that half of all offenders are arrested in more than one state during their criminal career, and that 17.8 percent are arrested in three or more states (Kelley, 1976: 43). Serial murderers wander from state to state killing their victims, and a centralized system of records can uncover patterns of similar crimes in different parts of the country. In response to this problem, the FBI in 1984 established the Violent Criminal Apprehension Program (VICAP) to collect and analyze standardized reports on violent crimes and missing persons.

The Courts

The primary way that the courts might reduce crime is by increasing the certainty of punishment. However, it is not obvious that certainty of punishment can be increased significantly in the United States without infringing on the constitutional rights of defendants or greatly expanding the resources of the criminal justice system.

SENTENCING STRATEGIES One proposal to reduce crime rates is to change sentencing procedures. Rather than providing indeterminate sentences, lawmakers might create a system of fixed sentences and thus increase the uniformity of sentences meted out to offenders. This would not necessarily increase the severity of sentences, but it would implement the principle of just deserts better than the current sentencing system does. It might also reduce the bitterness that now exists among inmates because of sentence disparity and parole board arbitrariness; this bitterness can impede rehabilitation. More uniform sentences might also be more certain in their application, and this could increase the deterrent effect of punishment. The federal government and several states have adopted this strategy in recent years.

Several policies have been implemented to punish offenders differently than in the past. For example, Pennsylvania has developed a package of reforms that combine various approaches: mandatory minimum sentences, the abolition of the parole board, the reduction of sentences for good behavior in prison, longer sentences for some crimes, a stronger department of corrections, and the construction of new prison cells. To increase the deterrent effect of these policies, television and radio advertisements have been used to educate the public about the increased risks of criminal activity.

MAKING PROSECUTION EASIER   Laws against sex offenses, such as forcible rape and child molestation, have traditionally included impediments to prosecution. One way to increase certainty of punishment would be to reform those laws to make prosecution easier and conviction more likely. For instance, in 1984 New York, Nebraska, and Washington, D.C., still required evidence to support a child's testimony in a case of child molestation. Because this offense usually occurs in private, the unwillingness of the courts to believe young victims made prosecution very difficult in those jurisdictions and thus made the certainty of punishment very low, thereby reducing the law's deterrent effect. Abolition of this corroboration requirement could reduce child molestation.

Some states have also required corroboration in cases of forcible rape, which has made prosecution of this crime difficult. Moreover, the testimony of a rape victim could be examined in court by asking her about her past sexual conduct, often making it seem that she, rather than the accused rapist, was on trial. Many states now have "shield laws" that protect rape victims from this kind of cross examination, even though critics claim this effort to protect victims has restricted the rights of rape defendants.

Another legal reform that has made the prosecution of rape defendants easier is the division of this crime into several degrees of rape and sexual assault, with different penalties specified for each of the three or four degrees of the offense. This might make it easier to get a conviction for rape from a jury that thinks that mitigating circumstances do not warrant the severe penalty that was previously attached to the single type of forcible rape.

PROSECUTING ORGANIZED CRIME   New legislation and increased resources have made it possible for the federal government and local district attorneys to prosecute the leaders of organized crime more successfully. The FBI began to devote more of its resources to the prosecution of organized crime beginning in the mid-1970s. The Racketeer Influenced and Corrupt Organizations law (RICO) is used by the federal government to prosecute defendants who engage in a series of crimes. This law also permits those who suffer losses due to financial fraud, either by organized crime or by white-collar offenders, to bring civil suits for triple damages.

More use of undercover agents and informers, the pooling of resources by law-enforcement agencies, and more FBI concentration on narcotics crimes have increased the prosecution and conviction of organized crime leaders. Witnesses have been given immunity and new identities in different parts of the country in return for testifying against suspects, and this has made prosecution easier.

Even though critics of these policies contend that imprisoned gangsters are replaced from within the organized crime "family," and that organized crime is not much affected by law-enforcement efforts, an intensive effort to prosecute leaders that is carried out over time might reduce this kind of criminal activity. One U.S. Attorney claims the following:

> The old-timers are not easily replaceable. The founders are now dying off, and we're dealing with the second, third and fourth level. They are not able to replenish themselves the way they could before. The ones they would have recruited are now in college and law school. (Rudolph Giuliani, cited in Werner, 1983: D18)

PROSECUTING WHITE-COLLAR CRIME   The rational nature of much white-collar crime suggests that it might be deterred by penalties that are more severe, more certain, and more promptly applied (Conklin, 1977; Clinard and Yeager, 1980). Federal and state agencies now lack the resources to prosecute very many cases, and those they select for prosecution sometimes require years of investigation. Consequently, certainty of punishment is low and even those offenders who are punished do not suffer any penalty for years.

Many people believe the penalties for corporate offenders are too lenient to deter white-collar crime. Fines levied against corporations are often minuscule compared with the company's total assets, and executives who are fined may be paid back by the company. Few corporate officers are imprisoned, and when they are it is usually for a short term in a minimum-security prison. Penalties could be made more harsh by requiring guilty corporations to take remedial action, by levying heavier fines, by prohibiting corporate recidivists from securing government contracts, and by sentencing more corporate officers to prison (Clinard and Yeager, 1980). Negative publicity might also affect corporate behavior, because firms are concerned with their public reputations and may make changes in response to adverse publicity (Fisse and Braithwaite, 1983). In extreme cases, an offending corporation might even be taken over by the federal government or prohibited from doing business.

JUVENILE COURTS Earlier in the book, we saw that many arrested suspects are juveniles. There is some evidence that juveniles have become increasingly prone to violence and that they are beginning to commit crime at an earlier age (Boffey, 1982). In addition, juvenile delinquents are more likely to go on to adult criminal careers than are nondelinquents. For these reasons, the search for solutions to the crime problem often focuses on young people.

One proposed reform would end the secrecy of juvenile court records, so that young adults with long records of serious offenses as juveniles could be sentenced as long-term criminals rather than as first-time offenders when they first appear in criminal court. This policy is in effect in Great Britain, in contrast to the "two-track" system in the Unites States. Another proposal would lower the age at which adolescents are legally prosecuted as adults. For instance, in 1982 New Jersey passed a law that allowed defendants fourteen or older to be tried as adults when they were charged with certain serious crimes.

Some have proposed that alternative sentences for juveniles should replace incarceration in reformatories, which might be reserved for those who repeatedly commit serious offenses. Placement in a group home, especially one in a different community, might have a greater impact in reducing criminal activity than does returning youths to their family's home. Group homes might provide a surrogate family, especially for juveniles from families that generate crime. Another innovative proposal is to treat the entire family of the youthful offender, rather than isolate the juvenile for treatment. The problems of juvenile delinquents frequently stem from poor relationships within the family, and as long as that problem remains untreated it is unlikely the juvenile's behavior will change.

The Prisons

Some criminologists support the idea that prisons are "schools for crime" — that is, that inmates learn to commit crimes from others while incarcerated. We have no solid evidence that inmates later engage in crimes they would not otherwise have committed because of what they have learned from other prisoners, but some information and skills that are useful in the pursuit of a life in crime may be exchanged among inmates.

Because there is no clear and consistent evidence that incarceration reduces crime through rehabilitation, some have suggested that the imprisonment of offenders should be based on the principle of just deserts. Treatment could be made optional during a fixed period of confinement. Whenever possible, pretrial diversion and sanctions of warnings or probation could be substituted for imprisonment, which is both expensive and ineffective in curbing crime.

Some criminologists have suggested that offenders who seem unlikely to commit additional dangerous crimes should be left in the community where they can maintain ties to families and jobs. This recommendation has several problems. First, leaving offenders in the community may continue to expose them to the influences that led them to violate the law in the first place. Second, predicting which offenders are likely to commit more crimes is difficult; research shows that we cannot accurately distinguish potentially dangerous offenders from those who are not potentially dangerous.

Situational Crime Prevention

A second general strategy for solving the crime problem — in addition to relying on the criminal justice system to deter, incapacitate, and rehabilitate — is *situational crime prevention.* This involves measures "(1) directed at highly specific forms of crime (2) that involve the management, design, or manipulation of the immediate environment in as systematic and permanent a way as possible (3) so as to reduce the opportunities for crime and increase its risks as perceived by a wide range of offenders" (Clarke, 1983: 225). This strategy involves "target hardening," self-protective measures, informal social control, and community crime prevention.

Target Hardening

One approach to reducing opportunities for crime is to make it more difficult for an offender to carry out a crime against a particular target. This policy is often referred to as *target hardening.* Included here are the installation of bars and locks on doors and windows, the use of spotlights, the purchase of guard dogs, and the use of alarms. These measures might reduce the chance that the target-hardened building will be burglarized, but it is likely that a burglar who is motivated to steal and who perceives a low risk of arrest will simply move to another, less well protected target.

One instance of target hardening that seemed to curb bank robbery was the installation in New York City banks during the early 1980s of bulletproof Plexiglass shields to protect tellers, who could press an alarm button and ignore the robber's demands. These barriers were in use in about half of the city's banks by early 1983 and were partly responsible for the decline in bank robberies in the city from 848 in 1979 to 447 in 1982. The robbery rate at banks with the protective shields was only one-fourth as high as the robbery rate at banks without the barriers (Buder, 1983).

A variation on target hardening is to remove from the home property that might be stolen by a burglar. In recent years, increasing prices of gold and silver and more investment in gems and artwork have led many people to place their valuables in safe-deposit boxes. In some cities, private depositories that store property have developed. These private firms meet a growing demand for the safe-keeping of goods that banks either cannot fulfill, because all safe-deposit

Target-hardening policies try to reduce opportunities for crime by making it more difficult to carry out offenses against particular targets. Here chains are used to prevent the shoplifting of jackets.   *Source: Cary Wolinsky/Stock Boston*

boxes have been rented, or are unwilling to fulfill, because of the inconvenience to the bank caused by depositors who make weekly or even daily trips to the box to get silverware or jewelry. Private depositories probably reduce the risk of a major loss in a burglary, but they do so at the cost of much inconvenience and expense to the property owner. Moreover, it is likely that burglars are simply displaced to less well protected targets. If everyone used these depositories, some marginal offenders might be deterred from crime altogether, but other thieves might develop methods to burglarize the depositories or rob people on their way to them.

Target-hardening measures have been proposed as a method to reduce computer crime. Traditional safeguards against unauthorized access to computerized information have been passwords and other electronic "locks," but these efforts to protect information have been neutralized by "hackers" and by more experienced professional computer operators who guess or steal passwords to gain access to the information. Passwords as a method of target hardening against computer crime have not been very successful, especially as the number of personal computers has grown. A new technique to make the computer more impermeable is being developed: encryption. This method translates information into code so that even someone who gains access to the information in the computer cannot interpret its meaning. So far, this method has not been widely used, because executives are often nonchalant about the possibility of computer crime and because it is expensive to code and decode information for use within a company. Some companies have chosen less burdensome methods to protect their computerized information, such as passwords that are more difficult to guess and systems in which a user is called back before being allowed access to the computer.

Self-Protective Measures

Some self-protective measures are much like target hardening, for they are designed to make it more difficult for offenders to perpetrate a crime successfully against an individual. The sale of firearms after urban riots and during crime waves is based on the belief that gun owners will be less likely to be victimized, or more likely to be able to resist successfully if they are attacked or robbed. People also buy dogs and take karate lessons to reduce their risk of victimization.

In the early 1980s, following several robbery-murders, many Californians enrolled in programs to train them how to use tear gas sprays against robbers, rapists, and assailants. However, tear gas may be ineffective in great heat, when the attacker is drunk or under the influence of drugs, or when the victim has difficulty getting the spray out and using it. The use of a tear gas spray may be dangerous to a victim if it does not work, because an offender may be more likely to use violence against a resisting victim. However, the widespread use of tear gas sprays may increase the public's sense of security and lead some people to go out when they otherwise would have feared to do so.

Informal Social Control

One way to reduce opportunities for crime is to increase informal social control over criminal behavior. This might be done through defensible space architecture, although we have seen that this method may be of limited value. Others have proposed improving street lighting, which makes public places more visible and draws to those places more people, who in turn enhance informal control. However, there is little research to support the idea that crime can be reduced by improving street lighting.

Another way to increase surveillance is to increase people's perception that the streets are safe and that incivil behavior in their community is rare. One unsuccessful attempt to do this was a controversial program in the South Bronx that stuck vinyl decals on burned-out buildings to improve community morale by making the area more attractive. Oakland, California, has adopted a more extensive program of this sort, seeking to erase signs of decay that create the impression of a dangerous community, including graffiti, broken windows, open prostitution and panhandling, and loitering on street corners. The long-run impact of this strategy is uncertain, but if these changes draw more people to the streets, they might reduce crime by enhancing informal social control.

Effective informal social control requires that people can be counted on to take action against criminals by intervening in a crime or by reporting an offense to the police. In the Using Criminology box, we look at one program that has succeeded in increasing citizen reporting of crime.

Community Crime Prevention

Another strategy of situational crime prevention involves the organization of the community. In 1976 a project was undertaken to reduce robbery and burglary in an area of Hartford, Connecticut, with the hope that changes in the community would reduce fear of crime and thereby enhance informal social control. This project altered the physical features of the community by changing roads to cul-de-sacs and one-way streets in order to reduce motorist traffic and to define the neighborhood more clearly in a visual sense. A neighborhood police team was organized, and better communication between the community and the local police was created. In addition, a formal neighborhood organization was established to deal with local problems.

In an evaluation of this project published six years later, the researchers concluded that environmental design can strengthen a neighborhood. By making a neighborhood more residential, the degree to which people exercise informal control over the area and the way they feel about their neighbors can be changed. By strengthening informal control, fear and concern about crime can be reduced. The evaluators of the Hartford project concluded that increased informal control in a neighborhood does not, by itself, necessarily reduce robbery and burglary, but in combination with aggressive and effective police practices it can help curb crime (Fowler and Mangione, 1982).

Using Criminology: Crime Stoppers

Crime Stoppers is a program initiated in Albuquerque, New Mexico, in 1976 that had grown to about 600 programs a decade later. Crime Stoppers tries to unite the news media, law-enforcement agencies, and the community to curb serious crime. To do this, "dead-end" crimes that the police have been unable to solve are reported in the media. Citizens are then encouraged to call in tips to help solve the crimes. Because of the fear of retaliation, the callers are guaranteed anonymity. They are paid for their information if it leads to an arrest and an indictment. The tipster is given an identification number on the telephone and collects the reward at a prearranged place. Money for the rewards is donated by private businesses and individuals, and in some cities funds have been raised through telethons and public appeals.

Crime Stoppers International claims that 92,339 felonies were solved, $562,219,371 in narcotics or stolen property was recovered, 20,992 defendants were convicted, and rewards of $6,728,392 were paid by the end of 1985 as a result of the program. What is not yet clear is whether Crime Stoppers has reduced the overall rate of crime in cities with programs. The deterrent effect is probably limited, because the solved cases are a small percentage of all serious offenses in those cities.

Most of the anonymous tips come from criminals, raising the possibility that Crime Stoppers may disrupt relationships among offenders, who fear their accomplices will turn them in for a reward.

Research indicates that the size of the reward is not related to a tipster's satisfaction with Crime Stoppers or with his or her willingness to participate in the program again. However, it seems that the payment of some reward is essential to the program's success in getting many citizens — especially criminals — to report crimes.

SOURCE: Based on Dennis P. Rosenbaum, Arthur J. Lurigio, and Paul J. Lavrakas, *Crime Stoppers — A National Evaluation*. Washington, D.C.: U.S. Department of Justice, September 1986.

Dealing with the Causes of Crime

Trying to reduce crime by relying on the criminal justice system is like relying on therapeutic or curative medicine rather than preventive medicine to deal with disease. Sick people do need help, but research into the causes of disease can lead to more effective treatment methods and may even suggest ways to prevent the disease from occurring in the first place. A search for the causes of a disease may in the short run be more costly than using traditional methods of treatment, but the long-term benefits of a successful search for the causes of a disease will be greater. Similarly, finding the causes of crime and attacking them is a more efficient way to reduce crime than waiting for crimes to occur and then using traditional methods to deal with offenders. The ineffectiveness of the criminal justice system in dealing with crime is suggested by James Q. Wilson, a political scientist who is an authority on crime and criminal justice; he says, "I doubt that a criminal justice system which I designed and I ran would have more than a small impact on the total crime rate" (cited in McCain, 1984: 2).

The causes of crime are not easily eradicated. As Gabriel Tarde said years ago, "If the tree of crime, with all its roots and rootlets, could ever be torn out of our society, it would leave a vast abyss" (cited in Radzinowicz and King, 1977: 84). Social conditions are not easily changed, but the solution to the crime problem seems to lie in policies that deal with the underlying causes of crime. One critic of this approach advises against this emphasis on causative factors such as "poverty, low education, youthful bravado, relative deprivation, social isolation, peer-group influence, family disorganization, habitual drug use, and so on," claiming that this approach would require "massive (and unlikely) social transformations" (Wilson, 1974: xvi). However, it is factors such as these that distinguish societies with high crime rates from those that have low crime rates. Consequently, making countries with high crime rates more like those with low crime rates would seem to be a useful strategy for reducing the crime rate. Doing this requires attention to the causes of crime and the development of policies that directly affect those causes.

Economic Factors

Countries undergoing economic development usually experience significant increases in crime rates, but neither China nor Japan seems to have had that experience. China has apparently avoided rising crime rates through careful social planning that has been implemented by an authoritarian regime. This has provided a full-employment economy in which people are trained and given rewarding jobs (Chiu, 1977; Cohen, 1977). In Japan, workers typically are employed by the same company for life; that company takes a great interest in the welfare of its employees. In recent years, job mobility has increased in Japan, but employee turnover is still much less common than in the United States (Bayley, 1976a, 1976b; Clifford, 1976).

In the United States, there is a need for policies that reduce unemployment, stabilize the economy, and provide technical skills and job counseling. We have seen that at the national level there is no clear relationship between the unemployment rate and the crime rate, but many people who commit conventional crimes are without job skills and are unemployed. Perhaps even more importantly, they lack the social bond to the conventional order that work provides. Income subsidies that maintain an ex-convict's incentive to find full-time employment might help reduce crime by creating such an attachment (Rossi, Berk, and Lenihan, 1980). To provide this bond to the social order, job training must include socialization in job-related skills as well as in the techniques of the work; these skills include promptness, an ability to cooperate with other workers, and a willingness to take orders from supervisors (Cook, 1975). Policies that reduce job turnover and encourage loyalty to an employer might reduce the crime rate by creating a stake in conformity for workers. Even more important than an ex-convict's getting a job is keeping a job over time and becoming habituated to a work routine.

Economic changes might also reduce white-collar crime. One strategy would be to require the federal chartering of corporations; this could make them more responsive to public needs. However, federal regulation of corporations in the twentieth century has not been very successful in reducing corporate crime, and so more regulation might have little impact on crime. Various corporate organizational changes that might reduce white-collar crime have been suggested, such as greater stockholder control of the company, but changes in the way that corporate decisions are made would be hard to achieve and might create new problems (Conklin, 1977; Clinard and Yeager, 1980). Conflict theorists claim that it is the capitalist system itself that is the source of white-collar crime, as well as conventional crime, and that only the elimination of privately held means of production can solve the problem of corporate crime. In a sense this may be true, but socialist alternatives create economic crimes of their own. The Soviet Union, in particular, has difficulties with crimes against socialist property, counterfeiting, and bribery that result from its efforts to curb capitalism (Chalidze, 1977; Simis, 1982).

Nations that have low crime rates commonly have less relative deprivation than nations with high crime rates. In China, control of the mass media limits access to information about the standard of living of the rest of the world and thus minimizes the "demonstration effect," which can increase expectations beyond the current level of well-being. The absolute level of economic well-being in a nation may be a less important influence on the crime rate than relative deprivation, the gap between current economic well-being and economic expectations. The Chinese are absolutely deprived compared with Americans, but they are largely unaware of this because their expectations have not been increased by constant exposure to higher standards of living.

In contrast to China, Americans at all economic levels are exposed to great wealth and are exhorted to work hard to achieve material success, which is seen as an indicator of individual worth. Thus, Americans who have higher absolute standards of living than most Chinese often see themselves as relatively disadvantaged compared with other Americans. These perceptions can lead to both conventional property crimes and white-collar crimes. Policies that reduce the emphasis of American culture on material well-being as a sign of personal worth might reduce crime. However, these policies could reduce the motivation to pursue material success through legitimate channels and could adversely affect the economy by lowering the demand for consumer goods.

One examination of inequality and crime predicted that "gross economic measures to reduce the gap between the poor and the rest of the population will reduce crime" (Braithwaite, 1979: 231). However, focusing only on the alleviation of poverty will not necessarily reduce inequality, because of problems with antipoverty programs:

1. They will not normally succeed in lifting people out of poverty.
2. They foster cynicism and disappointment by raising expectations which they cannot fulfill.
3. They label people as disreputable and inferior.

> Even if they do succeed in lifting people out of poverty, in a capitalist economy they typically do so at the expense of other people who are thrust into poverty. Even if they do reduce the total number of poor people in a city, this is unlikely to reduce crime because cities with smaller numbers of poor people do not have lower crime rates. (Braithwaite, 1979: 232)

In sum, relative deprivation and people's expectations seem to motivate them to break the law to a greater extent than does absolute poverty, and policies to reduce poverty, although beneficial in other ways, may not curb the crime rate in any dramatic way. Indeed, official crime rates in the United States increased significantly during and just after the War on Poverty in the 1960s, even though this federal effort did substantially reduce the proportion of Americans living in poverty.

The Process of Social Change

Crime might be reduced by policies that minimize the disruptive effects of social change. In recent decades, both China and Japan have experienced internal migration and urbanization, trends commonly associated with rising crime rates. In China, migration from rural areas to large cities is carefully planned so that those who move are provided with jobs in their new communities. Japan has experienced urbanization without increased crime rates, apparently because group influence in inducing conformity continues to exist, and is perhaps even enhanced, in large cities. Switzerland has also avoided a high crime rate through a slow process of urbanization that has minimized the disruption of individual lives (Clinard, 1978).

Countries such as China, Japan, and Switzerland that have experienced social change without increased crime rates seem to have maintained groups that have traditionally provided people with bonds to relatives, friends, neighbors, and others who encourage conformity to the law. This is consistent with control theory, which proposes that crime and delinquency will be less common when people have a stake in conformity and are concerned with the good opinion of those who are close to them.

Political Factors

The political ideology of China seems conducive to low crime rates. Prior to the Communist Revolution in 1949, China was a country composed of relatively autonomous regions; today it is a more integrated nation that commands its citizens' loyalty. People thus have an attachment to an institution with authority — the state — and this attachment reduces their motivation to engage in crime for selfish reasons.

The situation in Japan is similar in some ways, even though the political ideology is quite different. As in China, individuals in Japan are subordinated to the nation, the family, the community, and the company for which they work. The Japanese are greatly concerned with the good opinion of other nations and censure behavior that brings shame on the country in the eyes of the rest of the world.

Because crimes are often committed to improve the situation of the individual perpetrator, crime rates seem to be low in nations where people learn supraindividual goals and high where people learn to pursue individual goals. It is difficult to suggest policies that might reduce the American culture's emphasis on individualism and increase its emphasis on national goals, but it is important to recognize that one cost of individualism may be a high crime rate.

Community Ties

Nations with low crime rates often have neighborhoods that are socially integrated, thereby increasing the attachment of individuals to each other and reducing crime by increasing their stake in conformity. Socially integrated neighborhoods make the surveillance of behavior more likely and can reduce crime through the fear of being observed, reported, and arrested. Local communities in Japan are closely knit, and attachment to community is also strong in Switzerland.

Programs that strengthen community ties might reduce crime rates, but it could be difficult to implement such policies in a nation such as the United States where the value of individualism is so strongly held and where geographic mobility is so common. A report on criminal violence in the United States suggested that crime might be reduced by implementing a program tried in Puerto Rico that created a sense of community in a slum by allowing poor people to take charge of their own lives and by requiring offenders to work to improve the local community (Silberman, 1978: 429–466).

The Family

Another group that is usually strong in nations that have low crime rates is the family. Chinese and Japanese families traditionally have stressed close attachments between children and their parents, whose "psychological presence" curbs the children's tendency toward delinquency. The Chinese family is organized on a hierarchical basis, emphasizing respect for elders while providing parental affection for children. As a result, the Chinese usually have low crime rates, whether they live in China or in other nations (Count-Van Manen, 1971). The Japanese family has similar characteristics. Japanese children learn to be concerned about the good opinion of their family and to avoid bringing shame on it; this creates an investment in conformity and keeps children from delinquency. Swiss children also learn to be concerned with the good opinion of others and to avoid law-violating behavior that would bring public censure on themselves and their families.

In the United States, people who violate the law typically come from families that differ from the Chinese, Japanese, and Swiss families that are conducive to low crime rates. Policies might be devised and implemented to strengthen the ability of American families to prevent children's involvement in delinquency and crime. The closeness of adolescents and their elders in Switzerland suggests the possibility of creating programs that integrate young people and adults in common activities (Clinard, 1978: 132–133). Family treatment programs could focus on child and spouse abuse, which are crimes in themselves and which also seem to lead to crimes by people who are abused as children. Laws that require police officers to take criminal complaints from the victims of child and spouse abuse, and to arrest abusing individuals, might prevent crime. The treatment of entire families when one member gets into trouble with the law might be more effective than programs that single out the offender for treatment. There is some evidence that family intervention strategies can reduce delinquency if they treat children when they first get into trouble, focus on the child's family and school experiences, and keep the child in the community. These methods teach family members to communicate better with each other and to resolve conflicts. However, these methods do not seem to work very well with children whose behavior is extremely disruptive or with severely disturbed families, and it may be those families that are most likely to produce delinquents and criminals (Gendreau and Ross, 1979: 470–472; also, see Garrett, 1985).

The family can also be changed through reforms of the welfare system and the income tax system. Crime might be reduced if the welfare system encouraged families to stay together, rather than taking a neutral stance toward family breakups or even encouraging family dissolution in order to become eligible for certain kinds of public assistance. A guaranteed minimum income might increase family stability and harmony. The income tax system might be redesigned to encourage family stability, which in turn would reduce crime. In addition, more flexible work hours and inexpensive day care centers—and tax incentives to encourage these programs—might provide better supervision of children and instill the "psychological presence" of adults that can inhibit violation of the law.

One possible policy is to provide instruction on child rearing to high school students or to prospective or new parents. Teachers and school administrators might also teach child rearing by example, because they interact with school children on a daily basis, monitor their behavior, and mete out punishment for misconduct (Hirschi, 1983). So far, it has proved difficult to teach methods of child rearing that are effective in curbing delinquent behavior, and it has been even harder to get parents to use those methods once they learn them (Wilson and Herrnstein, 1985). Nevertheless, there is some evidence that parent-training programs can curb some delinquent behavior, with the impact on aggressive acts apparently greater than the impact on theft (Patterson, Chamberlain, and Reid, 1982).

The School

In China, the family's influence is reinforced by schools and government-run play centers, which tie children to adults who have authority. Schools and play centers also reduce the time available for children to engage in delinquency and minimize the boredom that has been cited as a cause of delinquency in the United States. In Japan, the tremendous academic pressure on students to succeed and not disappoint their families has been cited as a cause of recent increases in delinquency, although Japanese schools also provide control over students' behavior.

Rates of crime and delinquency might be reduced through changes in the school system. The school is an institution that cuts across all communities, classes, and racial and ethnic groups, and it is often a center of social activity for community residents. Because young people are economically superfluous and are isolated in school, it is a particularly good place to provide them with a legitimate identity and social attachments (Empey, 1974; Figueira-McDonough, 1987).

Most schools need smaller classes so that students can be dealt with on an individual basis by teachers (Rubel, 1978). Reforms that tie students more closely to the school and its teachers may create a "psychological presence" that keeps young people from violating the law. Revision of school curricula could also help reduce crime and delinquency. Courses might be made more relevant to the interests and needs of students in order to strengthen their attachment to the school. School curricula should provide students with the skills to achieve legitimate success and should be designed to fit the needs, values, and institutions of the specific community.

Nonacademic programs might also help reduce the crime problem. For instance, experiences such as survival training in the wilderness or contact with elderly people in the community might broaden students' perspectives and develop their self-confidence. Programs that strengthen a sense of personal responsibility and create empathy with others could reduce crime and delinquency by undermining the ability to use techniques of neutralization to justify violations of the law.

Juveniles might also be provided with access to the goods and services they now seek through criminal behavior. For example, "car libraries" might allow adolescents to rent cars, reducing their incentive to steal cars and possibly teaching them to drive and to repair cars (Morris and Hawkins, 1970: 171). Much delinquency is a search for "rep" or prestige among peers, and efforts to change the basis on which prestige is awarded might reduce violations of the law. This might be done by expanding athletic programs or by creating programs that offer different kinds of rewards to those who rely on delinquent peers for prestige.

Discrimination

Efforts to eliminate the racial and ethnic discrimination that denies minority groups equal access to valued opportunities can help solve the crime problem, because these minority groups often contribute disproportionately to a society's crime rate. Discrimination weakens a group's attachment to the conventional social order, increasing the chance that it will have a high crime rate. Disenfranchisement or obstacles placed in the way of the right to vote deny political power to a minority group and thus weaken its ties to the political system. Schools that are segregated or poorly funded provide minorities with an inadequate education and leave them unprepared for good jobs; this reduces their attachment to teachers and schools and makes it less likely that they will find jobs to which they can form strong ties. Job discrimination that means that minority-group members are the "last hired and the first fired" may keep them from developing loyalty to an employer. Housing discrimination that relegates minorities to the most run-down areas of the city may weaken their ties to the community.

Discrimination in education, work, and housing are sources of high rates of poverty among minority groups. When this poverty is combined with a cultural emphasis on material success, as it is in the United States, there is a strong motivation for committing property crimes. Eliminating discrimination would open legitimate opportunities and create bonds to the conventional order among groups that traditionally have had high crime rates, and thus help reduce the overall crime rate.

Conclusion

Eliminating the motivation to commit crime may be the most effective way to reduce crime in the long run. In the short run, the expression of this motivation may be minimized by developing informal control mechanisms that induce people to conform to the law (Toby, 1974). By creating a legitimate identity, a sense of competence and personal responsibility, and links to school and work, social policies can create a stake in conformity that makes the rewards of a law-abiding way of life and the risks of criminal behavior great enough to reduce violations of the law (Schrag, 1974). Increasingly harsh or certain punishment seems less likely to reduce crime than policies that make it more rewarding to abide by the law. Policies that strengthen the institutions that tie people to others whose good opinion matters to them are likely to be especially effective in reducing the crime rate in the long run.

Summary

Three approaches to solving the crime problem differ in their ideas about crime causation and their recommendations for reducing the crime rate. The conservative approach focuses on index crimes, which are attributed to the poor and to people who have been improperly socialized. Its solution focuses on the criminal justice system to deter and incapacitate criminals, rather than on eliminating poverty or strengthening the family. The liberal approach emphasizes conventional crime, suggesting that it can be reduced by policies that alleviate poverty and provide legitimate opportunities for everyone. The radical approach looks at both conventional crime and white-collar crime, which are attributed to the structure of a capitalist system. According to this perspective, only the elimination of capitalism can solve the crime problem.

Since the 1960s, several national commissions have studied crime and recommended changes in the criminal justice system, rather than changes in the larger society, as the way to reduce crime. The Law Enforcement Assistance Administration failed in its attempt to reduce crime by changing the criminal justice system; it was disbanded in 1982. Crime was a major issue in the 1968 and 1972 presidential campaigns, contributing in an important way to the victory of Richard Nixon in both elections. Since 1972, crime has faded as a major political issue for several reasons, including the involvement of some law-and-order politicians in crimes of their own. President Reagan has occasionally raised the crime issue, and in 1984 he signed into law a sweeping set of reforms aimed at curbing crime. Two years later, the Anti-Drug Abuse Act was passed and signed into law, allocating $1.7 billion to curb drug abuse, though only three months later President Reagan proposed cutbacks in funds to deal with illegal drugs.

The first of three general recommendations for reducing the crime rate is to change the criminal justice system. One way to do this would be to reduce the overreach of the criminal law, so that limited resources could be concentrated on the most serious crimes. The number of police officers in a city does not seem to make a difference in its crime rate, but the kind of action the police take might make a difference; for instance, arrest can deter domestic disputes, and better communication with the public may increase crime reporting. The federal government has tried to curb drug importation for years, but the amount of drugs entering the country does not seem to have decreased as a result. The federal government has developed computerized record systems to assist local law-enforcement agencies in their investigations. The courts might try to curb crime by increasing the certainty of punishment, but it is not clear that this can be done within the constraints of existing constitutional rights. According to some sources, concentrated efforts to imprison organized crime leaders have had an impact on gangsters' activities in recent years. Reforms of the legal system might make it easier to prosecute white-collar crime and thus deter it. There have been proposals to prevent crime by opening the juvenile court's records for use by criminal court judges and by lowering the age at which offenders are prosecuted as adults. The impact of prisons on reducing crime seems limited; rehabilitation has not been shown to be effective in prison settings.

A second strategy is situational crime prevention. This involves target hardening to make buildings and property less vulnerable to theft. Self-protective measures may reduce the chance that an individual will be victimized; the carrying of tear gas sprays is an example. Strategies to increase informal social control can reduce crime, and community crime prevention has had some effect in curbing crime, especially when it is used in conjunction with aggressive police practices.

The third strategy is to deal with the causes of crime. This may involve economic policies that provide offenders with work, and thus with a bond to the conventional social order. It may mean changing the role of the corporation in the economy to prevent white-collar crime. Crime can also be curbed by policies that minimize the disruptive effects of social change. Attachment to the nation might help to keep a country's crime rate low, as it has in China and Japan, and strong ties to the local community may have the same effect. Policies that strengthen the family and teach parents how to raise law-abiding children can reduce crime. Schools can reduce delinquency and crime by helping young people establish close ties to their teachers and by providing them with the skills to succeed in legitimate careers. Eliminating discrimination can reduce the crime rate by strengthening the attachment to the conventional order of minority groups that have traditionally had high crime rates. In general, providing stronger ties to conventional people and institutions seems to be an effective strategy for solving the crime problem.

Important Terms

conservative approach
liberal approach
radical approach

situational crime prevention
target hardening

Suggested Readings

WILLIAM CLIFFORD. *Crime Control in Japan.* Lexington, Mass.: D. C. Heath, 1976. A detailed examination of a society that has crime rates much lower than those of the United States

THOMAS E. CRONIN, TANIA Z. CRONIN, AND MICHAEL E. MILAKOVICH. *U.S. v. Crime in the Streets.* Bloomington: Indiana University Press, 1981. A comprehensive study of federal crime-reduction efforts since the 1960s.

ERIKA S. FAIRCHILD AND VINCENT J. WEBB, EDS. *The Politics of Crime and Criminal Justice.* Beverly Hills, Calif.: Sage Publications, 1985. A collection of papers that deal with ideology and the political context of the crime issue.

DAVID M. GORDON. "Capitalism, Class, and Crime in America," *Crime and Delinquency* 19 (April 1973), 163–186. A succinct statement of the radical perspective on crime.

JAMES Q. WILSON. *Thinking about Crime,* rev. ed. New York: Basic Books, 1983. An exploration of crime in the United States that focuses on the criminal justice system and its capacity to deal with crime.

Glossary

Absolute deterrence   The effect of punishment that leads people to refrain entirely from committing crime because of the perceived threat of a penalty.

Age-specific arrest rate   The number of arrests per 100,000 people in a given age category.

Aggravated assault   An unlawful attack by one person on another in which the purpose is to inflict severe bodily injury and in which a weapon typically is used.

Amenability issue   The possibility that certain kinds of offenders are amenable or suited to a particular type of treatment.

Anomie   Normlessness, or a disjunction between institutionalized means and culturally approved goals.

Appeal to higher loyalties   A technique of neutralization that justifies a violation of the law by the demands of a group that is smaller than the whole society but that requires of its members conformity to standards that may be incompatible with the law.

Arson   The willful burning of the building, motor vehicle, aircraft, or personal property of another person.

Assault   An unlawful attack by one person on another.

Atavism   A person "born out of time" and similar to primitive people or lower animals in his or her biological makeup; the basis of Lombroso's theory of the "born criminal."

Bail   A system of pretrial release designed to ensure that defendants will show up to face charges when the trial is scheduled, at the same time allowing them to remain free until the trial takes place.

Behavior modification   A treatment program that tries to change behavior, rather than personality, by rewarding desirable actions and punishing undesirable ones.

Biographical method   A research strategy in which the experiences of a single individual are examined in detail.

Brawner rule   The legal rule that a person will be found not guilty by reason of insanity "if at the time of such conduct as a result of mental disease or mental defect, he lacks substantial capacity either to appreciate the criminality of his conduct or to conform his conduct to the requirements of the law."

"Brutalization effect"   An increase in the homicide rate as a result of the administration of the death penalty.

Burglary   Unlawful entry of a building to commit a serious crime, usually the theft of property.

Cartography   An approach to the study of crime that uses official data to map or chart patterns of crime.

Case attrition   A funnel or sieve effect that characterizes the criminal justice system, with cases being sorted out as they proceed through the system and with relatively few crimes that occur ending up with a perpetrator being convicted and imprisoned.

Casework   A treatment program designed to help offenders cope with specific problems they face.

Certification   The social verification by the criminal justice system or by conventional people that an offender is rehabilitated.

Child savers   A late-nineteenth-century movement of people committed to providing delinquent adolescents with help rather than punishment.

Class   Social standing based on economic resources, occupational prestige, political power, or life style.

Classical conditioning   Conditioning that is a result of the contiguity of stimuli.

Classical school   An approach to crime that emphasizes free will and the deterrence of criminal behavior by the fear of punishment.

Clearance rate   The proportion of cases the police solve to their satisfaction.

Cohort   A carefully defined group of people who are in a common situation at one time.

Collective incapacitation   A policy of giving the same prison sentence to everyone convicted of a particular offense, in order to reduce the crime rate.

Comparative research   A research strategy that looks at crime in societies with different cultures and social structures.

Compensation   A system in which the state repays crime victims for their financial losses or physical injuries.

Computer crime   Any violation of the law in which a computer is the target or the means.

Concentric-zone model   A model of metropolitan areas that identifies concentric rings that have distinctive characteristics.

Concordance rate   A measure of the similarity of criminal behavior that is used in studies of twins.

Condemnation of the condemners   A technique of neutralization that asserts that it is the motives and behavior of the people who are condemning the offender, rather than the motives and behavior of the offender, that should be condemned.

Conflict gang   A gang that provides a way for adolescents to achieve prestige in the eyes of their peers through fighting.

Conflict perspective   An approach that sees the criminal law as closely intertwined with the distribution of political power and economic resources in a society.

Conformity   A mode of adaptation in which both cultural goals and the institutional means to reach those goals are accepted.

Consensus perspective   An approach that claims that the criminal law represents social consensus or agreement about what kinds of behavior should be punished by the state.

Conservative approach   An approach that seeks to preserve the status quo from criminals, who are seen as challengers to the existing social order.

Containment theory   The theory that people are insulated to various degrees against pressures to commit deviant acts by external and internal factors.

Contingency A factor that determines movement from one criminal role to another, or from one crime to another.

Control theory The theory that people who engage in crime or delinquency are relatively free of intimate attachments, aspirations, and moral beliefs that bind them to a conventional and law-abiding way of life.

Costs related to criminal violence The financial losses that result from violent crimes in which victims are physically hurt.

Crime An act that violates the criminal law and is punishable by the state.

Crime index The total number of eight serious crimes, which are defined by the FBI.

Crime rate The number of reported crimes divided by the number of people in an area, often expressed as a rate of crimes per 100,000 people.

Criminal career A sequence of criminal acts over time by one person.

Criminal career incapacitation An approach that would reduce crime by identifying and incarcerating classes of offenders who seem to be especially likely to remain active in crime.

Criminal gang A gang that seeks material gain, power, and prestige through illegitimate means such as theft.

Criminal intent The willed or conscious desire to commit an act that violates a criminal law.

Criminology A discipline that gathers and analyzes empirical data to explain violations of the criminal law and societal reactions to those violations.

Dark figure The number of crimes that actually occur but are not recorded by the police.

Defensible space The subdivision and design of housing to allow residents to distinguish stranger from neighbor and thus elicit a sense of territoriality, which can reduce crime by informal social control.

Denial of injury The technique of neutralization that claims that no one is hurt by an offender's crime, even if it technically violates the law.

Denial of responsibility The technique of neutralization that involves the denial of personal responsibility for actions that violate the criminal law.

Denial of the victim The technique of neutralization that claims that a crime is justified as a rightful retaliation against the victim.

Deterrence The inhibition of criminal activity by state-imposed penalties.

Deviance The violation of a norm.

Differential association-reinforcement theory A theory of crime and delinquency that states that learning occurs through operant conditioning in both nonsocial and social situations, even though most learning results from interaction with others.

Differential association theory A theory that proposes that crime and delinquency are learned in face-to-face interaction and occur when there is an excess of definitions favorable to violation of the law over definitions unfavorable to violation of the law.

Differential identification theory The theory that people engage in criminal or delinquent behavior because they identify with real or imaginary persons from whose perspective their crime or delinquency seems acceptable.

Differential opportunity theory A theory of delinquency that focuses on the discrepancy between aspirations and access to both legitimate and illegitimate means to reach those goals.

Diffusion of responsibility The situation that exists among groups of witnesses to an emergency or a crime, when people say that someone should act but that it need not be themselves because other potential helpers are present.

Direct loss The result of a crime in which the stock of useful things is reduced, as in arson or vandalism.

Discretion The use of judgment to decide what action to take.

Displacement effect A change in the pattern of crime without a reduction in the total amount of crime that results from criminals' efforts to avoid punishment; displacement may be from one target to another, from one area to another, or from one kind of offense to another.

Drift A condition of limbo between a conventional life style and a criminal life style with no strong attachment to either.

Economist's model A model of criminal behavior that focuses on instrumental rather than expressive offenses and sees crime as purposefully chosen by offenders to achieve certain ends.

EFT crime Any violation of the law that would not have occurred except for the presence of an electronic fund transfer system.

Enforcement costs The kind of financial cost of crime that results from the money spent on various criminal justice agencies.

Exiting A successful disengagement from a previous pattern of criminal behavior.

Experiment A controlled study in which people are treated in different ways to determine the effects of that treatment on their attitudes and behavior.

Expressive crime An offense in which the act itself fulfills an emotional need for the offender.

Focal concern A value or area of interest that elicits widespread, persistent attention and emotional involvement.

Forcible rape Carnal knowledge of a female forcibly and against her will.

Formal social control An effort to bring about conformity to the law by agents of the criminal justice system such as the police, the courts, and correctional institutions.

Fraud The crime of obtaining money or property by false pretenses.

General deterrence The inhibition of the desire to engage in crime among the general population through the punishment of certain offenders.

Good Samaritan problem The issue of how bystanders respond to emergencies such as crimes.

Group counseling A treatment program that allows several inmates to be treated at the same time and at a low cost; it involves the discussion of feelings and attitudes in an effort to create mutual acceptance and a supportive environment.

Historical research A research strategy that examines the same society at different times and looks at the way crime has changed with economic and social development.

Illegal expenditures The costs of crimes that divert money from the legitimate economy and represent a loss of potential revenue for people who produce and supply legal goods and services.

Incapacitation The custodial control of

convicted offenders so that they cannot commit crimes that affect the general public.

Indeterminate sentence A penalty imposed under a system that establishes long maximum sentences for different crimes and allows judges to impose any penalty up to the maximum; sentences are often a range of years to be served in prison.

Individual therapy A method of treatment commonly used in prison in which psychiatrists, psychologists, or psychiatric social workers help offenders solve psychological problems that are thought to be the cause of criminal behavior.

Informal social control The reactions of individuals and groups that bring about conformity to norms and laws; it includes peer and community pressure, bystander intervention in a crime, and collective responses such as citizen patrol groups.

Innovation The mode of adaptation in which cultural goals are accepted, but means are used that society regards as unacceptable.

Instrumental crime A crime in which the offender gets satisfaction from the product of the crime.

Intensive offender A person who engages in criminal activity that begins at an early age and is sustained over time, consciously planned, persistent, skilled, and frequent.

Interest group People who organize to further their shared economic, political, or moral goals.

Intermittent offender A person who engages in irregular and opportunistic crimes with low payoffs and great risks, and does not think of himself or herself as a professional criminal.

Just deserts The idea that offenders should be punished because they deserve to suffer for the harm they have caused.

Juvenile delinquent A person below a legally specified age who has been adjudged by a juvenile court to have violated the law or committed a juvenile status offense.

Labeling perspective The perspective on deviant behavior that emphasizes the effects that a socially imposed label has on a person who breaks a social rule.

Larceny The unlawful taking, carrying, leading, or riding away of property from the possession of another.

Law A kind of norm that is written down and formalized by the political system.

Learning disabilities An impairment in sensory and motor functioning that leads to deviant classroom performance and is the result of an abnormal physical condition.

Lex talionis The principle of "an eye for an eye, a tooth for a tooth."

Liberal approach The perspective that crime can be reduced by attacking its underlying causes through social reforms.

Machismo The demonstration of masculinity through the manipulation and exploitation of women.

M'Naghten rule The legal rule that a person will be found not guilty by reason of insanity if at the time of the crime the person was under a defect of reason so as to be unable to know the nature and the quality of the act, or if the person was aware of the nature of the act, he or she did not know that wrong was being done.

Marginal deterrent effect The extent to which crime rates respond to incremental changes in the threat of sanctions.

Mass murder The willful killing of several human beings at the same time.

Master status The situation in which other aspects of a person's behavior become submerged in a particular social identity, such as that of a deviant.

Mechanical solidarity A unity based on shared values and norms and on the similarity of functions performed by all members of the society.

Methadone maintenance A treatment program for heroin addicts that uses an addictive drug (methadone) that does not produce euphoria if taken orally in regulated doses, but that does block the euphoric effects of any heroin that is used.

Milieu therapy A treatment method that introduces the idea of rehabilitation into all aspects of an institution, including relations between inmates and staff members.

Mode of adaptation A way that individuals who occupy a particular social position adapt to cultural goals and the institutionalized means to reach those goals.

Moral entrepreneurs People who promote the idea that certain behavior is harmful and should be punished.

Motor vehicle theft The theft of an automobile.

Murder and nonnegligent manslaughter The willful killing of a human being.

Norm A rule that makes explicit certain social expectations about what is appropriate behavior for a particular person in a specific situation.

Obscene material Material, often pornographic in nature, that has been declared illegal because it poses a threat to the state or to organized religion, violates common morality, has no redeeming social value, or appeals to the prurient or lascivious interest.

Observation A research strategy that involves the careful and systematic watching of behavior.

Operant conditioning theory A theory that emphasizes the interaction of the person and the environment, and sees people's behavior as affecting the world around them in ways that in turn influence their future behavior.

Organic solidarity A unity based on an interdependence of functions, much as in a complex biological organism.

Organized crime Criminal activity by a formal organization developed and devoted primarily to the pursuit of profits through illegal means.

Parole A system under which inmates are released before they complete their full sentences and are then supervised on the street and sent back to prison if they violate the conditions of their release.

Patterns of crime A research strategy that involves the use of data to determine where crime is committed, who commits crime, who is victimized, and what are the major dimensions of the criminal act.

Plea bargaining An informal but structured process of negotiation in which the prosecutor and the defense attorney agree about a guilty plea and the sentence that the prosecutor will recommend to the judge.

Pluralistic ignorance A situation in which witnesses in a group fail to help the victim of an emergency or a crime because they interpret the failure of other witnesses to help as a sign that no help is needed.

Police diversion A program that allows the police to recommend to juvenile suspects that they enroll in a program that offers counseling or training.

Police probation A program that requires juvenile troublemakers to report to the police regularly, attend school, make restitution, and maintain a neat personal appearance.

Pornography   Material that is intended to arouse people sexually by portraying sexual matters in visual or verbal terms.

Positivism   A perspective that relies on the scientific method to quantify and measure behavior and the social conditions associated with behavior.

Premenstrual syndrome (PMS)   A set of symptoms associated with the onset of menstruation, including tension, nervousness, irritability, fatigue, headaches, cramps, and depressed moods.

Presumptive sentence   A specified sentence that is presumed for someone with a particular criminal record who is convicted of an offense of a certain degree of harmfulness.

Pretrial diversion   A program that allows a district attorney to recommend to a judge that a criminal proceeding be suspended while a suspect participates in a treatment program.

Prevention and protection costs   The financial costs of crimes that result from expenditures on alarm systems, spotlights, locks, bars, and other "target-hardening" devices, as well as the money that people spend on insurance premiums to cover their losses through theft.

Preventive detention   A system in which some defendants are held without bail while awaiting trial.

Primary deviation   An initial act of deviance that has not been socially labeled as deviant.

Prisoners' rights movement   A social movement led by ex-convicts and attorneys on behalf of people still in prison.

Proactive police work   Efforts by the police to discover and deal with crime on their own initiative.

Probation   A form of supervised release imposed on convicted offenders by judges, without any time being served in jail or prison.

Protective neighboring   A combination of cooperative surveillance and willingness to intervene in a crime by the residents of a community.

Psychoanalytic perspective   A psychological approach to crime causation that sees crime as the behavior of people who are inadequately socialized.

Psychopath   A person who has a specific cluster of personality traits; is asocial, aggressive, highly impulsive, and unable to form lasting bonds of affection with others; and feels little or no guilt for antisocial activities.

Radical approach   A perspective that focuses on crime by both the underprivileged and the privileged, and attributes crime by both groups to the conditions of a capitalist society.

Radical nonintervention   A policy to minimize official reaction to delinquency in order to prevent the labeling of adolescents that could drive them into criminal careers.

Reaction-formation   A repudiation of goals to which a person is emotionally attached but unable to attain, such as a reversal of middle-class goals by lower- or working-class delinquents.

Reactive police work   Efforts in which the police respond to a citizen's report of a crime.

Rebellion   A mode of adaptation in which people reject cultural goals and develop a new set of goals, and reject institutionalized means to reach cultural goals and develop a new set of means; behavior in which a person seeks to create a new social structure that will more effectively allow people to meet what the rebel considers appropriate goals.

Recidivism rate   The percentage of offenders who, during a specific period after their treatment has ended, are arrested and convicted of new offenses or have their punishment made more restrictive because they have failed to meet the conditions of a less restrictive sentence.

Rehabilitation   The restoration of criminals to a law-abiding way of life through treatment; the result of any planned intervention focused on the offender that reduces criminal activity.

Relative deprivation   The discrepancy between people's expectations about the goods and conditions of life to which they are rightfully entitled, and their capabilities, or the goods and conditions of life they believe they can attain and maintain under the current social system.

Restitution   A system that requires offenders to make monetary payments or provide services, either to the victim or to the community at large.

Restrictive deterrence   The effect of a penalty that causes people to limit their violations of the law in order to minimize the risk of punishment.

Retreatism   A mode of adaptation in which cultural goals are abandoned and institutionalized means are also rejected.

Retreatist gang   A gang formed by juveniles who have failed to use both legitimate and illegitimate means to achieve success, and which usually engages in the use of drugs or alcohol.

Retribution   The idea that offenders should be punished because they deserve to suffer for the harm they have caused.

Reward-risk model   A model that assumes that everyone, including criminals, chooses how to behave in a rational way,

and that everyone's actions are influenced by the consequences of his or her behavior.

Ritualism   A mode of adaptation in which cultural goals are scaled down or given up, while norms about the institutionalized means to reach cultural goals are accepted.

Robbery   The theft of property from another person by force or threat of force.

Routine activities approach   A perspective that sees crime as a function of people's everyday behavior, and stresses motivated offenders, target suitability, and guardianship.

Sanction   An effort to ensure future conformity to a norm and punish past nonconformity.

Schizophrenia   A psychosis that involves disordered thought patterns characterized by fantasy, delusion, and incoherence.

Secondary deviation   Deviant behavior that is the result of the labeling process.

Selective incapacitation   A system of predictive restraint in which only those offenders who are the most likely to commit more crime if released are held.

Self-report study   Research that measures crime by having respondents report their own violations in confidential interviews or on anonymous self-administered questionnaires.

Sentence disparity   The difference in the criminal sanctions that are meted out to people who are convicted of similar offenses and who have similar criminal records.

Serial murder   The willful killing of several human beings over a period of time.

Simple assault   An unlawful attack by one person on another in which no weapon is used and no serious injury results.

Simultaneity   A reciprocal cause-and-effect

relationship between two variables; for instance, sanctions by the criminal justice system may affect the crime rate, but the crime rate may also affect the sanctions that are meted out by the criminal justice system.

Situational crime prevention Measures that involve the management, design, or manipulation of the environment in order to reduce opportunities for crime and increase the perceived risks of committing crime.

Social control A process that brings about conformity to society's norms and laws.

Somatotype A body type that results from embryonic development and that is thought to be associated with a particular temperament and propensity to crime and delinquency.

Specific deterrence The effect of a penalty that causes an individual who is punished for a crime not to commit that crime again because his or her reward-risk calculations have been altered by the punishment.

Status offense An act defined as unacceptable for people below a given age and used as a basis for juvenile court proceedings; included are underage drinking, running away from home, and truancy.

Subculture A patterned way of life similar in some ways but different in others from the dominant culture of a society.

Subculture-of-violence theory The theory that the norms shared by a group of people may define violence as an appropriate response to certain circumstances and lead members of the group to engage in violent crime in order to conform to others' expectations.

Subterranean value A value or ideal that is subordinate or below the surface in the dominant value system and is sought by

most people only occasionally and in appropriate circumstances.

Survey A research strategy in which a sample of people who are representative of a larger population are asked a series of prepared questions.

Target hardening A policy of reducing opportunities for crime by making it more difficult for offenders to carry out crimes against particular targets.

Technique of neutralization A justification used prior to a crime by an offender to render inoperative the social controls that would otherwise check law-violating behavior.

Tort A civil wrong in which a plaintiff, or complaining party, can sue a defendant who is alleged to have caused the plaintiff harm.

Transfer of property The cost of crimes in which property is transferred from one person to another, such as from the victim of a theft to the thief.

Tutelage Instruction or socialization in criminal motives and skills, including how to spot opportunities for theft, how to plan thefts, and how to carry out thefts.

Typology A set of categories of crimes or criminal careers.

Value Something that is considered worthy, desirable, or proper.

Vandalism The willful or malicious destruction, injury, disfigurement, or defacement of property without consent of the owner.

Vengeance A private and personal response to a wrong; it does not involve an established authority such as the state.

Victim impact statement A detailed written report based on an interview with a victim about the effects of a crime on him or her.

Victim precipitation The situation that exists when a person who suffers eventual harm from a crime plays a direct role in causing the crime to be perpetrated.

Victim proneness The tendency for certain people to be victimized repeatedly.

Victimization survey A systematic effort to measure the experiences of the victims of crime by interviewing a cross section of a population.

Victimless crime An offense that is consensual and lacks a complaining participant.

White-collar crime An illegal act, punishable by a criminal sanction, that is committed in the course of a legitimate occupation or pursuit by a corporation or by an otherwise respectable individual of high social status.

Working personality The police officer's distinctive approach to the situations and events that are encountered on the job.

XYY chromosome A rare biological trait of some men that has been linked to a tendency to violate the law, or at least to be arrested for such violations.

Bibliography

ABT ASSOCIATES, INC. *American Prisons and Jails,* Vol. 2: *Population Trends and Projections.* Washington, D.C.: U.S. Government Printing Office, 1980.

ADAMS, VIRGINIA. "Studies Relate Physical Causes to Delinquency," *The New York Times,* June 26, 1979, pp. C1, C3.

ADLER, FREDA. *Nations Not Obsessed with Crime.* Littleton, Colo.: Fred B. Rothman, 1983.

ADLER, PATRICIA A. *Wheeling and Dealing: An Ethnography of an Upper-Level Drug Dealing and Smuggling Community.* New York: Columbia University Press, 1985.

———, AND PETER ADLER. "Shifts and Oscillations in Deviant Careers: The Case of Upper-Level Drug Dealers and Smugglers," *Social Problems* 31 (December 1983), 195–207.

AGETON, SUZANNE S., AND DELBERT S. ELLIOTT. "The Effects of Legal Processing on Self-Concept." Boulder: Institute of Behavioral Science, University of Colorado, 1973.

AGNEW, ROBERT. "Social Control Theory and Delinquency: A Longitudinal Test," *Criminology* 23 (February 1985), 47–61.

AICHHORN, AUGUST. *Wayward Youth.* New York: Viking, 1935, 1951.

AKERS, RONALD L. *Deviant Behavior: A Social Learning Approach,* 3rd ed. Belmont, Calif.: Wadsworth, 1985.

———. "Socioeconomic Status and Delinquent Behavior: A Re-Test," *Journal of Research in Crime and Delinquency* 1 (January 1964), 38–46.

———, ET AL. "Social Learning and Deviant Behavior: A Specific Test of a General Theory," *American Sociological Review* 44 (August 1979), 635–655.

AL-THAKEB, FAHAD. "Crime Trends in Kuwait," International Criminological Symposium, Stockholm, Sweden, 1978.

ALBRECHT, PETER-ALEXIS, CHRISTIAN PFEIFFER, AND KLAUS ZAPKA. "Reactions of the Agencies of Social Control to Crimes of Young Foreigners in the Federal Republic of Germany," *International Summaries.* Washington, D.C.: U.S. Department of Justice, 1978.

ALDER, CHRISTINE. "An Exploration of Self-Reported Sexually Aggressive Behavior," *Crime and Delinquency* 31 (April 1985), 306–331.

ALLEN, FRANCIS A. "Criminal Justice, Legal Values and the Rehabilitative Ideal," in Stanley E. Grupp, ed., *Theories of Punishment.* Bloomington: Indiana University Press, 1971, pp. 317–330.

549

ALLEN, VERNON L., AND DAVID B. GREENBERGER. "An Aesthetic Theory of Vandalism," *Crime and Delinquency* 24 (July 1978), 309–321.

ALTHEIDE, DAVID L., ET AL. "The Social Meanings of Employee Theft," in John M.
Johnson and Jack D. Douglas, eds., *Crime at the Top: Deviance in Business and the
Professions.* Philadelphia: Lippincott, 1978, pp. 90–124.

ALTMAN, LAWRENCE K. "Drug Abuse Found in Medical Training," *The New York
Times,* August 19, 1983a, p. A8.

———. "The Private Agony of an Addicted Physician," *The New York Times,* June 7,
1983b, pp. C1, C8.

AMERICAN FRIENDS SERVICE COMMITTEE. *Struggle for Justice: A Report on Crime and
Punishment in America.* New York: Hill and Wang, 1971.

AMIR, MENACHEM. *Patterns in Forcible Rape.* Chicago: University of Chicago Press, 1971.

ANDELMAN, DAVID A. "City Crime Wave Spreading to Suburbs," *The New York Times,*
January 30, 1972, p. 49.

ANDENAES, JOHANNES. "General Prevention—Illusion or Reality," *Journal of Criminal
Law, Criminology and Police Science* 43 (July–August 1952), 176–198.

———. *Punishment and Deterrence.* Ann Arbor: University of Michigan Press, 1974.

ANDERSON, OSCAR E. *The Health of a Nation: Harvey E. Wiley's Fight for Pure Food.*
Chicago: University of Chicago Press, 1958.

ANGEL, ARTHUR, ET AL. "Preventive Detention: An Empirical Analysis," *Harvard
Civil Rights Civil Liberties Law Review* 6 (March 1971), 300–396.

ANGLIN, M. DOUGLAS, AND YIH-ING HSER. "Addicted Women and Crime," *Criminology*
25 (May 1987), 359–397.

APPLEBOME, PETER. "Juvenile Crime: The Offenders Are Younger and the Offenses
More Serious," *The New York Times,* February 3, 1987, p. A16.

ARCHER, DANE, AND ROSEMARY GARTNER. *Violence and Crime in Cross-National Perspective.* New Haven, Conn.: Yale University Press, 1984.

———, AND ROSEMARY GARTNER. "Violent Acts and Violent Times: A Comparative
Approach to Postwar Homicide Rates," *American Sociological Review* 41 (December 1976), 937–963.

———, ROSEMARY GARTNER, AND MARC BEITTEL. "Homicide and the Death Penalty:
A Cross-National Test of a Deterrence Hypothesis," *Journal of Criminal Law
and Criminology* 74 (Fall 1983), 991–1013.

ARMS, ROBERT L., GORDON W. RUSSELL, AND MARK L. SANDILANDS. "Effects of Viewing Aggressive Sports on the Hostility of Spectators," *Social Psychology Quarterly*
42 (September 1979), 275–279.

ARMSTRONG, K. G. "The Retributivist Hits Back," in Stanley E. Grupp, ed., *Theories
of Punishment.* Bloomington: Indiana University Press, 1971, pp. 19–40.

AULETTA, KEN. *The Underclass.* New York: Random House, 1982.

AUSTIN, JAMES, AND BARRY KRISBERG. "The Unmet Promise of Alternatives to Incarceration," *Crime and Delinquency* 28 (July 1982), 374–409.

AUSTIN, ROY L. "Race, Father-Absence, and Female Delinquency," *Criminology* 15
(February 1978), 487–504.

———. "Women's Liberation and Increases in Minor, Major, and Occupational
Offenses," *Criminology* 20 (November 1982), 407–430.

AUSTIN, WILLIAM. "Sex Differences in Bystander Intervention in a Theft," *Journal of
Personality and Social Psychology* 37 (November 1979), 2110–2120.

AXENROTH, JOSEPH B. "Social Class and Delinquency in Cross-Cultural Perspective,"
Journal of Research in Crime and Delinquency 20 (July 1983), 164–182.

BACON, MARGARET K., IRVIN L. CHILD, AND HERBERT BARRY 3D. "A Cross-Cultural Study of Correlates of Crime," *Journal of Abnormal and Social Psychology* 66 (April 1963), 291–300.

BAILEY, WALTER C. "An Evaluation of 100 Studies of Correctional Outcome," *Journal of Criminal Law, Criminology and Police Science* 57 (June 1966), 153–160.

BAILEY, WILLIAM C. "Disaggregation in Deterrence and Death Penalty Research: The Case of Murder in Chicago," *Journal of Criminal Law and Criminology* 74 (Fall 1983), 827–859.

BAKER, MARY HOLLAND, ET AL. "The Impact of a Crime Wave: Perceptions, Fear, and Confidence in the Police," *Law and Society Review* 17 (1983), 319–335.

BALDWIN, JOHN. "Ecological and Areal Studies in Great Britain and the United States," in Norval Morris and Michael Tonry, eds., *Crime and Justice: An Annual Review of Research,* Vol. 1. Chicago: University of Chicago Press, 1979, pp. 29–66.

———, AND MICHAEL MCCONVILLE. "Criminal Juries," in Norval Morris and Michael Tonry, eds., *Crime and Justice: An Annual Review of Research,* Vol. 2. Chicago: University of Chicago Press, 1980, pp. 269–319.

BALDWIN, JOHN D. "Thrill and Adventure Seeking and the Age Distribution of Crime: Comment on Hirschi and Gottfredson," *American Journal of Sociology* 90 (May 1985), 1326–1330.

BALKAN, SHEILA, RONALD J. BERGER, AND JANET SCHMIDT. *Crime and Deviance in America: A Critical Approach.* Belmont, Calif.: Wadsworth, 1980.

BALL-ROKEACH, SANDRA J. "Values and Violence: A Test of the Subculture of Violence Thesis," *American Sociological Review* 38 (December 1973), 736–749.

BANDURA, ALBERT, DOROTHEA ROSS, AND SHEILA A. ROSS. "Transmission of Aggression through Imitation of Aggressive Models," *Journal of Abnormal and Social Psychology* 62 (1961), 575–582.

BARBANEL, JOSH. "Half Guilty under Gun Law Get Mandated Term," *The New York Times,* November 11, 1984, p. B4.

BARIDON, PHILIP C. *Addiction, Crime, and Social Policy.* Lexington, Mass.: D.C. Heath, 1976.

BARNETT, RANDY E. "Restitution: A New Paradigm of Criminal Justice," in Randy E. Barnett and John Hagel 3d, eds., *Assessing the Criminal: Restitution, Retribution, and the Legal Process.* Cambridge, Mass.: Ballinger, 1977, pp. 349–383.

BARTH, ALAN. "The Vanishing Samaritan," in James M. Ratcliffe, ed., *The Good Samaritan and the Law.* Garden City, N.Y.: Doubleday, 1966, pp. 159–169.

BASLER, BARBARA. "State's Gun Law: Impact and Intent Uncertain," *The New York Times,* April 11, 1982, pp. 1, 41.

BAUMRIND, DIANA. "Parental Disciplinary Patterns and Social Competence in Children," *Youth and Society* 9 (1978), 239–276.

BAYER, RONALD. "Crime, Punishment, and the Decline of Liberal Optimism," *Crime and Delinquency* 27 (April 1981), 169–190.

BAYLEY, DAVID H. *Forces of Order: Police Behavior in Japan and the United States.* Berkeley: University of California Press, 1976a.

———. "Learning about Crime—The Japanese Experience," *The Public Interest* No. 44 (Summer 1976b), 55–68.

———. "Police: History," in Sanford H. Kadish, ed., *Encyclopedia of Crime and Justice,* Vol. 3. New York: Free Press, 1983, pp. 1120–1125.

BECCARIA, CESARE. *On Crimes and Punishments.* Indianapolis, Ind.: Bobbs-Merrill, 1764, 1963.

BECK, ALLEN J., AND THOMAS HESTER. *Prison Admissions and Releases, 1983.* Washington, D.C.: U.S. Department of Justice, March 1986.

BECKER, HOWARD S. *Outsiders: Studies in the Sociology of Deviance.* New York: Free Press, 1973.

BEDAU, HUGO ADAM. "Concessions to Retribution in Punishment," in J. B. Cederblom and William L. Blizek, eds., *Justice and Punishment.* Cambridge, Mass.: Ballinger, 1977, pp. 51–73.

———. "Review of Walter Berns, *For Capital Punishment: Crime and the Morality of the Death Penalty,*" *Ethics* 90 (April 1980), 457–466.

———, AND MICHAEL L. RADELET. "Miscarriages of Justice in Potentially Capital Cases," *Stanford Law Review* 40 (November 1987), 21–179.

BEHN, NOEL. *Big Stick-Up at Brinks!* New York: G. P. Putnam's Sons, 1977.

BEIRNE, PIERS. "Adolphe Quetelet and the Origins of Positivist Criminology," *American Journal of Sociology* 92 (March 1987), 1140–1169.

———. "Generalization and Its Discontents: The Comparative Study of Crime," in Israel L. Barak-Glantz and Elmer H. Johnson, eds., *Comparative Criminology.* Beverly Hills, Calif.: Sage Publications, 1983, pp. 19–38.

BELL, DANIEL. "Crime as an American Way of Life: A Queer Ladder of Social Mobility," in *The End of Ideology: On the Exhaustion of Political Ideas in the Fifties,* rev. ed. New York: Free Press, 1962, pp. 127–150.

BELSON, WILLIAM A. *Juvenile Theft: The Causal Factors.* London: Harper & Row, 1975.

BENNETT, RICHARD R. "Constructing Cross-Cultural Theories in Criminology: Application of the Generative Approach," *Criminology* 18 (August 1980), 252–268.

BENNETTS, LESLIE. "Do the Arts Inspire Violence in Real Life?" *The New York Times,* April 26, 1981, pp. H1, H25.

BERG, ERIC N. "The Credit-Card Fraud Battle," *The New York Times,* December 29, 1986, p. D7.

BERISTAIN, ANTONIO. "Capital Punishment and Catholicism," *International Journal of Criminology and Penology* 5 (November 1977), 321–335.

BERK, RICHARD A., AND PHYLLIS J. NEWTON. "Does Arrest Really Deter Wife Battery? An Effort to Replicate the Findings of the Minneapolis Spouse Abuse Experiment," *American Sociological Review* 50 (April 1985), 253–262.

BERKOWITZ, LEONARD. "Some Determinants of Impulsive Aggression: Role of Mediated Associations with Reinforcements for Aggression," *Psychological Review* 81 (March 1974), 165–176.

———, AND JACQUELINE MACAULAY. "The Contagion of Criminal Violence," *Sociometry* 34 (June 1971), 238–260.

BERNS, WALTER C. *For Capital Punishment: Crime and the Morality of the Death Penalty.* New York: Basic Books, 1979.

BIDERMAN, ALBERT D. "Sources of Data for Victimology," *Journal of Criminal Law and Criminology* 72 (Summer 1981), 789–817.

BISHOP, DONNA M. "Legal and Extralegal Barriers to Delinquency: A Panel Analysis," *Criminology* 22 (August 1984), 403–419.

BITTNER, EGON. "The Police on Skid-Row: A Study of Peace Keeping," *American Sociological Review* 32 (October 1967), 699–715.

BLACK, DONALD J. *The Behavior of Law.* New York: Academic Press, 1976.

———. "Crime as Social Control," *American Sociological Review* 48 (February 1983), 34–35.

———. *The Manners and Customs of the Police.* New York: Academic Press, 1980.

———. "Production of Crime Rates," *American Sociological Review* 35 (August 1970), 733–748.

———, AND ALBERT J. REISS, JR. "Police Control of Juveniles," *American Sociological Review* 35 (February 1970), 63–78.

BLACKMORE, JOHN, AND JANE WELSH. "Selective Incapacitation: Sentencing According to Risk," *Crime and Delinquency* 29 (October 1983), 504–528.

BLAU, JUDITH, AND PETER BLAU. "The Cost of Inequality: Metropolitan Structure and Violent Crime," *American Sociological Review* 47 (February 1982), 114–129.

BLOCH, HERBERT A., AND ARTHUR NIEDERHOFFER. *The Gang: A Study in Adolescent Behavior.* New York: Philosophical Library, 1958.

BLOCK, ALAN A., AND FRANK R. SCARPITTI. *Poisoning for Profit: The Mafia and Toxic Waste in America.* New York: Morrow, 1985.

BLOCK, MICHAEL KENT, FREDERICK CARL NOLD, AND JOSEPH GREGORY SIDAK. "The Deterrent Effect of Antitrust Enforcement," *Journal of Political Economy* 89 (June 1981), 429–445.

BLOCK, RICHARD. "Victim-Offender Dynamics in Violent Crime," *Journal of Criminal Law and Criminology* 72 (Summer 1981), 743–761.

———. *Violent Crime: Environment, Interaction, and Death.* Lexington, Mass.: D. C. Heath, 1977.

———, AND CAROLYN R. BLOCK. "Decisions and Data: The Transformation of Robbery Incidents into Official Robbery Statistics," *Journal of Criminal Law and Criminology* 71 (Winter 1980), 622–636.

BLUMBERG, ABRAHAM S. "Crime and the Social Order," in Abraham S. Blumberg, ed., *Current Perspectives on Criminal Behavior: Original Essays on Criminology.* New York: Knopf, 1974, pp. 3–34.

———. *Criminal Justice: Issues & Ironies,* 2nd ed. New York: New Viewpoints, 1979.

BLUMENTHAL, MONICA, ET AL. *Justifying Violence: Attitudes of American Men.* Ann Arbor, Mich.: Institute for Social Research, 1972.

BLUMSTEIN, ALFRED. "On the Racial Disproportionality of United States' Prison Populations," *Journal of Criminal Law and Criminology* 73 (Fall 1982), 1259–1281.

———. "Prisons: Population, Capacity, and Alternatives," in James Q. Wilson, ed., *Crime and Public Policy.* San Francisco: ICS Press, 1983, pp. 229–250.

———, AND JACQUELINE COHEN. "Estimation of Individual Crime Rates from Arrest Records," *Journal of Criminal Law and Criminology* 70 (Winter 1979), 561–585.

———, AND JACQUELINE COHEN. "Sentencing of Convicted Offenders: An Analysis of the Public's View," *Law and Society Review* 14 (Winter 1980), 223–261.

———, JACQUELINE COHEN, AND WILLIAM GOODING. "The Influence of Capacity on Prison Population: A Critical Review of Some Recent Evidence," *Crime and Delinquency* 29 (January 1983), 1–51.

———, JACQUELINE COHEN, AND DANIEL NAGIN. *Deterrence and Incapacitation: Estimating the Effects of Criminal Sanctions on Crime Rates.* Washington, D.C.: National Academy of Sciences, 1978.

———, DAVID P. FARRINGTON, AND SOUMYO MOITRA. "Delinquency Careers: Innocents, Desisters, and Persisters," in Michael Tonry and Norval Morris, eds., *Crime and Justice: An Annual Review of Research,* Vol. 6. Chicago: University of Chicago Press, 1985, pp. 187–219.

———, AND ELIZABETH GRADDY. "Prevalence and Recidivism in Index Arrests: A Feedback Model," *Law and Society Review* 16 (1981–82), 265–290.

————, AND DANIEL NAGIN. "The Deterrent Effect of Legal Sanctions on Draft Evasion," *Stanford Law Review* 29 (January 1977), 241–276.

————, ET AL. *Criminal Careers and "Career Criminals",* Vols. 1 and 2. Washington, D.C.: National Academy Press, 1986.

BLUNDELL, WILLIAM E. "Equity Funding: 'I Did It for the Jollies,'" in Donald Moffitt, ed., *Swindled! Classic Business Frauds of the Seventies.* Princeton, N.J.: Dow Jones Books, 1976, pp. 42–89.

BOFFEY, PHILIP M. "Youth Crime Puzzle Defies a Solution," *The New York Times,* March 5, 1982, pp. B1, B4.

BOGGS, SARAH L. "Formal and Informal Crime Control: An Exploratory Study of Urban, Suburban, and Rural Orientations," *Sociological Quarterly* 12 (Summer 1971), 319–327.

BOHANNAN, PAUL, ED. *African Homicide and Suicide.* Princeton, N.J.: Princeton University Press, 1960.

BOLAND, BARBARA, AND JAMES Q. WILSON. "Age, Crime, and Punishment," *The Public Interest* No. 51 (Spring 1978), 22–34.

BOOKIN-WEINER, HEDY, AND RUTH HOROWITZ. "The End of the Youth Gang: Fad or Fact?" *Criminology* 21 (November 1983), 585–602.

BOOTH, ALAN. "The Built Environment as a Crime Deterrent: A Reexamination of Defensible Space," *Criminology* 18 (February 1981), 557–570.

————, DAVID R. JOHNSON, AND HARVEY M. CHOLDIN. "Correlates of City Crime Rates: Victimization Surveys versus Official Statistics," *Social Problems* 25 (December 1977), 187–197.

BORTNER, M. A. "Traditional Rhetoric, Organizational Realities: Remand of Juveniles to Adult Court," *Crime and Delinquency* 32 (January 1986), 53–73.

[The Boston Globe.] "Alcohol Use Linked to Violent Crimes," *The Boston Globe,* November 4, 1985, p. 12.

————. "Ask the Globe," *The Boston Globe,* May 7, 1980, p. 86.

————. "Childhood Aggressiveness, Adult Criminality Linked," *The Boston Globe,* August 28, 1983, p. 7.

————. "Hyperactivity Tied to Crime," *The Boston Globe,* November 26, 1982, p. 11.

————. "Panel Says Criminals Launder Up to $150b," *The Boston Globe,* December 30, 1986, p. 10.

————. "Senate Panel Told Gang Problem Is Spreading," *The Boston Globe,* July 10, 1981, p. 11.

————. "Study: Pornography Affects Attitude on Rape," *The Boston Globe,* November 21, 1982, p. 5.

————. Study Shows 25% Back in Prison within 2 Years," *The Boston Globe,* December 3, 1984, p. 9.

————. "20% of Americans in Study Said to Admit Tax-Cheating," *The Boston Globe,* March 25, 1985, p. 12.

BOWERS, WILLIAM J. "The Pervasiveness of Arbitrariness and Discrimination under Post-*Furman* Capital Statutes," *Journal of Criminal Law and Criminology* 74 (Winter 1983), 1067–1100.

————, AND GLENN L. PIERCE. "Arbitrariness and Discrimination under Post-*Furman* Capital Statutes," *Crime and Delinquency* 26 (October 1980a), 563–635.

————, AND GLENN L. PIERCE. "Deterrence or Brutalization: What Is the Effect of Executions?" *Crime and Delinquency* 26 (October 1980b), 453–484.

———, WITH GLENN L. PIERCE AND JOHN F. McDEVITT. *Legal Homicide: Death as Punishment in America, 1864–1982.* Boston: Northeastern University Press, 1984.

BOWKER, LEE H. "Crime and the Use of Prisons in the United States: A Time Series Analysis," *Crime and Delinquency* 27 (April 1981), 206–212.

BOYDSTUN, JOHN E. *San Diego Field Interrogation: Final Report.* Washington, D.C.: Police Foundation, 1975.

BRADY, JAMES P. "Arson, Fiscal Crisis, and Community Action: Dialectics of an Urban Crime and Popular Response," *Crime and Delinquency* 28 (April 1982), 247–270.

———. "Arson, Urban Economy, and Organized Crime: The Case of Boston," *Social Problems* 31 (October 1983a), 1–27.

———. "Behind the Burning of Boston," *The Boston Globe Magazine,* October 23, 1983b, pp. 9–11, 49–66.

BRAITHWAITE, JOHN. "Challenging Just Deserts: Punishing White-Collar Criminals," *Journal of Criminal Law and Criminology* 73 (Summer 1982), 723–763.

———. *Inequality, Crime, and Public Policy.* London: Routledge and Kegan Paul, 1979.

———. "*The Myth of Social Class and Criminality* Reconsidered," *American Sociological Review* 46 (February 1981), 36–57.

———, AND GILBERT GEIS. "On Theory and Action for Corporate Crime Control," *Crime and Delinquency* 28 (April 1982), 292–314.

BRANTINGHAM, PAUL, AND PATRICIA BRANTINGHAM. *Patterns in Crime.* New York: Macmillan, 1984.

BRIAR, SCOTT, AND IRVING PILIAVIN. "Delinquency, Situational Inducements, and Commitment to Conformity," *Social Problems* 13 (Summer 1965), 35–45.

BRIDGES, JAMES H., JOHN T. GANDY, AND JAMES D. JORGENSEN. "The Case for Creative Restitution in Corrections," *Federal Probation* 43 (September 1979), 28–35.

British Journal of Criminology 22 (July 1982), Special Issue on Dangerousness.

BRODY, JANE E. "Researchers Trace Key Factors in Profiles of Assassins on the American Scene," *The New York Times,* April 1, 1981, p. A26.

BROWN, BAILEY. "Community Service as a Condition of Probation," *Federal Probation* 41 (December 1977), 7–9.

BROWN, JULIA S. "A Comparative Study of Deviations from Sexual Mores," *American Sociological Review* 17 (April 1952), 135–146.

BROWN, RICHARD MAXWELL. "The American Vigilante Tradition," in Hugh Davis Graham and Ted Robert Gurr, eds., *Violence in America: Historical and Comparative Perspectives.* Staff Report to the National Commission on the Causes and Prevention of Violence, Vol. 1. Washington, D.C.: U.S. Government Printing Office, 1969, pp. 121–169.

———. *The South Carolina Regulators.* Cambridge, Mass.: Belknap Press of Harvard University Press, 1963.

BROWNMILLER, SUSAN. *Against Our Will: Men, Women and Rape.* New York: Simon and Schuster, 1975.

BROZAN, NADINE. "Jurors in Rape Trials Studied," *The New York Times,* June 17, 1985, p. C13.

BUDER, LEONARD. "Sharp Drop in Bank Robberies Cited by New York City Police," *The New York Times,* January 30, 1983, p. A22.

BUREAU OF JUSTICE STATISTICS. *Capital Punishment 1985.* Washington, D.C.: U.S. Department of Justice, October 1986.

————. *Crime and Seasonality: National Crime Survey Report.* Washington, D.C.: U.S. Department of Justice, May 1980.

————. *Crime Prevention Measures.* Washington, D.C.: U.S. Department of Justice, March 1986.

————. *Criminal Justice "Hot" Files.* Washington, D.C.: U.S. Department of Justice, November 1986.

————. *Criminal Victimization in the United States, 1981.* Washington, D.C.: U.S. Department of Justice, November 1983a.

————. *Criminal Victimization 1986.* Washington, D.C.: U.S. Department of Justice, October 1987.

————. *The Economic Cost of Crime to Victims.* Washington, D.C.: U.S. Department of Justice, April 1984.

————. *Electronic Fund Transfer and Crime.* Washington, D.C.: U.S. Department of Justice, February 1984.

————. *Households Touched by Crime, 1983.* Washington, D.C.: U.S. Department of Justice, May 1984.

————. *Justice Expenditure and Employment,* Washington, D.C.: U.S. Department of Justice, March 1987.

————. *Prisoners and Alcohol.* Washington, D.C.: U.S. Department of Justice, January 1983.

————. *Prisoners and Drugs.* Washington, D.C.: U.S. Department of Justice, March 1983.

————. *Prisoners in 1986.* Washington, D.C.: U.S. Department of Justice, May 1987.

————. *Prisoners in State and Federal Institutions on December 31, 1984.* Washington, D.C.: U.S. Department of Justice, February 1987.

————. *Probation and Parole 1985.* Washington, D.C.: U.S. Department of Justice, January 1987.

————. *Report to the Nation on Crime and Justice: The Data.* Washington, D.C.: U.S. Department of Justice, October 1983.

————. *Reporting Crimes to the Police.* Washington, D.C.: U.S. Department of Justice, December 1985.

————. *Tracking Offenders.* Washington, D.C.: U.S. Department of Justice, November 1983b.

BURGESS, ANN WOLBERT, AND LYNDA LYTLE HOLMSTROM. "Rape: Its Effect on Task Performance at Varying Stages in the Life Cycle," in Marcia J. Walker and Stanley L. Brodsky, eds., *Sexual Assault.* Lexington, Mass.: D. C. Heath, 1976, pp. 23–33.

BURGESS, ROBERT L., AND RONALD L. AKERS. "A Differential Association-Reinforcement Theory of Criminal Behavior," *Social Problems* 14 (Fall 1966), 128–147.

BURNHAM, DAVID. "F.B.I. Arrest Data Found Inaccurate," *The New York Times,* July 29, 1984, p. 17.

————. F.B.I. Says 12,000 Faulty Reports on Suspects Are Issued Each Day," *The New York Times,* August 25, 1985a, pp. 1, 30.

————. "Fear of Muggers Looms Large in Public Concern over Crime," *The New York Times,* May 20, 1968, p. 52.

————. "Plan for Crime Data Overhaul," *The New York Times,* June 20, 1985b.

BURSIK, ROBERT J., JR., AND JIM WEBB. "Community Change and Patterns of Delinquency," *American Journal of Sociology* 88 (July 1982), 24–42.

BUTTERFIELD, FOX. "How the Chinese Police Themselves," *The New York Times Magazine,* April 18, 1982, pp. 32, 36–40, 50–56.

BYNUM, TIM S., GARY W. CORDNER, AND JACK R. GREENE. "Victim and Offense Characteristics: Impact on Police Investigative Decision-Making," *Criminology* 20 (November 1982), 301–318.

BYRNE, HARRY J. "'Society Needs Draconian Justice,'" *The New York Times,* November 20, 1979, p. A23.

CAHALAN, MARGARET WERNER. *Historical Corrections Statistics in the United States, 1850–1984.* Washington, D.C.: U.S. Department of Justice, December 1986.

———. "Trends in Incarceration in the United States since 1880: A Summary of Reported Rates and the Distribution of Offenses," *Crime and Delinquency* 25 (January 1979), 9–41.

CAMERON, MARY OWEN. *The Booster and the Snitch: Department Store Shoplifting.* New York: Free Press, 1964.

CAMPBELL, ANNE. *The Girls in the Gang: A Report from New York City.* New York: Basil Blackwell, 1984.

CANTER, RACHELLE. "Family Correlates of Male and Female Delinquency," *Criminology* 20 (August 1982), 149–167.

CAPLAN, LINCOLN. "Annals of Law: The Insanity Defense," *The New Yorker,* July 2, 1984, pp. 45–78.

CAPOTE, TRUMAN. *In Cold Blood: A True Account of a Multiple Murder and Its Consequences.* New York: Random House, 1965.

CARMODY, DEIRDRE. "Law Graduate Held in $607,000 Fraud," *The New York Times,* February 20, 1974, pp. 1, 45.

CARROLL, LEO, AND MARGARET E. MONDRICK. "Racial Bias in the Decision to Grant Parole," *Law and Society Review* 11 (Fall 1976), 93–107.

CASPER, JONATHAN D. "Having Their Day in Court: Defendant Evaluations of the Fairness of Their Treatment," *Law and Society Review* 12 (Winter 1978), 237–249.

CATER, DOUGLASS, AND STEPHEN STRICKLAND. *TV Violence and the Child: The Evolution and Fate of the Surgeon General's Report.* New York: Russell Sage Foundation, 1975.

CERNKOVICH, STEPHEN A. "Conceptual and Empirical Ambiguity in Class-Oriented Theories of Crime and Delinquency," *International Journal of Criminology and Penology* 6 (May 1978a), 105–120.

———. "Evaluating Two Models of Delinquency Causation: Structural Theory and Control Theory," *Criminology* 16 (November 1978b), 335–352.

———. "Value Orientations and Delinquency Involvement," *Criminology* 15 (February 1978c), 443–458.

———, PEGGY C. GIORDANO, AND MEREDITH D. PUGH. "Chronic Offenders: The Missing Cases in Self-Report Delinquency Research," *Journal of Criminal Law and Criminology* 76 (Fall 1985), 705–732.

CHAIKEN, JAN M., AND MARCIA R. CHAIKEN. "Crime Rates and the Active Criminal," in James Q. Wilson, ed., *Crime and Public Policy.* San Francisco: ICS Press, 1983, pp. 11–29.

———, AND MARCIA R. CHAIKEN. *Varieties of Criminal Behavior.* Santa Monica, Calif.: Rand, 1982a.

———, AND MARCIA R. CHAIKEN, WITH JOYCE E. PETERSON. *Varieties of Criminal Behavior: Summary and Policy Implications.* Santa Monica, Calif.: Rand, 1982b.

——, Michael W. Lawless, and Keith A. Stevenson. *The Impact of Police Activity on Crime: Robberies in the New York City Subway System.* New York: Rand, 1974.

Chaiken, Marcia R., and Jan M. Chaiken. "Offender Types and Public Policy," *Crime and Delinquency* 30 (April 1984), 195–226.

Chalidze, Valery. *Criminal Russia: Crime in the Soviet Union.* New York: Random House, 1977.

Chambers, Marcia. "Adult-Jailing of West's Young Fought," *The New York Times,* October 13, 1986, p. A15.

——. "Life in City's Gangs: Some Things Have Changed, but It's Still a Dead End," *The New York Times,* September 27, 1983, pp. B1, B4.

Chambliss, William J., ed. *Crime and the Legal Process.* New York: McGraw-Hill, 1969, pp. 360–378.

——. *On the Table: From Petty Crooks to Presidents.* Bloomington: Indiana University Press, 1978.

——. "Vice, Corruption, Bureaucracy, and Power," *Wisconsin Law Review* No. 4 (1971), 1130–1155.

Chapman, William. "Rising Delinquency in Japanese Junior High Schools," *The Boston Globe,* April 5, 1983, p. 3.

Chein, Isidor, et al. *The Road to H: Narcotics, Delinquency, and Social Policy.* New York: Basic Books, 1964.

Chesney-Lind, Meda. "Judicial Enforcement of the Female Sex Role: The Family Court and the Female Delinquent," *Issues in Criminology* 8 (Fall 1973), 51–69.

Chevalier, Louis. *Laboring Classes and Dangerous Classes in Paris during the First Half of the Nineteenth Century.* New York: Howard Fertig, 1973.

Chibnall, Steve. *Law-and-Order News: An Analysis of Crime Reporting in the British Press.* London: Tavistock, 1977.

Chilton, Roland J. "Delinquency Area Research in Baltimore, Detroit, and Indianapolis," *American Sociological Review* 29 (February 1964), 71–83.

——. "Persistent Problems of Crime Statistics," in Simon Dinitz and Walter C. Reckless, eds., *Critical Issues in the Study of Crime: A Book of Readings.* Boston: Little, Brown, 1968, pp. 89–95.

Chiu, Hungdah. "Criminal Punishment in Mainland China: A Study of Some Yunnan Province Documents," *Journal of Criminal Law and Criminology* 68 (September 1977), 374–398.

Christiansen, Karl O. "A Preliminary Study of Criminality among Twins," in Sarnoff A. Mednick and Karl O. Christiansen, eds., *Biosocial Bases of Criminal Behavior.* New York: Gardner Press, 1977, pp. 89–108.

——. "Seriousness of Criminality and Concordance among Danish Twins," in Roger Hood, ed., *Crime, Criminology, and Public Policy: Essays in Honour of Sir Leon Radzinowicz.* New York: Free Press, 1974, pp. 63–77.

Christianson, Scott. "Our Black Prisons," *Crime and Delinquency* 27 (July 1981), 364–375.

Clark, John P., and Edward H. Haurek. "Age and Sex Roles of Adolescents and Their Involvement in Misconduct: A Reappraisal," *Sociology and Social Research* 50 (July 1966), 496–508.

——, and Larry L. Tifft. "Polygraph and Interview Validation of Self-Reported Deviant Behavior," *American Sociological Review* 31 (August 1966), 516–523.

Clarke, Ronald V. "Situational Crime Prevention: Its Theoretical Basis and Practical Scope," in Michael Tonry and Norval Morris, eds., *Crime and Justice: An*

Annual Review of Research, Vol. 4. Chicago: University of Chicago Press, 1983, pp. 225–256.

————, AND DEREK B. CORNISH. "Modeling Offenders' Decisions: A Framework for Research and Policy," in Michael Tonry and Norval Morris, eds., *Crime and Justice: An Annual Review of Research,* Vol. 6. Chicago: University of Chicago Press, 1985, pp. 147–185.

CLARKE, STEVENS H., AND GARY G. KOCH. "The Influence of Income and Other Factors on Whether Criminal Defendants Go to Prison," *Law and Society Review* 11 (Fall 1976), 57–92.

CLEAVER, ELDRIDGE. *Soul on Ice.* New York: Dell, 1968.

CLECKLEY, HERVEY. *The Mask of Sanity,* 4th ed. St. Louis: C. V. Mosby, 1964.

CLELLAND, DONALD, AND TIMOTHY J. CARTER. "The New Myth of Class and Crime," *Criminology* 18 (November 1980), 319–336.

CLENDINEN, DUDLEY. "Crowded Prisons in South Lead to Tests of Other Punishments," *The New York Times,* December 18, 1985, p. A18.

CLIFFORD, WILLIAM. *Crime Control in Japan.* Lexington, Mass.: D. C. Heath, 1976.

————. "Culture and Crime—In Global Perspective," *International Journal of Criminology and Penology* 6 (February 1978), 61–80.

CLINARD, MARSHALL B. *The Black Market: A Study of White Collar Crime.* Montclair, N.J.: Patterson Smith, 1952, 1969.

————, *Cities with Little Crime: The Case of Switzerland.* Cambridge, Eng.: Cambridge University Press, 1978.

————. *Corporate Ethics and Crime: The Role of Middle Management.* Beverly Hills, Calif.: Sage Publications, 1983.

————. "The Process of Urbanization and Criminal Behavior," *American Journal of Sociology* 48 (September 1942), 202–213.

————. "Rural Criminal Offenders," *American Journal of Sociology* 50 (July 1944), 38–45.

————, AND DANIEL J. ABBOTT. *Crime in Developing Countries: A Comparative Perspective.* New York: Wiley, 1973.

————, AND PETER C. YEAGER. *Corporate Crime.* New York: Free Press, 1980.

CLOWARD, RICHARD A., AND LLOYD E. OHLIN. *Delinquency and Opportunity: A Theory of Delinquent Gangs.* New York: Free Press, 1960.

COATES, ROBERT B., ALDEN D. MILLER, AND LLOYD E. OHLIN. *Diversity in a Youth Correctional System: Handling Delinquents in Massachusetts.* Cambridge, Mass.: Ballinger, 1978.

COCOZZA, JOSEPH J., AND HENRY J. STEADMAN. "Prediction in Psychiatry: An Example of Misplaced Confidence in Experts," *Social Problems* 25 (February 1978), 265–276.

COHEN, ALBERT K. *Delinquent Boys: The Culture of the Gang.* New York: Free Press, 1955.

COHEN, JACQUELINE. *Incapacitating Criminals: Recent Research Findings.* Washington, D.C.: National Institute of Justice, U.S. Department of Justice, December 1983a.

————. "Incapacitation as a Strategy for Crime Control: Possibilities and Pitfalls," in Michael Tonry and Norval Morris, eds., *Crime and Justice: An Annual Review of Research,* Vol. 5. Chicago: University of Chicago Press, 1983b, pp. 1–84.

COHEN, JEROME ALAN. "Reflections on the Criminal Process in China," *Journal of Criminal Law and Criminology* 68 (September 1977), 323–355.

COHEN, LAWRENCE E. "Modeling Crime Trends: A Criminal Opportunity Perspective," *Journal of Research in Crime and Delinquency* 18 (January 1981), 138–162.

————, AND DAVID CANTOR. "The Determinants of Larceny: An Empirical and Theoretical Study," *Journal of Research in Crime and Delinquency* 17 (July 1980), 140–159.

————, AND DAVID CANTOR. "Residential Burglary in the United States: Life-Style and Demographic Factors Associated with the Probability of Victimization," *Journal of Research in Crime and Delinquency* 18 (January 1981), 113–127.

————, AND MARCUS FELSON. "Social Change and Crime Rate Trends: A Routine Activity Approach," *American Sociological Review* 44 (August 1979), 588–608.

————, AND JAMES R. KLUEGEL. "Determinants of Juvenile Court Disposition: Ascriptive and Achieved Factors in Two Metropolitan Courts," *American Sociological Review* 43 (April 1978), 162–176.

————, JAMES R. KLUEGEL, AND KENNETH C. LAND. "Social Inequality and Predatory Criminal Victimization: An Exposition and Test of a Formal Theory," *American Sociological Review* 46 (October 1981), 505–524.

————, AND KENNETH C. LAND. "Age Structure and Crime: Symmetry versus Asymmetry and the Projection of Crime Rates through the 1990s," *American Sociological Review* 52 (April 1987), 170–183.

COLEMAN, JAMES S., THOMAS HOFFER, AND SALLY KILGORE. *High School Achievement: Public, Catholic, and Private Schools Compared.* New York: Basic Books, 1982.

COLEMAN, JAMES W. *The Criminal Elite: The Sociology of White Collar Crime.* New York: St. Martin's Press, 1985.

COLLINS, GLENN. "A Study Assesses Traits of Women Who Kill," *The New York Times,* July 7, 1986, p. C18.

————. "The Violent Child: Some Patterns Emerge," *The New York Times,* September 27, 1982, p. B10.

COLLINS, JAMES J., JR. *Alcohol Use and Criminal Behavior: An Executive Summary.* Washington, D.C.: U.S. Department of Justice, National Institute of Justice, 1981a.

————, ED. *Drinking and Crime: Perspectives on the Relationships between Alcohol Consumption and Criminal Behavior.* New York: Guilford Press, 1981b.

————, ROBERT L. HUBBARD, AND J. VALLEY RACHAL. "Expensive Drug Use and Illegal Income: A Test of Explanatory Hypotheses," *Criminology* 23 (November 1985), 743–764.

COLTON, KENT W., ET AL. *Computer Crime: Electronic Fund Transfer Systems and Crime.* Washington, D.C.: U.S. Government Printing Office, 1982.

COLVIN, MARK. "The 1980 New Mexico Prison Riot," *Social Problems* 29 (June 1982), 449–463.

CONKLIN, JOHN E., ED. *The Crime Establishment: Organized Crime and American Society.* Englewood Cliffs, N.J.: Prentice-Hall, 1973.

————. *"Illegal but Not Criminal": Business Crime in America.* Englewood Cliffs, N.J.: Prentice-Hall, 1977.

————. *The Impact of Crime.* New York: Macmillan, 1975.

————. *Robbery and the Criminal Justice System.* Philadelphia: Lippincott, 1972.

CONRAD, PETER, AND JOSEPH W. SCHNEIDER. *Deviance and Medicalization: From Badness to Sickness.* St. Louis: C. V. Mosby, 1980.

COOK, PHILIP J. "The Correctional Carrot: Better Jobs for Parolees," *Policy Analysis* 1 (1975), 11–54.

————. "The Influence of Gun Availability on Violent Crime Patterns," in Michael

Tonry and Norval Morris, eds., *Crime and Justice: An Annual Review of Research,* Vol. 4. Chicago: University of Chicago Press, 1983, pp. 49–89.

———. "Robbery Violence," *Journal of Criminal Law and Criminology* 78 (Summer 1987), 357–376.

COOK. R. F., AND J. A. ROEHL. *Preventing Crime and Arson—A Review of Community-Based Strategies.* Reston, Va.: Institute for Social Analysis, 1983.

CORDILIA, ANN. *The Making of an Inmate: Prison as a Way of Life.* Cambridge, Mass.: Schenkman, 1983.

COUNT-VAN MANEN, GLORIA. "A Deviant Case of Deviance: Singapore," *Law and Society Review* 5 (February 1971), 389–406.

CRESSEY, DONALD R. *Criminal Organization.* New York: Harper & Row, 1972.

———. *Other People's Money: A Study in the Social Psychology of Embezzlement.* Belmont, Calif.: Wadsworth, 1953, 1971.

———. *Theft of the Nation: The Structure and Operations of Organized Crime in America.* New York: Harper & Row, 1969.

———, AND ROBERT A. MCDERMOTT. *Diversion from the Juvenile Justice System.* Washington, D.C.: U.S. Government Printing Office, 1973.

CRIMINAL DIVISION, U.S. DEPARTMENT OF JUSTICE. Cited in *Congressional Record—Senate* 114 (July 18, 1968), 21986.

CRONIN, THOMAS E., TANIA Z. CRONIN, AND MICHAEL E. MILAKOVICH. *U.S. v. Crime in the Streets.* Bloomington: Indiana University Press, 1981.

CRUTCHFIELD, ROBERT D., MICHAEL R. GEERKEN, AND WALTER R. GOVE. "Crime Rate and Social Integration: The Impact of Metropolitan Mobility," *Criminology* 20 (November 1982), 467–478.

CSIKSZENTMIHALYI, MIHALY, AND REED LARSON. "Intrinsic Rewards in School Crime," *Crime and Delinquency* 24 (July 1978), 322–335.

CULLEN, FRANCIS T., AND KAREN E. GILBERT. *Reaffirming Rehabilitation.* Cincinnati, Ohio: Anderson, 1982.

———, BRUCE G. LINK, AND CRAIG W. POLANZI. "The Seriousness of Crime Revisited: Have Attitudes toward White-Collar Crime Changed?" *Criminology* 20 (May 1982), 83–102.

———, WILLIAM J. MAAKESTAD, AND GRAY CAVENDER. *Corporate Crime under Attack: The Ford Pinto Case and Beyond.* Cincinnati, Ohio: Anderson, 1987.

———, WILLIAM J. MAAKESTAD, AND GRAY CAVENDER. "The Ford Pinto Case and Beyond: Corporate Crime, Moral Boundaries, and the Criminal Sanction," in Ellen Hochstedler, ed., *Corporations as Criminals.* Beverly Hills, Calif.: Sage Publications, 1984, pp. 107–130.

———., ET AL. "Public Support for Punishing White-Collar Crime: Blaming the Victim Revisited?" *Journal of Criminal Justice* 11 (1983), 481–493.

CURRAN, DEBRA A. "Judicial Discretion and Defendant's Sex," *Criminology* 21 (February 1983), 41–58.

CURRIE, ELLIOTT. *Confronting Crime: An American Challenge.* New York: Pantheon, 1985.

CURTIS, LYNN A. *Criminal Violence: National Patterns and Behavior.* Lexington, Mass.: D. C. Heath, 1974.

———. *Violence, Race and Culture.* Lexington, Mass.: D. C. Heath, 1975.

CURWOOD, STEVE. "Study Finds More Rape Where Violence Is 'Accepted,'" *The Boston Globe,* June 24, 1985, p. 16.

Cushman, Paul, Jr. "Relationship between Narcotic Addiction and Crime," *Federal Probation* 38 (September 1974), 38–43.

Dalgard, Odd Steffen, and Einar Kringlen. "A Norwegian Twin Study of Criminality," *British Journal of Criminology* 16 (June 1976), 213–232.

Dannefer, Dale, and Russell K. Schutt. "Race and Juvenile Justice Processing in Court and Police Agencies," *American Journal of Sociology* 87 (March 1982), 1113–1132.

Danziger, Sheldon, and David Wheeler. "The Economics of Crime: Punishment or Income Redistribution," *Review of Social Economy* 33 (October 1975), 113–131.

Darley, John M., and C. Daniel Batson. "'From Jerusalem to Jericho': A Study of Situational and Dispositional Variables in Helping Behavior," *Journal of Personality and Social Psychology* 27 (July 1973), 100–108.

Datesman, Susan K., and Mikel Aickin. "Offense Specialization and Escalation among Status Offenders," *Journal of Criminal Law and Criminology* 75 (Winter 1984), 1246–1275.

Davies, Christie. "Crime, Bureaucracy, and Equality," *Policy Review* 23 (Winter 1983), 89–105.

Davis, John A. "Justification for No Obligation: Views of Black Males toward Crime and the Criminal Law," *Issues in Criminology* 9 (Fall 1974), 69–87.

Decker, David L., David Shichor, and Robert M. O'Brien. *Urban Structure and Victimization.* Lexington, Mass.: D. C. Heath, 1982.

Decker, Scott H., and Barbara Salert. "Predicting the Career Criminal: An Empirical Test of the Greenwood Scale," *Journal of Criminal Law and Criminology* 77 (Spring 1986), 215–236.

DeFleur, Lois B. "Biasing Influences on Drug Arrest Records: Implications for Deviance Research," *American Sociological Review* 40 (February 1975), 88–103.

DeFranco, Edward J. *Anatomy of a Scam: A Case Study of a Planned Bankruptcy by Organized Crime.* Washington, D.C.: U.S. Government Printing Office, 1973.

Della Fave, L. Richard. "The Culture of Poverty Revisited: A Strategy for Research," *Social Problems* 21 (June 1974), 609–621.

Deming, Romine R. "Correctional Restitution: A Strategy for Correctional Conflict Management," *Federal Probation* 40 (September 1976), 27–32.

Dentler, Robert A., and Lawrence J. Monroe. "Social Correlates of Early Adolescent Theft," *American Sociological Review* 26 (October 1961), 733–743.

Dietz, Jean. "Study: 1 in 4,000 Acquitted by Insanity," *The Boston Globe,* April 29, 1984, p. 32.

Dietz, Mary Lorenz. *Killing for Profit: The Social Organization of Felony Homicide.* Chicago: Nelson-Hall, 1983.

Dinitz, Simon, Frank R. Scarpitti, and Walter C. Reckless. "Delinquency Vulnerability: A Cross Group and Longitudinal Analysis," *American Sociological Review* 27 (August 1962), 515–517.

Dirks, Raymond L., and Leonard Gross. *The Great Wall Street Scandal.* New York: McGraw-Hill, 1974.

Dodge, Richard W. *Locating City, Suburban, and Rural Crime.* Washington, D.C.: U.S. Department of Justice, December 1985.

Doerner, William G. "The Index of Southernness Revisited: The Influence of Wherefrom upon Whodunnit," *Criminology* 16 (May 1978), 47–56.

DONNERSTEIN, EDWARD, DANIEL LINZ, AND STEVEN PENROD. *The Question of Pornography: Research Findings and Policy Implications.* New York: Free Press, 1987.

DOWD, MAUREEN. "20 Years after Kitty Genovese's Murder, Experts Study Bad Samaritanism," *The New York Times,* March 12, 1984, pp. B1, B4.

DuBOW, FRED, EDWARD McCABE, AND GAIL KAPLAN. *Reactions to Crime: A Critical Review of the Literature.* Evanston, Ill.: Northwestern University, 1979.

DUFFY, MIKE. "The Medium's Message: Call It Distorted," *The Boston Globe,* December 13, 1982, p. 35.

DURKHEIM, EMILE. *The Division of Labor in Society,* trans. by George Simpson. Glencoe, Ill.: Free Press, 1895, 1933.

———. *The Rules of the Sociological Method,* trans. by Sarah A. Solovay and John H. Mueller; ed. by George E. G. Catlin. New York: Free Press, 1895, 1938.

DUSTER, TROY. "Crime, Youth Unemployment, and the Black Underclass," *Crime and Delinquency* 33 (April 1987), 300–316.

EBERTS, PAUL, AND KENT P. SCHWIRIAN. "Metropolitan Crime Rates and Relative Deprivation," *Criminologica* 5 (February 1968), 43–52.

ECK, JOHN. "Solving Crimes," *NIJ Reports.* Washington, D.C.: U.S. Department of Justice, March 1984, pp. 4–8.

EDELHERTZ, HERBERT. *The Nature, Impact and Prosecution of White-Collar Crime.* Washington, D.C.: U.S. Government Printing Office, 1970.

EDWARDS, ANNE. "Sex and Area Variations in Delinquency Rates in an English City," *British Journal of Criminology* 13 (April 1973), 121–137.

EGAN, JOHN W. "The Internal Revenue Service and Corporate Slush Funds: Some Fifth Amendment Problems," *Journal of Criminal Law and Criminology* 69 (Spring 1978), 59–74.

EHRLICH, ISAAC. "The Deterrent Effect of Capital Punishment: A Question of Life and Death," *American Economic Review* 65 (June 1975), 397–417.

ELIAS, ROBERT. "Alienating the Victim: Compensation and Victim Attitudes," *Journal of Social Issues* 40 (1984), 103–116.

———. *Victims of the System: Crime Victims and Compensation in American Politics and Criminal Justice.* New Brunswick, N.J.: Transaction Books, 1983.

ELIFSON, KIRK W., DAVID M. PETERSEN, AND C. KIRK HADAWAY. "Religiosity and Delinquency: A Contextual Analysis," *Criminology* 21 (November 1983), 505–527.

ELLIOTT, DELBERT S., AND SUZANNE S. AGETON. "Reconciling Race and Class Differences in Self-Reported and Official Estimates of Delinquency," *American Sociological Review* 45 (February 1980), 95–110.

———, AND DAVID HUIZINGA. "Social Class and Delinquent Behavior in a National Youth Panel: 1976–1980," *Criminology* 21 (May 1983) 149–177.

———, DAVID HUIZINGA, AND SUZANNE S. AGETON. *Explaining Delinquency and Drug Use.* Beverly Hills, Calif.: Sage Publications, 1985.

———, AND HARWIN L. VOSS. *Delinquency and Dropout.* Lexington, Mass.: D. C. Heath, 1974.

ELLIS, LEE. "Genetics and Criminal Behavior: Evidence through the End of the 1970s," *Criminology* 20 (May 1982), 43–66.

———. "Religiosity and Criminality: Evidence and Explanations of Complex Relationships," *Sociological Perspectives* 28 (October 1985), 501–520.

ELLSWORTH, PHOEBE C., AND LEE ROSS. "Public Opinion and Capital Punishment: A Close Examination of the Views of Abolitionists and Retentionists," *Crime and Delinquency* 29 (January 1983), 116–169.

ELMHORN, KERSTIN. "Study in Self-Reported Delinquency among Schoolchildren in Stockholm," in Karl O. Christiansen, ed., *Scandinavian Studies in Criminology*, Vol. 1. London: Tavistock, 1965, pp. 117–146.

EMPEY, LaMAR T. "Crime Prevention: The Fugitive Utopia," in Daniel Glaser, ed., *Handbook of Criminology*. Chicago: Rand McNally, 1974, pp. 1095–1123.

———, AND MAYNARD L. ERICKSON. "Hidden Delinquency and Social Status," *Social Forces* 44 (June 1966), 546–554.

———, AND STEVEN G. LUBECK, WITH RONALD L. LaPORTE. *Explaining Delinquency: Construction, Test, and Reformulation of a Sociological Theory*. Lexington, Mass.: D. C. Heath, 1971.

ENNIS, PHILIP H. *Criminal Victimization in the United States: A Report of a National Survey*. Field Surveys II of the President's Commission on Law Enforcement and the Administration of Justice. Washington, D.C.: U.S. Government Printing Office, 1967.

EPSTEIN, EDWARD JAY. "The Krogh File—The Politics of 'Law and Order,'" *The Public Interest* No. 39 (Spring 1975), 99–124.

———. "Methadone: The Forlorn Hope," *The Public Interest* No. 36 (Summer 1974), 3–24.

EREZ, EDNA. "Planning of Crime and the Criminal Career: Official and Hidden Offenses," *Journal of Criminal Law and Criminology* 71 (Spring 1980), 73–76.

ERICKSON, MAYNARD L., AND LaMAR T. EMPEY. "Court Records, Undetected Delinquency and Decision Making," *Journal of Criminal Law, Criminology and Police Science* 54 (December 1963), 456–469.

———, AND JACK P. GIBBS. "Objective and Perceptual Properties of Legal Punishment and the Deterrence Doctrine," *Social Problems* 25 (February 1978), 253–264.

———, AND JACK P. GIBBS. "On the Perceived Severity of Legal Penalties," *Journal of Criminal Law and Criminology* 70 (Spring 1979), 102–116.

———, JACK P. GIBBS, AND GARY F. JENSEN. "Conventional and Special Crime and Delinquency Rates," *Journal of Criminal Law and Criminology* 68 (September 1977), 440–453.

———, AND GARY F. JENSEN. "'Delinquency Is Still Group Behavior!': Toward Revitalizing the Group Premise in the Sociology of Deviance," *Journal of Criminal Law and Criminology* 68 (June 1977), 262–273.

ERICKSON, PATRICIA G., AND MICHAEL S. GOODSTADT. "Legal Stigma for Marijuana Possession," *Criminology* 17 (August 1979), 208–216.

ERIKSON, KAI T. *Wayward Puritans: A Study in the Sociology of Deviance*. New York: Wiley, 1966.

ERLANGER, HOWARD S. "The Empirical Status of the Subculture of Violence Thesis," *Social Problems* 22 (December 1974), 280–292.

———. "Is There a 'Subculture of Violence' in the South?" *Journal of Criminal Law and Criminology* 66 (December 1975), 483–490.

ERMANN, M. DAVID, AND RICHARD J. LUNDMAN. *Corporate Deviance*. New York: Holt, Rinehart and Winston, 1982.

ERVIN, SAM J., JR. "Foreword: Preventive Detention—A Step Backward for Criminal Justice," *Harvard Civil Rights Civil Liberties Law Review* 6 (March 1971), 291–299.

EVANS, SANDRA S., AND JOSEPH E. SCOTT. "The Seriousness of Crime Cross-Culturally: The Impact of Religiosity," *Criminology* 22 (February 1984), 39–59.

EVE, RAYMOND A. "A Study of the Efficacy and Interactions of Several Theories for Explaining Rebelliousness among High School Students," *Journal of Criminal Law and Criminology* 69 (Spring 1978), 115–125.

EYSENCK, HANS. *Crime and Personality.* London: Routledge and Kegan Paul, 1977.

FAIRCHILD, ERIKA S., AND VINCENT J. WEBB, EDS. *The Politics of Crime and Criminal Justice.* Newbury Park, Calif.: Sage Publications, 1985.

FARBER, M. A. "Big Push on Crime Merely Pushes It Elsewhere, Many Officers Feel," *The New York Times,* June 1, 1982a, pp. B1, B6.

———. "Decade after Knapp Inquiry, a Sense of 'Revolution' Pervades Police Dept.," *The New York Times,* November 29, 1982b, pp. B1, B5.

FARNSWORTH, CLYDE H. "Imitation Goods Costly to the U.S.," *The New York Times,* February 5, 1984, p. 4.

FARRELL, RONALD A., AND JAMES F. NELSON. "A Sequential Analysis of Delinquency," *International Journal of Criminology and Penology* 6 (August 1978), 255–268.

———, AND VICTORIA LYNN SWIGERT. "Prior Offense Record as a Self-Fulfilling Prophecy," *Law and Society Review* 12 (Spring 1978), 437–453.

FARRINGTON, DAVID P. "Self Reports of Deviant Behavior: Predictive and Stable?" *Journal of Criminal Law and Criminology* 64 (March 1973), 99–110.

———, LLOYD E. OHLIN, AND JAMES Q. WILSON. *Understanding and Controlling Crime: Toward a New Research Strategy.* New York: Springer-Verlag, 1986.

FEDERAL BUREAU OF INVESTIGATION. *Crime in the United States, 1986: Uniform Crime Reports.* Washington, D.C.: U.S. Government Printing Office, 1987.

FEENEY, FLOYD, AND ADRIANNE WEIR, EDS. *The Prevention and Control of Robbery.* Davis: Center on Administration of Criminal Justice, University of California at Davis, 1973.

FELD, BARRY C. "Delinquent Careers and Criminal Policy: Just Deserts and the Waiver Decision," *Criminology* 21 (May 1983), 195–212.

FELSON, MARCUS. "Routine Activities and Crime Prevention in the Developing Metropolis," *Criminology* 25 (November 1987), 911–931.

FELSON, RICHARD B., AND HENRY J. STEADMAN. "Situational Factors in Disputes Leading to Criminal Violence," *Criminology* 21 (February 1983), 59–74.

FERRACUTI, FRANCO, SIMON DINITZ, AND ESPERANZA ACOSTA DE BRENES. *Delinquents and Nondelinquents in the Puerto Rican Slum Culture.* Columbus: Ohio State University Press, 1975.

FERRI, ENRICO. "The Positive School of Criminology," in Stanley E. Grupp, ed., *Theories of Punishment.* Bloomington: Indiana University Press, 1901, 1971, pp. 229–242.

FIGUEIRA-MCDONOUGH, JOSEFINA. "Discrimination or Sex Differences? Criteria for Evaluating the Juvenile Justice System's Handling of Minor Offenses," *Crime and Delinquency* 33 (July 1987), 403–424.

———, AND ELAINE SELO. "A Reformulation of the 'Equal Opportunity' Explanation of Female Delinquency," *Crime and Delinquency* 26 (July 1980), 333–343.

FINCKENAUER, JAMES O. "Scared Crooked," *Psychology Today* 13 (August 1979), 6, 10–11.

———. *Scared Straight! and the Panacea Phenomenon.* Englewood Cliffs, N.J.: Prentice-Hall, 1982.

FINESTONE, HAROLD. "Cats, Kicks and Color," in Howard S. Becker, ed., *The Other Side: Perspectives on Deviance.* New York: Free Press, 1964, pp. 281–297.

FISHBEIN, DIANA H., AND ROBERT W. THATCHER. "New Diagnostic Methods in Criminology: Assessing Organic Sources of Behavioral Disorders," *Journal of Research in Crime and Delinquency* 23 (August 1986), 240–267.

FISHER, JOSEPH C. "Homicide in Detroit: The Role of Firearms," *Criminology* 14 (November 1976), 387–400.

FISHMAN, MARK. "Crime Waves as Ideology," *Social Problems* 25 (June 1978), 531–543.

FISSE, BRENT, AND JOHN BRAITHWAITE. *The Impact of Publicity on Corporate Offenders.* Albany: State University of New York Press, 1983.

FLEMING, MACKLIN. "The Law's Delay: The Dragon Slain Friday Breathes Fire Again Monday," *The Public Interest* No. 32 (Summer 1973), 13–33.

FLOUD, JEAN, AND WARREN YOUNG. *Dangerousness and Criminal Justice.* Totowa, N.J.: Barnes and Noble, 1981.

FOREMAN, JUDY. "How to Tell If You Are 'Muggable,'" *The Boston Globe,* January 20, 1981, pp. 20, 21.

――――. "Violence Called Top Killer of Youth," *The Boston Globe,* June 26, 1987, pp. 1, 84.

FORST, BRIAN E., AND JOLENE C. HERNON. *The Criminal Justice Response to Victim Harm.* Washington, D.C.: U.S. Department of Justice, June 1985.

FOSTER, JACK D., SIMON DINITZ, AND WALTER C. RECKLESS. "Perceptions of Stigma Following Public Intervention for Delinquent Behavior," *Social Problems* 20 (Fall 1972), 202–209.

FOUCAULT, MICHEL. *Discipline and Punish,* trans. by Alan Sheridan. New York: Pantheon, 1978.

FOWLER, FLOYD J., JR., AND THOMAS W. MANGIONE. *Neighborhood Crime, Fear and Social Control: A Second Look at the Hartford Program.* Washington, D.C.: National Institute of Justice, U.S. Department of Justice, 1982.

FOWLER, GLENN. "More 'Career Criminals' Convicted in State Effort," *The New York Times,* January 8, 1981, p. B7.

FOX, JAMES ALAN, ED. *Methods in Quantitative Criminology.* New York: Academic Press, 1981a.

――――. *Models in Quantitative Criminology.* New York: Academic Press, 1981b.

FRANKLIN, ALICE. "Criminality in the Work Place: A Comparison of Male and Female Offenders," in Freda Adler and Rita James Simon, eds., *The Criminology of Deviant Women.* Boston: Houghton Mifflin, 1979, pp. 167–170.

FRANKLIN, JAMES L. "The Churches and the Death Penalty," *The Boston Globe,* March 14, 1982, p. 30.

――――. "Why Bishops are Trying to Halt Execution of Sullivan," *The Boston Globe,* November 30, 1983, p. 18.

FRAZIER, CHARLES E. *Theoretical Approaches to Deviance: An Evaluation.* Columbus, Ohio: Charles E. Merrill, 1976.

FREEDMAN, LAWRENCE ZELIC. "No Response to the Cry for Help," in James M. Ratcliffe, ed., *The Good Samaritan and the Law.* Garden City, N.Y.: Doubleday, 1966, pp. 171–182.

――――. "Presidential Assassins Strike Out More at the Symbols Than the Man," *The Boston Globe,* April 5, 1981, p. A3.

FREEMAN, RICHARD B. "Crime and Unemployment," in James Q. Wilson, ed., *Crime and Public Policy.* San Francisco: ICS Press, 1983, pp. 89–106.

FREUD, SIGMUND. *Civilization and Its Discontents,* trans. by James Strachey. New York: Norton, 1930, 1962.

_____. *New Introductory Lectures on Psycho-analysis,* ed. and trans. by James Strachey. New York: Norton, 1933.

FYFE, JAMES J. "Observations on Police Deadly Force," *Crime and Delinquency* 27 (July 1981), 376–389.

GAES, GERALD G. "The Effects of Overcrowding in Prison," in Michael Tonry and Norval Morris, eds., *Crime and Justice: An Annual Review of Research,* Vol. 6. Chicago: University of Chicago Press, 1985, pp. 95–146.

GAGNON, JOHN H. "Sexual Conduct and Crime," in Daniel Glaser, ed., *Handbook of Criminology.* Chicago: Rand McNally, 1974, pp. 233–272.

GALLUP, GEORGE. "Safety Fears Swelled Nixon Vote," *The Boston Globe,* November 11, 1972, p. 7.

GARDINER, MURIEL. *The Deadly Innocents: Portraits of Children Who Kill.* New Haven, Conn.: Yale University Press, 1985.

GARFINKEL, HAROLD. "Conditions of Successful Degradation Ceremonies," *American Journal of Sociology* 61 (March 1956), 420–424.

GARGAN, EDWARD A. "The Nation's Prisoners Join the Labor Force," *The New York Times,* August 28, 1983, pp. F6–F7.

GAROFALO, JAMES. "Crime and the Mass Media—A Selective Review of Research," *Journal of Research in Crime and Delinquency* 18 (July 1981), 319–350.

GARRETT, CAROL J. "Effects of Residential Treatment on Adjudicated Delinquents: A Meta-Analysis," *Journal of Research in Crime and Delinquency* 22 (November 1985), 287–308.

GARTNER, ALLAN, COLIN GREER, AND FRANK REISSMAN, EDS. *The New Assault on Equality.* New York: Harper & Row, 1973.

GASTIL, RAYMOND D. "Homicide and a Regional Culture of Violence," *American Sociological Review* 36 (June 1971), 412–427.

GEBHARD, PAUL H., ET AL. *Sex Offenders.* New York: Harper & Row, 1965.

GEIS, GILBERT. "Avocational Crime," in Daniel Glaser, ed., *Handbook of Criminology.* Chicago: Rand McNally, 1974, pp. 273–298.

_____. "The Crime Intervenor: Samaritan or Superman?" Lecture presented February 5, 1981 at University of California, Irvine.

_____. "White Collar Crime: The Heavy Electrical Equipment Antitrust Cases of 1961," in Marshall B. Clinard and Richard Quinney, eds., *Criminal Behavior Systems: A Typology.* New York: Holt, Rinehart and Winston, 1967, pp. 139–151.

GELBSPAN, ROSS. "FBI's Arrest Files Often Do Injustice," *The Boston Globe,* October 19, 1986, p. 99.

GELFAND, DONNA M., ET AL. "Who Reports Shoplifters?" *Journal of Personality and Social Psychology* 25 (February 1973), 276–283.

GELLER, WILLIAM, AND KEVIN J. KARALES. "Shootings of and by Chicago Police: Uncommon Crises. Part I: Shootings by Chicago Police," *Journal of Criminal Law and Criminology* 72 (Winter 1981), 1813–1866.

GELLES, RICHARD J. "Domestic Criminal Violence," in Marvin E. Wolfgang and Neil Alan Weiner, eds., *Criminal Violence.* Beverly Hills, Calif.: Sage Publications, 1982, pp. 201–235.

GENDREAU, PAUL, AND BOB ROSS. "Effective Correctional Treatment: Bibliotherapy for Cynics," *Crime and Delinquency* 25 (October 1979), 463–489.

GEORGES-ABEYIE, DANIEL E., AND KEITH D. HARRIES, EDS. *Crime: A Spatial Perspective.* New York: Columbia University Press, 1980.

GERBNER, GEORGE, AND LARRY GROSS. "Living with Television: The Violence Profile," *Journal of Communication* 26 (Spring 1976), 173–199.

GERETY, PIERCE, JR. "A French Program to Reduce Pretrial Detention: Contrôle Judiciare," *Crime and Delinquency* 26 (January 1980), 22–34.

GIBBONS, DON C. "Crime and Punishment: A Study of Social Attitudes," *Social Forces* 47 (June 1969), 391–397.

————. *Society, Crime, and Criminal Behavior,* 5th ed. Englewood Cliffs, N.J.: Prentice-Hall, 1987.

GIBBS, JACK P. "Crime, Punishment, and Deterrence," *Social Science Quarterly* 48 (March 1968), 515–530.

————. *Crime, Punishment, and Deterrence.* New York: Elsevier, 1975.

GIBBS, JOHN J., AND PEGGY L. SHELLY. "Life in the Fast Lane: A Retrospective View by Commercial Thieves," *Journal of Research in Crime and Delinquency* 19 (July 1982), 299–330.

GILLESPIE, ROBERT W. *Economic Factors in Crime and Delinquency: A Critical Review of the Empirical Evidence.* Washington, D.C.: National Institute of Law Enforcement and Criminal Justice, Department of Justice, 1975.

GILLIS, A. R., AND JOHN HAGAN. "Density, Delinquency, and Design: Formal and Informal Control and the Built Environment," *Criminology* 19 (February 1982), 514–529.

GIORDANO, PEGGY C. "Girls, Guys and Gangs: The Changing Social Context of Female Delinquency," *Journal of Criminal Law and Criminology* 69 (Spring 1978), 126–132.

————, STEPHEN A. CERNKOVICH, AND M. D. PUGH. "Friendships and Delinquency," *American Journal of Sociology* 91 (March 1986), 1170–1202.

GLASER, DANIEL. "The Classification of Offenses and Offenders," in Daniel Glaser, ed., *Handbook of Criminology.* Chicago: Rand McNally, 1974, pp. 45–83.

————. *Crime in Our Changing Society.* New York: Holt, Rinehart and Winston, 1978.

————. "Criminal Theories and Behavioral Images," *American Journal of Sociology* 61 (March 1956), 433–444.

————. "A Review of Crime-Causation Theory and Its Application," in Norval Morris and Michael Tonry, eds., *Crime and Justice: An Annual Review of Research,* Vol. 1. Chicago: University of Chicago Press, 1979, pp. 203–237.

————. *Social Deviance.* Chicago: Markham, 1971.

GLUECK, SHELDON, AND ELEANOR GLUECK. *Physique and Delinquency.* New York: Harper & Brothers, 1956.

————. *Unraveling Juvenile Delinquency.* Cambridge, Mass.: Harvard University Press, 1950.

GOLD, MARTIN. *Delinquent Behavior in an American City.* Belmont, Calif.: Brooks/Cole, 1970.

GOLDKAMP, JOHN S. "Questioning the Practice of Pretrial Detention: Some Empirical Evidence from Philadelphia," *Journal of Criminal Law and Criminology* 74 (Winter 1983), 1556–1588.

GOLDMAN, NATHAN. *The Differential Selection of Juvenile Offenders for Court Appearance.* New York: National Council on Crime and Delinquency, 1963.

GOLDSTEIN, JEFFREY H. *Aggression and Crimes of Violence,* 2nd ed. New York: Oxford University Press, 1986.

GOLDSTEIN, MICHAEL J., AND HAROLD S. KANT. *Pornography and Sexual Deviance.* Berkeley: University of California Press, 1973.

GOLEMAN, DANIEL. "Brutal Sports and Brutal Fans," *The New York Times,* August 13, 1985a, pp. C1, C3.

———. "Researchers Dispute Pornography Report on Its Use of Data," *The New York Times,* May 17, 1986, pp. 1, 6.

———. "Study Lists Ways to Deter Rapists," *The New York Times,* May 5, 1985b, p. 35.

———. "Violence against Women in Films," *The New York Times,* August 28, 1984, pp. C1, C5.

GOODE, ERICH. "The Criminology of Drugs and Drug Use," in Abraham S. Blumberg, ed., *Current Perspectives on Criminal Behavior: Original Essays on Criminology.* New York: Knopf, 1974, pp. 165–191.

GOODSTADT, MICHAEL S. "Legal Stigma for Marijuana Possession," *Criminology* 17 (August 1979), 208–216.

GOODSTEIN, LYNNE. "Psychological Effects of the Predictability of Prison Release: Implications for the Sentencing Debate," *Criminology* 18 (November 1980), 363–384.

GORDON, DAVID M. "Capitalism, Class, and Crime in America," *Crime and Delinquency* 19 (April 1973), 163–186.

GORING, CHARLES. *The English Convict: A Statistical Study.* London: His Majesty's Stationery Office, 1913.

GOTTFREDSON, DON M. "Probation and Parole: Release and Revocation," in Sanford H. Kadish, ed., *Encyclopedia of Crime and Justice,* Vol. 3. New York: Free Press, 1983, pp. 1247–1255.

GOTTFREDSON, MICHAEL R. "Parole Board Decision Making: A Study of Disparity Reduction and the Impact of Institutional Behavior," *Journal of Criminal Law and Criminology* 70 (Spring 1979a), 77–88.

———. "Parole Guidelines and the Reduction of Sentencing Disparity: A Preliminary Study," *Journal of Research in Crime and Delinquency* 16 (July 1979b), 218–231.

———. "Treatment Destruction Techniques," *Journal of Research in Crime and Delinquency* 16 (January 1979c), 39–54.

GOULD, LEROY, ET AL. *Crime as a Profession.* Washington, D.C.: U.S. Department of Justice, 1966.

GOVE, WALTER R., MICHAEL HUGHES, AND MICHAEL GEERKEN. "Are Uniform Crime Reports a Valid Indicator of the Index Crimes? An Affirmative Answer with Minor Qualifications," *Criminology* 23 (August 1985), 451–501.

GRAHAM, MARY G. "Controlling Drug Abuse and Crime: A Research Update," *NIJ Reports,* March/April 1987, pp. 2–7.

GRASMICK, HAROLD G., AND DONALD E. GREEN. "Legal Punishment, Social Disapproval and Internalization as Inhibitors of Illegal Behavior," *Journal of Criminal Law and Criminology* 71 (Fall 1980), 325–335.

———, AND STEVEN D. MCLAUGHLIN. "Comment: Deterrence and Social Control," *American Sociological Review* 43 (April 1978), 272–278.

GREEN, EDWARD. "Race, Social Status, and Criminal Arrest," *American Sociological Review* 35 (June 1970), 476–490.

GREEN, GARY S. "Citizen Gun Ownership and Criminal Deterrence: Theory, Research, and Policy," *Criminology* 25 (February 1987), 63–81.

GREEN, PENNY A., AND H. DAVID ALLEN. "Severity of Societal Response to Crime: A Synthesis of Models," *Law and Society Review* 16 (1981–82), 181–205.

GREENBERG, DAVID F. "The Correctional Effects of Corrections: A Survey of Evaluations," in David F. Greenberg, eds., *Corrections and Punishment.* Beverly Hills, Calif.: Sage Publications, 1977a, pp. 111–148.

————. "Delinquency and the Age Structure of Society," *Contemporary Crises* 1 (April 1977b), 189–223.

————. "The Incapacitative Effect of Imprisonment: Some Estimates," *Law and Society Review* 9 (Summer 1975), 541–580.

————. "Methodological Issues in Survey Research on the Inhibition of Crime," *Journal of Criminal Law and Criminology* 72 (Fall 1981), 1094–1101.

————, AND DREW HUMPHRIES. "Economic Crisis and the Justice Model: A Skeptical View," *Crime and Delinquency* 28 (October 1982), 601–609.

————, AND RONALD C. KESSLER. "The Effects of Arrests on Crime: A Multivariate Panel Analysis," *Social Problems* 60 (March 1982), 771–790.

————, RONALD C. KESSLER, AND COLIN LOFTIN. "The Effects of Police Employment on Crime," *Criminology* 21 (August 1983), 375–394.

————, RONALD C. KESSLER, AND COLIN LOFTIN. "Social Inequality and Crime Control," *Journal of Criminal Law and Criminology* 76 (Fall 1985), 684–704.

GREENBERG, STEPHANIE W. "Alcohol and Crime: A Methodological Critique of the Literature," in James J. Collins, Jr., ed., *Drinking and Crime: Perspectives on the Relationships between Alcohol Consumption and Criminal Behavior.* New York: Guilford Press, 1981, pp. 71–109.

————, AND FREDA ADLER. "Crime and Addiction: An Empirical Analysis of the Literature, 1920–1973," *Contemporary Drug Problems* 3 (Summer 1974), 221–269.

GREENWOOD, PETER W. "Career Criminal Prosecution: Potential Objectives," *Journal of Criminal Law and Criminology* 71 (Summer 1980), 85–88.

————. "Controlling the Crime Rate through Imprisonment," in James Q. Wilson, ed., *Crime and Public Policy.* San Francisco: ICS Press, 1983, pp. 251–269.

————. "Differences in Criminal Behavior and Court Responses among Juvenile and Young Adult Defendants," in Michael Tonry and Norval Morris, eds., *Crime and Justice: An Annual Review of Research,* Vol. 7. Chicago: University of Chicago Press, 1986, pp. 151–187.

————. "Selective Incapacitation: A Method of Using Our Prisons More Effectively," *NIJ Reports,* January 1984, pp. 4–7.

————, AND FRANKLIN E. ZIMRING. *One More Chance: The Pursuit of Promising Intervention Strategies for Chronic Juvenile Offenders.* Santa Monica, Calif.: Rand, May 1985.

————, WITH ALLAN ABRAHAMSE. *Selective Incapacitation.* Santa Monica, Calif.: Rand, 1982.

GREER, WILLIAM R. "Most Burglars Look for Easy Ways to Slip Unseen into Empty Homes and Head Straight for the Bedroom," *The New York Times,* July 10, 1986, pp. C1, C6.

GRILLO, E. G. *Delincuencia en Caracas.* Caracas, Venezuela: Universidad del Zulia, 1970.

GRINNELL, RICHARD M., JR., AND CHERYL A. CHAMBERS. "Broken Homes and Middle-Class Delinquency: A Comparison," *Criminology* 17 (November 1979), 395–400.

GROPPER, BERNARD A. "Probing the Links between Drugs and Crime," *NIJ Reports,* November 1984, pp. 4–8.

GROSS, SAMUEL R., AND ROBERT MAURO. "Patterns of Death: An Analysis of Racial Disparity in Criminal Sanctioning and Homicide Victimization," *Stanford Law Review* 37 (November 1984), 27–153.

GROTH, A. NICHOLAS. *Men Who Rape: The Psychology of the Offender.* New York: Plenum Press, 1979.

———, ROBERT E. LONGO, AND J. BRADLEY McFADIN. "Undetected Recidivism among Rapists and Child Molesters," *Crime and Delinquency* 28 (July 1982), 450–458.

GURR, TED ROBERT. "Historical Trends in Violent Crime: A Critical Review of the Evidence," in Michael Tonry and Norval Morris, eds., *Crime and Justice: An Annual Review of Research,* Vol. 3. Chicago: University of Chicago, 1981, pp. 295–353.

———. *Why Men Rebel.* Princeton, N.J.: Princeton University Press, 1970.

GUSFIELD, JOSEPH R. *Symbolic Crusade: Status Politics and the American Temperance Movement.* Urbana: University of Illinois Press, 1963.

HABERMAN, CLYDE. "In Japan, A Crime Wave Is Measured in Drops," *The New York Times,* August 2, 1983, p. 2.

HACKNEY, SHELDON. "Southern Violence," in Hugh Davis Graham and Ted Robert Gurr, eds., *Violence in America: Historical and Comparative Perspectives.* Staff Report to the National Commission on the Causes and Prevention of Violence, Vol. 2. Washington, D.C.: U.S. Government Printing Office, 1969, pp. 387–404.

HAGAN, JOHN, AND KRISTEN BUMILLER. "Making Sense of Sentencing: A Review and Critique of Sentencing Research," in Alfred Blumstein et al., eds., *Research on Sentencing: The Search for Reform,* Vol. 2. Washington, D.C.: National Academy Press, 1983, pp. 1–54.

HAKIM, SIMON, AND GEORGE F. RENGERT, EDS. *Crime Spillover.* Beverly Hills, Calif.: Sage Publications, 1981a.

———. "Introduction," in Simon Hakim and George F. Rengert, eds., *Crime Spillover.* Beverly Hills, Calif.: Sage Publications, 1981b, pp. 7–19.

HALL, ANDY. *Systemwide Strategies to Alleviate Jail Crowding.* Washington, D.C.: U.S. Department of Justice, January 1987.

HALLECK, SEYMOUR L., AND ANN D. WITTE. "Is Rehabilitation Dead?" *Crime and Delinquency* 23 (October 1977), 372–382.

HAMILTON, V. LEE, AND LAURENCE ROTKIN. "Interpreting the Eighth Amendment: Perceived Seriousness of Crime and Severity of Punishment," in Hugo Adam Bedau and Chester M. Pierce, eds., *Capital Punishment in the United States.* New York: AMS Press, 1976, pp. 502–524.

———, AND STEVE RYTINA. "Social Consensus on Norms of Justice: Should the Punishment Fit the Crime?" *American Journal of Sociology* 85 (March 1980), 1117–1144.

HAMPARIAN, DONNA MARTIN, ET AL. *The Young Criminal Years of the Violent Few.* Washington, D.C.: U.S. Department of Justice, June 1985.

HANEY, CRAIG, CURTIS BANKS, AND PHILIP ZIMBARDO. "Interpersonal Dynamics in a Simulated Prison," *International Journal of Criminology and Penology* 1 (February 1973), 69–97.

HARLOW, CAROLINE WOLF. *Robbery Victims.* Washington, D.C.: U.S. Department of Justice, April 1987.

HARMETZ, ALJEAN. "'Jedi' Prints Stolen for Cassette Piracy, Movie Industry Says," *The New York Times,* July 9, 1983, pp. 1, 10.

HARRING, SIDNEY L. "Policing a Class Society: The Expansion of the Urban Police in the Late Nineteenth and Early Twentieth Centuries," in David F. Greenberg, ed., *Crime & Capitalism.* Palo Alto, Calif.: Mayfield, 1981, pp. 292–313.

————. *Policing a Class Society: The Experience of American Cities, 1865–1915.* New Brunswick, N.J.: Rutgers University Press, 1983.

HARTJEN, CLAYTON A., AND DON C. GIBBONS. "An Empirical Investigation of a Criminal Typology," *Sociology and Social Research* 54 (October 1969), 56–62.

HATHAWAY, STARKE R., AND ELIO D. MONACHESI. *Analyzing and Predicting Juvenile Delinquency with the MMPI.* Minneapolis: University of Minnesota Press, 1953.

HAWKINS, GORDON. "God and the Mafia," *The Public Interest* No. 14 (Winter 1969), 24–51.

HEINZ, ANNE M., AND WAYNE A. KERSTETTER. "Pretrial Settlement Conference: Evaluation of a Reform in Plea Bargaining," in Burt Galaway and Joe Hudson, eds., *Perspectives on Crime Victims.* St. Louis: C. V. Mosby, 1981, pp. 266–276.

HEINZELMANN, FRED. "Crime Prevention and the Physical Environment," in Dan A. Lewis, ed., *Reactions to Crime.* Beverly Hills, Calif.: Sage Publications, 1981, pp. 87–101.

HELLMAN, DARYL A. *The Economics of Crime.* New York: St. Martin's Press, 1980.

HENNESSY, MICHAEL, PAMELA J. RICHARDS, AND RICHARD A. BERK. "Broken Homes and Middle Class Delinquency," *Criminology* 15 (February 1978), 505–528.

HENRY, ANDREW F., AND JAMES F. SHORT, JR. *Suicide and Homicide: Some Economic, Sociological, and Psychological Aspects of Aggression.* New York: Free Press, 1954.

HEPBURN, JOHN R. "The Impact of Police Intervention upon Juvenile Delinquents," *Criminology* 15 (August 1977), 225–262.

HERBERS, JOHN. "Fear of Crime Leads in Survey of Reasons to Leave Big Cities," *The New York Times,* May 16, 1981, p. 8.

HILL, GARY D., FRANK M. HOWELL, AND ERNEST T. DRIVER. "Gender, Fear, and Protective Handgun Ownership," *Criminology* 23 (August 1985), 541–552.

HILLS, STUART L. *Demystifying Social Deviance.* New York: McGraw-Hill, 1980.

HINDELANG, MICHAEL J. "Causes of Delinquency: A Partial Replication and Extension," *Social Problems* 20 (Spring 1973), 471–487.

————. "Class and Crime," in Sanford H. Kadish, ed., *Encyclopedia of Crime and Justice,* Vol. 1. New York: Free Press, 1983, pp. 175–181.

————. *Criminal Victimization in Eight American Cities: A Descriptive Analysis of Common Theft and Assault.* Cambridge, Mass.: Ballinger, 1976.

————. "Race and Involvement in Common Law Personal Crimes," *American Sociological Review* 43 (February 1978), 93–109.

————, MICHAEL R. GOTTFREDSON, AND JAMES GAROFALO. *Victims of Personal Crime: An Empirical Foundation for a Theory of Personal Victimization.* Cambridge, Mass.: Ballinger, 1978.

————, TRAVIS HIRSCHI, AND JOSEPH G. WEIS. "Correlates of Delinquency: The Illusion of Discrepancy between Self-Report and Official Measures," *American Sociological Review* 44 (December 1979), 995–1014.

HIRSCHI, TRAVIS. *Causes of Delinquency.* Berkeley: University of California Press, 1969.

————. "Crime and the Family," in James Q. Wilson, ed., *Crime and Public Policy.* San Francisco: ICS Press, 1983, pp. 53–68.

————, AND MICHAEL GOTTFREDSON. "All Wise after the Fact Learning Theory, Again: Reply to Baldwin," *American Journal of Sociology* 90 (May 1985), 1330–1333.

————, AND MICHAEL J. HINDELANG. "Intelligence and Delinquency: A Revisionist Review," *American Sociological Review* 42 (August 1977): 571–587.

HOCHSTEDLER, ELLEN. *Crime against the Elderly in 26 Cities.* Washington, D.C.: Department of Justice, Bureau of Justice Statistics, 1981.

HOFFMAN-BUSTAMANTE, DALE. "The Nature of Female Criminality," *Issues in Criminology* 8 (Fall 1973), 117–136.

HOLLINGER, RICHARD C., AND JOHN P. CLARK. *Theft by Employees.* Lexington, Mass.: D. C. Heath, 1983.

HOLZMAN, HAROLD R. "Learning Disabilities and Juvenile Delinquency: Biological and Sociological Theories," in C. R. Jeffery, ed., *Biology and Crime.* Beverly Hills, Calif.: Sage Publications, 1979, pp. 77–86.

———. "The Rationalistic Opportunity Perspective on Criminal Behavior: Toward a Reformulation of the Theoretical Basis for the Notion of Property Crime as Work," *Crime and Delinquency* 28 (April 1982), 233–246.

HOOTON, EARNEST A. *The American Criminal: An Anthropological Study.* Cambridge, Mass.: Harvard University Press, 1939.

HOPKINS, ANDREW. "Controlling Corporate Deviance," *Criminology* 18 (August 1980), 198–214.

HORN, PATRICE, AND THE EDITORS OF *Psychology Today.* "Newsline," *Psychology Today* 7 (September 1973), 17.

HORNING, DONALD N. M. "Blue-Collar Theft: Conceptions of Property, Attitudes toward Pilfering, and Work Group Norms in a Modern Industrial Plant," in Erwin O. Smigel and H. Laurence Ross, eds., *Crimes against Bureaucracy.* New York: Van Nostrand Reinhold, 1970, pp. 46–64.

HOROWITZ, RUTH. *Honor and the American Dream: Culture and Social Identity in a Chicano Community.* New Brunswick, N.J.: Rutgers University Press, 1983.

———, AND GARY SCHWARTZ. "Honor, Normative Ambiguity and Gang Violence," *American Sociological Review* 39 (April 1974), 238–251.

HOSPERS, JOHN. "Retribution: The Ethics of Punishment," in Randy E. Barnett and John Hagel 3d, eds., *Assessing the Criminal: Restitution, Retribution, and the Legal Process.* Cambridge, Mass.: Ballinger, 1977, pp. 181–209.

HOWARD, JAN, AND PHILLIP BORGES. "Needle-Sharing in the Haight: Some Social and Psychological Functions," in David E. Smith and George R. Gay, eds., *"It's So Good, Don't Even Try It Once": Heroin in Perspective.* Englewood Cliffs, N.J.: Prentice-Hall, 1972, pp. 125–136.

HSU, MARLENE. "Cultural and Sexual Differences in the Judgment of Criminal Offenses: A Replication Study of the Measurement of Delinquency," *Journal of Criminal Law and Criminology* 64 (September 1973), 348–353.

HUMPHREYS, LAUD. *Tearoom Trade: Impersonal Sex in Public Places,* enlarged ed. Chicago: Aldine, 1975.

HUNT, LEON GIBSON, AND CARL D. CHAMBERS. *The Heroin Epidemics: A Study of Heroin Use in the U.S., 1965–75.* New York: Spectrum, 1976.

HUTCHISON, ROBERT A. *Vesco.* New York: Praeger, 1974.

HYLTON, JOHN H. "Rhetoric and Reality: A Critical Appraisal of Community Correctional Programs," *Crime and Delinquency* 28 (July 1982), 341–373.

HYMAN, HERBERT A. "The Value Systems of Different Classes," in Reinhard Bendix and Seymour Martin Lipset, eds., *Class, Status and Power: Social Stratification in Comparative Perspective,* 2nd ed. New York: Free Press, 1966, pp. 488–499.

IANNI, FRANCIS A. J., WITH ELIZABETH REUSS-IANNI. *A Family Business: Kinship and Social Control in Organized Crime.* New York: Russell Sage Foundation, 1972.

IGNATIEFF, MICHAEL. *A Just Measure of Pain: The Penitentiary in the Industrial Revolution, 1750–1850.* New York: Pantheon, 1978.

INCIARDI, JAMES A. *Careers in Crime.* Chicago: Rand McNally, 1975.

————. "Heroin Use and Street Crime," *Crime and Delinquency* 25 (July 1979), 335–346.

————. "Problems in the Measurement of Criminal Behavior," in Delos H. Kelly, ed., *Criminal Behavior: Readings in Criminology*. New York: St. Martin's Press, 1980a, pp. 59–68.

————, ED. *Radical Criminology: The Coming Crises*. Beverly Hills, Calif.: Sage Publications, 1980b.

IRWIN, JOHN. "Adaptation to Being Corrected: Corrections from the Convict's Perspective," in Daniel Glaser, ed., *Handbook of Criminology*. Chicago: Rand McNally, 1974, pp. 971–993.

————. *The Felon*. Englewood Cliffs, N.J.: Prentice-Hall, 1970.

————. *Prisons in Turmoil*. Boston: Little, Brown, 1980.

JACKSON, BRUCE. *A Thief's Primer*. New York: Macmillan, 1969.

JACKSON, PAMELA IRVING, AND LEO CARROLL. "Race and the War on Crime: The Sociopolitical Determinants of Municipal Police Expenditures in 90 Non-Southern U.S. Cities," *American Sociological Review* 46 (June 1981), 290–305.

JACOB, HERBERT, AND MICHAEL J. RICH. "The Effects of the Police on Crime: A Rejoinder," *Law and Society Review* 16 (1981–82), 171–172.

JACOBS, JANE. *The Death and Life of Great American Cities*. N.Y.: Vintage, 1961.

JAMES, JENNIFER, AND WILLIAM THORNTON. "Women's Liberation and the Female Delinquent," *Journal of Research in Crime and Delinquency* 17 (July 1980), 230–244.

JAQUITH, SUSAN M. "Adolescent Marijuana Use: An Empirical Test of Differential Association Theory," *Criminology* 19 (August 1981), 271–280.

JARVIS, G. K., AND H. B. MESSINGER. "Social and Economic Correlates of Juvenile Delinquency Rates: A Canadian Case," *Canadian Journal of Criminology and Corrections* 16 (1974), 361–372.

JASPAN, NORMAN. *Mind Your Own Business*. Englewood Cliffs, N.J.: Prentice-Hall, 1974.

JEFFERY, C. R. "Biology and Crime: The New Neo-Lombrosians," in C. R. Jeffery, ed., *Biology and Crime*. Beverly Hills, Calif.: Sage Publications, 1979, pp. 7–18.

————. *Crime Prevention through Environmental Design*, rev. ed. Beverly Hills, Calif.: Sage Publications, 1977.

JENKINS, RICHARD L. "Adaptive and Maladaptive Delinquency," *Nervous Child* 2 (October 1955), 9–11.

JENSEN, GARY F. "Inner Containment and Delinquency," *Journal of Criminal Law and Criminology* 64 (December 1973), 464–470.

JENSEN, MICHAEL C. "Business Students Disagree on Bribes," *The New York Times*, March 27, 1976, p. 37.

JOE, DELBERT, AND NORMAN ROBINSON. "Chinatown's Immigrant Gangs: The New Young Warrior Class," *Criminology* 18 (November 1980), 337–345.

JOHNSON, ELMER H., AND ISRAEL L. BARAK-GLANTZ. "Introduction," in Israel L. Barak-Glantz and Elmer H. Johnson, eds., *Comparative Criminology*. Beverly Hills, Calif.: Sage Publications, 1983, pp. 7–17.

JOHNSON, KIRK ALAN, AND PATRICIA L. WASIELEWSKI. "A Commentary on Victimization Research and the Importance of Meaning Structures," *Criminology* 20 (August 1982), 205–222.

JOHNSON, RICHARD E. "Social Class and Delinquent Behavior: A New Test," *Criminology* 18 (May 1980), 86–93.

JOINT COMMITTEE ON NEW YORK DRUG LAW EVALUATION. *The Nation's Toughest Drug Law: Evaluating the New York Experience.* Washington, D.C.: U.S. Government Printing Office, 1978.

JONES, ALFRED WINSLOW. *Life, Liberty and Property.* New York: Octagon, 1941, 1964.

JOYCE, FAY S. "Some Victims' Families Find Relief in Executions," *The New York Times,* January 19, 1984, p. A18.

JUDSON, HORACE FREELAND. *Heroin Addiction in Britain: What Americans Can Learn from the English Experience.* New York: Harcourt Brace Jovanovich, 1974.

KAISER, GUENTHER. "The Comparative Method in Criminology," trans. by Sybille Jobin. *International Summaries.* Washington, D.C.: U.S. Department of Justice, National Institute of Justice, 1978.

KALVEN, HARRY, JR., AND HANS ZEISEL. *The American Jury.* Boston: Little, Brown, 1966.

KANDEL, DENISE B., AND ISRAEL ADLER. "Socialization into Marijuana Use among French Adolescents: A Cross-Cultural Comparison with the United States," *Journal of Health and Social Behavior* 23 (December 1982), 295–309.

KAPLAN, HOWARD B., STEVEN S. MARTIN, AND ROBERT J. JOHNSON. "Self-Rejection and the Explanation of Deviance: Specification of the Structure among Latent Constructs," *American Journal of Sociology* 92 (September 1986), 384–411.

KARACKI, LARRY, AND JACKSON TOBY. "The Uncommitted Adolescent: Candidate for Gang Socialization," *Sociological Inquiry* 32 (Spring 1962), 203–215.

KASSEBAUM, GENE, DAVID A. WARD, AND DANIEL M. WILNER. *Prison Treatment and Parole Survival: An Empirical Assessment.* New York: Wiley, 1971.

KATES, DON B., JR., ED. *Firearms and Violence: Issues of Public Policy.* Cambridge, Mass.: Ballinger, 1984.

KELLEY, CLARENCE M. *Crime in the United States, 1975: Uniform Crime Reports.* Washington, D.C.: U.S. Government Printing Office, 1976.

KELLEY, THOMAS M. "Status Offenders Can Be Different: A Comparative Study of Delinquent Careers," *Crime and Delinquency* 29 (July 1983), 365–380.

KELLING, GEORGE L., ET AL. *The Kansas City Preventive Patrol Experiment.* Washington, D.C.: Police Foundation, 1974.

KEMPF, KIMBERLY L. "Specialization and the Criminal Career," *Criminology* 25 (May 1987), 399–420.

KENNEY, DENNIS JAY. *Crime, Fear, and the New York City Subways: The Role of Citizen Action.* New York: Praeger, 1987.

KERR, PETER. "Crime Study Finds High Use of Drugs at Time of Arrest," *The New York Times,* January 22, 1988, pp. A1, B4.

————. "Drug Tests Losing Most of Court Cases," *The New York Times,* December 11, 1986, pp. A1, D35.

KESSLER, RONALD. "Heroin Deaths on the Increase," *The Boston Globe,* July 6, 1983, p. 10.

KIHSS, PETER. "Limited Heroin Use Is Urged by Expert," *The New York Times,* September 26, 1982, p. 36.

KING, HARRY, AND WILLIAM J. CHAMBLISS. *Harry King: A Professional Thief's Journey.* New York: Wiley, 1984.

KITCHENER, HOWARD, ANNESLEY K. SCHMIDT, AND DANIEL GLASER. "How Persistent Is Post-Prison Success?" *Federal Probation* 41 (March 1977), 9–15.

KITSUSE, JOHN I., AND AARON V. CICOUREL. "A Note on the Use of Official Statistics," *Social Problems* 11 (Fall 1963), 131–138.

KITTRIE, NICHOLAS N. *The Right to Be Different: Deviance and Enforced Therapy.* Baltimore, Md.: Johns Hopkins University Press, 1971.

KLECK, GARY. "Racial Discrimination in Criminal Sentencing: A Critical Evaluation of the Evidence with Additional Evidence on the Death Penalty," *American Sociological Review* 46 (December 1981), 783–805.

KLEMKE, LLOYD W. "Does Apprehension for Shoplifting Amplify or Terminate Shoplifting Activity?" *Law and Society Review* 12 (Spring 1978), 391–403.

KLOCKARS, CARL B. *The Professional Fence.* New York: Free Press, 1974.

The Knapp Commission Report on Police Corruption. New York: George Braziller, 1972.

KNIGHT, MICHAEL. "Boston Study Finds Gun Law Is Working," *The New York Times,* June 18, 1979, p. D14.

KNORR, STEPHEN J. "Deterrence and the Death Penalty: A Temporal Cross-Sectional Approach," *Journal of Criminal Law and Criminology* 70 (Summer 1979), 235–254.

KOBRIN, SOLOMON. "The Conflict of Values in Delinquency Areas," *American Sociological Review* 16 (October 1951), 653–661.

KOHLMEIER, LOUIS M. "The Bribe Busters," *The New York Times Magazine,* September 26, 1976, pp. 47–60.

KRAJICK, KEVIN. "The Growing Crisis in Prison Crowding," *The Boston Globe,* June 13, 1982, p. A3.

KRAMER, JOHN H., AND ROBIN L. LUBITZ. "Pennsylvania's Sentencing Reform: The Impact of Commission-Established Guidelines," *Crime and Delinquency* 31 (October 1985), 481–500.

KRAMER, RONALD C. "Corporate Crime: An Organizational Perspective," in Peter Wickman and Timothy Dailey, eds., *White-Collar and Economic Crime.* Lexington, Mass.: D. C. Heath, 1982, pp. 75–94.

KRANTZ, SHELDON. "Prisoners, Legal Rights Of," in Sanford H. Kadish, ed., *Encyclopedia of Crime and Justice,* Vol. 3. New York: Free Press, 1983, pp. 1190–1197.

KRISBERG, BARRY. *Crime and Privilege: Toward a New Criminology.* Englewood Cliffs, N.J.: Prentice-Hall, 1975.

KROHM, GREGORY. "The Pecuniary Incentives of Property Crime," in Simon Rotenberg, ed., *The Economics of Crime and Punishment.* Washington, D.C.: American Enterprise Institute for Public Policy Research, 1973, pp. 31–34.

KROHN, MARVIN D., ET AL. "Social Status and Deviance: Class Context of School, Social Status, and Delinquent Behavior," *Criminology* 18 (November 1980), 303–318.

———, JAMES P. CURRY, AND SHIRLEY NELSON-KILGER. "Is Chivalry Dead? An Analysis of Changes in Police Dispositions of Males and Females," *Criminology* 21 (August 1983), 417–437.

KROST, JACK. "He Tries to Determine What Makes Criminals Tick," *The Boston Globe,* October 24, 1982, p. 8.

KRUTTSCHNITT, CANDACE. "Women, Crime, and Dependency: An Application of the Theory of Law," *Criminology* 19 (February 1982), 495–513.

KVÅLSETH, TARALD O. "Seriousness of Offenses: An Experimental Study Based on a Psychological Scaling Technique," *Criminology* 18 (August 1980), 237–244.

LAB, STEVEN P. "Patterns in Juvenile Misbehavior," *Crime and Delinquency* 30 (April 1984), 293–308.

LaFREE, GARY D. "Adversarial and Nonadversarial Justice: Comparison of Guilty Pleas and Trials," *Criminology* 23 (May 1985), 289–312.

_____. "The Effect of Sexual Stratification by Race on Official Reactions to Rape," *American Sociological Review* 45 (October 1980), 842–854.

_____. "Official Reactions to Social Problems: Police Decisions in Sexual Assault Cases," *Social Problems* 28 (June 1981), 582–594.

LaGRANGE, RANDY L., AND HELENE RASKIN WHITE. "Age Differences in Delinquency: A Test of Theory," *Criminology* 23 (February 1985), 19–45.

LANDIS, DYLAN. "Insurance Fraud: Billions in Losses," *The New York Times,* July 6, 1982, pp. D1, D2.

LANE, ROGER. *Policing the City: Boston 1822–1885.* Cambridge, Mass.: Harvard University Press, 1967.

LANGAN, PATRICK A. "Racism on Trial: New Evidence to Explain the Racial Composition of Prisons in the United States," *Journal of Criminal Law and Criminology* 76 (Fall 1985), 666–683.

_____, AND DAVID P. FARRINGTON. "Two-Track or One-Track Justice? Some Evidence from an English Longitudinal Survey," *Journal of Criminal Law and Criminology* 74 (Summer 1983), 519–546.

LANGER, SIDNEY. *The Rahway State Prison Lifers' Group: A Critical Analysis.* Union, N.J.: Kean College Department of Sociology, October, 1979.

LANGLEY, MICHAEL H. "The Juvenile Court: The Making of a Delinquent," *Law and Society Review* 7 (Winter 1972), 273–298.

LARSON, RICHARD C. "What Happened to Patrol Operations in Kansas City? A Review of the Kansas City Preventive Patrol Experiment," *Journal of Criminal Justice* 3 (Winter 1975), 267–297.

LATANÉ, BIBB, AND JOHN M. DARLEY. *The Unresponsive Bystander: Why Doesn't He Help?* New York: Appleton-Century-Crofts, 1970.

LAUDON, KENNETH C. *Dossier Society: Value Choices in the Design of National Information Systems.* New York: Columbia University Press, 1986.

_____. "A Risky Index of Crime," *The New York Times,* July 24, 1981, p. A27.

LAVRAKAS, PAUL J., AND ELICIA J. HERZ. "Citizen Participation in Neighborhood Crime Prevention," *Criminology* 20 (November 1982), 479–498.

LeBLANC, MARC, AND LOUISE BIRON. "Status Offenses: A Legal Term without Meaning: An Empirical Demonstration," *Journal of Research in Crime and Delinquency* 17 (January 1980), 114–125.

LEFKOWITZ, MONROE M., ET AL. *Growing Up to Be Violent: A Longitudinal Study of the Development of Aggression.* New York: Pergamon, 1977.

LEJEUNE, ROBERT. "The Management of a Mugging," *Urban Life* 6 (July 1977), 123–148.

LEJINS, PETER P. "Uniform Crime Reports," *Michigan Law Review* 64 (April 1966), 1011–1030.

LEMERT, EDWIN M. *Instead of Court: Diversion in Juvenile Justice.* Washington D.C.: U.S. Government Printing Office, 1971.

_____. "Isolation and Closure Theory of Naive Check Forgery," *Journal of Criminal Law, Criminology and Police Science* 44 (September–October 1953), 293–307.

_____. *Social Pathology.* New York: McGraw-Hill, 1951.

LEMPERT, RICHARD. "The Effect of Executions on Homicides: A New Look in an Old Light," *Crime and Delinquency* 29 (January 1983), 88–115.

_____. "Organizing for Deterrence: Lessons from a Study of Child Support," *Law and Society Review* 16 (1981–82), 513–568.

LEONARD, EILEEN B. *Women, Crime, and Society: A Critique of Criminology Theory.* New York: Longman, 1982.

LEONARD, WILLIAM N., AND MARVIN GLENN WEBER. "Automakers and Dealers: A Study of Criminogenic Market Forces," *Law and Society Review* 4 (February 1970), 407–424.

LETKEMANN, PETER. *Crime as Work.* Englewood Cliffs, N.J.: Prentice-Hall, 1973.

LEVI, MICHAEL. *The Phantom Capitalists—The Organization and Control of Long-Firm Fraud.* London: Heinemann, 1981.

LEVIN, JACK, AND JAMES ALAN FOX. *Mass Murder: America's Growing Menace.* New York: Plenum, 1985.

LEVINE, JAMES P. "Jury Toughness: The Impact of Conservatism on Criminal Court Verdicts," *Crime and Delinquency* 29 (January 1983), 71–87.

———. "The Potential for Crime Overreporting in Criminal Victimization Surveys," *Criminology* 14 (November 1976), 307–330.

———. "Reply to Singer," *Criminology* 16 (May 1978), 99–103.

LEWIS, C. S. "The Humanitarian Theory of Punishment," in Stanley E. Grupp, ed., *Theories of Punishment.* Bloomington: Indiana University Press, 1971, pp. 301–308.

LEWIS, DAN A., AND GRETA SALEM. "Community Crime Prevention: An Analysis of a Developing Strategy," *Crime and Delinquency* 27 (July 1981), 405–421.

———. *Fear of Crime: Incivility and the Production of a Social Problem.* New Brunswick, N.J.: Transaction Books, 1986.

LEYTON, ELLIOTT. *Compulsive Killers: The Story of Modern Multiple Murder.* New York: Washington Mews Books, 1986.

LICHTER, LINDA S., AND S. ROBERT LICHTER. *Prime Time Crime: Criminals and Law Enforcers in TV Entertainment.* Washington, D.C.: Media Institute, 1983.

LIEBERT, ROBERT M., AND ROBERT A. BARON. "Some Immediate Effects of Televised Violence on Children's Behavior," *Developmental Psychology* 6 (1972), 469–475.

LIN, JENNIFER. "Theft Takes Some of the Joy out of Holiday for Retailers," *The Boston Globe,* December 1, 1985, p. A7.

LIND, ANDREW W. "Some Ecological Patterns of Community Disorganization in Honolulu," *American Journal of Sociology* 36 (September 1930), 206–220.

LINDESMITH, ALFRED R. *Addiction and Opiates.* Chicago: Aldine, 1968.

———. *Opiate Addiction.* Bloomington, Ind.: Principia Press, 1947.

———. "Problems in the Social Psychology of Addiction," in Daniel M. Wilner and Gene C. Kassebaum, eds., *Narcotics.* New York: McGraw-Hill, 1965, pp. 118–139.

———. "A Reply to McAuliffe and Gordon's 'A Test of Lindesmith's Theory of Addiction,'" *American Journal of Sociology* 81 (July 1975), 147–153.

———. "A Sociological Theory of Drug Addiction," *American Journal of Sociology* 43 (January 1938), 593–613.

LIPTON, DOUGLAS, ROBERT MARTINSON, AND JUDITH WILKS. *The Effectiveness of Correctional Treatment: A Survey of Treatment Evaluation Studies.* New York: Praeger, 1975.

LISKA, ALLEN E., AND MARK D. REED. "Ties to Conventional Institutions and Delinquency: Estimating Reciprocal Effects," *American Sociological Review* 50 (August 1985), 547–560.

LITTLE, CRAIG B., AND CHRISTOPHER P. SHEFFIELD. "Frontiers and Criminal Justice: English Private Prosecution Societies and American Vigilantism in the Eighteenth and Nineteenth Centuries," *American Sociological Review* 48 (December 1983), 796–808.

LOFTIN, COLIN, MILTON HEUMANN, AND DAVID McDOWALL. "Mandatory Sentencing and Firearms Violence: Evaluating an Alternative to Gun Control," *Law and Society Review* 17 (1983), 287–318.

———, AND ROBERT H. HILL. "Regional Subculture and Homicide: An Examination of the Gastil-Hackney Thesis," *American Sociological Review* 39 (October 1974), 714–724.

———, AND DAVID McDOWALL. "The Deterrent Effects of the Florida Felony Firearm Law," *Journal of Criminal Law and Criminology* 75 (Spring 1984), 250–259.

———, AND DAVID McDOWALL. "'One with a Gun Gets You Two': Mandatory Sentencing and Firearms Violence in Detroit," *Annals of the American Academy of Political and Social Science* 455 (May 1981), 150–167.

———, AND DAVID McDOWALL. "The Police, Crime, and Economic Theory: An Assessment," *American Sociological Review* 47 (June 1982), 393–401.

LOGAN, CHARLES H. "Arrest Rates and Deterrence," *Social Science Quarterly* 56 (December 1975), 376–389.

LUCKENBILL, DAVID F. "Criminal Homicide as a Situated Transaction," *Social Problems* 25 (December 1977), 176–186.

———, AND JOEL BEST. "Careers in Deviance and Respectability: The Analogy's Limitations," *Social Problems* 29 (December 1981), 197–206.

LUNDQUIST, JOHN H., AND JANICE M. DUKE. "The Elderly Victim at Risk: Explaining the Fear-Victimization Paradox," *Criminology* 29 (May 1982), 115–126.

LUNDSGAARDE, HENRY P. *Murder in Space City: A Cultural Analysis of Houston Homicide Patterns.* New York: Oxford University Press, 1977.

LUPSHA, PETER A. "Individual Choice, Material Culture, and Organized Crime," *Criminology* 19 (May 1981), 3–24.

MacANDREW, CRAIG, AND ROBERT B. EDGERTON. *Drunken Comportment: A Social Explanation.* Chicago: Aldine, 1969.

McAULIFFE, WILLIAM E., AND ROBERT A. GORDON. "Issues in Testing Lindesmith's Theory," *American Journal of Sociology* 81 (July 1975), 154–168.

———. "A Test of Lindesmith's Theory of Addiction: The Frequency of Euphoria among Long-Term Addicts," *American Journal of Sociology* 79 (January 1974), 795–840.

McBRIDE, DUANE C., AND CLYDE B. McCOY. "Crime and Drug-Using Behavior: An Areal Analysis," *Criminology* 19 (August 1981), 281–302.

McCAGHY, CHARLES H. "Child Molesters: A Study of Their Careers as Deviants," in Marshall B. Clinard and Richard Quinney, eds., *Criminal Behavior Systems: A Typology.* New York: Holt, Rinehart and Winston, 1967, pp. 75–88.

———. "Drinking and Deviance Disavowal: The Case of Child Molesters," *Social Problems* 16 (Summer 1968), 43–49.

———, PEGGY C. GIORDANO, AND TRUDY KNICELY HENSON. "Auto Theft: Offender and Offense Characteristics," *Criminology* 15 (November 1977), 367–385.

McCAIN, NINA. "James Q. Wilson Talks about Crime and Punishment in the U.S.," *The Boston Globe,* August 11, 1984, p. 2.

McCARTHY, JOHN D., AND DEAN R. HOGE. "The Dynamics of Self-Esteem and Delinquency," *American Journal of Sociology* 90 (September 1984), 396–410.

McCLEARY, RICHARD, BARBARA C. NIENSTEDT, AND JAMES M. ERVEN. "Uniform Crime Reports as Organizational Outcomes: Three Time Series Experiments," *Social Problems* 29 (April 1982), 361–372.

McClintock, F. H., and Evelyn Gibson. *Robbery in London.* London: Macmillan & Co., Ltd., 1961.

Maccoby, Eleanor E., and Carol Nagy Jacklin. "Sex Differences in Aggression: A Rejoinder and a Reprise," *Child Development* 51 (December 1980), 964–980.

———, Joseph P. Johnson, and Russell M. Church. "Community Integration and the Social Control of Juvenile Delinquency," *Journal of Social Issues* 14 (June 1958), 38–51.

McCord, Joan. "A Longitudinal Perspective on Patterns of Crime," *Criminology* 19 (August 1981), 211–218.

———. "Some Child-Rearing Antecedents of Criminal Behavior in Adult Men," *Journal of Personality and Social Psychology* 37 (1979), 1477–1486.

———. "A Thirty-Year Followup of Treatment Effects," *American Psychologist* 33 (March 1978), 284–289.

McCord, William. "Psychopathy," in Sanford H. Kadish, ed., *Encyclopedia of Crime and Justice,* Vol. 4. New York: Free Press, 1983, pp. 1315–1318.

———, and Joan McCord. *Origins of Crime: A New Evaluation of the Cambridge-Somerville Youth Study.* New York: Columbia University Press, 1959.

———, and Joan McCord. *The Psychopath: An Essay on the Criminal Mind.* Princeton, N.J.: D. Van Nostrand, 1964.

McDonald, Lynn. *Social Class and Delinquency.* Hamden, Conn.: Archon, 1969.

McFarland, Sam G. "Is Capital Punishment a Short-Term Deterrent to Homicide? A Study of the Effects of Four Recent American Executions," *Journal of Criminal Law and Criminology* 74 (Winter 1983), 1014–1032.

McGahey, Richard M. "Economic Conditions, Neighborhood Organization, and Urban Crime," in Albert J. Reiss, Jr., and Michael Tonry, eds., *Communities and Crime.* Chicago: University of Chicago Press, 1986, pp. 231–270.

McGarrell, Edmund F., and Timothy J. Flanagan. "Measuring and Explaining Legislator Crime Control Ideology," *Journal of Research in Crime and Delinquency* 24 (May 1987), 102–118.

McGlothin, William H., M. Douglas Anglin, and Bruce D. Wilson. "Narcotic Addiction and Crime," *Criminology* 16 (November 1978), 293–315.

McGuire, William J., and Richard G. Sheehan. "Relationships between Crime Rates and Incarceration Rates: Further Analysis," *Journal of Research in Crime and Delinquency* 20 (January 1983), 73–85.

McIntosh, Mary. *The Organisation of Crime.* London: The Macmillan Press, Ltd., 1975.

McKay, Robert. "Riots: Prison Riots," in Sanford H. Kadish, ed., *Encyclopedia of Crime and Justice,* Vol. 4. New York: Free Press, 1983, pp. 1394–1398.

McNamara, John H. "Uncertainty in Police Work: The Relevance of Police Recruits' Backgrounds and Training," in David J. Bordua, ed., *The Police: Six Sociological Essays.* New York: Wiley, 1967, pp. 163–252.

McNamara, Joseph D. "Preface," in George L. Kelling et al., *The Kansas City Preventive Patrol Experiment.* Washington, D.C.: Police Foundation, 1974, pp. iii–iv.

McPheters, Lee R. "Criminal Behavior and the Gains from Crime," *Criminology* 14 (May 1976), 137–152.

———. "Measuring the Costs of Homicide," in Charles M. Gray, ed., *The Costs of Crime.* Beverly Hills, Calif.: Sage, 1979, pp. 33–46.

McVisk, William. "Toward a Rational Theory of Criminal Liability for the Corporate Executive," *Journal of Criminal Law and Criminology* 69 (Spring 1978), 75–91.

Mahoney, Anne Rankin. "The Effect of Labeling upon Youths in the Juvenile Justice

System: A Review of the Evidence," *Law and Society Review* 8 (Summer 1974), 583–614.

MAITLAND, LESLIE. "U.S. Tries New Tack in Drug Fight as Global Supply and Use Mount," *The New York Times,* January 30, 1983, pp. 1, 18.

MALTZ, MICHAEL D. "Crime Statistics: A Historical Perspective," *Crime and Delinquency* 23 (January 1977), 32–40.

MANN, DAVID W. "Age and Differential Predictability of Delinquent Behavior," *Social Forces* 60 (September 1981), 97–113.

MARKHAM, JAMES M. "Soaring Urban Crime Troubling Spaniards," *The New York Times,* December 18, 1977, p. 16.

MARS, GERALD. "Dock Pilferage: A Case Study in Occupational Theft," in Paul Rock and Mary McIntosh, eds., *Deviance and Social Control.* London: Tavistock, 1974, pp. 209–228.

MARTIN, SUSAN E. "Policing Career Criminals: An Examination of an Innovative Crime Control Program," *Journal of Criminal Law and Criminology* 77 (Winter 1986), 1159–1182.

———, AND LAWRENCE R. SHERMAN. "Selective Apprehension: A Police Strategy for Repeat Offenders," *Criminology* 24 (February 1986), 155–173.

MARTINSON, ROBERT. "New Findings, New Views: A Note of Caution Regarding Sentencing Reform," *Hofstra Law Review* 7 (Winter 1979), 243–258.

———. "What Works?—Questions and Answers about Prison Reform," *The Public Interest* No. 35 (Spring 1974), 22–54.

MARX, GARY T., AND DANE ARCHER. "Citizen Involvement in the Law Enforcement Process: The Case of Community Police Patrols," *American Behavioral Scientist* 15 (September–October 1971), 52–72.

———. "Picking Up the Gun: Some Organizational and Survey Data on Community Police Patrols." A paper presented at the Symposium on Studies of Public Experience, Knowledge and Opinion of Crime and Justice. Washington, D.C.: Bureau of Social Science Research, Inc., March 1972.

———. "The Urban Vigilante," *Psychology Today* 6 (January 1973), 45–50.

MATZA, DAVID. *Delinquency and Drift.* New York: Wiley, 1964.

———, AND GRESHAM M. SYKES. "Juvenile Delinquency and Subterranean Values," *American Sociological Review* 26 (October 1961), 712–719.

MAURER, DAVID W. *The American Confidence Man.* Springfield, Ill.: Charles C. Thomas, 1974.

———. *Whiz Mob: A Correlation of the Technical Argot of Pickpockets with Their Behavior Pattern.* New Haven, Conn.: College & University Press, 1955, 1964.

MAWBY, R. I. "Overcoming the Barriers of Privacy: Police Strategies against Nonvisible Crime," *Criminology* 18 (February 1981), 501–521.

MAYNARD, DOUGLAS W. "The Structure of Discourse in Misdemeanor Plea Bargaining," *Law and Society Review* 18 (1984), 75–104.

MAYO, PATRICIA ELTON. *The Making of a Criminal: A Comparative Study of Two Delinquency Areas.* London: Weidenfeld and Nicolson, 1969.

MEADOW, ARNOLD, ET AL. "Self-Concept, Negative Family Affect, and Delinquency: A Comparison across Mexican Social Classes," *Criminology* 19 (November 1981), 434–448.

MEDINNUS, GENE R. "Delinquents' Perceptions of Their Parents," *Journal of Consulting Psychology* 29 (December 1965), 592–593.

MEDNICK, SARNOFF A., AND JAN VOLAVKA. "Biology and Crime," in Norval Morris and Michael Tonry, eds., *Crime and Justice: An Annual Review of Research,* Vol. 2. Chicago: University of Chicago Press, 1980, pp. 85–158.

————, ET AL. "Biology and Violence," in Marvin E. Wolfgang and Neil Alan Weiner, eds., *Criminal Violence.* Beverly Hills, Calif.: Sage Publications, 1982, pp. 21–80.

————, ET AL. "EEG as a Predictor of Antisocial Behavior," *Criminology* 19 (August 1981), 219–229.

MEGARGEE, EDWIN I. "Psychological Determinants and Correlates of Criminal Violence," in Marvin E. Wolfgang and Neil Alan Weiner, eds., *Criminal Violence.* Beverly Hills, Calif.: Sage Publications, 1982, pp. 81–170.

————, AND MARTIN J. BOHN. *Classifying Criminal Offenders: A New System Based on the MMPI.* Beverly Hills, Calif.: Sage Publications, 1979.

MEISENHELDER, THOMAS. "An Exploratory Study of Exiting from Criminal Careers," *Criminology* 15 (November 1977), 319–334.

MEISLER, STANLEY. "The Mounties Went Forth," *The Boston Globe,* June 20, 1981, p. 3.

MENARD, SCOTT, AND BARBARA J. MORSE. "A Structuralist Critique of the IQ-Delinquency Hypothesis: Theory and Evidence," *American Journal of Sociology* 89 (May 1984), 1347–1378.

MERRY, SALLY ENGLE. *Urban Danger: Life in a Neighborhood of Strangers.* Philadelphia: Temple University Press, 1981.

MERTON, ROBERT K. "Social Structure and Anomie," in *Social Theory and Social Structure,* 1968 enlarged ed. New York: Free Press, 1968, pp. 185–214.

MESSNER, STEVEN F. "Poverty, Inequality, and the Urban Homicide Rate: Some Unexpected Findings," *Criminology* 20 (May 1982), 103–114.

————. "Regional and Racial Effects on the Urban Homicide Rate: The Subculture of Violence Revisited," *American Journal of Sociology* 88 (March 1983a), 997–1007.

————. "Regional Differences in the Economic Correlates of the Urban Homicide Rate: Some Evidence on the Importance of Cultural Context," *Criminology* 21 (November 1983b), 477–488.

————, AND KENNETH TARDIFF. "The Social Ecology of Urban Homicide: An Application of the 'Routine Activities' Approach," *Criminology* 23 (May 1985), 241–267.

MIETHE, TERANCE D., MARK C. STAFFORD, AND J. SCOTT LONG. "Social Differentiation in Criminal Victimization: A Test of Routine Activities/Lifestyle Theories," *American Sociological Review* 52 (April 1987), 184–194.

MILAN, MICHAEL A., AND JOHN M. McKEE. "Behavior Modification: Principles and Applications in Corrections," in Daniel Glaser, ed., *Handbook of Criminology.* Chicago: Rand McNally, 1974, pp. 745–776.

MILGRAM, STANLEY. "The Experience of Living in Cities: A Psychological Analysis," *Science* 167 (March 13, 1970), 1461–1468.

————, AND PAUL HOLLANDER. "The Murder They Heard," in Renatus Hartogs and Eric Artzt, eds., *Violence: Causes & Solutions.* New York: Dell, 1970, pp. 206–212.

MILLER, J. L., PETER H. ROSSI, AND JON E. SIMPSON. "Perceptions of Justice: Race and Gender Differences in Judgments of Appropriate Prison Sentences," *Law and Society Review* 20 (1986), 313–334.

MILLER, NORMAN C. *The Great Salad Oil Swindle.* New York: Coward-McCann, 1965.

MILLER, STUART J., SIMON DINITZ, AND JOHN P. CONRAD. *Careers of the Violent: The Dangerous Offender and Criminal Justice.* Lexington, Mass.: D. C. Heath, 1982.

MILLER, WALTER, B. "American Youth Gangs: Past and Present," in Abraham S. Blumberg, ed., *Current Perspectives on Criminal Behavior: Original Essays in Criminology.* New York: Knopf, 1974, pp. 210–239.

———. "Ideology and Criminal Justice Policy: Some Current Issues," *Journal of Criminal Law and Criminology* 64 (June 1973), 141–162.

———. "Lower Class Culture as a Generating Milieu of Gang Delinquency," *Journal of Social Issues* 14 (No. 3, 1958), 5–19.

MILLS, C. WRIGHT. *The Power Elite.* New York: Oxford University Press, 1956.

MINOR, W. WILLIAM. "Techniques of Neutralization: A Reconceptualization and Empirical Examination," *Journal of Research in Crime and Delinquency* 18 (July 1981), 295–318.

———, AND MICHAEL COURLANDER. "The Postrelease Trauma Thesis: A Reconsideration of the Risk of Early Parole Failure," *Journal of Research in Crime and Delinquency* 16 (July 1979), 273–293.

———, AND JOSEPH HARRY. "Deterrent and Experiential Effects in Perceptual Deterrence Research: A Replication and Extension," *Journal of Research in Crime and Delinquency* 19 (July 1982), 190–203.

MINSKY, TERRI. "The Odds on Being Slain—Worse for Young Black Males," *The Boston Globe,* February 23, 1984, pp. 1, 47.

MITFORD, JESSICA. *Kind & Usual Punishment: The Prison Business.* New York: Knopf, 1973

MOELLER, H. G. "Community-Based Correctional Services," in Daniel Glaser, ed., *Handbook of Criminology.* Chicago: Rand McNally, 1974, pp. 895–907.

MOLOTSKY, IRVIN. "The Hidden Costs of the Cashless Society," *The New York Times,* March 4, 1984, p. E3.

MONACHESI, ELIO D., AND STARKE R. HATHAWAY. "The Personality of Delinquents," in J. N. Butcher, ed., *MMPI: Research Developments and Clinical Applications.* New York: McGraw-Hill, 1969, pp. 207–219.

MORAN, RICHARD. "Insanity Defense Survives Tinkering," *The Boston Globe,* June 21, 1987, pp. A3, A4.

MORASH, MERRY. "Establishment of a Juvenile Police Record: The Influence of Individual and Peer Group Characteristics," *Criminology* 22 (February 1984), 97–111.

MORRIS, NORVAL. "Punishment, Desert, and Rehabilitation," in Hyman Gross and Andrew Von Hirsch, eds., *Sentencing.* New York: Oxford University Press, 1981, pp. 257–271.

———, AND GORDON HAWKINS. *The Honest Politician's Guide to Crime Control.* Chicago: University of Chicago Press, 1970.

MURRAY, CHARLES A. "The Physical Environment and Community Control of Crime," in James Q. Wilson, ed., *Crime and Public Policy.* San Francisco: ICS Press, 1983, pp. 107–122.

———, AND LOUIS A. COX, JR. *Beyond Probation: Juvenile Corrections and the Chronic Delinquent.* Beverly Hills, Calif.: Sage Publications, 1979.

MUSON, HOWARD. "Teenage Violence and the Telly," *Psychology Today* 11 (March 1978), 50–54.

NAGEL, ILENE H., AND JOHN HAGAN. "Gender and Crime: Offense Patterns and Criminal Court Sanctions," in Michael Tonry and Norval Morris, eds., *Crime and Justice: An Annual Review of Research,* Vol. 4. Chicago: University of Chicago, 1983, pp. 91–144.

NAGIN, DANIEL. "Crime Rates, Sanction Levels, and Constraints on Prison Population," *Law and Society Review* 12 (Spring 1978), 341–366.

NATIONAL ADVISORY COMMISSION ON CRIMINAL JUSTICE STANDARDS AND GOALS. *A National Strategy to Reduce Crime.* Washington, D.C.: U.S. Government Printing Office, 1973.

NATIONAL INSTITUTE OF MENTAL HEALTH. *Television and Behavior: Ten Years of Scientific Progress and Implications for the Eighties,* Vol. 1: *Summary Report.* Washington, D.C.: U.S. Department of Health and Human Services, 1982.

NELSON, BRYCE. "Children Who Kill: Personality Patterns Are Identified," *The New York Times,* October 11, 1983, pp. C1, C8.

NELSON, JAMES F. "Multiple Victimization in American Cities: A Statistical Analysis of Rare Events," *American Journal of Sociology* 85 (January 1980), 870–891.

NETTLER, GWYNN. *Explaining Crime,* 2nd ed. New York: McGraw-Hill, 1978.

———. *Explaining Crime,* 3rd ed. New York: McGraw-Hill, 1984.

NEUBAUER, DAVID W. *Criminal Justice in Middle America.* Morristown, N.J.: General Learning Press, 1974.

NEVARES-MUNIZ, DORA. "The Eighth Amendment Revisited: A Model of Weighted Punishments," *Journal of Criminal Law and Criminology* 75 (Spring 1984), 272–289.

[The New York Times.] "British Clinics are Struggling as Heroin Addiction Climbs," *The New York Times,* April 11, 1985, p. A15.

———. "Group Finds Gain in Rehabilitation," *The New York Times,* October 2, 1983, p. 30.

———. "I.R.S. Once Used Embarrassment as Delinquents' Penalty in Idaho," *The New York Times,* November 24, 1980, p. A24.

———. "Morgenthau Says Data Link a Third of Crimes to the Career Criminal," *The New York Times,* April 9, 1981, p. B3.

———. "On the Wild Side: Women in Gangs," *The New York Times,* January 2, 1986, p. C8.

———. "Study Cites Lack of Programs for Retarded Inmates in U.S.," *The New York Times,* June 14, 1982, p. A17.

———. "Study Says Hedges May Stop Burglars," *The New York Times,* November 17, 1983, p. C11.

———. "Study Stresses Link between Heroin Dependence and Incidence of Crime," *The New York Times,* March 22, 1981, p. 22.

NEWMAN, GRAEME. *Comparative Deviance: Perception and Law in Six Cultures.* New York: Elsevier, 1976.

———. *The Punishment Response.* Philadelphia: Lippincott, 1978.

NEWMAN, OSCAR. *Architectural Design for Crime Prevention.* Washington, D.C.: U.S. Government Printing Office, 1973.

———. *Defensible Space: Crime Prevention through Urban Design.* New York: Macmillan, 1972.

———, AND K. A. FRANCK. "The Effects of Building Size on Personal Crime and Fear of Crime," *Population and Environment* 5 (1982), 203–220.

———, AND K. A. FRANCK. *Factors Influencing Crime and Instability in Urban Housing Developments.* Washington, D.C.: U.S. Government Printing Office, 1980.

[Newsweek.] "Justice: The Woman's Touch," *Newsweek,* January 6, 1975, p. 35.

NORMANDEAU, ANDRÉ. *Trends and Patterns in Crimes of Robbery.* Ph.D. dissertation. Philadelphia: University of Pennsylvania, 1968.

NYE, F. IVAN. *Family Relationships and Delinquent Behavior.* Westport, Conn.: Greenwood Press, 1958.

———, JAMES F. SHORT, JR., AND VIRGIL L. OLSON. "Socioeconomic Status and Delinquent Behavior," *American Journal of Sociology* 63 (January 1958), 381–389.

O'BRIEN, ROBERT M. "The Interracial Nature of Violent Crimes: A Reexamination," *American Journal of Sociology* 92 (January 1987), 817–835.

O'CONNOR, JAMES F., AND ALAN LIZOTTE. "The 'Southern Subculture of Violence' Thesis and Patterns of Gun Ownership," *Social Problems* 25 (April 1978), 420–429.

OFFICE OF YOUTH DEVELOPMENT. *Juvenile Court Statistics, 1972.* Washington, D.C.: U.S. Department of Health, Education, and Welfare, 1974.

OPPENLANDER, NAN. "Coping or Copping Out: Police Service Delivery in Domestic Disputes," *Criminology* 20 (November 1982), 449–465.

ORSAGH, THOMAS, AND ANN DRYDEN WITTE. "Economic Status and Crime: Implications for Offender Rehabilitation," *Journal of Criminal Law and Criminology* 72 (Fall 1981), 1055–1071.

OSBUN, LEE ANN, AND PETER A. RODE. "Prosecuting Juveniles as Adults: The Quest for 'Objective' Decisions," *Criminology* 22 (May 1984), 187–202.

OSTROW, RONALD J. "Meese Backs Death Penalty for Young in Capital Crimes," *The Boston Globe,* September 17, 1985, p. 10.

———. "US Panel Lists Ill Effects of Mob on the Economy," *The Boston Globe,* April 1, 1986, p. 8.

PACE, ERIC. "Crime's Lingering Allure," *The New York Times,* June 6, 1982, p. F9.

PALMER, TED. "Martinson Revisited," *Journal of Research in Crime and Delinquency* 12 (July 1975), 133–152.

PARISI, NICOLETTE. "Are Females Treated Differently? A Review of the Theories and Evidence on Sentencing and Parole Decisions," in Nicole Hahn Rafter and Elizabeth Anne Stanko, eds., *Judge, Lawyer, Victim, Thief: Women, Gender Roles, and Criminal Justice.* Boston: Northeastern University Press, 1982, pp. 205–220.

———. "A Taste of the Bars?" *Journal of Criminal Law and Criminology* 72 (Fall 1981), 1109–1123.

PARKER, DONN B. *Crime by Computer.* New York: Scribner's, 1976.

———. *Fighting Computer Crime.* New York: Scribner's, 1983.

PATE, TONY, GEORGE L. KELLING, AND CHARLES BROWN. "A Response to 'What Happened to Patrol Operations in Kansas City?'" *Journal of Criminal Justice* 3 (Winter 1975), 299–320.

PATERNOSTER, RAYMOND. "Race of Victim and Location of Crime: The Decision to Seek the Death Penalty in South Carolina," *Journal of Criminal Law and Criminology* 74 (Winter 1983), 754–785.

———, ET AL. "Perceived Risk and Social Control: Do Sanctions Really Deter?" *Law and Society Review* 17 (1983), 457–479.

PATTERSON, GERALD R. "Children Who Steal," in Travis Hirschi and Michael Gottfredson, eds., *Understanding Crime: Current Theory and Research.* Beverly Hills, Calif.: Sage Publications, 1980, pp. 73–90.

———, P. CHAMBERLAIN, AND J. B. REID. "A Comparative Evaluation of a Parent-Training Program," *Behavior Therapy* 13 (1982), 638–650.

———, AND THOMAS J. DISHION. "Contributions of Families and Peers to Delinquency," *Criminology* 23 (February 1985), 63–79.

PEPINSKY, HAROLD E. *Crime Control Strategies: An Introduction to the Study of Crime.* New York: Oxford University Press, 1980.

PERRY, JOSEPH B., JR., AND ERDWIN H. PFUHL, JR. "Adjustment of Children in 'Solo' and 'Remarriage' Homes," *Marriage and Family Living* 25 (May 1963), 221–223.

PETERSILIA, JOAN. "Criminal Career Research: A Review of Recent Evidence," in Norval Morris and Michael Tonry, eds., *Crime and Justice: An Annual Review of Research,* Vol. 2. Chicago: University of Chicago Press, 1980, pp. 321–379.

———. *Racial Disparities in the Criminal Justice System.* Santa Monica, Calif.: Rand, 1983.

———, PETER W. GREENWOOD, AND MARVIN LAVIN. *Criminal Careers of Habitual Felons.* Santa Monica, Calif.: Rand, 1977.

PETERSON, MARK A., AND HARRIET BRAIKER, WITH SUZANNE M. POLICH. *Who Commits Crimes: A Survey of Prison Inmates.* Boston: Oelgeschlager, Gunn & Hain, 1981.

PETERSON, RUTH D., AND JOHN HAGAN. "Changing Conceptions of Race: Towards an Account of Anomalous Findings of Sentencing Research," *American Sociological Review* 49 (February 1984), 56–70.

PETTIGREW, THOMAS F., AND ROSALIND B. SPIER. "The Ecological Structure of Negro Homicide," *American Journal of Sociology* 67 (May 1962), 621–629.

PFUHL, ERDWIN H., JR. "Police Strikes and Conventional Crime: A Look at the Data," *Criminology* 21 (November 1983), 489–503.

PHILLIPS, DAVID P. "The Deterrent Effect of Capital Punishment: New Evidence on an Old Controversy," *American Journal of Sociology* 86 (July 1980), 139–148.

———. "The Impact of Mass Media Violence on U.S. Homicides," *American Sociological Review* 48 (August 1983), 560–568.

———, AND JOHN E. HENSLEY. "When Violence Is Rewarded or Punished: The Impact of Mass Media Stories on Homicide," *Journal of Communication* 34 (Summer 1984), 101–116.

PHILLIPS, JOEL, AND CHARLSEY CARTWRIGHT. "The California Career Criminal Prosecution Program One Year Later," *Journal of Criminal Law and Criminology* 71 (Summer 1980), 107–112.

PHILLIPS, LLAD, AND HAROLD L. VOTEY, JR. "An Economic Analysis of the Deterrent Effect of Law Enforcement on Criminal Activity," *Journal of Criminal Law, Criminology and Police Science* 63 (September 1972), 330–342.

———. *The Economics of Crime Control.* Beverly Hills, Calif.: Sage Publications, 1981.

PHILLIPS, PHILLIP D. "Characteristics and Typology of the Journey to Crime," in Daniel E. Georges-Abeyie and Keith D. Harries, eds., *Crime: A Spatial Perspective.* New York: Columbia University Press, 1980, pp. 167–180.

PIERCE, GLENN, AND WILLIAM J. BOWERS. "The Bartley-Fox Gun Law's Short-Term Impact on Crime in Boston," *Annals of the American Academy of Political and Social Science* 455 (May 1981), 120–137.

PILIAVIN, IRVING, AND SCOTT BRIAR. "Police Encounters with Juveniles," *American Journal of Sociology* 70 (September 1964), 206–214.

PINES, MAYA. "Violence Termed Hard to Foretell," *The New York Times,* June 27, 1982, p. 25.

PITTMAN, DAVID J. "Drugs, Addiction, and Crime," in Daniel Glaser, ed., *Handbook of Criminology.* Chicago: Rand McNally, 1974, pp. 209–232.

PLATT, ANTHONY M. *The Child Savers: The Invention of Delinquency,* 2nd ed. Chicago: University of Chicago Press, 1977.

———. "Prospects for a Radical Criminology in the USA," in Ian Taylor, Paul Walton, and Jock Young, eds., *Critical Criminology.* London: Routledge and Kegan Paul, 1975, pp. 95–112.

————, AND PAUL TAKAGI, EDS. *Crime and Social Justice.* London: The Macmillan Press, Ltd., 1981.

PODOLEFSKY, AARON, AND FREDRIC DUBOW. *Strategies for Community Crime Prevention: Collective Responses to Crime in Urban America.* Springfield, Ill.: Charles C. Thomas Publisher, 1981.

POLK, KENNETH. "Delinquency and Adult Criminal Careers," in Delos H. Kelly, eds., *Criminal Behavior: Readings in Criminology.* New York: St. Martin's Press, 1980, pp. 143–150.

POLLOCK, VICKI, SARNOFF A. MEDNICK, AND WILLIAM F. GABRIELLI, JR. "Crime Causation: Biological Theories," in Sanford H. Kadish, ed., *Encyclopedia of Crime and Justice,* Vol. 1. New York: Free Press, 1983, pp. 308–315.

POOLE, ERIC D., AND ROBERT M. REGOLI. "Parental Support, Delinquent Friends, and Delinquency: A Test of Interaction Effects," *Journal of Criminal Law and Criminology* 70 (Summer 1979), 188–193.

————. "Race, Institutional Rule Breaking, and Disciplinary Response: A Study of Discretionary Decision Making in Prison," *Law and Society Review* 14 (Summer 1980), 931–946.

PORTERFIELD, AUSTIN L. *Youth in Trouble: Studies in Delinquency and Despair, with Plans for Prevention.* Fort Worth, Tex.: Leo Potishman Foundation, 1946.

POUND, ROSCOE. "The Future of Criminal Law," *Columbia Law Review* 21 (January 1921), 1–16.

POWERS, EDWIN, AND HELEN L. WITMER. *An Experiment in the Prevention of Delinquency: The Cambridge-Somerville Youth Study.* New York: Columbia University Press, 1951.

PREBLE, EDWARD, AND JOHN J. CASEY, JR. "Taking Care of Business: The Heroin User's Life on the Street," in David E. Smith and George R. Gay, eds., *"It's So Good, Don't Even Try It Once": Heroin in Perspective.* Englewood Cliffs, N.J.: Prentice-Hall, 1972, pp. 97–118.

THE PRESIDENT'S COMMISSION ON LAW ENFORCEMENT AND ADMINISTRATION OF JUSTICE. *The Challenge of Crime in a Free Society.* Washington, D.C.: U.S. Government Printing Office, 1967a.

————. *Crime and Its Impact—An Assessment.* Washington, D.C.: U.S. Government Printing Office, 1967b.

THE PRESIDENT'S COMMISSION ON OBSCENITY AND PORNOGRAPHY. *Report.* Washington, D.C.: U.S. Government Printing Office, 1970.

PRIAL, FRANK J. "Ex-Treasury Chief Gets 1-Month Term in Illegal-Bank Case," *The New York Times,* June 26, 1987, pp. A1, A27.

PRUGH, JEFF. "In Atlanta, a Pall of Fear," *The Boston Globe,* February 14, 1981, p. 3.

PRUITT, CHARLES R., AND JAMES Q. WILSON. "A Longitudinal Study of the Effect of Race on Sentencing," *Law and Society Review* 17 (1983), 613–635.

QUINNEY, RICHARD. *The Social Reality of Crime.* Boston: Little, Brown, 1970.

RADELET, MICHAEL L. "Racial Characteristics and the Imposition of the Death Penalty," *American Sociological Review* 46 (December 1981), 918–927.

————, AND GLENN L. PIERCE. "Race and Prosecutorial Discretion in Homicide Cases," *Law and Society Review* 19 (1985), 587–621.

RADZINOWICZ, SIR LEON, AND JOAN KING. *The Growth of Crime: The International Experience.* New York: Basic Books, 1977.

RAND, MICHAEL, ET AL. *The Use of Weapons in Committing Crimes.* Washington, D.C.: U.S. Department of Justice, January 1986.

RANKIN, JOSEPH H. "The Family Context of Delinquency," *Social Problems* 30 (April 1983), 466–479.

RATCLIFFE, JAMES M., ED. *The Good Samaritan and the Law.* Garden City, N.Y.: Doubleday, 1966.

RAUSCH, SHARLA. "Court Processing versus Diversion of Status Offenders: A Test of Deterrence and Labeling Theories," *Journal of Research in Crime and Delinquency* 20 (January 1983), 39–54.

RAWLS, WENDELL, JR. "Fear Linked to Killings Rises among Atlanta Youths," *The New York Times,* March 22, 1981, p. 24.

RECKLESS, WALTER C. "Containment Theory," in Barry Krisberg and James Austin, eds., *The Children of Ishmael: Critical Perspectives on Juvenile Justice.* Palo Alto, Calif.: Mayfield, 1978, pp. 187–193.

———. *The Crime Problem,* 5th ed. New York: Appleton-Century-Crofts, 1973.

REED, JOHN P., AND ROBIN S. REED. " 'Doctor, Lawyer, Indian Chief': Old Rhymes and New on White Collar Crime," *International Journal of Criminology and Penology* 3 (August 1975), 279–293.

REED, JOHN SHELTON. "To Live—and Die—in Dixie: A Contribution to the Study of Southern Violence," *Political Science Quarterly* 86 (September 1971), 429–443.

REIMAN, JEFFREY H. "Marxist Explanations and Radical Misinterpretations: A Reply to Greenberg and Humphries," *Crime and Delinquency* 28 (October 1982), 610–617.

———. *The Rich Get Richer and the Poor Get Prison: Ideology, Class, and Criminal Justice,* 2nd ed. New York: Wiley, 1984.

———, AND SUE HEADLEE. "Marxism and Criminal Justice Policy," *Crime and Delinquency* 27 (January 1981), 24–47.

REISS, ALBERT J., JR. "Foreword: Towards a Revitalization of Theory and Research on Victimization by Crime," *Journal of Criminal Law and Criminology* 72 (Summer 1981), 704–713.

———. "Inappropriate Theories and Inadequate Methods as Policy Plagues: Self-Reported Delinquency and the Law," in N. J. Demerath 3d, Otto Larsen, and Karl F. Schuessler, eds., *Social Policy and Sociology.* New York: Academic Press, 1975, pp. 211–222.

———. *The Police and the Public.* New Haven, Conn.: Yale University Press, 1971.

———. "Police Brutality—Answers to Key Questions," *Trans-Action* 5 (July/August 1968), 10–19.

———, AND DAVID J. BORDUA. "Environment and Organization: A Perspective on the Police," in David J. Bordua, ed., *The Police: Six Sociological Essays.* New York: Wiley, 1968, pp. 25–55.

———, AND ALBERT LEWIS RHODES. "The Distribution of Juvenile Delinquency in the Social Class Structure," *American Sociological Review* 26 (October 1961), 720–732.

REPPETTO, THOMAS A. *Residential Crime.* Cambridge, Mass.: Ballinger, 1974.

RETTIG, RICHARD P., MANUAL J. TORRES, AND GERALD R. GARRETT. *Manny: A Criminal-Addict's Story.* Boston: Houghton Mifflin, 1977.

REUSS-IANNI, ELIZABETH. *Two Cultures of Policing: Street Cops and Management Cops.* New Brunswick, N.J.: Transaction Books, 1983.

REUTER, PETER. *Disorganized Crime: The Economics of the Visible Hand.* Cambridge, Mass.: MIT Press, 1983.

———, AND JONATHAN B. RUBINSTEIN. "Fact, Fancy, and Organized Crime," *The Public Interest* No. 53 (Fall 1978), 45–67.

RHODES, WILLIAM C. *Behavioral Threat and Community Response.* New York: Behavioral Publications, 1972.

RICHARDS, PAMELA, RICHARD A. BERK, AND BRENDA FOSTER. *Crime as Play: Delinquency in a Middle Class Suburb.* Cambridge, Mass.: Ballinger, 1979.

ROBERTS, SAM. "Mafia Infiltration of Business Costing Consumers Millions," *The New York Times,* December 19, 1985, p. B13.

ROBIN, GERALD D. "Patterns of Department Store Shoplifting," *Crime and Delinquency* 9 (April 1963), 163–172.

ROBISON, JAMES, AND GERALD SMITH. "The Effectiveness of Correctional Programs," *Crime and Delinquency* 17 (January 1971), 67–80.

ROGERS, JOSEPH W. *Why Are You Not a Criminal?* Englewood Cliffs, N.J.: Prentice-Hall, 1977.

ROJEK, DEAN G., AND MAYNARD L. ERICKSON. "Delinquent Careers: A Test of the Career Escalation Model," *Criminology* 20 (May 1982), 5–28.

——. "Reforming the Juvenile Justice System: The Diversion of Status Offenders," *Law and Society Review* 16 (1981–82), 241–264.

ROSENBAUM, DENNIS P. "The Theory and Research behind Neighborhood Watch: Is It a Sound Fear and Crime Reduction Strategy?" *Crime and Delinquency* 33 (January 1987), 103–134.

ROSENBAUM, MARSHA. *Women on Heroin.* New Brunswick, N.J.: Rutgers University Press, 1981.

——. "Work and the Addicted Prostitute," in Nicole Hahn Rafter and Elizabeth Ann Stanko, eds., *Judge, Lawyer, Victim, Thief: Women, Gender Roles, and Criminal Justice.* Boston: Northeastern University Press, 1982, pp. 131–150.

ROSENQUIST, CARL M., AND EDWIN I. MEGARGEE. *Delinquency in Three Cultures.* Austin: University of Texas Press, 1969.

ROSETT, ARTHUR, AND DONALD R. CRESSEY. *Justice by Consent: Plea Bargains in the American Courthouse.* Philadelphia: Lippincott, 1976.

ROSS, R. R., AND H. B. MCKAY. "Behavioural Approaches to Treatment in Corrections: Requiem for a Panacea," *Canadian Journal of Criminology* 20 (1978), 279–298.

ROSSI, PETER H., RICHARD A. BERK, AND KENNETH J. LENIHAN. *Money, Work, and Crime: Experimental Evidence.* New York: Academic Press, 1980.

ROTH, JEFFREY A. "Prosecutor Perceptions of Crime Seriousness," *Journal of Criminal Law and Criminology* 69 (Summer 1978), 232–242.

ROTHMAN, DAVID J. *Conscience and Convenience: The Asylum and Its Alternatives in Progressive America.* Boston: Little, Brown, 1980.

——. *The Discovery of the Asylum.* Boston: Little, Brown, 1971.

ROWE, DAVID C. "Biometrical Genetic Models of Self-Reported Delinquent Behavior: A Twin Study," *Behavior Genetics* 13 (1983), 473–489.

——, AND D. WAYNE OSGOOD. "Heredity and Sociological Theories of Delinquency: A Reconsideration," *American Sociological Review* 49 (August 1984), 526–540.

RUBEL, ROBERT J. "Analysis and Critique of HEW's *Safe School Study Report to the Congress*," *Crime and Delinquency* 24 (July 1978), 257–265.

RUSSELL, DIANA E. H. *The Politics of Rape: The Victim's Perspective.* New York: Stein and Day, 1975.

——. *Rape in Marriage.* New York: Macmillan, 1982.

RUSSELL, DONALD H., AND G. P. HARPER. "Who Are Our Assaultive Juveniles? A Study of 100 Cases," *Journal of Forensic Sciences* 18 (October 1973), 387–393.

RUTTER, MICHAEL, ET AL. *Fifteen Thousand Hours: Secondary Schools and Their Effects on Children.* Cambridge, Mass.: Harvard University Press, 1979.

SALAS, LUIS, AND WILLIAM WILBANKS. "Latin American Homicide Statistics: A Critique of Available Statistics." Paper presented at the American Society of Criminology Meeting, Washington, D.C., November 1981.

SALTZMAN, LINDA, ET AL. "Deterrent and Experiential Effects: The Problem of Causal Order in Perceptual Deterrence Research," *Journal of Research in Crime and Delinquency* 19 (July 1982), 172–189.

SAMENOW, STANTON E. *Inside the Criminal Mind.* New York: Times Books, 1984.

SAMPSON, ROBERT J. "Crime in Cities: The Effects of Formal and Informal Social Control," in Albert J. Reiss, Jr., and Michael Tonry, eds., *Communities and Crime.* Chicago: University of Chicago Press, 1986, pp. 271–311.

————. "Structural Sources of Variation in Race-Age-Specific Rates of Offending across Major U.S. Cities," *Criminology* 23 (November 1985), 647–673.

SAMUEL, WILLIAM, AND ELIZABETH MOULDS. "The Effect of Crime Severity on Perceptions of Fair Punishment: A California Case Study," *Journal of Criminal Law and Criminology* 77 (Fall 1986), 931–948.

SANDERS, WILLIAM B. *Detective Work.* New York: Free Press, 1977.

SAVITZ, LEONARD D. *Delinquency and Migration.* Ph.D. dissertation. Philadelphia: University of Pennsylvania, 1960.

SCHAFER, STEPHEN. *The Political Criminal: The Problem of Morality and Crime.* New York: Free Press, 1974.

————. *The Victim and His Criminal: A Study in Functional Responsibility.* Englewood Cliffs, N.J.: Prentice-Hall, 1968.

SCHLESINGER, STEVEN R. "Prison Crowding in the United States: The Data," *Criminal Justice Research Bulletin* 3 (1987), 1–3.

SCHMECK, HAROLD M., JR. "Brain Defects Seen in Those Who Repeat Violent Acts," *The New York Times,* September 17, 1985, pp. C1, C3.

SCHMIDT, WILLIAM E. "Pressure for Gun Control Rises and Falls, but Ardor for Arms Seems Constant," *The New York Times,* October 25, 1987, p. E5.

SCHNEIDER, ANNE L., AND PETER R. SCHNEIDER. *Private and Public Minded Citizen Responses to a Neighborhood-Based Crime Prevention Strategy.* Eugene, Ore.: Institute of Policy Analysis, 1978.

SCHRAG, CLARENCE. "Theoretical Foundations for a Social Science of Corrections," in Daniel Glaser, ed., *Handbook of Criminology.* Chicago: Rand McNally, 1974, pp. 705–743.

SCHRAGER, LAURA SHILL, AND JAMES F. SHORT, JR. "How Serious a Crime? Perceptions of Organizational and Common Crimes," in Gilbert Geis and Ezra Stotland, eds., *White-Collar Crime: Theory and Research.* Beverly Hills, Calif.: Sage Publications, 1980, pp. 14–31.

————. "Toward a Sociology of Organizational Crime," *Social Problems* 25 (April 1978), 407–419.

SCHUESSLER, KARL F., AND DONALD R. CRESSEY. "Personality Characteristics of Criminals," *American Journal of Sociology* 55 (July–August 1953), 166–176.

SCHULTZ, LEROY G. "Why the Negro Carries Weapons," *Journal of Criminal Law, Criminology and Police Science* 53 (December 1962), 476–483.

SCHUR, EDWIN M. *Crimes without Victims: Deviant Behavior and Public Policy.* Englewood Cliffs, N.J.: Prentice-Hall, 1965.

_____. *Interpreting Deviance: A Sociological Introduction*. New York: Harper & Row, 1979.

_____. *Labeling Deviant Behavior: Its Sociological Implications*. New York: Harper & Row, 1971.

_____. *Narcotic Addiction in Britain & America*. London: Tavistock, 1962.

_____. *Our Criminal Society: The Social and Legal Sources of Crime in America*. Englewood Cliffs, N.J.: Prentice-Hall, 1969.

_____. *Radical Nonintervention: Rethinking the Delinquency Problem*. Englewood Cliffs, N.J.: Prentice-Hall, 1973.

SCHWARTZ, RICHARD D. "Law in the Kibbutz: A Response to Professor Shapiro," *Law and Society Review* 10 (Spring 1976), 439–442.

_____. "Social Factors in the Development of Legal Controls: A Case Study of Two Israeli Settlements," *Yale Law Journal* 63 (February 1954), 471–491.

_____, AND JEROME H. SKOLNICK. "Two Studies of Legal Stigma," *Social Problems* 10 (Fall 1962), 133–142.

SCHWENDINGER, HERMAN, AND JULIA SCHWENDINGER. "Defenders of Order or Guardians of Human Rights?" in Ian Taylor, Paul Walton, and Jock Young, eds., *Critical Criminology*. London: Routledge and Kegan Paul, 1975, pp. 113–146.

SCHWENDINGER, JULIA R., AND HERMAN SCHWENDINGER. *Rape and Inequality*. Beverly Hills, Calif.: Sage Publications, 1983.

SCIMECCA, JOSEPH A. "Labeling Theory and Personal Construct Theory: Toward the Measurement of Individual Variation," *Journal of Criminal Law and Criminology* 68 (December 1977), 652–659.

SCOTT, JOSEPH E., AND FAHAD AL-THAKEB. "The Public's Perceptions of Crime: Scandinavia, Western Europe, the Middle East, and the United States," in C. Ronald Huff, ed., *Contemporary Corrections: Social Control and Conflict*. Beverly Hills, Calif.: Sage Publications, 1977, pp. 77–88.

SEBBA, LESLIE. "Crime Seriousness and Criminal Intent," *Criminology* 30 (April 1984), 227–244.

_____. "Is Mens Rea a Component of Perceived Offense Seriousness?" *Journal of Criminal Law and Criminology* 71 (Summer 1980), 124–135.

SECHREST, LEE, SUSAN O. WHITE, AND ELIZABETH D. BROWN, EDS. *The Rehabilitation of Criminal Offenders: Problems and Prospects*. Washington, D.C.: National Academy of Sciences, 1979.

SEIDMAN, DAVID, AND MICHAEL COUZENS. "Getting the Crime Rate Down: Political Pressure and Crime Reporting," *Law and Society Review* 8 (Spring 1974), 457–493.

SEIDMAN, ROBERT B. "Witch Murder and *Mens Rea:* A Problem of Society under Radical Social Change," *Modern Law Review* 28 (January 1965), 46–61.

SEITZ, STEVEN THOMAS. "Firearms, Homicides, and Gun Control Effectiveness," *Law and Society Review* 6 (May 1972), 595–613.

SELLIN, THORSTEN. "The Basis of a Crime Index," *Journal of Criminal Law and Criminology* 22 (September 1931), 335–356.

_____. *Culture Conflict and Crime*. New York: Social Science Research Council, 1938.

_____, AND MARVIN E. WOLFGANG. *The Measurement of Delinquency*. New York: Wiley, 1964.

SELZNICK, PHILIP. *Law, Society, and Industrial Justice*. New York: Russell Sage Foundation, 1969.

SERRILL, MICHAEL S. "A Cold New Look at the Criminal Mind," *Psychology Today* 11 (February 1978), 86–92, 106.

SHAH, SALEEM A., AND LOREN H. ROTH. "Biological and Psychophysiological Factors in Criminality," in Daniel Glaser, ed., *Handbook of Criminology*. Chicago: Rand McNally, 1974, pp. 101–173.

SHANLEY, FRED J. "Middle-Class Delinquency as a Social Problem," *Sociology and Social Research* 51 (January 1967), 185–198.

SHANNON, LYLE W. *Assessing the Relationship of Adult Criminal Careers to Juvenile Careers: A Summary*. Washington, D.C.: U.S. Government Printing Office, June 1982.

SHAW, CLIFFORD R., AND HENRY D. MCKAY. *Juvenile Delinquency and Urban Areas*, rev. ed. Chicago: University of Chicago Press, 1942, 1969.

SHELEFF, LEON SHASKOLSKY, AND DAVID SHICHOR. "Victimological Aspects of Bystander Involvement," *Crime and Delinquency* 26 (April 1980), 193–201.

SHELLEY, LOUISE I. *Crime and Modernization: The Impact of Industrialization and Urbanization on Crime*. Carbondale: Southern Illinois University Press, 1981a.

––––––. "Urbanization and Crime: The Soviet Case in Cross-Cultural Perspective," in Louise I. Shelley, ed., *Readings in Comparative Criminology*. Carbondale: Southern Illinois University Press, 1981b, pp. 141–152.

SHENON, PHILIP. "The Mobsters Who Lurk behind the Corporate Veil," *The New York Times*, December 8, 1985, p. E4.

––––––. "One Price of High Bail: Overcrowded City Prisons," *The New York Times*, November 13, 1983, p. E6.

––––––. "Pornography in U.S. Linked to Violence, Meese Panel Asserts," *The New York Times*, May 14, 1986, pp. A1, B13.

SHERMAN, LAWRENCE W. "Policing Communities: What Works?" in Albert J. Reiss, Jr., and Michael Tonry, eds., *Communities and Crime*. Chicago: University of Chicago Press, 1986, pp. 343–386.

––––––, AND RICHARD A. BERK. "The Specific Deterrent Effects of Arrest for Domestic Assault," *American Sociological Review* 49 (April 1984), 261–272.

––––––, ET AL. *Citizens Killed by Big City Police, 1970–1984*. Washington, D.C.: Crime Control Institute, 1986.

SHILS, EDWARD. "The Sanctity of Life," *Encounter* 28 (January 1967), 39–49.

SHORT, JAMES F., JR. "Introduction to the Revised Edition," in Clifford R. Shaw and Henry D. McKay, *Juvenile Delinquency and Urban Areas*, rev. ed. Chicago: University of Chicago Press, 1942, 1969, pp. xxv–liv.

––––––, AND F. IVAN NYE. "Extent of Unrecorded Juvenile Delinquency: Tentative Conclusions," *Journal of Criminal Law, Criminology and Police Science* 49 (December 1958), 296–302.

––––––, AND F. IVAN NYE. "Reported Behavior as a Criterion of Deviant Behavior," *Social Problems* 5 (Winter 1957), 207–213.

––––––, AND FRED L. STRODTBECK. *Group Process and Gang Delinquency*. Chicago: University of Chicago Press, 1965.

SHOVER, NEAL. *Aging Criminals*. Beverly Hills, Calif.: Sage Publications, 1985.

––––––. "The Later Stages of Ordinary Property Offender Careers," *Social Problems* 31 (December 1983), 208–218.

––––––. "The Social Organization of Burglary," *Social Problems* 20 (Spring 1973), 499–514.

SILBERMAN, CHARLES E. *Criminal Violence, Criminal Justice*. New York: Random House, 1978.

SILVER, ALLAN. "The Demand for Order in Civil Society: A Review of Some Themes in the History of Urban Crime, Police, and Riot," in David J. Bordua, ed., *The Police: Six Sociological Essays.* New York: Wiley, 1967, pp. 1–24.

SIMIS, KONSTANTIN M. *USSR: The Corrupt Society.* New York: Simon and Schuster, 1982.

SIMON, RITA JAMES. *The Jury and the Defense of Insanity.* Boston: Little, Brown, 1967.

SINCLAIR, UPTON. *The Jungle.* New York: New American Library, 1906, 1960.

SINGER, SIMON I. "A Comment on Alleged Overreporting," *Criminology* 16 (May 1978), 99–103.

SKOGAN, WESLEY G. "Citizen Reporting of Crime: Some National Panel Data," *Criminology* 13 (February 1976a), 535–549.

———. "Crime and Crime Rates," in Wesley G. Skogan, eds., *Sample Surveys of the Victims of Crime.* Cambridge, Mass.: Ballinger, 1976b, pp. 105–119.

———. "Fear of Crime and Neighborhood Change," in Albert J. Reiss, Jr., and Michael Tonry, eds., *Communities and Crime.* Chicago: University of Chicago Press, 1986, pp. 203–229.

———. "On Attitudes and Behaviors," in Dan A. Lewis, ed., *Reactions to Crime.* Beverly Hills, Calif.: Sage Publications, 1981, pp. 19–45.

———. "Reporting Crimes to the Police: The Status of World Research," *Journal of Research in Crime and Delinquency* 21 (May 1984), 113–137.

———, AND MICHAEL G. MAXFIELD. *Coping with Crime: Individual and Neighborhood Reactions.* Beverly Hills, Calif.: Sage Publications, 1981.

SKOLNICK, JEROME H. *Justice without Trial: Law Enforcement in Democratic Society,* 2nd ed. New York: Wiley, 1975.

SMIGEL, ERWIN O. "Public Attitudes toward Stealing as Related to the Size of the Victim Organization," *American Sociological Review* 21 (June 1956), 320–327.

———, AND H. LAURENCE ROSS. "Introduction," in *Crimes against Bureaucracy.* New York: Van Nostrand Reinhold, 1970, pp. 1–14.

SMITH, DAVID E., AND GEORGE R. GAY, EDS. *"It's So Good, Don't Even Try It Once": Heroin in Perspective.* Englewood Cliffs, N.J.: Prentice-Hall, 1972.

SMITH, DOUGLAS A. "The Plea Bargaining Controversy," *Journal of Criminal Law and Criminology* 77 (Fall 1986), 949–967.

———, AND CHRISTY A. VISHER. "Street-Level Justice: Situational Determinants of Police Arrest Decisions," *Social Problems* 29 (December 1981), 167–177.

SOROKIN, PITIRIM A. "An Experimental Study of Efficiency of Work under Various Specified Conditions," *American Journal of Sociology* 35 (March 1930), 765–782.

SPARKS, RICHARD F. "Criminal Opportunities and Crime Rates," in Stephen E. Fienberg and Albert J. Reiss, Jr., eds., *Indicators of Crime and Criminal Justice: Quantitative Studies.* Washington, D.C.: Bureau of Justice Statistics, U.S. Department of Justice, 1980a, pp. 18–28.

———. "A Critique of Marxist Criminology," in Norval Morris and Michael Tonry, eds., *Crime and Justice: An Annual Review of Research,* Vol 2. Chicago: University of Chicago Press, 1980b, pp. 159–210.

———. "Multiple Victimization: Evidence, Theory, and Future Research," *Journal of Criminal Law and Criminology* 72 (Summer 1981), 762–778.

———. *Research on Victims of Crime: Accomplishments, Issues, and New Directions.* Washington, D.C.: U.S. Government Printing Office, 1982.

SPITZER, STEVEN. "The Political Economy of Policing," in David E. Greenberg, ed., *Crime & Capitalism.* Palo Alto, Calif.: Mayfield, 1981, pp. 314–340.

SPIVACK, GORDON B. "Antitrust Enforcement in the United States: A Primer," *Connecticut Bar Journal* 37 (September 1963), 375–389.

SPOHN, CASSIA, JOHN GRUHL, AND SUSAN WELCH. "The Effect of Race on Sentencing: A Reexamination of an Unsettled Question," *Law and Society Review* 16 (1981–82), 71–88.

STACK, STEVEN. "Income Inequality and Property Crime: A Cross-National Analysis of Relative Deprivation Theory," *Criminology* 22 (May 1984), 229–257.

———. "Publicized Executions and Homicide, 1950–1980," *American Sociological Review* 52 (August 1987), 532–540.

———. "Social Structure and Swedish Crime Rates: A Time-Series Analysis, 1950–1979," *Criminology* 20 (November 1982), 499–513.

STAFFORD, MARK C., AND OMER R. GALLE. "Victimization Rates, Exposure to Risk, and Fear of Crime," *Criminology* 22 (May 1984), 173–185.

STANKO, ELIZABETH ANNE. "The Impact of Victim Assessment on Prosecutors' Screening Decisions: The Case of the New York County District Attorney's Office," *Law and Society Review* 16 (1981–82), 225–239.

STARK, RODNEY. "Whose Status Counts?" *American Sociological Review* 44 (August 1979), 668–669.

———, ET AL. "Crime and Delinquency in the Roaring Twenties," *Journal of Research in Crime and Delinquency* 20 (January 1983), 4–23.

STEBBINS, ROBERT A. *Commitment to Deviance: The Nonprofessional Criminal in the Community.* Westport, Conn.: Greenwood, 1971.

STEFFENSMEIER, DARRELL J. "Assessing the Impact of the Women's Movement on Sex-Based Differences in the Handling of Adult Criminal Defendants," *Crime and Delinquency* 26 (July 1980), 344–357.

———. *The Fence: In the Shadow of Two Worlds.* Totowa, N.J.: Rowman and Littlefield, 1986.

———. "Organization Properties and Sex-Segregation in the Underworld: Building a Sociological Theory of Sex Differences in Crime," *Social Forces* 61 (June 1983), 1010–1032.

———, AND MICHAEL J. COBB. "Sex Differences in Urban Arrest Patterns," *Social Problems* 29 (October 1981), 37–50.

———, AND MILES D. HARER. "Is the Crime Rate Really Falling? An 'Aging' U.S. Population and Its Impact on the Nation's Crime Rate, 1980–1984," *Journal of Research in Crime and Delinquency* 24 (February 1987), 23–48.

———, AND RENEE HOFFMAN STEFFENSMEIER. "Trends in Female Delinquency: An Examination of Arrest, Juvenile Court, Self-Report, and Field Data," *Criminology* 18 (May 1980), 62–85.

STEINMETZ, SUZANNE K., AND MURRAY A. STRAUS. "The Family as a Cradle of Violence," in Delos H. Kelly, ed., *Criminal Behavior: Readings in Criminology.* New York: St. Martin's Press, 1980, pp. 130–142.

STENROSS, BARBARA. "Police Response to Residential Burglaries: Dusting for Prints as a Negative Rite," *Criminology* 22 (August 1984), 389–402.

STEPHENS, RICHARD C., AND ROSALIND D. ELLIS. "Narcotic Addicts and Crime: Analysis of Recent Trends," *Criminology* 12 (February 1975), 474–488.

STERNGOLD, JAMES. "Firms Act in Wake of 2 Scandals," *The New York Times,* June 7, 1986, pp. 33, 36.

STINCHCOMBE, ARTHUR L. "Institutions of Privacy in the Determination of Police Administration," *American Journal of Sociology* 69 (September 1963), 150–160.

STONE, CHRISTOPHER D. *Where the Law Ends.* New York: Harper & Row, 1974.

STOOKEY, JOHN ALAN. "A Cost Theory of Victim Justice," in Burt Galaway and Joe Hudson, eds., *Perspectives on Crime Victims.* St. Louis: C. V. Mosby, 1981, pp. 80–89.

STRASBURG, PAUL A. *Violent Delinquents: A Report to the Ford Foundation from the Vera Institute of Justice.* New York: Monarch, 1978.

STUART, REGINALD. "Atlanta Deaths: Fear Felt by Young," *The New York Times,* January 26, 1981, pp. A1, A12.

SUDNOW, DAVID. "Normal Crimes: Sociological Features of the Penal Code in a Public Defender Office," *Social Problems* 12 (Winter 1965), 255–276.

SUTHERLAND, EDWIN H. "The Diffusion of Sexual Psychopath Laws," *American Journal of Sociology* 56 (September 1950), 142–148.

———. *The Professional Thief.* Chicago: University of Chicago Press, 1937.

———. *White Collar Crime: The Uncut Version.* New Haven, Conn.: Yale University Press, 1949, 1983.

———, AND DONALD R. CRESSEY. *Criminology,* 10th ed. Philadelphia: Lippincott, 1978.

SUTTLES, GERALD D. *The Social Order of the Slum: Ethnicity and Territory in the Inner City.* Chicago: University of Chicago Press, 1968.

SVIRIDOFF, MICHELLE, AND JAMES W. THOMPSON. "Links between Employment and Crime: A Qualitative Study of Rikers Island Releasees," *Crime and Delinquency* 29 (April 1983), 195–212.

SWIGERT, VICTORIA LYNN, AND RONALD A. FARRELL. *Murder, Inequality, and the Law.* Lexington, Mass.: D. C. Heath, 1976.

———. "Normal Homicides and the Law," *American Sociological Review* 42 (February 1977), 16–32.

SYKES, GRESHAM M. *The Society of Captives: A Study of a Maximum Security Prison.* Princeton, N.J.: Princeton University Press, 1958.

———, AND DAVID MATZA. "Techniques of Neutralization: A Theory of Delinquency," *American Sociological Review* 22 (December 1957), 664–670.

SZASZ, ANDREW. "Corporations, Organized Crime, and the Disposal of Hazardous Waste: An Examination of the Making of a Criminogenic Regulatory Structure," *Criminology* 24 (February 1986), 1–27.

TAYLOR, IAN, PAUL WALTON, AND JOCK YOUNG, EDS. *Critical Criminology.* London: Routledge and Kegan Paul, 1975a.

———. "Critical Criminology in Britain: Review and Prospects," in Ian Taylor, Paul Walton, and Jock Young, eds., *Critical Criminology.* London: Routledge and Kegan Paul, 1975b, pp. 6–62.

———. *The New Criminology: For a Social Theory of Deviance.* London: Routledge and Kegan Paul, 1973.

TAYLOR, RALPH B., AND STEVEN GOTTFREDSON. "Environmental Design, Crime, and Prevention: An Examination of Community Dynamics," in Albert J. Reiss, Jr., and Michael Tonry, eds., *Communities and Crime.* Chicago: University of Chicago Press, 1986, pp. 387–416.

———, STEPHEN D. GOTTFREDSON, AND SIDNEY BROWER. "Block Crime and Fear: Defensible Space, Local Social Ties, and Territorial Functioning," *Journal of Research in Crime and Delinquency* 21 (November 1984), 303–331.

———, STEPHEN D. GOTTFREDSON, AND SIDNEY BROWER. "The Defensibility of Defensible Space: A Critical Review and a Synthetic Framework for Future Research," in Travis Hirschi and Michael Gottfredson, eds., *Understanding Crime: Current Theory and Research*. Beverly Hills, Calif.: Sage Publications, 1980, pp. 53–71.

———, AND MARGARET HALE. "Testing Alternative Models of Fear of Crime," *Journal of Criminal Law and Criminology* 77 (Spring 1986), 151–189.

THOMAS, CHARLES W., AND DONNA M. BISHOP. "The Effect of Formal and Informal Sanctions on Delinquency: A Longitudinal Comparison of Labeling and Deterrence Theories," *Journal of Criminal Law and Criminology* 75 (Winter 1984), 1222–1245.

THOMPSON, JAMES W., ET AL. *Employment and Crime: A Review of Theories and Research*. Washington, D.C.: National Institute of Justice, U.S. Department of Justice, 1981.

THORNBERRY, TERENCE P. "Race, Socioeconomic Status and Sentencing in the Juvenile Justice System," *Journal of Criminal Law and Criminology* 64 (March 1973), 90–98.

———. "Sentencing Disparities in the Juvenile Justice System," *Journal of Criminal Law and Criminology* 70 (Summer 1979), 164–171.

———, AND R. L. CHRISTENSON. "Unemployment and Criminal Involvement: An Investigation of Reciprocal Causal Structures," *American Sociological Review* 49 (June 1984), 398–411.

———, AND MARGARET FARNWORTH. "Social Correlates of Criminal Involvement: Further Evidence on the Relationship between Social Status and Criminal Behavior," *American Sociological Review* 47 (August 1982), 505–518.

THORSELL, BERNARD A., AND LLOYD W. KLEMKE. "The Labeling Process: Reinforcement and Deterrent?" *Law and Society Review* 6 (February 1972), 393–403.

THRASHER, FREDERIC M. *The Gang: A Study of 1,313 Gangs in Chicago*, abridged ed. Chicago: University of Chicago Press, 1927, 1963.

TIEN, JAMES M., THOMAS F. RICH, AND MICHAEL F. CAHN. *Electronic Fund Transfer Systems Fraud: Computer Crime*. Washington, D.C.: U.S. Department of Justice, April, 1986.

TIMNICK, LOIS. "Psychic Trauma Follows Chowchilla Kidnaping," *The Boston Globe*, January 24, 1981, p. 3.

TIMROTS, ANITA D., AND MICHAEL R. RAND. *Violent Crime by Strangers and Nonstrangers*. Washington, D.C.: U.S. Department of Justice, January 1987.

TITTLE, CHARLES R. "Social Class and Criminal Behavior: A Critique of the Theoretical Foundation," *Social Forces* 62 (December 1983), 334–358.

———, AND ALAN R. ROWE. "Certainty of Arrest and Crime Rates: A Further Test of the Deterrence Hypothesis," *Social Forces* 52 (June 1974), 455–462.

———, WAYNE J. VILLEMEZ, AND DOUGLAS A. SMITH. "The Myth of Social Class and Criminality: An Empirical Assessment of the Empirical Evidence," *American Sociological Review* 43 (October 1978), 643–656.

TOBIAS, J. J. *Crime and Industrial Society in the 19th Century*. New York: Schocken, 1967.

TOBY, JACKSON. "Affluence and Adolescent Crime," in The President's Commission on Law Enforcement and Administration of Justice, *Task Force Report: Juvenile Delinquency and Youth Crime*. Washington, D.C.: U.S. Government Printing Office, 1967, pp. 132–144.

———. "The Differential Impact of Family Disorganization," *American Sociological Review* 22 (October 1957), 505–512.

———. "The Socialization and Control of Deviant Motivation," in Daniel Glaser, ed., *Handbook of Criminology*. Chicago: Rand McNally, 1974, pp. 85–100.

TRACY, PAUL E., MARVIN E. WOLFGANG, AND ROBERT M. FIGLIO. *Delinquency in Two Birth Cohorts: Executive Summary.* Washington, D.C.: U.S. Department of Justice, September 1985.

TREBACH, ARNOLD S. *The Heroin Solution.* New Haven, Conn.: Yale University Press, 1982.

TURK, AUSTIN T. *Political Criminality: The Defiance and Defense of Authority.* Beverly Hills, Calif.: Sage Publications, 1982.

TURNER, STANLEY. "The Ecology of Delinquency," in Thorsten Sellin and Marvin E. Wolfgang, eds., *Delinquency: Selected Studies.* New York: Wiley, 1969, pp. 27–60.

TYLER, TOM R., AND RENEE WEBER. "Support for the Death Penalty: Instrumental Response to Crime, or Symbolic Attitude?" *Law and Society Review* 17 (1982), 21–45.

UHLMAN, THOMAS M., AND N. DARLENE WALKER. " 'He Takes Some of My Time; I Take Some of His': An Analysis of Sentencing Patterns in Jury Cases," *Law and Society Review* 14 (Winter 1980), 323–341.

U.S. DEPARTMENT OF JUSTICE, ATTORNEY GENERAL'S TASK FORCE ON VIOLENT CRIME. *Final Report.* Washington, D.C.: U.S. Government Printing Office, 1981.

[U.S. News & World Report.] "American Justice: ABC's of How It Really Works," *U.S. News & World Report,* November 1, 1982, pp. 35–58.

UNNEVER, JAMES D. "Direct and Organizational Discrimination in the Sentencing of Drug Offenders," *Social Problems* 30 (December 1982), 212–225.

USEEM, BERT. "Disorganization and the New Mexico Prison Riot of 1980," *American Sociological Review* 50 (October 1985), 677–688.

VAN DEN HAAG, ERNEST. "For the Death Penalty," *The New York Times,* October 17, 1983, p. A21.

———. *Punishing Criminals: Concerning a Very Old and Painful Question.* New York: Basic Books, 1975.

———, AND JOHN P. CONRAD. *The Death Penalty: A Debate.* New York: Plenum, 1983.

VAN DINE, STEVE, JOHN P. CONRAD, AND SIMON DINITZ. "The Incapacitation of the Chronic Thug," *Journal of Criminal Law and Criminology* 70 (Spring 1979), 125–135.

VELLENGA, JACOB J. "Is Capital Punishment Wrong?" *Christianity Today* 4 (October 12, 1959), 7–9.

VERA INSTITUTE OF JUSTICE. *Felony Arrests,* rev. ed. New York: Vera Institute of Justice and Longman, 1981.

VIDMAR, NEIL, AND DALE T. MILLER. "Socialpsychological Processes Underlying Attitudes toward Legal Punishment," *Law and Society Review* 14 (Spring 1980), 565–602.

VISCUSI, W. KIP. "Market Incentives for Criminal Behavior," in Richard B. Freeman and Harry J. Holzer, eds., *The Black Youth Employment Crisis.* Chicago: University of Chicago Press, 1986, pp. 301–346.

VISHER, CHRISTY A. "The Rand Inmate Survey: A Reanalysis," in Alfred Blumstein et al., eds., *Criminal Careers and "Career Criminals",* Vol. 2. Washington, D.C.: National Academy Press, 1986, pp. 161–211.

VOLAVKA, JAN, ET AL. "EEGs of XYY and XXY Men Found in a Large Birth Cohort," in Sarnoff A. Mednick and Karl O. Christiansen, eds., *Biosocial Bases of Criminal Behavior.* New York: Gardner Press, 1977, pp. 189–198.

VOLD, GEORGE B., AND THOMAS J. BERNARD. *Theoretical Criminology,* 3rd ed. New York: Oxford University Press, 1986.

VON HIRSCH, ANDREW. *Doing Justice: The Choice of Punishments.* New York: Hill and Wang, 1976.

——. "The Ethics of Selective Incapacitation: Observations on the Contemporary Debate," *Crime and Delinquency* 30 (April 1984a), 175–194.

——. *Past or Future Crimes: Deservedness and Dangerousness in the Sentencing of Criminals.* New Brunswick, N.J.: Rutgers University Press, 1985.

——. "Selective Incapacitation: A Critique," *NIJ Reports,* January 1984b, pp. 5–8.

——. "Utilitarian Sentencing Resuscitated: The American Bar Association's Second Report on Criminal Sentencing," *Rutgers Law Review* 33 (Spring 1981), 772–789.

——, AND KATHLEEN HANRAHAN. *Abolish Parole?* Washington, D.C.: U.S. Government Printing Office, 1978.

VORENBERG, JAMES, AND IRVING F. LUKOFF. "Addiction, Crime, and the Criminal Justice System," *Federal Probation* 37 (December 1973), 3–7.

VOSS, HARWIN L. "Ethnic Differentials in Delinquency in Honolulu," *Journal of Criminal Law, Criminology and Police Science* 54 (September 1963), 322–327.

——, AND JOHN R. HEPBURN. "Patterns in Criminal Homicide in Chicago," *Journal of Criminal Law, Criminology and Police Science* 59 (December 1968), 499–508.

VOTEY, HAROLD L., JR., AND LLAD PHILLIPS. "The Control of Criminal Activity: An Economic Analysis," in Daniel Glaser, ed., *Handbook of Criminology.* Chicago: Rand McNally, 1974, pp. 1055–1093.

WAEGEL, WILLIAM B. "The Use of Lethal Force by Police: The Effect of Statutory Change," *Crime and Delinquency* 30 (January 1984), 121–140.

WALDO, GORDON P., AND SIMON DINITZ. "Personality Attributes of the Criminal: An Analysis of Research Studies, 1950–1965," *Journal of Research in Crime and Delinquency* 4 (July 1967), 185–201.

WALKER, NIGEL. "Lost Causes in Criminology," in Roger Hood, ed., *Crime, Criminology and Public Policy: Essays in Honour of Sir Leon Radzinowicz.* New York: Free Press, 1974, pp. 47–62.

WALLERSTEIN, JAMES S., AND CLEMENT J. WYLE. "Our Law-Abiding Law-Breakers," *Probation* 35 (April 1947), 107–112.

WALLIS, C. P., AND R. MALIPHANT. "Delinquent Areas in the County of London: Ecological Factors," *British Journal of Criminology* 7 (July 1967), 250–284.

WALSH, ANTHONY. "Placebo Justice: Victim Recommendations and Offender Sentences in Sexual Assault Cases," *Journal of Criminal Law and Criminology* 77 (Winter 1986), 1126–1141.

——. "The Sexual Stratification Hypothesis and Sexual Assault in Light of the Changing Conceptions of Race," *Criminology* 25 (February 1987), 153–173.

WARD, DAVID A. "Sweden: The Middle Way to Prison Reform?" in Marvin E. Wolfgang, eds., *Prisons: Present and Possible.* Lexington, Mass.: D. C. Heath, 1979, pp. 89–167.

WARREN, DONALD I. "Neighborhood Structure and Riot Behavior in Detroit: Some Exploratory Findings," *Social Problems* 16 (Spring 1969), 464–484.

WEIS, JOSEPH G. "Crime Statistics: Reporting Systems and Methods," in Sanford H.

Kadish, ed., *Encyclopedia of Crime and Justice,* Vol. 1. New York: Free Press, 1983, pp. 378–392.

WEIS, KURT, AND SANDRA S. BORGES. "Victimology and Rape: The Case of the Legitimate Victim," *Issues in Criminology* 8 (Fall 1973), 71–115.

WELCH, SUSAN, JOHN GRUHL, AND CASSIA SPOHN. "Sentencing: The Influence of Alternative Measures of Prior Record," *Criminology* 22 (May 1984), 215–227.

WELLS, L. EDWARD, AND JOSEPH H. RANKIN. "The Broken Home Model of Delinquency: Analytic Issues," *Journal of Research in Crime and Delinquency* 23 (February 1986), 68–93.

WERNER, LESLIE MAITLAND. "U.S. Officials Cite Key Successes in War against Organized Crime," *The New York Times,* November 7, 1983, pp. A1, D18.

WEST, D. J. *Delinquency: Its Roots, Careers and Prospects.* Cambridge, Mass.: Harvard University Press, 1982.

———. *Present Conduct and Future Delinquency.* London: Heinemann, 1969.

———, AND D. P. FARRINGTON. *The Delinquent Way of Life.* London: Heinemann, 1977.

———, AND D. P. FARRINGTON. *Who Becomes Delinquent?* London: Heinemann, 1973.

WHITING, RICHARD A. "Antitrust Enforcement and the Corporate Executive II," *Virginia Law Review* 48 (January 1962), 1–49.

WIATROWSKI, MICHAEL D., DAVID B. GRISWOLD, AND MARY K. ROBERTS. "Social Control Theory and Delinquency," *American Sociological Review* 46 (October 1981), 525–541.

WIEHOFEN, HENRY. "Punishment and Treatment: Rehabilitation," in Stanley E. Grupp, ed., *Theories of Punishment.* Bloomington: Indiana University Press, 1971, pp. 255–263.

WILBANKS, WILLIAM. "Does Alcohol Cause Homicide?" *Journal of Crime and Justice* 4 (1981), 149–170.

———. *Murder in Miami.* Lanham, Md.: University Press of America, 1984.

WILEY, NORBERT. "The Ethnic Mobility Trap and Stratification Theory," *Social Problems* 15 (Fall 1967), 147–159.

WILKINSON, KAREN. "The Broken Home and Delinquent Behavior: An Alternative Interpretation of Contradictory Findings," in Travis Hirschi and Michael Gottfredson, eds., *Understanding Crime: Current Theory and Research.* Beverly Hills, Calif.: Sage Publications, 1980, pp. 21–42.

WILLIAMS, HERBERT, AND ANTONY M. PATE. "Returning to First Principles: Reducing the Fear of Crime in Newark," *Crime and Delinquency* 33 (January 1987), 53–70.

WILLIAMS, JAY R., AND MARTIN GOLD. "From Delinquent Behavior to Official Delinquency," *Social Problems* 20 (Fall 1972), 209–229.

WILSON, JAMES Q. "Foreword," in Thomas A. Reppetto, *Residential Crime.* Cambridge, Mass.: Ballinger, 1974, pp. xv–xvi.

———. *Thinking about Crime,* rev. ed. New York: Basic Books, 1983.

———. *Varieties of Police Behavior: The Management of Law and Order in Eight Communities.* Cambridge, Mass.: Harvard University Press, 1968.

———, AND BARBARA BOLAND. "Crime," in William Gorham and Nathan Glazer, eds., *The Urban Predicament.* Washington, D.C.: Urban Institute, 1976, pp. 179–230.

———, AND BARBARA BOLAND. "The Effect of the Police on Crime," *Law and Society Review* 12 (Spring 1978), 367–390.

———, AND BARBARA BOLAND. "The Effects of the Police on Crime: A Response to Jacob and Rich," *Law and Society Review* 16 (1981–82), 163–169.

————, AND RICHARD J. HERRNSTEIN. *Crime & Human Nature.* New York: Simon and Schuster, 1985.

WINICK, CHARLES. "Physician Narcotic Addicts," in Howard S. Becker, ed., *The Other Side: Perspectives on Deviance.* New York: Free Press, 1964, pp. 261–279.

WISE, NANCY BARTON. "Juvenile Delinquency among Middle-Class Girls," in Edmund W. Vaz, ed., *Middle-Class Juvenile Delinquency.* New York: Harper & Row, 1967, pp. 179–188.

WITKIN, HERMAN A., ET AL. "Criminality in XYY and XXY Men," *Science* 193 (August 13, 1976), 547–555.

WOLFGANG, MARVIN E. "Crime in a Birth Cohort," in Roger Hood, ed., *Crime, Criminology and Public Policy: Essays in Honour of Sir Leon Radzinowicz.* New York: Free Press, 1974, pp. 79–92.

————. *Patterns in Criminal Homicide.* Philadelphia: University of Pennsylvania Press, 1958.

————. "Urban Crime," in James Q. Wilson, ed., *The Metropolitan Enigma.* Garden City, N.Y.: Doubleday, 1968, pp. 270–311.

————, AND FRANCO FERRACUTI. *The Subculture of Violence: Towards an Integrated Theory in Criminology.* Beverly Hills, Calif.: Sage Publications, 1967, 1982.

————, ROBERT M. FIGLIO, AND THORSTEN SELLIN. *Delinquency in a Birth Cohort.* Chicago: University of Chicago Press, 1972.

————, AND SIMON I. SINGER. "Victim Categories of Crime," *Journal of Criminal Law and Criminology* 69 (Fall 1978), 379–394.

————, ET AL. *The National Survey of Crime Severity.* Washington, D.C.: U.S. Department of Justice, June 1985.

WOLPIN, KENNETH I. "An Economic Analysis of Crime and Punishment in England and Wales, 1894–1967," *Journal of Political Economy* 86 (October 1978), 815–840.

WOOTTON, BARBARA. *Social Science and Social Pathology.* London: George Allen and Unwin, 1959.

WRIGHT, JAMES D., AND PETER H. ROSSI. *Armed and Considered Dangerous: A Survey of Felons and Their Firearms.* New York: Aldine de Gruyter, 1986.

————, PETER H. ROSSI, AND KATHLEEN DALY. *Under the Gun: Weapons, Crime, and Violence in America.* New York: Aldine, 1983.

YIN, PETER. "Fear of Crime as a Problem for the Elderly," *Social Problems* 30 (December 1982), 240–245.

YOCHELSON, SAMUEL, AND STANTON E. SAMENOW. *The Criminal Personality,* Vol. 1: *A Profile for Change.* New York: Jason Aronson, 1976.

————. *The Criminal Personality,* Vol 2: *The Change Process.* New York: Jason Aronson, 1977.

YODER, STEPHEN A. "Criminal Sanctions for Corporate Illegality," *Journal of Criminal Law and Criminology* 69 (Spring 1978), 40–58.

YOUNG, ROBERT L., DAVID McDOWALL, AND COLIN LOFTIN. "Collective Security and the Ownership of Firearms for Protection," *Criminology* 25 (February 1987), 47–62.

YUNKER, JAMES A. "The Relevance of the Identification Problem to Statistical Research on Capital Punishment," *Crime and Delinquency* 28 (January 1982), 96–124.

ZARR, GERALD H. "Liberia," in Alan Milner, ed., *African Penal Systems*. London: Routledge and Kegan Paul, 1969.

ZATZ, MARJORIE S. "The Changing Forms of Racial/Ethnic Biases in Sentencing," *Journal of Research in Crime and Delinquency* 24 (February 1987), 69–92.

———. "Race, Ethnicity, and Determinate Sentencing: A New Dimension to an Old Controversy," *Criminology* 22 (May 1984), 147–171.

ZEISEL, HANS. "A Comment on 'The Deterrent Effect of Capital Punishment' by Phillips," *American Journal of Sociology* 88 (July 1982), 167–169.

———. "An International Experiment on the Effects of the Good Samaritan Law," in James M. Ratcliffe, ed., *The Good Samaritan and the Law*. Garden City, N.Y.: Doubleday, 1966, pp. 209–212.

———. "Race Bias in the Administration of the Death Penalty: The Florida Experience," *Harvard Law Review* 95 (December 1981), 456–468.

ZEITLIN, LAWRENCE R. "A Little Larceny Can Do a Lot for Employee Morale," *Psychology Today* 5 (June 1971), 22–26, 64.

ZIMBARDO, PHILIP G. "Pathology of Imprisonment," *Society* 9 (April 1972), 4–8.

———. "The Prison Game," Hearings before Subcommittee #3 of the Committee on the Judiciary, House of Representatives, 92nd Congress, 1st Session, Part II, Serial No. 15, October 25, 1971, pp. 110–113. Reprinted in Norman Johnston and Leonard D. Savitz, eds., *Legal Process and Corrections*. New York: Wiley, 1982, pp. 105–108.

———, ET AL. "A Pirandellian Prison," *The New York Times Magazine*, April 8, 1973, pp. 38–60.

ZIMRING, FRANKLIN E., AND GORDON J. HAWKINS. *Deterrence: The Legal Threat in Crime Control*. Chicago: University of Chicago Press, 1973.

NAME INDEX

SUBJECT INDEX